DIVERSITY
AND SOCIETY

4 EDITION

This book is dedicated to my mother, Alice T. Healey.
May she rest in peace.

DIVERSITY
AND SOCIETY
Race, Ethnicity, and Gender

4 EDITION

Joseph F. Healey
Christopher Newport University

Los Angeles | London | New Delhi
Singapore | Washington DC

Los Angeles | London | New Delhi
Singapore | Washington DC

FOR INFORMATION:

SAGE Publications, Inc.
2455 Teller Road
Thousand Oaks, California 91320
E-mail: order@sagepub.com

SAGE Publications Ltd.
1 Oliver's Yard
55 City Road
London EC1Y 1SP
United Kingdom

SAGE Publications India Pvt. Ltd.
B 1/I 1 Mohan Cooperative Industrial Area
Mathura Road, New Delhi 110 044
India

SAGE Publications Asia-Pacific Pte. Ltd.
3 Church Street
#10-04 Samsung Hub
Singapore 049483

Acquisitions Editor: David Repetto
Editorial Assistant: Lauren Johnson
Production Editor: Brittany Bauhaus
Copy Editor: Alison Hope
Typesetter: C&M Digitals (P) Ltd.
Proofreader: Jennifer Gritt
Indexer: Molly Hall
Cover Designer: Bryan Fishman
Marketing Manager: Erica DeLuca
Permissions Editor: Karen Ehrmann

Cover artwork: Olga Storms, www.olgastorms.com

Printed in the United States of America

Library of Congress Cataloging-in-Publication Data

Healey, Joseph F., 1945-

Diversity and society : race, ethnicity, and gender / Joseph F. Healey. — Fourth edition.

pages cm
Includes bibliographical references and index.

ISBN 978-1-4129-9245-9 (paper : acid-free paper)
1. Minorities—United States. 2. Ethnicity—United States.
3. Racism—United States. 4. Group identity—United States.
5. Social conflict—United States. 6. United States—Race relations. 7. United States—Ethnic relations. 8. United States—Social conditions. I. Title.

E184.A1H415 2013
305.800973—dc23   2012037725

This book is printed on acid-free paper.

13 14 15 16 17 10 9 8 7 6 5 4 3 2 1

Brief Contents

Detailed Contents

Preface

❖

Of all the challenges confronting the United States today, those relating to minority groups continue to be among the most urgent and the most daunting. Discrimination and racial and ethnic inequality are part of our national heritage and—along with equality, freedom, and justice—prejudice and racism are among our oldest values. Minority group issues penetrate every aspect of society, and virtually every item on the national agenda—welfare and health-care reform, crime and punishment, safety in the streets, the future of the family, even defense spending, foreign policy, and terrorism—has some connection with dominant-minority relations.

These issues will not be resolved easily or quickly. Feelings are intense, and controversy and bitter debate often swamp dispassionate analysis and calm reason. As a society, we have little hope of resolving these dilemmas unless we confront them openly and honestly; they will not disappear, and they will not resolve themselves.

This textbook contributes to the ongoing discussion by presenting information, raising questions, and probing issues. My intent is to help students increase their knowledge, improve their understanding of the issues, and clarify their thinking regarding matters of race and ethnicity. This text has been written for undergraduate students—sociology majors and nonmajors alike. It makes minimal assumptions about students' knowledge of history or sociological concepts, and presents material in a way that students will find accessible and coherent.

For example, a unified set of themes and concepts is used throughout the text. The analysis is consistent and continuous, even as multiple perspectives and various points of view are examined. The bulk of the conceptual framework is introduced in the first four chapters. These concepts and analytical themes are then used in a series of case studies of minority groups in contemporary America and are also used to investigate group relations in various societies around the globe. In the final chapter, main points and themes are summarized and reviewed, the analysis is brought to a conclusion, and some speculations are made regarding the future.

The analysis in this text is generally macro and comparative. It is focused on groups and larger social structures—institutions and stratification systems, for example—and systematically compares and contrasts the experiences and situations of America's many minorities. The text is in the tradition of conflict theory, but it is not a comprehensive statement of that tradition. Other perspectives are introduced and applied, but no attempt is made to give equal attention to all current sociological paradigms. The text does not try to explain everything, nor does it attempt to include all possible analytical points of view. Rather, the goals are (a) to present the sociology of minority group relations in a way that students will find understandable as well as intellectually challenging, and (b) to deal with the issues and tell the stories behind the issues in a textbook that is both highly readable and a demonstration of the power and importance of thinking sociologically.

Every chapter (except the last) begins with a recounting of personal experiences that compellingly and dramatically foreshadows the material. These introductions include the experiences and thoughts of a wide variety of people: immigrants, journalists, sociologists, and slaves, among others. Also, each chapter (except the last) includes a section called "Focus on Contemporary Issues," which addresses a specific issue in U.S. society that readers will find current and relevant to their lives.

This text also explores the diversity of experiences within each minority group, particularly gender differences. Too often, minority groups (and the dominant group, for that matter) are seen as single, undifferentiated entities. The text acknowledges the variety of experiences within each group and, in particular, explores differences in the experiences of minority group males and females. The analysis explores the ways in which gender differences cut across ethnic and racial differences and stresses that these sources of inequality and injustice are independent of each other. Solving one set of problems (e.g., prejudice and racial discrimination) will not automatically or directly solve the other (e.g., sexism and gender inequalities).

The text focuses on the experiences of minority groups in the United States, but a considerable amount of comparative, cross-national material has also been included. A series of boxed inserts called "Comparative Focus" explores group relations in other societies.

Finally, this text stresses the ways in which American minority groups are inseparable from the American experience, from the early days of colonial settlements to tomorrow's headlines. The relative success of this society is due no less to the contributions of minority groups than it is to those of the dominant group. The nature of the minority group experience has changed as the larger society has changed, and to understand America's minority groups is to understand some elemental truths about America. To raise the issues of race and ethnicity is to ask what it means, and what it has meant, to be an American.

This text is an abridged and updated version of *Race, Ethnicity, Gender, and Class: The Sociology of Group Conflict and Change* (6th edition), also published by SAGE. The larger volume includes a number of additional features, more detail, and a separate chapter on prejudice. This volume takes a more macro approach and deemphasizes individual prejudice, but retains the overall format, case study approach, and conceptual framework of the larger text.

Changes in the Fourth Edition of *Diversity and Society*

Many changes have been made in this edition, most designed to make the material as current as possible and to respond to the ever-changing landscape of minority issues.

- Research findings and all data have been updated. In particular, this edition relies on the latest information from the U.S. Census Bureau, particularly the 2010 census.
- There is an increased emphasis on immigration, particularly in chapters 1 and chapters 7–9.

- The "Comparative Focus" features have been updated and shortened to make them more appealing and to increase their impact. A new "Comparative Focus" feature can be found in chapter 9.

- A new set of "Internet Research Projects" has been included for every chapter. In these assignments, students gather information and data from the Internet and apply concepts and ideas from the chapter. Each project has an "Optional Group Discussion" component.

- The topics of the "Focus on Contemporary Issues" box in chapters 1, 8, and 9 have been changed. The other "Focus on Contemporary Issues" have been updated.

- In chapter 4, the section on gender inequality has been reorganized into two subsections, one focused on the United States and the other on global changes. Coverage of the glass ceiling has been expanded. The section on "Modern Institutional Discrimination" has also been reorganized into subsections, and the coverage of "past-in-present" discrimination has been expanded.

- In chapter 5, the section on "Black–White Relations Since the 1960s: Issues and Trends" has been reorganized. A new section on "Modern Institutional Discrimination" has been added, along with a subsection on the recent recession's differential effects on blacks and whites.

- In chapter 7, the sections addressing recent immigration from Mexico have been expanded and updated and the section on "New Hispanic Groups" has been moved to chapter 9. The material on the Cuban enclave has been updated to include important new research and data. New material on Mexican American values has been added.

- In chapter 8, the case studies in the "Contemporary Immigration from Asia" section have been moved to chapter 9, but the section now includes mention of several more Asian groups, including the Hmong. There is more material on the diversity of Asian American groups and the inadequacy of the "model minority" label. More material on Asian American intermarriage has been added. New material on Asian American values has been added, as has material on gender and physical acculturation, and the effect of nativity on poverty.

- Chapter 9 now includes discussion of recent immigrants from Central and South America and from Asia. A photo essay on Arab Americans in Michigan has been added. Information on American attitudes about immigration has been updated, along with the material on "Costs and Benefits" and "Undocumented Immigrants." The "Segmented Assimilation" section has been updated to include important new research on the second generation.

Acknowledgments

All textbooks, even those with a single author's name on the title page, are profoundly collaborative efforts. This book has been shaped by more than 40 years of teaching minority relations and by the thoughts and reactions of hundreds of students. My approach to this subject has grown from years of "field testing" ideas, concepts, theories, and research, and constant monitoring of what seemed to help the students make sense of the world they live in. I acknowledge and thank my students for their myriad contributions.

When I was a student, I had the good fortune of learning from faculty members who were both accomplished scholars and exceptionally dedicated teachers. Each of them contributed to my interest in and commitment to sociology, but two stand out in my memory as mentors and intellectual role models: Professors Edwin H. Rhyne and Charles S. Green. Dr. Rhyne encouraged me as a young scholar and quite literally introduced me to the world of ideas and the life of the mind. Later in my career, Dr. Green showed me what it means to be a professional scholar, a sociologist, and a teacher. Their influence on my life was profound, and I thank them deeply.

I am no less indebted to my colleagues, past and present, in the Department of Sociology and Anthropology at Christopher Newport University: Stephanie Byrd, Cheri Chambers, Robert Durel, Marcus Griffin, Mai Lan Gustafsson, Kai Heidemann, Michael Lewis, Marion Manton, Eileen O'Brien, Lea Pellett, Eduardo Perez, Virginia Purtle, Andria Timmer, and Linda Waldron. They have been unflagging in their support of this project, and I thank them for their academic, logistical, and intellectual assistance. I would also like to thank Iris Price, Tracey Rausch, and Ellen Whiting for their indispensable help and support.

I thank Dave Repetto of SAGE for his invaluable assistance in the preparation of this manuscript and Ben Penner and Steve Rutter, formerly of SAGE, for their help in the development of this project.

This text has benefited in innumerable ways from the reactions and criticisms of a group of reviewers who proved remarkably insightful about the subject matter and about the challenges of college teaching. I can no longer even estimate the number of points in the process of writing and research where the comments of the reviewers led to significant improvements in scholarship, clarity, and more meaningful treatments of the subject. The shortcomings that remain are, of course, my responsibility, but whatever quality this text has is a direct result of the insights and expertise of these reviewers. I thank the following people:

Fourth Edition Reviewers

Janice Kelly, *Molloy College*

Teri Moran, *Jackson Community College*

Creaig Dunton, *SUNY College at Plattsburgh*

C. Douglas Johnson, *Gwinnett College of Business*

Margaret Vaughan, *Metropolitan State University–Saint Paul*

Enid Lyne Logan, *University of Minnesota–Twin Cities*

Lisa Eargle, *Francis Marion University*

Tennille Allen, *Lewis University*

Gerald Tichener, *Des Moines Area Community College–Ankeny*

Elijah Ward, *Saint Xavier University*

Elsa Valdez

Kimberly Fortin, *Cayuga Community College*

Deidre Tyler, *Salt Lake Community College–Redwood*

Leslie Baker-Kimmons, *Chicago State University*

Melanie Deffendall, *Delgado Community College*

Ami Moore, *University of North Texas*

Steven Arxer, *University of Texas at Dallas*

Patricia Literte, *California State University–Fullerton*

Kathy Westman, *Waubonsee Community College*

Chris Keegan, *SUNY College at Oneonta*

Marci Littlefield, *Indiana Univeristy/Purdue University at Indianapolis*

PART I

An Introduction to the Study of Minority Groups in the United States

✦

❦ ❧

❦ ❧

The United States is a nation of groups as well as individuals. These groups vary along a number of dimensions, including size, wealth, education, race, culture, religion, and language. Some of these groups have been part of American society since colonial days, and others have formed in the past few years.

How should all these groups relate to one another? Who should be considered American? Should we preserve the multitude of cultural heritages and languages that currently exists and stress our diversity? Should we encourage everyone to adopt Anglo

American culture and strive to become more similar and unified? Should we emphasize our similarities or celebrate our differences? Is it possible to do both?

Questions of unity and diversity are among the most pressing to face the United States today and we begin to address these issues and many other issues in chapters 1 and 2 of this text. Our goal is to develop a broader, more informed understanding of the past and present forces that have created and sustained the groups that compose U.S. society. We will sustain this focus throughout the text.

Diversity in the United States: Questions and Concepts

Who am I?...Where do I fit into American society?...For most of my 47 years, I have struggled to find answers to these questions. I am an American of multiracial descent and culture [Native American, African American, Italian American, and Puerto Rican]. In this aspect, I am not very different from many Americans [but] I have always felt an urge to feel and live the intermingling of blood that runs through my veins. American society has a way of forcing multiracial and biracial people to choose one race over the other. I personally feel this pressure every time I have to complete an application form with instructions to check just one box for race category.

—Butch, a 47-year-old male[1]

Actually, I don't feel comfortable being around Asians except for my family...I couldn't relate to...other Asians [because] they grew up in [wealthier neighborhoods]. I couldn't relate to the whole "I live in a mansion" [attitude]. This summer, I worked in a media company and it was kind of hard to relate to them [other Asians] because we all grew up in a different place...the look I would get when I say "Yeah, I'm from [a less affluent neighborhood"] they're like, "Oh, Oh" like, "That's unfortunate for your parents, I'm sorry they didn't make it."

—Rebecca, a 19-year-old Macanese-
Chinese-Portuguese female[2]

Yeah, my people came from all over—Italy, Ireland, Poland, and others too. I don't really know when they got here or why they came and, really, it doesn't matter much to me. I mean, I'm just an American . . . I'm from everywhere . . . I'm from here!

—Jennifer, a 25-year-old white American female[3]

What do these people have in common? How do they differ? They think about their place in U.S. society in very different ways. All are connected to a multitude of groups and traditions but not all find this fact interesting or important. One feels alienated from the more affluent members of her group, one seeks to embrace his multiple memberships, and one dismisses the issue of ancestry as irrelevant and is comfortable and at ease being "just an American."

Today, the United States is growing more diverse in culture, race, religion, and language. The number of people who can connect themselves to different cultural traditions is increasing, as is the number of Americans of mixed race. Where will this lead us? Will increasing diversity lead to greater tolerance and respect for one another? Can we overcome the legacies of racism and inequality that stretch back to colonial days? Will we fragment along these lines of difference and dissolve into warring ethnic enclaves (the fate of more than one modern, apparently unified nation)?

This text raises a multitude of questions about the past, present, and future of group relationships in U.S. society. What historical, social, political, and economic forces shaped those relationships in the past? How do racial and ethnic groups relate to each other today? What issues and problems can we expect in the years to come? Why do some people struggle with their identity? What is an American?

The United States is a nation of immigrants and groups and we have been arguing, often passionately, about what this means, about inclusion and exclusion, and about unity and diversity, since the infancy of this society. Every member of our society is in some sense an immigrant or the descendant of immigrants. Even American Indians migrated to this continent, albeit thousands of years ago. We are all from someplace else, with roots in another part of the globe. Some came here in chains, others came on ocean liners, on jet planes, or on foot. Some arrived last week and others have had family here for centuries. Each wave of newcomers has altered the social landscape of the United States. As many have observed, our society is continually becoming, permanently unfinished.

Today, the United States is remaking itself yet again. Large numbers of immigrants are arriving from all over the world, and their presence has raised questions about who belongs, what it means to be a U.S. citizen, and how much diversity we can tolerate. Even as we debate the implications of immigration, other long-standing issues of belonging, fairness, and justice remain unresolved. American Indians and African Americans have been a part of this society since its inception but largely as "others," slaves and outsiders, servants and laborers—groups outside the mainstream, not "true Americans" or full citizens. The legacies of racism and exclusion continue to affect these groups today and, as we shall see in chapters to come, they and other American minority groups continue to suffer from inequality, discrimination, and marginalization.

Today, the definition of "American" seems up for grabs. After all, in 2008 we elected a black man to the most powerful position in the society (and, arguably, in the world). To many Americans, this was proof that the United States had finally become what it so often claimed to be: a truly open society, the last, best hope for all of humanity. Yet, even a casual glance at our schools, courts, neighborhoods, churches, corporate board rooms—indeed, at any nook or cranny of our society—reveals pervasive patterns of inequality, differential opportunity, injustice, and unfairness. Which is the real America: the land of tolerance and opportunity, or the sinkhole of narrow-mindedness and inequity?

We may be at a crossroads in this era of growing diversity and, perhaps, we have an opportunity to reexamine the fundamental questions of citizenship and inclusion in this society: What is an American? Can we incorporate all groups while avoiding fragmentation and chaotic disunity? What can hold us together? Should we celebrate our diversity or stress the need for unity?

Our understanding of these issues and our answers to these questions is partly affected by the groups to which we belong. Some of us feel intensely connected to our people and identify closely with our heritage(s). Others are uncertain about who they are exactly, where they fit in the social landscape. Still others feel no particular connection with any tradition, group, or homeland. Still, these elements of our identity influence our lives and perceptions. They help to shape who we are and how we relate to the larger society. They affect the ways others perceive us, the opportunities available to us, the way we think about ourselves, and our view of American society and the larger world. They affect our perception of what it means to be American.

The Increasing Variety of American Minority Groups: Trends and Questions

Our group memberships also shape the choices we make in the voting booth and in other areas of social life. We face important decisions that will affect our lives and the lives of countless millions, and we need to contemplate these choices systematically and thoroughly. We also need to be aware that members of different groups will evaluate these decisions in different ways. The issues will be filtered through the screens of divergent experiences, group histories, and present situations. The debates over which direction our society should take are unlikely to be meaningful or even mutually intelligible without some understanding of the variety of ways of being American.

Increasing Diversity

The choices about the future of our society are especially urgent because the diversity of U.S. society is increasing dramatically, largely due to high rates of immigration. Since the 1960s, the number of immigrants arriving in the United States each year has tripled and includes groups, literally, from all over the globe (U.S. Department of Homeland Security, 2011).

Can our society deal successfully with this diversity of cultures, languages, and races? Concerns about increasing diversity are compounded by other long-standing minority issues and grievances that remain unresolved. For example, charts and graphs presented in part 3 of this text document continuing gaps in income, poverty rates, and other measures of affluence and equality between minority groups and national norms. In fact, in many ways the problems of African Americans, American Indians, Hispanic Americans, and Asian Americans today are just as formidable as they were a generation ago.

As one way of gauging the dimensions of diversity in our nation, consider the changing makeup of U.S. society. Exhibit 1.1 presents the percentage of the total U.S. population in each of five groups. We will first consider this information "on its face" and analyze some of its implications. Then we consider (and question) the terms in which this information is framed.

Exhibit 1.1   Racial and Ethnic Groups

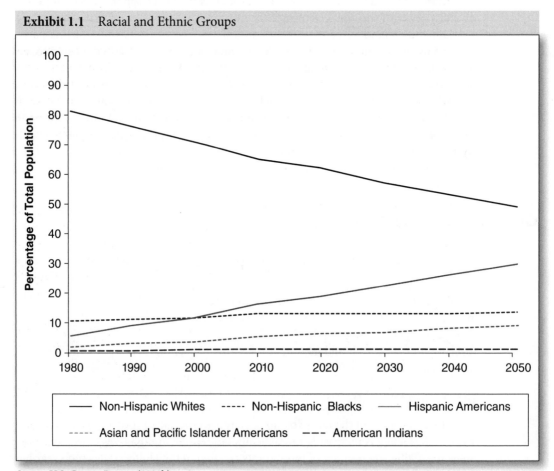

Source: U.S. Census Bureau (2008b).

Note: "Hispanics" may be of any race.

The exhibit reports the actual relative sizes of the groups for 1980 through 2010 and the projected relative sizes through 2050. Note how the increasing diversity of U.S. society is reflected in the declining numerical predominance of Non-Hispanic whites. As recently as 1980, more than 8 out of 10 Americans were members of this group but, by the middle of this century, non-Hispanic whites are projected to become a numerical minority. Several states (California, Hawaii, New Mexico, and Texas) are already majority-minority, and seven more are less than 60% white (Arizona, Florida, Georgia, Maryland, Mississippi, Nevada, and New York) ("A Changing Population," 2010). These states are a preview of what the nation as a whole will look like within several decades.

African Americans and American Indians will grow in absolute numbers, but will remain stable in their relative size, according to projections. Hispanic Americans and Asian Americans and Pacific Islanders will grow dramatically. Asian Americans and Pacific Islander groups made up only 2% of the population in 1980 but will grow to almost 10% by mid-century. The most dramatic growth, however, will be for Hispanic Americans, who became the largest minority group in 2002, surpassing African Americans. This group will grow to slightly more than 30% of the population by mid-century.

The projections into the future are just educated guesses, of course, but they presage profound change for the United States. As this century unfolds, our society will grow more diverse racially, culturally, and linguistically. The United States will become less white, less European, and more like the world as a whole. Some see these changes as threats to traditional white middle-class American values and lifestyles. Others see them as providing an opportunity for the emergence of other equally legitimate value systems and lifestyles.

What's in a Name?

Let's take a moment to reflect on the categories in exhibit 1.1. The group names I used are arbitrary and none of these groups has clear or definite boundaries. I use these terms because they are convenient, familiar, and consistent with the labels found in census reports, much of the sociological research literature, and other sources of information. This does not mean that the labels are "true" in any absolute sense or equally useful in all circumstances. In fact, these group names have some serious shortcomings, several of which I note here.

First, the people within these groups may have very little in common with each other. Any two people in one of these categories might be as different from each other as any two people selected from different categories. They may share some general, superficial physical or cultural traits, but they will also vary by social class, religion, and gender, and in thousands of other ways. People in the "Asian American and Pacific Islander" group, for example, represent scores of different national and linguistic backgrounds (Japanese, Pakistanis, Samoans, Vietnamese, and so forth), and the category "American Indian or Alaska Native" includes people from hundreds of different tribal groups.

Second, people do not necessarily use these labels when they think about their identity or who they are. In this sense, the labels are not "real" or important for all of the people in these categories. For example, many whites in the United States (like Jennifer, quoted in the opening of this chapter) think of themselves as "just an American." A Hispanic American may think of herself more in national terms, as a Mexican or a Cuban, or, even more specifically, she may identify with a particular region or village in her homeland. Thus, the labels do not always reflect the ways people think about themselves, their families, or where they come from. The categories are statistical classifications created by researchers and census takers: they do not grow out of or always reflect the everyday realities of the people who happen to be in the category.

Third, even though the categories in exhibit 1.1 are broad, they provide no place for a number of groups. For example, where should we place Arab Americans and recent immigrants from Africa? These groups are relatively small in size (about 1 million people each), but there is no clear place for them in these categories. Should Arab Americans be classified as "Asian"? Should recent immigrants from Africa be placed in the same category as African Americans? Of course, we don't need to have a category for every person, but we should recognize that classification schemes like the one used in exhibit 1.1 (and in many other contexts) have fuzzy boundaries and limited utility and application.

A related problem with this classification scheme will become increasingly apparent in the years to come: there is no category for the growing number of people who (like Butch, quoted in the opening of this chapter) are members of more than one racial or ethnic group. The number of "mixed-group" Americans is relatively small today, slightly less than 3% of the total population. However, the number of people who chose more than one racial or ethnic category to describe themselves increased by 32% (from 2.4% to 2.9% of the total population) between 2000 and 2010 (Humes, Jones, & Ramirez, 2011, p. 4) and is likely to continue to increase rapidly because of the growing number of marriages across group lines. To illustrate, exhibit 1.2 is based on an analysis of census data and shows dramatic increases in the percentage of "new" marriages (couples that got married in the year prior to the survey date) and all marriages that unite members of different racial or ethnic groups (Wang, 2012, p. 5). Obviously, the greater the number of mixed marriages, the greater the number of mixed Americans. One study estimates that 21% of the population will claim membership in this category by 2050 (J. Smith & Edmonston, 1997, p. 119).

Finally, we should note that these categories and group names are **social constructions**, fabricated in particular historical circumstances and reflective of particular power relationships.[4] For example, the group called "American Indians" today didn't exist prior to the period of European exploration and colonization of North America (and, in some ways, it doesn't exist today). Before the arrival of Europeans, there were hundreds of separate societies spread across the North American continent, each with its own language and culture. American Indians thought of themselves primarily in terms of their tribe and had no sense of a common identity with the other peoples that inhabited North America. They became a group first in the perceptions of European conquerors, who stressed their similarities and cast them as an enemy out-group. The fact that American Indians are often defined as a single group today reflects their

Exhibit 1.2   Percentage of New and All Marriages Involving a Spouse of Different Race or Ethnicity

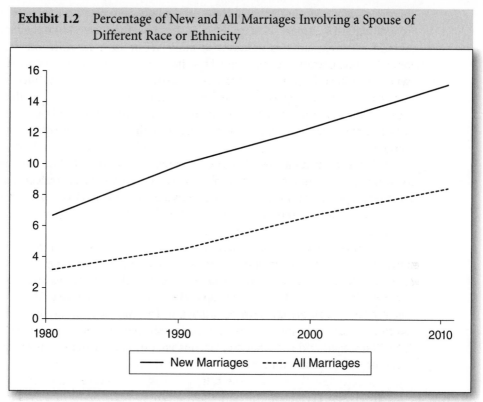

Source: Wang (2012, p. 5).

defeat and subordination and their status as a minority group: they became the "others" in contrast to the dominant group.

In the same way (although through different processes), African, Hispanic, and Asian Americans came to be seen as separate groups not by their own choices, but as one outcome of an unequal interaction with white Americans. These groups have become "real" and much of this text is organized around a consideration of each of them (e.g., see the chapter titles in part 3). Nonetheless, we use the terms and labels as a convenience, not as a reflection of some unchangeable reality. These groups are real because they are seen as real from a particular perspective—that of the dominant group in this society: white Americans.

Questions about the Future, Sociology, and the Plan of this Book

Even though the labels used in exhibit 1.1 are arbitrary, the trends displayed have important implications for the future of the United States. What kind of society are we becoming? What should it mean to be American? In the past, opportunity and success have been far more available to white Anglo-Saxon Protestant males than to members of other groups. Most of us, even those who would be favored, would agree that a narrow definition of American is undesirable, but how inclusive should the definition be? Should we stress unity or celebrate diversity? How wide can the limits be stretched before national unity is threatened? How narrow can they be before the desire to preserve cultural and linguistic diversity is unjustly and unnecessarily stifled?

These first few pages have raised a lot of questions. The purpose of this book is to help you develop some answers and some thoughtful, informed positions on these issues. You should be aware from the beginning that the questions addressed here are complex and that the answers we seek are not obvious or easy. Indeed, there is no guarantee that we as a society will be able or willing to resolve all the problems of intergroup relations in the United States. However, we will never make progress in this area unless we confront the issues honestly and with an accurate base of knowledge and understanding. Certainly, these issues will not resolve themselves or disappear if we ignore them.

In the course of our investigation, we will rely on sociology and other social sciences for concepts, theory, and information. The first two chapters of this text introduce and define many of the ideas that will guide our investigation. Part 2 explores how relations between the dominant group and minority groups have evolved in American society. Part 3 analyzes the current situation of U.S. minority groups. In part 4, the final section of the book, we explore many of the challenges and issues facing our society (and the world) and see what conclusions we can glean from our investigations and how they might shape the future.

What Is a Minority Group?

Before we can begin to sort out the issues, we need common definitions and a common vocabulary for discussion. We begin with the term **minority group**. Taken literally, the mathematical connotation of this term is a bit misleading because it implies that minority groups are small. In reality, a minority group can be quite large and can even be a numerical majority of the population. Women, for example, are sometimes considered to be a separate minority group, but they are a numerical majority of the U.S. population. In South Africa, as in many nations created by European colonization, whites are a numerical minority (fewer than 10% of the population), but they have been by far the most powerful and affluent group and, despite recent changes, they retain their advantages in many ways.

Minority status has more to do with the distribution of resources and power than with simple numbers. The definition of minority group used in this book is based on Wagley and Harris (1958). According to this definition, a minority group has five characteristics:

1. The members of the group experience a pattern of *disadvantage or inequality*.

2. The members of the group share a *visible trait or characteristic* that differentiates them from other groups.

3. Minority groups are *self-conscious social units*.

4. Membership in the group is usually *determined at birth*.

5. Members tend to *marry within their own groups*.

We will examine each of the defining characteristics here and, a bit later, we will return to examine the first two—inequality and visibility—in greater detail, because they are the most important characteristics of minority groups.

The first and most important defining characteristic of a minority group is *disadvantage or inequality*—that is, some pattern of disability and disadvantage. The nature of the disability and the degree of disadvantage are variable and can range from exploitation, slavery, and **genocide** to slight irritants such as a lack of desks for left-handed students or a policy of racial or religious exclusion at an expensive country club. (Note, however, that you might not agree that the irritant is slight if you are a left-handed student awkwardly taking notes at a right-handed desk or if you are a golf aficionado who happens to be African American or Jewish American.)

Whatever its scope or severity, whether it extends to wealth, jobs, housing, political power, police protection, or health care, the pattern of disadvantage is the key characteristic of a minority group. Because the group has less of what is valued by society, the term "subordinate group" is sometimes used instead of minority group. The pattern of disadvantage is the result of the actions of another group, often in the distant past, that benefits from and tries to sustain the unequal arrangement. This group can be called the **core group** or the **dominant group**. The latter term is used most frequently in this book because it reflects the patterns of inequality and the power realities of minority group status.

The second defining characteristic of a minority group is some *visible trait or characteristic* that sets members of the group apart and that the dominant group holds in low esteem. The trait can be cultural (language, religion, speech patterns, or dress styles), physical (skin color, stature, or facial features), or both. Groups that are defined primarily by their cultural characteristics are called **ethnic minority groups**. Examples of such groups are Irish Americans and Jewish Americans. Groups defined primarily by their physical characteristics are **racial minority groups**, such as African Americans or American Indians. Note that these categories overlap. So-called ethnic groups may have (or may be thought to have) distinguishing physical characteristics (for example, the stereotypical Irish red hair or Jewish nose), and racial groups commonly have (or are thought to have) cultural traits that differ from the dominant group (for example, differences in dialect, religious values, or cuisine).

These distinguishing traits set boundaries and separate people into distinct groups. The traits are outward signs that identify minority group members and help to maintain the patterns of disadvantage. The dominant group has (or at one time had) sufficient power to create the distinction between groups and thus solidify a higher position for itself. These markers of group membership are crucial. Without these visible signs, it would be difficult or impossible to identify who was in which group, and the system of minority group oppression would soon collapse. (A partial exception to this generalization, the Burakumin of Japan, is considered in chapter 8.)

It is important to realize that the characteristics that mark the boundaries between groups usually are not significant in and of themselves. They are selected for their visibility and convenience, and, objectively, they may be quite trivial and unimportant. For example, scientists have concluded that skin color and other so-called racial traits have little scientific, evolutionary, medical, or biological importance. As we shall see, skin color is an important marker of group membership in our society because it was selected during a complex and lengthy historical process, not because it has any inherent significance. These markers are social constructions that become important because we attribute significance to them.

A third characteristic of minority groups is that they are *self-conscious social units*, aware of their differentiation from the dominant group and of their shared disabilities. This shared social status can provide the basis for strong intragroup bonds and a sense of solidarity, and can lead to views of the world that are quite different from those of the dominant group and other minority groups: minority and dominant groups can live in different cultural worlds. For example, public opinion polls frequently show sizeable differences between dominant and minority groups in their views of the seriousness and extent of discrimination in American society. Exhibit 1.3 shows persistent and sizeable gaps in the percentage of nationally representative samples of whites and blacks who agree that blacks and whites have equal job opportunities. As would be expected, given their different histories, experiences, and locations in the social structure, blacks have much more negative views of racial equality, even though both groups have become somewhat more optimistic over the years. Even after the election of President Barack Obama, the percentage of black Americans who perceived that racial opportunity was equal was about half the corresponding percentage of white Americans.

A fourth characteristic of minority groups is that, in general, membership is an **ascribed status**, or a status that is *determined at birth*. The traits that identify minority group membership are typically not easy to change, and minority group status is usually involuntary and for life.

Finally, minority group members tend to *marry within their own groups*. This pattern can be voluntary, or the dominant group can dictate it. For example, interracial marriages have traditionally been illegal in many states. Laws against **miscegenation** were declared unconstitutional only 40 years ago, in the late 1960s, by the U.S. Supreme Court (Bell, 1992).

This is a lengthy definition, but note how inclusive it is. Although it encompasses "traditional" minority groups such as African Americans and American Indians, it also could be applied to other groups (with perhaps a little stretching). For instance, women arguably fit the first four criteria and can be analyzed with many of the same concepts and ideas that guide the analysis of other minority groups. Also, Americans who are gay, lesbian, and transgendered; Americans who are disabled; Americans who are left-handed; Americans who are aged; and Americans who are very short, very tall, or very obese could fit the definition of minority group without much difficulty. Although we should not be whimsical or capricious about definitions, it is important to note that the analyses developed in this book can be applied

Exhibit 1.3 Percentage of White and Black Americans Who Believe that There Is Equal Opportunity in Their Community, 1963–2009

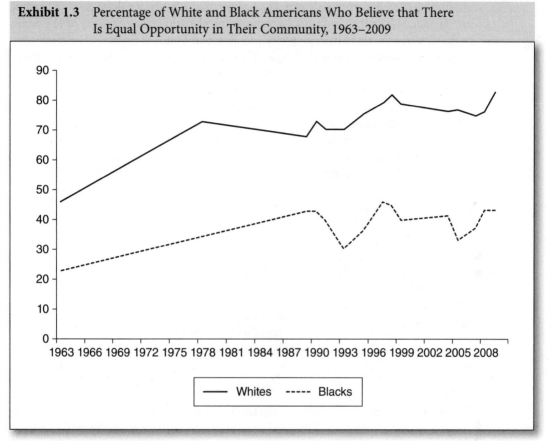

Source: Gallup Organization (2010).

more generally than you might realize at first and so may lead to some fresh insights about a wide variety of groups and people.

Patterns of Inequality

As I mentioned earlier, the most important defining characteristic of minority group status is inequality. As documented in later chapters, minority group membership can affect access to jobs, education, wealth, health care, and housing. It is associated with a lower (often much lower) proportional share of valued goods and services and more limited (often much more limited) opportunities for upward mobility.

Stratification, or the unequal distribution of valued goods and services, is a basic feature of society. Every human society, except perhaps the simplest hunter–gatherer societies, is stratified to some degree; that is, the resources of the society are distributed so that some get more and others get less of whatever is valued. Societies are divided into horizontal layers (or strata), often called **social classes**, that differ from one another by the amount of resources they command. Many criteria (such as education, age, gender, and talent) may affect a person's social class position and his or her access to goods and services. Minority group membership is one of these criteria, and it has a powerful impact on the distribution of resources in the United States and in many other societies.

This section begins with a brief consideration of theories about the nature and important dimensions of stratification. It then focuses on how minority group status relates to stratification. During the discussion, I identify several concepts and themes used throughout this book.

Theoretical Perspectives

Sociology and the other social sciences have been concerned with stratification and human inequality since the formation of the discipline in the 19th century. An early and important contributor to our understanding of the nature and significance of social inequality was Karl Marx, the noted social philosopher and revolutionary. Half a century later, a sociologist named Max Weber, a central figure in the development of sociology, critiqued and elaborated on Marx's view of inequality. Here, we will also consider the views of Gerhard Lenski, a contemporary sociologist whose ideas about the influence of economic and technological development on social stratification have considerable relevance when comparing societies and understanding the evolution of intergroup relations. We close with a consideration of the views of another contemporary sociologist, Patricia Hill-Collins, who argues that we need to view class, racial, gender, and other inequalities as a single, interlocking pattern.

Karl Marx. Although best known as the father of modern Communism, Karl Marx was also the primary architect of a political, economic, and social philosophy that has played a major role in world affairs for more than 150 years. Marxism is a complex theory of history and social change in which inequality is a central concept and concern.

Marx argued that the most important source of inequality in society was the system of economic production. More specifically, he focused on the **means of production**, or the materials, tools, resources, and social relationships by which the society produces and distributes goods and services. In an agricultural society, the means of production include land, draft animals, and plows. In an industrial society, the means of production include factories, commercial enterprises, banks, and transportation systems, such as railroads.

All societies include two main social classes that struggle over the means of production. One class owns or controls the means of production and the other is exploited and oppressed in order to sustain the advantage of the dominant class. In an industrial society, the two classes are the **bourgeoisie**, or the capitalists who own the means of production; and the **proletariat**, or the working class. Marx believed that conflict between these classes was inevitable and that ultimately the working class would successfully revolt against the bourgeoisie and create a utopian society without exploitation, coercion, or inequality: in other words, a classless society.

Marxism has been extensively revised and modified over the past century and a half. Still, modern social science owes a great deal to Marx's views on inequality and his insights on class struggle and social conflict. As you shall see, Marxism remains an important body of work and a rich source of insight into group relations in industrial society.

Max Weber. One of Marx's major critics was Max Weber, a German sociologist who did most of his work around the turn of the 20th century. Weber thought that Marx's view of inequality was too narrow. Marx saw social class as a matter of economic position or relationship to the means of production, but Weber argued that inequality was more complex and included dimensions other than just the economic. Individuals could be members of the elite in some ways but not in others. For example, an aristocratic family that has fallen on hard financial times might belong to the elite in terms of family lineage but not in terms of wealth. To use a more contemporary example, a major figure in the illegal drug trade could enjoy substantial wealth but be held in low esteem otherwise.

Weber expanded on Marx's view of inequality by identifying three separate stratification systems. First, economic inequality is based on ownership or control of property, wealth, and income. This is similar to Marx's concept of class, and in fact Weber used the term "class" to identify this form of inequality.

A second system of stratification revolves around differences in **prestige** between groups, or the amount of honor, esteem, or respect given to us by others. Class position is one factor that affects the amount of prestige enjoyed by a person. Other factors might include family lineage, athletic ability, and physical appearance. In the United States and other societies, prestige is affected by the groups to which people belong, and members of minority groups typically receive less prestige than members of the dominant group. A wealthy minority group member might be ranked high on class or control of property, wealth, and income, but low on status or prestige.

Weber's third stratification system is **power,** or the ability to influence others, have an impact on the decision-making process of society, and pursue and protect one's self-interest and achieve one's goals. One source of power is a person's standing in politically active organizations, such as labor unions or pressure groups, that lobby state and federal legislatures. Some politically active groups have access to great wealth and can use their riches to promote their causes. Other groups may rely more on their size and their ability to mobilize large demonstrations to achieve their goals. Political groups and the people they represent vary in their abilities to affect the political process and control decision making; that is, they vary in the amount of power they can mobilize.

Typically, these three dimensions of stratification go together: wealthy, prestigious groups will be more powerful (more likely to achieve their goals or protect their self-interest) than low-income groups or groups with little prestige. It is important to realize, however, that power is a separate dimension: even very impoverished groups have sometimes found ways to express their concerns and pursue their goals.

Gerhard Lenski. Gerhard Lenski is a contemporary sociologist who follows Weber and distinguishes between class (or property), prestige, and power. Lenski expands on Weber's ideas, however, by analyzing stratification in the context of societal evolution or the **level of development** of a society (Nolan & Lenski, 2004). He argues that the nature of inequality (the degree of inequality or the specific criteria affecting a group's position) is closely related to **subsistence technology**, the means by which the society satisfies basic needs such as hunger and thirst. A preindustrial agricultural society relies on human and animal labor to generate the calories necessary to sustain life. Inequality in this type of society centers on control of land and labor because they are the most important means of production at that level of development.

In a modern industrial society, however, land ownership is not as crucial as control of manufacturing and commercial enterprises. At the industrial level of development, control of capital is more important than control of land, and the nature of inequality will change accordingly.

The United States and other societies have recently entered still another stage of development, often referred to as "postindustrial society." In this type of society, economic growth is powered by developments in new technology, computer-related fields, information processing, and scientific research. In the postindustrial era, economic success will be closely related to specialized knowledge, familiarity with new technologies, and education in general (Chirot, 1994, p. 88; see also Bell, 1973).

These changes in subsistence technology, from agriculture to industrialization to the "information society," alter the stratification system. As the sources of wealth, success, and power change, so do the relationships between minority and dominant groups. For example, the shift to an information-based, "hi-tech," postindustrial society means that the advantages conferred by higher levels of education will be magnified and that groups that have less access to schooling are likely to rank low on all dimensions of stratification.

Patricia Hill-Collins. Sociologist Patricia Hill-Collins calls for a new approach to the study of inequality and group relations. She argues that it is insufficient to examine the dimensions of inequality—class, race, and gender—separately or one at a time. Rather, they need to be seen as interlocked and mutually reinforcing. Traditionally, inequality tends to be viewed by social scientists as a series of dichotomies: elite versus masses, powerful versus powerless, men versus women, blacks versus whites, and so forth. Intersectionality theorists urge us to analyze how these statuses are linked to each other and form a "matrix of domination." For example, white Americans should not be seen as simply the "dominant group," undifferentiated and homogenous. Some segments of this group, such as women or poor whites, may occupy a privileged status in terms of their **race** but be subordinate on other dimensions, as defined by their gender or economic status. In the same way, minority groups are internally differentiated along lines of class and gender and members of some segments are more privileged than others. Who is oppressed and who is oppressor changes across social contexts, and people can occupy both statuses simultaneously.

All groups experience some relative degree of advantage and disadvantage and Hill urges us to focus on how the separate systems of domination and subordination crosscut and overlap each other, how opportunity and individual experience are shaped by the matrix of domination. In this text, one of our main concerns will be to explore how minority group experience is mediated by class and gender, but you should be aware that this approach can be applied to many other dimensions of power and inequality including disability, sexual preference, and religion.

Minority Group Status and Stratification

The theoretical perspectives we have just reviewed raise three important points about the connections between minority group status and stratification. First, as already noted, minority group status affects access to wealth and income, prestige, and power. A society in which minority groups systematically receive less of these valued goods is stratified, at least partly, by race and ethnicity. In the United States, minority group status has been and continues to be one of the most important and powerful determinants of life chances, health and wealth, and success. These patterns of inequality are documented and explored in part 3, but even casual observation of U.S. society will reveal that minority groups control proportionately fewer resources and that minority group status and stratification are intimately and complexly intertwined.

Second, although social classes and minority groups are correlated, they are separate social realities. The degree to which one is dependent on the other varies from group to group. Some groups, such as Irish or Italian Americans, enjoy considerable **social mobility** or easy access to opportunities, even though they faced considerable discrimination in the past. Furthermore, as stressed by the intersectionality approach, degrees of domination and subordination are variable and all groups are subdivided by crosscutting lines of differentiation.

Social class and minority group status are different dimensions of inequality and they can vary independently. Some members of a minority group can be successful economically, wield great political power, or enjoy high prestige even though the vast majority of their group languishes in poverty and powerlessness. Each minority group is internally divided by systems of inequality based on class, status, or power; in the same way, members of the same social class may be separated by ethnic or racial differences.

The third point concerning the connections between stratification and minority groups brings us back to group conflict. Dominant-minority group relationships are created by struggle over the control of valued goods and services. Minority group structures (such as slavery) emerge so that the dominant group can control commodities such as land or labor, maintain its position in the stratification system, or eliminate a perceived threat to its well-being. Struggles over property, wealth, prestige, and power lie at the heart of every dominant-minority relationship. Karl Marx believed that all aspects of society and culture were shaped to benefit the elite or ruling class and sustain the economic system that underlies its privileged position. The treatment of minority groups throughout American history provides a good deal of evidence to support Marx's point.

Visible Distinguishing Traits

In this section, we focus on the second defining characteristic of minority groups: the visible traits that denote membership. The boundaries between dominant and minority groups have been established along a wide variety of lines including religion, language, and occupation. Here we consider race and gender, two of the more physical and permanent—and thus more socially visible—markers of group membership.

Race

In the past, race has been widely misunderstood, but the false ideas and exaggerated importance attached to race have not been mere errors of logic, subject to debate and refutation. At various times and place, they have been associated with some of the greatest tragedies in human history: massive exploitation and mistreatment, slavery, and genocide. Many myths about race survive today, although perhaps in diluted or muted form, and it is important to cultivate accurate understandings (although the scientific knowledge that has accumulated about race is no guarantee that it will not be used to instigate or justify further tragedies in the future).

Thanks to advances in the sciences of genetics, biology, and physical anthropology, we know more about what race is and, more importantly, what race it is not. We cannot address all of the confusion in these few pages, but we can establish a basic framework and use the latest scientific research to dispel some of the myths.

Race and Human Evolution. Our species first appeared in East Africa about 100,000 years ago. Our ancient ancestors were hunters and gatherers who gradually wandered away from their ancestral region in search of food and other resources. Over the millennia, our ancestors traveled across the entire globe, first to what is now the Middle East and then to Asia, Europe, Australia, and North and South America.

Human "racial" differences evolved during this period of dispersion, as our ancestors adapted, physically as well as culturally, to different environments and ecological conditions. For example, consider skin color, the most visible "racial" characteristic. Skin color is derived from a pigment called melanin. In areas with intense sunlight, at or near the equator, melanin screens out the ultraviolet rays of the sun that cause sunburn and, more significantly, protects against skin cancer. Thus, higher levels of melanin and darker skin colors are found in peoples who are adapted to equatorial ecologies.

In peoples adapted to areas with less-intense sunlight, the amount of melanin is lower, and skin color is lighter. The lower concentration of melanin may also be an adaptation to a particular ecology. It maximizes the synthesis of vitamin D, which is important for the absorption of calcium and protection against disorders such as rickets. Thus the skin color (amount of melanin) of any group balances the need for vitamin D against the need to protect against ultraviolet rays.

The map in exhibit 1.4 shows the distribution of skin color for indigenous people. Note the rough correlation with proximity to the equator: peoples with darker skin are generally found within 20 degrees of the equator whereas peoples with lighter skin are found primarily in the northern hemisphere, in locales distant from tropical sunlight.

Exhibit 1.4 The Distribution of Skin Color

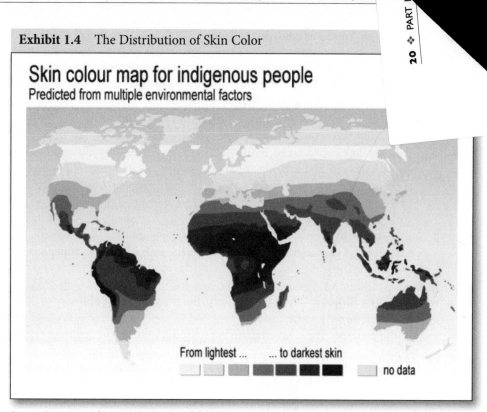

Skin colour map for indigenous people
Predicted from multiple environmental factors

From lightest ...   ... to darkest skin   no data

Source: Bournay and UNEP/GRID-Arendal (2012).

Note also that our oldest ancestors were adapted to the equatorial sun of Africa. This almost certainly means that they were dark skinned (had a high concentration of melanin) and that lighter skin colors are the more recent adaptation.

The period of dispersion and differentiation began to end about 10,000 years ago when some of our hunting and gathering ancestors developed a new subsistence technology and settled down in permanent agricultural villages. Over the centuries, some of these settlements grew into larger societies and kingdoms and empires that conquered and absorbed neighboring societies, some of which differed culturally, linguistically, and racially from each other. The great agricultural empires of the past—Roman, Egyptian, Chinese, Aztec—united different peoples, reversed the process of dispersion and differentiation, and began a phase of consolidation and merging of human cultures and genetics. Over the 10,000 years following the first settlements, human genes were intermixed and spread around the globe, eliminating any "pure" races (if such ever existed).

The differentiation created during the period of global dispersion was swamped by the consolidation that continues in the present. In our society, consolidation manifests itself in the increasing numbers of mixed race folks; similar patterns are common across the globe and throughout more recent human history. The consolidation phase accelerated beginning about 500 years ago with the expansion of European power that resulted in the exploration and conquest of much of the rest of the world.

Race and Western Traditions. The U.S. concept of race has its origins in Western Europe. Race became a matter of concern in the Western European tradition beginning in the 1400s when Europeans, aided by breakthroughs in navigation and ship design, began to travel to Africa, Asia and eventually North and South America. They came into continuous contact with the peoples of these continents and became more aware of and curious about the physical differences they saw.

Europeans also conquered, colonized, and sometimes destroyed the peoples and cultures they encountered. From the beginning, the European awareness of the differences between the races was linked to notions of inferior and superior (conquered versus conquering) peoples. For centuries, the European tradition has been to see race in this political and military context and to intermix biological and physical variation with judgments about the relative merits of the various races. Racist thinking has been used to justify military conquest, genocide, exploitation, and slavery. The especially toxic form of racism that bloomed during the expansion of European power continues to haunt the world today.

Race and Biology. While Europeans generally used race primarily to denigrate, reject, and exclude non-whites, some attempted to apply the principles of scientific research to the concept. These investigations focused on the construction of typologies or taxonomies, systems of classification that were intended to provide a category for every race and every person. Some of these typologies were quite elaborate and included scores of races and subraces. For example, the Caucasian race was often subdivided into Nordics (blond, fair-skinned Northern Europeans), Mediterraneans (dark-haired Southern Europeans), and Alpines (those falling between the first two categories).

One major limitation of these systems of classification was that the dividing lines between the so-called racial groups are arbitrary and blurred. There is no clear or definite point where, for example, "black" skin color stops and "white" skin color begins. The characteristics used to define race blend imperceptibly into each other, and one racial trait (skin color) can be blended with others (e.g., hair texture) in an infinite variety of ways. A given individual might have a skin color that is associated with one race, the hair texture of a second, the nasal shape of a third, and so forth. Even the most elaborate racial typologies could not handle the fact that many individuals fit into more than one category or none at all. Although people undeniably vary in their physical appearance, these differences do not sort themselves out in a way that permits us to divide people up as we do species of animals: the differences between the so-called human races are not at all like the differences between elephants and butterflies. The ambiguous and continuous nature of racial characteristics makes it impossible to establish categories that have clear, nonarbitrary boundaries.

Over the past several decades, rapid advances in genetics have provided additional information and new insights into race that continue to refute many racial myths and further undermine the validity of racial typologies. Perhaps the most important single finding of modern research is that genetic variation *within* the "traditional" racial groups is greater than the variation *between* those groups (American Sociological Association, 2003). In other words, any two randomly selected members of, say, the "black" race are likely to vary genetically from each other at least as much as they do from a randomly selected member of the "white" race. No single finding could be more destructive of traditional racial categories that are, after all, intended to group people into homogenous categories. Just as certainly, the traditional American perception of race based primarily on skin color has no scientific validity.

The Social Construction of Race. Despite its limited scientific uselessness, race continues to animate intergroup relations in the United States and around the world. It continues to be socially important and a significant way of differentiating among people. Race, along with gender, is one of the first things people notice about one another. In the United States, we still tend to see race as a simple, unambiguous matter of skin color alone and to judge everyone as belonging to one and only one group, ignoring the realities of multiple ancestry and ambiguous classification.

How can such an unimportant scientific concept retain its relevance? Because of the way it developed, Western concepts of race have a social as well as a biological or scientific dimension. To sociologists, race is a social construction and its meaning has been created and sustained not by science, but by historical, social, economic, and political processes (see Omi & Winant, 1986; and Smedley, 2007). For example, in chapter 3 we will analyze the role of race in the creation of American slavery and will see that the physical differences between blacks and whites became important *as a result of* the creation of that system of inequality. The elites of colonial society needed to justify their unequal treatment of Africans and seized on the obvious differences in skin color, elevated it to a matter of supreme importance, and used it to justify the enslavement of blacks. In other words, the importance of race was socially constructed as the result of a particular historical conflict. Race remains important not because of objective realities, but because of the widespread, shared social perception that it is important.

Gender

You have already seen that minority groups can be internally divided by social class and other factors. An additional source of differentiation is gender. Like race, gender has both a biological and a social component and can be a highly visible and convenient way of judging and sorting people. From birth, the biological differences between the sexes form the basis for different **gender roles**, or societal expectations about proper behavior, attitudes, and personality traits. Generally, nurturance, interpersonal skills, and "emotion work" tend to be stressed for girls while assertiveness and independence are stressed for boys.

Gender roles and relationships vary across time and from society to society, but gender and inequality have usually been closely related, and men typically claim more property, prestige, and power. Exhibit 1.5 provides some perspective on the variation in gender inequality across the globe. The map shows the distribution of a statistic called the gender development index, which measures the amount of inequality between men and women across a range of variables including education, health, and

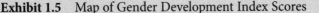

Exhibit 1.5   Map of Gender Development Index Scores

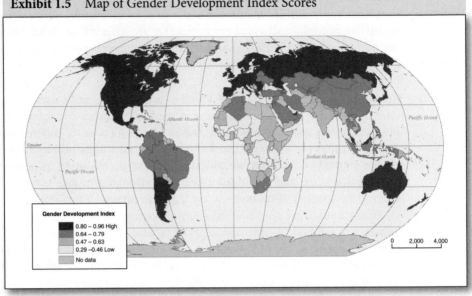

Source: Nationmaster.com (n.d.).

income. As you can see, gender equality is generally highest in the more developed, industrialized nations of North America and Western Europe and lowest in the less developed, more agricultural nations of Sub-Saharan Africa.

Although they rank relatively high on gender equality, the societies of Western Europe and North American have strong traditions of **patriarchy**, or male dominance. In a patriarchal society, men have more control over the economy and more access to leadership roles in religion, politics, and other institutions. In these societies, women possess many characteristics of a minority group (namely, a pattern of disadvantage based on group membership marked by physical stigma). Thus, women could be, and in many ways should be, treated as a separate minority group.

In this text, however, rather than discussing women as a separate group, I will focus on the divergent experiences of men and women within each minority group. This approach will permit us to analyze the ways in which race, ethnicity, gender, and class combine, overlap, and crosscut each other to form a "matrix of domination" (Hill-Collins, 1991, pp. 225–227). We will consider how the interests and experiences of females of different groups and classes coincide with and diverge from each other and from the men in their groups. For example, on some issues African American females might have interests identical to white females and opposed to African American males, and on other issues the constellations of interests might be reversed. As you shall see, the experience of minority group membership varies by gender, and the way gender is experienced is not the same for every group.

History generally has been and is written from the standpoint of the "winners," that is, those in power. The voices of minority groups have generally been repressed, ignored, forgotten, or trivialized. Much of the history of slavery in America, for instance, has been told from the viewpoint of the slave owners. Slaves were kept illiterate by law and had few mechanisms for recording their thoughts or experiences. A more balanced and accurate picture of slavery began to emerge only in the past few decades, when scholars began to dig beneath the written records and memoirs of the slave owners and reconstruct the experiences of African Americans from nonwritten materials such as oral traditions and the physical artifacts left by the slaves.

However, our understanding of the experiences of minority groups is often based almost entirely on the experiences of minority group males alone, and the experiences of minority group females are much less well known and documented. If the voices of minority groups have been hushed, those of female minority group members have been virtually silenced. One of the important trends in contemporary scholarship is to adjust this skewed focus and systematically incorporate gender as a factor in the minority group experience (Baca Zinn & Dill, 1994; Espiritu, 1997).

The Social Construction of Gender. Social scientists see race as a social construction formulated in certain historical circumstances (such as the era of European colonialism) when it was needed to help justify the unequal treatment of non-white groups. What about gender? Is it also merely a social creation designed to rationalize the higher status of men and their easier access to power, prestige, and property? Exhibit 1.5 shows that all contemporary nations have some degree of gender inequality. Is this because—as many people believe—boys and men are "naturally" more aggressive and independent and girls and women are more emotional and expressive? What is the basis of these distinctions? What connection, if any, do they have with biology and genetics?

First, the traits commonly seen as "typical" of men or women—aggressiveness or emotional expressiveness, for example—are not discrete, separate categories. Every person has them to some degree and, to the extent that gender differences exist at all, they are manifested not in absolutes but in averages, tendencies, and probabilities. Aggressiveness is often thought of as a male characteristic, but many women are more aggressive than many men. Likewise, emotionality tends to be associated with women but many males are more expressive and emotional than many females. Second, the fact that gender is a social construction is illustrated by the wide variation is what is thought to be "appropriate" gender behavior from time to time and society to society. The behavior expected of a female in Victorian England would be thoroughly out of place in 21st-century America, and the typical behavior of a contemporary male would be regarded as outrageously scandalous in Puritan America. This variability makes it difficult to argue that the differences between the genders are "hard-wired" in the genetic code: if they were, the variations over time and place would be nonexistent.

Third, the essentially social nature of gender roles is further illustrated by the relationship between subsistence technology and gender inequality. As we noted previously, our species evolved in East Africa and relied on hunting and gathering to satisfy their need for food. Our distant ancestors lived in small, nomadic bands that relied on cooperation and sharing for survival. Societies at this level of development typically divide adult labor roles by gender (with men hunting and women gathering) and, although they may tend toward patriarchy, women and women's work are highly valued and gender inequality is minimal. The subordination of women is more associated with settled agricultural communities, the first of which appeared in what is now the Middle East about 10,000 years ago. Survival in preindustrial farming societies requires the combined efforts of many people thus large families are valued as a cheap labor force. Women are consigned to household and domestic duties, with a strong emphasis on producing and raising children. Since the infant mortality rate in these societies is high (perhaps 50% or more), women spend much of their lives confined and secluded, pregnant or nursing young children, far removed from the possibility of contending for leadership roles in their communities.

Industrialization and urbanization, linked processes that began in the mid-1700s in Great Britain, changed the cost–benefit ratios for child bearing. The expenses associated with having children rise in the city and the nature of industrial work increasingly required education and literacy, qualities and abilities available to both genders. Thus, gender inequality probably reached its peak in preindustrial agrarian societies and has tended to decline as societies industrialized. It is no accident of timing that the push for gender equality and the women's liberation movement is associated with industrial societies and that gender equality is highest today in industrial and postindustrial societies (see exhibit 1.5).

To be sure, biology shapes the production of personality and researchers continue to explore the links between genetics and gender roles (e.g., see Hopcroft, 2009; Huber, 2007; and Udry, 2000) but the key to understanding gender is social and experiential, not biological (Booth, Granger, Mazur, & Kivligham, 2006, pp. 167–191; see also Ridgeway, 2011, pp. 18–23). Gender, like race, is a social construction, especially when the supposed differences between men and women are treated as categorical, "natural," and fixed, and then used to deny opportunity and equality to women.

Key Concepts in Dominant-Minority Relations

Whenever sensitive issues such as dominant-minority group relations are raised, the discussion turns to (or on) matters of prejudice and discrimination. We will be very much concerned with these subjects in this book, so we need to clarify what we mean by these terms. This section introduces and defines four concepts that will help you understand dominant-minority relations in the United States.

This book addresses how individuals from different groups interact, as well as how groups interact with each other. Thus, we need to distinguish between what is true for individuals (the more psychological level of analysis) and what is true for groups or society as a whole (the more sociological level of analysis). Beyond that, we must attempt to trace the connections between the two levels of analysis.

We also need to make a further distinction on both the individual and the group levels. At the individual level, what people think and feel about other groups and how they actually behave toward members of that group may differ. A person might express negative feelings about other groups in private but deal fairly with members of the group in face-to-face interactions. Groups and entire societies may display this same kind of inconsistency. A society may express support for equality in its official documents or formal codes of law and simultaneously treat minority groups in unfair and destructive ways. An example of this kind of inconsistency is the contrast between the commitment to equality stated in the Declaration of Independence ("All men are created equal") and the actual treatment of black slaves, Anglo American women, and American Indians at that time.

At the individual level, social scientists refer to the "thinking/feeling" part of this dichotomy as prejudice and the "doing" part as discrimination. At the group level, the term **ideological racism** describes the "thinking/feeling" dimension and **institutional discrimination** describes the "doing" dimension. Exhibit 1.6 depicts the differences among these four concepts.

Prejudice

Prejudice is the tendency of an individual to think about other groups in negative ways, to attach negative emotions to those groups, and to prejudge individuals on the basis of their group memberships. Individual prejudice has two aspects: **cognitive prejudice**, or the thinking aspect, and **affective prejudice**, or the feeling part. A prejudiced person thinks about other groups in terms of **stereotypes** (cognitive prejudice), generalizations that he or she thinks apply to group members. Examples of familiar stereotypes include notions such as "women are emotional," "Jews are stingy," "blacks are lazy," "the Irish are drunks," and "Germans are authoritarian." A prejudiced person also experiences negative emotional responses to other groups (affective prejudice), including contempt, disgust, arrogance, and hatred. People vary in their levels of prejudice, and levels of prejudice vary in the same person from one time to another and from one group to another. We can say that a person is prejudiced to the extent that he or she uses stereotypes in his or her thinking about other groups or has negative emotional reactions to other groups.

Generally, the two dimensions of prejudice are highly correlated with each other. However, they are also distinct and separate aspects of prejudice and can vary independently. One person may think entirely in stereotypes but feel no particular negative emotional response to any group. Another person may feel a very strong aversion toward a group but be unable to articulate a clear or detailed stereotype of that group.

We should note here that individual prejudice, like all aspects of society, evolves and changes. In the past, American prejudice was strongly felt, baldly expressed, and

Exhibit 1.6 Four Concepts in Dominant-Minority Relations

	Level of Analysis	
Dimension	*Individual*	*Group or Societal*
Thinking/feeling	Prejudice	Ideological racism
Doing	Discrimination	Institutional discrimination

laced with clear, detailed stereotypes. Today, in the modern atmosphere of "political correctness," prejudice tends to be expressed in subtle, indirect ways. For example, it might be manifested in code words, as when people disparage "welfare cheats" or associate criminality with certain minority groups. We will explore the "modern" forms of prejudice further but we need to be clear that the relative absence of blatant stereotyping or expressions of strong public emotions against minority groups in modern society does not mean that we have eliminated individual prejudice in the United States.

Causes of Prejudice

American social scientists of all disciplines have made prejudice a primary concern and have produced literally thousands of articles and books on the topic. They have approached the subject from a variety of theoretical perspectives and have asked a wide array of different questions. One firm conclusion that has emerged is that prejudice is not a single, unitary phenomenon. It has a variety of possible causes (some more psychological and individual, others more sociological and cultural) and can present itself in a variety of forms (some blatant and vicious, others subtle and indirect). No single theory has emerged that can explain prejudice in all its complexity. In keeping with the macrosociological approach of this text, we will focus primarily on the theories that stress the causes of prejudice that are related to culture, social structure, and group relationships.

Competition Between Groups and the Origins of Prejudice. Every form of prejudice—even the most ancient—started at some specific point in history. If we go back far enough in time, we can find a moment that predates anti-black prejudice, anti-Semitism, negative stereotypes about American Indians or Hispanic Americans, or antipathy against Asian Americans. What sorts of conditions create prejudice?

Perhaps the most important single factor in the origin of prejudice is competition between groups: prejudice originates in the heat of that competition and is used to justify and rationalize the privileged status of the winning group. If we go back far enough, we can always find some episode in which one group successfully dominates, takes resources from, or eliminates a threat from some other group. The successful group becomes the dominant group, and the other group becomes the minority group.

Why is group competition associated with the emergence of prejudice? Typically, prejudice is more a result of the competition than a cause. Its role is to help mobilize emotional energy for the contest, justify rejection and attack, and rationalize the structures of domination, like slavery or segregation, which result from the competition. Groups react to the competition and to the threat presented by other groups with antipathy and stereotypes about the "enemy" group. Prejudice emerges from the heat of the contest but then can solidify and persist for years (even centuries) after the end of the conflict.

The relationship between prejudice and competition has been demonstrated in a variety of settings and situations ranging from labor strikes to international war to social psychology labs. In the chapters to come, we will examine the role of prejudice during the creation of slavery in North America, as a reaction to periods of high immigration, and as an accompaniment to myriad forms of group competition. Here, to illustrate our central point about group competition and prejudice, we will examine a classic experiment from the sociological literature. The experiment was conducted in the 1950s at a summer camp for 11- and 12-year-old boys known as Robber's Cave.

The camp director, social psychologist Muzafer Sherif, divided the campers into two groups, the Rattlers and the Eagles (M. Sherif, Harvey, White, Hood, & C. Sherif, 1961). The groups lived in different cabins and were continually pitted against each other in a wide range of activities. Games, sports, and even housekeeping chores were set up on a competitive basis. The boys in each group developed and expressed negative feelings (prejudice) against the other group. Competition and prejudicial feelings grew quite intense and were manifested in episodes of name-calling and raids on the "enemy" group.

Sherif attempted to reduce the harsh feelings he had created by bringing the campers together in various pleasant situations featuring food, movies, and other treats. But the rival groups only used these opportunities to express their enmity. Sherif then came up with some activities that required the members of the rival groups to work cooperatively with each other. For example, the researchers deliberately sabotaged some plumbing to create an emergency that required the efforts of everyone to resolve. As a result of these cooperative activities, intergroup "prejudice" was observed to decline, and, eventually, friendships formed across groups.

In the Robber's Cave experiment, as in many actual group relationships, prejudice (negative feelings and stereotypes about other campers) arose to help mobilize feelings and to justify rejection and attacks, both verbal and physical, against the out-group. When group competition was reduced, the levels of prejudice abated and eventually disappeared, again demonstrating that competition causes prejudice, and not the other way around.

Although the Robber's Cave experiment illustrates our central point, we must be cautious in generalizing from these results. The experiment was conducted in an artificial environment with young boys (all white) who had no previous acquaintance with each other and no history of grievances or animosity. Thus, these results may be only partially generalizable to group conflicts in the "real world." Nonetheless, Robber's Cave illustrates a fundamental connection between group competition and prejudice that we will observe repeatedly in the chapters to come. Competition and the desire to protect resources and status and to defend against threats—perceived as well as real—from other groups are the primary motivations for the construction of traditions of prejudice and structures of inequality that benefit the dominant group.

Culture, Socialization, and the Persistence of Prejudice. Prejudice originates in group competition of some sort but often outlives the conditions of its creation. It can persist, full-blown and intense, long after the episode that sparked its creation has faded from memory. How does prejudice persist through time? How is it passed on to succeeding generations?

In his classic analysis of American race relations, *An American Dilemma* (1944/1962), Swedish economist Gunnar Myrdal proposed the idea that prejudice is perpetuated through time by a self-fulfilling prophecy or a **vicious cycle of prejudice**, as illustrated in exhibit 1.7. The dominant group uses its power to force the minority group into an inferior status, such as slavery, as shown in the diagram in area (1). Partly to motivate the construction of a system of racial stratification and partly to justify its existence, individual prejudice and racist belief systems are invented and accepted by the dominant group, as shown in area (2). Individual prejudices are reinforced by the everyday observation of the inferior status of the minority group. The fact that the minority group is in fact impoverished, enslaved, or otherwise exploited, confirms and strengthens the attribution of inferiority. The belief in inferiority motivates further discrimination and unequal treatment, as shown in area (3) of the diagram, which reinforces the inferior status, which validates the prejudice and racism, which justifies further discrimination, and so on. Over not too many generations, a stable, internally reinforced system of racial inferiority and an elaborate, widespread set of prejudiced beliefs and feelings can become an integral, unremarkable, and (at least for the dominant group) accepted part of everyday life.

Culture is conservative, and, once created, prejudice will be sustained over time just like any set of attitudes, values, and beliefs. Future generations will learn prejudice in the same way and for the same reasons that they learn any other aspect of their culture. Thus, prejudice and racism come to us through our cultural heritage as a package of stereotypes, emotions, and ideas. We learn which groups are "good" and which are "bad" in the same way we learn table manners and religious beliefs (Pettigrew, 1958, 1971, p. 137; Simpson & Yinger, 1985, pp. 107, 108). When prejudice is part of the cultural heritage, individuals learn to think and feel negatively toward other groups as a routine part of socialization. Much of the prejudice expressed by Americans—and the people of many other societies—is the normal result of a typical socialization in families, communities, and societies that are, to some degree, racist. Given our long history of intense racial and ethnic exploitation, it is not surprising that Americans continue to manifest antipathy toward and stereotypical ideas about other groups.

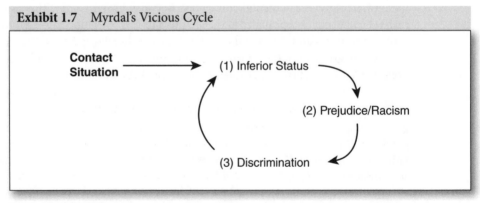

Exhibit 1.7 Myrdal's Vicious Cycle

Source: Myrdal (1962).

The Development of Prejudice in Children. The idea that prejudice is learned during socialization is reinforced by studies of the development of prejudice in children. Research generally shows that children become aware of group differences (e.g., black versus white) at a very early age, perhaps as early as six months (Katz, 2003, p. 898). By age three or younger, they recognize the significance and the permanence of racial groups and can accurately classify people on the basis of skin color and other cues (Brown, 1995, pp. 121–136; Katz, 1976, p. 126). Once the racial or group categories are mentally established, the child begins the process of learning the "proper" attitudes and stereotypes to associate with the various groups; both affective and cognitive prejudice begin to grow at an early age.

It is important to note that children can acquire prejudice even when parents and other caregivers do not teach it overtly or directly. Adults control the socialization process and valuable resources (food, shelter, praise), and children are motivated to seek their approval and conform to their expectations (at least in the early years). There are strong pressures on the child to learn and internalize the perceptions of the older generation, and even a casual comment or an overheard remark can establish or reinforce negative beliefs or feelings about members of other groups (Ashmore & DelBoca, 1976). Children need not be directly instructed about presumed minority group characteristics; it is often said that racial attitudes are "caught and not taught."

Research also shows that children are actively engaged in their learning and that their levels of prejudice reflect their changing intellectual capabilities. Children as young as five to six months old can make some simple distinctions (e.g., by gender or race) between categories of people. The fact that this capability emerges so early in life suggests that it is not simply a response to adult teaching. "Adults use categories to simplify and make sense of their environment; apparently children do the same" (Brown, 1995, p. 126). Gross, simplistic distinctions between people may help very young children organize and understand the world around them. The need for such primitive categorizations may decline as the child becomes more experienced in life and more sophisticated in his or her thinking. Doyle and Aboud (1995), for example, found that prejudice was highest for younger children and actually decreased between kindergarten and the third grade. The decline was related to increased awareness of racial similarities (as well as differences) and diverse perspectives on race (see also Black-Gutman & Hickson, 1996; Bronson & Merryman, 2009; Brown, 1995, pp. 149–159; Cristol & Gimbert, 2008; Powlishta, Serbin, Doyle, & White, 1994; and Van Ausdale & Feagin, 2001). Thus, changing levels of prejudice in children may reflect an interaction between children's changing mental capacities and their environment rather than a simple or straightforward learning of racist cultural beliefs or values.

Social Distance Scales. Further evidence for the cultural nature of prejudice is provided by research on the concept of **social distance**, which is related to prejudice but is not quite the same thing. Social distance is the degree of intimacy that a person is willing to accept in his or her relations with members of other groups. On this scale, the most intimate relationship would be close kinship, and the most distant relationship would be exclusion from the country. The inventor of the social distance scale was Emory Bogardus (1933), who specified a total of seven degrees of social distance:

1. To close kinship by marriage

2. To my club as personal chums

3. To my street as neighbors

4. To employment in my occupation

5. To citizenship in my country

6. As visitors only to my country

7. Would exclude from my country

Research using social distance scales demonstrates that Americans rank other groups in similar ways across time and space. The consistency indicates a common frame of reference or set of perceptions, a continuity of vision possible only if perceptions have been standardized by socialization in a common culture.

Exhibit 1.8 presents some results of seven administrations of the scale to samples of Americans from 1926 to 2001. The groups are listed by the rank order of their scores for 1926. In that year, the sample expressed the least social distance from the English and the most distance from Asian Indians. While the average social distance score for the English was 1.02, indicating virtually no sense of distance, the average score for Indians was 3.91, indicating a distance between "to my street as neighbors" to "to employment in my occupation."

Exhibit 1.8 Rank on Social Distance for Selected Groups, 1926–2001

Group	1926	1946	1956	1966	1977	1993	2001
English	1	3	3	2	2	2	4
American whites	2	1	1	1	1	—	1
Canadians	3	2	2	3	3	—	3
Irish	5	4	5	5	7	1	5
Germans	7	10	8	10	11	10	8
Norwegians	10	7	10	7	12	8	—
Russians	13	13	24	24	29	13	20
Italians	14	16	12	8	5	3	2
Poles	15	14	13	16	18	12	14
American Indians	18	20	18	18	10	16	12
Jews	19	19	16	15	15	15	11
Mexicans	21	24	28	28	26	18	25
Japanese	22	30	26	25	25	19	22

Group	1926	1946	1956	1966	1977	1993	2001
Filipinos	23	23	21	21	24	—	16
African Americans	24	29	27	29	17	17	9
Turks	25	25	23	26	28	22	—
Chinese	26	21	25	22	23	20	17
Koreans	27	27	30	27	30	21	24
Asian Indians	28	28	29	30	27	—	26
Vietnamese	—	—	—	—	—	—	28
Muslims	—	—	—	—	—	—	29
Arabs	—	—	—	—	—	—	30
Mean (all scores)	2.14	2.12	2.08	1.92	1.93	1.43	1.44
Range	2.85	2.57	1.75	1.56	1.38	1.07	0.87
Total number of groups included	28	30	30	30	30	24	30
Correlation with 1926 rankings	—	.95	.93	.90	.84	.92	.76

Source: 1926–1977, T. Smith and Dempsey (1983), p. 588; 1993, Kleg and Yamamoto (1998); Parrillo (2003).

Note: Scores are the group's rank for the year in question. For example, the Irish were ranked fifth of 28 groups in 1926, rose to fourth of 30 in 1946, and so forth. To conserve space, some groups and ranks have been eliminated.

Note, first, the stability in the rankings. The actual *scores* (not shown) generally decrease from decade to decade, indicating less social distance and presumably a decline in prejudice over the years. The *rankings* of the various groups, however, tend to be the same year after year. This stability is clearly displayed in the bottom row of the table, which shows correlations between the group rankings for each year and the 1926 ranking. If any of the lists of scores had been identical, this statistic in this row would have shown its maximum value of 1.00. Although they weaken over time, the actual correlations approach that maximum value and indicate that the rank order of the groups from year to year has been substantially the same. Considering the changes that society has experienced between 1926 and 2001 (the Great Depression; World War II, the Korean War, and other wars; the Cold War with the former Soviet Union; the civil rights movement; the resumption of large-scale immigration, etc.), this overall continuity in group rankings is remarkable.

Second, note the nature of the ranking: groups with origins in Northern and Western Europe are ranked highest, followed by groups from Southern and Eastern Europe, with racial minorities near the bottom. These preferences reflect the relative status of these groups in the U.S. hierarchy of racial and ethnic groups. The rankings also reflect the relative amount of exploitation and prejudice directed at each group over the course of U.S. history.

Although these patterns of social distance scores support the general point that prejudice is cultural, this body of research has some important limitations. The respondents were generally college students from a variety of campuses, not representative samples of the population, and the differences in scores from group to group are sometimes very small. Still, the stability of the patterns cannot be ignored: the top two or three groups are always Northern European, Poles and Jews are always ranked in the middle third of the groups, and Koreans and Japanese always fall in the bottom third. African Americans and American Indians were also ranked toward the bottom until the most recent rankings.

Finally, note how the relative positions of some groups change with international and domestic relations. For example, both Japanese and Germans fell in the rankings at the end of World War II (1946). Comparing 1966 with 1946, Russians fell and Japanese rose, reflecting changing patterns of alliance and enmity in the global system of societies. The dramatic rise of American Indians and African Americans since the 1966 ranking may reflect declining levels of overt prejudice in American society. In 2001, the scale was administered in the weeks following the terrorist attacks on 9/11, and the low ranking of Arabs reflects the societal reaction toward those traumatic events.

How do we explain the fact that group rankings generally remain stable from the 1920s to 2001? The stability strongly suggests that Americans view the various groups through the same culturally shaped lens. A sense of social distance, a perception of some groups as "higher" or "better" than others, is part of the cultural package of intergroup prejudices we acquire from socialization into American society. The social distance patterns illustrate the power of culture to shape individual perceptions and preferences and attest to the deep streak of prejudice and racism built into American culture.

Modern Racism. A large and growing body of research demonstrates that prejudice evolves as group relations and cultural beliefs and information change. The harsh, blatant forms of prejudice that typified U.S. society in its first several centuries have become muted in recent decades, leading some people to conclude that individual prejudice is no longer a significant problem in American life. However, sociological research clearly demonstrates that prejudice has not disappeared. Rather, it has assumed a more subtle and indirect form, consistent with the growing sensitivity of Americans, the success of the civil rights campaign of the 1950s and 1960s and the resultant societal rejection of blatant prejudice, and the growing resources of minority groups and their enhanced ability to protect themselves from attacks.

The new forms of prejudice have been described with a variety of terms including **modern racism, color-blind racism,** and **symbolic racism.** People who are prejudiced in these ways typically reject "old-fashioned" blatant prejudice and the traditional view that racial inferiority is innate or biological. They often proclaim their allegiance to the ideals of equality of opportunity and treatment for all. Analysis of their thinking, however, reveals prejudice lurking just beneath the surface of these egalitarian sentiments, powerfully influencing their views of racial issues.

To illustrate, sociologist Eduardo Bonilla-Silva argues that the new form of prejudice is often expressed in seemingly neutral language or "objective" terms. For example, the modern racist might attribute the underrepresentation of people of color in high-status positions to cultural rather than biological factors ("*they* don't emphasize education enough") or explain continuing residential and school segregation by the "natural" choices people make ("*they* would rather be with their own kind"). This kind of thinking rationalizes the status quo and permits dominant group members to live in segregated neighborhoods and send their children to segregated schools without guilt or hesitation (Bonilla-Silva, 2006, p. 28).

What makes this belief system racist? First, it encourages people to take for granted the realities around them—the legacies of centuries of segregation, racism, and exclusion—much like, in earlier times, Americans were encouraged to accept ideas about innate racial inferiority as an explanation for black slavery or segregation. More importantly, this framework obscures the myriad, not-so-subtle social forces that created segregated schools, neighborhoods, and other manifestations of racial inequality in the first place and maintains them in the present. That is, residential and school segregation are not the results of some abstract and benign tendency of people to seek out others like themselves: these patterns were *created* by the deliberate, conscious actions of real estate boards, school boards, city councils, zoning boards and other local, state, and national institutions. (See Satter, 2009, for an example of how black ghettos in Chicago were created.) The naturalization framework permits people to ignore the social, political, and economic realities that actually create and sustain racial inequality and, by this selective perception, to support a kind of racism without appearing to be a racist. We will return to the subject of modern racism frequently, and especially in chapter 5.

The Sociology of Individual Prejudice. The sociological approach to prejudice used in this text stresses several points. Individual prejudice has its origins in competition between groups but is more a result of that competition than a cause. It is created at a certain time in history to help mobilize feelings and emotional energy for competition and to rationalize the consignment of a group to minority status. It then becomes a part of the cultural heritage and is passed on to later generations as part of their "taken-for-granted" world, where it helps to shape their perceptions and reinforce the very group inferiority that was its original cause. Although it has evolved into a more subtle form, prejudice remains an important force in U.S. society and will continue as long as there are patterns of inequality and systems of group privilege and disadvantage that require justification.

Discrimination

Discrimination is defined as the unequal treatment of a person or persons based on group membership. An example of discrimination is an employer who decides not to hire an individual because he or she is African American (or Puerto Rican, Jewish, Chinese, etc.). If the unequal treatment is based on the group membership of the individual, the act is discriminatory.

Just as the cognitive and affective aspects of prejudice can be independent, discrimination and prejudice do not necessarily occur together. Even highly prejudiced individuals may not act on their negative thoughts or feelings. In social settings regulated by strong egalitarian codes or laws (for example, restaurants and other public facilities), people who are highly bigoted in their private thoughts and feelings may abide by the codes in their public roles.

On the other hand, social situations in which prejudice is strongly approved and supported might evoke discrimination in otherwise unprejudiced individuals. In the Southern United States during the height of segregation or in South Africa during the period of state-sanctioned racial inequality, it was usual and customary for whites to treat blacks in discriminatory ways. Regardless of a person's actual level of prejudice, he or she faced strong social pressure to conform to the official patterns of racial superiority and participate in acts of discrimination.

Ideological Racism

Ideological racism, a belief system that asserts that a particular group is inferior, is the group or societal equivalent of individual prejudice. These ideas and beliefs are used to legitimize or rationalize the inferior status of minority groups and are incorporated into the culture of a society and passed on from generation to generation during socialization.

Because it is a part of the cultural heritage, ideological racism exists apart from the individuals who inhabit the society at a specific time (Andersen, 1993, p. 75; See & Wilson, 1988, p. 227). An example of a racist ideology is the elaborate system of beliefs and ideas that attempted to justify slavery in the American South. The exploitation of slaves was "explained" in terms of the innate racial inferiority of blacks and the superiority of whites.

Distinguishing between individual prejudice and societal racist ideologies naturally leads to a consideration of the relationship between these two phenomena. We will explore this relationship in later chapters, but for now I can make what is probably an obvious point: people socialized into societies with strong racist ideologies are very likely to absorb racist ideas and be highly prejudiced. It should not surprise us that a high level of personal prejudice existed among whites in the antebellum American South or in other highly racist societies, such as in South Africa. At the same time, we need to remember that ideological racism and individual prejudice are different phenomena with different causes and different locations in the society. Racism is not a prerequisite for prejudice; prejudice may exist even in the absence of an ideology of racism.

Institutional Discrimination

The final concept is the societal equivalent of individual discrimination. Institutional discrimination refers to a pattern of unequal treatment based on group membership that is built into the daily operations of society, whether or not it is consciously intended. The public schools, the criminal justice system, and political and economic institutions can operate in ways that put members of some groups at a disadvantage.

Institutional discrimination can be obvious and overt. For many years following the Civil War, African Americans in the American South were prevented from voting by practices such as poll taxes and rigged literacy tests. For nearly a century, well into the 1960s, elections and elected offices in the South were confined to whites only. The purpose of this blatant pattern of institutional discrimination was widely understood by African American and white Southerners alike: it existed to disenfranchise the African American community and keep it politically powerless.

At other times, institutional discrimination may operate more subtly and without conscious intent. If public schools use aptitude tests that are biased in favor of the dominant group, decisions about who does and who does not take college preparatory courses may be made on racist grounds, even if everyone involved sincerely believes that they are merely applying objective criteria in a rational way. If a decision-making process has unequal consequences for dominant and minority groups, institutional discrimination may well be at work.

Note that although a particular discriminatory policy may be implemented and enforced by individuals, the policy is more appropriately thought of as an aspect of the operation of the institution as a whole. Election officials in the South during segregation did not and public school administrators today do not have to be personally prejudiced themselves to implement these discriminatory policies.

However, a major thesis of this book is that both racist ideologies and institutional discrimination are created to sustain the positions of dominant and minority groups in the stratification system. The relative advantage of the dominant group is maintained from day to day by widespread institutional discrimination. Members of the dominant group who are socialized into communities with strong racist ideologies and a great deal of institutional discrimination are likely to be personally prejudiced and to routinely practice acts of individual discrimination. The respective positions of dominant and minority groups are preserved over time through the mutually reinforcing patterns of prejudice, **racism**, and discrimination on both the individual and the institutional levels. Institutional discrimination is but one way in which members of a minority group can be denied access to valued goods and services, opportunities, and rights (such as voting). That is, institutional discrimination helps to sustain and reinforce the unequal positions of racial and ethnic groups in the stratification system.

A Global Perspective

In the chapters that follow, we will focus on developing a number of concepts and theories and applying those ideas to the minority groups of the United States. However, it is important to expand our perspective beyond the experiences of just a single nation. Just as you would not accept an interview with a single person as an adequate test of a psychological theory, you should not accept the experiences of a single nation as proof for the sociological perspective developed in this text. Thus, we will take time, throughout this text, to apply our ideas to other societies and non-American minority groups. If the ideas and concepts developed in this text can help us make sense of these situations, we will have some assurance that they have some general applicability and that the dynamics of intergroup relations in the United States are not unique.

On another level, we must also take account of the ways in which group relations in the United States are shaped by economic, social, and political forces beyond our borders. As we will see, the experiences of this society cannot be understood in isolation. We are part of the global system of societies and now, more than ever, we must systematically take account of the complex interconnections between the domestic and the international, particularly with respect to issues related to immigration. The world is indeed growing smaller and we must see our society as one part of a larger system. I explore one connection between the global and the local in the "Focus on Contemporary Issues" box.

FOCUS ON CONTEMPORARY ISSUES:
Immigration and Globalization

Immigration is a major concern in our society today and we will address the issue on a number of occasions in the pages to come. Here, we will point out that immigration is a global phenomenon that affects virtually every nation in the world. About 214 million people—a little more than 3% of the world's population—live outside their countries of birth and the number of migrants has increased steadily over the past several decades (United Nations, 2012).

What has caused this massive population movement? People leave their homelands for many reasons, but one very important underlying cause is globalization, or the increasing interconnectedness of people, groups, organizations, and nations. This process is complex and multidimensional and includes communication (e.g., the Internet), easier and faster travel, and the spread of a common culture that makes international icons of everything from Disney movie characters to rock stars to Big Macs. Perhaps the most powerful dimension of globalization—especially for understanding contemporary immigration—is economic, and the movement of jobs and opportunity from place to place. People flow from areas of lower opportunity to areas with greater opportunity, much as air flows between high- to low-pressure systems.

To illustrate, consider the southern border of the United States. For the past several decades, there has been an influx of people from Mexico as well as from Central American nations to the United States. The presence of these newcomers has generated a great deal of emotional and political heat, especially since much of this migration is illegal. For many Americans, especially those living in the border states and most especially for those living in Arizona, there is no more intensely felt or important issue than undocumented immigration.

Some Americans see these newcomers as threats to Anglo culture and the English language, and others associate them with crime, violence, and drug smuggling. Still others see them as simply people trying to survive as best they can, desperate to support themselves and their families. Few, however, see these immigrants as the human consequences of the economic globalization of the world.

What is the connection between globalization and this immigrant stream? The population pressure on the southern border is in large part a result of the North American Free Trade Agreement (NAFTA), implemented in 1994. NAFTA united the three North American nations into a single trading bloc—economically "globalizing" the region—and permitted goods and capital (but not people) to move freely between Canada, the United States, and Mexico. Among many other consequences, NAFTA opened Mexico to the importation of food products produced at very low cost by the agribusinesses of Canada and the United States. This cheap food (corn in particular) destroyed the livelihoods of many rural Mexicans and forced them to leave their villages in search of work. Millions pursued the only survival strategy that seemed even remotely sensible: migration to the North. Even the meanest job in the United States can pay many times more than the average Mexican wage. Of course, the grimmest calculation for many is simply this: even a very-low-wage job in the United States is infinitely better than no wage at all.

NAFTA changed the economic landscape of North America and created enormous pressure to move from Mexico to *el Norte*. At the same time, the United States became increasingly concerned with the security of its borders (especially after the terrorist attacks of 9/11) and attempted to stem the flow of people, partly by building fences and increasing the size of the Border Patrol. The easier border crossings were quickly sealed but this did not stop the pressure from the south. Migrants moved to more difficult and dangerous crossing routes, including the deadly, forbidding Sonoran Desert in southern Arizona, resulting in an untold number of deaths on the border since the mid-1990s.

Exhibit 1.9 displays one count of deaths in southern Arizona for a 5-year period: each of the 650 red dots represents a migrant death. These are only the bodies that were discovered: some estimates are that there have been 10 deaths for every recovered corpse. The map shows only a segment of the southern border for a few years. A wider and longer view suggests that there have been thousands of deaths along the border between the mid-1990s and the present.

The relationship between NAFTA and immigration to the United States is just one aspect of a complex, global relationship. Around the globe, people are moving in huge numbers from less-developed nations to more-developed, affluent economies. The wealthy nations of Western Europe, including Germany, Ireland, France, and the Netherlands, are also receiving large numbers of immigrants and the citizens of these

(Continued)

(Continued)

Exhibit 1.9   Deaths in the Desert, 2000–2004

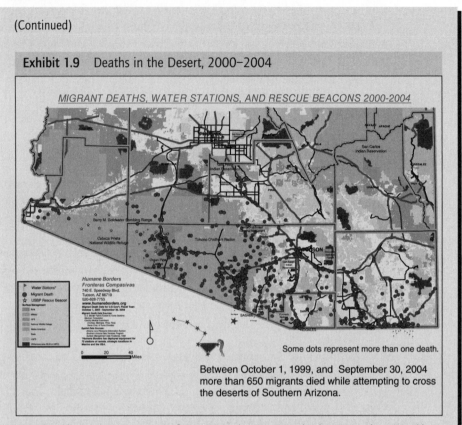

MIGRANT DEATHS, WATER STATIONS, AND RESCUE BEACONS 2000-2004

Some dots represent more than one death.

Between October 1, 1999, and September 30, 2004 more than 650 migrants died while attempting to cross the deserts of Southern Arizona.

Source: Death Maps appear courtesy of Humane Borders, Inc. Data development and cartographic design by John F. Chamblee, Michael Malone, and Matthew Reynolds.

nations are concerned about their jobs and communities, housing, language, and the integrity of the national culture in much the same ways as Americans. The world is changing and contemporary immigration must be understood in terms of changes that affect many nations and, indeed, the entire global system of societies.

Conclusion

This chapter raises a lot of questions. Let me assure you that this text will not answer them, at least not in any permanent or final sense. However, by applying the sociological perspective and the concepts, theories, and body of research developed over the years, we can illuminate and clarify the issues and, in many cases, identify some approaches and ideas that are simply wrong and others that hold promise. Sociology can't answer all questions, but it does supply research tools and ideas that can help us think more clearly and with greater depth and nuance about the issues that face our society.

Notes

1. Schwartzbaum, S. E., & Thomas, A. J. (2008). *Dimensions of multicultural counseling*. Thousand Oaks, CA: SAGE Publications, p. 92.

2. O'Brien, E. (2008). *The racial middle: Latinos and Asian Americans living beyond the racial divide*. New York: New York University Press, p. 45.

3. Personal communication, June 2009.

4. Boldface terms in the text are defined in the glossary at the end of the book.

Main Points

- The United States faces enormous problems in dominant-minority relationships. Although many historic grievances of minority groups remain unresolved, our society is becoming increasingly diverse.
- The United States is a nation of immigrants, and many different groups and cultures are represented in its population.
- A minority group has five defining characteristics: a pattern of disadvantage, identification by some visible trait, awareness of its minority status, a membership determined at birth, and a tendency to marry within the group.
- A stratification system has three different dimensions (class, prestige, and power), and the nature of inequality in a society varies by its level of development. Minority groups and social class are correlated in numerous and complex ways.
- Race is a criterion widely used to identify minority group members. As a biological concept, race has been largely abandoned, but as a social category, race maintains a powerful influence on the way we think about one another.
- Minority groups are internally differentiated by social class, age, region of residence, and many other variables. In this book, I focus on gender as a source of variation within minority groups.
- Four crucial concepts for analyzing dominant-minority relations are prejudice, discrimination, ideological racism, and institutional discrimination.

Study Site on the Web

Don't forget the interactive quizzes and other resources and learning aids at www.sagepub.com/healeyds4e.

For Further Reading

Allport, G. (1954). *The nature of prejudice*. Reading, MA: Addison-Wesley.

A classic work on individual prejudice.

Baca Zinn, M., & Dill, B. T. (1994). *Women of color in U.S. society*. Philadelphia: Temple University Press.

A wide-ranging collection of articles examining the intersecting forces of race, class, and gender in the United States.

Feagin, J. (2001). *Racist America.* New York: Routledge.

A passionate analysis of the pervasiveness of racism and antiblack prejudice in America.

Omi, M., & Winant, H. (1986). *Racial formation in the United States from the 1960s to the 1980s.* New York: Routledge and Kegan Paul.

An adept analysis of the social and political uses of race.

Smedley, A. (1999). Race in North American: Origin and evolution of a worldview. Boulder, CO: Westview Press.

An analysis of the origins of the American view of race.

Takaki, R. (1993). *A different mirror: A History of multicultural America.* Boston: Little, Brown.

A highly readable look at minority groups and cultural diversity in American life.

New York Times. (2001). *How race is lived in America.* New York: Times Books.

An in-depth look at the continuing importance of race in American life conducted by correspondents of the New York Times. *Based on the Pulitzer-Prize winning television documentary.*

Questions for Review and Study

1. What kind of society should the United States strive to become? In your view, does the increasing diversity of American society represent a threat or an opportunity? Should we acknowledge and celebrate our differences, or should we strive for more unity and conformity? What possible dangers and opportunities are inherent in increasing diversity? What are the advantages and disadvantages of stressing unity and conformity?

2. What groups should be considered "minorities"? Using each of the five criteria included in the definition presented in this chapter, should Americans who are gay and lesbian be considered a minority group? How about people who are left-handed or people who are very overweight? Explain and justify your answers.

3. What is a social construction? How do race and gender differ in this regard? What does it mean to say, "Gender becomes a social construction—like race—when it is treated as an unchanging, fixed difference and then used to deny opportunity and equality to women"?

4. Define and explain each of the terms in exhibit 1.6. Cite an example of each from your own experiences. How does "ideological racism" differ from prejudice? Which concept is more sociological? Why? How does institutional discrimination differ from discrimination? Which concept is more sociological? Why?

Internet Research Project

In this chapter we discussed race—arguably the most consequential concept in the history of this nation (and the globe). To extend the discussion, we can utilize some readily available resources on the Internet. One very useful website was created to accompany a PBS-sponsored (2003) documentary on race entitled, "The Power of an Illusion." The series is well worth viewing on its own and the website includes a vast array of richly detailed insights on the phenomenon of race.

The single major point of the website (as in this text) is that race is a social construction, a cultural and political perception invented during particular historical eras, largely to justify and rationalize the differential treatment of others. Once established and passed from generation to generation, race becomes hugely consequential in the lives of all U.S. citizens—it becomes its own reality, shaping and controlling peoples' lives.

The website has six subsections and you are encouraged to explore them all. As you do, look for answers to each of the questions below and use this information (and others) to discuss the concept of race with others.

1. In what ways should race be considered a "modern" idea?

2. In what ways is race NOT a biological concept?

3. How have ideas about race evolved and changed since ancient times?

4. What are some U.S. examples of how public policy has treated people differently based on race? What are some of the consequences?

5. How have definitions of black and white changed over the years? How has U.S. Census Bureau definitions of race changed? Why?

6. Try the "Sorting People" exercise and record your number of "correct" classifications here: ____. What does this exercise make you think about race as a concept? Can you accurately tell someone's race by looking at them? If not, what does this say about the concept of race?

7. Take the quiz under the "Human Diversity" tab and record the number of correct answers here: ____. Was your information accurate? Where did you get this information?

8. Click on the "Explore Diversity" button under "Human Diversity" and explore the activities. Does this information support the idea that "race isn't biological?" How?

Optional Group Discussion

Select three of the questions above to discuss with classmates. (*Your instructor may have more-specific or different instructions.*) Add your own topic if you wish. Bring your information and reactions from the website and the text to class and be prepared to discuss the issues with your classmates. To aid the discussion, develop a concise statement or summary of what you learned by visiting the website and what you think was most important about the experience.

2

Assimilation and Pluralism: From Immigrants to White Ethnics

The shaman is in the living room . . . He uses his . . . powers to help people who are physically or emotionally sick . . . and must communicate directly with the spirit world in order to diagnose ills and determine how to cure them.

The shaman . . . faces an altar [and wears] a black veil that separates him from the material world. He is straddling a bench, riding it as though it were a horse, his whole body shaking as he sits aside his spiritual "charger." His body is present but he is really off in the other world, galloping to find a spirit . . . who will tell him why Ghia's stepfather is sick and what must be done to cure him. . . .

Three feet away from the shaman the television set is playing an old rerun of a Flintstones cartoon. Five little children sit pressed against each other in front of the set, giggling at every "Yabba, dabba, doo."

(Faderman, 1998, pp. 102–104)

The Hmong are one of the newest immigrant groups to the United States. Refugees from the wars in Southeast Asia, they face more-severe challenge than most immigrants. The older Hmong grew up in remote farming villages with almost no contact with the wider world. They knew nothing of the technologies that Americans take for granted (flush toilets, radios, aspirin); coming to the United States took them across centuries as well as miles. The passage above focuses on one of the innumerable cultural tensions they face daily: the contrast between a world in which illness is caused by spirits and one in which animated cartoons are completely unremarkable. How do groups like these adjust to American culture? How do they retain connections with their traditions and history? Can they preserve a part of who they are in the face of assimilation?

This chapter continues to look at the ways in which ethnic and racial groups in the United States relate to each other. Two concepts, assimilation and pluralism, are at the core of the discussion. Each includes a variety of possible group relations and pathways along which group relations might develop.

Assimilation is a process in which formerly distinct and separate groups come to share a common culture and merge together socially. As a society undergoes assimilation, differences among groups decrease. **Pluralism**, on the other hand, exists when groups maintain their individual identities. In a pluralistic society, groups remain separate, and their cultural and social differences persist over time.

In some ways, assimilation and pluralism are contrary processes, but they are not mutually exclusive. They may occur together in a variety of combinations within a particular society or group. Some groups in a society may be assimilating as others are maintaining (or even increasing) their differences. As we shall see in part 3, virtually every minority group in the United States has, at any given time, some members who are assimilating and others who are preserving or reviving traditional cultures. Some American Indians, for example, are pluralistic. They live on or near reservations, are strongly connected to their heritage, practice the old ways as much as they can, and speak their traditional language. Other American Indians are very much assimilated into the dominant society: they live in urban areas, speak English only, and know relatively little about their traditional cultures. Both assimilation and pluralism are important forces in the everyday lives of American Indians and most other minority groups.

Over the past century, American sociologists have been very concerned with these processes, especially assimilation. This concern was stimulated by the massive population movement from Europe to the United States that occurred between the 1820s and the 1920s. More than 31 million people crossed the Atlantic during this time, and a great deal of energy has been devoted to documenting, describing, and understanding the experiences of these immigrants and their descendants. These efforts have resulted in the development of a rich and complex literature that I will refer to as the "traditional" perspective on how newcomers are incorporated into U.S. society.

This chapter begins with a consideration of the traditional perspective on both assimilation and pluralism and a brief examination of several other possible group relationships. The concepts and theories of the traditional perspective are then applied to European immigrants and their descendants, and we develop a model of American assimilation based on these experiences. This model will be used in our analysis of other minority groups throughout the text and especially in part 3.

A particularly important issue is whether the theories, concepts, and models based on the first mass immigration to the United States (from the 1820s to the 1920s) apply to the second (post-1965) mass immigration. The newest arrivals differ in many ways from those who came earlier, and ideas and theories based on the earlier experiences will not necessarily apply to the present. We will briefly note some of the issues in this chapter and explore them in more detail in the case study chapters in part 3.

Finally, at the end of this chapter, I briefly consider the implications of these first two chapters for the exploration of intergroup relations. By the end of this chapter, you will be familiar with many of the concepts that will guide us throughout this text as we examine the variety of possible dominant-minority group situations and the directions our society (and the groups within it) can take.

Assimilation

We begin with assimilation because the emphasis in U.S. group relations has historically been on this goal rather than on pluralism. This section presents some of the most important sociological theories and concepts that have been used to describe and analyze the assimilation of the 19th-century immigrants from Europe.

Types of Assimilation

Assimilation is a general term for a process that can follow a number of different pathways. One form of assimilation is expressed in the metaphor of the **melting pot**, a process in which different groups come together and contribute in roughly equal amounts to create a common culture and a new, unique society. People often think of the American experience of assimilation in terms of the melting pot. This view stresses the ways in which diverse peoples helped to construct U.S. society and made contributions to American culture. The melting-pot metaphor sees assimilation as benign and egalitarian, a process that emphasizes sharing and inclusion.

Although it is a powerful image in our society, the melting pot is not an accurate description of how assimilation actually proceeded for American minority groups (Abrahamson, 1980, pp. 152–154). Some groups—especially the racial minority groups—have been largely excluded from the "melting" process. Furthermore, the melting-pot brew has had a distinctly Anglocentric flavor: "For better or worse, the white Anglo-Saxon Protestant tradition was for two centuries—and in crucial respects still is—the dominant influence on American culture and society" (Schlesinger, 1992, p. 28).

Contrary to the melting-pot image, assimilation in the United States generally has been a largely one-sided process better described by the terms **Americanization** or **Anglo-conformity**. Rather than an equal sharing of elements and a gradual blending of diverse peoples, assimilation in the United States was designed to maintain the predominance of the English language and the British-type institutional patterns created during the early years of American society.

This stress on Americanization continues today, as reflected in recent public opinion polls. For example, in one recent survey 77% of respondents—the overwhelming majority—agreed that "the United States should require immigrants to be proficient in English as a condition of remaining in the United States." Interestingly, about 60% of Hispanic Americans (versus 80% of non-Hispanic whites and 76% of blacks) also agreed with this statement (Carroll, 2007). We should note that the apparent agreement between Hispanic and white Americans for learning English may come from very different thought processes. The white responses may mix prejudice and rejection with the support for Americanization whereas the Hispanic responses may be based on direct experiences with the difficulties of negotiating the monolingual institutions of American society.

Under Anglo-conformity, immigrant and minority groups are expected to adapt to Anglo American culture as a precondition for acceptance and access to better jobs, education, and other opportunities. Assimilation has meant that minority groups have had to give up their traditions and adopt Anglo American culture. To be sure, many groups and individuals were (and continue to be) eager to undergo Anglo-conformity, even if it meant losing much or all of their heritage. For other groups, Americanization created conflict, anxiety, demoralization, and resentment. We assess these varied reactions in our examination of America's minority groups in part 3.

The "Traditional" Perspective on Assimilation: Theories and Concepts

American sociologists developed a rich body of thought based on their studies of the immigrants who came from Europe between the 1820s and 1920s, and we shall refer to this body of work as the traditional perspective on assimilation. As you will see, the scholars working in this tradition have made invaluable contributions, and their thinking is impressively complex and comprehensive. This does not mean, of course, that they have exhausted the possibilities or answered (or asked) all the questions. Theorists working in the pluralist tradition and contemporary scholars studying the experiences of more recent immigrants have questioned many aspects of traditional assimilation theory and have made a number of important contributions of their own.

Robert Park. Many theories of assimilation are grounded in the work of Robert Park. He was one of a group of scholars who had a major hand in establishing sociology as a discipline in the United States in the 1920s and 1930s.

Park believed that intergroup relations go through a predictable set of phases that he called a **race relations cycle**. When groups first come into contact (through immigration, conquest, etc.), relations are conflictual and competitive. Eventually, however, the process, or cycle, moves toward assimilation, or the "interpenetration and fusion" of groups (Park & Burgess, 1924, p. 735).

Park argued that assimilation is inevitable in a democratic and industrial society. In a political system based on democracy, fairness, and impartial justice, all groups will eventually secure equal treatment under the law. In an industrial economy, people tend to be judged on rational grounds—that is, on the basis of their abilities and talents—and not by ethnicity or race. Park believed that as American society continued to modernize, urbanize, and industrialize, ethnic and racial groups would gradually lose their importance. The boundaries between groups would eventually dissolve, and a more "rational" and unified society would emerge (see also Geschwender, 1978, pp. 19–32; and Hirschman, 1983).

Social scientists have examined, analyzed, and criticized Park's conclusions for decades. One frequently voiced criticism is that he did not specify a time frame for the completion of assimilation, and therefore his idea that assimilation is "inevitable" cannot be tested. Until the exact point in time when assimilation is deemed complete, we will not know whether the theory is wrong or whether we just have not waited long enough.

An additional criticism of Park's theory is that he does not describe the nature of the assimilation process in much detail. How would assimilation proceed? How would everyday life change? Which aspects of the group would change first?

Milton Gordon. To clarify some of the issues left unresolved by Park, we turn to the works of sociologist Milton Gordon, who made a major contribution to theories of assimilation in his book *Assimilation in American Life* (1964). Gordon broke down the overall process of assimilation into seven subprocesses; we will focus on the first three. Before considering these phases of assimilation, we need to consider some new concepts and terms.

Gordon makes a distinction between the cultural and the structural components of society. **Culture** encompasses all aspects of the way of life associated with a group of people. It includes language, religious beliefs, customs and rules of etiquette, and the values and ideas people use to organize their lives and interpret their existence. The **social structure**, or structural components of a society, includes networks of social relationships, groups, organizations, stratification systems, communities, and families. The social structure organizes the work of the society and connects individuals to one another and to the larger society.

It is common in sociology to separate the social structure into primary and secondary sectors. The **primary sector** includes interpersonal relationships that are intimate and personal, such as families and groups of friends. Groups in the primary sector are small. The **secondary sector** consists of groups and organizations that are more public, task oriented, and impersonal. Organizations in the secondary sector often are very large and include businesses, factories, schools and colleges, and bureaucracies.

Now we can examine Gordon's earliest stages of assimilation, which are summarized in exhibit 2.1.

Exhibit 2.1 Gordon's Stages of Assimilation

Stage	Process
1. Acculturation	The group learns the culture of the dominant group, including language and values.
2. Integration (structural assimilation)	
a. At the secondary level	Members of the group enter the public institutions and organizations of the dominant society.
b. At the primary level	Members of the group enter the cliques, clubs, and friendship groups of the dominant society.
3. Intermarriage (marital assimilation)	Members of the group marry with members of the dominant society on a large scale.

Source: Adapted from Gordon (1964, p. 71).

1. **Cultural Assimilation, or Acculturation**. Members of the minority group learn the culture of the dominant group. **Acculturation** to the dominant Anglo American culture may include changes both great and small, including learning the English language, changing eating habits, adopting new value systems, and altering the spelling of the family surname.

2. **Structural Assimilation, or Integration**. The minority group enters the social structure of the larger society. Integration typically begins in the secondary sector and gradually moves into the primary sector. That is, before people can form friendships with members of other groups (integration into the primary sector), they must first become acquaintances. The initial contact between groups often occurs in public institutions such as schools and workplaces (integration into the secondary sector). The greater their integration into the secondary sector, the more nearly equal the minority group will be to the dominant group in income, education, and occupational prestige. Once a group has entered the institutions and public sectors of the larger society, according to Gordon, integration into the primary sector and the other stages of assimilation will follow inevitably (although not necessarily quickly). Measures of integration into the primary sector include the extent to which people have acquaintances, close friends, or neighbors from other groups.

3. **Marital Assimilation, or Intermarriage**. When integration into the primary sector becomes substantial, the basis for Gordon's third stage of assimilation is established. People are most likely to select spouses from among their primary relations, and thus, in Gordon's view, primary structural integration typically precedes intermarriage.

Gordon argued that acculturation was a prerequisite for integration. Given the stress on Anglo-conformity, a member of an immigrant or minority group would not be able to compete for jobs or other opportunities in the secondary sector of the social structure until he or she had learned the dominant group's culture. Gordon recognized, however, that successful acculturation does not automatically ensure that a group will begin the integration phase. The dominant group may still exclude the minority group from its institutions and limit the opportunities available to the group. Gordon argued that "acculturation without integration" (or Americanization without equality) is a common situation in the United States for many minority groups, especially racial minority groups.

In Gordon's theory, movement from acculturation to integration is the crucial step in the assimilation process. Once that step is taken, all the other subprocesses will occur inevitably, although movement through the stages can be very slow. Gordon's idea that assimilation runs a certain course in a certain order echoes Park's conclusion regarding the inevitability of the process.

Over the decades since Gordon published his analysis, some of his conclusions about American assimilation have been called into question. For example, the individual subprocesses of assimilation that Gordon saw as linked in a certain order are often found to occur independently of one another (Yinger, 1985, p. 154). A group may integrate before acculturating or combine the subprocesses in other ways. Also, many researchers no longer think of the process of assimilation as necessarily linear or one-way (Greeley, 1974). Groups (or segments thereof) may "reverse direction" and become less assimilated over time, revive their traditional cultures, relearn their old language, or revitalize ethnic organizations or associations.

Nonetheless, Gordon's overall model continues to guide our understanding of the process of assimilation, to the point that a large part of the research agenda for contemporary studies of immigrants involves assessment of the extent to which their experiences can be described in Gordon's terms (Alba & Nee, 1997). In fact, Gordon's model will provide a major organizational framework for the case study chapters presented in part 3 of this text.

Human Capital Theory. Why did some European immigrant groups acculturate and integrate more rapidly than others? Although not a theory of assimilation per se, **human capital theory** offers one possible answer to this question. This theory argues that status attainment, or the level of success achieved by an individual in society, is a direct result of educational levels, personal values and skills, and other individual characteristics and abilities. Education is seen as an investment in human capital, not unlike the investment a business might make in machinery or new technology. The greater the investment in a person's human capital, the higher the probability of success. Blau and Duncan (1967), in their pioneering statement of status attainment theory, found that even the relative advantage conferred by having high-status parents is largely mediated through education. In other words, high levels of affluence and occupational prestige are not so much a result of being born into a privileged status as they are the result of the superior education that affluence makes possible.

Human capital theory answers questions about immigrant group mobility in terms of the resources and cultural characteristics of the members of the groups, especially their levels of education and familiarity with English. Success is seen as a direct result of individual effort and the wise investment of personal resources. People or groups who fail have not tried hard enough, have not made the right kinds of educational investments, or have values or habits that limit their ability to compete.

More than most sociological theories, human capital theory is quite consistent with traditional American culture and values. Both tend to see success as an individual phenomenon, a reward for hard work, sustained effort, and good character. Both tend to assume that success is equally available to all and that the larger society is open and neutral in its distribution of rewards and opportunity. Both tend to see assimilation as a highly desirable, benign process that blends diverse peoples and cultures into a strong, unified whole. Thus, people or groups that resist Americanization or question its benefits are seen as threatening or illegitimate.

On one level, human capital theory is an important theory of success and upward mobility, and we will on occasion use the theory to analyze the experiences of minority and immigrant groups. On another level, the theory is so resonant with American "commonsensical" views of success and failure that we may tend to use it uncritically.

A final judgment on the validity of the theory will be more appropriately made at the end of the text, but you should be aware of the major limitations of the theory from the beginning. First, as an explanation of minority group experience, human capital theory is not so much "wrong" as it is incomplete. In other words, it does not take account of all the factors that affect mobility and assimilation. Second, as we shall see, the assumption that U.S. society is equally open and fair to all groups is simply wrong. We will point out other strengths and limitations of this perspective as we move through the text.

Pluralism

Sociological discussions of pluralism often begin with a consideration of the work of Horace Kallen. In articles published in the *Nation* magazine in 1915, Kallen argued that people should not have to surrender their culture and traditions to become full participants in American society. He rejected the Anglo-conformist, assimilationist model and contended that the existence of separate ethnic groups, even with separate cultures, religions, and languages, was consistent with democracy and other core American values. In Gordon's terms, Kallen believed that integration and equality were possible without extensive acculturation and that American society could be a federation of diverse groups, a mosaic of harmonious and interdependent cultures and peoples (Kallen, 1915a, 1915b; see also Abrahamson, 1980; and Gleason, 1980).

Assimilation has been such a powerful theme in U.S. history that in the decades following the publication of Kallen's analysis, support for pluralism remained somewhat marginalized. In more recent decades, however, interest in pluralism and ethnic diversity has increased, in part because the assimilation predicted by Park (and implicit in the conventional wisdom of many Americans) has not fully materialized. Perhaps we simply have not waited long enough, but as the 21st century unfolds, distinctions among the racial minority groups in our society show few signs of disappearing, and, in fact, some members of these groups are questioning the very desirability of assimilation. Also, more surprising perhaps, is that white ethnicity maintains a stubborn persistence, although it continues to change in form and decrease in strength.

An additional reason for the growing interest in pluralism, no doubt, is the everyday reality of the increasing diversity of U.S. society, as reflected in exhibit 1.1. Controversies over issues such as "English-only" language policies, bilingual education, and welfare rights for immigrants are common and often bitter. Many Americans believe that diversity or pluralism has exceeded acceptable limits and that the unity of the nation is at risk (for example, visit http://www.us-english.org/, the home page of a group that advocates for English-only legislation).

Finally, interest in pluralism and ethnicity in general has been stimulated by developments around the globe. Several nation-states have disintegrated into smaller units based on language, culture, race, and ethnicity. Recent events in India, the Middle East, Eastern Europe, the former Soviet Union, Canada, and Africa, just to mention a few, have provided dramatic and often tragic evidence of how ethnic identities and enmities can persist across decades or even centuries of submergence and suppression in larger national units.

In contemporary debates, discussions of diversity and pluralism are often couched in the language of **multiculturalism**, a general term for a variety of programs and ideas that stress mutual respect for all groups and for the multiple heritages that have shaped the United States. Some aspects of multiculturalism are controversial and have evoked strong opposition. In many ways, however, these debates merely echo a recurring argument about the character of American society, a debate that will be revisited throughout this text.

Types of Pluralism

We can distinguish various types of pluralism by using some of the concepts introduced in the discussion of assimilation. **Cultural pluralism** exists when groups have not acculturated and each maintains its own identity. The groups might speak different languages, practice different religions, and have different value systems. The groups are part of the same society and might even live in adjacent areas, but in some ways they live in different worlds. Some American Indian tribal groupings are culturally pluralistic and maintain traditional languages and cultures and live on isolated reservations. The Amish, a religious community sometimes called the Pennsylvania Dutch, are also a culturally pluralistic group. They are committed to a way of life organized around farming, and they maintain a culture and an institutional life that is separate from the dominant culture (see Hostetler, 1980; Kephart & Zellner, 1994; and Kraybill & Bowman, 2001).

Following Gordon's subprocesses, a second type of pluralism exists when a group has acculturated but not integrated. That is, the group has adopted the Anglo American culture but does not have full and equal access to the institutions of the larger society. In this situation, called **structural pluralism**, cultural differences are minimal, but the groups occupy different locations in the social structure. The groups may speak with the same accent, eat the same food, pursue the same goals, and subscribe to the same values, but they may also maintain separate organizational systems, including different churches, clubs, schools, and neighborhoods.

Under structural pluralism, groups practice a common culture but do so in different places and with minimal interaction across group boundaries. An example of structural pluralism can be found on any Sunday morning in the Christian churches of the United States. Not only are local parishes separated by denomination, but they also are often identified with specific ethnic groups or races. What happens in the various churches—the rituals, expressions of faith, statements of core values and beliefs—is similar and expresses a common, shared culture. Structurally, however, this common culture is expressed in separate buildings and by separate congregations.

A third type of pluralism reverses the order of Gordon's first two phases: integration without acculturation. This situation is exemplified by groups that have had some material success (measured by wealth or income, for example) but have not become Americanized (learned English, adopted American values and norms, etc.). Some immigrant groups have found niches in American society in which they can survive and occasionally prosper economically without acculturating very much.

Two different situations can be used to illustrate this pattern. An **enclave minority group** establishes its own neighborhood and relies on a set of interconnected businesses, each of which is usually small in scope, for its economic survival. Some of these businesses serve the group, whereas others serve the larger society. The Cuban

American community in South Florida and Chinatowns in many larger American cities are examples of ethnic enclaves.

A similar pattern of adjustment, the **middleman minority group**, also relies on small shops and retail firms, but the businesses are more dispersed throughout a large area rather than concentrated in a specific locale. Some Chinese American communities fit this second pattern, as do Korean American greengroceries and Indian American–owned motels (Portes & Manning, 1986). These types of minority groups are discussed further in part 3.

The economic success of enclave and middleman minorities is partly due to the strong ties of cooperation and mutual aid within their groups. The ties are based, in turn, on cultural bonds that would weaken if acculturation took place. In contrast with Gordon's idea that acculturation is a prerequisite to integration, whatever success these groups enjoy is due in part to the fact that they have *not* Americanized. At various times and places, Jewish, Chinese, Japanese, Korean, and Cuban Americans have been enclave or middleman minorities (see Bonacich & Modell, 1980; and Kitano & Daniels, 2001).

The situation of enclave and middleman minorities, integration without acculturation, can be considered either a type of pluralism (emphasizing the absence of acculturation) or a type of assimilation (emphasizing the relatively high level of economic equality). Keep in mind that assimilation and pluralism are not opposites but can occur in a variety of combinations. It is best to think of acculturation, integration, and the other stages of assimilation (or pluralism) as independent processes.

FOCUS ON CONTEMPORARY ISSUES:
Language and Assimilation

A bumper sticker expresses a common sentiment: "Welcome to America. Now Speak English." Many Americans are concerned about the increase in the number of non-English speakers in their communities, and the bumper sticker succinctly—if crudely—expresses the opinion that newcomers should learn English as a condition for acceptance. In Gordon's terms, the slogan expresses support for Anglo-conformity, the model that guided the assimilation of immigrants in the past.

The bumper sticker also reflects a common concern: How can we manage a multilingual society? Americans from all walks of life and political persuasions wonder about the difficulties of everyday communication and the problems created when people speak multiple languages. Also, people wonder if increasing language diversity will weaken social solidarity and the sense of unity that every society requires in order to function effectively. In 2007, about 20% of the population spoke a language other than English at home and there were almost 400 different languages being spoken in the United States (Shinn & Kominski, 2010, p. 3). Of course, most of these languages,

(Continued)

(Continued)

except Spanish, have few speakers but, still, people wonder if this multiplicity of tongues is a threat to unity and efficiency. What does sociological research reveal about language acculturation for today's immigrants?

First, for the first great wave of immigrants to the United States—those who came from Europe between the 1820s and the 1920s—language acculturation happened by generation. The first generation largely lived and died speaking their native language. Their children learned English in school and often served as bilingual go-betweens for their parents and the larger society. However, they largely failed to pass on the language of their parents to their children and the third generation tended to grow up in nonethnic settings and speak English as their first and only language. Thus, by the third (or fourth) generation, English had replaced the old language, especially after immigration from Europe ended in the 1920s and 1930s and few newcomers arrived to keep the old ways alive.

Today, 80 years after the first wave of immigration ended, the importance of language is not lost on immigrants and language acculturation seems to be following, more or less, the generational pattern described in Gordon's model. Exhibit 2.2 displays

Exhibit 2.2   Percent of Each Generation Speaking English Only

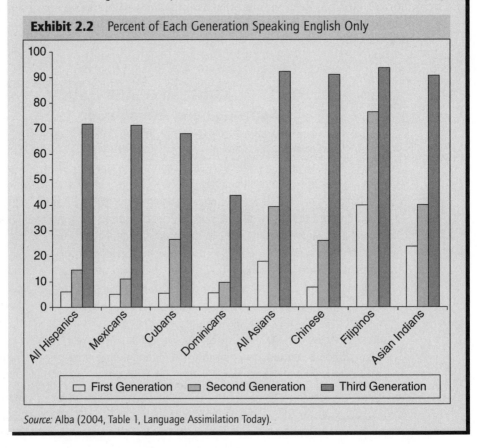

Source: Alba (2004, Table 1, Language Assimilation Today).

the generational switch to English for all Hispanic and all Asian immigrants and for some of the largest contemporary immigrant groups. The data come from the 2000 U.S. census (Alba, 2004).Although there is quite a bit of variation from group to group, the pattern in the graph is clear: the third generation of recent immigrant groups in over-whelmingly monolingual is English, just as European immigrant groups were. Asian immigrant groups are quite close to complete language acculturation. Hispanic groups are less acculturated, but virtually all bilingual Hispanics also speak English "very well." As in the past, "the immigrant generation makes some progress but remains dominant in their native tongue, the second generation is bilingual, and the third generation speaks English only" (Waters & Jimenez, 2005, p. 110).

For many Americans, the finding that language acculturation is occurring now much as it did in the past will seem counterintuitive. Their everyday experience in their communities tells them that the strength of non-English languages (particularly Spanish) is *not* waning over the years, but is growing more common. How can we reconcile this impression with the information presented in exhibit 2.2?

The persistence of the "old" language reflects the continuing high rate of immigration. Even as the children and grandchildren of immigrants learn English, the old language is replenished by newcomers. In other words, assimilation and pluralism are occurring simultaneously in the United States today: the movement of the second and third generations towards English is counterbalanced by continuing immigration. The assimilation of European immigrant groups was sharply reinforced by the cessation of immigration after the 1920s (see exhibit 2.4). Language diversity today is sustained by the continuing flow of new immigrants. This is an important difference in the assimilation experience of the two waves and we will explore it more in chapters to come. For now, we can say that immigration today will continue, newcomers will keep the "old" language alive, and language diversity will continue to be perceived as a problem and, for some, as a threat.

Given these trends, it seems likely that language will continue to be an important political issue in the years ahead. Although Americans espouse a variety of opinions on the issue, one widely supported proposal is to make English the official language of the United States (much as suggested by the bumper sticker slogan). Generally, "English Only" laws require that the official business of the society (including election ballots, court proceedings, public school assemblies, and street signs) be conducted in *only* English.

Some questions come to mind about these laws. First, are these laws necessary? Would such laws speed up the acquisition of English in the first generation? This seems unlikely since a large percentage of immigrants arrive with little formal education and low levels of literacy in their native language, as we will see in chapters to come. Furthermore, the laws would have little impact on the second and third generation, since they are already learning English at the "normal," generational pace.

(Continued)

(Continued)

Second, is there something behind the support for these laws besides concern for language diversity? Is support for English Only laws an expression of prejudice? Recall the concept of modern racism (disguised ways of expressing disdain for other groups without appearing to be racist) from chapter 1. Support for English Only laws provides a perfect cover for "nonracist racism." It permits people to express their fears and act on their stereotypes in language that is neutral and that even seems patriotic. Does the English Only movement hide a deeper, more exclusionist agenda? Is it a way of sustaining the dominance of Anglo culture, a manifestation of the ideological racism we discussed in chapter 1?

Of course, not all supporters of English Only laws are racist or prejudiced. My point is that some (many?) of those feelings and ideas are prejudicial and that we must be careful to sort out the real challenges created by language diversity from the more hysterical and racist concerns. There are many good reasons to be concerned about immigration and assimilation and many issues that need to be addressed, but language acculturation doesn't seem to justify the degree of worry that is common across the society.

Other Group Relationships

This book concentrates on assimilation and pluralism, but there are, of course, other possible group relationships and goals. Two commonly noted goals for minority groups are separatism and revolution (Wirth, 1945). The goal of **separatism** is for the group to sever all ties (political, cultural, and geographic) with the larger society. Thus, separatism goes well beyond pluralism. American Indians have expressed both separatist and pluralist goals, and separatism has also been pursued by some African American organizations, such as the Black Muslims. In the contemporary world, there are separatist movements among groups in Chechnya, Cyprus, Hawaii, southern Mexico, Quebec, Scotland, and scores of other places.

A minority group promoting **revolution** seeks to switch places with the dominant group and become the ruling elite or create a new social order, perhaps in alliance with members of the dominant group. As a goal, revolution has been relatively rare for U.S. minority groups, although revolutionary activity sometime can be found among groups such as the Black Panthers. Revolutionary minority groups are more commonly found in situations such as those in colonial Africa, in which one nation conquered and controlled another racially or culturally different nation.

The dominant group may also pursue goals other than assimilation and pluralism, including forced migration or expulsion, extermination or genocide, and continued subjugation of the minority group. Chinese immigrants were the victims of a policy of expulsion, beginning in the 1880s, when the Chinese Exclusion Act (1882) closed the door on further immigration and concerted efforts were made to encourage those in the country to leave (see chapter 8). American Indians have also been the victims of expulsion. In 1830, all tribes living east of the Mississippi were forced to migrate to a new territory in the West (see chapter 3). The most infamous example of genocide is the Holocaust in Nazi Germany, during which 6 million Jews were murdered. The dominant group pursues "continued subjugation" when, as with slavery in the antebellum South, it attempts to maintain the powerlessness and exploitation of the minority group. A dominant group may simultaneously pursue different policies with different minority groups and may, of course, change policies over time.

From Immigrants to White Ethnics

In this section, we will explore the experiences of the minority groups that stimulated the development of what I have called the traditional perspective on assimilation. A massive immigration from Europe began in the 1820s, and over the next century millions of people made the journey from the Old World to the New. They came from every corner of the continent: Germany, Greece, Ireland, Italy, Poland, Portugal, Russia, Ukraine, and scores of other nations and provinces. They came as young men and women seeking jobs, as families fleeing religious persecution, as political radicals fleeing the police, as farmers seeking land and a fresh start, and as paupers barely able to scrape together the cost of the passage. They came as immigrants, became minority groups upon their arrival, experienced discrimination and prejudice in all its forms, went through all the varieties and stages of assimilation and pluralism, and eventually merged into the society that had rejected them so viciously upon their arrival. Exhibit 2.3 shows the major European sending nations.

This first mass wave of immigrants shaped the United States in countless ways. When the immigration started in the 1820s, the United States was not yet 50 years old, an agricultural nation clustered along the East Coast. The nation was just coming into contact with Mexicans in the Southwest, immigration from China had not begun, slavery was flourishing in the South, and conflict with American Indians was intense and brutal. When the immigration ended in the 1920s, the population of the United States had increased from fewer than 10 million to more than 100 million, and the society had industrialized, become a world power, and stretched from coast to coast, with colonies in the Pacific and the Caribbean.

It was no coincidence that European immigration, American industrialization, and the rise to global prominence occurred simultaneously. These changes were intimately interlinked, the mutual causes and effects of each other. Industrialization fueled the growth of U.S. military and political power, and the industrial machinery of the nation depended heavily on the flow of labor from Europe. By World War I, for example, 25% of the nation's total labor force was foreign-born, and more than half of the workforce in New York, Detroit, and Chicago consisted of immigrant men. Immigrants were the majority of the workers in many important sectors of the economy, including coal mining, steel manufacturing, the garment industry, and meatpacking (Martin & Midgley, 1999, p. 15; Steinberg, 1981, p. 36).

In the sections that follow, we explore the experiences of these groups, beginning with forces that caused them to leave Europe and come to the United States, and ending with an assessment of their present status in American society.

Exhibit 2.3   Major European Sending Nations, Immigration to the United States, 1820–1920

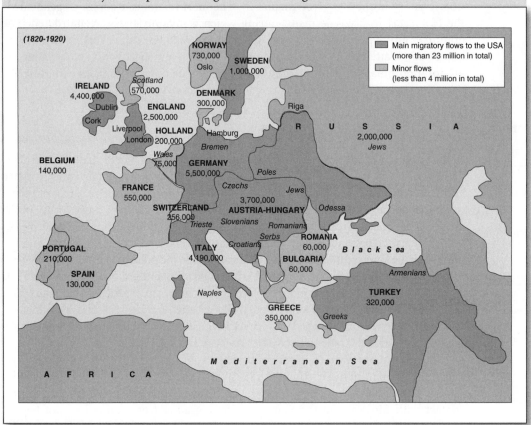

Source: Encyclopedia of Immigration (2011).

Industrialization and Immigration

What forces stimulated this mass movement of people? Like any complex phenomenon, immigration from Europe had a multitude of causes, but underlying the process was a massive and fundamental shift in subsistence technology: the **Industrial Revolution**. I mentioned the importance of subsistence technology in chapter 1. Dominant-minority relations are intimately related to the system a society uses to satisfy its basic needs, and they change as that system changes. The immigrants were pushed out of Europe as industrial technology wrecked the traditional agricultural way of life, and they were drawn to the United States by the jobs created by the spread of the very same technology. We will consider the impact of this fundamental transformation of social structure and culture in some detail.

Industrialization began in England in the mid-1700s, spread to other parts of Northern and Western Europe and then, in the 19th century, to Eastern and Southern

Europe. As it rolled across the continent, the Industrial Revolution replaced people and animal power with machines and new forms of energy (steam, coal, and eventually oil and gas), causing an exponential increase in the productive capacity of society. At the dawn of the Industrial Revolution, most Europeans lived in small, rural villages and survived by traditional farming practices that had changed very little over the centuries. The work of production was **labor intensive** or done by hand or with the aid of draft animals. Productivity was low, and the tasks of food production and survival required the efforts of virtually the entire family working ceaselessly throughout the year.

Industrialization destroyed this traditional way of life as it introduced new technology, machines, and new sources of energy to the tasks of production. The new technology was **capital intensive** or dependent on machine power, and it reduced the need for human labor in rural areas as it modernized agriculture. Also, farmland was consolidated into larger and larger tracts for the sake of efficiency, further decreasing the need for human laborers. At the same time, even as survival in the rapidly changing rural economy became more difficult, the rural population began to grow.

In response, peasants began to leave their home villages and move toward urban areas. Factories were being built in or near the cities, opening up opportunities for employment. The urban population tended to increase faster than the job supply, however, and many migrants had to move on. Many of these former peasants responded to opportunities available in the New World, especially in the United States, where the abundance of farmland on the frontier kept people moving out of the cities and away from the East Coast, thereby sustaining a fairly constant demand for labor in the very areas that were easiest for Europeans to reach. As industrialization took hold on both continents, the population movement to European cities and then to North America eventually grew to become one of the largest in human history.

The timing of immigration from Europe followed the timing of industrialization. The first waves of immigrants, often called the **Old Immigration**, came from Northern and Western Europe starting in the 1820s. A second wave, the **New Immigration**, began arriving from Southern and Eastern Europe in the 1880s. Exhibit 2.4 shows both waves and the rates of legal immigration up to 2010. Note that the New Immigration was much more voluminous than the Old Immigration, and that the number of immigrants declined drastically after the 1920s. We will explore the reasons for this decline later in this chapter and discuss in detail in chapters 7 through 9 the more recent (post-1965) increase in immigration.

European Origins and Conditions of Entry

The immigrants from Europe varied from each other in innumerable ways. They followed a variety of pathways into the United States, and their experiences were shaped by their cultural and class characteristics, their countries of origin, and the timing of their arrival. Some groups encountered much more resistance than others, and different groups played different roles in the industrialization and urbanization of America. To discuss these diverse patterns systematically, I distinguish three subgroups

Exhibit 2.4 Legal Immigration to the United States, 1820–2010

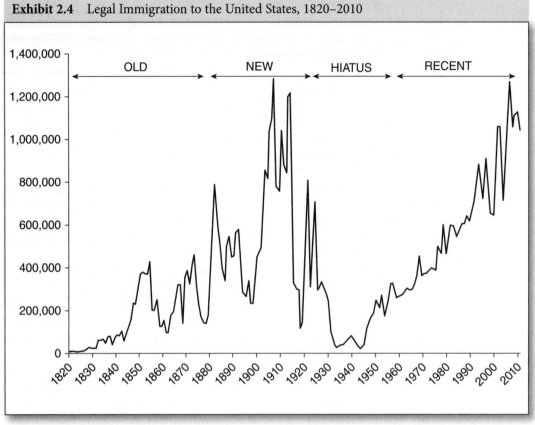

Source: U. S. Department of Homeland Security (2011).

of European immigrants: Protestants from Northern and Western Europe, the largely Catholic immigrant laborers from Ireland and from Southern and Eastern Europe, and Jewish immigrants from Eastern Europe. We look at these subgroups in roughly the order of their arrival. In later sections, we will consider other sociological variables (social class, gender) that further differentiated these groups.

Northern and Western Protestant Europeans. Northern and Western European immigrants included Danes, Dutch, English, French, Germans, Norwegians, Swedes, and Welsh. These groups were similar to the dominant group in their racial and religious characteristics and also shared many cultural values with the host society, including the Protestant ethic—which stressed hard work, success, and individualism—and support for the principles of democratic government. These similarities eased their acceptance into a society that was highly intolerant of religious and racial differences until well into the 20th century, and these immigrant groups generally experienced a lower degree of ethnocentric rejection and racist disparagement than did the Irish and the immigrants from Southern and Eastern Europe.

Northern and Western European immigrants came from nations that were just as developed as the United States. Thus, these immigrants tended to be more skilled and educated than other immigrant groups, and often brought money and other resources with which to secure a comfortable place for themselves in their new society. Many settled in the sparsely populated Midwest and in other frontier areas, where they farmed the fertile land that had become available after the conquest and removal of American Indians and Mexican Americans (see chapter 3). By dispersing throughout the midsection of the country, they lowered their visibility and their degree of competition with dominant group members. Two brief case studies, first Norwegians and then Germans, outline the experiences of these groups.

Immigrants from Norway. Norway had a small population base, and immigration from this Scandinavian nation was never sizable in absolute numbers. However, "America fever" struck here as it did elsewhere in Europe, and on a per capita basis Norway sent more immigrants to the United States before 1890 than did any European nation except Ireland (Chan, 1990, p. 41).

The first Norwegian immigrants were moderately prosperous farmers searching for cheap land. They found abundant acreage in upper-Midwest states, such as Minnesota and Wisconsin, and then found that the local labor supply was too small to effectively cultivate the available land. Many turned to their homeland for assistance and used their relatives and friends to create networks and recruit a labor force. Thus, chains of communication and migration linking Norway to the Northern Plains were established, supplying immigrants to these areas for decades (Chan, 1990, p. 41). Today, a strong Scandinavian heritage is still evident in the farms, towns, and cities of the upper Midwest.

Immigrants from Germany. The stream of immigration from Germany was much larger than that from Norway, and German Americans left their mark on the economy, political structure, and cultural life of their new land. In the last half of the 19th century, at least 25% of the immigrants each year were German (Conzen, 1980, p. 406), and today more Americans (about 15%) trace their ancestries to Germany than to any other country (Brittingham & de la Cruz, 2004).

The German immigrants who arrived earlier in the 1800s moved into the newly opened farmland and the rapidly growing cities of the Midwest, as had many Scandinavians. By 1850, large German communities could be found in Milwaukee, St. Louis, and other Midwestern cities (Conzen, 1980, p. 413). Some German immigrants followed the trans-Atlantic route of the cotton trade between Europe and the Southern United States, and entered through the port of New Orleans, moving from there to the Midwest and Southwest.

German immigrants arriving later in the century were more likely to settle in urban areas, in part because fertile land was less available. Many of the city-bound German immigrants were skilled workers and artisans, and others found work as laborers in the rapidly expanding industrial sector. The double penetration of German immigrants into the rural economy and the higher sectors of the urban economy is reflected by the fact that by 1870 most employed German Americans were involved in skilled labor (37%) or farming (25%) (Conzen, 1980, p. 413).

German immigrants took relatively high occupational positions in the U.S. labor force, and their sons and daughters were able to translate that relative affluence into economic mobility. By the dawn of the 20th century, large numbers of second-generation German Americans were finding their way into white-collar and professional careers. Within a few generations, German Americans had achieved parity with national norms in education, income, and occupational prestige.

Assimilation Patterns. By and large, assimilation for Norwegian, German, and other Protestant immigrants from Northern and Western Europe was consistent with the traditional views discussed earlier in this chapter. Although members of these groups felt the sting of rejection, prejudice, and discrimination, their movement from acculturation to integration and equality was relatively smooth, especially when compared with the experiences of racial minority groups. Their relative success and high degree of assimilation is suggested in exhibits 2.7 and 2.8, presented later in this chapter.

Immigrant Laborers From Ireland and Southern and Eastern Europe. The relative ease of assimilation for Northern and Western Europeans contrasts sharply with the experiences of non-Protestant, less-educated, and less-skilled immigrants. These "immigrant laborers" came in two waves. The Irish were part of the Old Immigration that began in the 1820s, but the bulk of this group—Bulgarians, Greeks, Hungarians, Italians, Poles, Russians, Serbs, Slovaks, Ukrainians, and scores of other Southern and Eastern European groups—made up the New Immigration that began in the 1880s. Most of the immigrants in these nationality groups (like many recent immigrants to the United States) were peasants or unskilled laborers, with few resources other than their willingness to work. They came from rural, village-oriented cultures in which family and kin took precedence over individual needs or desires. Family life for them tended to be autocratic, males dominated, and children were expected to subordinate their personal desires and to work for the good of the family as a whole. Arranged marriages were common. This cultural background was less consistent with the industrializing, capitalistic, individualistic, Protestant, Anglo American culture of the United States and was a major reason that these immigrant laborers experienced a higher level of rejection and discrimination than the immigrants from Northern and Western Europe.

The immigrant laborers were much less likely to enter the rural economy than were the Northern and Western European immigrants. Much of the better frontier land had already been claimed by the time most new immigrant groups began to arrive, and a large number of them had been permanently soured on farming by the oppressive and exploitative agrarian economies from which they were trying to escape. They settled in the cities of the industrializing Northeast and found work in plants, mills, mines, and factories. They supplied the armies of laborers needed to power the Industrial Revolution in the United States, although their view of this process was generally from the bottom looking up. They arrived during the decades in which the American industrial and urban infrastructure was being constructed. They built roads, canals, and railroads, as well as the buildings that housed the machinery of industrialization. For example, the first tunnels of the New York City subway system were dug, largely by hand, by laborers from Italy. Other immigrants found work in the coalfields of Pennsylvania and West Virginia and the steel mills of Pittsburgh, and they flocked by the millions to the factories of the Northeast.

Like other low-skilled immigrant groups, these newcomers took jobs in which strength and stamina were more important than literacy or skilled craftsmanship. In fact, the minimum level of skills required for employment actually declined as industrialization proceeded through its early phases. To keep wages low and take advantage of what seemed like an inexhaustible supply of cheap labor, industrialists and factory owners developed technologies and machines that required few skills and little knowledge of English to operate. As mechanization proceeded, unskilled workers replaced skilled workers in the workforce. Not infrequently, women and children replaced men because they could be hired for lower wages (Steinberg, 1981, p. 35).

Eventually, as the generations passed, the prejudice, systematic discrimination, and other barriers to upward mobility for the immigrant laborer groups weakened, and their descendants began to rise out of the working class. Although the first and second generations of these groups were largely limited to jobs at the unskilled or semiskilled level, the third and later generations rose in the American social class system. As exhibits 2.7 and 2.8 show (later in this chapter), the descendants of the immigrant laborers achieved parity with national norms by the latter half of the 20th century.

Eastern European Jewish Immigrants and the Ethnic Enclave. Jewish immigrants from Russia and other parts of Eastern Europe followed a third pathway into U.S. society. These immigrants were a part of the New Immigration and began arriving in the 1880s. Unlike the immigrant laborer groups, who were generally economic refugees and included many young, single males, Eastern European Jews were fleeing religious persecution and arrived as family units intending to settle permanently and become citizens. They settled in the urban areas of the Northeast and Midwest. New York City was the most common destination, and the Lower East Side became the best-known Jewish American neighborhood. By 1920, about 60% of all Jewish Americans lived in the urban areas between Boston and Philadelphia, with almost 50% living in New York City alone. Another 30% lived in the urban areas of the Midwest, particularly in Chicago (Goren, 1980, p. 581).

In Russia and other parts of Eastern Europe, Jews had been barred from agrarian occupations and had come to rely on the urban economy for their livelihoods. When they immigrated to the United States, they brought these urban skills and job experiences with them. For example, almost two thirds of the immigrant Jewish men had been tailors and other skilled laborers in Eastern Europe (Goren, 1980, p. 581). In the rapidly industrializing U.S. economy of the early 20th century, they were able to use these skills to find work.

Other Jewish immigrants joined the urban working class and took manual labor and unskilled jobs in the industrial sector (Morawska, 1990, p. 202). The garment industry in particular became the lifeblood of the Jewish community and provided jobs to about one third of all Eastern European Jews residing in the major cities (Goren, 1980, p. 582). Women as well as men were involved in the garment industry. Jewish women, like the women of more recent immigrant laborer groups, found ways to combine their jobs and their domestic responsibilities. As young girls, they worked in factories and sweatshops, and after marriage, they did the same work at home, sewing precut garments together or doing other piecework such as wrapping cigars or making artificial flowers, often assisted by their children (Amott & Matthaei, 1991, p. 115).

Unlike most European immigrant groups, Jewish Americans became heavily involved in commerce and often found ways to start their own businesses and become self-employed. Drawing on their experience in the old country, many started businesses and small independent enterprises and developed an enclave economy. The Jewish neighborhoods were densely populated and provided a ready market for services of all kinds. Some Jewish immigrants became street peddlers or started bakeries, butcher and candy shops, or any number of other retail enterprises.

Capitalizing on their residential concentration and close proximity, Jewish immigrants created dense networks of commercial, financial, and social cooperation. The Jewish American enclave survived because of the cohesiveness of the group; the willingness of wives, children, and other relatives to work for little or no monetary compensation; and the commercial savvy of the early immigrants. Also, a large pool of cheap labor and sources of credit and other financial services were available within the community. The Jewish American enclave grew and provided a livelihood for many of the children and grandchildren of the immigrants (Portes & Manning, 1986, pp. 51–52). As has been the case with other enclave groups that we will discuss in future chapters, including Chinese Americans and Cuban Americans, economic advancement preceded extensive acculturation, and Jewish Americans made significant strides toward economic equality before they became fluent in English or were otherwise Americanized.

One obvious way in which an enclave immigrant group can improve its position is to develop an educated and acculturated second generation. The Americanized, English-speaking children of the immigrants used their greater familiarity with the dominant society and their language facility to help preserve and expand the family enterprise. Furthermore, as the second generation appeared, the American public school system was expanding, and education through the college level was free or inexpensive in New York City and other cities (Steinberg, 1981, pp. 128–138). There was also a strong push for the second and third generations to excel in school and enter the professions. Predictably, their academic and occupational success stimulated resistance and discrimination. By the 1920s, many elite colleges and universities, such as Dartmouth, had established quotas that limited the number of Jewish students they would admit (Dinnerstein, 1977, p. 228). These quotas were not abolished until after World War II.

The enclave economy and the Jewish neighborhoods established by the immigrants proved to be an effective base from which to integrate into American society. The descendants of the Eastern European Jewish immigrants moved out of the ethnic neighborhoods years ago, and their positions in the economy—their pushcarts, stores, and jobs in the garment industry—have been taken over by more-recent immigrants.

When they left the enclave economy, many second- and third-generation Eastern European Jews did not enter the mainstream occupational structure at the bottom, as the immigrant laborer groups tended to do. They used the resources generated by the entrepreneurship of the early generations to gain access to prestigious and advantaged social class positions (Portes & Manning, 1986, p. 53). Studies show that Jewish Americans today, as a group, surpass national averages in income, levels of education, and occupational prestige (Sklare, 1971, pp. 60–69; see also S. Cohen, 1985; and Massarik & Chenkin, 1973). The relatively higher status of Russian Americans shown in exhibits 2.7 and 2.8 (later in this chapter) is due in part to the fact that many Jewish Americans are of Russian descent.

Chains of Immigration

All of the immigrant groups tended to follow "chains" established and maintained by the members of their groups. Some versions of the traditional assimilation perspective (especially human capital theory) treat immigration and status attainment as purely the result of individual effort. To the contrary, scholars have demonstrated that immigration to the United States was in large measure a group (sociological) phenomenon. Immigrant chains stretched across the oceans, held together by the ties of kinship, language, religion, culture, and a sense of common peoplehood (Bodnar, 1985; Tilly, 1990). The networks supplied information, money for passage, family news, and job offers.

Here is how chain immigration worked (and, although modified by modern technology, continues to work today): Someone from a village in, say, Poland, would make it to the United States. The successful immigrant would send word to the home village, perhaps by hiring a letter writer. Along with news and stories of his adventures, he would send his address. Within months, another immigrant from the village, perhaps a brother or other relative, would show up at the address of the original immigrant. After his months of experience in the new society, the original immigrant could lend assistance, provide a place to sleep, help with job hunting, and orient the newcomer to the area.

Before long, others would arrive from the village in need of the same sort of introduction to the mysteries of America. The compatriots would tend to settle close to one another, in the same building or on the same block. Soon, entire neighborhoods were filled with people from a certain village, province, or region. In these ethnic enclaves, the old language was spoken and the old ways observed. Businesses were started, churches or synagogues were founded, families were begun, and mutual aid societies and other organizations were formed. There was safety in numbers and comfort and security in a familiar, if transplanted, set of traditions and customs.

Immigrants often responded to U.S. society by attempting to recreate as much of their old world as possible. Partly to avoid the harsher forms of rejection and discrimination and partly to band together for solidarity and mutual support, immigrants created their own miniature social worlds within the bustling metropolises of the industrializing Northeast and the West Coast. These Little Italys, Little Warsaws, Little Irelands, Greektowns, Chinatowns, and Little Tokyos were safe havens that insulated the immigrants from the larger society and allowed them to establish bonds with one another, organize a group life, pursue their own group interests, and have some control over the pace of their adjustment to American culture. For some groups and in some areas, the ethnic subcommunity was a short-lived phenomenon. For others (the Jewish enclave discussed earlier, for example), the neighborhood became the dominant structure of their lives, and the networks continued to function long after the arrival of group members in the United States.

The Campaign against Immigration: Prejudice, Racism, and Discrimination

Today, it may be hard to conceive of the bitterness and intensity of the prejudice that greeted the Irish, Italians, Jews, Poles, and other new immigrant groups. Even as they were becoming an indispensable segment of the American workforce, they were castigated, ridiculed, attacked, and disparaged. The Irish were the first immigrant laborers to arrive and thus the first to feel this intense prejudice and discrimination. Campaigns against immigrants were waged, Irish neighborhoods were attacked by mobs, and Roman Catholic churches and convents were burned. Some employers blatantly refused to hire the Irish, often advertising their ethnic preferences with signs that read "No Irish Need Apply." Until later arriving groups pushed them up, the Irish were mired at the bottom of the job market. Indeed, at one time they were referred to as the "niggers of Boston" (Blessing, 1980; Potter, 1973; Shannon, 1964).

Other groups felt the same sting of rejection as they arrived. Italian immigrants were particularly likely to be the victims of violent attacks, one of the most vicious of which took place in New Orleans in 1891. The city's police chief was assassinated, and rumors of Italian involvement in the murder were rampant. Hundreds of Italians were arrested, and nine were brought to trial. All were acquitted. Anti-Italian sentiment was running so high, however, that a mob lynched eleven Italians while police and city officials did nothing (Higham, 1963).

Anti-Catholicism. Much of the prejudice against the Irish and the new immigrants was expressed as anti-Catholicism. Prior to the mid-19th century, Anglo American society had been almost exclusively Protestant. Catholicism, with its celibate clergy, Latin masses, and cloistered nuns, seemed alien, exotic, and threatening. The growth of Catholicism, especially because it was associated with non-Anglo immigrants, raised fears that the Protestant religions would lose status. There were even rumors that the Pope was planning to move the Vatican to America and organize a takeover of the U.S. government.

Although Catholics were often stereotyped as single groups, they also varied along a number of dimensions. For example, the Catholic faith as practiced in Ireland differed significantly from that practiced in Italy, Poland, and other countries. Catholic immigrant groups often established their own parishes, with priests who could speak the old language. These cultural and national differences often separated Catholic groups, despite their common faith (Herberg, 1960).

Anti-Semitism. Jews from Russia and Eastern Europe faced intense prejudice and racism (or **anti-Semitism**) as they began arriving in large numbers in the 1880s. Biased sentiments and negative stereotypes of Jews have been a part of Western tradition for centuries and, in fact, have been stronger and more vicious in Europe than in the United States. For nearly two millennia, European Jews have been chastised and persecuted as the "killers of Christ" and stereotyped as materialistic moneylenders and crafty business owners. The stereotype that links Jews and money lending has its origins in the fact that in premodern Europe, Catholics were forbidden by the church to engage in usury (charging interest for loans). Jews were under no such restriction, and they filled the gap thus created in the economy. The most dreadful episode in the long history of European anti-Semitism was, of course, the Nazi Holocaust, in which 6 million Jews died. European anti-Semitism did not end with the demise of the Nazi regime, and it remains a prominent concern throughout Europe and Russia.

Before the mass immigration of Eastern European Jews began in the late 19th century, anti-Semitism in the United States was relatively mild, perhaps because the group was so small. As the immigration continued, anti-Semitism increased in intensity and viciousness, fostering the view of Jews as cunning but dishonest merchants. In the late 19th century, Jews began to be banned from social clubs and the boardrooms of businesses and other organizations. Summer resorts began posting notices such as, "We prefer not to entertain Hebrews" (Goren, 1980, p. 585).

By the 1920s and 1930s, anti-Semitism had become quite prominent among American prejudices and was being preached by the Ku Klux Klan and other extreme racist groups. Also, because many of the political radicals and labor leaders of the time were Jewish immigrants, anti-Semitism became fused with a fear of Communism and other anticapitalist doctrines. Some prominent Americans espoused anti-Semitic views, among them Henry Ford, the founder of Ford Motor Company; Charles Lindbergh, the aviator who was the first to fly solo across the Atlantic; and Father Charles Coughlin, a Catholic priest with a popular radio show (Selzer, 1972).

Anti-Semitism reached a peak before World War II and tapered off in the decades following the war, but it remains part of U.S. society (Anti-Defamation League, 2000). Anti-Semitism also has a prominent place in the ideologies of a variety of extremist groups that have emerged in recent years, including "skinheads" and various contemporary incarnations of the Ku Klux Klan. Some of this targeting of Jews seems to increase during economic recession and may be related to the stereotypical view of Jewish Americans as extremely prosperous and materialistic.

A Successful Exclusion. The prejudice and racism directed against the immigrants also found expression in organized, widespread efforts to stop the flow of immigration. A variety of anti-immigrant organizations appeared almost as soon as the mass European immigration started in the 1820s. The strength of these campaigns waxed and waned, largely in harmony with the strength of the economy and the size of the job supply. Anti-immigrant sentiment increased in intensity, and the strength of its organized expressions increased during hard times and depressions and tended to soften when the economy improved. The campaign ultimately triumphed with the passage of the National Origins Act in 1924. This act drastically reduced the overall number of immigrants that would be admitted each year. The effectiveness of the numerical restrictions is clearly apparent in exhibit 2.4.

The National Origins Act established a quota system that limited the number of immigrants that would be accepted each year from each sending nation, a system that was openly racist. For example, the size of the quota for European nations was based on the proportional representation of each nationality in the United States as of 1890. This year was chosen because it predated the bulk of the New Immigration and gave the most generous quotas to Northern and Western European nations. Immigration from western hemisphere nations was not directly affected by this legislation, but immigration from Asian nations was banned altogether. At this time, almost all parts of Africa were still the colonial possessions of various European nations and received no separate quotas. In other words, the quota for immigrants from Africa was zero.

The result was that the quota system allocated nearly 70% of the available immigration slots to the nations of Northern and Western Europe, despite the fact that immigration from those regions had largely ended by the 1920s. The National Origins Act was very effective, and by the time the Great Depression took hold of the American economy, immigration had dropped to the lowest level in a century. The National Origins Act remained in effect until 1965.

Patterns of Assimilation

In this section, we will explore some of the common patterns in the process of assimilation followed by European immigrants and their descendants. These patterns have been well established by research conducted in the traditional perspective and are consistent with the model of assimilation developed by Gordon. They include assimilation by generation, ethnic succession, and structural mobility. We discuss each separately in this section.

The Importance of Generations

People today—social scientists, politicians, and ordinary citizens—often fail to recognize the time and effort it takes for a group to become completely Americanized. For most European immigrant groups, the process took generations, and it was the grandchildren or the great-grandchildren (or even great-great-grandchildren) of the immigrants who finally completed acculturation and integration. Mass immigration from Europe ended in the 1920s, but the assimilation of some European ethnic groups was not completed until late in the 20th century.

Here is a rough summary of how assimilation proceeded for these European immigrants: The first generation, the actual immigrants, settled in ethnic neighborhoods, such as Little Italy in New York City, and made only limited movement toward acculturation and integration. They focused their energies on the network of family and social relationships encompassed within their own groups. Of course, many of them—most often the men—had to leave their neighborhoods for work and for other reasons, and these excursions required some familiarity with the larger society. Some English had to be learned, and taking a job outside the neighborhood is, almost by definition, a form of integration. Nonetheless, the first generation lived and died largely within the context of the old country, which had been recreated within the new.

The second generation, or the children of the immigrants, found themselves in a position of psychological or social marginality: They were partly ethnic and partly American but full members of neither group. They were born in America but in households and neighborhoods that were ethnic, not American. They learned the old language first and were socialized in the old ways. As they entered childhood, however, they entered the public schools, where they were socialized into the Anglo American culture.

Very often, the world the second generation learned about at school conflicted with the world they inhabited at home. For example, the old country family values often expected children to subordinate their self-interests to the interests of their elders and of the family as a whole. Parents arranged marriages, or at least they heavily influenced them; marriages were subject to parents' approval. Needless to say, these customs conflicted sharply with American ideas about individualism and romantic love. Differences of this sort often caused painful conflict between the ethnic first generation and their Americanized children.

As the second generation progressed toward adulthood, they tended to move out of the old neighborhoods. Their geographic mobility was often motivated by social mobility. They were much more acculturated than their parents, spoke English fluently, and enjoyed a wider range of occupational choices and opportunities. Discriminatory policies in education, housing, and the job market sometimes limited them, but they were upwardly mobile, and in their pursuit of jobs and careers they left behind the ethnic subcommunity and many of the customs of their parents.

The members of the third generation, or the grandchildren of the immigrants, were typically born and raised in nonethnic settings. English was their first (and often their only) language, and their values and perceptions were thoroughly American. Although family and kinship ties with grandparents and the old neighborhood often remained strong, ethnicity for this generation was a relatively minor part of their daily realities and their self-images. Visits on weekends and holidays and family rituals revolving around the cycles of birth, marriage, and death—these activities might have connected the third generation to the world of their ancestors, but in terms of their everyday lives, they were American, not ethnic.

The pattern of assimilation by generation progressed as follows:

- The first generation began the process and was at least slightly acculturated and integrated.
- The second generation was very acculturated and highly integrated (at least into the secondary sectors of the society).
- The third generation finished the acculturation process and enjoyed high levels of integration at both the secondary and primary levels.

Exhibit 2.5 illustrates these patterns in terms of the structural assimilation of Italian Americans. The educational and occupational characteristics of this group converge with those of white Anglo-Saxon Protestants (WASPs) as the generations change. For example, the percentage of Italian Americans with some college shows a gap of more than 20 points between the first and second generations and WASPs. Italians of the third and fourth generations, though, are virtually identical to WASPs on this measure of integration in the secondary sector. The other differences between Italians and WASPs shrink in a similar fashion from generation to generation.

Indicators one through five in exhibit 2.5 illustrate the generational patterns of integration or structural assimilation. The sixth indicator, however, measures marital assimilation, or intermarriage. It displays the percentage of males of "unmixed," or 100%, Italian heritage who married females outside the Italian community. Note once more the tendency for integration, now at the primary level, to increase across the generations. The huge majority of first-generation males married within their group (only 21.9% married non-Italians). By the third generation, 67.3% of the males were marrying non-Italians.

Of course, this model of step-by-step, linear assimilation by generation fits some groups better than others. For example, immigrants from Northern and Western Europe (with the exception of the Irish) were generally more similar, racially and culturally, to the dominant group and tended to be more educated and skilled. They experienced relatively easier acceptance and tended to complete the assimilation process in three generations or less. In contrast, immigrants from Ireland and from Southern and Eastern Europe were mostly uneducated, unskilled peasants who were more likely to join the huge army of industrial labor that manned the factories, mines, and mills. These groups were more likely to remain at the bottom of the American class

Exhibit 2.5 Some Comparisons Between Italians and WASPs

	Indicators:	WASPs*	First	Second	Third and Fourth
				Generation	
1	Percentage with some college	42.4%	19.0%	19.4%	41.7%
2	Average years of education	12.6	9.0	11.1	13.4
3	Percentage white collar	34.7%	20.0%	22.5%	28.8%
4	Percentage blue collar	37.9%	65.0%	53.9%	39.0%
5	Average occupational prestige	42.5	34.3	36.8	42.5
6	Percentage of "unmixed" Italian males marrying non-Italian females		21.9%	51.4%	67.3%

Source: Adapted from Alba (1985, Tab. 5-3, 5-4, 6-2). Data are originally from the NORC General Social Surveys (1975–1980) and the Current Population Survey (1979). Copyright © 1985 Richard D. Alba.

Note: *White Anglo-Saxon Protestants (WASPs) were not separated by generation, and some of the differences between groups may be the result of factors such as age. That is, older WASPs may have levels of education more comparable to first-generation Italian Americans than they are to WASPs as a whole.

structure for generations and to have risen to middle-class prosperity only in the recent past. As mentioned earlier, Eastern European Jews formed an enclave and followed a distinctly different pathway of assimilation, using the enclave as a springboard to launch the second and third generations into the larger society (although their movements were circumscribed by widespread anti-Semitic sentiments and policies).

It is important to keep this generational pattern in mind when examining immigration to the United States today. It is common for contemporary newcomers (especially Hispanics) to be criticized for their "slow" pace of assimilation, but their "progress" takes on a new aspect when viewed in the light of the generational time frame for assimilation followed by European immigrants. Especially with modern forms of transportation, immigration can be very fast. Assimilation, on the other hand, is by nature slow.

Ethnic Succession

A second factor that shaped the assimilation experience is captured in the concept of **ethnic succession**, or the myriad ways in which European ethnic groups unintentionally affected each other's position in the social class structure of the larger society. The overall pattern was that each European immigrant group tended to be pushed to higher social class levels and more favorable economic situations by the groups that arrived after them. As more experienced groups became upwardly mobile and began to move out of the neighborhoods that served as their "ports of entry," they were often replaced by a new group of immigrants who would begin the process all over again. Some neighborhoods in the cities of the Northeast served as the ethnic neighborhood— the first safe haven in the new society—for a variety of successive groups. Some neighborhoods continue to fill this role today.

This process can be understood in terms of the second stage of Gordon's model: integration at the secondary level (see exhibit 2.1) or entry into the public institutions and organizations of the larger society. Three pathways of integration tended to be most important for European immigrants: politics, labor unions, and the church. We will cover each in turn, illustrating with the Irish, the first immigrant laborers to arrive in large numbers, but the general patterns apply to all white ethnic groups.

Politics. The Irish tended to follow the Northern and Western Europeans in the job market and social class structure and were, in turn, followed by the wave of new immigrants. In many urban areas of the Northeast they moved into the neighborhoods and took jobs left behind by German laborers. After a period of acculturation and adjustment, the Irish began to create their own connections with the mainstream society and to improve their economic and social positions. They were replaced in their neighborhoods and at the bottom of the occupational structure by Italians, Poles, and other immigrant groups arriving after them.

As the years passed and the Irish gained more experience, they began to forge more links to the larger society; in particular, they allied themselves with the Democratic Party and helped to construct the political machines that came to dominate many city governments in the 19th and 20th centuries. Machine politicians were often corrupt and even criminal, regularly subverting the election process, bribing city and state officials, using city budgets to fill the pockets of the political bosses and their cronies, and passing out public jobs as payoffs for favors and faithful service. Although not exactly models of good government, the political machines performed a number of valuable social services for their constituents and loyal followers. Machine politicians, such as Boss Tweed of Tammany Hall in New York City, could find jobs, provide food and clothing for the destitute, aid victims of fires and other calamities, and intervene in the criminal and civil courts.

Much of the power of the urban political machines derived from their control of the city payroll. The leaders of the machines used municipal jobs and the city budget as part of a "spoils" system (as in "to the victor go the spoils") and as rewards for their supporters and allies. The faithful Irish party worker might be rewarded for service to the machine with a job in the police department (thus the stereotypical Irish cop) or some other agency. Private businesspeople might be rewarded with lucrative contracts to supply services or perform other city business.

The political machines served as engines of economic opportunity and linked Irish Americans to a central and important institution of the dominant society. Using the resources controlled by local government as a power base, the Irish (and other immigrant groups after them) began to integrate themselves into the larger society and carve out a place in the mainstream structures of American society.

Labor Unions. The labor movement provided a second link between the Irish, other European immigrant groups, and the larger society. Although virtually all white ethnic groups had a hand in the creation and eventual success of the movement, many of the founders and early leaders were Irish. For example, Terence Powderly, an Irish Catholic, founded one of the first U.S. labor unions, and in the early years of the 20th century, about one third of union leaders were Irish, and more than 50 national unions had Irish presidents (Bodnar, 1985, p. 111; Brody, 1980, p. 615).

As the labor movement grew in strength and gradually acquired legitimacy, the leaders of the movement also gained status, power, and other resources, while the rank-and-file membership gained job security, increased wages, and improved fringe benefits. The labor movement provided another channel through which resources, power, status, and jobs flowed to the white ethnic groups.

Because of the way in which jobs were organized in industrializing America, union work typically required communication and cooperation across ethnic lines. The American workforce at the turn of the 20th century was multiethnic and multilingual, and union leaders had to coordinate and mobilize the efforts of many different language and cultural groups to represent the interest of the workers as a social class. Thus, labor union leaders became important intermediaries between the larger society and European immigrant groups.

Women were also heavily involved in the labor movement. Immigrant women were among the most exploited segments of the labor force, and they were involved in some of the most significant events in American labor history. For example, one of the first victories of the union movement occurred in New York City in 1909. The

Uprising of the 20,000 was a massive strike of mostly Jewish and Italian women (many in their teens) against the garment industry. The strike lasted 4 months despite attacks by thugs hired by the bosses and abuses by the police and the courts. The strikers eventually won recognition of the union from many employers, a reversal of a wage decrease, and a reduction in the 56- to 59-hour week they were expected to work (Goren, 1980, p. 584).

One of the great tragedies in the history of labor relations in the United States also involved European immigrant women. In 1911, a fire swept through the Triangle Shirtwaist Company, a garment industry shop located on the 10th floor of a building in New York City. The fire spread rapidly, and the few escape routes were quickly cut off. About 140 young immigrant women died, and many chose to leap to their deaths rather than be consumed by the flames. The disaster outraged the public, and the funerals of the victims were attended by more than a quarter of a million people. The incident fueled a drive for reform and improvement of work conditions and safety regulations (Amott & Matthaei, 1991, pp. 114–116; see also Schoener, 1967).

European immigrant women also filled leadership roles in the labor movement and served as presidents and in other offices, although usually in female-dominated unions. One of the most colorful union activists was Mother Jones, an Irish immigrant who worked tirelessly to organize miners:

> Until she was nearly one hundred years old, Mother Jones was where the danger was greatest— crossing militia lines, spending weeks in damp prisons, incurring the wrath of governors, presidents, and coal operators—she helped to organize the United Mine Workers with the only tools she felt she needed: "convictions and a voice." (Forner, 1980, p. 281)

Women workers often faced opposition from men as well as from employers. The major unions were not only racially discriminatory, but also hostile to organizing women. For example, women laundry workers in San Francisco at the start of the 20th century were required to live in dormitories and work from 6 a.m. until midnight. When they applied to the international laundry workers union for a charter, they were blocked by the male members. They eventually went on strike and won the right to an eight-hour workday in 1912 (Amott & Matthaei, 1991, p. 117).

The Church. A third avenue of mobility for the Irish and other white ethnic groups was provided by religious institutions. The Irish were the first large group of Catholic immigrants and were thus in a favorable position to eventually dominate the church's administrative structure. The Catholic priesthood became largely Irish; as these priests were promoted through the hierarchy, they eventually became bishops and cardinals. The Catholic faith was practiced in different ways in different nations. As other Catholic immigrant groups began to arrive, conflict within the Irish-dominated church increased. Both Italian and Polish Catholic immigrants demanded their own parishes in which they could speak their own languages and celebrate their own customs and festivals. Dissatisfaction was so intense that some Polish Catholics broke with Rome and formed a separate Polish National Catholic Church (Lopata, 1976, p. 49).

The other Catholic immigrant groups eventually began to supply priests and other religious functionaries and to occupy leadership positions within the church. Although the church continued to be disproportionately influenced by the Irish, other white ethnic groups also used the Catholic church as part of their power base for gaining acceptance and integration into the larger society.

Other Pathways. Besides party politics, the union movement, and religion, European immigrant groups forged other not-so-legitimate pathways of upward mobility. One alternative to legitimate success was offered by crime, a pathway that has been used by every ethnic group to some extent. Crime became particularly lucrative and attractive when Prohibition, the attempt to eliminate all alcohol use in the United States, went into effect after ratification of the 18th amendment in 1919. The criminalization of liquor failed to lower the demand, and Prohibition created a golden economic opportunity for those willing to take the risks involved in manufacturing and supplying alcohol to the American public. Italian Americans headed many of the criminal organizations that took advantage of Prohibition. Criminal leaders and organizations with roots in Sicily, a region with a long history of secret antiestablishment societies, were especially important (Alba, 1985, pp. 62–64). The connection between organized crime, Prohibition, and Italian Americans is well known, but it is not so widely recognized that ethnic succession operated in organized crime as it did in the legitimate opportunity structures. The Irish and Germans had been involved in organized crime for decades before the 1920s, and the Italians competed with these established gangsters and with Jewish crime syndicates for control of bootlegging and other criminal enterprises. The pattern of ethnic succession continued after the repeal of Prohibition in 1933, and members of groups newer to urban areas, including African Americans, Jamaicans, and Hispanic Americans, have recently challenged the Italian-dominated criminal "families."

Ethnic succession also can be observed in the institution of sports. Since the beginning of the 20th century, sports have offered a pathway to success and affluence that has attracted countless millions of young men and women. Success in many sports requires little in the way of formal credentials, education, or English fluency, and sports have been particularly appealing to the young men in minority groups that have few other resources or opportunities.

For example, at the turn of the century the Irish dominated the sport of boxing, but boxers from the Italian American community and other new immigrant groups eventually replaced them. Each successive wave of boxers reflected the concentration of a particular ethnic group at the bottom of the class structure. The succession of minority groups continues to this day, with boxing now dominated by African American and Latino fighters (Rader, 1983, pp. 87–106). A similar progression, or "layering," of ethnic and racial groups can be observed in other sports and in the entertainment industry.

The institutions of American society, both legitimate and illegal, reflect the relative positions of minority groups at a particular moment in time. Just a few generations ago, European immigrant groups dominated both crime and sports because they were blocked from legitimate opportunities. Now, the colonized racial minority groups still excluded from the mainstream job market and mired in the urban underclass are supplying disproportionate numbers of young people to these alternative opportunity structures.

Continuing Industrialization and Structural Mobility

We have already mentioned that dominant-minority relations tend to change along with changes in subsistence technology, and we can find an example of this relationship in the history of the European immigrant groups across the 20th century. Industrialization is a continuous process, and as it proceeded, the nature of work in America evolved and changed and created opportunities for upward mobility for the white ethnic groups. One important form of upward mobility throughout the 20th century, called **structural mobility**, resulted more from changes in the structure of the economy and the labor market than from any individual effort or desire to "get ahead."

Structural mobility is the result of the continuing mechanization and automation of the workplace. As machines replaced people in the workforce, the supply of manual, blue-collar jobs that had provided employment for so many first- and second-generation European immigrant laborers dwindled. At the same time, the supply of white-collar jobs increased, but access to the better jobs depended heavily on educational credentials. For white ethnic groups, a high school education became much more available in the 1930s, and college and university programs began to expand rapidly in the late 1940s, spurred in large part by the educational benefits made available to World War II veterans. Each generation of white ethnics, especially those born after 1925, was significantly more educated than the previous generation, and many were able to translate their increased human capital into upward mobility in the mainstream job market (Morawska, 1990, pp. 212–213).

The descendants of European immigrants became upwardly mobile not only because of their ambitions and efforts, but also because of the changing location of jobs and the progressively greater opportunities for education available to them. Of course, the pace and timing of this upward movement was highly variable from group to group and place to place. Ethnic succession continued to operate, and the descendants of the most recent immigrants from Europe (Italians and Poles, for example) tended to be the last to benefit from the general upgrading in education and the job market. Still, structural mobility is one of the keys to the eventual successful integration of all white ethnic groups that is displayed in exhibits 2.7 and 2.8 (later in this chapter). During these same years, the racial minority groups, particularly African Americans, were excluded from the dominant group's educational system and from the opportunity to compete for better jobs.

Variations in Assimilation

In the previous section, we discussed patterns that were common to European immigrants and their descendants. Now we address some of the sources of variation and diversity in assimilation, a complex process that is never exactly the same for any two groups. Sociologists have paid particular attention to the way that degree of similarity, religion, social class, and gender shaped the overall assimilation of the descendants of the mass European immigration. They have also investigated the way in which immigrants' reasons for coming to this country have affected the experiences of different groups.

Degree of Similarity

Since the dominant group consisted largely of Protestants with ethnic origins in Northern and Western Europe and especially in England, it is not surprising to learn that the degree of resistance, prejudice, and discrimination encountered by the different European immigrant groups varied in part by the degree to which they differed from these dominant groups. The most significant differences related to religion, language, cultural values, and, for some groups, physical characteristics. Thus, Protestant immigrants from Northern and Western Europe experienced less resistance than the English-speaking Catholic Irish, who in turn were accepted more readily than the new immigrants, who were both non–English speaking and overwhelmingly non-Protestant.

The preferences of the dominant group correspond roughly to the arrival times of the immigrants. The most similar groups immigrated earliest, and the least similar tended to be the last to arrive. Because of this coincidence, resistance to any one group of immigrants tended to fade as new groups arrived. For example, anti-German prejudice and discrimination never became particularly vicious or widespread (except during the heat of the world wars), because the Irish began arriving in large numbers at about the same time. Concerns about the German immigrants were swamped by the fear that the Catholic Irish could never be assimilated. Then, as the 19th century drew to a close, immigrants from Southern and Eastern Europe—even more different from the dominant group—began to arrive and made concerns about the Irish seem trivial.

In addition, the New Immigration was far more voluminous than the Old Immigration (see exhibit 2.4). Southern and Eastern Europeans arrived in record numbers in the early 20th century, and the sheer volume of the immigration raised fears that American cities and institutions would be swamped by hordes of what were seen as racially inferior, unassimilable immigrants (a fear with strong echoes in the present).

Thus, a preference hierarchy was formed in American culture that privileged Northern and Western Europeans over Southern and Eastern Europeans, and Protestants over Catholics and Jews. These rankings reflect the ease with which the groups have been assimilated and made their way into the larger society. This hierarchy of ethnic preference is still a part of American prejudice, as we saw in the social distance scores displayed in exhibit 1.8, although it is much more muted today than in the heyday of immigration.

Religion

A major differentiating factor in the experiences of the European immigrant groups, recognized by Gordon and other students of American assimilation, was religion. Protestant, Catholic, and Jewish immigrants lived in different neighborhoods, occupied different niches in the workforce, formed separate networks of affiliation and groups, and chose their marriage partners from different pools of people.

One important study that documented the importance of religion for European immigrants and their descendants (and also reinforced the importance of generations) was conducted by sociologist Ruby Jo Kennedy (1944). She studied intermarriage patterns in New Haven, Connecticut, over a 70-year period ending in the 1940s and found that the immigrant generation chose marriage partners from a pool whose boundaries were marked by ethnicity and religion. For example, Irish Catholics married other Irish Catholics, Italian Catholics married Italian Catholics, Irish Protestants married Irish Protestants, and so forth across all the ethnic and religious divisions she studied.

The pool of marriage partners for the children and grandchildren of the immigrants continued to be bounded by religion but not as much by ethnicity. Thus, later generations of Irish Catholics continued to marry other Catholics but were less likely to marry other Irish. As assimilation proceeded, ethnic group boundaries faded (or "melted"), but religious boundaries did not. Kennedy described this phenomenon as a **triple melting pot**: a pattern of structural assimilation within each of the three religious denominations (Kennedy, 1944, 1952).

Will Herberg (1960), another important student of American assimilation, also explored the connection between religion and ethnicity. Writing in the 1950s, he noted that the pressures of acculturation did not affect equally all aspects of ethnicity. European immigrants and their descendants were strongly encouraged to learn English, but they were not as pressured to change their religious beliefs. Very often, their religious faith was the strongest connection between later generations and their immigrant ancestors. The American tradition of religious tolerance allowed the descendants of the European immigrants to preserve this tie to their roots without being seen as "un-American." As a result, the Protestant, Catholic, and Jewish faiths eventually came to occupy roughly equal degrees of legitimacy in American society.

Thus, for the descendants of the European immigrants, religion became a vehicle through which their ethnicity could be expressed. For many members of this group, religion and ethnicity were fused, and ethnic traditions and identities came to have a religious expression.

Social Class

Social class is a central feature of social structure, and it is not surprising that it affected the European immigrant groups in a number of ways. First, social class combined with religion to shape the social world of the descendants of the European immigrants. In fact, Gordon (1964) concluded that U.S. society in the 1960s actually incorporated not three, but four melting pots (one for each of the major ethnic or religious groups and one for black Americans), each of which were internally subdivided by social class. In his view, the most significant structural unit within American society was the **ethclass**, defined by the intersection of the religious, ethnic, and social class boundaries (e.g., working-class Catholic, upper-class Protestant, etc.). Thus, people were not "simply American," but tended to identify with, associate with, and choose their spouses from within their ethclasses.

Second, social class affected structural integration. The huge majority of the post-1880s European immigrants were working class, and because they "entered U.S. society at the bottom of the economic ladder, and . . . stayed close to that level for the next half century, ethnic history has been essentially working class history" (Morawska, 1990, p. 215; see also Bodnar, 1985). For generations, many groups of Eastern and Southern European immigrants did not acculturate to middle-class American culture, but to an urban working-class, blue-collar set of lifestyles and values. Even today, ethnicity for many groups remains interconnected with social class factors, and a familiar stereotype of white ethnicity is the hard-hat construction worker.

Gender

Anyone who wants to learn about the experience of immigration will find a huge body of literature incorporating every imaginable discipline and genre. The great bulk of this material, however, concerns the immigrant experience in general or focuses specifically on male immigrants. The experiences of female immigrants have been much less recorded and hence far less accessible. Many immigrant women came from cultures with strong patriarchal traditions, and they had much less access to leadership roles, education, and prestigious, high-paying occupations. As is the case with women of virtually all minority groups, the voices of immigrant women have been muted. The research that has been done, however, documents that immigrant women played multiple roles both during immigration and during the assimilation process. As would be expected in patriarchal societies, the roles of wife and mother were central, but immigrant women were involved in myriad other activities as well.

In general, male immigrants tended to precede women, and it was common for the males to send for the women only after they had secured lodging, jobs, and a certain level of stability. However, women immigrants' experiences were quite varied, often depending on the economic situation and cultural traditions of their home societies. In some cases, women were not only prominent among the "first wave" of immigrants, but also began the process of acculturation and integration. During the 19th century, for example, a high percentage of Irish immigrants were young single women. They came to America seeking jobs and often wound up employed in domestic work, a role that permitted them to live "respectably" in a family setting. In 1850, about 75% of all employed Irish immigrant women in New York City worked as servants, and the rest were employed in textile mills and factories. As late as 1920, 81% of employed Irish-born women in the United States worked as domestics. Factory work was the second-most-prevalent form of employment (Blessing, 1980; see also Steinberg, 1981).

Because the economic situation of immigrant families was typically precarious, it was common for women to be involved in wage labor. The type and location of the work varied from group to group. Whereas Irish women were concentrated in domestic work and factories and mills, this was rare for Italian women. Italian culture had strong norms of patriarchy, and "one of the culture's strongest prohibitions was directed against contact between women and male strangers" (Alba, 1985, p. 53). Thus, acceptable work situations for Italian women were likely to involve tasks that could be done at home: doing laundry, taking in boarders, and doing piecework for the garment industry. Italian women who worked outside the home were likely to find themselves in single-sex settings among other immigrant women. Thus, women immigrants from Italy tended to be far less acculturated and integrated than those from Ireland.

Eastern European Jewish women represent a third pattern of assimilation. They were refugees from religious persecution, and most came with their husbands and children in intact family units. According to Steinberg (1981), "Few were independent bread-winners, and when they did work, they usually found employment in the . . . garment industry. Often they worked in small shops as family members" (p. 161).

Generally, immigrant women, like working-class women in general, were expected to work until they married, after which time it was expected that their husbands would support them and their children. In many cases, however, immigrant men could not earn enough to support their families, and their wives and children were required by necessity to contribute to the family budget. Immigrant wives sometimes continued to work outside the home, or they found other ways to make money. They took in boarders, did laundry or sewing, tended gardens, and were involved in myriad other activities that permitted them to contribute to the family budget and still stay home and attend to family and child-rearing responsibilities. A 1911 report on Southern and Eastern European households found that about half kept lodgers and that the income from this activity amounted to about 25% of the husbands' wages. Children also contributed to the family income by taking after-school and summertime jobs (Morawska, 1990, pp. 211–212). Compared with the men, immigrant women were more closely connected to home and family, less likely to learn to read or speak English or otherwise acculturate, and significantly more influential in preserving the heritage of their groups.

When they sought employment outside the home, they found opportunities in the industrial sector and in clerical and sales work, occupations that were quickly stereotyped as "women's work." Women were seen as working only to supplement the family treasury, and this assumption was used to justify a lower wage scale. Evans (1989) reports that in the late 1800s, "Whether in factories, offices, or private homes . . . women's wages were about half of those of men" (p. 135).

Sojourners

Some versions of the traditional perspective and the "taken-for-granted" views of many Americans assume that assimilation is desirable and therefore desired. However, immigrant groups from Europe were highly variable in their interest in Americanization, a factor that greatly shaped their experiences.

Some groups were very committed to Americanization. Eastern European Jews, for example, came to America because of religious persecution and planned to make America their home from the beginning. They left their homeland in fear for their lives and had no plans and no possibility of returning. They intended to stay, for they had nowhere else to go. (The nation of Israel was not founded until 1948.) These immigrants committed themselves to learning English, becoming citizens, and familiarizing themselves with their new society as quickly as possible.

Other immigrants had no intention of becoming American citizens and therefore had little interest in Americanization. These **sojourners**, or "birds of passage," were oriented to the old country and intended to return once they had accumulated enough capital to be successful in their home villages or provinces. Because immigration records are not very detailed, it is difficult to assess the exact numbers of immigrants who returned to the old country (see Wyman, 1993). We do know, for example, that a large percentage of Italian immigrants were sojourners. It is estimated that although 3.8 million Italians landed in the United States between 1899 and 1924, around 2.1 million departed during the same interval (Nelli, 1980, p. 547).

The Descendants of the Immigrants Today

Geographic Distribution

Exhibit 2.6 shows the geographical distribution of 8 racial and ethnic groups across the United States. The map displays the single largest group in each state.

First, the single largest ancestry group is German American, and this is reflected by the predominance of white from Pennsylvania to the west coast. Note also how the

---

Exhibit 2.6 Ancestry with Largest Population in Each County, 2000

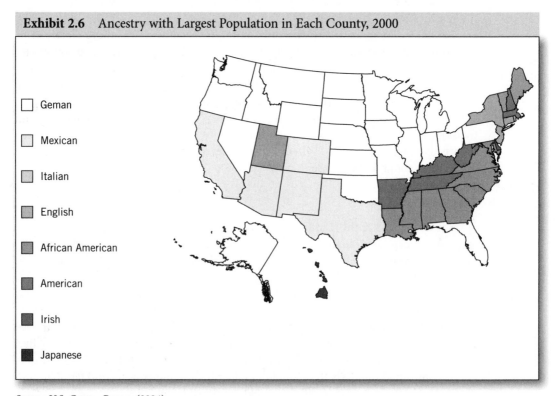

Source: U.S. Census Bureau (2004).

map reflects the original settlement areas for this group, especially in the Midwest. Although the map does not show it, Norwegian Americans (and Swedish Americans) are numerically dominant in some sections of the upper Midwest (e.g., northwestern Minnesota and northern North Dakota), Irish Americans and Italian Americans are also concentrated in their original areas of settlement, with the Irish more concentrated in Massachusetts and Italians more concentrated around New York City.

Thus, almost a century after the end of mass immigration from Europe, many of the descendants of the immigrants have not wandered far from their ancestral locales. Of course, the map shows that the same point could be made for other groups, including blacks (concentrated in the "black belt" across the states of the old Confederacy), Mexican Americans (concentrated along the southern border from Texas to California), and American Indians (their concentration in the upper Midwest, eastern Oklahoma, and the Southwest reflects the locations of the reservations into which they were forced after the end of the Indian wars).

Given all that has changed in American society over the past century—industrialization, population growth, urbanization, and massive mobility—the stable location of white ethnics (and other ethnic and racial groups) seems remarkable. Why aren't people distributed more randomly across the nation's landscape?

The stability is somewhat easier to explain for some groups. African Americans, Mexican Americans, and American Indians have been limited in their geographic as well as their social mobility by institutionalized discrimination, racism, and limited resources. We will examine the power of these constraints in detail in later chapters.

For white ethnics, on the other hand, the power of exclusion and rejection waned as the generations passed and the descendants of the immigrants assimilated and integrated. Their current locations are perhaps more a reflection of the fact that the United States is a nation of groups as well as of individuals. Our group memberships, especially family and kin, exert a powerful influence on our decisions about where to live and work and, despite the transience and mobility of modern American life, can keep people connected to their relatives, the old neighborhood, their ethnic roots, and the sites of their ancestors' struggles.

Integration and Equality

Perhaps the most important point, for our purposes, about white ethnic groups (the descendants of the European immigrants) is that they are today on the verge of being completely assimilated. Even the groups that were the most despised and rejected in earlier years are acculturated, integrated, and thoroughly intermarried.

To illustrate this point, consider exhibits 2.7 and 2.8, which illustrate the degree to which a variety of white ethnic groups had been integrated as long ago as 1990. The exhibits display data for nine of the more than 60 white ethnic groups that people mentioned when asked to define their ancestries. The groups include the two largest white ethnic groups (German and Irish Americans) and seven more chosen to represent a range of geographic regions of origin and times of immigration (U.S. Census Bureau, 2008a).

The graphs show that by 1990 all nine of the groups selected were at or above national norms ("all persons") for all measures of equality. There is some variation among the groups, of course, but exhibit 2.7 shows that all exceeded the national averages for both high school and college education. Exhibit 2.8 shows that all nine groups had dramatically lower poverty rates (see the line in the graph and refer to the right-hand axis for values), usually less than half the national average. The bars in exhibit 2.8 show median household income (refer to the left-hand axis for values). All nine groups exceed the national average, and some—Russians, for example, many of whom are Jewish—exceeded it by a considerable margin.

In other areas, the evidence for assimilation and equality is also persuasive. For example, the distinct ethnic neighborhoods that these groups created in American cities (Little Italy, Greektown, Little Warsaw, etc.) have faded away or been taken over by other groups, and the rate of intermarriage between members of different white ethnic groups is quite high. For example, based on data from the 1990 census, about 56% of all married whites have spouses whose ethnic backgrounds do not match their own (Alba, 1995, pp. 13–14).

Exhibit 2.7   Educational Attainment for Selected White Ethnic Groups, 1990

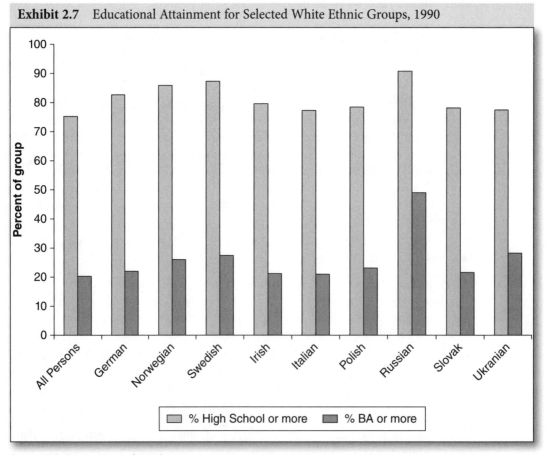

Source: U.S. Census Bureau (2008a).

Exhibit 2.8   Median Household Income and Percent of Families Living in Poverty for Selected White Ethnic Groups, 1990

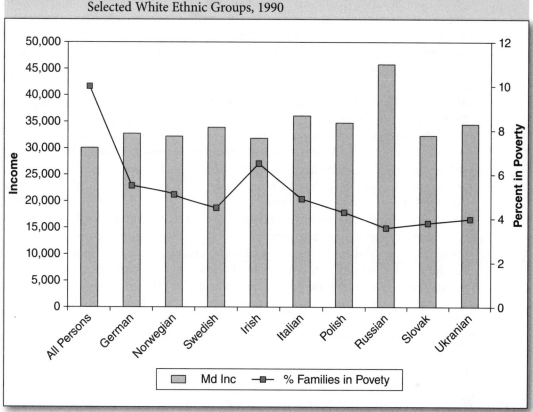

Source: U.S. Census Bureau (2008a).

The Evolution of White Ethnicity

Absorption into the American mainstream was neither linear nor continuous for the descendants of European immigrants. Over the generations, white ethnic identity sporadically reasserted itself in many ways, two of which are especially notable. First, there was a tendency for later generations to be more interested in their ancestry and ethnicity than were earlier generations. Marcus Hansen (1952) captured this phenomenon in his **principle of third-generation interest**: "What the second generation tries to forget, the third generation tries to remember" (p. 495). Hansen observed that the children of immigrants tended to minimize or deemphasize ("forget") their ethnicity to avoid the prejudice and intolerance of the larger society and compete on more favorable terms for jobs and other opportunities. As they became adults and started families of their own, the second generation tended to raise their children in nonethnic settings, with English as their first and only language.

By the time the third generation reached adulthood, especially the New Immigrant groups that arrived last, the larger society had become more tolerant of white ethnicity and diversity; having little to risk, the third generation tried to reconnect with its grandparents and roots. These descendants wanted to remember their ethnic heritage and understand it as part of their personal identities, their sense of who they were and where they belonged in the larger society. Thus, interest in the "old ways" and the strength of the identification with the ancestral group was often stronger in the more Americanized third generation than in the more ethnic second. Ironically, of course, the grandchildren of the immigrants could not recover much of the richness and detail of their heritage because their parents had spent their lives trying to forget it. Nonetheless, the desire of the third generation to reconnect with its ancestry and recover its ethnicity shows that assimilation is not a simple, one-dimensional, or linear process. In addition to this generational pattern, the strength of white ethnic identity also responded to the changing context of American society and the activities of other groups. For example, in the late 1960s and early 1970s, there was a notable increase in the visibility of, and interest in, white ethnic heritage, an upsurge often referred to as the **ethnic revival**. The revival manifested itself in a variety of ways. Some people became more interested in their families' genealogical roots, and others increased their participation in ethnic festivals, traditions, and organizations. The white ethnic vote became a factor in local, state, and national politics, and appearances at the churches, meeting halls, and neighborhoods associated with white ethnic groups became almost mandatory for candidates for office. Demonstrations and festivals celebrating white ethnic heritages were organized, and buttons and bumper stickers proclaiming the ancestry of everyone from Irish to Italians were widely displayed. The revival was also endorsed by politicians, editorialists, and intellectuals (e.g., see Novak, 1973), reinforcing the movement and giving it additional legitimacy.

The ethnic revival may have been partly fueled, à la Hansen's principle, by the desire to reconnect with ancestral roots, even though most groups were well beyond their third generations by the 1960s. More likely, the revival was a reaction to the increase in pluralistic sentiment in the society in general and the pluralistic, even separatist assertions of other groups. In the 1960s and 1970s, virtually every minority group generated a protest movement (Black Power, Red Power, Chicanismo, etc.) and proclaimed a recommitment to its own heritage and to the authenticity of its own culture and experience. The visibility of these movements for cultural pluralism among racial minority groups helped make it more acceptable for European Americans to express their own ethnicity and heritage.

Besides the general tenor of the times, the resurgence of white ethnicity had some political and economic dimensions that bring us back to issues of inequality and competition for resources. In the 1960s, a white ethnic urban working class made up largely of Irish and Southern and Eastern European groups still remained in the neighborhoods of the industrial Northeast and Midwest and continued to breathe life into the old networks and traditions (see Glazer & Moynihan, 1970; and Greeley, 1974). At the same time that cultural pluralism was coming to be seen as more legitimate, this ethnic working class was feeling increasingly threatened by minority groups of color. In the industrial cities, it was not unusual for white ethnic neighborhoods to adjoin black and Hispanic neighborhoods, putting these groups in direct competition for housing, jobs, and other resources.

Many members of the white ethnic working class saw racial minority groups as inferior and perceived the advances being made by these groups as unfair, unjust, and threatening. They also reacted to what they saw as special treatment and attention being accorded on the basis of race, such as school busing and affirmative action. They had problems of their own (the declining number of good, unionized jobs; inadequate schooling; and deteriorating city services) and believed that their problems were being given lower priority and less legitimacy because they were white. The revived sense of ethnicity in the urban working-class neighborhoods was in large part a way of resisting racial reform and expressing resentment for the racial minority groups. Thus, among its many other causes and forms, the revival of white ethnicity that began in the 1960s was fueled by competition for resources and opportunities. As we will see throughout this text, such competition commonly leads to increased prejudice and a heightened sense of cohesion among group members.

The Twilight of White Ethnicity?[1]

As the conflicts of the 1960s and 1970s faded and white ethnic groups continued to leave the old neighborhoods and rise in the class structure, the strength of white ethnic identity resumed its slow demise. Today, several more generations removed from the tumultuous 1960s, white ethnic identity has become increasingly nebulous and largely voluntary. It is often described as **symbolic ethnicity** or as an aspect of self-identity that symbolizes one's roots in the "old country" but otherwise is minor. The descendants of the European immigrants feel vaguely connected to their ancestors, but this part of their identities does not affect their lifestyles, circles of friends and neighbors, job prospects, eating habits, or other everyday routines (Gans, 1979; Lieberson & Waters, 1988). For the descendants of the European immigrants today, ethnicity is an increasingly minor part of their identities that is expressed only occasionally or sporadically. For example, they might join in ethnic or religious festivals (e.g., St. Patrick's Day for Irish Americans, Columbus Day for Italian Americans), but these activities are seasonal or otherwise peripheral to their lives and self-images. The descendants of the European immigrants have choices, in stark contrast with their ancestors, members of racial minority groups, and recent immigrants: they can stress their ethnicity, ignore it completely, or maintain any degree of ethnic identity they choose. Many people have ancestors in more than one ethnic group and may change their sense of affiliation over time, sometimes emphasizing one group's traditions and sometimes another's (Waters, 1990).

In fact, white ethnic identity has become so ephemeral that it may be on the verge of disappearing altogether. For example, based on a series of in-depth interviews with white Americans from various regions of the nation, Gallagher (2001) found a sense of ethnicity so weak that it did not even rise to the level of "symbolic." His respondents were the products of ancestral lines so thoroughly intermixed and intermarried that any trace of a unique heritage from a particular group was completely lost. They had virtually no knowledge of the experiences of their immigrant ancestors or of the life and cultures of the ethnic communities they had inhabited, and for many their ethnic ancestries were no more meaningful to them than their states of birth. Their lack of interest in and information about their ethnic heritage was so complete that it led Gallagher (2001) to propose an addendum to Hansen's principle: "What the grandson wished to remember, the great-granddaughter has never been told."

At the same time that more specific white ethnic identities are disappearing, they are also evolving into new shapes and forms. In the view of many analysts, a new identity is developing that merges the various "hyphenated" ethnic identities (German American, Polish American, etc.) into a single, generalized European American identity based on race and a common history of immigration and assimilation. This new identity reinforces the racial lines of separation that run through contemporary society, but it does more than simply mark group boundaries. Embedded in this emerging identity is an understanding, often deeply flawed, of how the white immigrant groups succeeded and assimilated in the past and a view, often deeply ideological, of how the racial minority groups should behave in the present. These understandings are encapsulated in "immigrant tales": legends that stress heroic individual effort and grim determination as key ingredients leading to success in the old days. These tales feature impoverished, victimized immigrant ancestors who survived and made a place for themselves and their children by working hard, saving their money, and otherwise exemplifying the virtues of the Protestant ethic and American individualism. They stress the idea that past generations became successful despite the brutal hostility of the dominant group and with no government intervention, and they equate the historical difficulties faced by immigrants from Europe with those suffered by racial minority groups (slavery, segregation, attempted genocide, etc.). They strongly imply—and sometimes blatantly assert—that the latter groups could succeed in America by simply following the example set by the former (Alba, 1990; Gallagher, 2001).

These accounts mix versions of human capital theory and traditional views of assimilation with prejudice and racism. Without denying or trivializing the resolve and fortitude of European immigrants, equating their experiences and levels of disadvantage with those of African Americans, American Indians, and Mexican Americans is widely off the mark, as we shall see in the remainder of this text. These views support an attitude of disdain and lack of sympathy for the multiple dilemmas faced today by the racial minority groups and by many contemporary immigrants. They permit a more subtle expression of prejudice and racism and allow whites to use these highly distorted views of their immigrant ancestors as a rhetorical device to express a host of race-based grievances without appearing racist (Gallagher, 2001).

Alba (1990) concludes as follows:

> The thrust of the [emerging] European American identity is to defend the individualistic view of the American system, because it portrays the system as open to those who are willing to work hard and pull themselves out of poverty and discrimination. Recent research suggests that it is precisely this individualism that prevents many whites from sympathizing with the need for African Americans and other minorities to receive affirmative action in order to overcome institutional barriers to their advancement. (p. 317)

What can we conclude? The generations-long journey from immigrant to white ethnic to European American seems to be drawing to a close. The separate ethnic identities are merging into a larger sense of "whiteness" that unites descendants of the immigrants with the dominant group and provides a rhetorical device for expressing disdain for other groups, especially African Americans.

Contemporary Immigrants: Does the Traditional Perspective Apply?

Does the traditional perspective—based as it is on the experiences of European immigrants and their descendants—apply to more recent immigrants? This is a key issue facing social scientists, government policymakers, and the general public today. Will contemporary immigrants duplicate the experiences of earlier groups? Will they acculturate before they integrate? Will religion, social class, and race be important forces in their lives? Will they take three generations to assimilate? More than three? Fewer? What will their patterns of intermarriage look like? Will they achieve socioeconomic parity with the dominant group? When? How?

Sociologists (as well as the general public and policymakers) are split in their answers to these questions. Some social scientists believe that the "traditional" perspective on assimilation does not apply and that the experiences of contemporary immigrant groups will differ greatly from those of European immigrants. They believe that assimilation today is fragmented (or **segmented assimilation**) and will have a number of different outcomes. Although some contemporary immigrant groups may integrate into the middle-class mainstream, others will find themselves permanently mired in the impoverished, alienated, and marginalized segments of racial minority groups. Still others may form close-knit enclaves based on their traditional cultures and become successful in the United States by resisting the forces of acculturation (Portes & Rumbaut, 2001, p. 45).

In stark contrast, other theorists believe that the traditional perspective on assimilation is still relevant and that contemporary immigrant groups will follow the established pathways of mobility and assimilation. Of course, the process will be variable from group to group and place to place, but even the groups that are today the most impoverished and marginalized will, in time, move into mainstream society.

How will the debate be resolved? We cannot say at the moment, but we can point out that this debate is reminiscent of the critique of Park's theory of assimilation. In both cases, the argument is partly about time: even the most impoverished and segmented groups may find their way into the economic mainstream eventually, at some unspecified time in the future. There are also other levels of meaning in the debate, however, related to one's perception of the nature of modern U.S. society. Is U.S. society today growing more tolerant of diversity, more open and equal? If so, this would seem to favor the traditionalist perspective. If not, this trend would clearly favor those who argue for the segmented-assimilation hypothesis. Although we will not resolve this argument in this text, we will use the debate between the traditional and segmented views on assimilation as a useful framework as we consider the experiences of these groups (see chapters 8, 9, and 10).

Implications for Examining Dominant-Minority Relations

Chapters 1 and 2 have introduced many of the terms, concepts, and themes that form the core of the rest of this text. Although the connections between the concepts are not simple, some key points can be made to summarize these chapters and anticipate the material to come.

First, minority group status has much more to do with power and the distribution of resources than it does with simple numbers or the percentage of the population in any particular category. We saw this notion expressed in chapter 1 in the definition of a minority group and in our exploration of inequality. The themes of inequality and differentials in status were also covered in our discussion of prejudice, racism, and discrimination. To understand minority relations, we must examine some very basic realities of human society: inequalities in wealth, prestige, and the distribution of power. To discuss changes in minority group status, we must be prepared to discuss changes in the way society does business, makes decisions, and distributes income, jobs, health care, and opportunity.

A second area that we will focus on in the rest of the book is the question of how our society should develop. Assimilation and pluralism, with all their variations, define two broad directions. Each has been extensively examined and discussed by social scientists, by leaders and decision makers in American society, and by ordinary people from all groups and walks of life. The analysis and evaluation of these two broad directions is a thread running throughout this book.

COMPARATIVE FOCUS:
Immigration, Emigration, and Ireland

Just as the United States has been a major receiver of immigrants for the past 200 years, Ireland has been a major supplier. Mass emigration from Ireland began with the potato famines of the 1840s and continued through the end of the 20th century, motivated by continuing hard times, political unrest, and unemployment. Combined with the death toll from the famines, this continuing exodus cut the 1840 Irish population of 7 million in half, and today the population of Ireland is still only about 4 million.

History rarely runs in straight lines, however. At the turn of the 21st century, after nearly 200 years of supplying immigrants, Ireland (along with other nations of Northern and Western Europe) became a consumer. As displayed in exhibit 2.9, the number of newcomers entering Ireland grew rapidly after the mid-1990s, increasing by a factor of five to more than 100,000 in 2007. At the same time, the number of people leaving decreased dramatically, to less than 25,000. In the most recent years, as the Irish economy soured and jobs became scarcer, immigration has resumed its historic pattern and the number of newcomers dropped precipitously. Still, the patterns of immigration from the 1990s through 2007 are a remarkable reversal of an historic trend and beg for an explanation.

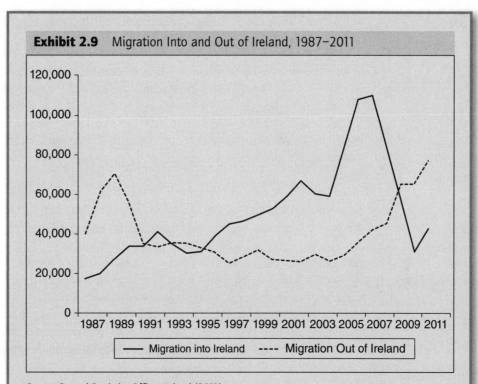

Exhibit 2.9 Migration Into and Out of Ireland, 1987–2011

Legend: —— Migration into Ireland   ---- Migration Out of Ireland

Source: Central Statistics Office, Ireland (2011).

We should note that the volume of in- and out-migration is minuscule compared with the United States, but the percentage of Ireland's population that is "non-Irish" (12%) is comparable to the percentage of the United States population that is foreign-born (13%) (Central Statistics Office, Ireland, 2011).

What explains the influx of population between the mid-1990s and 2007? The answers are not hard to find. After decades of unemployment and depression, the Irish economy entered a boom phase in the early 1990s. Spurred by investments from multinational corporations and the benefits of joining the European Economic Union, the Irish economy and the job supply grew rapidly.

Irish nationals who had left Ireland to find work returned in large numbers, and people from Europe and other parts of the globe also arrived. In addition, Ireland received refugees and people seeking asylum. In 2009, for example, roughly 32% of the people entering Ireland were of Irish origin, 47% were from the United Kingdom or other nations of the European Union, and 20% were from "the rest of the world," a category that includes the Middle East, Nigeria, and various "trouble spots" around the globe (Central Statistics Office, Ireland, 2011).

The immigration is changing the racial composition of Irish society. Although still a small minority of the total population, the number of Irish residents of African descent

(Continued)

(Continued)

has increased by a factor of seven since 1996, from less than 5,000 to more than 35,000. Also, the number of Irish residents of Asian descent has increased by a factor of six, from about 8,000 to about 47,000. Each group is about 1% of the total population.

What awaits these newcomers when they arrive on the Emerald Isle? Will they be subjected to the Irish version of Anglo-conformity? Will Irish society become a melting pot? Will Gordon's ideas about assimilation be applicable to their experiences? Will the Irish, such immigrants themselves, be especially understanding of the traumas faced by the newcomers?

Although many Irish are very sympathetic to the immigrants and refugees, others have responded with racist sentiments and demands for exclusion, reactions that ironically echo the rejection Irish immigrants in the United States experienced in the 19th century. Irish radio and TV talk shows commonly discuss issues of immigration and assimilation and frequently evoke prejudiced statements from the audience, and there are also reports of racism and discrimination.

The rejection of non-Irish newcomers was manifested in the passage of the Citizenship Amendment to the Irish Constitution, which was overwhelmingly supported (80% in favor) by the Irish electorate in June 2004. Prior to the passage of the amendment, any baby born in Ireland had the right to claim Irish citizenship. The amendment denied the right of citizenship to any baby that did not have at least one Irish parent; it was widely interpreted as a hostile rejection of immigrants (see Fanning, 2003). One poll suggested that people supported the amendment because they believed that there were simply too many immigrants in Ireland (Neissen, Schibel, & Thompson, 2005).

Like the United States, Ireland finds itself dealing with diversity and debating what kind of society it should become. It is too early to predict ultimate outcomes, but we can be sure that Irish society will deal with questions of unity and acceptance, assimilation and pluralism, in much the same way as U.S. society has done.

Note

1. The phrase comes from Alba (1990).

Main Points

- Assimilation and pluralism are two broad pathways of development for intergroup relations. Assimilation and pluralism are in some ways contrary processes but may appear together in a variety of combinations.
- Two types of assimilation are the melting pot and Anglo-conformity. The latter has historically been the dominant value in the United States.

- Gordon theorized that assimilation occurs through a series of stages, with integration being the crucial stage. In his view, it is common for American minority groups, especially racial minority groups, to be acculturated but not integrated. Once a group has begun to integrate, all other stages will follow in order.
- In the past few decades, there has been increased interest in pluralism. There are three types of pluralistic situations: cultural, or full, pluralism; structural pluralism; and enclave, or middleman, minority groups.
- According to many scholars, white ethnic groups survived decades of assimilation, albeit in altered forms. New ethnic (and racial) minority groups continue to appear, and old ones change form and function as society changes. As the 21st century unfolds, however, white ethnicity may well be fading in salience for most people, except perhaps as a context for criticizing other groups.
- In the United States today, assimilation may be segmented and have outcomes other than equality with and acceptance into the middle class.

Study Site on the Web

Don't forget the interactive quizzes and other resources and learning aids at www.sagepub.com/healeyds4e.

For Further Reading

Alba, R. (1990). *Ethnic identity: The transformation of White America*. New Haven, CT: Yale University Press.

A useful analysis of the changing meanings of ethnic identity for the descendants of European immigrants.

Alba, R., & Nee, V. (2003). *Remaking the American mainstream: Assimilation and contemporary immigration.* Cambridge, MA: Harvard University Press.
Bean, F., & Stevens, G. (2003). *America's newcomers and the dynamics of diversity*. New York: Russell Sage.

Two recent works that argue that the "traditional" model of assimilation remains viable.

Foner, N. (2005). *In a new land: A comparative view of immigration*. New York: NYU Press.

A masterful analysis of immigration across time and space.

Gordon, M. (1964). *Assimilation in American life: The role of race, religion and national origins*. New York: Oxford University Press.
Herberg, W. (1960). Protestant-Catholic-Jew: *An essay in American religious sociology*. New York: Anchor.

Two classic works of scholarship on assimilation, religion, and white ethnic groups.

Perlman, J. (2005). *Italians then, Mexicans now*. New York: Russell Sage.

A detailed, intriguing, and rigorous comparison of immigrant groups from two different eras.

Portes, A., & Rumbaut, R. (2001). *Ethnicities: Children of immigrants in America*. New York: Russell Sage Foundation.
Portes, A., & Rumbaut, R. (2001). *Legacies: The story of the immigrant second generation*. Berkeley: University of California Press.

Zhou, M., & Bankston, C. (1998). *Growing up American: How Vietnamese children adapt to life in the United States.* New York: Russell Sage.

Three outstanding works analyzing the new immigrants and the concept of segmented assimilation.

Questions for Review and Study

1. Summarize Gordon's model of assimilation. Identify and explain each stage and how the stages are linked together. Explain exhibit 2.5 in terms of Gordon's model.

2. "Human capital theory is not so much wrong as it is incomplete." Explain this statement. What does the theory leave out? What are the strengths of the theory? What questionable assumptions does it make?

3. What are the major dimensions along which the experience of assimilation varies? Explain how and why the experience of assimilation can vary.

4. Define pluralism and explain the ways in which it differs from assimilation. Why has interest in pluralism increased? Explain the difference between and cite examples of structural and cultural pluralism. Describe enclave minority groups in terms of pluralism and in terms of Gordon's model of assimilation. How have contemporary theorists added to the concept of pluralism?

5. Define and explain segmented assimilation and explain how it differs from Gordon's model. What evidence is there that assimilation for recent immigrants is not segmented? What is the significance of this debate for the future of U.S. society? For other minority groups (e.g., African Americans)? For the immigrants themselves?

6. Do American theories and understandings of assimilation apply to Ireland?

Internet Research Project

American society incorporates scores of ethnic groups. In this exercise, you will use the U.S. census to gather information about the relative assimilation of five different ethnic groups of your own choosing. We will consider racial minority groups in other "Internet Research Projects." Choose groups so that you include a variety of places of origin, and times of immigration (i.e., choose some that arrived before the 1920s restrictions and some that arrived more recently).

Get information by following these steps:

1. Go to the official U.S. Census Bureau website at www.census.gov.

2. Click on "Data" in the list of choices at the top of the screen and then click "American Fact Finder" on the menu that drops down.

3. Click the "Race and Ethnic Groups" tab on the left of the next screen. A new window will open. Find the list of "Racial and Ethnic Group Results" on the right of the screen and click on the box next to "Total Population" (Code 001). Next, click the "Add" button above the "Racial and Ethnic Group Results" window and "Total Population" will be added to the "Your selections" box in the top-left-hand corner of the screen.

4. Find the "Race/Ethnic Group Filter Options" window in the middle of the screen and click on "Ancestry Group." Now the "Racial and Ethnic Group Results" window will display a list of ethnic or ancestry groups. The list of white ethnic groups—the subject of this chapter—begins at the bottom of the first screen and continues across the next several screens. You may choose any groups from the list, but be sure to include at least three white ethnic groups.

5. You will choose a total of five groups from this list. To choose a group, click the box next to the group name and then click the "Add" button to transfer the group name to the "Your Selection" box. When you have included "Total Population" and your five groups in the "Your Selections" window, you are ready to proceed to the next step.

6. Close the "Select Race and Ethnic Group" window by clicking the "Close" button on the top-right-hand corner of the window.

7. The "Search Results" window on the right of the screen lists all of the tables that are currently available from the complete census of 2010 and the yearly American Community Survey (ACS). For this project, we will use the 2011 ACS 1-year estimates. Look in either the "ID" column on the left for "Table S0201" or in the Dataset column on the right for the "2011 ACS 1-year estimates." Click the box next to the file name and then click "View" from the menu above the window.

8. The table that will be displayed lists the total population and your five groups along the top, Scroll down the table until you get to the heading "EDUCATIONAL ATTAINMENT." Find the subheadings "High school graduate or higher" and "Bachelor's degree or higher" and copy the percentages for each of your groups in the table below. Percentages for the total population have already been entered.

9. Continuing scrolling down the table until you get to the heading "PLACE OF BIRTH, CITIZENSHIP STATUS AND YEAR OF ENTRY." Fill in the table below with information for your groups.

10. Scroll down a little more until you come to "LANGAUGE SPOKEN AT HOME AND ABILITY TO SPEAK ENGLISH." Fill in the table with information for your groups.

	Variables	Total Population	Your Groups _____	_____	_____	_____	_____
1	Educational Attainment						
	Percent HS graduate or higher	85.9%					
	Percent BA degree or higher	28.5%					
2	Number foreign-born	40,377,960					
	% foreign-born who are						
	Male	48.9%					
	Female	49.7% 51.1%					

(Continued)

(Continued)

	Variables	Total Population	Your Groups _____	_____	_____	_____	_____
3	% foreign-born who are naturalized citizens (Divide the number of foreign-born who are naturalized by the total number of foreign-born and multiply by 100.)	44.9%					
4	Foreign-born: % that entered U.S.						
	2000 or later	35.7%					
	1990–1999	26.7%					
	Before 1990	37.6%					
5	Language spoken at home and ability to speak English						
	% English only	79.2%					
	% who speak English Less than "Very Well"	8.7%					

Questions

1. How do these variables measure assimilation? What stage of Gordon's model (see exhibit 2.1) do they relate to?

2. Which of your groups is most or least assimilated? Based on this chapter and what you know about these groups at this point, what factors might explain their relative position?

3. Compare the percentage of each group that entered the United States after 2000 with the percentage of the group that speaks only English. Do you see any trends here? Are the newest arrivals least likely to be speaking English only? Is there evidence that language acculturation is taking place?

Optional Group Discussion

Bring this information to class and, in groups of four to six people, compare your results with the information collected by others. Consider the issues raised in the questions above and in the chapter and develop some ideas about why these groups are where they are relative to each other and to the total population. (*Note: Your instructor may have different instructions for this step of the project.*)

PART 2

The Evolution of Dominant-Minority Relations in the United States

❖

☙ ❧

Chapter 3 The Development of Dominant-Minority Group Relations in Preindustrial America: The Origins of Slavery

Chapter 4 Industrialization and Dominant-Minority Relations: From Slavery to Segregation and the Coming of Postindustrial Society

☙ ❧

The chapters in part 2 explore several questions: Why do some groups become minorities? How and why do dominant-minority relations change over time? These questions are more than casual or merely academic. Understanding the dynamics that created and sustained prejudice, racism, discrimination, and inequality in the past will build understanding about group relations in the present and future, and such understanding is crucial if we are ever to deal effectively with these problems.

Both chapters in part 2 use African Americans as the primary case study. Chapter 3 focuses on the preindustrial United States and the creation of slavery but also considers the fate of American Indians and Mexican Americans during the same period. Chapter 4 analyzes the changes in group relations that were caused by the Industrial Revolution and focuses on the shift from slavery to segregation for African Americans and their migration out of the South. Throughout the 20th century, industrial technology continued to evolve and shape American society and group relationships. We begin to explore the consequences of these changes in chapter 4, and we continue the investigation in the case studies of contemporary minority groups in part 3.

The concepts introduced in part 1 are used throughout chapters 3 and 4, and some very important new concepts and theories are introduced as well. By the end of part 2, you will be familiar with virtually the entire conceptual framework that will guide us through the remainder of this text.

A Note on the Morality and the History of Minority Relations in America: Guilt, Blame, Understanding, and Communication

Consider a conversation that occurred recently on a popular social networking site. Danny, my nephew, posted a link to some maps that illustrated the loss of land suffered by American Indians over the past 400 years (http://www.stupidgifs.com/view/326/). He made no comment about the maps and was simply sharing what he thought was some interesting information. However, his post provoked an almost immediate response from his friend Jason: "So, we Caucasian-Americans should just pack up and move back to Europe? We're not responsible for the crimes of our ancestors."

Danny responded, "I think we need to realize that the inequalities between people today are determined by history . . . we've got to know our history to even start to understand the present. . . . When you see maps that show the historic genocide of entire indigenous nations you should think about it for a minute and realize the place we're in because of that genocide."

What strikes you about this interchange? What messages are stated and implied? Was Jason shutting himself off from a meaningful conversation about American Indians by dismissing the maps and suggesting the "solution" of moving back to Europe? Was Danny merely mouthing pious platitudes about the past? Is there any chance that these two could have a dialogue on the topic?

In the next few chapters, we will examine the creation of several American minority groups. Very often, when people confront this material, they react on a personal level. Some, like Jason, respond with denial or indifference and argue that the events discussed in chapters 3 and 4 are so distant in time that they have no importance today. Others might feel a sense of guilt for America's less-than-wholesome history of group relations, and still others might get angry about the injustice and unfairness that remains in American society.

These reactions—denial, guilt, anger, and indifference—are common, and I ask you to think about them as you read these chapters. First, the awful things I will discuss did happen, and they were done largely by members of a particular racial and ethnic group: white Europeans and their descendants in what became the United States. No amount of denial, distancing, or disassociation can make these facts go away. African Americans, American Indians, Mexican Americans, and other groups were victims, and they paid a terrible price for the early growth and success of white American society.

Second, the successful domination and exploitation of these groups was made easier by the cooperation of members of the victimized groups. The slave trade relied on black African agents; some American Indians aided the cause of white society, and some Mexicans helped to cheat other Mexicans. There is plenty of guilt to go around, and European Americans do not have a monopoly on greed, bigotry, or viciousness. Indeed, some white Southerners opposed slavery and fought for the abolition of the "peculiar institution." Similarly, some whites were appalled at the treatment of American Indians and Mexicans and attempted to stop it. Many of the ideas and values on which the United States was founded (justice, equality, liberty) had their origins in European intellectual traditions, and minority group protest has often involved little more than insisting that the nation live up to these ideals. Some members of the dominant group devoted (and sometimes gave) their lives to end the oppression, bigotry, and racial stratification examined in the next few chapters.

My point is to urge you to avoid, insofar as is possible, a "good guy/bad guy" approach to this subject matter. Guilt, anger, denial, and indifference are common reactions to this material, but these emotions do little to advance understanding, and often they impede communication. I—like my nephew Danny—believe that an understanding of America's racial past is vitally important for understanding the present. Historical background gives us a perspective on the present and allows us to identify important concepts and principles that we can use to disentangle the intergroup complexities surrounding us.

The goal of these chapters is not to make you feel any particular emotion. I will try to present the often-ugly facts neutrally and without extraneous editorializing. As scholars, your goal should be to absorb the material, understand the principles, and apply them to your own life and the society around you—not to indulge yourself in elaborate moral denunciations of American society, develop apologies for the past, or deny the realities of what happened. By dealing as objectively as we can with this material, we can begin to liberate our perspectives and build an understanding of the realities of American society and American minority groups.

3

The Development of Dominant-Minority Group Relations in Preindustrial America: The Origins of Slavery

I now entered on my fifteenth year—a sad epoch in the life of a slave girl. My master began to whisper foul words in my ear. Young as I was, I could not remain ignorant of their import. . . .

He was a crafty man, and resorted to many means to accomplish his purposes. . . . He tried his utmost to corrupt the pure principles my grandmother had instilled. . . . I turned from him with disgust and hatred. But he was my master. I was compelled to live under the same roof with him, where I saw a man forty years my senior daily violating the most sacred commandments of nature. He told me I was his property; that I must be subject to his will in all things. My soul revolted against the mean tyranny. But where could I turn for protection?

No matter whether the slave girl be as black as ebony or as fair as her mistress. In either case, there is no shadow of law to protect her from insult, from violence, or even from death; all these are inflicted by fiends who bear the shape of men. . . . The degradation, the wrongs,

> the vices that grow out of slavery, are more than I can describe. They are greater than you
> would willingly believe.
>
> —Harriet Jacobs (2012/1861, p. 35)*

This passage is taken from the memoirs of Harriet Jacobs, an escaped slave. It illustrates some
of the features of Southern slavery. She grew up as a slave in Edenton, North Carolina, and, in
this excerpt she recounts the sexual harassment she suffered at the hand of her master. Her
narrative illustrates the dynamics of power and sex in the "peculiar institution" and the very
limited options she had for defending herself from the advances of her master. To escape, she
hid in her grandmother's house for nearly 17 years before making her way to the North.

From the first settlements in the 1600s until the 19th century, most people living in what
was to become the United States relied directly on farming for food, shelter, and other
necessities of life. In an agricultural society, land and labor are central concerns, and the
struggle to control these resources led directly to the creation of minority group status for
three groups: African Americans, American Indians, and Mexican Americans. Why did
the colonists create slavery? Why were Africans but not American Indians or Europeans
enslaved? Why did American Indians lose their land and most of their population by the
1890s? How did the Mexican population in the Southwest become "Mexican Americans"?
How did the experience of becoming a subordinated minority group vary by gender?

In this chapter, the concepts introduced in part 1 will be used to answer these questions. Some new ideas and theories will also be introduced, and by the end of the chapter
we will have developed a theoretical model of the process that leads to the creation of a
minority group. The creation of black slavery in colonial America, arguably the single
most significant event in the early years of this nation, will be used to illustrate the process of minority group creation. We will also consider the subordination of American
Indians and Mexican Americans—two more historical events of great significance—as
additional case studies. We will follow the experiences of African Americans through the
days of segregation (chapter 4) and into the contemporary era (chapter 5). The story of
the development of minority group status for American Indians and Mexican Americans
will be picked up again in chapters 6 and 7, respectively.

Two broad themes underlie this chapter and, indeed, the remainder of the text:

1. The nature of dominant-minority group relations at any point in time is largely
a function of the characteristics of the society as a whole. The situation of a minority
group will reflect the realities of everyday social life and particularly the subsistence
technology (the means by which the society satisfies basic needs such as food and
shelter). As explained by Gerhard Lenski (see chapter 1), the subsistence technology of

---

The Trials of Girlhood, reprinted by permission of the publishers from *Incidents in the Life of a Slave Girl: Written
by Herself* by Harriet A. Jacobs, edited and with an Introduction by Jean Fagan Yellin: pp. 27–30, Cambridge,
Mass.: Harvard University Press, copyright © 1987, 2000 by the President and Fellows of Harvard College.

a society acts as a foundation, shaping and affecting every other aspect of the social structure, including minority group relations.

2. The contact situation—the conditions under which groups first come together—is the single most significant factor in the creation of minority group status. The nature of the contact situation has long-lasting consequences for the minority group and the extent of racial or ethnic stratification, the levels of racism and prejudice, the possibilities for assimilation and pluralism, and virtually every other aspect of the dominant-minority relationship.

The Origins of Slavery in America

By the early 1600s, Spanish explorers had conquered much of Central and South America, and the influx of gold, silver, and other riches from the New World had made Spain a powerful nation. Following Spain's lead, England proceeded to establish its presence in the western hemisphere, but its efforts at colonization were more modest than those of Spain. By the early 1600s, the English had established only two small colonies: Plymouth, settled by pious Protestant families, and Jamestown, populated primarily by males seeking their fortunes.

By 1619, the British colony at Jamestown, Virginia, had survived for more than a decade. The residents of the settlement had fought with the local natives and struggled continuously to eke out a living from the land. Starvation, disease, and death were frequent visitors, and the future of the enterprise continued to be in doubt.

In August of that year, a Dutch ship arrived. The master of the ship needed provisions and offered to trade his only cargo: about 20 black Africans. Many of the details of this transaction have been lost, and we probably will never know exactly how these people came to be chained in the hold of a ship. Regardless, this brief episode was a landmark event in the formation of what would become the United States. In combination with the strained relations between the English settlers and American Indians, the presence of these first few Africans raised an issue that has never been fully resolved: How should different groups in this society relate to each other?

The colonists at Jamestown had no ready answer. In 1619, England and its colonies did not practice slavery, so these first Africans were probably incorporated into colonial society as **indentured servants**, contract laborers who are obligated to serve a master for a specific number of years. At the end of the indenture, or contract, the servant became a free citizen. The colonies depended heavily on indentured servants from the British Isles for labor, and this status apparently provided a convenient way of defining the newcomers from Africa, who were, after all, treated as commodities and exchanged for food and water.

The position of African indentured servants in the colonies remained ambiguous for several decades. American slavery evolved gradually and in small steps; in fact, there was little demand for African labor during the years following 1619. By 1625, there still were only 23 blacks in Virginia, and that number had increased to perhaps 300 by mid-century (Franklin & Moss, 1994, p. 57). In the decades before the dawn of slavery in the British colonies, we know that some African indentured servants did become free citizens. Some became successful farmers and landowners and, like their white neighbors, purchased African and white indentured servants themselves (Smedley, 2007, p. 104). By the 1650s, however, many African Americans (and their offspring) were being treated as the property of others, or in other words, as slaves (Morgan, 1975, p. 154).

It was not until the 1660s that the first laws defining slavery were enacted. In the century that followed, hundreds of additional laws were passed to clarify and formalize the status of Africans in colonial America. By the 1750s, slavery had been clearly defined in law and in custom, and the idea that a person could own another person—not just the labor or the energy or the work of a person, but also the actual person—had been thoroughly institutionalized.

What caused slavery? The gradual evolution and low demand for indentured servants from Africa suggest that slavery was not somehow inevitable or preordained. Why did the colonists deliberately create this repressive system? Why did they reach out all the way to Africa for their slaves? If they wanted to create a slave system, why didn't they enslave the American Indians nearby or the white indentured servants already present in the colonies?

The Labor Supply Problem

American colonists of the 1600s saw slavery as a solution to several problems they faced. The business of the colonies was agriculture, and farm work at this time was labor intensive, performed almost entirely by hand. The Industrial Revolution was two centuries in the future, and there were few machines or labor-saving devices available to ease the everyday burden of work. A successful harvest depended largely on human effort.

As colonial society grew and developed, a specific form of agricultural production began to emerge. The **plantation system** was based on cultivating crops such as sugar, tobacco, and rice on large tracts of land using a large, cheap labor force, then exporting those crops. Profit margins tended to be small, so planters sought to stabilize their incomes by keeping the costs of production as low as possible. Profits in the labor-intensive plantation system could be maximized if a large, disciplined, and cheap workforce could be maintained by the landowners (Curtin, 1990; Morgan, 1975).

At about the same time the plantation system began to emerge, the supply of white indentured servants from the British Isles began to dwindle. Furthermore, the white indentured servants who did come to the colonies had to be released from their indenture every few years. Land was available, and these newly freed citizens tended to strike out on their own. Thus, landowners who relied on white indentured servants had to deal with high turnover rates in their workforces and faced a continually uncertain supply of labor.

Attempts to solve the labor supply problem by using American Indians failed. The tribes closest to the colonies were sometimes exploited for manpower. However, by the time the plantation system had evolved, the local tribes had dwindled in numbers as a result of disease and, to a lesser extent, warfare. Other Indian nations across the continent retained enough power to resist enslavement, and it was relatively easy for American Indians to escape back to their kinfolk.

This left black Africans as a potential source of manpower. The slave trade from Africa to the Spanish and Portuguese colonies of South America had been established in the 1500s and could be expanded to fill the needs of the British colonies as well. The colonists came to see slaves imported from Africa as the most logical, cost-effective way to solve their vexing shortage of labor and entered into the Atlantic slave trade, the system that eventually kidnapped millions of people from Africa (see exhibit 3.1). The colonists created slavery to cultivate their lands and generate profits, status, and success. The paradox at the core of U.S. society had been established: the construction of a social system devoted to freedom and individual liberty "in the New World was made possible only by the revival of an institution of naked tyranny foresworn for centuries in the Old" (Lacy, 1972, p. 22).

Exhibit 3.1 The African Diaspora

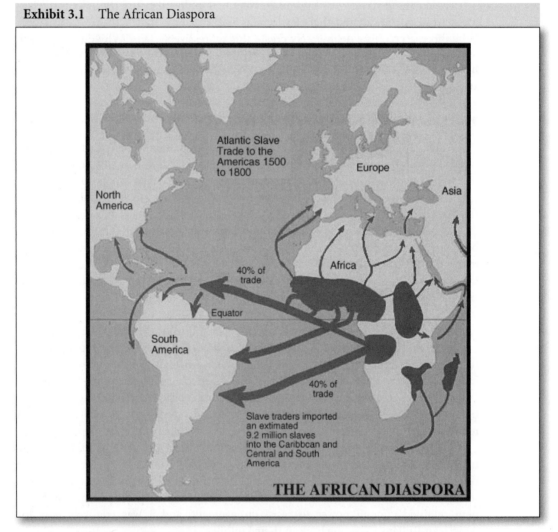

Source: From Williams. *Macmillan Encyclopedia of World Slavery, 1e.* © 1998 Gale, a part of Cengage Learning, Inc. Reproduced by permission. www.cengage.com/permissions.

Note: The size of the arrows is proportional to the number of slaves. Note that the bulk went to South America and that there were also flows to Europe and Asia.

The Contact Situation

The conditions under which groups first come into contact determine the immediate fate of the minority group and shape intergroup relations for years to come. We discussed the role of group competition in creating prejudice in chapter 1. Here, I expand on some these ideas by introducing two theories that will serve as analytical guides in understanding the contact situation.

The Noel Hypothesis. Sociologist Donald Noel (1968) identifies three features of the contact situation that in combination lead to some form of inequality between groups. The **Noel hypothesis** states, "*If two or more groups come together in a contact situation characterized by ethnocentrism, competition, and a differential in power, then some form of racial or ethnic stratification will result*" (p. 163; italics added). If the contact situation has all three characteristics, some dominant-minority group structure will be created.

Noel's first characteristic, **ethnocentrism**, is the tendency to judge other groups, societies, or lifestyles by the standards of one's own culture. Ethnocentrism is probably a universal component of human society, and some degree of ethnocentrism is essential to the maintenance of social solidarity and cohesion. Without some minimal level of pride in and loyalty to one's own society and cultural traditions, there would be no particular reason to observe the norms and laws, honor the sacred symbols, or cooperate with others in doing the daily work of society.

Regardless of its importance, ethnocentrism can have negative consequences. At its worst, it can lead to the view that other cultures and peoples are not just different, but also inferior. At the very least, ethnocentrism creates a social boundary line that members of the groups involved will recognize and observe. When ethnocentrism exists in any degree, people will tend to sort themselves out along group lines and identify characteristics that differentiate "us" from "them."

Competition is a struggle over a scarce commodity. As we saw in chapter 1, competition between groups often leads to harsh negative feelings (prejudice) and hostile actions (discrimination). In competitive contact situations, the victorious group becomes the dominant group, and the losers become the minority group. The competition may center on land, labor, jobs, housing, educational opportunities, political office, or anything else that is mutually desired by both groups or that one group has and the other group wants. Competition provides the eventual dominant group with the motivation to establish superiority. The dominant group serves its own interests by ending the competition and exploiting, controlling, eliminating, or otherwise dominating the minority group.

The third feature of the contact situation is a **differential in power** between the groups. Power, as you recall from chapter 1, is the ability of a group to achieve its goals even in the face of opposition from other groups. The amount of power commanded by a group is a function of three factors. First, the size of the group can make a difference, and, all other things being equal, larger groups are more powerful. Second, in addition to raw numbers, the degree of organization, discipline, and the quality of group leadership can make a difference in the ability of a group to pursue its goals.

A third component of power is resources, or anything that can be used to help the group achieve its goals. Depending on the context, resources might include anything from land to information to money. The greater the number and variety of resources at the disposal of a group, the greater that group's potential ability to dominate other groups. Thus, a larger, better-organized group with more resources at its disposal will generally be able to impose its will on smaller, less-well-organized groups with fewer resources. The Noel hypothesis is diagrammed in exhibit 3.2.

Note the respective functions of each of the three factors in shaping the contact situation and the emergence of inequality. If ethnocentrism is present, the groups will recognize their differences and maintain their boundaries. If competition is also present, the group that eventually dominates will attempt to maximize its share of scarce commodities by controlling or subordinating the group that eventually becomes the "minority" group. The differential in power allows the dominant group to succeed in establishing a superior position. Ethnocentrism tells the dominant group whom to dominate, competition tells the dominant group why it should establish a structure of dominance, and power is how the dominant group's will is imposed on the minority group.

The Noel hypothesis can be applied to the creation of minority groups in a variety of situations. We will also use the model to analyze changes in dominant-minority structures over time.

The Blauner Hypothesis. The contact situation also has been analyzed by sociologist Robert Blauner in his book *Racial Oppression in America* (1972). Blauner identifies two different initial relationships: colonization and immigration. His analysis is complex and nuanced but, for our purposes, we can summarize his thinking in terms of what we will call the **Blauner hypothesis**: *Minority groups created by colonization will experience more intense prejudice, racism, and discrimination than those created by immigration.*

Exhibit 3.2   A Model of the Establishment of Minority Group Status

Characteristics of Contact Situation	Result	
Ethnocentrism	→ Group boundaries established (who to dominate)	
Competition	→ Motivation to establish superiority (why dominate)	→ Ethnic or racial stratification
Differential in power	→ Dominant group imposes its will on minority group (how to dominate)	

Source: Based on Noel (1968).

Furthermore, the disadvantaged status of colonized groups will persist longer and be more difficult to overcome than the disadvantaged status faced by groups created by immigration (Blauner, 1972, pp. 52–75).

Colonized minority groups, such as African Americans, are forced into minority status by the superior military and political power of the dominant group. At the time of contact with the dominant group, colonized groups are subjected to massive inequalities and attacks on their cultures. They are assigned to positions, such as slave status, from which any form of assimilation is extremely difficult and perhaps even forbidden by the dominant group. Frequently, members of the minority group are identified by highly visible racial or physical characteristics that maintain and reinforce the oppressive system. Thus, minority groups created by colonization experience harsher and more-persistent rejection and oppression than groups created by immigration.

Immigrant minority groups are at least in part voluntary participants in the host society. That is, although the decision to immigrate may be motivated by extreme pressures, such as famine or political persecution, immigrant groups have at least some control over their destinations and their positions in the host society. As a result, they do not occupy positions that are as markedly inferior as those of colonized groups. They retain enough internal organization and resources to pursue their own self-interests, and they commonly experience more rapid acceptance and easier movement to equality. The boundaries between groups are not so rigidly maintained, especially when the groups are racially similar. In discussing European immigrant groups, for example, Blauner (1972) states that entering into American society

> involved a degree of choice and self-direction that was for the most part denied to people of color. Voluntary immigration made it more likely that . . . European . . . ethnic groups would identify with America and see the host culture as a positive opportunity. (p. 56)

Acculturation and, particularly, integration were significantly more possible for European immigrant groups than for the groups formed under conquest or colonization.

Blauner stresses that the initial differences between colonized and immigrant minority groups have consequences that persist long after the original contact. For example, based on measures of equality—or integration into the secondary sector, the second step in Gordon's model of assimilation (see chapter 2)—such as average income, years of education, and unemployment rate, descendants of European immigrants are equal with national norms today (see chapter 2 for specific data). In contrast, descendants of colonized and conquered groups (e.g., African Americans) are, on the average, below the national norms on virtually all measures of equality and integration (see chapters 5–8 for specific data).

Blauner's two types of minority groups lie at opposite ends of a continuum, but there are intermediate positions between the extremes. Enclave and middleman minorities (see chapter 2) often originate as immigrant groups who bring some resources and thus have more opportunities than colonized minority groups to carve out places for themselves in the host society. Unlike European groups, however, many of these minorities are also racially distinguishable, and certain kinds of opportunities may be closed to them. For instance, U.S. citizenship was expressly forbidden to immigrants from China until World War II. Federal laws restricted the entrance of Chinese immigrants, and state and local laws restricted their opportunities for education, jobs, and housing. For these and other reasons, the Asian immigrant experience cannot be equated with European immigrant patterns (Blauner, 1972, p. 55). Because they combine characteristics of both the colonized and the immigrant minority group experience, we can predict that in terms of equality, enclave and middleman minority groups will occupy an intermediate status between the more assimilated white ethnic groups and the colonized racial minorities.

Blauner's typology has proven to be an extremely useful conceptual tool for the analysis of U.S. dominant-minority relations, and it is used extensively throughout this text. In fact, the case studies that compose part 3of this text are arranged in approximate order from groups created by colonization to those created by immigration. Of course, it is difficult to measure such things as the extent of colonization objectively or precisely, and the exact order of the groups is somewhat arbitrary.

The Creation of Slavery in the United States

The Noel hypothesis helps explain why colonists enslaved black Africans instead of white indentured servants or American Indians. First, all three groups were the objects of ethnocentric feelings on the part of the elite groups that dominated colonial society. Black Africans and American Indians were perceived as being different on religious as well as racial grounds. Many white indentured servants were Irish Catholics, criminals, or paupers. They not only occupied a lowly status in society, but also were perceived as different from the British Protestants who dominated colonial society.

Second, competition of some sort existed between the colonists and all three groups. The competition with American Indians was direct and focused on control of land. Competition with indentured servants, white and black, was more indirect; these groups were the labor force that the landowners needed to work on their plantations and become successful in the New World.

Noel's third variable, differential in power, is the key variable that explains why Africans instead of the other groups were enslaved (see exhibit 3.3). During the first several decades of colonial history, the balance of power between the colonists and American Indians was relatively even and, in fact, often favored American Indians (Lurie, 1982, pp. 131–133). The colonists were outnumbered, and their muskets and cannons were only marginally more effective than bows and spears. The American Indian tribes were well-organized social units capable of sustaining resistance to and mounting reprisals against the colonists, and it took centuries for the nascent United States to finally defeat American Indians militarily.

White indentured servants, on the one hand, had the advantage of being preferred over black indentured servants (Noel, 1968, p. 168). Their greater desirability gave

Exhibit 3.3 The Noel Hypothesis Applied to the Origins of Slavery

	Three Causal Factors		
Potential Sources of Labor	Ethnocentrism	Competition	Differential in Power
White indentured servants	Yes	Yes	No
American Indians	Yes	Yes	No
Black indentured servants	Yes	Yes	Yes

Source: From "A Theory of the Origin of Ethnic Stratification" by Donald Noel in *Social Problems,* vol. 16, no. 2, Autumn 1968, Copyright © 1968. Reprinted by permission of The University of California Press, via the Copyright Clearance Center.

them bargaining power and the ability to negotiate better treatment and more lenient terms than could black indentured servants. If the planters had attempted to enslave white indentured servants, this source of labor would have dwindled even more rapidly.

Africans, on the other hand, had become indentured servants by force and coercion. In Blauner's terms, they were a colonized group that did not freely choose to enter the British colonies. Thus, they had no bargaining power. Unlike American Indians, they had no nearby relatives, no knowledge of the countryside, and no safe havens to which to escape. Exhibit 3.3 summarizes the impact of these three factors on the three potential sources of labor in colonial America.

Paternalistic Relations

Recall the first theme stated at the beginning of this chapter: the nature of intergroup relationships will reflect the characteristics of the larger society. The most important and profitable unit of economic production in the colonial South was the plantation, and the region was dominated by a small group of wealthy landowners. A society with a small elite class and a plantation-based economy will often develop a form of minority relations called **paternalism** (van den Berghe, 1967; Wilson, 1973). The key features of paternalism are vast power differentials and huge inequalities between dominant and minority groups, elaborate and repressive systems of control over the minority group, caste-like barriers between groups, elaborate and highly stylized codes of behavior and communication between groups, and low rates of overt conflict. Each of these characteristics will be considered in turn.

As slavery evolved in the colonies, the dominant group shaped the system to fit its needs. To solidify control of the labor of their slaves, the plantation elite designed and enacted an elaborate system of laws and customs that gave masters nearly total legal power over slaves. In these laws, slaves were defined as **chattel**, or personal property, rather than as persons, and they were accorded no civil or political rights. Slaves could not own property, sign contracts, bring lawsuits, or even testify in court (except against another slave). The masters were given the legal authority to determine almost every aspect of a slave's life, including work schedules, living arrangements, diets, and even names (Elkins, 1959; Franklin & Moss, 1994; Genovese, 1974; Jordan, 1968; Stampp, 1956).

The law permitted the master to determine the type and severity of punishment for misbehavior. Slaves were forbidden by law to read or write, and marriages between slaves were not legally recognized. Masters could separate husbands from wives and parents from children if it suited them. Slaves had little formal decision-making ability or control over their lives or the lives of their loved ones.

In colonial America, slavery became synonymous with race. Race, slavery, inferiority, and powerlessness became intertwined in ways that, according to many analysts, still affect the ways black and white Americans think about one another (Hacker, 1992). Slavery was a **caste system**, or closed stratification system. In a caste system, there is no mobility between social positions, and the social class you are born into (your ascribed status) is permanent. Slave status was for life and was passed on to any children a slave might have. Whites, no matter what they did, could not become slaves.

Interaction between members of the dominant and minority groups in a paternalistic system is governed by a rigid, strictly enforced code of etiquette. Slaves were expected to show deference and humility and visibly display their lower status when interacting with whites. These rigid behavioral codes made it possible for blacks and whites to work together, sometimes intimately, sometimes for their entire lives, without threatening the power and status differentials inherent in the system. Plantation and farm work required close and frequent contact between blacks and whites, and status differentials were maintained socially rather than physically.

The frequent but unequal interactions allowed the elites to maintain a pseudotolerance, an attitude of benevolent despotism, toward their slaves. Their prejudice and racism were often expressed as positive emotions of affection for their black slaves. The attitude of the planters toward their slaves was often paternalistic and even genteel (Wilson, 1973, pp. 52–55).

For their part, black slaves often could not hate their owners as much as they hated the system that constrained them. The system defined slaves as pieces of property owned by their masters—yet they were, undeniably, human beings. Thus, slavery was founded, at its heart, on a contradiction.

> The master learned to treat his slaves both as property and as men and women, the slaves learned to express and affirm their humanity even while they were constrained in much of their lives to accept their status as chattel. (Parish, 1989, p. 1)

The powerlessness of slaves made it difficult for them to openly reject or resist the system. Slaves had few ways in which they could directly challenge the institution of slavery or their position in it. Open defiance was ineffective and could result in punishment or even death. In general, masters would not be prosecuted for physically abusing their slaves.

One of the few slave revolts that occurred in the United States illustrates both the futility of overt challenge and the degree of repression built into the system. In 1831, in Southampton County, Virginia, a slave named Nat Turner led an uprising during which 57 whites were killed. The revolt was starting to spread when the state militia met and routed the growing slave army. More than 100 slaves died in the armed encounter, and Nat Turner and 13 others were later executed. Slave owners and white Southerners in general were greatly alarmed by the uprising and consequently tightened the system of control over slaves, making it even more repressive (Franklin & Moss, 1994, p. 147). Ironically, the result of Nat Turner's attempt to lead slaves to freedom was greater oppression and control by the dominant group.

Others were more successful in resisting the system. Runaway slaves were a constant problem for slave owners, especially in the states bordering the free states of the North. The difficulty of escape and the low likelihood of successfully reaching the North did not deter thousands from attempting the feat, some of them repeatedly. Many runaway slaves received help from the Underground Railroad, an informal network of safe houses supported by African Americans and whites involved in **abolitionism**, the movement to abolish slavery. These escapes created colorful legends and heroic figures, including Frederick Douglass, Sojourner Truth, and Harriet Tubman.

Besides running away and open rebellion, slaves used the forms of resistance most readily available to them: sabotage, intentional carelessness, dragging their feet, and work slowdowns. As historian Peter Parish (1989) points out, it is difficult to separate "a natural desire to avoid hard work [from a] conscious decision to protest or resist" (p. 73), and much of this behavior may fall more into the category of noncooperation than of deliberate political rebellion. Nonetheless, these behaviors were widespread and document the rejection of the system by its victims.

On an everyday basis, the slaves managed their lives and families as best they could. Most slaves were neither docile victims nor unyielding rebels. As the institution of slavery developed, a distinct African American experience accumulated, and traditions of resistance and accommodation developed side by side. Most slaves worked to create a world for themselves within the confines and restraints of the plantation system, avoiding the more vicious repression as much as possible while attending to their own needs and those of their families. An African American culture was forged in response to the realities of slavery and was manifested in folklore, music, religion, family and kinship structures, and other aspects of everyday life (Blassingame, 1972; Genovese, 1974; Gutman, 1976).

The Dimensions of Minority Group Status

The situation of African Americans under slavery can be more completely described by applying some of the concepts developed in part 1.

Power, Inequality, and Institutional Discrimination. The key concepts for understanding the creation of slavery are power, inequality, and institutional discrimination. The plantation elite used its greater power resources to consign black Africans to an inferior status. The system of racial inequality was implemented and reinforced by institutionalized discrimination; it became a central aspect of everyday life in the antebellum South. The legal and political institutions of colonial society were shaped to benefit the landowners and give them almost total control over their slaves.

Prejudice and Racism. What about the attitudes and feelings of the people involved? What was the role of personal prejudice? How and why did the ideology of anti-black racism start? As we discussed in chapter 1, individual prejudice and ideological racism are not as important as causes of the creation of minority group status, but are more the results of systems of racial inequality (Jordan, 1968, p. 80; Smedley, 2007, pp. 100–104). The colonists did not enslave black indentured servants because they were prejudiced or because they disliked blacks or thought them inferior. The decision to enslave black Africans was an attempt to resolve a labor supply problem. The primary roles of prejudice and racism in the creation of minority group status are to rationalize and "explain" the emerging system of racial and ethnic advantage (Wilson, 1973, pp. 76–78).

Prejudice and racism help to mobilize support for the creation of minority group status and to stabilize the system as it emerges. Prejudice and racism can provide convenient and convincing justifications for exploitation. They can help insulate a system like slavery from questioning and criticism and make it appear reasonable and even desirable. Thus, the intensity, strength, and popularity of anti-black Southern racism actually reached its height almost 200 years after slavery began to emerge. During the early 1800s, the American abolitionist movement brought slavery under heavy attack, and in response the ideology of anti-black racism was strengthened (Wilson, 1973, p. 79). The greater the opposition to a system of racial stratification or the greater the magnitude of the exploitation, the greater the need of the beneficiaries and their apologists to justify, rationalize, and explain.

Once created, dominant group prejudice and racism become widespread and common ways of thinking about the minority group. In the case of colonial slavery, anti-black beliefs and feelings became part of the standard package of knowledge, understanding, and truths shared by members of the dominant group. As the decades wore on and the institution of slavery solidified, prejudice and racism were passed on from generation to generation. For succeeding generations, anti-black prejudice became just another piece of information and perspective on the world learned during socialization. Anti-black prejudice and racism began as part of an attempt to control the labor of black indentured servants, became embedded in early American culture, and were established as integral parts of the socialization process for succeeding generations (see Myrdal's "vicious cycle" in chapter 1).

These conceptual relationships are presented in exhibit 3.4. Racial inequality arises from the contact situation, as specified in the Noel hypothesis. As the dominant-minority relationship begins to take shape, prejudice and racism develop as rationalizations. Over

Exhibit 3.4   A Model for the Creation of Prejudice and Racism

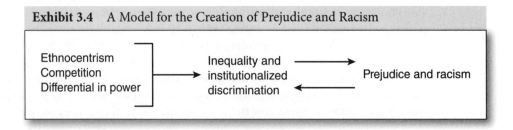

Ethnocentrism
Competition
Differential in power

Inequality and
institutionalized
discrimination

Prejudice and racism

time, a vicious cycle develops as prejudice and racism reinforce the pattern of inequality between groups, which was the cause of prejudice and racism in the first place. Thus, the Blauner hypothesis states, the subordination of colonized minority groups is perpetuated through time.

Assimilation. There is an enormous literature on American slavery, and research on the nature and meaning of the system continues to this day. Many issues remain unsettled, however, and one of the more controversial, consequential, and interesting of these concerns the effect of slavery on the slaves.

Apologists for the system of slavery and some historians of the South writing early in the 20th century accepted the rationalizations inherent in anti-black prejudice and argued that slavery was actually beneficial for black Africans. According to this view, British American slavery operated as a "school for civilization" (Phillips, 1918) that rescued savages from the jungles of Africa and exposed them to Christianity and Western civilization. Some argued that slavery was benevolent because it protected slaves from the evils and exploitation of the factory system of the industrial North. These racist views were most popular a century ago, early in the development of the social sciences. Since that time, scholars have established a number of facts (e.g., Western Africa, the area from which most slaves came, had been the site of a number of powerful, advanced civilizations) that make this view untenable by anyone but the most dedicated racist thinkers.

At the opposite extreme, slavery has been compared with Nazi concentration camps and likened to a "perverted patriarchy" that brainwashed, emasculated, and dehumanized slaves, stripping them of their heritage and culture. Historian Stanley Elkins provocatively argued this interpretation, now widely regarded as overstated, in his book *Slavery: A Problem in American Institutional and Intellectual Life* (1959). Although his conclusions might be overdrawn, Elkins' argument and evidence are important for any exploration of the nature of American slavery. In fact, much of the scholarship on slavery since the publication of Elkins' book has been an attempt to refute or at least modify the points he made.

Still a third view of the impact of slavery maintains that through all the horror and abuse of enslavement, slaves retained a sense of self and a firm anchor in their African traditions. This point of view stresses the importance of kinship, religion, and culture in helping African Americans cope; it has been presented most poignantly in Alex Haley's semifictional family history *Roots* (1976), but it is also represented in the scholarly literature on slavery since Elkins (see Blassingame, 1972; and Genovese, 1974).

The debate over the impact of slavery continues, and we cannot hope to resolve the issues here. However, it is clear that African Americans, in Blauner's terms, were a "colonized" minority group who were extensively—and coercively—acculturated. Language acculturation began on the slave ships, where different tribal and language groups were mixed together to inhibit communication and lower the potential for resistance and revolt (Mannix, 1962).

The plantation elite and their agents needed to communicate with their workforce and insisted on using English. Within a generation or two, African language use died out. Some scholars argue that some African words and language patterns persist to the present day, but even if this is true the significance of this survival is trivial compared with the coerced adoption of English. To the extent that culture depends on language, Africans under slavery experienced massive acculturation.

Acculturation through slavery was clearly a process that was forced on African Americans. Because they were a colonized minority group and unwilling participants in the system, they had little choice but to adjust to the conditions established by the plantation elite as best they could. Their traditional culture was suppressed, and their choices for adjustment to the system were sharply constrained. Black slaves developed new cultural forms and social relationships, but they did so in a situation with few options or choices (Blauner, 1972, p. 66). The extent to which any African cultural elements survived the institution of slavery is a matter of some controversy, but given the power differentials inherent in the system, African Americans had few choices regarding their manner of adjustment.

Gender Relations. Southern agrarian society developed into a complex social system stratified by race and gender as well as by class. The plantation elite, small in number but wealthy and politically powerful, was at the top of the structure. Most whites in the South were small farmers, and relatively few of them owned slaves. In 1860, for example, only 25% of all Southern whites owned slaves (Franklin & Moss, 1994, p. 123).

The principal line of differentiation in the antebellum South was, of course, race, which was largely synonymous with slave versus nonslave status. Each of the racial groups was, in turn, stratified by gender. White women were subordinate to the males of the plantation elite, and the slave community echoed the patriarchal pattern of Southern society, except that the degree of gender inequality among blacks was sharply truncated by the fact that slaves had little autonomy and few resources. At the bottom of the system were African American female slaves. Minority women are generally in double jeopardy, oppressed through their gender as well as their race. For black female slaves, the constraints were triple: "Black in a white society, slave in a free society, women in a society ruled by men, female slaves had the least formal power and were perhaps the most vulnerable group of antebellum America" (White, 1985, p. 15).

The race and gender roles of the day idealized Southern white women and placed them on a pedestal. A romanticized conception of femininity was quite inconsistent with the roles women slaves were required to play. Besides domestic roles, female slaves also worked in the fields and did their share of the hardest, most physically demanding, least "feminine" farm work. Southern ideas about feminine fragility and daintiness were quickly abandoned when they interfered with work and the profit to be made from slave labor (Amott & Matthaei, 1991, p. 146).

Reflecting their vulnerability and powerlessness, women slaves were sometimes used to breed more slaves to sell. They were raped and otherwise abused by the males of the dominant group. John Blassingame (1972) expresses their vulnerability to sexual victimization:

> Many white men considered every slave cabin a house of ill-fame. Often through "gifts" but usually by force, white overseers and planters obtained the sexual favors of black women. Generally speaking, the women were literally forced to offer themselves "willingly" and receive a trinket for their compliance rather than a flogging for their refusal. (p. 83)

Note the power relationships implicit in this passage: female slaves had little choice but to feign willing submission to their white owners.

The routines of work and everyday life differed for male and female slaves. Although they sometimes worked with the men, especially during harvest time, women more often worked in sex-segregated groups organized around domestic as well as farm chores. In addition to working in the fields, they attended the births and cared for the children of both races, cooked and cleaned, wove cloth and sewed clothes, and did the laundry. The women often worked longer hours than the men, doing housework and other chores long after the men had retired for the night (Robertson, 1996, p. 21; White, 1985, p. 122).

The group-oriented nature of their tasks gave female slaves an opportunity to develop same-sex bonds and relationships. Women cooperated in their chores, in caring for their children, in the maintenance of their quarters, and in myriad other domestic and family chores. These networks and interpersonal bonds could be used to resist the system. For example, slave women sometimes induced abortions rather than bring more children into bondage. They often controlled the role of midwife and were able to effectively deceive slave owners and disguise the abortions as miscarriages (White, 1985, pp. 125–126). The networks of relationships among the female slaves provided mutual aid and support for everyday problems, solace and companionship during the travails of a vulnerable and exploited existence, and some ability to buffer and resist the influence and power of the slave owners (Andersen, 1993, pp. 164–165).

Slaves in the American system were brutally repressed and exploited, but females were even more subordinated than males. Also, their oppression and exclusion sharply differentiated female slaves from white females. The white "Southern belle," chaste, untouchable, and unremittingly virtuous, had little in common with African American women under slavery.

FOCUS ON CONTEMPORARY ISSUES:
Slavery and Indentured Servitude Today

You might think of slavery as a distant piece of history, remote and bizarre. The idea that a person could be owned by another person, and bought and sold like livestock, might seem hopelessly alien, especially in a culture so devoted to individual happiness and personal well-being. Yet, this ancient institution is not as remote as it might seem and, in fact, can be found around the world, in advanced industrial nations, including in the United States.[1] The "Internet Research Project" at the end of this chapter will expose you to the realities of modern slavery in some detail. Here, I will provide a general overview.

It is impossible to know the dimensions of modern slavery but it is estimated that the number of slaves today ranges up to 30 million or more. Contemporary slavery takes a variety of forms, but all feature dynamics similar to those noted in the Noel hypothesis:

(Continued)

(Continued)

the motivation is supplied by a desire for profits, and the populations from which slaves are taken are relatively powerless and lack the resources to defend themselves. Furthermore, ethnocentrism is often a factor as slaves and owners are frequently from different language, culture, racial, or religious groups.

Many modern-day slaves are laborers living within their country of birth. They are forced into bondage by various means, including debt bondage. In this system, individuals are not owned outright as slaves. Rather, they are required to work for little or no wages until some debt is paid off and their unfree status is maintained through time by high interest rates. For example, Skinner (2008) reports the case of a man in India working to pay off a debt of $0.62 cents incurred by his great-grandfather in 1958. With interest rates of 100% per year, he is forced to work in a quarry for no wage, three generations after the debt was originally incurred. It is thought that most forced labor slaves are in Southeast Asia, especially India and China.

Other slaves are part of an international system of trafficking in people, aided by globalization, instantaneous communication, and rapid, cheap travel. A large part of this trafficking is connected to commercial sexual enterprises such as prostitution and pornography. Sex trafficking involves children as well as women. The traffickers find their victims in less-developed nations in which many women (and children) have been displaced from their village communities and are no longer protected by their traditional familial, religious, or political institutions. Women are often duped into believing that they are being hired for legitimate jobs (domestic work or childcare) in a more-developed nation. When they arrive at their destination, their travel documents are taken and they are forced into sex work. They are isolated and kept powerless by their lack of documents, their illegal status, and their inability to speak the language of their new country. The huge power differentials between "slaves and masters" are reminiscent of American slavery, as is the masters' ability to treat their slaves any way they please.

The United States is one of the prime destinations for victims of sex trafficking and for a variety of other workers who are bound by various forms of debt bondage. Some of these modern slaves provide the unskilled labor that keeps enclaves like Chinatown functioning, while others work in agriculture, the seafood industry, landscaping, construction, and other areas. Many of these workers enter the United States legally as "guest workers." Once they are in the country, however, there is little federal or state oversight of their situation. According to one report, these workers are often abused, forced to live and work in horrible conditions, and cheated of their wages by the brokers that brought them into the country (Bauer, 2008).

Some of these modern forms of involuntary servitude are quite different from the system of American slavery. Instead of a journey from Africa that could last months, modern slaves can be shipped around the globe in hours or days. Instead of cotton plantations, slaves today work in factories and brothels. Like all forms of slavery, however, the modern versions are involuntary, coercive, and maintained by violence and force.

The Creation of Minority Status for American Indians and Mexican Americans

Two other groups became minorities during the preindustrial period. In this section, we will review the dynamics of these processes and make some comparisons with African Americans. As you will see, both the Noel and Blauner hypotheses provide some extremely useful insights into these experiences.

American Indians

As Europeans began to penetrate the areas of North America that became the United States, they encountered hundreds of societies that had lived on this land for thousands of years. American Indian societies were highly variable in culture, language, size, and subsistence technology. Some were small, nomadic hunter–gatherer bands, and others were more-developed societies in which people lived in settled villages and tended large gardens. Regardless of their exact nature, the inexorable advance of white society eventually devastated them all. Contact began in the East and established a pattern of conflict and defeat for American Indians that continued until the last of the tribes were finally defeated in the late 1800s. The continual expansion of white society into the West allowed many settlers to fulfill their dreams of economic self-sufficiency, but American Indians, who lost not only their lives and their land, but also much of their traditional way of life, paid an incalculable price.

An important and widely unrecognized point about American Indians is that there is no such thing as the American Indian. Rather, there were—and are—hundreds of different tribes or nations, each with its own language, culture, home territory, and unique history. There are, of course, similarities from tribe to tribe, but there are also vast differences between, for example, the forest-dwelling tribes of Virginia, who lived in longhouses and cultivated gardens, and the nomadic tribes of the Great Plains, who relied on hunting to satisfy their needs. Each tribe was and remains a unique blend of language, values, and social structure. Because of space constraints, we will not always be able to take all these differences into account. Nonetheless, it is important to be aware of the diversity and to be sensitive to the variety of peoples and histories subsumed within the general category of American Indian.

A second important point is that many American Indian tribes no longer exist or are vastly diminished in size. When Jamestown was established in 1607, it is estimated that there were anywhere from several million to 10 million or more American Indians living in what became the United States. By 1890, when the Indian wars finally ended, the number of American Indians had fallen to fewer than 250,000. By the end of the nearly 300-year-long "contact situation," American Indian populations had declined by at least 75%, perhaps as much as 95% (Mann, 2011, pp. 105–109). Very little of this population loss was due directly to warfare and battle casualties. The greatest part was caused by European diseases brought over by the colonists and by the destruction of the food supplies on which American Indian societies relied. American Indians died by the thousands from measles, influenza, smallpox, cholera, tuberculosis, and a variety of other infectious diseases (Wax, 1971, p. 17; see also Oswalt & Neely, 1996; and Snipp,

1989). Traditional hunting grounds and garden plots were taken over by the expanding American society, and game such as the buffalo was slaughtered to the point of extinction. The result of the contact situation for American Indians very nearly approached genocide.

American Indians and the Noel and Blauner Hypotheses. We have already used the Noel hypothesis to analyze why American Indians were not enslaved during the colonial era. Their competition with whites centered on land, not labor, and the Indian nations were often successful in resisting domination (at least temporarily). As American society spread to the West, competition over land continued, and the growing power, superior technology, and greater resource base of the dominant group gradually pushed American Indians to near extinction.

Various attempts were made to control the persistent warfare, the most important of which occurred before independence from Great Britain. In 1763, the British Crown ruled that the various tribes were to be considered "sovereign nations with inalienable rights to their land" (see Lurie, 1982, p. 136; McNickle, 1973; and Wax, 1971). In other words, each tribe was to be treated as a nation-state, like France or Russia, and the colonists could not simply expropriate tribal lands. Rather, negotiations had to take place, and treaties of agreement had to be signed by all affected parties. The tribes had to be compensated for any loss of land.

This policy was often ignored but was continued by the newborn federal government after the American Revolution. The principle of sovereignty is important because it established a unique relationship between the federal government and American Indians. The fact that white society ignored the policy and regularly broke the treaties gives American Indians legal claims against the federal government that are also unique.

East of the Mississippi River, the period of open conflict was brought to a close by the Indian Removal Act of 1830, which dictated to the tribes a policy of forced emigration. The law required all tribes in the East to move to lands west of the Mississippi. Some of the affected tribes did not resist, others fought, and still others fled to Canada rather than move to the new territory. Regardless, the Indian Removal Act "solved" the Indian problem in the East. The relative scarcity of American Indians in the eastern United States continues to the present, and the majority of American Indians live in the western two-thirds of the nation.

In the West, the grim story of competition for land accompanied by rising hostility and aggression repeated itself. Wars were fought, buffalo were killed, territory was expropriated, atrocities were committed on both sides, and the fate of the tribes became more and more certain. By 1890, the greater power and resources of white society had defeated the Indian nations. All of the great warrior chiefs were dead or in prison, and almost all American Indians were living on reservations controlled by agencies of the federal government. The reservations consisted of land set aside for the tribes by the government during treaty negotiations. Often, these lands were not the traditional homelands and were hundreds or even thousands of miles away from what the tribe considered to be "home." It is not surprising that the reservations were usually on undesirable, often worthless, land.

The 1890s mark a low point in American Indian history, a time of great demoralization and sadness. The tribes had to find a way to adapt to reservation life and new forms of subordination to the federal government. Although elements of the tribal way of life have survived, the tribes were impoverished and without resources and had little ability to pursue their own interests.

American Indians, in Blauner's terms, were a colonized minority group who faced high levels of prejudice, racism, and discrimination. Like African Americans, they were controlled by paternalistic systems (the reservations) and in a variety of ways were coercively acculturated. Furthermore, according to Blauner, the negative consequences of colonized minority group status will persist long after the contact situation has been resolved. As we will see in chapter 6, there is a great deal of evidence to support this prediction.

Gender Relations. In the centuries before contact with Europeans, American Indian societies distributed resources and power in a wide variety of ways. At one extreme, some American Indian societies were highly stratified, and many practiced various forms of slavery. Others stressed equality, sharing of resources, and respect for the autonomy and dignity of each individual, including women and children (Amott & Matthaei, 1991, p. 33). American Indian societies were generally patriarchal and followed a strict gender-based division of labor, but this did not necessarily mean that women were subordinate. In many tribes, women held positions of great responsibility and controlled the wealth. For example, among the Iroquois (a large and powerful federation of tribes located in the Northeast), women controlled the land and the harvest, arranged marriages, supervised the children, and were responsible for the appointment of tribal leaders and decisions about peace and war (Oswalt & Neely, 1996, pp. 404–405). It was not unusual for women in many tribes to play key roles in religion, politics, warfare, and the economy. Some women even became highly respected warriors and chiefs (Amott & Matthaei, 1991, p. 36).

Gender relations were affected in a variety of ways during the prolonged contact period. In some cases, the relative status and power of women rose. For example, the women of the Navajo tribe (located mainly in what is now Arizona and New Mexico) were traditionally responsible for the care of herd animals and livestock. When the Spanish introduced sheep and goats into the region, the importance of this sector of the subsistence economy increased, and the power and status of women grew along with it.

In other cases, women were affected adversely. The women of the tribes of the Great Plains, for example, suffered a dramatic loss as a result of contact. The sexual division of labor in these tribes was that women were responsible for gardening, whereas men handled the hunting. When horses were introduced from Europe, the productivity of the male hunters was greatly increased. As their economic importance increased, males became more dominant and women correspondingly lost status and power. Women in the Cherokee nation—a large tribe whose original homelands were in the Southeast—similarly lost considerable status and power under the pressure to assimilate. Traditionally, Cherokee land was cultivated, controlled, and passed down from generation to generation by the women. This matrilineal pattern was abandoned in favor of the European pattern of male ownership when the Cherokee attempted (futilely, as it turned out) to acculturate and avoid relocation under the Indian Removal Act of 1830 (Evans, 1989, pp. 12–18).

Summary. By the end of the contact period, the surviving American Indian tribes were impoverished, powerless, and clearly subordinate to white society and the federal government. Like African Americans, American Indians were sharply differentiated from the dominant group by race, and in many cases the tribes were internally stratified by gender. As was the case with African American slaves, the degree of gender inequality within the tribes was limited by their overall lack of autonomy and resources.

COMPARATIVE FOCUS:
Hawaii

In 1788, while American Indians and whites continued their centuries-long struggle, white Europeans first made contact with the indigenous people of Hawaii (see map in Exhibit 3.5). The contact situation and the system of group relations that evolved on the island nation provide an interesting and instructive contrast with the history of American Indians.

In Hawaii, contact was not immediately followed by conquest and colonization. Early relations between Europeans and Hawaiians were organized around trade and

Exhibit 3.5   Map of the Hawaiian Islands

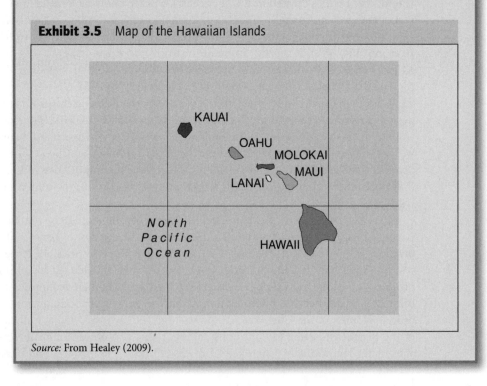

Source: From Healey (2009).

commerce, not competition over the control of land or labor. Also, Hawaiian society was large and highly developed, and it had sufficient military strength to protect itself from the relatively few Europeans who came to the islands in the early days. Thus, two of the three conditions stated in the Noel hypothesis for the emergence of a dominant-minority situation were not present in the early days of European–Hawaiian contact and, consistent with the hypothesis, overt structures of conquest or dominance did not emerge until decades after first contact.

Contact with Europeans did bring other consequences, of course, including smallpox and other diseases to which native Hawaiians had no immunity. Death rates rose, and the population of native Hawaiians, which numbered about 300,000 in 1788, fell to less than 60,000 a century later (Kitano & Daniels, 1995, p. 137). White Europeans gradually turned the land to commercial agriculture, and by the mid-1800s white planters had established large sugar plantations, an enterprise that is extremely labor intensive and that has often been associated with systems of enforced labor and slavery (Curtin, 1990). By that time, however, there were not enough native Hawaiians to fill the demand for labor, and the planters began to recruit abroad, mostly in China, Japan, Korea, the Philippines, Portugal, and Puerto Rico. The numbers of Native Hawaiians continued to shrink, and they were gradually pushed off their land and to the margins of the emerging society.

The white plantation owners began to dominate the island economy and political structure. Other groups, however, were not excluded from schools or jobs and no segregation laws were enacted. Americans of Japanese ancestry, for example, have been very powerful in politics and have produced many of the leading Hawaiian politicians. Most other groups have taken advantage of the relative openness of Hawaiian society and carved out niches for themselves in the institutional structure.

In terms of primary relations, rates of intermarriage among the various groups have been much higher than on the mainland, reflecting the openness to intimacy across group lines that characterized Hawaii since first contact. In particular, Native Hawaiians have intermarried freely with other groups (Kitano & Daniels, 1995, pp. 138–139).

Hawaii did not experience the most blatant and oppressive forms of group domination. However, all is not perfect in this reputed racial paradise, and there is continuing ethnic and racial stratification, as well as prejudice and discrimination. In particular, Native Hawaiians today retain their minority group status. The group is quite small and numbers about 157,000, an increase from the historic lows of the 19th century but still only about 12% of the state's population and a tiny minority of the U.S. population.

On the other hand, Native Hawaiians compare favorably with both American Indians and black Americans in terms of education, income, and poverty (see exhibit 3.6). This relatively higher status today is consistent with both the Noel and Blauner hypotheses: Native Hawaiians were not subjected to the harsh conditions (slavery, segregation, near genocide, and massive institutional discrimination) of the other two groups.

(Continued)

(Continued)

Exhibit 3.6 Native Hawaiians Compared with Total Population, Black Americans, and American Indians, 2010

INDICATOR	Total U.S. Population	Native Hawaiians	Black Americans	American Indians
Percent high school graduate or more	85.3%	89.2%	81.5%	80.1%
Percent college graduate or more	28.0%	15.8%	18.1%	16.3%
Median household income	$51,222	$59,055	$34,937	$38,382
Percent of families in poverty	10.5%	11.7%	21.9%	19.4%

Source: U.S. Census Bureau (2010).

Notes: Black Americans and Native Americans are "Alone and in Combination."

Although they compare favorably to the two colonized and conquered groups, Native Hawaiians tend to be the poorest of the various ethnic and racial groups on the island, and a protest movement of Native Hawaiians that stresses self-determination and the return of illegally taken land has been in existence since at least the 1960s.

Mexican Americans

As the population of the United States increased and spread across the continent, contact with Mexicans inevitably occurred. Spanish explorers and settlers had lived in what is now the southwestern United States long before the wave of American settlers broke across this region. For example, Santa Fe, now in the state of New Mexico, was founded in 1598, nearly a decade before Jamestown. As late as the 1820s, Mexicans and American Indians were almost the sole residents of the region.

In the early 1800s, four areas of Mexican settlement had developed, roughly corresponding to what was to become Arizona, California, New Mexico, and Texas. These areas were sparsely settled, and most Mexicans lived in what was to become New Mexico (Cortes, 1980, p. 701). The economy of the regions was based on farming and herding. Most people lived in villages and small towns or on ranches and farms. Social and political life was organized around family and the Catholic church and tended to be dominated by an elite class of wealthy landowners.

Texas. Some of the first effects of U.S. expansion to the West were felt in Texas early in the 1800s. Mexico was no military match for its neighbor to the north, and the farmland of East Texas was a tempting resource for the cotton-growing interests in the American South. Anglo Americans began to immigrate to Texas in sizable numbers in the 1820s, and by 1835 they outnumbered Mexicans six to one. The attempts by the Mexican government to control these immigrants were clumsy and ineffective and eventually precipitated a successful revolution by the Anglo Americans, with some Mexicans also joining the rebels. At this time, competition between Anglos and Texans of Mexican descent (called Tejanos) was muted by the abundance of land and opportunity in the area. Population density was low, fertile land was readily available for all, and the "general tone of the time was that of inter-cultural cooperation" (Alvarez, 1973, p. 922).

Competition between Anglo-Texans and Tejanos became increasingly intense. When the United States annexed Texas in the 1840s, full-scale war broke out and Mexico was defeated. Under the Treaty of Guadalupe Hidalgo in 1848, Mexico ceded much of the Southwest to the United States. In the Gadsden Purchase of 1853, the United States acquired the remainder of the territory that now composes the southwestern United States. As a result of these treaties, the Mexican population of this region had become, without moving an inch from their traditional villages and farms, both a conquered people and a minority group.

Following the war, intergroup relations continued to sour, and the political and legal rights of the Tejano community were often ignored in the hunger for land. Increasingly impoverished and powerless, the Tejanos had few resources with which to resist the growth of Anglo American domination. They were badly outnumbered and stigmatized by the recent Mexican military defeat. Land that had once been Mexican increasingly came under Anglo control, and widespread violence and lynchings reinforced the growth of Anglo dominance (Moquin & Van Doren, 1971, p. 253).

California. In California, the Gold Rush of 1849 spurred a massive population movement from the East. Early relations between Anglos and Californios (native Mexicans in the state) had been relatively cordial, forming the basis for a multiethnic, bilingual state. The rapid growth of an Anglo majority after statehood in 1850 doomed these efforts, however, and the Californios, like the Tejanos, lost their land and political power.

Laws were passed encouraging Anglos to settle on land traditionally held by Californios. In such situations, the burden was placed on the Californios (or Mexican American) landowners to show that their deeds were valid. The Californios protested the seizure of their land but found it difficult to argue their cases in the English-speaking, Anglo-controlled court system. By the mid-1850s, a massive transfer of land to Anglo American hands had taken place in California (Mirandé, 1985, pp. 20–21; see also Pitt, 1970).

Other laws passed in the 1850s made it increasingly difficult for Californios to retain their property and power as Anglo Americans became the dominant group as well as the majority of the population. The area's Mexican heritage was suppressed and eliminated from public life and institutions such as schools and local government. For example, in 1855 California repealed a requirement in the state constitution that all laws be published in Spanish as well as English (Cortes, 1980, p. 706). Anglo Americans used violence, biased laws, discrimination, and other means to exploit and repress Californios, and the new wealth generated by gold mining flowed into Anglo hands.

Arizona and New Mexico. The Anglo immigration into Arizona and New Mexico was less voluminous than that into Texas and California, and both states retained Mexican numerical majorities for a number of decades. In Arizona, which became a state in 1912, most of the Mexican population were immigrants themselves, seeking work on farms, on ranches, in the mines, and on railroads. The economic and political structures of the state quickly came under the control of the Anglo population.

Only in New Mexico did Mexican Americans retain some political power and economic clout, mostly because of the relatively large size of the group and their skill in mobilizing for political activity. New Mexico became a state in 1912, and Mexican Americans continued to play a prominent role in governmental affairs even after statehood (Cortes, 1980, p. 706).

Thus, the contact situation for Mexican Americans was highly variable by region. Although some areas were affected more rapidly and more completely than others, the ultimate result was the creation of minority group status for Mexican Americans (Acuna, 1999; Alvarez, 1973; McLemore, 1973; McWilliams, 1961; Moore, 1970; Stoddard, 1973).

Mexican Americans and the Noel and Blauner Hypotheses. The causal model we have applied to the origins of slavery and the domination of American Indians also provides a way of explaining the development of minority group status for Mexican Americans. Ethnocentrism was clearly present from the very first contact between Anglo immigrants and Mexicans. Many American migrants to the Southwest brought with them the prejudices and racism they had acquired with regard to African Americans and American Indians. In fact, many of the settlers who moved into Texas came directly from the South in search of new lands for the cultivation of cotton. They readily transferred their prejudiced views to at least the poorer Mexicans, who were stereotyped as lazy and shiftless (McLemore, 1973, p. 664). The visibility of group boundaries was heightened and reinforced by physical and religious differences. Mexicans were "racially" a mixture of Spaniards and American Indians, and the differences in skin color and other physical characteristics provided a convenient marker of group membership. In addition, the vast majority of Mexicans were Roman Catholic, whereas the vast majority of Anglo Americans were Protestant.

Competition for land began with the first contact between the groups. However, for many years population density was low in the Southwest, and the competition did not immediately or always erupt into violent domination and expropriation. Nonetheless, the loss of land and power for Mexican Americans was inexorable, although variable in speed.

The size of the power differential between the groups was variable and partly explains why domination was established faster in some places than in others. In both Texas and California, the subordination of the Mexican American population followed quickly after a rapid influx of Anglos and the military defeat of Mexico. Anglo

Americans used their superior numbers and military power to acquire control of the political and economic structures and expropriate the resources of the Mexican American community. In New Mexico, the groups were more evenly matched in size, and Mexican Americans were able to retain a measure of power for decades.

Unlike the case of American Indians, however, the labor as well as the land of the Mexicans was coveted. On cotton plantations, ranches, and farms, and in mining and railroad construction, Mexican Americans became a vital source of inexpensive labor. During times of high demand, this labor force was supplemented by workers who were encouraged to emigrate from Mexico. When demand for workers decreased, these laborers were forced back to Mexico. Thus began a pattern of labor flow that continues to the present.

As in the case of African Americans and American Indians, the contact period clearly established a colonized status for Mexican Americans in all areas of the Southwest. Their culture and language were suppressed even as their property rights were abrogated and their status lowered. In countless ways, they, too, were subjected to coercive acculturation. For example, California banned the use of Spanish in public schools, and severely restricted bullfighting and other Mexican sports and recreational activities (Moore, 1970, p. 19; Pitt, 1970). In contrast to African Americans, however, Mexican Americans were in close proximity to their homeland and maintained close ties with villages and families. Constant movement across the border with Mexico kept the Spanish language and much of the Mexican heritage alive in the Southwest. Nonetheless, 19th-century Mexican Americans fit Blauner's category of a colonized minority group, and the suppression of their culture was part of the process by which the dominant culture was established.

Anglo American economic interests benefited enormously from the conquest of the Southwest and the colonization of the Mexican people. Growers and other business people came to rely on the cheap labor provided by Mexican Americans and immigrant and day laborers from Mexico. The region grew in affluence and productivity, but Mexican Americans were now outsiders in their own land and did not share in the prosperity. In the land grab of the 1800s and the conquest of the indigenous Mexican population lies one of the roots of Mexican American relations with the dominant U.S. society today.

Gender Relations. Prior to the arrival of Anglo Americans, Mexican society in the Southwest was patriarchal and maintained a clear gender-based division of labor. These characteristics tended to persist after the conquest and the creation of minority group status.

Most Mexican Americans lived in small villages or on large ranches and farms. The women devoted their energies to the family, child rearing, and household tasks. As Mexican Americans were reduced to a landless labor force, women along with men suffered the economic devastation that accompanied military conquest by a foreign power. The kinds of jobs available to the men (mining, seasonal farm work, railroad construction) often required them to be away from home for extended periods, and women, by default, began to take over the economic and other tasks traditionally performed by men.

Poverty and economic insecurity placed the family structures under considerable strain. Traditional cultural understandings about male dominance and patriarchy became moot when the men were absent for long periods and the decision-making power of Mexican American women increased. Also, women were often forced to work outside the household for the family to survive economically. The economics of conquest led to increased matriarchy and more mothers who worked outside the home (Becerra, 1988, p. 149).

For Mexican American women, the consequences of contact were variable even though the ultimate result was a loss of status within the context of the conquest and colonization of the group as a whole. Like black female slaves, Mexican American women became the most vulnerable part of the social system.

Comparing Minority Groups

American Indians and black slaves were the victims of the explosive growth of European power in the western hemisphere that began with Columbus' voyage in 1492. Europeans needed labor to fuel the plantations of the mid-17th-century American colonies and settled on slaves from Africa as the most logical, cost-effective means of resolving their labor supply problems. Black Africans had a commodity the colonists coveted (labor), and the colonists subsequently constructed a system to control and exploit this commodity.

To satisfy the demand for land created by the stream of European immigrants to North America, the threat represented by American Indians had to be eliminated. Once their land was expropriated, American Indians ceased to be of much concern to Anglo Americans. The only valuable resource they possessed—their land—was under the control of white society by 1890, and American Indians were thought to be unsuitable as a source of labor.

Mexico, like the United States, had been colonized by a European power, in this case Spain. In the early 1800s, the Mexican communities in the Southwest were a series of outpost settlements, remote and difficult to defend. Through warfare and a variety of other aggressive means, Mexican citizens living in this area were conquered and became an exploited minority group.

African Americans, American Indians, and Mexican Americans, in their separate ways, became involuntary players in the growth and development of European and, later, American economic and political power. None of these groups had much choice in their respective fates; all three were overpowered and relegated to an inferior, subordinate status. Many views of assimilation (such as the "melting pot" metaphor discussed in chapter 2) have little relevance to these situations. These minority groups had little control over their destinies, their degree of acculturation, or even their survival as groups. These three groups were coercively acculturated in the context of paternalistic relations in an agrarian economy. Meaningful integration (structural assimilation) was not a real possibility, especially for African Americans and American Indians. In Milton Gordon's (1964) terms (see chapter 2), we might characterize these situations as "acculturation without integration" or structural pluralism. Given the grim realities described in this chapter, Gordon's terms seem a little antiseptic, and Blauner's concept of colonized minority groups seems far more descriptive.

COMPARATIVE FOCUS:
Mexico, Canada, and the United States

Dominant-minority relations are profoundly shaped by the contact situation and by the characteristics of the groups involved (especially their subsistence technologies).[2] In this chapter, we saw how these factors shaped the fate of African Americans, American Indians, and Mexican Americans. How do the experiences of the Spanish and the French in the western hemisphere compare with those of the British in what became the United States? What roles did the contact situation and subsistence technology play in the development of group relations in these two neighbors of the United States?

The Spanish were the first of the three European nations to invade the western hemisphere, and they conquered much of what is now Central and South America about a century before Jamestown was founded. In 1521, they defeated the Aztec Empire, located in what is now central Mexico. The Aztec Empire was large, highly organized, and complex. The Aztec emperor ruled over scores of subject nations; the great majority of his subjects were peasants or agricultural laborers who farmed small plots of land owned by members of the elite classes, to whom they paid rents. Peasants are a fundamental part of any labor-intensive, preindustrial agrarian society, in Aztec society just as in Spain.

When the Spanish defeated the Aztecs, they did not destroy the social structure; rather, they absorbed it and used it for their own benefit. For example, the Aztec Empire had financed its central government by collecting taxes and rents from citizens and tribute from conquered tribes. The Spanish simply grafted their own tax collection system onto this structure and diverted the flow from the Aztec elite classes to themselves (Russell, 1994, pp. 29–30).

The Spanish tendency to absorb rather than destroy operated at many levels. Aztec peasants became Spanish (and then Mexican) peasants, occupying roughly the same role in the new society that they had in the old, save for paying their rents to different landlords. There was also extensive interbreeding between the Spanish and the conquered tribes of Mexico but, unlike the English, the Spanish recognized the resultant racial diversity and developed an elaborate system for classifying people by race. They recognized as many as 56 racial groups, including whites, **mestizos** (mixed European–Indian), and mulattoes (mixed European–African) (Russell, 1994, p. 35). The society that emerged was highly race conscious, and race was highly correlated with social class: the elite classes were white and the lower classes were non-white. However, the large-scale intermarriage and the official recognition of mixed-race peoples did establish the foundation for a racially mixed society. Today, the huge majority of the Mexican population is mestizo, although there remains a very strong correlation between race and class, and the elite positions in the society tend to be monopolized by people of "purer" European ancestry.

(Continued)

(Continued)

The French colonized Canada at about the same time the English established their colonies farther south. The dominant economic enterprise in the early days was not farming, but trapping and the fur trade. The French developed a lucrative trade by allying themselves with some American Indian tribes. The Indians produced the furs and traded them to the French, who, in turn, sold them on the world market. Like the Spanish in Mexico, the French in Canada tended to link to and absorb Native American social structures. There was also a significant amount of intermarriage between the French and American Indians, resulting in a mixed-race group, called Métis, who had their own identities and, indeed, their own settlements along the Canadian frontier (Russell, 1994, p. 39).

Note the profound differences in these three contact situations. The Spanish confronted a large, well-organized social system and found it expeditious to adapt Aztec practices to their own benefit. The French developed an economy that required cooperation with at least some of the Native American tribes they encountered, and they, too, found benefits in adaptation. The tribes encountered by the English were much smaller and much less developed than the Aztecs, and there was no particular reason for the English to adapt to or absorb these social structures. Furthermore, because the business of the English colonies was agriculture (not trapping), the competition at the heart of the contact situation was for land, and American Indians were seen as rivals. Thus, the English tended to confront and exclude American Indians, keeping them on the outside of their emerging society and building strong boundaries between their own "civilized" world and the "savages" that surrounded them. The Spanish and French colonists had to adapt their societies to fit with American Indians, but the English faced no such restraints. They could create their institutions and design their social structure to suit themselves (Russell, 1994, p. 30).

Slavery was practiced throughout the New World but the institution evolved in very different ways in Spanish and French colonies and never assumed the importance that it did in English colonies. Why? As you might suspect, the answer has a lot to do with the nature of the contact situation. Like the English, both the Spanish and French attempted large-scale agricultural enterprises that might have created a demand for imported slave labor. In the case of New Spain, however, there was a ready supply of Native American peasants available to fill the role played by blacks in the English colonies. Although Africans became a part of the admixture that shaped modern Mexico racially and socially, demand for black slaves never matched that of the English colonies. Similarly, in Canada, slaves from Africa were sometimes used, but farmers there tended to rely on labor from France to fill their agricultural needs. The British opted for slave labor from Africa over indentured labor from Europe, and the French made the opposite decision.

Another important difference was that, compared with England, Spain and France were more traditional and feudalistic in their cultures and social structures. This meant that they had to shape their agricultural enterprises in the New World around the ancient social relations between peasants and landlords they brought from the Old World. Thus, the Spanish and French colonists were limited in their actions by these ancient customs, traditions, and understandings. Whereas the Spanish and French had to shape their colonial societies to fit both American Indian social patterns and European traditions, the English could improvise and attend only to their own needs and desires. The closed, complex, and repressive institution of American slavery—designed and crafted from scratch in the New World—was one result.

Finally, we should note that many of the modern racial characteristics of these three neighboring societies were foreshadowed in their colonial origins (for example, the greater concentration of African Americans in the United States and the more racially intermixed population of Mexico). The differences run much deeper than race alone, of course, and include differences in class structure and relative levels of industrialization and affluence. For our purposes, however, this brief comparison of the origins of dominant-minority relations underscores the importance of the contact situation in shaping group relations for centuries to come.

Notes

1. For a powerful account of how a form of slavery in the United States survived the Civil War, see Blackmon (2008).

2. This section is largely based on Russell (1994).

Main Points

- Dominant-minority relations are shaped by the characteristics of society as a whole, particularly by subsistence technology. The contact situation is the single most important factor in the development of dominant-minority relations.
- The Noel hypothesis states that when a contact situation is characterized by ethnocentrism, competition, and a differential in power, ethnic or racial stratification will result. The colonists in America enslaved Africans instead of white indentured servants or American Indians because only the Africans fit all three conditions. American slavery was a paternalistic system.
- The Blauner hypothesis states that minority groups created by colonization will experience greater, more long-lasting disadvantages than minority groups created by immigration.
- Prejudice and racism are more the results of systems of racial and ethnic inequality than they are the causes. They serve to rationalize, "explain," and stabilize these systems.

- The competition with American Indians centered on control of the land. American Indian tribes were conquered and pressed into a paternalistic relationship with white society. American Indians became a colonized minority group and were subjected to forced acculturation.
- Mexican Americans were the third minority group created during the preindustrial era. Mexican Americans competed with white settlers over both land and labor. Like Africans and American Indians, Mexican Americans were a colonized minority group subjected to forced acculturation.
- Conquest and colonization affected men and women differently. Women's roles changed, and they sometimes were less constrained by patriarchal traditions. These changes were always in the context of increasing powerlessness and poverty for the group as a whole, however, and minority women have been doubly oppressed by their gender roles as well as their minority group status.

Study Site on the Web

Don't forget the interactive quizzes and other resources and learning aids at www.sagepub.com/healeyds4e.

For Further Reading

Genovese, E. D. (1974). *Roll, Jordan, roll: The world the slaves made*. New York: Pantheon.
Gutman, H. G. (1976). *The black family in slavery and freedom, 1750–1925*. New York: Vintage.
Levine, L. (1977). *Black culture and black consciousness*. New York: Oxford University Press.
Rawick, G. P. (1972). *From sundown to sunup: The making of the black community*. Westport, CT: Greenwood Press.
Stuckey, S. (1987). *Slave culture: Nationalist theory and the foundations of black America*. New York: Harper & Row.

A short list of five vital sources on the origins and psychological and cultural impact of slavery in America.

Brown, D. (1970). *Bury my heart at Wounded Knee*. New York: Holt, Rinehart & Winston.

An eloquent and moving account of the conquest of American Indians.

Nabakov, P. (Ed.). (1999). *Native American testimony* (rev. ed.). New York: Penguin.

A collection of valuable and insightful American Indian accounts of the past 500 years.

Wax, M. (1971). *Indian Americans: Unity and diversity*. Englewood Cliffs, NJ: Prentice Hall.

A compact and informative analysis of the history and present situation of American Indians.

McWilliams, C. (1961). *North from Mexico: The Spanish-speaking people of the United States*. New York: Monthly Review Press.

A classic overview of the historical development of Mexican Americans.

Acuna, R. (1999). *Occupied America* (4th ed.). New York: Harper & Row.

Acuna examines a broad sweep of Mexican American experiences and argues that their status is comparable to that of other colonized groups.

Mirandé, A. (1985). *The Chicano experience: An alternative perspective*. Notre Dame, IN: University of Notre Dame Press.

A passionate argument for a new sociological approach to the study of Mexican Americans. Many useful insights into Mexican American family structures, the problem of crime, and other areas.

Questions for Review and Study

1. State and explain the two themes presented at the beginning of the chapter. Apply each to the contact situations between white European colonists, African Americans, American Indians, and Mexican Americans. Identify and explain the key differences and similarities between the three situations.

2. Explain what a plantation system is and why this system of production is important for understanding the origins of slavery in colonial America. Why are plantation systems usually characterized by (a) paternalism, (b) huge inequalities between groups, (c) repressive systems of control, (d) rigid codes of behavior, and (e) low rates of overt conflict?

3. Explain the Noel and Blauner hypotheses and explain how they apply to the contact situations covered in this chapter. Explain each of the following key terms: ethnocentrism, competition, power, colonized minority group, immigrant minority group. How did group conflict vary when competition was over land rather than over labor?

4. Explain the role of prejudice and racism in the creation of minority group status. Do prejudice and racism help cause minority group status, or are they caused by minority group status? Explain.

5. Compare and contrast gender relations in regard to each of the contact situations discussed in this chapter. Why do the relationships vary?

6. What does it mean to say that, under slavery, acculturation for African Americans was coerced? What are the implications for assimilation, inequality, and African American culture?

7. Compare and contrast the contact situations of Native Hawaiians with American Indians. What were the key differences in the contact situations, and how are these differences reflected in the current situations of the groups?

8. Compare and contrast the contact situations in colonial America, Canada, and Mexico. What groups were involved in each situation? What was the nature of the competition, and what were the consequences?

Internet Research Project

Americans today might look at slavery as a distant relic of history, remote and bizarre. The idea that a person could be owned by another person, defined as a piece of property, and bought and sold like livestock probably seems hopelessly alien to people who live in a culture devoted to individual happiness and personal well-being. Yet, this ancient institution can still be found around the world, on every continent, in advanced industrial societies, including in the United States.

In this project, you will use sources of information readily available on the Internet to gather facts and estimate the volume and scope of modern slavery. You will also collect some case studies or personal examples of slavery, analyze the nature of the practice today, compare it to American slavery, and gather information about what is being done to combat the practice. This project will also provide an opportunity to review some of the important points and ideas presented in this chapter.

To begin, consider the list of questions below. Next, visit the websites listed here and search for answers to the questions. Also, search the Internet for additional sources that may help you develop an understanding of modern slavery. (*Note: Your instructor may have additional or different instructions for gathering information.*)

As you search the Internet, remember that you will need to practice a healthy skepticism about the information, ideas, and arguments that you will find—including the information on the websites listed for this project. Of course, you should always be careful and critical when doing research but, as you know, the Internet is notorious for spreading incomplete, deeply biased, or false information and an extra note of caution is justified. Also, recognize at the outset that many of the facts you gather (e.g., the number of people currently enslaved) will consist of approximations and, in some case, will be mere guesswork. So, do the best you can and don't expect to find exact numbers.

1. Scope and volume
   a. About how many people are currently enslaved or in a condition of involuntary servitude? (*Note: You might want to cite both high and low estimates.*)
   b. Describe this population in terms of gender, age, race, and nationality. What percentage are women? Children?
   c. Where in the world are modern slaves most numerous or common?
   d. For the slave population that is transported across national lines, what are the major sending areas or nations and what are the most important destination areas and nations?

2. Experiences
   a. Describe the mechanisms and practices by which slave status is enforced. What is the role of debt bondage? How often are coercion and violence used? How do these practices vary across different types of slavery (e.g., sex trafficking versus involuntary labor)?
   b. Find at least three to five case studies of people who have been victimized by modern slavery.
   c. Sociologically, what do these people have in common? That is, what important social characteristics (age, gender, social class, race, and ethnicity) do they share?

3. Dynamics and causes
   a. American slavery was shaped by the level of development and labor-intensive subsistence technology of the colonial era. Can you find ways in which similar factors shape modern slavery?
   b. Can you apply elements of the Noel hypothesis to modern slavery? Does ethnocentrism, prejudice, or sexism play a role? How? What resources and abilities do modern slaves have that make them the objects of competition? What role does power play in shaping and maintaining these practices?

4. Markets: Supply and Demand
   a. What roles do modern slaves play in the job market? What economic niches are being filled? Who profits? Who loses? Describe the minority-dominant group situations you find in your search for facts.

5. Enforcement Efforts, Legal Considerations, Human Rights
   a. Find at least three national and international programs aimed at stopping modern slavery and describe what they are doing
   b. What specific human rights are at stake here? Is slavery illegal? Where? By what authority?

Websites for this Project

1. http://www.freetheslaves.net/Page.aspx?pid=584

   Home Page of "Free the Slaves." Includes information, resources for teachers, and a description of the organization's efforts to combat modern slavery.

2. http://www.ijm.org/?gclid=CJ__pezm56YCFVln5QodCTD_0w

   Home Page for the International Justice Mission, a Christian advocacy and activist group dedicated to combating slavery

3. http://www.state.gov/g/tip/rls/tiprpt/2010/

   U.S. Department of State's annual Trafficking in Persons report. The report can be downloaded in pdf format.

Optional Group Discussion

Bring your findings to class and discuss with classmates. Focus your discussion on comparing and contrasting modern and colonial American slavery, especially the roles of ethnocentrism and power, subsistence technology, demand and supply, human rights, and enforcement efforts. (*Your instructor may have more-specific or different instructions.*)

4

Industrialization and Dominant-Minority Relations: From Slavery to Segregation and the Coming of Postindustrial Society

A war sets up in our emotions: one part of our feelings tells us it is good to be in the city, that we have a chance at life here, that we need but turn a corner to become a stranger, that we need no longer bow and dodge at the sight of the Lords of the Land. Another part of our feelings tells us that, in terms of worry and strain, the cost of living in the kitchenettes is too high, that the city heaps too much responsibility on us and gives too little security in return. . . .

The kitchenette, with its filth and foul air, with its one toilet for thirty or more tenants, kills our black babies so fast that in many cities twice as many of them die as white babies. . . .

The kitchenette scatters death so widely among us that our death rate exceeds our birth rate, and if it were not for the trains and autos bringing us daily into the city from the plantations, we black folk who dwell in northern cities would die out entirely over the course of a few years. . . .

The kitchenette throws desperate and unhappy people into an unbearable closeness of association, thereby increasing latent friction, giving birth to never-ending quarrels of recrimination, accusation, and vindictiveness, producing warped personalities.

The kitchenette injects pressure and tension into our individual personalities, making many of us give up the struggle, walk off and leave wives, husbands, and even children behind to shift for themselves....

The kitchenette reaches out with fingers of golden bribes to the officials of the city, persuading them to allow old firetraps to remain standing and occupied long after they should have been torn down.

The kitchenette is the funnel through which our pulverized lives flow to ruin and death on the city pavement, at a profit.

—Richard Wright (1941, pp. 105–111)*

Richard Wright (1908–1960), one of the most powerful writers of the 20th century, lived through and wrote about many of the social changes discussed in this chapter. He grew up in the South during the height of the Jim Crow system, and his passionate hatred for segregation and bigotry is expressed in his major works, *Native Son* (1940) and the autobiographical *Black Boy* (1945). In 1941, Wright helped to produce *Twelve Million Black Voices*, a folk history of African Americans. A combination of photos and brief essays, the work is a powerful commentary on three centuries of oppression.

The selection above is adapted from "Death on the City Pavement," which expresses Wright's view of the African American migration out of the South that began in the early 1900s as a reaction to Jim Crow segregation. Wright himself moved from the South to the North, a bittersweet journey that often traded harsh, rural repression for overcrowded, anonymous ghettos. Housing discrimination, both overt and covert, confined African American migrants to the least desirable, most overcrowded areas of the city—in many cases, the neighborhoods that had first housed immigrants from Europe. Unscrupulous landlords subdivided buildings into the tiniest possible apartments ("kitchenettes"), and as impoverished newcomers who could afford no better, African American migrants were forced to cope with overpriced, substandard housing as best they could.

One theme stated at the beginning of chapter 3 was that a society's subsistence technology shapes dominant-minority group relations. A corollary of this theme, explored in this chapter, is that *dominant-minority group relations change as the subsistence technology* changes. We saw in chapter 3 that dominant-minority relations in the formative years of the United States were profoundly shaped by agrarian technology and the desire to control land and labor. The agrarian era ended in the 1800s, and the United States has experienced two major transformations in subsistence technology since then, each of which has transformed dominant-minority relations and required the creation of new structures and processes to maintain racial stratification and white privilege.

---

*From *Twelve Million Back Voices* by Richard Wright. Copyright © 1941 by Richard Wright. Published by Thunder's Mouth Press, an imprint of Avalon Publishing Group Incorporated.

The first transformation, the industrial revolution, began in the early 19th century when machine-based technologies began to develop, especially in the North. In the agrarian era, work was labor-intensive, done by hand or with the aid of draft animals. During industrialization, work became capital-intensive and machines replaced people and animals.

The new industrial technology rapidly increased the productivity and efficiency of the U.S. economy and quickly began to change all other aspects of society, including the nature of work, politics, communication, transportation, family life, birth rates and death rates, the system of education, and, of course, dominant-minority relations. The groups that had become minorities during the agrarian era (African Americans, American Indians, and Mexican Americans) faced new possibilities and new dangers, but industrialization also created new minority groups, new forms of exploitation and oppression and, for some, new opportunities to rise in the social structure and succeed in America. In this chapter, we will explore this transformation and illustrate its effects on the status of African Americans, including the construction of Jim Crow segregation in the South. The impact of industrialization on other minority groups will be considered in the case studies presented in part 3.

The second transformation in subsistence technology brings us to more recent times. In the mid-20th century, the United States (and other advanced industrial societies) entered the postindustrial era, also called **deindustrialization**. This shift in subsistence technology was marked by (1) a decline in the manufacturing sector of the economy and a decrease in the supply of secure, well-paid, blue-collar, manual-labor jobs; and (2) an expansion in the service and information-based sectors of the economy and an increase in the relative proportion of white-collar and "high-tech" jobs. Like the 19th-century industrial revolution, these changes have profound implications for every aspect of modern society, not just for dominant-minority relations. Work, family, politics, popular culture—indeed, every characteristic of American society is being transformed as the subsistence technology continues to develop and modernize. In the latter part of this chapter, we examine this most recent transformation in general terms and point out some of its implications for minority groups. We will examine some new concepts—especially the concept of **modern institutional discrimination**—to help us understand group relations in this new era. We will also establish some important groundwork for the case studies in part 3, in which we will consider the implication of postindustrial society for America's minority groups in detail.

Exhibit 4.1 summarizes the characteristics of the three major subsistence technologies considered in this text. As U.S. society has moved through these stages, group relations and the nature of racial and ethnic stratification have continuously changed.

Exhibit 4.1   Three Subsistence Technologies and the United States

Technology	Key Trends and Characteristics	Dates
Agrarian	Labor-intensive agriculture. Control of land and labor are central.	1607 to early 1800s
Industrial	Capital-intensive manufacturing. Machines replace animal and human labor.	Early 1800s to mid-1900s
Postindustrial	Shift away from manufacturing to a service economy. The "information society."	Mid-1900s to the present

Industrialization and the Shift from Paternalistic to Rigid Competitive Group Relations

As we noted in chapter 2, the Industrial Revolution began in England in the mid-1700s and spread from there to the rest of Europe, to the United States, and eventually to the rest of the world. The key innovations associated with this change in subsistence technology were the application of machine power to production and the harnessing of inanimate sources of energy, such as steam and coal, to fuel the machines. As machines replaced humans and animals, work became many times more productive, the economy grew, and the volume and variety of goods produced increased dramatically.

In an industrial economy, the close, paternalistic control of minority groups found in agrarian societies becomes irrelevant. Paternalistic relationships such as slavery are associated with labor-intensive technologies and are designed to organize and control a large, involuntary, geographically immobile labor force. An industrial economy, in contrast, requires a workforce that is geographically and socially mobile, skilled, and literate. Furthermore, with industrialization comes urbanization, and close, paternalistic controls are difficult to maintain in a city.

Thus, as industrialization progresses, agrarian paternalism tends to give way to **rigid competitive group** relations (see exhibit 4.6 below). Under this system, minority group members are freer to compete for jobs and other valued commodities with dominant group members, especially the lower-class segments of the dominant group. As competition increases, the threatened members of the dominant group become more hostile, and attacks on the minority groups tend to increase. While paternalistic systems were designed to directly dominate and control the minority group (and its labor), rigid competitive systems are more defensive in nature. Segments of the dominant group seek to minimize or eliminate minority group encroachment on jobs, housing, or other valuable goods or services (van den Berghe, 1967; Wilson, 1973).

Paternalistic systems such as slavery required members of the minority group to be active, if involuntary, participants. Rigid competitive systems, in contrast, seek to handicap the minority group's ability to compete effectively or, in some cases, eliminate competition from the minority group altogether. We have already considered an example of a dominant group attempt to protect itself from a threat. As you recall, the National Origins Act was passed in the 1920s to stop the flow of cheaper labor from Europe and protect jobs and wages (see chapter 2). In this chapter, we consider dominant group attempts to keep African Americans powerless and impoverished and to maintain black–white racial stratification as the society shifted from an agricultural to an industrial base.

The Impact of Industrialization on the Racial Stratification of African Americans: From Slavery to Segregation

Industrial technology began to transform American society in the early 1800s, but its effects were not felt equally in all regions. The Northern states industrialized first, while the Southern states remained primarily agrarian. This economic diversity was one of the underlying causes of the regional conflict that led to the Civil War. Because of its more productive technology, the North had more resources and defeated the Confederacy in a bloody war of attrition. Slavery was abolished, and black–white relations in the South entered a new era when the Civil War ended in April 1865.

The Southern system of race relations that ultimately emerged after the Civil War was designed in part to continue the control of African American labor institutionalized under slavery. It was also intended to eliminate any political or economic threat from the African American community. This rigid competitive system grew to be highly elaborate and inflexible, partly because of the high racial visibility and long history of inferior status and powerlessness of African Americans in the South and partly because of the particular needs of Southern agriculture. In this section, we look at black–white relations from the end of the Civil War through the coming of segregation in the South and the mass migration of African Americans to the cities of the industrializing North.

Reconstruction

The period of **Reconstruction**, from 1865 to the 1880s, was a brief respite in the long history of oppression and exploitation of African Americans. The Union Army and other agencies of the federal government, such as the Freedman's Bureau, were used to enforce racial freedom in the defeated Confederacy. Black Southerners took advantage of the 15th Amendment to the Constitution, passed in 1870, which states that the right to vote cannot be denied on the grounds of "race, color, or previous condition of servitude." They registered to vote in large numbers and turned out on Election Day, and some were elected to high political office. Schools for the former slaves were opened, and African Americans purchased land and houses and founded businesses.

The era of freedom was short, however, and Reconstruction began to end when the federal government demobilized its armies of occupation and turned its attention to other matters. By the 1880s, the federal government had withdrawn from the South, Reconstruction was over, and black Southerners began to fall rapidly into a new system of exploitation and inequality.

Reconstruction was too brief to change two of the most important legacies of slavery. First, the centuries of bondage left black Southerners impoverished, largely illiterate and uneducated, and with few power resources. When new threats of racial oppression appeared, African Americans found it difficult to defend their group interests. These developments are consistent with the Blauner hypothesis: colonized minority groups face greater difficulties in improving their disadvantaged status because they confront greater inequalities and have fewer resources at their disposal.

Second, slavery left a strong tradition of racism in the white community. Antiblack prejudice and racism originated as rationalizations for slavery but had taken on lives of their own over the generations. After two centuries of slavery, the heritage of prejudice and racism was thoroughly ingrained in Southern culture. White Southerners were predisposed by this cultural legacy to see racial inequality and exploitation of

African Americans as normal and desirable. They were able to construct a social system based on the assumption of racial inferiority after Reconstruction ended and the federal government withdrew.

De Jure Segregation

The system of race relations that replaced slavery in the South was **de jure segregation**, sometimes referred to as the **Jim Crow system**. Under segregation, the minority group is physically and socially separated from the dominant group and consigned to an inferior position in virtually every area of social life. The term "de jure" (meaning "by law") means that the system is sanctioned and reinforced by the legal code; the inferior status of African Americans was actually mandated or required by state and local laws. For example, Southern cities during this era had laws requiring African Americans to ride at the back of the bus. If an African American refused to comply with this seating arrangement, he or she could be arrested.

De jure segregation came to encompass all aspects of Southern social life. Neighborhoods, jobs, stores, restaurants, and parks were segregated. When new social forms, such as movie theaters, sports stadiums, and interstate buses appeared in the South, they, too, were quickly segregated.

The logic of segregation created a vicious cycle. The more African Americans were excluded from the mainstream of society, the greater their objective poverty and powerlessness became. The more inferior their status and the greater their powerlessness, the easier it was to mandate more inequality. High levels of inequality reinforced racial prejudice and made it easy to use racism to justify further separation. The system kept turning on itself, finding new social niches to segregate and reinforcing the inequality that was its starting point. For example, at the height of the Jim Crow era, the system had evolved to the point that some courtrooms maintained separate Bibles for African American witnesses to swear on. Also, in Birmingham, Alabama, it was against the law for blacks and whites to play checkers or dominoes together (Woodward, 1974, p. 118).

What were the causes of this massive separation of the races? Once again, the concepts of the Noel hypothesis prove useful. Because strong anti-black prejudice was already in existence when segregation began, we do not need to account for ethnocentrism. The post-Reconstruction competition between the racial groups was reminiscent of the origins of slavery in that black Southerners had something that white Southerners wanted: labor. In addition, a free black electorate threatened the political and economic dominance of the elite segments of the white community. Finally, after the withdrawal of federal troops and the end of Reconstruction, white Southerners had sufficient power resources to end the competition on their own terms and construct repressive systems of control for black Southerners.

The Origins of De Jure Segregation. Although the South lost the Civil War, its basic class structure and agrarian economy remained intact. The plantation elite remained the dominant class and was able to use its power to build a system of racial stratification to replace slavery.

Control of Black Labor. The plantation elite retained ownership of huge tracts of land, and cotton remained the primary cash crop in the South. As was the case before the Civil War, the landowners needed a workforce to farm the land. Because of the depredations and economic disruptions of the war, the old plantation elite were short on cash and liquid capital and could not always hire workers for wages. In fact, almost as soon as the war ended, Southern legislatures attempted to force African Americans back into involuntary servitude by passing a series of laws known as the "Black Codes." Only the beginning of Reconstruction and the active intervention of the federal government halted the implementation of this legislation (Geschwender, 1978, p. 158; Wilson, 1973, p. 99).

The plantation elite solved their manpower problem this time by developing a system of **sharecropping**, or tenant farming. The sharecroppers worked the land, which was actually owned by the planters, in return for payment in shares of the profit when the crop was taken to market. The landowner would supply a place to live and food and clothing on credit. After the harvest, tenant and landowner would split the profits (sometimes very unequally), and the tenant's debts would be deducted from his share. The accounts were kept by the landowner who could cheat and take advantage of the tenants with great impunity. With few or no political and civil rights, black sharecroppers found it difficult to keep unscrupulous white landowners honest. The landowner could inflate the indebtedness of the sharecropper and claim that he was still owed money even after profits had been split. Under this system, sharecroppers had few opportunities to improve their situations and could be bound to the land until their "debts" were paid off (Geschwender, 1978, p. 163).

By 1910, more than half of all employed African Americans worked in agriculture, and more than half of the remainder (25% of the total) worked in domestic occupations, such as maid or janitor (Geschwender, 1978, p. 169). The manpower shortage in Southern agriculture was solved, and the African American community once again found itself in a subservient status.

At the same time, the white Southern working class was protected from direct job competition with African Americans. As the South began to industrialize, white workers were able to exclude black workers and reserve the better-paying jobs using a combination of whites-only labor unions and strong anti-black laws and customs. White workers took advantage of the new jobs created by industrialization, while black Southerners remained a rural peasantry, excluded from participation in the modernizing job structure.

In some sectors of the changing Southern economy, the status of African Americans actually fell lower than it had been during slavery. For example, in 1865, 83% of the artisans, or skilled craftsmen, in the South were African Americans; by 1900, this percentage had fallen to 5% (Geschwender, 1978, p. 170). The Jim Crow system confined African Americans to the agrarian and domestic sectors of the labor force, denied them the opportunity for a decent education, and excluded them from politics. The system was reinforced by still more laws and customs that drastically limited the options and life opportunities available to black Southerners.

Political and Civil Rights Under Jim Crow. A final force behind the creation of de jure segregation was political. As the 19th century drew to a close, a wave of agrarian radicalism known as populism spread across the country. This anti-elitist movement was a reaction to changes in agriculture caused by industrialization. The movement attempted to unite poor whites and blacks in the rural South against the traditional elite classes. The economic elite were frightened by the possibility of a loss of power and split the incipient coalition between whites and blacks by fanning the flames of racial hatred. The strategy of "divide and conquer" proved to be effective (as it often has both before and since this time), and the white elite classes in states throughout the South eliminated the possibility of future threats by depriving African Americans of the right to vote (Woodward, 1974).

The disenfranchisement of the black community was accomplished by measures such as literacy tests, poll taxes, and property requirements. The literacy tests were officially justified as promoting a better-informed electorate but were shamelessly rigged to favor white voters. The requirement that voters pay a tax or prove ownership of a certain amount of property could also disenfranchise poor whites, but again, the implementation of these policies was racially biased.

The policies were extremely effective, and by the early 20th century the political power of the Southern black community was virtually nonexistent. For example, as late as 1896 in Louisiana there had been more than 100,000 registered African American voters; African American voters were a majority in 26 parishes (counties). In 1898, the state adopted a new constitution containing stiff educational and property requirements for voting unless the voter's father or grandfather had been eligible to vote as of January 1, 1867. At that time, the 14th and 15th Amendments, which guaranteed suffrage for black males, had not yet been passed. Such "grandfather clauses" made it easy for white males to register while disenfranchising blacks. By 1900, only about 5,000 African Americans were registered to vote in Louisiana, and African American voters were not a majority in any parish. A similar decline occurred in Alabama, where an electorate of more than 180,000 African American males was reduced to 3,000 by provision of a new state constitution. This story repeated itself throughout the South, and African American political powerlessness was a reality by 1905 (Franklin & Moss, 1994, p. 261).

This system of legally mandated racial privilege was approved by the U.S. Supreme Court, which ruled in the case of *Plessy v. Ferguson* (1896) that it was constitutional for states to require separate facilities (schools, parks, etc.) for African Americans as long as the separate facilities were fully equal. The Southern states paid close attention to "separate" but ignored "equal."

Reinforcing the System. Under de jure segregation, as under slavery, the subordination of the African American community was reinforced and supplemented by an elaborate system of racial etiquette. Everyday interactions between blacks and whites proceeded according to highly stylized and rigidly followed codes of conduct intended to underscore the inferior status of the African American community. Whites were addressed as "mister" or "ma'am," whereas African Americans were called by their first names or, perhaps, by an honorific title such as "aunt," "uncle," or "professor." Blacks were expected to assume a humble and deferential manner, remove their hats, cast their eyes downward, and enact the role of the subordinate in all interactions with whites. If an African American had reason to call on anyone in the white community, he or she was expected to go to the back door.

These expectations and "good manners" for black Southerners were systematically enforced. Anyone who ignored them ran the risk of reprisal, physical attacks, and even death by lynching. During the decades in which the Jim Crow system was being imposed, there were thousands of lynchings in the South. From 1884 until the end of the century, lynchings averaged almost one every other day in the South (Franklin & Moss, 1994, p. 312). The bulk of this violent terrorism was racial and intended to reinforce the system of racial advantage or punish real or imagined transgressors. Also, various secret organizations, such as the Ku Klux Klan, engaged in terrorist attacks against the African American community and anyone else who failed to conform to the dictates of the system.

Increases in Prejudice and Racism. As the system of racial advantage formed and solidified, levels of prejudice and racism increased (Wilson, 1973, p. 101). The new system needed justification and rationalization, just as slavery did, and anti-black sentiment, stereotypes, and ideologies of racial inferiority grew stronger. At the start of the 20th century, the United States in general—not just the South—was a very racist and intolerant society. This spirit of rejection and scorn for all out-groups coalesced with the need for justification of the Jim Crow system and created an especially negative brand of racism in the South.

The Great Migration

Although African Americans lacked the power resources to withstand the resurrection of Southern racism and oppression, they did have one option that had not been available under slavery: freedom of movement. African Americans were no longer legally tied to a specific master or to a certain plot of land. In the early 20th century, a massive population movement, often called the Great Migration, out of the South began. Slowly at first, African Americans began to move to other regions of the nation and from the countryside to the city. The movement increased when hard times hit Southern agriculture and slowed down during better times. It has been said that African Americans voted against Southern segregation with their feet.

As exhibits 4.2 and 4.3 show, an urban black population living outside the South is a 20th century phenomenon. A majority of African Americans continues to live in the South, but the group is more evenly distributed across the nation and much more urbanized than it was a century ago.

The significance of this population redistribution is manifold. Most important, perhaps, was the fact that by moving out of the South and from rural to urban areas, African Americans moved from areas of great resistance to racial change to areas of lower resistance. In the Northern cities, for example, it was far easier to register and

Exhibit 4.2   Regional Distribution of African American Population, 1890–2010

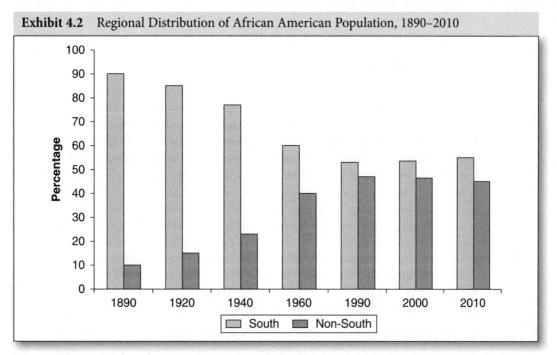

Source: 1890–1960: Geschwender (1978); 1990: Heaton, Chadwick, and Jacobson (2000); 2000, 2010: Rastogi, Johnson, Hoeffel, and Drewery (2011, p. 7).

Exhibit 4.3   Percentage of African American Population Living in Urban Areas, 1890–2000

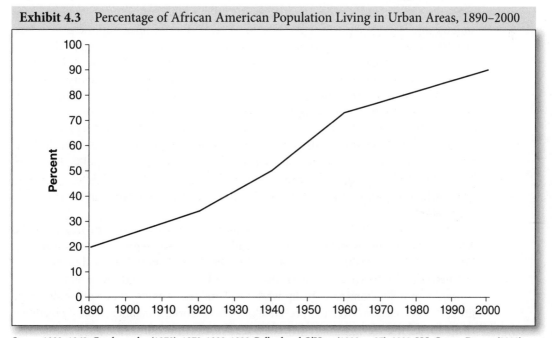

Source: 1890–1960: Geschwender (1978); 1970, 1980, 1990: Pollard and O'Hare (1999, p. 27); 2000: U.S. Census Bureau (2000).

vote. Black political power began to grow and eventually provided many of the crucial resources that fueled the civil rights movement of the 1950s and 1960s.

Life in the North

What did African American migrants find when they got to the industrializing cities of the North? There is no doubt that life in the North was better for the vast majority of African American migrants. The growing Northern African American communities relished the absence of Jim Crow laws and oppressive racial etiquette, the relative freedom to pursue jobs, and the greater opportunities to educate their children. Inevitably, however, life in the North fell far short of utopia. Many aspects of African American culture—literature, poetry, music—flourished in the heady new atmosphere of freedom, but on other fronts Northern African American communities faced massive discrimination in housing, schools, and the job market. Along with freedom and such cultural flowerings as the Harlem Renaissance came black ghettos and new forms of oppression and exploitation. We will explore these events and the workings of what has been called **de facto segregation** in chapter 5.

Competition with White Ethnic Groups

It is useful to see the movement of African Americans out of the South in terms of their resultant relationships with other groups. Southern blacks began to move to the North at about the same time as the New Immigration from Europe (see chapter 2) began to end. By the time substantial numbers of black Southerners began arriving in the North, European immigrants and their descendants had had years, decades, and even generations to establish themselves in the job markets, political systems, labor unions, and neighborhoods of the North. Many of the European ethnic groups had also been the victims of discrimination and rejection, and, as we discussed in chapter 2, their hold on economic security and status was tenuous for much of the 20th century. They often saw the newly arriving black migrants as a threat to their status, a perception that was reinforced by the fact that industrialists and factory owners often used African Americans as strikebreakers and scabs during strikes. The white ethnic groups responded by developing defensive strategies to limit the dangers presented by these migrants from the South. They tried to exclude African Americans from their labor unions and other associations and limit their impact on the political system. They also attempted, often successfully, to maintain segregated neighborhoods and schools (although the legal system outside the South did not sanction overt de jure segregation).

This competition led to hostile relations between black Southern migrants and white ethnic groups, especially the lower- and working-class segments of those groups. Ironically, however, in another chapter of the ethnic succession discussed in chapter 2, the newly arriving African Americans actually helped white ethnic groups become upwardly mobile. Dominant group whites became less contemptuous of white ethnic groups as their alarm over the presence of African Americans increased. The greater antipathy of the white community toward African Americans made the immigrants more desirable and thus hastened their admission to the institutions of the larger society. For many white ethnic groups, the increased tolerance of the larger society coincided happily with the coming of age of the more educated and skilled descendants of the original immigrants, further abetting the rise of these groups in the U.S. social class structure (Lieberson, 1980).

For more than a century, each new European immigrant group had helped to push previous groups up the ladder of socioeconomic success and out of the old, ghettoized neighborhoods. Black Southerners got to the cities after immigration from Europe had been curtailed, and no newly arrived immigrants appeared to continue the pattern of succession for Northern African Americans. Instead, American cities developed concentrations of low-income blacks who were economically vulnerable and politically weak and whose position was further solidified by anti-black prejudice and discrimination (Wilson, 1987, p. 34).

The Origins of Black Protest

As I pointed out in chapter 3, African Americans have always resisted their oppression and protested their situation. Under slavery, however, the inequalities they faced were so great and their resources so meager that the protest was ineffective. With the increased freedom that followed slavery, a national African American leadership developed and spoke out against oppression and founded organizations that eventually helped to lead the fight for freedom and equality. Even at its birth, the **black protest movement** was diverse and incorporated a variety of viewpoints and leaders.

Booker T. Washington was the most prominent African American leader prior to World War I. Washington had been born in slavery and was the founder and president of Tuskegee Institute, a college in Alabama dedicated to educating African Americans. His public advice to African Americans in the South was to be patient, to accommodate to the Jim Crow system for the time being, to raise their levels of education and job skills, and to take full advantage of whatever opportunities became available. This nonconfrontational stance earned Washington praise and support from the white community and widespread popularity in the nation. Privately, he worked behind the scenes to end discrimination and implement full racial integration and equality (Franklin & Moss, 1994, pp. 272–274; Hawkins, 1962; Washington, 1965).

Washington's most vocal opponent was W. E. B. Du Bois, an intellectual and activist who was born in the North and educated at some of the leading universities of the day. Among his many other accomplishments, Du Bois was part of a coalition of blacks and white liberals who founded the National Association for the Advancement of Colored People (NAACP) in 1909. Du Bois rejected Washington's accommodationist stance and advocated immediate pursuit of racial equality and a direct assault on de jure segregation. Almost from the beginning of its existence, the NAACP filed lawsuits that challenged the legal foundations of Jim Crow segregation (Du Bois, 1961). As we shall see in chapter 6, this legal strategy was eventually successful and led to the demise of the Jim Crow system.

Washington and Du Bois may have differed on matters of strategy and tactics, but they agreed that the only acceptable goal for African Americans was an integrated, racially equal United States. A third leader who emerged early in the 20th century called for a very different approach to the problems of U.S. race relations. Marcus Garvey was born in Jamaica and immigrated to the United States during World War I. He argued that the white-dominated U.S. society was hopelessly racist and would never truly support integration and racial equality. He advocated separatist goals, including a return to Africa. Garvey founded the Universal Negro Improvement Association in 1914 in his native Jamaica and founded the first U.S. branch in 1916. Garvey's organization was very popular for a time in African American communities outside the South, and he helped to establish some of the themes and ideas of black nationalism and pride in African heritage that would become prominent again in the pluralistic 1960s (Essien-Udom, 1962; Garvey, 1969, 1977; Vincent, 1976).

These early leaders and organizations established some of the foundations for later protest movements, but prior to the mid-20th century they made few actual improvements in the situation of African Americans in the North or South. Jim Crow was a formidable opponent, and the African American community lacked the resources to successfully challenge the status quo until the century was well along and some basic structural features of American society had changed.

Applying Concepts

Acculturation and Integration

During this era of Southern segregation and migration to the North, assimilation was not a major factor in the African American experience. Rather, the black–white relations of the time are better described as a system of structural pluralism combined with great inequality. Excluded from the mainstream but freed from the limitations of slavery, African Americans constructed a separate subsociety and subculture. In all regions of the nation, African Americans developed their own institutions and organizations, including separate neighborhoods, churches, businesses, and schools. Like immigrants from Europe in the same era, they organized their communities to cater to their own needs and problems and pursue their agenda as a group.

During segregation, a small African American middle class emerged based on leadership roles in the church, education, and business. A network of black colleges and universities was constructed to educate the children of the growing middle class, as well as other classes. Through this infrastructure, African Americans began to develop the resources and leadership that in the decades ahead would attack, head on, the structures of racial inequality.

Gender and Race

For African American men and women, the changes wrought by industrialization and the population movement to the North created new possibilities and new roles. However, as African Americans continued to be the victims of exploitation and exclusion in both the North and the South, African American women continued to be among the most vulnerable groups in society.

Following Emancipation, there was a flurry of marriages and weddings among African Americans, as they were finally able to legitimate their family relationships (Staples, 1988, p. 306). African American women continued to have primary responsibility for home and children. Historian Herbert Gutman (1976) reports that it was common for married women to drop out of the labor force and attend solely to household and family duties, because a working wife was too reminiscent of a slave role. This pattern became so widespread that it created serious labor shortages in many areas (Gutman, 1976; see also Staples, 1988, p. 307).

The former slaves were hardly affluent, however, and as sharecropping and segregation began to shape race relations in the South women often had to return to the fields or to domestic work for the family to survive. One former slave woman noted that women "do double duty, a man's share in the field and a woman's part at home" (Evans, 1989, p. 121). During the bleak decades following the end of Reconstruction, Southern black families and black women in particular lived "close to the bone" (Evans, 1989, p. 121).

In the cities and in the growing African American neighborhoods in the North, African American women played a role that in some ways paralleled the role of immigrant women from Europe. The men often moved north first and sent for the women after they had attained some level of financial stability or after the pain of separation became too great (Almquist, 1979, p. 434). In other cases, African American women by the thousands left the South to work as domestic servants; they often replaced European immigrant women, who had moved up in the job structure (Amott & Matthaei, 1991, p. 168).

In the North, discrimination and racism created constant problems of unemployment for the men, and families often relied on the income supplied by the women to make ends meet. It was comparatively easy for women to find employment, but only in the low-paying, less-desirable areas, such as domestic work. In both the South and the North, African American women worked outside the home in larger proportions than did white women. For example, in 1900 41% of African American women were employed, compared with only 16% of white women (Staples, 1988, p. 307).

In 1890, more than a generation after the end of slavery, 85% of all African American men and 96% of African American women were employed in just two occupational categories: agriculture and domestic or personal service. By 1930, 90% of employed African American women were still in these same two categories, whereas the corresponding percentage for employed African American males had dropped to 54% (although nearly all of the remaining 46% were unskilled workers) (Steinberg, 1981, pp. 206–207). Since the inception of segregation, African American women have had consistently higher unemployment rates and lower incomes than African American men and white women (Almquist, 1979, p. 437). These gaps, as we shall see in chapter 6, persist to the present day.

During the years following the Civil War some issues did split men and women, within both the African American community and the larger society. Prominent among these was suffrage, or the right to vote, which was still limited to men only. The abolitionist movement, which had been so instrumental in ending slavery, also supported universal suffrage. Efforts to enfranchise women, though, were abandoned by the

Republican Party and large parts of the abolitionist movement to concentrate on efforts to secure the vote for African American males in the South. Ratification of the 15th Amendment in 1870 extended the vote, in principle, to African American men, but the 19th Amendment enfranchising women would not be passed for another 50 years (Almquist, 1979, pp. 433–434; Evans, 1989, pp. 121–124).

COMPARATIVE FOCUS:
South African Apartheid

Legally sanctioned racial segregation can be found in many nations, but perhaps the

Exhibit 4.4 Map of Africa Showing South Africa

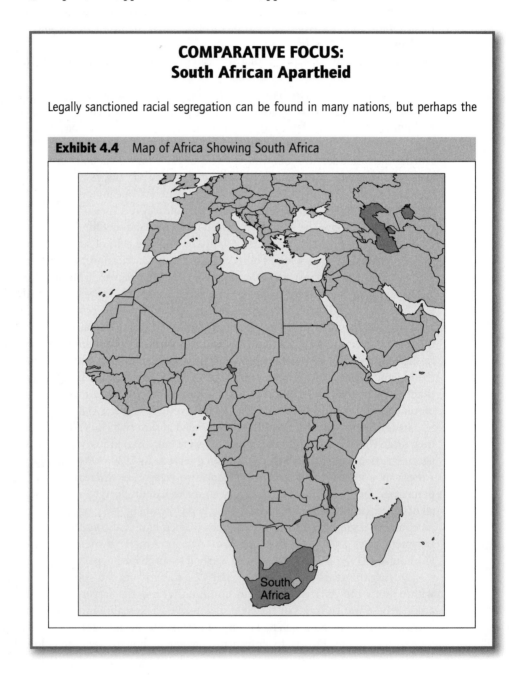

most infamous system was constructed in South Africa (see exhibit 4.4). As in the Southern United States, South African segregation was intended to control the labor of the black population and eliminate all political and economic threats from the group. The white dominant group enjoyed a level of race-based privilege rarely equaled in the history of the world. Today, although enormous problems of inequality and racism remain, South Africa has officially dismantled the machinery of racial oppression, has enfranchised non-whites, and has elected three black presidents as of this writing.

South Africa has a long and bloody history of racial oppression but the system known as **apartheid** dates only from the late 1940s. The word "apartheid" means "separate" or "apart" in Afrikaans, one of the two languages of white South Africans (the other language is English). The logic of the system was to separate whites and blacks in every area of life: schools, neighborhoods, jobs, buses, churches, and so forth. Apartheid resembled the Jim Crow system of segregation in the United States except it was even more repressive, elaborate, and unequal. By keeping blacks poor and powerless, white South Africans created a pool of cheap, highly controlled labor. Of the dominant-minority situations considered in this text, perhaps only American slavery rivals apartheid for its naked, unabashed subjugation of one group for the benefit of another.

Note that the coming of apartheid reverses the relationship between modernization and control of minority groups in the Southern United States. As the United States industrialized and modernized, group relations evolved from paternalistic (slavery) to the looser rigid competitive form (de jure segregation). In South Africa, the structures of minority group control became stronger and more oppressive. Why the difference?

One reason for the increasing repression was that South African blacks in the late 1940s were extremely powerless. Protest organizations existed, but they were illegal and had to operate underground or from exile and under conditions of extreme repression. In the United States, in contrast, blacks living outside the South were able to organize and pool their resources to assist in the campaign against Jim Crow, and these activities were protected (more or less) by the national commitment to civil liberties and political freedom.

Perhaps more important than the power differential was the extreme sense of threat felt by white South Africans. Blacks were the great majority of the population in the society and whites feared that they would be "swamped" unless black powerlessness was perpetuated. This strong sense of threat helped to create a "fortress" mentality among white South Africans: the feeling that they were defending a small (but luxurious) outpost surrounded and besieged by savage hordes who threatened their immediate and total destruction.

Apartheid lasted about 40 years. Through the 1970s and 1980s, changes within South Africa and in the world in general built up pressure against the system. Internally, protests against apartheid by blacks began in the 1960s and continued to build in

(Continued)

(Continued)

intensity, in spite of the brutal, violent repression of the South African government. Internationally, other nations established trade embargoes and organized boycotts of South African goods. Many of these efforts were more symbolic than real and had only minor impact on everyday social life, but they sustained an outcast status for South Africa and helped create an atmosphere of uncertainty among its economic and political elite.

By the late 1980s, these various pressures made it impossible to ignore the need for reform. In 1990, President F. W. de Klerk began a series of changes that eventually ended apartheid. He lifted the ban on many outlawed black African protest organizations, and released Nelson Mandela from prison. Mandela was the leader of the African National Congress (ANC), one of the oldest and most important black organizations, and he had served a 27-year prison term for actively protesting apartheid. Together, de Klerk and Mandela helped to ease South Africa through a period of rapid racial change that saw the franchise being extended to blacks, the first open election in South African history, and, in 1994, Mandela's election to a 5-year term as president. Mandela has been succeeded by two other black South Africans: Thabo M. Mbeki, first elected in 1999, and Jacob Zuma, who became president in 2009.

The future of South Africa remains unclear. Although the majority black population now has political power, deep racial divisions remain and much of the black population lives in apartheid–era townships—pockets of deep, grinding poverty with no running water, poor or nonexistent medical care, and grossly overcrowded and understaffed schools. To illustrate, the average annual income (in U.S. dollars) for white households in 2006 was about $38,000 whereas black households averaged about $5,000 (Statistics South Africa, 2008, p. 9)

The problems of racial and class inequality facing South Africa are enormous and this experiment in racial reform might still fail. However, should it succeed in meeting these challenges, the dramatic transition away from massive racism and institutionalized discrimination could still provide a model of change for other racially divided societies.

Industrialization, the Shift to Postindustrial Society, and Dominant-Minority Group Relations: General Trends

The processes of industrialization that began in the 19th century continued to shape the larger society and dominant-minority relations throughout the 20th century. Today, the United States bears little resemblance to the society it was a century ago. The population has more than tripled in size and has urbanized even more rapidly than it has grown. New organizational forms (bureaucracies, corporations, multinational businesses) and new technologies (nuclear power, computers) dominate everyday life. Levels of education have risen, and the public schools have produced one of the most literate populations and best-trained workforces in the history of the world.

Minority groups also grew in size during this period, and most became even more urbanized than the general population. Minority group members have come to participate in an increasing array of occupations, and their average levels of education also have risen. Despite these real improvements, however, virtually all U.S. minority groups continue to face racism, poverty, discrimination, and exclusion. As industrialization proceeded, the mechanisms for maintaining racial stratification also evolved, morphing into forms that are subtle, indirect, but, in their way, as formidable as Jim Crow segregation.

In this section, I outline the social processes that began in the industrial era and continue to shape the postindustrial stage. I note the ways in which these processes have changed American society and examine some of the general implications for minority groups. I then summarize these changes in terms of a transition from the rigid competitive Jim Crow era to a new stage of group relations called **fluid competitive system**. The treatment here is broad and intended to establish a general framework for the examination of the impacts of industrialization and deindustrialization on group relations in the case studies that make up part 3 of this text.

Urbanization

We have already noted that urbanization made close, paternalistic controls of minority groups irrelevant. For example, the racial etiquette required by Southern de jure segregation, such as African Americans deferring to whites on crowded sidewalks, tended to disappear in the chaos of an urban rush hour.

Besides weakening dominant group controls, urbanization also created the potential for minority groups to mobilize and organize large numbers of people. As stated in chapter 1, the sheer size of a group is a source of power. Without the freedom to organize, however, size means little, and urbanization increased both the concentration of populations and the freedom to organize.

Occupational Specialization

One of the first and most important results of industrialization, even in its earliest days, was an increase in occupational specialization and the variety of jobs available in the workforce. The growing needs of an urbanizing population increased the number of jobs available in the production, transport, and sale of goods and services. Occupational specialization was also stimulated by the very nature of industrial production. Complex manufacturing processes could be performed more efficiently if they were broken down into the narrower component tasks. It was easier and more efficient to train the workforce in the simpler, specialized jobs. Assembly lines were invented, work was subdivided, the division of labor became increasingly complex, and the number of different occupations continued to grow.

The sheer complexity of the industrial job structure made it difficult to maintain rigid, caste-like divisions of labor between dominant and minority groups. Rigid competitive forms of group relations, such as Jim Crow segregation, became less viable as the job market became more diversified and changeable. Simple, clear rules about which groups could do which jobs disappeared. As the more repressive systems of control weakened, job opportunities for minority group members sometimes increased. However, conflict between groups also increased as the relationships between group memberships and positions in the job market became more blurred. For example, as we have noted, African Americans moving from the South often found themselves in competition for jobs with members of white ethnic groups, labor unions, and other elements of the dominant group.

Bureaucracy and Rationality

As industrialization continued, privately owned corporations and businesses came to have workforces numbering in the hundreds of thousands. Gigantic factories employing thousands of workers became common. To coordinate the efforts of these huge workforces, bureaucracy became the dominant form of organization in the economy and, indeed, throughout the society.

Bureaucracies are large-scale, impersonal, formal organizations that run "by the book." They are governed by rules and regulations (i.e., "red tape") and are "rational" in that they attempt to find the most efficient ways to accomplish their tasks. Although they typically fail to attain the ideal of fully rational efficiency, bureaucracies tend to recruit, reward, and promote employees on the basis of competence and performance (Gerth & Mills, 1946).

The stress on rationality and objectivity can counteract the more blatant forms of racism and increase the array of opportunities available to members of minority groups. Although they are often nullified by other forces (see Blumer, 1965), these antiprejudicial tendencies do not exist at all or are much weaker in preindustrial economies.

The history of the concept of race illustrates the impact of rationality and scientific ways of thinking. Today, virtually the entire scientific community regards race as a biological triviality, a conclusion based on decades of research. This scientific finding undermined and contributed to the destruction of the formal systems of privilege based solely on race (e.g., segregated school systems) and traditional prejudice, which is based on the assumption that race is a crucial personal characteristic.

Growth of White-Collar Jobs and the Service Sector

Industrialization changed the composition of the labor force. As work became more complex and specialized, the need to coordinate and regulate the production process increased, and as a result bureaucracies and other organizations grew larger still. Within these organizations, white-collar occupations—those that coordinate, manage, and deal with the flow of paperwork—continued to expand. As industrialization progressed, mechanization and automation reduced the number of manual or blue-collar workers, and white-collar occupations became the dominant sector of the job market in the United States.

The changing nature of the workforce can be illustrated by looking at the proportional representation of three different types of jobs:

1. **Extractive (primary) occupations** are those that produce raw materials, such as food and agricultural products, minerals, and lumber. The jobs in this sector often involve unskilled manual labor, require little formal education, and are generally low paying.

2. **Manufacturing (secondary) occupations** transform raw materials into finished products ready for sale in the marketplace. Like jobs in the extractive sector, these blue-collar jobs involve manual labor, but they tend to require higher levels of skill and are more highly rewarded. Examples of occupations in this sector include the assembly line jobs that transform steel, rubber, plastic, and other materials into finished automobiles.

3. **Service (tertiary) occupations** do not produce "things"; rather, they provide services. As urbanization increased and self-sufficiency decreased, opportunities for work in this sector grew. Examples of tertiary occupations include police officer, clerk, waiter, teacher, nurse, doctor, and cabdriver.

The course of industrialization is traced in the changing structure of the labor market depicted in exhibit 4.5. In 1840, when industrialization was just beginning in the United States, most of the workforce (70%) was in the extractive sector, with

Exhibit 4.5 The Changing U.S. Workforce: The Distribution of Jobs from 1840 to 2010

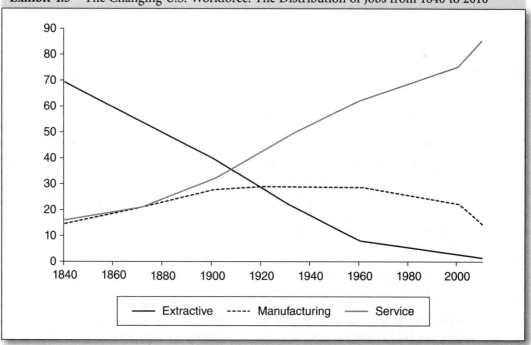

Source: 1840–1990: Adapted from Lenski, Nolan, and Lenski (1995); 2000: Calculated from U.S. Census Bureau (2005, pp. 385–388); 2010: Calculated from U.S. Census Bureau (2012b, pp. 393–396).

agriculture being the dominant occupation. As industrialization progressed, the manufacturing, or secondary, sector grew, reaching a peak after World War II. Today, in the postindustrial era, the large majority of U.S. jobs are in the service, or tertiary, sector.

This shift away from blue-collar jobs and manufacturing since the 1960s is sometimes referred to as deindustrialization or discussed in terms of the emergence of postindustrial society. The U.S. economy has lost millions of unionized, high-paying factory jobs since the 1960s, and the downward trend continues. The industrial jobs that sustained so many generations of American workers have moved to other nations where wages are considerably lower than in the United States, or have been eliminated by robots or other automated manufacturing processes (see Rifkin, 1996).

The changing structure of the job market helps to clarify the nature of intergroup competition and the sources of wealth and power in society. Job growth in the United States today is largely in the service sector, and these occupations are highly variable. At one end are low-paying jobs with few, if any, benefits or chances for advancement (e.g., washing dishes in a restaurant). At the other end are high-prestige, lucrative positions, such as Supreme Court justice, scientist, and financial analyst. The new service sector jobs are either highly desirable technical, professional, or administrative jobs with demanding entry requirements (e.g., physician or nurse) or low-paying, low-skilled jobs with few benefits and little security (e.g., receptionist, nurse's aide). For the past half century, job growth in the United States has been either in areas in which educationally deprived minority group members find it difficult to compete or in areas that offer little compensation, upward mobility, or security. As we will see in part 3, the economic situation of contemporary minority groups reflects these fundamental trends.

The Growing Importance of Education

Education has been an increasingly important prerequisite for employability in the United States and in other advanced industrial societies. A high school or, increasingly, a college degree has become the minimum entry-level requirement for employment. However, opportunities for high-quality education are not distributed equally across the population. Some minority groups, especially those created by colonization, have been systematically excluded from the schools of the dominant society, and today they are less likely to have the educational backgrounds needed to compete for better jobs.

Access to education is a key issue for all U.S. minority groups, and the average educational levels of these groups have been rising since World War II. Still, minority children continue to be much more likely to attend segregated, underfunded, deteriorated schools and to receive inferior educations (see Orfield & Lee, 2007).

A Dual Labor Market

The changing composition of the labor force and increasing importance of educational credentials has split the U.S. labor market into two segments or types of jobs. The **primary labor market** includes jobs usually located in large, bureaucratic organizations. These positions offer higher pay, more security, better opportunities for advancement, health and retirement benefits, and other amenities. Entry requirements include college degrees, even when people with fewer years of schooling could competently perform the work.

The **secondary labor market**, sometimes called the competitive market, includes low-paying, low-skilled, insecure jobs. Many of these jobs are in the service sector. They do not represent a career and offer little opportunity for promotion or upward mobility. Very often, they do not offer health or retirement benefits, have high rates of turnover, and are part-time, seasonal, or temporary.

Many American minority groups are concentrated in the secondary job market. Their exclusion from better jobs is perpetuated not so much by direct or overt discrimination as by their lack of access to the educational and other credentials required to enter the primary sector. The differential distribution of educational opportunities, in the past as well as in the present, effectively protects workers in the primary sector from competition from minority groups.

Globalization

Over the past century, the United States became an economic, political, and military world power with interests around the globe. These worldwide ties have created new minority groups through population movement and have changed the status of others. Migration to this country has been considerable for the past three decades. The American economy is one of the most productive in the world, and jobs, even those in the low-paying secondary sector, are the primary goals for millions of newcomers. For other immigrants, this country continues to play its historic role as a refuge from political and religious persecution.

Many of the wars, conflicts, and other disputes in which the United States has been involved have had consequences for American minority groups. For example, both Puerto Ricans and Cuban Americans became U.S. minority groups as the result of processes set in motion during the Spanish-American War of 1898. Both World War I and World War II created new job opportunities for many minority groups, including African Americans and Mexican Americans. After the Korean War in the early 1950s, international ties were forged between the United States and South Korea, and this led to an increase in immigration from that nation. In the 1960s and 1970s, the military involvement of the United States in Southeast Asia led to the arrival of Vietnamese, Cambodians, Hmong, and other immigrant and refugee groups. The most recent war in Iraq has also produced new communities of immigrants and refugees.

Dominant-minority relations in the United States have been increasingly played out on an international stage as the world has effectively "shrunk" in size and become more interconnected by international organizations, such as the United Nations; by ties of trade and commerce; and by modern means of transportation and communication. In a world in which two thirds of the population is non-white and many important nations (such as China, India, and Nigeria) are composed of peoples of color, the treatment of racial minorities by the U.S. dominant group has come under increased scrutiny. It is difficult to preach principles of fairness, equality, and justice—which the United States claims as its own—when domestic realities suggest an embarrassing failure to fully implement these standards. Part of the pressure for the United States to end blatant systems of discrimination such as de jure segregation came from the desire to maintain a leading position in the world.

Postindustrial Society and the Shift from Rigid to Fluid Competitive Relationships

The coming of postindustrial society brought changes so fundamental and profound that they are often described in terms of a revolution: from an industrial society, based on manufacturing, to a postindustrial society, based on information processing and computer-related or other new technologies. As the subsistence technology evolved, so did American dominant-minority relations. The rigid competitive systems (such as Jim Crow) associated with earlier phases of industrialization gave way to fluid competitive systems of group relations. In fluid competitive relations, formal or legal barriers to competition—such as Jim Crow laws or South African apartheid—no longer exist. Both geographic and social mobility are greater in the newer system, and the limitations imposed by minority group status are less restrictive and burdensome. Rigid caste systems of stratification (in which group membership determines opportunities, adult statuses, and jobs) are replaced by more open class systems, in which there are weaker relationships between group membership and wealth, prestige, and power. Because fluid competitive systems are more open and the position of the minority group is less fixed, the fear of competition from minority groups becomes more widespread for the dominant group, and intergroup conflict increases. Exhibit 4.6 compares the characteristics of the three systems of group relations.

Exhibit 4.6   Characteristics of Three Systems of Group Relationships

	Systems of Group Relations		
		Competitive	
	Paternalistic	*Rigid*	*Fluid*
Subsistence Technology	**Agrarian**	**Industrial**	**Postindustrial**
Stratification	**Caste**. Group determines status.	**Mixed**. Elements of caste and class. Status largely determined by group.	**Variable**. Status strongly affected by group. Inequality varies within groups.
Division of labor	**Simple**. Determined by group.	**More complex**. Job largely determined by group, but some sharing of jobs by different groups.	**Most complex**. Group and job are less related. Complex specialization and great variation within groups.
Contact between groups	**Common**, but statuses unequal.	**Less common**, and mostly unequal.	**More common**. Highest rates of equal status contact.
Overt intergroup conflict	**Rare**.	**More common**.	**Common**.
Power differential	**Maximum**. Minority groups have little ability to pursue self-interests.	**Less**. Minority groups have some ability to pursue self-interests.	**Least**. Minority groups have more ability to pursue self-interests.

Source: Based on J. Farley (2000, p. 109).

Compared with previous systems, the fluid competitive system is closer to the American ideal of an open, fair system of stratification in which effort and competence are rewarded and race, ethnicity, gender, religion, and other "birthmarks" are irrelevant. However, as we will see in chapters to come, race and ethnicity continue to affect life chances and limit opportunities for minority group members even in fluid competitive systems. As suggested by the Noel hypothesis, people continue to identify themselves with particular groups (ethnocentrism), and competition for resources continues to play out along group lines. Consistent with the Blauner hypothesis, the minority groups that were formed by colonization remain at a disadvantage in the pursuit of opportunities, education, prestige, and other resources.

Gender Inequality in a Globalizing, Postindustrial World

Deindustrialization and globalization are transforming gender relations along with relations between racial and ethnic groups. Everywhere, even in the most patriarchal, male-dominated societies, women are moving away from their traditional role as wives and mothers, taking on new responsibilities, and facing new challenges. Some women are also encountering new dangers and new forms of exploitation that perpetuate their lower status and extend it into new areas.

Trends in the United States

In the United States, the transition to a postindustrial society has changed gender relations and the status of women on a number of levels. Women and men are now equal in terms of levels of education (U.S. Census Bureau, 2012b, p. 151) and the shift to fluid competitive group relations has weakened the barriers to gender equality along with the barriers to racial equality, although formidable obstacles remain. The changing role of women is also shaped by other characteristics of a modern society: smaller families, high divorce rates, and rising numbers of single mothers who must work to support their children as well as themselves. Here, we will look at the ways in which the shift to a postindustrial subsistence technology has raised the status of women relative to men and then examine some of the barriers and challenges that remain.

Many of these trends have coalesced to motivate women to enter the paid labor force in unprecedented numbers over the past half century. Women are now employed at almost the same levels as men. In the year 2010, for example, 63% of single women (versus about 67% of single men) and about 61% of married women (versus about 76% of married men) had jobs outside the home (U.S. Census Bureau, 2012a, p. 384). Furthermore, between 1970 and 2009 the participation of married women with children in the workforce increased from a little less than 40% to almost 70% (U.S. Census Bureau, 2012a, p. 385).

These "new" women workers are entering a wider variety of careers. In the past, women were largely concentrated in a relatively narrow range of female-dominated jobs such as nurse and elementary school teacher. Exhibit 4.7 focuses on four pairs of careers and illustrates both traditional patterns and recent changes. Each pair includes

Exhibit 4.7   Percentage Female in Selected Occupations for Selected Years

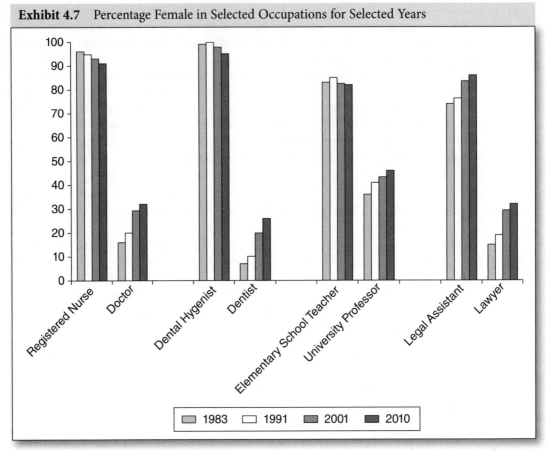

Source: 1983 and 1991: U.S. Census Bureau (1992, pp. 392–393); 2001: U.S. Census Bureau (2002, pp. 587–588); 2010: U.S. Census Bureau (2012b, pp. 393–394).

a female-dominated occupation and a comparable but higher-status, more-lucrative, traditionally male-dominated occupation. While the "women's" careers remain largely female, the percentage of females in higher-status occupations has increased dramatically (even though, except for university professor, the more lucrative careers remain overwhelmingly male).

Some women enter the paid labor force to compensate for the declining earning power of men. Before deindustrialization began to transform U.S. society, men monopolized the more desirable, higher-paid, unionized jobs in the manufacturing sector. For much of the last century, these blue-collar jobs paid well enough to subsidize a comfortable lifestyle, a house in the suburbs, and vacations, with enough money left over to save for a rainy day or for college for the kids.

However, when deindustrialization began, many of these desirable jobs were lost to automation and to cheaper labor forces outside the United States and were replaced, if at all, by lower-paying jobs in the service sector. Thus, deindustrialization tended to drive men's wages down, and many women took jobs outside the home to supplement the family income. Women have taken jobs in sectors of the economy that tended to be relatively unaffected by the shift to an information society (such as elementary school teacher) or in areas that actually benefitted from this shift (finance, insurance, and real estate—the "FIRE" sector).

The rising aspirations of women and their movement into more lucrative and higher status careers have resulted in much greater gender equality in earning power. Exhibit 4.8 shows median income for male and female full-time, year-round workers. Note that the comparison is limited to full-time workers: this eliminates any difference in income caused by the fact that women tend to be less involved in the paid labor force. Also, income is expressed in 2010 dollars and this eliminates the effects of inflation on wages.

The graph reflects the impact of deindustrialization on men: their average wages have been stagnant or actually declining since the early 1970s. Women's wages, in contrast, have been steadily rising. In 1955, women's income was less than two thirds of men's income. By 2007, the percentage had risen to 78% but then declined slightly to 77% in 2010.

The large-scale, macrolevel forces associated with deindustrialization have tended to raise the status of women and narrow the income gap but they have not equalized gender relations. Far from it! Even though women and men are now equal in terms of

Exhibit 4.8 Median Incomes for Full-Time, Year-Round Workers by Gender, 1955–2010 (2010 dollars)

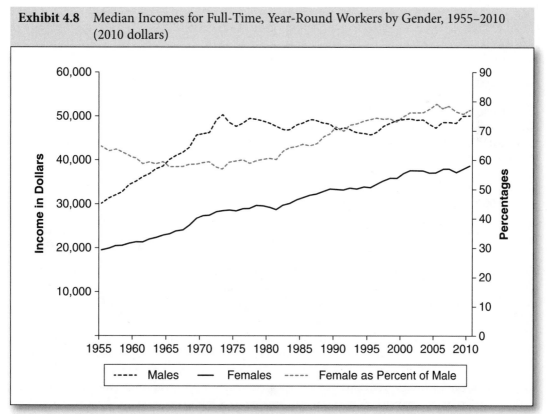

Source: U.S. Census Bureau (2012c).

education, women tend to get lower returns for their investment in human capital. Exhibit 4.9 compares men and women who were full-time workers in 2010 and shows a wage gap at every level of education. Wages rise as education rises for both sexes but the wage gap tends to increase as education increases. The least-educated women earned 71% of what the least-educated men earned, and women with a high-school education earned 73% of what comparably educated men earned. Women college graduates ("BA degree only") earned only 70% of what the men college graduates earned. Among people with a college degree or more ("BA degree or more"), women earned only 68% of what men earned. The wage gap is greatest (60%) for people with professional degrees (doctors, lawyers, etc.)

Exhibit 4.9   Mean Income for Full-Time, Year-Round Workers by Gender and Level of Education, 2010

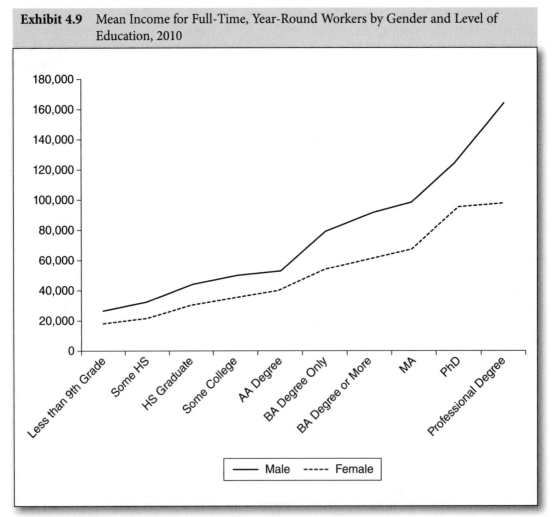

Source: U.S. Census Bureau (2012d).

Furthermore, the gender wage gap persists across occupational areas. Exhibit 4.10 compares men and women in 10 types of occupations in 2010 and, like exhibit 4.9, shows a substantial wage gap. The gender wage gap is smallest for nurses and social workers—two traditionally female-dominated jobs—and largest for the most prestigious and lucrative jobs (management and the professions).

The continuing gender income gap is related to the continuing concentration of women in less-well-paid occupations illustrated in exhibit 4.7, which, in turn, is partly a result of outright occupational discrimination and a pervasive pressure to funnel young women into "appropriate" jobs. This pattern is also a result of the choices women make to balance the demands of their jobs with their family obligations. Whereas men are expected to make a total commitment to their jobs and careers,

Exhibit 4.10 Median Earnings for Full-Time, Year-Round Workers by Gender, for Selected Occupational Categories, 2009

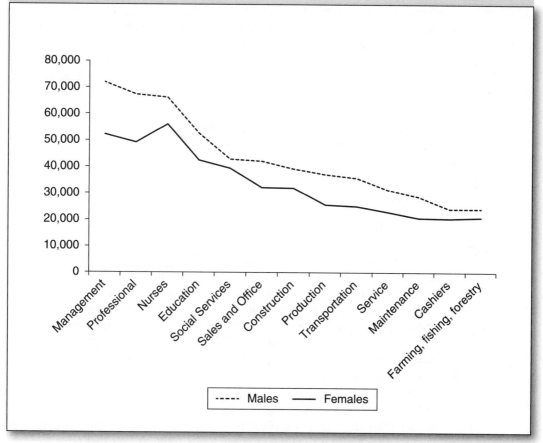

Source: U.S. Census Bureau (2012e).

women have been expected to find ways to continue to fulfill their domestic roles even while working full-time, and many "female" jobs offer some flexibility in this area. For example, some women become elementary school teachers because the job offers long summer breaks, which can help women meet their childcare and other family responsibilities. This pattern of gender occupational segregation testifies to the persistence of minority status for women and the choices they make to reconcile the demands of career and family.

Women, along with minority groups in general, are also limited by the **glass ceiling**, or the discriminatory practices that limit opportunities to rise to higher levels in their careers, qualify for promotions, and earn higher salaries. These practices, today, are usually subtle, unspoken, and unwritten, but effective in maintaining gender inequality, including income inequality. Decisions about promotions or raises will not overtly mention gender but the glass ceiling is maintained, for example, by giving women less access to key mentors or sponsors and fewer opportunities for training and other experiences needed to qualify for higher-level jobs (Federal Glass Ceiling Commission, 1995, p. 8; Ridgeway, 2011, pp. 109–117).

One recent cross-national study demonstrated the reality of gender discrimination in business. The researchers followed a group of men and women who held MBAs from prestigious universities and found that the women in the sample started in lower positions, earned less over the course of their careers, and were far less likely to rise to the top of their companies (Carter & Silva, 2010). Another recent study of the Fortune 500 largest corporations found that women were woefully underrepresented among top business leaders and absent from the executive suites and board rooms. Women made up almost half of the total work force in these companies but were only about 15% of executive officers and board members and fewer than 8% of top earners (Soares, Combopiano, Regis, Shut, & Wong, 2010).

Global Trends

How have deindustrialization and globalization affected women around the world? In part, these trends parallel those in the United States. According to the United Nations (2010), indicators such as rising education levels for women and lower rates of early marriage and childbirth show that women around the world are moving out of their traditional (and often highly controlled and repressed) status. Levels of education for women are rising worldwide and women are approaching educational parity with men, although progress has been slowed by the recent global economic crisis. They are entering the labor force in unprecedented numbers virtually everywhere, and women now make up about 40% of the paid global workforce. Still, women are concentrated in lower-status, less-lucrative, and more-insecure jobs everywhere (United Nations, 2010, pp. 20–23).

Although the status of women is generally rising, the movement away from traditional gender roles also brings exposure to new forms of exploitation. Around the globe, women have become a source of cheap labor, often in jobs that have recently been exported from the U.S. economy. For example, many manufacturing jobs formerly held by men in the United States have migrated just south of the border to Mexico, where they are held by women. Maquiladoras are assembly plants built by corporations (often headquartered in the United States) to take advantage of the plentiful supply of working-class females who will work for low wages and in conditions that workers in the United States would not tolerate.

The weakening of traditional gender roles has increased women's vulnerability in other areas, as well. A global sex trade in prostitution and pornography is flourishing and accounts for a significant portion of the economy of the Philippines, Thailand, and other nations. This international industry depends on impoverished women (and children) pushed out of the subsistence rural economy by industrialization and globalization and made vulnerable for exploitation by their lack of resources and power (Poulan, 2003; see also Ehrenreich & Hochschild, 2004; and Kristof & WuDunn, 2010).

Across all these changes and around the globe, women commonly face the challenge of reconciling their new work demands with their traditional family responsibilities. Also, women face challenges and issues such as sexual harassment and domestic violence, which clearly differentiate their status from that of men. In this context, minority group women face a double disadvantage because the issues they face as women are complicated by the barriers created by racial and ethnic prejudice and discrimination. As we will see in part 3, minority group and immigrant women often form the poorest, most vulnerable, and most exploited groups in U.S. society and around the globe.

Modern Institutional Discrimination

Virtually all American minority groups continue to lag behind national averages in income, employment, and other measures of equality, despite the greater fluidity of group relations, the end of legal barriers such as Jim Crow laws, the dramatic declines in overt prejudice, and the introduction of numerous laws designed to ensure that all people are treated without regard to race, gender, or ethnicity. After all this change, shouldn't there be less minority group inequality and racial stratification?

As we will discuss in chapter 5, many Americans attribute the persisting patterns of inequality to the minority groups' lack of willpower or motivation to get ahead. In the remaining chapters of this text, however, I argue that the major barriers facing minority groups in postindustrial, post–Jim Crow America are pervasive, subtle, but still powerful forms of discrimination that together can be called modern institutional discrimination.

As you read in chapter 1, institutional discrimination is built into the everyday operation of the social structure of society. The routine procedures and policies of institutions and organizations are arranged so that minority group members are automatically put at a disadvantage. In the Jim Crow era in the South, for example, African Americans were deprived of the right to vote by overt institutional discrimination and could acquire little in the way of political power.

The forms of institutional discrimination that persist in the present are more subtle and difficult to document than the blatant, overt customs and laws of the Jim

Crow system. In fact, they are sometimes unintentional or unconscious and are manifested more in the results for minority groups than in the intentions or prejudices of dominant group members. Modern institutional discrimination is not necessarily linked to prejudice, and the decision makers who implement it may sincerely think of themselves as behaving rationally and in the best interests of their organizations.

The Continuing Power of the Past

Many forces conspire to maintain racial stratification in the present. Some are the legacies of past discriminatory practices. Consider, for example, **past-in-present institutional discrimination**, which involves practices in the present that have discriminatory consequences because of some pattern of discrimination or exclusion in the past (Feagin & Feagin, 1986, p. 32). One form of this discrimination is found in workforces organized around the principle of seniority. In these systems, which are quite common, workers who have been on the job longer have higher incomes, more privileges, and other benefits, such as longer vacations. The "old-timers" often have more job security and are designated in official, written policy as the last to be fired or laid off in the event of hard times. Workers and employers alike may think of the privileges of seniority as just rewards for long years of service, familiarity with the job, and so forth.

Personnel policies based on seniority may seem perfectly reasonable, neutral, and fair. However, they can have discriminatory results in the present because in the past members of minority groups and women were excluded from specific occupations by racist or sexist labor unions, discriminatory employers, or both. As a result, minority group workers and women may have fewer years of experience than dominant group workers and may be the first to go when layoffs are necessary. The adage "last hired, first fired" describes the situation of minority group and female employees who are more vulnerable not because of some overtly racist or sexist policy in the present, but because of the routine operation of the seemingly neutral principle of seniority.

Racial differences in home ownership provide a second example of the myriad ways in which the past shapes the present and maintains racial stratification. Today, about 70% of whites own their own home, and these houses have a median value of $182,000. In contrast, only 44% of blacks are homeowners and the median value of their homes is $134,000 (U.S. Census Bureau, 2012b). Home ownership is an important source of family wealth because home equity can be used to establish credit; finance businesses, other purchases, and investments; and fund education and other sources of human capital for the next generation. What is the origin of these huge differences in family wealth?

Part of answer lies in events that date back 80 years. As you know, President Franklin D. Roosevelt's administration responded to the Great Depression of the 1930s, in part, by instituting the New Deal—a variety of programs that provided assistance to distressed Americans. What is not as widely known is that these programs were racially discriminatory and provided few or no benefits to African Americans (Massey, 2007, p. 60; see also Katznelson, 2005; and Lieberson, 1998). One of the New Deal programs was administered by the Federal Housing Administration (FHA): the agency offered low-interest mortgages and made home ownership possible for millions of families. However, the FHA sanctioned racially restrictive covenants, which forbade whites to sell to blacks, and helped to institutionalize the practice of "redlining" black neighborhoods, which prevented banks from making home loans in these areas. Together, these and other discriminatory practices effectively excluded black Americans from home ownership (Massey, 2007, pp. 60–61; Massey & Denton, 1993, pp 53–54) Thus, another racial divide was created that, over the generations, has helped countless white families develop wealth and credit but made it impossible for black families to qualify for home ownership, the "great engine of wealth creation" (Massey, 2007, p. 61).

More broadly, racial residential segregation—which is arguably the key factor in preserving racial stratification in the present—provides a third illustration of modern institutional discrimination. The overt, Jim Crow–era laws and customs that created racially segregated neighborhoods and towns in the past were abolished decades ago, and racial discrimination in selling and renting houses has been illegal since the passage of the Fair Housing Act in 1968. However, blacks continue to be concentrated in all- or mostly black neighborhoods, many of which are also characterized by inadequate services and high levels of poverty and crime. How is racial residential segregation maintained in an era of fair housing laws?

Some of the practices that preserve racial residential segregation have been documented by audit studies. In this technique, black and white (and sometimes Latino and Asian) customers are prepared with carefully matched background credentials (education, employment and credit histories, and finances) and sent to test the market for racial fairness. Characteristically, the black customer is steered away from white neighborhoods, required to furnish larger down payments or deposits, charged higher interest rates, or otherwise discouraged from a successful sale or rental. Sometimes, the black customer may be told that a unit is already sold or rented, or otherwise given false or misleading information.

The result is that blacks are discouraged from breaking the housing color line, but not directly, blatantly, or in ways that clearly violate the fair housing laws. The gatekeepers (real estate agents, landlords, mortgage bankers) base their behavior not on race per se but on characteristics associated with race—accent, dialect, home address, and so forth—to make decisions about what levels of service and responsiveness to provide to customers. Sociologist Douglas Massey has even demonstrated racially biased treatment based on the use of "black English" in telephone contacts (Massey, 2000, p.4).

Audit studies have also documented racial discrimination in the job market (for example, see Bertrand & Mullainathan, 2004). Other forms of modern institutional discrimination include the use of racially and culturally biased standardized tests in school systems, the pattern of drug arrests that sends disproportionate numbers of black teenage boys and young men to jail and prison (see chapter 5 for more), and decisions by businesspeople to move their operations away from center-city neighborhoods. Part of what makes modern institutional discrimination so challenging to document is that race, ethnicity, or gender may not be a conscious or overt part of these decision-making processes. Still, the results are that blacks and other minorities—in the past as in the present—are filtered away from opportunities and resources and racial stratification is maintained, even in the new age of a supposedly color-blind society.

Modern institutional discrimination routinely places black Americans in less desirable statuses in education, residence and home ownership, jobs, the criminal justice system—indeed, across the entire expanse of the socioeconomic system. The result is racial stratification maintained not by monolithic Jim Crow segregation or slavery, but by a subtle and indirect system that is the "new configuration of inequality" (Katz & Stern, 2008, p. 100). We will apply the concept of modern institutional discrimination throughout the case study chapters in part 3 of this text.

Affirmative Action

By its nature, modern institutional discrimination is more difficult to identify, measure, and eliminate. Some of the most heated disputes in recent group relations have concerned public policy and law in this area. Among the most controversial issues is **affirmative action**, a group of programs that attempt to reduce the effects of past discrimination or increase diversity in the workplace or in schools. In the 1970s and 1980s, the Supreme Court found that programs designed to favor minority employees as a strategy for overcoming past discrimination were constitutional (e.g., *Firefighters Local Union No. 1784 v. Stotts*, 1984; *Sheet Metal Workers v. EEOC*, 1986; *United Steelworkers of America, AFL-CIO-CLC v. Weber*, 1979). Virtually all these early decisions concerned blatant policies of discrimination, which are becoming increasingly rare as we move farther away from the days of Jim Crow. Even so, the decisions were based on narrow margins (votes of five to four) and featured acrimonious and bitter debates. More recently, the Supreme Court narrowed the grounds on which such past grievances could be redressed (e.g., *Adarand Constructors Inc. v. Peña*, 1995).

A Case of Discrimination? The most recent case involving affirmative action programs in the work place is *Ricci v. DeStefano*, 2009, involving firefighters in New Haven, Connecticut. In 2003, the city administered a test for promotion in the city's fire department. More than 100 people took the test but no African American scored high enough to qualify for promotion. The city decided to throw out the test results on the grounds that its dramatically unequal racial results strongly suggested that it was biased against African Americans. This decision is consistent with the legal concept of "disparate impact": if a practice has unequal results, federal policy and court precedents tend to assume that the practice is racially biased. The city feared that using these possibly "tainted" test scores might result in lawsuits by black and other minority firefighters. Instead, a lawsuit was filed by several white and Hispanic firefighters who *had* qualified for promotion, claiming that invalidating the test results amounted to reverse racial discrimination. In yet another five to four ruling, the Supreme Court ruled in favor of the white and Hispanic plaintiffs in 2009. This case illustrates some of the difficult issues that accompany attempts to address modern institutional discrimination.

The issue in *Ricci v. Stefano* is not overt Jim Crow discrimination, but a test that might be discriminatory in its results, although not in its intent. New Haven was attempting to avoid racial discrimination: How far do employers need to go to ensure racial fairness? Should policies and procedures be judged by the outcomes or their intents? What does "fairness" and "equal treatment" mean in a society in which minority groups have only recently won formal equality and still have lower access to quality schooling and jobs in the mainstream economy? Did the city of New Haven go too far in its attempt to avoid discrimination? (Five of the Supreme Court Justices thought so.) Can there be a truly fair, race-neutral policy for employment and promotion in the present when opportunities and resources have been allocated on the basis of race for so long in the past? If the problem is color-coded, can the solution be color-neutral?

Higher Education and Affirmative Action. Colleges and universities have been another prominent battleground for affirmative action programs. Since the 1960s, many institutions of higher education have implemented programs to increase the number of minority students on campus at both the undergraduate and graduate levels, sometimes admitting minority students who had lower grade point averages or test scores than dominant group students who were turned away. In general, advocates of these programs have justified them in terms of redressing the discriminatory practices of the past or increasing diversity on campus and making the student body a more accurate representation of the surrounding society. To say the least, these programs have been highly controversial and the targets of frequent lawsuits, some of which have found their way to the highest courts in the land.

Recent decisions by the U.S. Supreme Court have limited the application of affirmative action to colleges and universities. In two lawsuits involving the University of Michigan in 2003 (*Grutter v. Bollinger* and *Gratz v. Bollinger*), the Supreme Court held that the university's law school *could* use race as one criterion in deciding admissions but that undergraduate admissions *could not* award an automatic advantage to minority applicants. In other words, universities could take account of an applicant's race but only in a limited way, as one factor among many.

In February 2012, the Supreme Court agreed to hear a case that challenges the partial use of minority status in determining college admissions (Liptak, 2012a). The case (*Fisher v University of Texas at Austin*) involves the University of Texas (UT), which uses a unique admissions system: the top 10% of the student body in each high school in Texas is automatically admitted to the university. Because of the residential segregation in towns and cities across the state, the student body at many high schools is disproportionately black, white, or Hispanic and the 10% rule guarantees substantial diversity in the UT student body. Some 80% of the students are selected by this method. The remaining 20% are selected using a variety of criteria, including race and ethnicity.

The case was brought by a white student who was not admitted to UT. She argues that some of the admitted minority students had lower grade point averages and test scores than hers. The university argues that the educational benefit of a diverse student body justifies its partial and limited use of race as an admission criterion. Like many other select universities, UT uses many criteria—not just test scores—to diversify the student body. The Supreme Court will hear arguments in the fall of 2012 and decide if such programs remain constitutional, probably by a narrow margin and in a split decision.

The Future of Affirmative Action. What lies ahead for affirmative action? On the one hand, there is a clear trend in court decisions to narrow the scope and applicability of these programs. Also, there is very little public support for affirmative action, especially for programs that are perceived as providing specific numerical quotas in jobs or university admissions for minority groups. For example, a representative sample of Americans was asked in a 2010 survey if they supported "preferential hiring and promotion of blacks." Only 12% of white respondents expressed support. More surprising, perhaps, preferences were supported by less than a majority of black respondents (44%) and only 18% of female respondents (National Opinion Research Council, 1972–2010).

On the other hand, although white (and many minority group) Americans object to fixed quotas or preferences, there is support for programs that expand the opportunities available to minority groups, including enhanced job training, education, and recruitment in minority communities (Wilson, 2009, p. 139). Programs of this sort are more consistent with traditional ideologies and value systems that stress individual initiative, personal responsibility, and equality of opportunity. Also, many businesses and universities are committed to the broad principles of affirmative action—the need to address past injustices and the importance of providing diversity in the workplace and classroom—and they are likely to sustain their programs (to the extent allowed by court decisions and legislation) into the future. By and large, it seems that affirmative action programs, especially those that stress equality of opportunity, will continue in some form, perhaps quite limited, into the foreseeable future.

Social Change and Minority Group Activism

This chapter has focused on the continuing Industrial Revolution and its impact on minority groups in general and black–white relations in particular. For the most part, changes in group relations have been presented as the results of the fundamental transformation of the U.S. economy from agrarian to industrial to postindustrial. However, the changes in the situation of African Americans and other minority groups did not "just happen" as society modernized. Although the opportunity to pursue favorable change was the result of broad structural changes in American society, the realization of these opportunities came from the efforts of the many who gave their time, their voices, their resources, and sometimes their lives in pursuit of racial justice in America. Since World War II, African Americans have often been in the vanguard of protest activity, and we focus on the contemporary situation of this group in the next chapter.

FOCUS ON CONTEMPORARY ISSUES:
Hate Crimes

Hate crimes are attacks or other acts of intimidation motivated by the group membership of the victim or victims. Victims can be chosen randomly and are often strangers to their assailants. They are chosen because they are taken as representatives of a group, not because of who they are as individuals. These crimes are expressions of hatred or disdain, strong prejudice, and blatant racism, and are not committed for profit or gain. In recent years, they have included homicides and assaults, arson against black churches, vandalism of Jewish synagogues, cross burnings, nooses prominently tied to office doors of black university professors, and other acts of intimidation and harassment. Furthermore, a number of violent, openly racist extremist groups—skinheads, the Ku Klux Klan (KKK), White Aryan Resistance (WAR), the Minutemen, and Aryan Nations—have achieved widespread notoriety and have a prominent presence not only in some local communities, but also on the Internet.

As we will see in chapters to come, racial violence, hate crimes, and extremist racist groups are hardly new to the United States. Violence between whites and non-whites began in the earliest days of this society (e.g., conflicts with American Indians, the kidnapping and enslavement of Africans) and has continued, in one form or another, to the present. Contemporary racist attacks and hate crimes, in all their manifestations, have deep roots in the American past.

Are hate crimes increasing or decreasing? It's difficult to answer this question, though the FBI (Federal Bureau of Investigation) has been collecting and compiling information on hate crimes since 1996. Not all localities report these incidents or classify them in the same way, and perhaps more important, not all hate crimes are reported. Thus, the actual volume of hate crimes may be many times greater than the "official" rate compiled by the FBI. (For a recent analysis, see Fears, 2007.)

Keeping these sharp limitations in mind, here is some of what is known. Exhibit 4.11 reports the breakdown of hate crimes in 2010 and shows that most incidents were motivated by race. In the great majority (70%) of these racial cases, the victims were black Americans. Most of the religious incidents (67%) involved Jewish victims, and most of the anti-ethnic attacks were against Hispanics (67%). The majority (57%) of the attacks motivated by the sexual orientation of the victims were directed against male homosexuals (FBI, 2012).

Exhibit 4.12 shows the number of hate crimes by the group membership of victims since the mid-1990s. For all categories, there has been a slight upward trend over the past several years. However, because our information on these crimes is so partial and untrustworthy, it is best not to make any hard-and-fast conclusions about trends.

Hate crimes and hate groups are not limited to a particular region. The Southern Poverty Law Center (SPLC) tracks hate groups and hate crimes around the nation and

(Continued)

(Continued)

Exhibit 4.11 Hate Crimes by Target, 2010

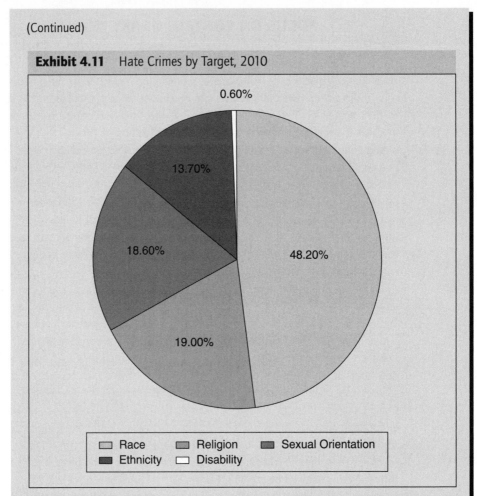

Source: FBI (2012).

estimates that there were 1,002 hate groups (defined as groups that "have beliefs or practices that attack or malign an entire class of people, typically for their immutable characteristics") active in the United States in 2010 (SPLC, 2012). These groups include the KKK, various skinhead and white power groups, and black groups such as the Nation of Islam. The SPLC maintains a map at its website showing the locations of the known hate groups (see exhibit 4.13). The map shows that although the greatest concentration is in the Southeast, Texas, and California, hate groups are spread across the nation and can be found in all states.

What causes hate crimes? One possible explanation for at least some hate crimes is that they are fueled by perceived frustration and fear. Some white Americans believe

Exhibit 4.12   Number of Hate Crime Victims by Target Group, 1996–2010

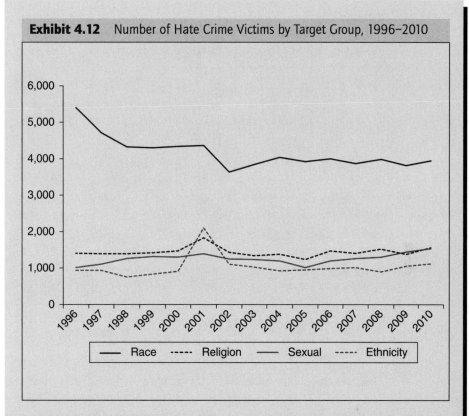

Source: From Healey (2009).

that minority groups are threatening their position in society and making unfair prog-ress at their expense. They feel threatened by what they perceive to be an undeserved rise in the status of minority groups and fear that they may lose their jobs, incomes, neighborhoods, and schools to what they see as "inferior" groups.

Given the nature of American history, it is logical to suppose that the white Americans who feel most threatened and angriest are those toward the bottom of the stratification system: lower-class and working-class whites. There is evidence that males from these classes commit the bulk of hate crimes and are the primary sources of membership for the extremist racist groups (Schafer & Navarro, 2004). In the eyes of the perpetrators, attacks on minorities may represent attempts to preserve status and privilege.

(Continued)

(Continued)

Exhibit 4.13 Distribution of Hate Groups, 2010

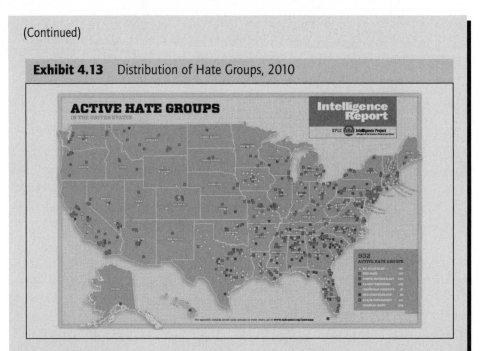

Source: SPLC (2012).

The connection between social class and hate crimes might also reflect some broad structural changes in the economy, especially the shift from an industrial, manufacturing economy to a postindustrial, information-processing economy. This change has meant a decline in the supply of secure, well-paying, blue-collar jobs. Many manufacturing jobs have been lost to other nations with cheaper workforces; others have been lost to automation and mechanization. The tensions resulting from the decline in desirable employment opportunities for people with lower levels of education have been exacerbated by industry downsizing, increasing inequality in the class structure, and rising costs of living. These economic forces have squeezed the middle and lower ranges of the dominant group's class system, creating considerable pressure and frustration, some of which may be directed at immigrants and minority groups.

Several studies support these ideas. One study found that at the state level, the rate of hate crimes increased as unemployment rose and as the percentage of the population between 15 and 19 years old increased. Also, the rate fell as average wages rose (Medoff, 1999, p. 970; see also Jacobs & Wood, 1999). Another study, based on county-level data gathered in South Carolina, found a correlation between white-on-black hate crimes and economic competition (D'Alessio, Stolzenberg, & Eitle, 2002). Finally, Arab Americans have been victimized by a rash of violent attacks after September 11, 2001 (Ibish, 2003). These patterns are exactly what one would expect if the perpetrators of hate crimes tended to be young men motivated by a sense of threat and economic distress.

Main Points

- Group relations change as the subsistence technology and the level of development of the larger society change. As nations industrialize and urbanize, dominant-minority relations change from paternalistic to rigid competitive forms.
- In the South, slavery was replaced by de jure segregation, a system that combined racial separation with great inequality. The Jim Crow system was motivated by a need to control labor and was reinforced by coercion and intense racism and prejudice.
- Black Southerners responded to segregation in part by moving to Northern urban areas. The Northern African American population enjoyed greater freedom and developed some political and economic resources, but a large concentration of low-income, relatively powerless African Americans developed in ghetto neighborhoods.
- In response to segregation, the African American community developed a separate institutional life centered on family, church, and community. An African American middle class emerged, as well as a protest movement.
- African American women remain one of the most exploited groups. Combining work with family roles, African American females were employed mostly in agriculture and domestic service during the era of segregation.
- Industrialization continued throughout the 20th century and has profoundly affected dominant-minority relations. Urbanization, specialization, bureaucratization, and other trends have changed the shape of race relations, as have the changing structure of the occupational sector and the growing importance of education. Group relations have shifted from rigid to fluid competitive. Modern institutional discrimination is one of the major challenges facing minority groups.

Study Site on the Web

Don't forget the interactive quizzes and other resources and learning aids at www.sagepub.com/healeyds4e.

For Further Reading

Bluestone, B., & Harrison, B. (1982). *The deindustrialization of America.* New York: Basic Books.

The classic analysis of the shift from a manufacturing to a service-based, information society.

Feagin, J. R., & Feagin, C. B. (1986). *Discrimination American style: Institutional racism and sexism.* Malabar, FL: Robert E. Krieger.
Feagin, Joe R. (2006). *Systematic racism: A theory of oppression.* New York: Routledge.

Two comprehensive and provocative looks at modern institutional discrimination.

Geschwender, J. A. (1978). *Racial stratification in America.* Dubuque, IA: William C. Brown.
Wilson, W. J. (1973). *Power, racism, and privilege: Race relations in theoretical and sociohistorical perspectives.* New York: Free Press.
Woodward, C. V. (1974). *The strange career of Jim Crow* (3rd ed., rev.). New York: Oxford University Press.

Three outstanding analyses of black–white relations in the United States, with a major focus on the historical periods covered in this chapter.

Pincus, F. (2003). *Reverse discrimination: Dismantling the myth.* Boulder, CO: Lynne Reiner.

A compact, masterful review of the myths and realities surrounding affirmative action.

Questions For Review and Study

1. A corollary to two themes from chapter 3 is presented at the beginning of chapter 4. How exactly does the material in this chapter illustrate the usefulness of this corollary?

2. Explain paternalistic and rigid competitive relations and link them to industrialization. How does the shift from slavery to de jure segregation illustrate the dynamics of these two systems?

3. What was the Great Migration to the North? How did it change American race relations?

4. Explain the transition from rigid competitive to fluid competitive relations and explain how this transition is related to the coming of postindustrial society. Explain the roles of urbanization, bureaucracy, the service sector of the job market, and education in this transition.

5. What is modern institutional discrimination? How does it differ from "traditional" institutional discrimination? Explain the role of affirmative action in combating each.

6. Explain the impact of industrialization and globalization on gender relations. Compare and contrast these changes with the changes that occurred for racial and ethnic minority groups.

7. What efforts have been made on your campus to combat modern institutional discrimination? How effective have these programs been?

Internet Research Project

In this project, you will extend the treatment of de jure segregation in this chapter by visiting a website entitled "The Rise and Fall of Jim Crow" at http://www.pbs.org/wnet/jimcrow/index.html. The website is related to a documentary series, which can be ordered from the website and is well worth viewing. The website has five subsections; you should explore each and take the "Jim Crow quiz" under the "Tools and Activities" link. As you browse the site, find answers to each of the questions below (*Note: Your instructor may have different or additional questions.*)

Questions

1. What "strange fruit" did Billie Holiday sing about?

2. In what year did Louisiana ban marriages between "White persons and persons of color?"

3. What state, in 1876, provided that schools could be segregated if there were 15 or more "colored" children?

4. In Florida in 1909, what was the fine for "occupying" a train car other than the one designated for one's race?

5. In what year was Wilberforce University in Ohio founded? Who was Wilberforce? What was the mission of this institution?

6. What were the following people best known for? Where did they live and what were their dates of birth and death?
   a. Sidney Bechet
   b. Madam C. J. Walker
   c. Ida B. Wells
   d. Walter White
   e. Ned Cobb

7. What was the Brownsville Affair of 1906? How does this incident illustrate the dynamics of the Jim Crow era?

8. Why is the *Plessy v. Ferguson* 1896 Supreme Court decision important? What was its relationship to the Jim Crow system? What events led to this decision?

9. What happened during the Red Summer of 1919? How do these events illustrate the dynamics of the Jim Crow system and American race relations in general?

10. What was the relevance of the following organizations for Jim Crow?
    a. The Democratic Party
    b. The Populist Party
    c. The National Urban League
    d. The Brotherhood of Sleeping Car Porters

Reactions

Using the information and insights you gathered from the website, along with the material in this chapter, write an essay in which you explain the legal, political, economic, and social dimensions of Jim Crow segregation, citing specific examples. How did the system control blacks, institutionalize racial stratification, and sustain the privilege of whites? (*Note: Your instructor may have more-specific or different instructions.*)

Optional Group Discussion

Discuss what you learned from the website and this chapter with a group of your classmates. Use your reaction essay to help guide your thoughts and focus the discussion. You might organize the discussion around questions such as these:

1. Why did de jure segregation happen? What was at stake? Who gained and who lost? Be sure to discuss class and gender differences in connection with these issues.

2. How was the Jim Crow system sustained across time? What was the role of prejudice and racism? Subsistence technology? Law and custom? How was violence used to enforce the system? What organizations were involved in the creation and persistence of segregation?

3. What does it mean to call this system "rigid competitive"? How did it differ from the paternalistic system of slavery?

4. How did the black community react to segregation? What means of resistance and escape were available? Were they effective? Why or why not?

5. Why did de jure segregation end? What macrolevel changes in subsistence technology made segregation untenable? Why?
(*Note: Your instructor may have more-specific or different instructions.*)

PART 3

Understanding Dominant-Minority Relations in the United States Today

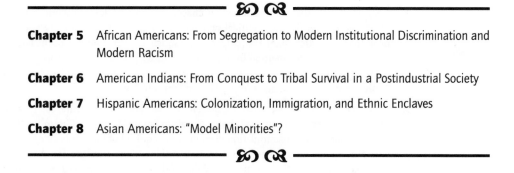

In part 3, we turn to contemporary intergroup relations. We emphasize the present situation of American minority groups, but also investigate the recent past to see how present situations developed. We explore the ways minority and dominant groups respond to a changing American society and to each other and how minority groups define and pursue their own self-interests in interaction with other groups, American culture and values, and the institutions of the larger society.

The themes and ideas developed in the first two parts of this text will continue to be central to the analysis. For example, the case studies are presented in an order that roughly follows the Blauner hypothesis: Colonized groups are presented first, and we end with groups created by immigration. Also, we will continue to rely on the concepts of the Noel hypothesis to analyze and explain contemporary dominant-minority patterns.

The history and present conditions of each minority group are unique, and no two groups have had the same experiences. To help identify and understand these differences, the concepts developed in the first two parts of this text and a common comparative frame of reference are used throughout part 3. We stress assimilation and pluralism; inequality and power; and prejudice, racism, and discrimination. For ease of comparison, the final sections of chapters 5 through 8 use the same headings and subheadings, in the same order. Much of the conceptual frame of reference used in these case studies can be summarized in six themes. The first five themes are based on material from previous chapters; the last is covered in the forthcoming chapters.

1. Consistent with the Noel hypothesis, the present conditions of America's minority groups reflect their contact situations, especially the nature of their competition with the dominant group (e.g., competition over land versus competition over labor) and the size of the power differential between groups at the time of contact.

2. Consistent with the Blauner hypothesis, minority groups created by colonization experience economic and political inequalities that have lasted longer and been more severe than those experienced by minority groups created by immigration.

3. Power and economic differentials and barriers to upward mobility are especially pronounced for groups identified by racial or physical characteristics, as opposed to cultural or linguistic traits.

4. Consistent with the themes stated in chapters 3 and 4, dominant-minority relations reflect the economic and political characteristics of the larger society and change as those characteristics change. Changes in the subsistence technology of the larger society are particularly consequential for dominant-minority relations. The shift from a manufacturing to a service economy (deindustrialization) is one of the key factors shaping dominant-minority relations in the United States today.

5. The development of group relations, both in the past and for the future, can be analyzed in terms of assimilation (more unity) and pluralism (more diversity). Group relations in the past (e.g., the degree of assimilation permitted or required of the minority group) reflected mainly dominant group needs and wishes. Although the pressure for Americanization remains considerable, there is more flexibility and variety in group relations today.

6. Since World War II, minority groups have gained significantly more control over the direction of group relationships. This trend reflects the decline of traditional prejudice in the larger society and the successful efforts of minority groups to protest, resist, and change patterns of exclusion and domination. These successes have been possible in large part because American minority groups have increased their share of political and economic resources.

5

African Americans: From Segregation to Modern Institutional Discrimination and Modern Racism

The children called home . . . "the projects" but [9-year-old] Pharoah called it "The graveyard." Nothing here, the children would tell you, was as it should be. . . .

If [Pharoah and his brother] had one guidepost in their young lives, . . . it was their mother, LaJoe. They depended on her; she depended on them. The boys would do anything for their mother. A shy, soft-spoken woman, LaJoe was known for her warmth and generosity, not only to her own children, but also to her children's friends. . . . LaJoe had often mothered children who needed advice or comforting. Many young men and women still called her "Mom." She let so many people through her apartment, sometimes just to use the bathroom, that she hid the toilet paper in the kitchen because it had often been stolen.

But the neighborhood, which hungrily devoured its children, had taken its toll of LaJoe as well. In recent years, she had become more tired as she questioned her ability to raise her children here. . . . LaJoe had watched and held on as the neighborhood slowly decayed . . . First, the middle-class whites fled to the suburbs. Then the middle-class blacks left for safer neighborhoods. Then, the businesses moved . . . Over the past 10 years, the city had lost a third of its manufacturing jobs. And there were few jobs left. . . .

To LaJoe, the neighborhood had become a black hole. She could more easily recite what wasn't there than what was. There were no banks, . . . no public libraries, movie theaters, skating rinks, or bowling alleys to entertain the neighborhood's children. For the infirm, there were two neighborhood clinics, both of which teetered on the edge of bankruptcy. . . . . The death rate of newborn babies exceeded infant mortality rates in a number of Third World countries, including Chile, Costa Rica, Cuba, and Turkey. And there was no rehabilitation center, though drug abuse was rampant.

According to a 1980 profile of the [area], 60,110 people lived there, 88% of them black, 46% of them below the poverty level. It was an area so impoverished that, when Mother Theresa visited in 1982, she assigned nuns from her Missionaries of Charity to work there. . . .

Alex Kotlowitz (1991, pp. 8–12)*

This housing project in Chicago has been demolished and replaced with low-rise buildings and town-house units. However, the grim realities of "concentrated poverty" illustrated in this passage live on in low-income, black, and minority neighborhoods across the nation. The story of the projects presented in Kotlowitzs' classic *There Are No Children Here* shows the bitter consequences of combining class and race, of compounding poverty with segregation, joblessness, inadequate schooling, and strong traditions of racism and rejection. In a nation led by a black man, a nation with many wealthy and powerful African Americans, there is another America: bleak, violent, rife with hopelessness, separate, marginal, and unequal.

A century ago, African Americans were primarily a Southern rural peasantry, oppressed by de jure segregation, exploited by the sharecropping system of agriculture, and blocked from the better-paying industrial and manufacturing jobs in urban areas. Segregation had disenfranchised them and stripped them of the legal and civil rights they had briefly enjoyed during Reconstruction. As we saw in chapter 4, the huge majority of African Americans had limited access to quality education, few political rights, few occupational choices, and few means of expressing their grievances to the larger society or the world.

Today, African Americans are highly urbanized, dispersed throughout the United States, and represented in every occupation. The single most significant sign of the progress African Americans have made is, without question, the election of Barack Obama to the presidency of the United States, but members of the group are visible across the board at the highest levels of American society: from the Supreme Court to corporate boardrooms to the most prestigious universities. Some of the best-known, most successful, most respected (and wealthiest) people in the world have been African Americans: Muhammad Ali, Maya Angelou, Mariah Carey, Bill Cosby, Michael Jordan, Martin Luther King Jr., Toni Morrison, Rosa Parks, Colin Powell, Condoleezza Rice, Malcolm X, and Oprah Winfrey, and to name just a few. Furthermore, some of the most important and prestigious American corporations (including Merrill Lynch, American Express, and Time Warner) have been led by African Americans.

---

*From THERE ARE NO CHILDREN HERE by Alex Kotlowitz, copyright © 1991 by Alex Kotlowitz. Used by permission of Doubleday, a division of Random House, Inc. Any third party use of this material, outside of this publication, is prohibited. Interested parties must apply directly to Random House, Inc. for permission.

Compared with 100 years ago, the situation of black Americans today is obviously much improved. The journey to racial equality, however, is far from accomplished. As we shall see in this chapter, a large percentage of black Americans remain on the margins of society: excluded, segregated, and victimized by persisting inequalities in opportunity, education, health care, housing, and jobs. Even the more fortunate segments of the black community remain in a tenuous situation: they have fewer resources to fall back on in hard times and weaker connections to the sources of power and privilege. The glittering success stories of the few obscure the continuing struggles of the many; anti-black racism and discrimination continue to be powerful forces in American society. Their greater vulnerability means that hard times for America can mean disaster for black Americans.

To understand black–white relations in the present, we must deal with the watershed events of the recent past: the end of de jure segregation, the triumph (and limitations) of the civil rights movement of the 1950s and 1960s, the urban riots and Black Power movement of the 1960s, and the continuing racial divisions within U.S. society since the 1970s. Behind these events, we can see the powerful pressures of industrialization and modernization, the shift from rigid to fluid competitive group relations, deindustrialization and modern institutional discrimination, changing distributions of power and forms of intergroup competition, the shift from traditional prejudice to modern racism, and new ideas about assimilation and pluralism. Black–white relations changed as a direct result of protest, resistance, and the concerted actions of thousands of individuals, both black and white.

The End of De Jure Segregation

A century ago, African Americans faced extreme inequality, relative powerlessness, and sharp limitations on their freedom. Their most visible enemy was the system of de jure segregation in the South, the rigid competitive system of group relations that controlled the lives of most African Americans.

Why and how did de jure segregation come to an end? Recall from chapter 4 that dominant-minority relationships change as the larger society and its subsistence technology change. As the United States industrialized and urbanized during the 20th century, a series of social, political, economic, and legal processes were set in motion that ultimately destroyed Jim Crow segregation.

The mechanization and modernization of agriculture in the South had a powerful effect on race relations. As farm-work became less labor intensive and machines replaced people, the need to maintain a large, powerless workforce declined (Geschwender, 1978, pp. 175–177). Thus, one of the primary motivations for maintaining Jim Crow segregation and the sharecropping system of farming lost force.

In addition, the modernization of Southern agriculture helped to spur the migration northward and to urban areas, as we discussed in chapter 4. African Americans found it easier to register to vote and pursue other avenues for improving their situations outside the rural South. The weight of the growing African American vote was first felt in the 1930s and was large enough to make a difference in local, state, and even national elections by the 1940s. In 1948, for example, President Harry S. Truman recognized that he could not be reelected without the support of African American voters.

As a result, the Democratic Party adopted a civil rights plank in the party platform, the first time since Reconstruction that a national political party had taken a stand on race relations (Wilson, 1973, p. 123).

The weight of these changes accumulated slowly, and no single date or specific event marks the end of de jure segregation. The system ended as it had begun: gradually and in a series of discrete episodes and incidents. By the mid-20th century, resistance to racial change was weakening, and the power resources of African Americans were increasing. This enhanced freedom and strength fueled a variety of efforts that accelerated the demise of Jim Crow segregation. Although a complete historical autopsy is not necessary here, a general understanding of the reasons for the death of Jim Crow segregation is essential for an understanding of modern black–white relations.

Wartime Developments

One of the first successful applications of the growing stock of black power resources occurred in 1941 as the United States was mobilizing for war against Germany and Japan. Despite the crisis atmosphere, racial discrimination was common, even in the defense industry. A group of African Americans, led by labor leader A. Philip Randolph, head of the Brotherhood of Sleeping Car Porters, threatened to march on Washington to protest the discriminatory treatment.

To forestall the march, President Franklin D. Roosevelt signed Executive Order No. 8802, banning discrimination in defense-related industries, and created a watchdog federal agency, the Fair Employment Practices Commission, to oversee compliance with the new antidiscriminatory policy (Franklin & Moss, 1994, pp. 436–437; Geschwender, 1978, pp. 199–200). President Roosevelt's actions were significant in two ways: First, a group of African Americans not only had their grievances heard at the highest level of society, but also succeeded in getting what they wanted. Underlying the effectiveness of the planned march was the rising political and economic power of the African American community outside the South and the need to mobilize all segments of the population for a world war. Second, the federal government made an unprecedented commitment to fair employment rights for African Americans. This alliance between the federal government and African Americans was tentative, but it foreshadowed some of the dynamics of racial change in the 1950s and 1960s.

The Civil Rights Movement

The **civil rights movement** was a multifaceted campaign to end legalized segregation and ameliorate the massive inequalities faced by African Americans. The campaign lasted for decades and included lawsuits and courtroom battles as well as protest marches and demonstrations. We begin our examination with a look at the movement's successful challenge to the laws of racial segregation.

Brown v. Board of Education of Topeka. Undoubtedly, the single most powerful blow to de jure segregation was delivered by the U.S. Supreme Court in *Brown v. Board of Education* *of Topeka* in 1954 (hereafter *Brown*). The Supreme Court reversed the *Plessy v. Ferguson* decision of 1896 and ruled that racially separate facilities are inherently unequal and therefore unconstitutional. Segregated school systems—and all other forms of legalized racial segregation—would have to end. The landmark *Brown* decision was the culmination of decades of planning and effort by the National Association for the Advancement of Colored People (NAACP) and individuals such as Thurgood Marshall, the NAACP's chief counsel (who was appointed to the Supreme Court in 1967).

The strategy of the NAACP was to attack Jim Crow by finding instances in which the civil rights of an African American had been violated and then bringing suit against the relevant governmental agency. These lawsuits were intended to extend far beyond the specific case being argued. The goal was to persuade the courts to declare segregation unconstitutional not only in the specific instance being tried, but also in all similar cases. The *Brown* (1954) decision was the ultimate triumph of this strategy. The significance of the Supreme Court's decision was not that Linda Brown—the child in whose name the case was argued—would attend a different school or even that the school system of Topeka, Kansas, would be integrated. Instead, the significance was in the rejection of the principle of de jure segregation in the South and, by implication, throughout the nation. The *Brown* decision changed the law and dealt a crippling blow to Jim Crow segregation.

The blow was not fatal, however. Southern states responded to the *Brown* decision by stalling and mounting campaigns of massive resistance. Jim Crow laws remained on the books for years. White Southerners actively defended the system of racial privilege and attempted to forestall change through a variety of means, including violence and intimidation. The Ku Klux Klan (KKK), largely dormant since the 1920s, reappeared, along with other racist and terrorist groups, such as the White Citizens' Councils. White politicians and other leaders competed with one another to express the most adamant statements of racist resistance (Wilson, 1973, p. 128). One locality, Prince Edward County in central Virginia, chose to close its public schools rather than integrate them. The schools remained closed for 5 years. During that time, the white children attended private, segregated academies, and the county provided no schooling at all for African American children) (Franklin, 1967, p. 644).

Nonviolent Direct Action Protest. The principle established by the *Brown* decision was assimilationist: it ordered the educational institutions of the dominant group to be opened up freely and equally to all. Southern states and communities overwhelmingly rejected the principle of equal access and shared facilities. Centuries of racist tradition and privilege were at stake, and considerable effort would be required to overcome Southern defiance and resistance. The central force in this struggle was a protest movement, the beginning of which is often traced to Montgomery, Alabama. There, on December 1, 1955, Rosa Parks, a seamstress and NAACP member, rode the city bus home from work, as she usually did. As the bus filled, she was ordered to surrender her seat to a white male passenger. When she refused, the police were called and Rosa Parks was jailed for violating a local segregation ordinance.

Although Mrs. Parks was hardly the first African American to be subjected to such indignities, her case stimulated a protest movement in the African American community, and a boycott of the city buses was organized. Participants in the boycott set up car pools, shared taxis, and walked (in some cases, for miles) to and from work. They stayed off the buses for more than a year, until victory was achieved and the city was ordered to desegregate its buses. The Montgomery boycott was led by the Reverend Martin Luther King Jr., the new minister of a local Baptist church.

From these beginnings sprang the protest movement that eventually defeated de jure segregation. The central strategy of the movement involved **nonviolent direct action**, a method by which the system of de jure segregation was confronted head on—not in the courtroom or in the state legislature, but in the streets. The movement's principles of nonviolence were adopted from the tenets of Christianity and from the teachings of Mohandas K. Gandhi, Henry David Thoreau, and others. Dr. King expressed the philosophy in a number of books and speeches (King, 1958, 1963, 1968). Nonviolent protest was intended to confront the forces of evil rather than the people who happened to be doing evil, and it attempted to win the friendship and support of its enemies rather than to defeat or humiliate them. Above all, nonviolent protest required courage and discipline; it was not a method for cowards (King, 1958, pp. 83–84).

The movement used different tactics for different situations, including sit-ins at segregated restaurants, protest marches and demonstrations, prayer meetings, and voter registration drives. The police and terrorist groups such as the KKK often responded to these protests with brutal repression and violence, and protesters were routinely imprisoned, beaten, and attacked by police dogs. The violent resistance sometimes escalated to acts of murder, including the 1963 bombing of a black church in Birmingham, Alabama that took the lives of four little girls, and the 1968 assassination of Dr. King. Resistance to racial change in the South was intense. It would take more than protests and marches to end de jure segregation, and the U.S. Congress finally provided the necessary tools (see D'Angelo, 2001; Killian, 1975; King, 1958, 1963, 1968; and Morris, 1984).

Landmark Legislation. The successes of the protest movement, combined with changing public opinion and the legal principles established by the Supreme Court, coalesced in the mid-1960s to stimulate the passage of two laws that together ended Jim Crow segregation. In 1964, at the urging of President Lyndon B. Johnson, the U.S. Congress passed the Civil Rights Act of 1964, banning discrimination on the grounds of race, color, religion, national origin, or gender. The law applied to publicly owned facilities such as parks and municipal swimming pools, businesses and other facilities open to the public, and any programs that received federal aid. Congress followed this up with the Voting Rights Act in 1965, also initiated by President Johnson, that required that the same standards be used to register all citizens in federal, state, and local elections. The act banned literacy tests, whites-only primaries, and other practices that had been used to prevent African Americans from registering to vote. This law gave the franchise back to black Southerners and laid the groundwork for increasing black political power. This landmark federal legislation, in combination with court decisions and the protest movement, finally succeeded in crushing Jim Crow.

The Success and Limitations of the Civil Rights Movement. Why did the civil rights movement succeed? A comprehensive list of reasons would be lengthy, but we can cite some of the most important causes of its success, especially those consistent with the general points about dominant-minority relations that have been made in previous chapters.

First, the continuing industrialization and urbanization of the society as a whole—and the South in particular—weakened the Jim Crow, rigid competitive system of minority group control and segregation. We made this point in chapter 4 when we discussed the impact of the changing subsistence technology and the end of paternalistic controls (see exhibit 4.6).

Second, following World War II the United States enjoyed a period of prosperity that lasted into the 1960s. Consistent with the Noel hypothesis, this was important, because it reduced the intensity of intergroup competition, at least outside the South. During prosperous times, resistance to change tends to weaken. If the economic "pie" is expanding, the "slices" claimed by minority groups can increase without threatening the size of anyone else's portions, and the prejudice generated during intergroup competition (à la Robber's Cave, chapter 1) is held in check. Thus, these "good times" muted the sense of threat experienced in the dominant group by the demands for equality made by the civil rights movement.

Third, some of the economic prosperity found its way into African American communities and increased their pool of economic and political resources. Networks of independent, African American–controlled organizations and institutions, such as churches and colleges, were created or grew in size and power. The increasingly elaborate infrastructure of the black community included protest organizations, such as the NAACP (see chapter 4), and provided material resources, leadership, and "people power" to lead the fight against segregation and discrimination.

Fourth, the goals of the civil rights movement were assimilationist: The movement embraced the traditional American values of liberty, equality, freedom, and fair treatment. It demanded civil, legal, and political rights for African Americans, rights available to whites automatically. Thus, many whites did not feel threatened by the movement because they saw it as consistent with mainstream American values, especially in contrast with the intense, often violent resistance of Southern whites.

Fifth, the perceived legitimacy of the goals of the movement also opened up the possibility of alliances with other groups (white liberals, Jews, college students). The support of others was crucial because black Southerners had few resources of their own other than their numbers and their courage. By mobilizing the resources of other, more powerful groups, black Southerners forged alliances and created sympathetic support that was brought to bear on their opposition.

Finally, widespread and sympathetic coverage from the mass media, particularly television, was crucial to the success of the movement. The oft-repeated scenario of African Americans being brutally attacked while demonstrating for their rights outraged many Americans and reinforced the moral consensus that eventually rejected overt racial prejudice along with Jim Crow segregation.

The Southern civil rights movement ended de jure segregation but found it difficult to survive the demise of its primary enemy. The confrontational tactics that had been so effective against the Jim Crow system proved less useful when attention turned to the actual distribution of jobs, wealth, political power, and other valued goods and services. Outside the South, the allocation of opportunity and resources always had been the central concern of the African American community. Let's take a look at these concerns.

Developments Outside the South

De Facto Segregation

Chapter 4 discussed some of the difficulties encountered by African Americans as they left the rural South. Discrimination by labor unions, employers, industrialists, and white ethnic groups was common. Racial discrimination outside the South was less overt but was still pervasive, especially in housing, education, and employment.

The pattern of racial separation and inequality outside the South is often called de facto segregation: segregation resulting from what seems to be, at first glance, the voluntary choices of dominant and minority group members alike. As opposed to the Jim Crow system in the South or apartheid in South Africa, there are no public laws mandating racial separation. It is often assumed that de facto segregation "just happened" as people and groups made decisions about where to live and work or that it resulted from some benign tendency of people to be "with their own kind."

On the contrary, de facto segregation was quite intentional and is best thought of as de jure segregation in thin disguise. Racial segregation outside the South was the direct result of intentionally racist decisions made by governmental and quasigovernmental agencies, such as real estate boards, school boards, and zoning boards (see Massey & Denton, 1993, pp. 74–114). De facto segregation was created when local and state authorities actively colluded with private citizens behind the scenes, ignored racist practices within their jurisdiction, and "simply refrained from enforcing black social, economic, and political rights so that private discriminatory practices could do their work" (Massey, 2007 p. 57). For example, shortly after World War I the real estate board in the city of Chicago adopted a policy that required its members, on penalty of "immediate expulsion," to enforce racial residential segregation (Cohen & Taylor, 2000, p. 33). The city itself passed no Jim Crow laws but the result was the same: black Americans were consigned to a separate and unequal status.

African Americans outside the South faced more poverty, higher unemployment, and lower-quality housing and schools than did whites, but there was no clear equivalent of Jim Crow to attack or blame for these patterns of inequality. Thus, the triumphs of the civil rights movement had little impact on their lives. In the 1960s, the African American community outside the South expressed its frustration over the slow pace of change in two ways: urban unrest and a movement for change that rose to prominence as the civil rights movement faded.

Urban Unrest

In the mid-1960s, the frustration and anger of urban African American communities erupted into a series of violent uprisings. The riots began in the summer of 1965 in Watts, a black neighborhood in Los Angeles, California, and over the next four years, virtually every large black urban community experienced similar outbursts. Racial violence was hardly a new phenomenon in America. Race riots had existed as early as the Civil War, and various periods had seen racial violence of considerable magnitude.

The riots of the 1960s were different, however. Most race riots in the past had been attacks by whites against blacks, often including the invasion and destruction of African American neighborhoods (e.g., see D'Orso, 1996; Ellsworth, 1982). The urban unrest of the 1960s, in contrast, consisted largely of attacks by blacks against the symbols of their oppression and frustration. The most obvious targets were white-owned businesses operating in black neighborhoods and the police, who were seen as an army of occupation and whose excessive use of force was often the immediate precipitator of riots (Conot, 1967; National Advisory Commission, 1968).

The Black Power Movement

The urban riots of the 1960s were an unmistakable sign that the problems of race relations had not been resolved with the end of Jim Crow segregation. Outside the South, the problems were different and called for different solutions. Even as the civil rights movement was celebrating its victory in the South, a new protest movement rose to prominence. The **Black Power movement** was a loose coalition of organizations and spokespersons that encompassed a variety of ideas and views, many of which differed sharply from those of the civil rights movement. Some of the central ideas included racial pride ("Black is beautiful" was a key slogan of the day), interest in African heritage, and Black Nationalism. In contrast to the assimilationist goals of the civil rights movement, Black Power groups worked to increase African American control over schools, police, welfare programs, and other public services operating in black neighborhoods.

Most adherents of the Black Power movement believed that white racism and institutional discrimination, forces buried deep in the core of American culture and society, were the primary causes of racial inequality in America. Thus, if African Americans were ever to be truly empowered, they would have to liberate themselves and do it on their own terms. Some Black Power advocates specifically rejected the goal of assimilation into white society, arguing that integration would require blacks to become part of the very system that had for centuries oppressed, denigrated, and devalued them and other peoples of color.

The Nation of Islam. The themes of Black Power voiced so loudly in the 1960s were decades, even centuries, old. Marcus Garvey had popularized many of these ideas in the 1920s, and they were espoused and further developed by the Nation of Islam, popularly known as the Black Muslims, in the 1960s.

The Black Muslims, one of the best-known organizations within the Black Power movement, were angry, impatient, and outspoken. They denounced the hypocrisy, greed, and racism of American society and advocated staunch resistance and racial separation. The Black Muslims did more than talk, however. Pursuing the goals of autonomy and self-determination, they worked hard to create a separate, independent African American economy within the United States. They opened businesses and stores in African American neighborhoods and tried to deal only with other Muslim-owned firms. Their goal was to develop the African American community economically and to supply jobs and capital for expansion solely by using their own resources (Essien-Udom, 1962; Lincoln, 1961; Malcolm X, 1964; Marable, 2011; Wolfenstein, 1993).

The Nation of Islam and other Black Power groups distinguished between racial separation and racial segregation. The former is a process of empowerment whereby a group becomes stronger as it becomes more autonomous and self-controlled. The latter is a system of inequality in which the African American community is powerless and is controlled by the dominant group. Thus, the Black Power groups were working to find ways in which African Americans could develop their own resources and deal with the dominant group from a more powerful position, a strategy similar to that followed by minority groups that form ethnic enclaves (see chapter 2).

The best-known spokesperson for the Nation of Islam was Malcolm X, one of the most charismatic figures of the 1960s. Malcolm X forcefully articulated the themes of the Black Power movement. Born Malcolm Little, he converted to Islam and joined the Nation of Islam while serving a prison term. He became the chief spokesperson for the Black Muslims and a well-known but threatening figure to the white community. After a dispute with Elijah Muhammad, the leader of the Nation of Islam, Malcolm X founded his own organization, in which he continued to express and develop the ideas of Black Nationalism. Like so many other protest leaders of the era, Malcolm X was assassinated, in 1965 (Marable, 2011).

Black power leaders such as Malcolm X advocated autonomy, independence, and a pluralistic direction for the African American protest movement. They saw the African American community as a colonized, exploited population in need of liberation from the unyielding racial oppression of white America, not integration into the system that was the source of its oppression.

Protest, Power, and Pluralism

The Black Power Movement in Perspective

By the end of the 1960s, the riots had ended, and the most militant and dramatic public manifestations of the Black Power movement had faded. In many cases, the passion of Black Power activists had been countered by the violence of the police and other agencies, and many of the most powerful spokespersons of the movement were dead; others were in jail or in exile. The nation's commitment to racial change wavered and weakened as other concerns, such as the Vietnam War, competed for attention.

Richard M. Nixon was elected president in 1968 and made it clear that his administration would not ally itself with the black protest movements. Pressure from the federal government for racial equality was reduced. The boiling turmoil of the mid-1960s faded, but the idea of Black Power had become thoroughly entrenched in the African American community.

In some part, the pluralistic themes of Black Power were a reaction to the failure of assimilation and integration in the 1950s and 1960s. Laws had been passed; court decisions had been widely publicized; and promises and pledges had been made by presidents, members of Congress, ministers, and other leaders. For many African Americans, though, little had changed. The problems of their parents and grandparents continued to constrain and limit their lives and, as far into the future as they could see, the lives of their children. The pluralistic Black Power ideology was a response to the failure to go beyond the repeal of Jim Crow laws and fully implement the promises of integration and equality.

Black Nationalism, however, was and remains more than simply a reaction to a failed dream. It was also a different way of defining what it means to be black in America. In the context of black–white relations in the 1960s, the Black Power movement served a variety of purposes. First, along with the civil rights movement, it helped carve out a new identity for African Americans. The cultural stereotypes of black Americans stressed laziness, irresponsibility, and inferiority. This image needed to be refuted, rejected, and buried. The black protest movements supplied a view of African Americans that emphasized power, assertiveness, seriousness of purpose, intelligence, and courage.

Second, Black Power served as a new rallying cry for solidarity and unified action. Following the success of the civil rights movement, these new themes and ideas helped to focus attention on "unfinished business": the black–white inequalities that remained in U.S. society.

Finally, the ideology provided an analysis of the problems of American race relations in the 1960s. The civil rights movement, of course, had analyzed race relations in terms of integration, equality of opportunity, and an end to exclusion. After the demise of Jim Crow, that analysis became less relevant. A new language was needed to describe and analyze the continuation of racial inequality. Black Power argued that the continuing problems of U.S. race relations were structural and institutional, not individual or legal. To take the next steps toward actualizing racial equality and justice would require a fundamental and far-reaching restructuring of the society. Ultimately, white Americans, as the beneficiaries of the system, would not support such restructuring. The necessary energy and commitment had to come from African Americans pursuing their own self-interests.

The nationalistic and pluralistic demands of the Black Power movement evoked defensiveness and a sense of threat in white society. By questioning the value of assimilation and celebrating a separate African heritage equal in legitimacy with white European heritage, the Black Power movement questioned the legitimacy and worth of Anglo American values. In fact, many Black Power spokespersons condemned Anglo American values fiercely and openly and implicated them in the creation and maintenance of a centuries-long system of racial repression. Today, almost 50 years after the success of the civil rights movement, assertive and critical demands by the African American community continue to be perceived as threatening.

Gender and Black Protest

Both the civil rights movement and the Black Power movement tended to be male dominated. African American women were often viewed as supporters of men rather than as equal partners in liberation. Although African American women were heavily involved in the struggle, they were often denied leadership roles or decision-making positions in favor of men. In fact, the women in one organization, the Student Nonviolent Coordinating Committee, wrote position papers to protest their relegation to lowly clerical positions and the frequent references to them as "girls" (Andersen, 1993, p. 284). The Nation of Islam emphasized female subservience, imposing a strict code of behavior and dress for women, and separating the sexes in many temple and community activities. Thus, the battle against racism and the battle against sexism were separate struggles with separate and often contradictory agendas, as the black protest movements continued to subordinate women (Amott & Matthaei, 1991, p. 177).

When the protest movements began, however, African American women were already heavily involved in community and church work, and they often used their organizational skills and energy to further the cause of black liberation. In the view of many, African American women were the backbone of the movement, even if they were often relegated to less glamorous but vital organizational work (Evans, 1979).

Fannie Lou Hamer of Mississippi, an African American who became a prominent leader in the black liberation movement, illustrates the importance of the role played by women. Born in 1917 to sharecropper parents, Hamer's life was so circumscribed that until she attended her first rally at the beginning of the civil rights movement she was unaware that blacks could—even theoretically—register to vote. The day after the rally, she quickly volunteered to register:

> I guess if I'd had any sense I'd a-been a little scared, but what was the point of being scared? The only thing they could do to me was kill me and it seemed like they'd been trying to do that a little bit at a time ever since I could remember. (Evans, 1989, p. 271)

As a result of her activism, Hamer lost her job, was evicted from her house, and was jailed and beaten on a number of occasions. She devoted herself entirely to the civil rights movement and founded the Freedom Party, which successfully challenged the racially segregated Democratic Party and the all-white political structure of the State of Mississippi (Evans, 1979; Hamer, 1967).

Much of the energy that motivated black protest was forged in the depths of segregation and exclusion, a system of oppression that affected all African Americans. Not all segments of the community had the same experience; the realities faced by the black community, as always, were differentiated by class as well as gender.

COMPARATIVE FOCUS:
Race in Another America

Traditional anti-black prejudice in the United States includes an array of stereotypes alleging biological inferiority and laziness along with feelings of contempt and dislike. These ideas and emotions reflect the particular history of black–white relations in the United States, especially the centuries of slavery and decades of legally sanctioned racial inferiority. Other nations, even close neighbors to the United States, have different experiences, different histories, different cultures, and different sets of stereotypes and emotions.

One of the key characteristics of traditional U.S. anti-black prejudice is a simple "two-race" view: everyone belongs to one and only one race, and a person is either black or white. This perception is a legacy of the assumption of black inferiority that was at the heart of both U.S. slavery and Jim Crow segregation in the South. The Southern states formalized the racial dichotomy in law as well as custom with the "one-drop rule": any trace of black ancestry, even "one drop" of African blood, meant that a person was legally black and subject to all the limitations of extreme racial inequality.

This two-race model lives on in the present, and many Americans continue to insist on a single racial category for everyone, regardless of actual racial inheritance. This rigid perception will be challenged by the increases in racial intermarriage and the number of mixed-race individuals, but, in fact, "racial mixing" always has been a part of the U.S. experience, and there always have been people of mixed-race heritage. In the past, especially under slavery, interracial unions were generally coercive, and following the one-drop rule the offspring were classified, socially and legally, as black. This nation has a long history of ignoring the reality that people can be both black *and* white.

The U.S. perception of race contrasts sharply with the racial sensibilities in many other nations. Throughout Central and South America, for example, race is perceived as a continuum of possibilities and combinations, not as a simple split between white and black. This does not mean that these societies are egalitarian, racially open utopias. To the contrary, they incorporate a strong sense of status and position and clear notions of who is higher and who is lower. However, other factors, especially social class, are considered more important than race as criteria for judging and ranking other people. In fact, social class can affect perceptions of skin color: people of higher status can be seen as "whiter" than those of lower status, regardless of actual skin color.

One interesting comparison is between the United States and Brazil, the largest nation in South America. The racial histories of Brazil and the United States run parallel in many ways, and prejudice, discrimination, and racial inequality are very much a part of Brazilian society, past and present. Like other Central and South Americans, however, Brazilians recognize many gradations of skin color and the different blends that are

(Continued)

(Continued)

possible in people of mixed-race heritage. Commonly used terms in Brazil include *branco* (white), *moreno* (brown), *moreno claro* (light brown), *claro* (light), *pardo* (mixed race), and *negro* and *preto* (black). Some reports count scores of Brazilian racial categories, but Telles (2004, p. 82) reports that fewer than 10 are in common use. Still, this system is vastly more complex than the traditional U.S. perception of race.

Why does Brazil have a more open-ended, less rigid system than the United States? In large part, the foundation for this perception was laid in the distant past. The Portuguese, the colonial conquerors of Brazil, were mostly single males, and they married into other racial groups, thereby producing a large class of mixed-race people. Also, slavery was not as thoroughly equated with race in Brazil as it was in the United States. Although slave status was certainly regarded as undesirable and unfortunate, it did not carry the presumption of racial inferiority as in North America, where slavery, blackness, and inferiority were tightly linked in the dominant ideology, an equation with powerful echoes in the present. Also, after slavery ended, Brazil did not go through a period of legalized racial segregation like the Jim Crow system in the U.S. South or apartheid in South Africa. Thus, there was less need politically, socially, or economically to divide people into rigid groups in Brazil.

I should stress that Brazil is not a racial utopia, as is sometimes claimed. Prejudice is an everyday reality, the legacy of slavery is strong, and there is a high correlation between skin color and social status. Compared to national norms, black Brazilians have much higher illiteracy, unemployment, and poverty rates, and are much less likely to have access to a university education. Whites dominate the more prestigious and lucrative occupations and the leadership positions in the economy and in politics, whereas blacks are concentrated at the bottom of the class system, with mixed-race people in between (Kuperman, 2001, p. 25). It would be difficult to argue that race prejudice in Brazil is less intense than in the United States. On the other hand, given the vastly different perceptions of race in the two societies, we can conclude that Brazilian prejudice has a different content and emotional texture and reflects a different contact situation and national history (Mikulak, 2011).

Black–White Relations Since the 1960s: Issues and Trends

Black–white relations have changed over the past five decades, of course, but the basic outlines of black inequality and white dominance have persisted. To be sure, some progress has been made in integrating society and eliminating racial inequality. The election of Barack Obama—unimaginable just a few decades ago (and maybe a few years ago)—stands as one unmistakable symbol of racial progress, a breakthrough so stunning that it has led many to conclude that America is now "postracial" and that people's fates are no longer connected to the color of their skin, an argument that is easily refuted by a consideration of the trends and statistics presented in this chapter.

Without denying the signs of progress, the situation of the African American community today has stagnated—or worsened—on many dimensions, and the problems that remain are deep-rooted and inextricably mixed with the structure and functioning of modern American society. As was the case in earlier eras, racism and racial inequality today cannot be addressed apart from the trends of change in the larger society, especially changes in subsistence technology. This section examines the racial separation that continues to characterize so many areas of U.S. society and applies many of the concepts from previous chapters to present-day black–white relations.

Continuing Separation

More than 40 years ago, a presidential commission charged with investigating black urban unrest warned that the United States was "moving towards two societies, one black, one white, separate and unequal" (National Advisory Commission, 1968, p. 1). We could object to the commission's use of the phrase "moving towards," with its suggestion that U.S. society was at one time racially unified, but the warning still seems prophetic. Without denying the progress toward integration that has been made, African Americans and white Americans continue to live in worlds that are indeed separate and unequal.

Each group has committed violence and hate crimes against the other, but the power differentials and the patterns of inequality that are the legacy of our racist past guarantee that African Americans will more often be seen as "invaders" pushing into areas where they do not belong and are not wanted. Sometimes the reactions to these perceived intrusions are immediate and bloody, but other, subtler attempts to maintain the exclusion of African Americans continue to be part of everyday life, even at the highest levels of society. For example, in a lawsuit reminiscent of Jim Crow days, a national restaurant chain was accused of discriminating against African American customers by systematically providing poor service. In 2004, the company agreed to pay $8.7 million to settle the lawsuit (McDowell, 2004). In another example, Matrix, a large janitorial service, agreed to pay $450,000 for discrimination against black employees. The company was alleged to require black employees to sit in the back of the cafeteria during breaks, barring them from the cafeteria altogether, and firing all black employees at a particular worksite and replacing them with non-black personnel (U.S. Equal Employment Opportunity Commission, 2012).

Many African Americans mirror the hostility of whites, and as the goals of full racial equality and justice continue to seem remote, frustration and anger continue to run high. While Obama's election stirred strong optimism and positive attitudes towards the future in the black community, the more typical mood is pessimistic. (Recall our discussion of public opinion poll results and the differences in black and white perceptions of U.S. race relations from chapter 1.)

The discontent and frustration of the black community has erupted into collective violence on a number of occasions since the riots of the 1960s. The most widely publicized incident followed the 1991 arrest and beating of Rodney King by police officers in Los Angeles. The attack on King by white police officers was videotaped and shown repeatedly on national and international news. When the officers were acquitted of almost all charges in April 1992, African American communities in several cities erupted in violence, with the worst disturbance occurring in the Watts section of Los Angeles, where 58 people lost their lives and millions of dollars of property was damaged or destroyed (see Wilkens, 1992; and Gooding-Williams, 1993).

This incident illustrates several of the common ingredients that have sparked black collective violence and protest since the 1960s: the behavior of the police and the ubiquity of recording devices. An illustrative incident occurred in Oakland, California on New Year's Day, 2009. Oscar Grant, a 23-year-old black man, was returning from New Year's Eve celebrations in San Francisco when he was caught up in an altercation at a subway station. Police had Grant down on the ground when Officer Johannes Mehserle shot him in the back. Grant was not handcuffed. Mehserle claimed that Grant was reaching for his waistband—possibly for a weapon—when Mehserle fired the fatal shot. In fact, Grant was unarmed. These events were recorded on multiple cameras and cell phones and quickly went viral in the Internet. To many, Grant's death appeared to be an intentional, unprovoked execution.

The black community responded with both peaceful protests and violent rioting. Mehserle was eventually convicted of involuntary manslaughter and sentenced to a 2-year prison term. The punishment seemed a mere slap on the wrist to many and provoked further protest, both peaceful and violent (Bulwa, 2010; Egelko, 2009)

In some ways, these events were similar to the 1960s riots. They were spontaneous and expressed diffuse but bitter discontent with the racial status quo. They signaled the continuing racial inequality, urban poverty and despair, and the reality of separate communities, unequal and hostile.

The Criminal Justice System and African Americans

As illustrated by the shooting of Oscar Grant, no area of race relations is more volatile and controversial than the relationship between the black community and the criminal justice system. There is considerable mistrust and resentment of the police among African Americans, and the perception that the entire criminal justice system is stacked against them is common. These perceptions are not without justification: The police and other elements of the criminal justice system have a long tradition of abuse, harassment, and mistreatment of black citizens. The perception of the police as the enemy and the entire criminal justice system as an occupying force remains widespread. For example, a 2008 nationally representative poll found that only 12% of black respondents—as opposed to 42% of white respondents—had a "great deal" of confidence that local police would treat blacks and whites equally. Furthermore, 67% of blacks—versus only 32% of whites—thought that the American justice system was biased against blacks (Gallup Organization, 2010).

The great majority of social science research in this area has documented the continuing bias of the criminal justice system, at all levels, against African Americans (and other minorities). In a comprehensive summary of this research, Rosich (2007) concludes that, while blatant and overt discrimination has diminished over the past few decades, the biases that remain have powerful consequences for the black community, even though they often are more subtle and harder to tease out. Even slight acts of discrimination against blacks can accumulate over the stages of processing in the criminal justice system and result in large differences in racial outcomes (Rosich, 2007). The magnitude of these racial differences is documented by a report that found that, while African Americans make up 13% of the population, they account for 28% of all arrests, 40% of all prison and jail inmates, and 42% of the population on death row (Hartney & Vuong, 2009, p. 2) Civil rights advocates and other spokespersons for the black community charge that there is a dual justice system in the United States and that blacks, adults as well as juveniles, are more likely to receive harsher treatment than are whites charged with similar crimes.

Perhaps the most important manifestation of these biases is that black males are much more likely than white males to be involved in the criminal justice system; in many major U.S. cities, well over half of black males have prison records (Alexander, 2012, p. 7). This phenomenal level of imprisonment is largely the result of a national "get tough" policy on drugs, especially on crack cocaine, that began in the 1980s. Crack cocaine is a cheap form of the drug and the street-level dealers who have felt the brunt of the national antidrug campaign have been disproportionately young African American males from less-affluent areas. Some see this crackdown as a not-so-subtle form of racial discrimination. For example, federal laws require a mandatory prison term of 5 years for possession of five grams of crack cocaine, a drug much more likely to be dealt by poor blacks. In contrast, comparable levels of sentencing for dealing powder cocaine—the more expensive form of the drug—are not reached until the accused possessed a minimum of 500 grams (Rosich, 2007).

Exhibit 5.1 shows the differential drug arrest rates for blacks and whites from 1980 to 2007. Note the spike in arrest rates for blacks in the late 1980s—when the "war on drugs" began—and the continuing large racial gap since that time. It should be stressed that there is considerable evidence that blacks and whites use illegal drugs at roughly the same rate: the difference in arrest rates does not reflect a proportional difference in use (National Center for Health Statistics, 2011, p. 232). The African American community suffered a double victimization from crack cocaine: first from the drug itself and then from the so-called "war on drugs."

The nature of the relationship between the African American community and the criminal justice system is further documented in two recent studies. The first (Pettit & Western, 2004) focused on men born between 1965 and 1969 and found that 3% of whites, compared with 20% of blacks, had been imprisoned by the time they were 30 years old. Also, the study found that education was a key variable affecting the probability of imprisonment: nearly 60% of African American men in this cohort who had not completed high school went to prison. The second study (Pew Charitable Trust, 2008) found that black men were imprisoned at far higher rates than white men: while fewer than 1% of all white men are in prison, the rate for black men is 7%. Furthermore, 11% of black men aged 20–34 are imprisoned.

Exhibit 5.1 Drug Arrest Rates by Race (Arrests per 100,000 Population), 1980–2007

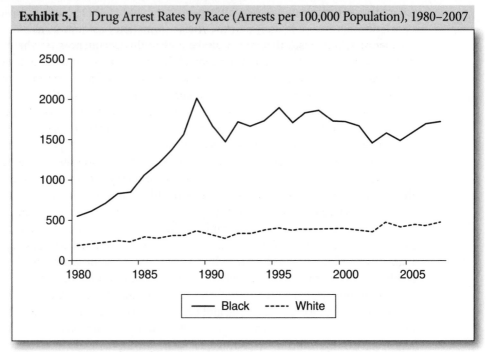

Source: National Center for Health Statistics (2010).

On another level, more pervasive if less dramatic, is the issue of racial profiling: the police use of race as an indicator when calculating whether a person is suspicious or dangerous (Kennedy, 2001, p. 3). The tendency to disproportionately focus on blacks and to stop, question, and follow them is a form of discrimination that generates resentment and increases the distrust (and fear) many African Americans feel toward their local police forces. According to some, humiliating encounters with police (for example, being stopped and questioned for "driving while black") are virtually a rite of passage for black men (Kennedy, 2001, p. 7). According to one national survey, more than half of all black men and 25% of black women believe they have been unfairly stopped by police (Morin & Cottman, 2001; see also Weitzer & Tuch, 2005).

The charges of racial profiling and discrimination in the war against drugs can be controversial but these patterns sustain the ancient perceptions of African Americans as dangerous outsiders, and feed the tradition of resentment and anger toward the police in the African American community.

Increasing Class Inequality

As black Americans moved out of the rural South and as the repressive force of de jure segregation receded, social class inequality within the African American population increased. Since the 1960s, the black middle class has grown, but black poverty continues to be a serious problem.

The Black Middle Class. A small African American middle class, based largely on occupations and businesses serving only the African American community, had been in existence since before the Civil War (Frazier, 1957). Has this more affluent segment benefited from increasing tolerance in the larger society, civil rights legislation, and affirmative action programs? Is the African American middle class growing in size and affluence?

The answers to these questions are not entirely clear, but research strongly suggests that the size and affluence of the African American middle class is less than is often assumed. For example, one study (Kochhar, 2004) found that between 1996 and 2002 the percentage of blacks that could be considered middle and upper class never exceeded 25% of the black population. The comparable figure for whites was almost 60%. Thus, by this definition, the black middle and upper classes were less than half the size of the white middle and upper classes.

Another recent study (Oliver & Shapiro, 2006) indicates that the African American middle class is not only smaller, but also much less affluent. The researchers studied racial differences in wealth, which includes not only income, but also all other financial assets: the value of houses, cars, savings, other property, and so forth. Exhibit 5.2 compares the wealth of blacks and whites, using two different definitions of "middle class" and two different measures of "wealth." Middle-class status is defined, first, in terms of level of education, with a college education indicating middle-class status and, second,

Exhibit 5.2   Wealth by Definition of Middle Class by Race

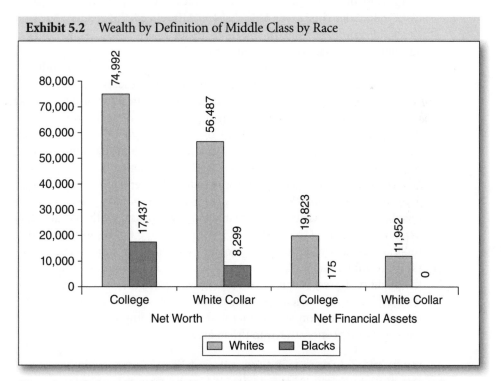

Source: From *Black Wealth, White Wealth: A New Perspective on Racial Inequality, 2nd ed.,* by Melvin L. Oliver and Thomas M. Shapiro. Copyright © 1995 by Routledge. Reprinted by permission of Routledge/Taylor & Francis.

in terms of occupation, with a white-collar occupation indicating middle-class status. Wealth is defined first in terms of net worth, which includes all assets (houses, cars, and so forth) minus debt. The second measure, net financial assets, is the same as net worth but excludes the value of a person's investments in home and cars. This second measure is a better indicator of the resources that are available to invest in educating the next generation or financing new businesses (Oliver & Shapiro, 2006, pp. 60–62).

By either definition, the black middle class is at a distinct disadvantage. There are huge differentials in net worth between blacks and whites, and even greater differences in net financial assets. Note, in fact, that the figure for net financial assets of blacks in white-collar occupations is exactly zero. Once their equity in houses and cars is subtracted out, they are left with no wealth at all, a statistic that strongly underscores the greater precariousness of middle-class standing for blacks. (For other studies that document the lower size and affluence of the black middle class, see Avery & Rendall, 2002; Pollard & O'Hare, 1999; and Shapiro, 2004.)

These economic differences are due partly to discrimination in the present and partly to the racial gaps in income, wealth, and economic opportunity inherited from past generations. As suggested by the concept of net financial assets in exhibit 5.2, economically more-advantaged white families have passed along a larger store of resources, wealth, and property to the present generation. Thus, the greater economic marginality of the African American middle class today is a form of "past-in-present" institutional discrimination (see chapter 4). It reflects the greater ability of white parents (and grandparents) to finance higher education and to subsidize business ventures and home mortgages (Oliver & Shapiro, 2006).

Not only is their economic position more marginal, but also middle-class African Americans commonly report that they are unable to escape the narrow straitjacket of race. No matter what their level of success, occupation, or professional accomplishments, race continues to be seen as their primary defining characteristic in the eyes of the larger society (Benjamin, 2005; Cose, 1993; Hughes & Thomas, 1998). Without denying the advances of some, many analysts argue that the stigma of race continues to set sharp limits on the life chances of African Americans.

There is also a concern that greater class differentiation may decrease solidarity and cohesion within the African American community. There is greater income inequality among African Americans than ever before, with the urban poor at one extreme and some of the wealthiest, most recognized figures in the world at the other: millionaires, celebrities, business moguls, politicians, and sports and movie stars. Will the more affluent segment of the African American community disassociate itself from the plight of the less fortunate and move away from the urban neighborhoods, taking with it its affluence, articulateness, and leadership skills? If this happens, it would reinforce the class division and further seal the fate of impoverished African Americans, who are largely concentrated in urban areas.

Urban Poverty. African Americans have become an urban minority group, and the fate of the group is inextricably bound to the fate of America's cities. The issues of black–white relations cannot be successfully addressed without dealing with urban issues, and vice versa.

As we saw in chapter 4, automation and mechanization in the workplace have eliminated many of the manual labor jobs that sustained city dwellers in earlier decades (Kasarda, 1989). The manufacturing, or secondary, segment of the labor force has declined in size, and the service sector has continued to expand (see exhibit 4.5). The more desirable jobs in the service sector have more and more demanding educational prerequisites. The service sector jobs available to people with lower educational credentials pay low wages, often less than the minimum necessary for the basics, including food and shelter, and offer few benefits, little security, and no links to more rewarding occupations. This form of past-in-present institutional discrimination constitutes a powerful handicap for colonized groups such as African Americans, who have been excluded from educational opportunities for centuries.

Furthermore, many of the blue-collar jobs that have escaped automation have migrated away from the cities. Industrialists have been moving their businesses to areas where labor is cheaper, unions have less power, and taxes are lower. This movement to the suburbs, to the Sunbelt, and offshore has been devastating for the inner city. Poor transportation systems, the absence of affordable housing outside the center city, and outright housing discrimination have combined to keep urban poor people of color confined to center-city neighborhoods, distant from opportunities for jobs and economic improvement (Feagin, 2001, pp. 159–160; Kasarda, 1989; Massey & Denton, 1993).

Sociologist Rogelio Saenz (2005) recently analyzed the situation of blacks in the 15 largest metropolitan areas in the nation and found that they are much more likely than whites to be living in highly impoverished neighborhoods, cut off from the "economic opportunities, services, and institutions that families need to succeed" (p. 1). Saenz found that the greater vulnerability and social and geographical isolation of blacks is pervasive, however, and includes not only higher rates of poverty and unemployment, but also large differences in access to cars and even phones, amenities taken for granted in the rest of society. In the areas studied by Saenz, blacks were as much as 3 times as likely not to have a car (and thus a means to get to jobs outside center-city areas) and as much as 8 times as likely not to have a telephone.

Some of these industrial and economic forces affect all poor urbanites, not just minority groups or African Americans in particular. The dilemma facing many African Americans is in some part not only racism or discrimination, but also the impersonal forces of evolving industrialization and social class. However, when immutable racial stigmas and centuries of prejudice (even disguised as modern racism) are added to these economic and urban developments, the forces limiting and constraining many African Americans become extremely formidable.

For the past 60 years, the African American poor have been increasingly concentrated in narrowly delimited urban areas (ghettos) in which the scourge of poverty has been compounded and reinforced by a host of other problems, including joblessness, high rates of school dropout, crime, drug use, teenage pregnancy, and welfare dependency. These increasingly isolated neighborhoods are fertile grounds for the development of oppositional cultures, which reject or invert the values of the larger society. The black urban counterculture may be most visible in music, fashion, speech, and other forms of popular culture, but it is also manifest in widespread lack of trust in the larger society, and whites in particular. An **urban underclass**, barred from the mainstream economy and the primary labor force and consisting largely of poor African Americans and other minority groups of color, has become a prominent and perhaps permanent feature of the American landscape (Kasarda, 1989; Massey & Denton, 1993; Wilson, 1987, 1996, 2009)

Consider the parallels and contrasts between the plight of the present urban underclass and black Southerners under de jure segregation:

- In both eras, a large segment of the African American population was cut off from opportunities for success and growth.
- In the earlier era, African Americans were isolated in rural areas; now they are isolated in urban areas, especially center cities.
- In the past, escape from segregation was limited primarily by political and legal restrictions and blatant racial prejudice; escape from poverty in the present is limited by economic and educational deficits and a more subtle and amorphous prejudice.

The result is the same: many African Americans remain as a colonized minority group, isolated, marginalized, and burdened with a legacy of powerlessness and poverty.

Modern Institutional Discrimination

The social processes that maintain racial inequality in the present are indirect and sometimes difficult to document and measure. They often flow from the patterns of blatant racial discrimination in the past but are not overtly racial in the present. They operate through a series of cumulative effects that tend to filter black Americans into less-desirable positions in education, housing, the criminal justice system, and the job market. Consider three instances where racial class inequalities are perpetuated, one by employment networks that were closed in the past and remain shut today, a second that is a reflection of the greater vulnerability of the black community to economic hardships, and a third that illustrates the concept of past-in-present discrimination introduced in chapter 4.

Closed Networks and Racial Exclusion. The continuing importance of race as a primary factor in the perpetuation of class inequality is dramatically illustrated in a recent research project. Royster (2003) interviewed black and white graduates of a trade school in Baltimore. Her respondents had completed the same curricula and earned similar grades. In other words, they were nearly identical in terms of the credentials they brought to the world of work. Nonetheless, the black graduates were employed less often in the trades for which they had been educated, had lower wages and fewer promotions, and experienced longer periods of unemployment. Virtually every white graduate found secure and reasonably lucrative employment. The black graduates, in stark contrast, usually were unable to stay in the trades and became, instead, low-skilled, low-paid workers in the service sector.

What accounts for these differences? Based on extensive interviews with the subjects, Royster (2003) concluded that the differences could not be explained by training or by personality characteristics. Instead, she found that what really mattered was not "what you know" but "who you know." The white graduates had access to networks of referrals and recruitment that linked them to the job market in ways that simply were not available to black graduates, largely because the unions had been racially discriminatory in the past. In their search for jobs, whites were assisted more fully by their instructors and were able to use intraracial networks of family and friends, connections so powerful that they "assured even the worst [white] troublemaker a solid place in the blue collar fold" (p. 78).

Needless to say, these results run contrary to some deeply held American values, most notably the widespread, strong support for the idea that success in life is due to individual effort, self-discipline, and the other attributes enshrined in the Protestant ethic. The strength of this faith is documented in survey that was administered in 2010 to a representative sample of adult Americans. The respondents were asked whether they thought people got ahead by hard work, luck, or a combination of the two. Fully 69% of the sample chose "hard work," and another 20% chose "hard work and luck equally" (National Opinion Research Council, 1972–2010). This overwhelming support for the importance of individual effort is echoed in human capital theory and many "traditional" sociological perspectives on assimilation (see chapter 2).

Royster's results demonstrate that American faith in the power of hard work alone is simply wrong. To the contrary, access to jobs is controlled by networks of personal relationships that are decidedly not open to everyone. These subtle patterns of exclusion and closed intraracial networks are more difficult to document than the blatant discrimination that was at the core of Jim Crow segregation, but they can be just as devastating in their effects and just as powerful as mechanisms for perpetuating racial gaps in income and employment.

The Differential Impact of Hard Times. Because of their greater vulnerability, African Americans are more likely to suffer the more virulent form of any trauma—economic, natural, or otherwise—that strikes the society: they tend to feel the impact earlier, experience higher levels of distress, and to be the last to recover. The recent downturn in the U.S. economy has affected almost everyone in one way or another. Americans everywhere have suffered from job loss, increasing poverty, home foreclosures, loss of health-care coverage, and other disasters. How has the recession affected the black community?

Consider the unemployment rate, which generally runs twice as high for blacks as for whites. During the recession, the rate rose for all groups but, as displayed in exhibit 5.3, it rose earlier for blacks, rose at a steeper angle to a much higher peak, and leveled off and began to fall later than for whites. The highest rate for whites was 9.4%, while the peak rate for blacks was 16.7%. The white unemployment rate began to fall in early 2010 but the rate for blacks didn't dip appreciably until the fall of 2011. These hard times affected all groups, across the board, but created a deeper economic hole for black Americans.

A similar pattern of greater difficulty for black Americans has affected home ownership over recent years. As we noted in chapter 4, home ownership is a crucial source

Exhibit 5.3   Monthly Unemployment Rate by Race, January 2001–January 2012

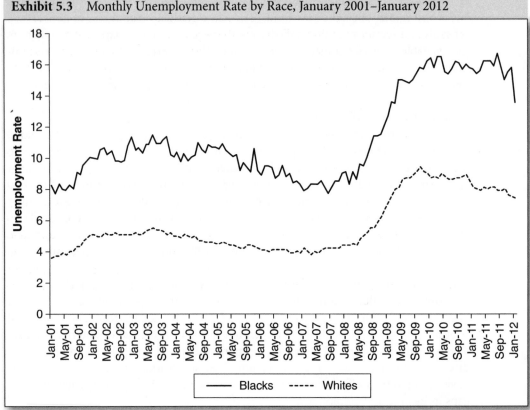

Source: U.S. Bureau of Labor (2012).

of wealth for the average American since home equity can be used to finance businesses, retirement, education, and for scores of other purposes. Income enables families to get along, but financial assets such as home ownership help families get ahead, escape poverty, and become socially mobile (Oliver & Shapiro, 2008, p. A9). The financial advantages of home ownership are particularly important for black Americans because of the long history of racial economic inequality and discrimination in the housing market. A recent report (Oliver & Shapiro, 2008) found that black Americans and other minority groups of color, compared with whites, were more than three times as likely to be victimized by toxic, so-called "subprime," home loans, and more than twice as likely to suffer foreclosure as a result. Subprime home loans were new financial instruments that enabled many previously ineligible people to qualify for home mortgages. Starting in about 2004, these loans were especially marketed to more vulnerable populations by predatory lenders; they had hidden costs, higher interest rates, and other features that made keeping up with payments difficult. The collapse of the housing market affected everyone but was especially devastating for the African American community which, in 2008, faced "the greatest loss of financial wealth in its history" (Oliver & Shapiro, 2008, p. A11).

Thus, a group that was already more vulnerable and economically marginal suffered the greatest proportional loss—an economic collapse from which it will take years to recover. Societal disasters such as the recent recession are not shared equally by everyone, but are especially severe for the groups that are the most vulnerable and have the most tenuous connections with prosperity and affluence. Thus, racial inequality persists decades after the end of blatant, direct, state-supported segregation.

Past-in-Present Discrimination. The effects of past discrimination on the present can be illustrated by the relatively low level of African American business ownership. From the beginning of slavery through the end of Jim Crow segregation in the 1960s, the opportunities for African Americans to start their own businesses were severely restricted (or even forbidden) by law. The black-owned businesses that did exist were confined to the relatively less-affluent market provided by the African American community, a market they had to share with firms owned by dominant group members. At the same time, customs and laws prevented the black-owned businesses from competing for more-affluent white customers. The lack of opportunity to develop and maintain a strong business base in the past—and the consequent inability to accumulate wealth, experience, and other resources—limits the ability of African Americans to compete successfully for economic opportunities in the present (Oliver & Shapiro, 2001, p. 239). These limitations are reinforced, as we have seen, by the lower home equities of black Americans and the consequent lower ability for them to amass the resources to finance new business ventures.

The Family Institution and the Culture of Poverty

The African American family institution has been a continuing source of concern and controversy. One line of analysis sees the African American family as structurally weak, a cause of continuing poverty and a variety of other problems. The most famous study in this tradition was the Moynihan (1965) report, which focused on the higher rates of divorce, separation, desertion, and illegitimacy among African American families and the fact that black families were far more likely to be female headed than were white families. Moynihan concluded that the fundamental barrier facing African Americans was a family structure that he saw as crumbling, a condition that would perpetuate the cycle of poverty entrapping African Americans (p. iii). Today, many of the differences between black and white families identified by Moynihan are even more pronounced. Exhibit 5.4, for example, compares the percentage of households headed by females (black and white) with the percentage of households headed by married couples. (Note that the trends seem to have stabilized since the mid-1990s.)

The Moynihan (1965) report locates the problem of urban poverty in the characteristics of the African American community, particularly in the African American family. These structures are "broken" in important ways and need to be "fixed." This argument is consistent with the **Culture of Poverty Theory**, which argues that poverty is perpetuated by the particular characteristics of the poor. Specifically, poverty is said to encourage **fatalism** (the sense that one's destiny is beyond one's control) and an

Exhibit 5.4 Percentage of Family Households with Married Couples and Headed by Females by Race, 1970–2010

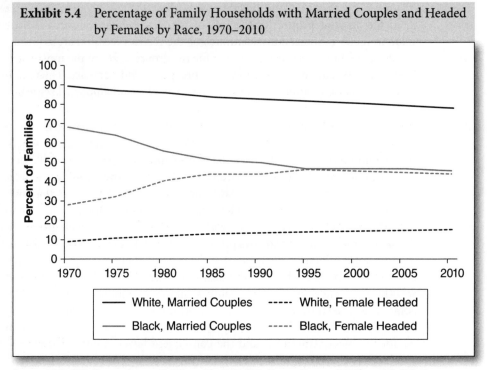

Source: 1977: U.S. Census Bureau (1978, p. 43); 2007: U.S. Census Bureau (2007b, p. 56); U.S. Census Bureau (2012b, p. 56).

orientation to the present rather than the future. The desire for instant gratification is a central trait of the culture of poverty, as opposed to the ability to defer gratification, which is thought to be essential for middle-class success. Other characteristics include violence, school failure, authoritarianism, and high rates of alcoholism and family desertion by males (Lewis, 1959, 1965, 1966; for a recent reprise of the debate over the culture of poverty concept, see Steinberg, 2011; and Small, Harding, & Lamont, 2010).

The Culture of Poverty Theory leads to the conclusion that the problem of urban poverty would be resolved if female-headed family structures and other cultural characteristics correlated with poverty could be changed, an approach that is consistent with the traditional assimilationist perspective and Human Capital Theory: The poor have "bad" or inappropriate values. If they could be equipped with "good" (i.e., white, middle-class) values, the problem would be resolved.

An opposed perspective, more consistent with the concepts and theories that underlie this text, sees the matriarchal structure of the African American family as the *result* of urban poverty—rather than a cause—and a reflection of pervasive, institutional racial discrimination and the scarcity of jobs for urban African American males. In impoverished African American urban neighborhoods, the supply of men able to support a family is reduced by high rates of unemployment, incarceration, and violence, conditions that are, in turn, created by the concentration of urban poverty and the growth of the "underclass" (Massey & Denton, 1993; W. Wilson, 1996, 2009). Thus, the burden of child rearing tends to fall on females, and female-headed households are more common than in more-advantaged neighborhoods.

Female-headed African American families tend to be poor, not because they are "weak," but because of the lower wages accorded to women in general and to African American women in particular, as documented in exhibit 5.5. Note that black female workers have the lowest wages throughout the period. Also note that the gap between black women and white men has narrowed over the years. In 1955, black women earned about a third of what white men earned. In 2010, the gap stood at about 67% (after shrinking to just under 70% in 2005), largely because male wages (for blacks as well as whites) have been relatively flat since the 1970s, while women's wages (again for whites and blacks) have risen. This pattern reflects the impact of deindustrialization: the shift away from manufacturing, which has eliminated many good blue-collar jobs, and the rise of employment sectors, in which women tend to be more concentrated. A similar pattern was documented in exhibit 4.8, which compared the wages of all full-time, year-round workers by sex.

The poverty associated with black female-headed households reflects the interactive effects of sexism and racism on black women, not some weakness in the black

Exhibit 5.5   Median Income for Full-Time, Year-Round Workers by Race and Sex, 1955–2010 (in 2010 dollars)

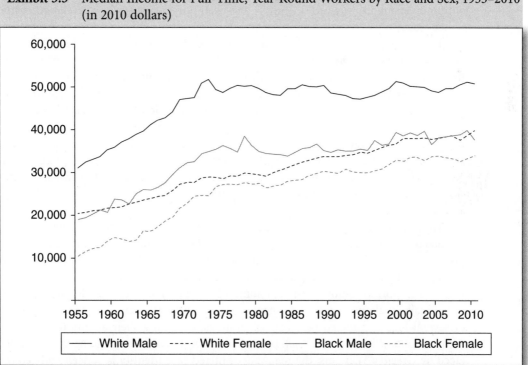

Source: U.S. Census Bureau (2012c).

family. African American urban poverty is the result of the complex forces of past and present institutional discrimination, American racism and prejudice, the precarious position of African American women in the labor force, and continuing urbanization and industrialization. The patterns of African American family life, as well as many of the attitudes and values characteristic of the urban underclass, are more the results of impoverishment than the causes. The solution to African American urban poverty lies in fundamental changes in the urban industrial economy and sweeping alterations in the distribution of resources and opportunities.

Mixed Race and New Racial Identities

As we have discussed, Americans traditionally see race as a simple dichotomy: people are either black or white, with no intermediate categories. In the past, the social convention of the "one-drop rule" meant that people of mixed racial descent were classified as black. To illustrate, consider the story of Gregory Williams (known then as Billy), a white boy growing up in the segregated South in the late 1940s and early 1950s (Williams, 1995). When Billy was 10, his father revealed that he was "half-colored." Under the one-drop rule, that made Billy black. He at first refused to believe his father: "I'm not colored, I'm white! I look white! I've always been white! I go to the 'whites only' school, 'whites only' movie theaters, and 'whites only' swimming pool" (p. 34). Gradually, he came to realize that his life—not just his life chances and his relations with others, but also his very identity—had been transformed by the revelation of his father's race.

In the past, Gregory Williams, and other mixed race people like him, had few choices: Others classified him as black and the rigid social conventions of the day forced him to accept that identity, with all its implications. Today, more than four decades after the formal end of Jim Crow segregation, Americans are confronting the limitations of this dichotomous racial convention. People of mixed race descent are increasing in number and, in fact, are some of the most prominent and well-known people in the nation (and the world). President Barack Obama is the obvious example of a highly visible mixed-race person, but others include Tiger Woods, the professional golfer (who defines himself—tongue in cheek—as Cablanasian: Caucasian, black, American Indian, and Asian), vocalist Mariah Carey, Yankee baseball star Derek Jeter, and actress Halle Berry.

How do people of multiracial descent define themselves today? How are they defined by others? Have the old understandings of race become irrelevant? Is there still pressure to place people in one and only one group? There has been a fair amount of research on this issue and we can begin to formulate some ideas.

One important study illustrates some of the possible identities for mixed race individuals. Rockquemore and Brunsma (2008; Brunsma, 2005) interviewed a sample of several hundred mixed-race college students, confining their attention to people who had one white and one black parent. They found that today, unlike the situation faced by Gregory Williams, the meaning of mixed race identity is conceptually complex and highly variable (Rockquemore & Brunsma, 2008, p. 50). They identified four main categories that their respondents used to understand their biracialism; I present these in order from most to least common. However, the sample they assembled was not representative and there is no reason to assume that these same percentages would characterize all biracial Americans.

1. The most common racial identity in the sample was the **border identity**. These respondents (58% of the sample), didn't consider themselves to be either black or white. They define themselves as members of a third, separate category that is linked to both groups but is unique in itself. One respondent declared, "I'm not black, I'm biracial" (Rockquemore & Brunsma, 2008, p. 43) The authors make a further distinction:

   a. Some border identities are "validated" or recognized and acknowledged by others. These respondents see themselves as biracial, and their family, friends, and the community also see them that way.
   b. Other border identities are "unvalidated" by others. These individuals see themselves as biracial but are classified by others as black. For example, one respondent said, "I consider myself biracial but I experience the world as a black person" (Rockquemore & Brunsma, 2008, p. 45). This disconnect may be the result of the persistence of traditional dichotomous racial thinking and the fact that some people lack the category of "biracial" in their thinking. According to the authors, people in this category are of special interest because of the tensions created by the conflict between their self-image and the way they are defined by others.

2. The second-most-common identity in the sample was the **singular identity**. These individuals saw themselves not as biracial, but as exclusively black (13%) or exclusively white (3%). As the case of Gregory Williams illustrated, the singular black identity is most consistent with American traditional thinking about race. The authors argue that the fact that this identity was *not* the most common in their sample illustrates the complexity of racial identity for biracial people today.

3. A third identity was the **transcendent identity** (15%). The respondents in this category rejected the whole notion of race, along with the traditional categories of black and white, and insisted that they should be seen as unique individuals and not placed in a category, especially since those categories carry multiple assumptions about character, personality, intelligence, attitudes, and a host of other characteristics. Respondents with the transcendent identity were in a constant battle to avoid classification in our highly race-conscious society. One respondent's remarks are illustrative:

   I'm just John, you know? . . . I'm a good guy, just like me for that . . . When I came here (to college), it was like I was almost forced to look at other people as being white, black, Asian, or Hispanic. And so now, I'm still trying to go "I'm just John," but uh, you gotta be something. (Rockquemore & Brunsma, 2008, p. 49)

4. The final racial identity is the least common (4%) but perhaps the most interesting. The authors describe the racial identity of these individuals as **protean**, or changing as the individual moves from group to group and through the various social

contexts of everyday life. There are different "ways of being" in groups of blacks versus groups of whites; individuals with the protean racial identity slip effortlessly from one mode to the next and are accepted by both groups as insiders. The authors point out that most people adjust their *behavior* to different situations (e.g., a fraternity party versus a family Thanksgiving dinner) but these individuals also change their *identity* and adjust who they are to different circumstances. Respondents with the protean identity felt empowered by their ability to fit in with different groups and felt they were endowed with a high degree of "cultural savvy" (Rockquemore & Brunsma, 2008, p. 47). In our increasingly diverse, multicultural, and multiracial society, the ability to belong easily to multiple groups may prove to be a unique strength.

What can we conclude? Racial identity, like so many other aspects of our society, is evolving and becoming more complex. Traditions such as the one-drop rule live on but in attenuated, weakened form. Also, racial identity, like other aspects of self-concept, can be situational or contingent on social context, not permanent or fixed. Given the world in which he lived, Gregory Williams had no choice but to accept a black racial identity. Today, in a somewhat more tolerant and pluralistic social environment, biracial people have choices and some space in which to carve out their own, unique identities. According to Rockquemore and Brunsma (2008), these identity choices are contingent on a number of factors, including personal appearance, but they are always made in the context of a highly race-conscious society with long and strong traditions of racism and prejudice.

Traditional Prejudice and Modern Racism

Public opinion polls and other sources of evidence document a dramatic decline in traditional, overt, anti-black prejudice since the mid-20th century. Exhibit 5.6 displays this trend using a number of survey items administered to representative samples of U.S. citizens. In 1942, the huge majority—more than 70%—of white Americans thought that black and white children should attend different schools. Forty years later, in 1982, support for separate schools had dropped to less than 10%. Similarly, support for the right of white people to maintain separate neighborhoods declined from 65% in 1942 to 18% in the early 1990s. In more recent decades, the percentage of white respondents who support laws against interracial marriage decreased from almost 40% in the early 1970s to about 10% in 2002, and the percentage that believe that blacks are inferior fell from 26% to less than 10% between the early 1970s and 2010.

The overall trend is unmistakable: There has been a dramatic decline in support for prejudiced statements since World War II. In the early 1940s, most white Americans supported prejudiced views. In recent years, only a small minority expresses such views.

These trends document changing American prejudice, but we should not accept these changes at face value and take them as proof that racial prejudice is no longer a problem in society. First, these survey items also show that prejudice has not vanished. A percentage of the white population continues to endorse highly prejudicial sentiments and opinions. Second, the polls show only what people *say* they believe and think,

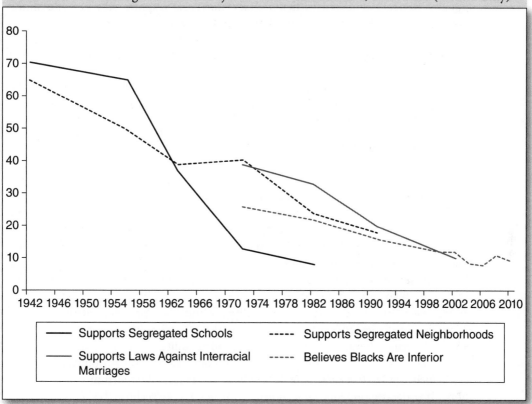

Exhibit 5.6   Declining Anti-Black Prejudice in the United States, 1942–2010 (Whites Only)

Legend:
— Supports Segregated Schools
----- Supports Segregated Neighborhoods
— Supports Laws Against Interracial Marriages
----- Believes Blacks Are Inferior

Source: 1942, 1956, 1963: Hyman and Sheatsley (1964); 1972–2010: National Opinion Research Council (1972–2010).

which can be different from what they truly believe. Exhibit 5.6 may document a decline in people's willingness to admit their prejudice as much as it does a genuine improvement in intergroup attitudes and feelings.

An additional possibility is that the exhibit is misleading and that prejudice remains substantial but has taken on new forms and modes of expression. I raised this possibility in chapter 1 when I introduced the concept of modern or color-blind racism. A number of researchers have been pursuing this more subtle, complex, and indirect way to express negative feelings toward minority groups and opposition to change in dominant-minority relations (see Bobo, 1988, 2001; Bonilla-Silva, 2001, 2006; Kinder & Sears, 1981; Kluegel & Smith, 1982; McConahy, 1986; and Sears, 1988; for a review, see Quillian, 2006).

People affected by modern racism have negative feelings (the affective aspect of prejudice) toward minority groups but reject the idea of genetic or biological inferiority and do not think in terms of the traditional stereotypes. Instead, their prejudicial feelings are expressed indirectly and subtly. The attitudes that define modern racism tend to be consistent with some tenets of the traditional assimilation perspective discussed in chapter 2, especially Human Capital Theory and the Protestant ethic—the traditional American value system that stresses individual responsibility and the importance of hard work. Specifically, modern racism assumes

- there is no longer any serious or important racial, ethnic, or religious discrimination in American society;
- any remaining racial or ethnic inequality is the fault of members of the minority group; who are simply not working hard enough; and
- demands for preferential treatment or affirmative action for minorities are unjustified. Minority groups (especially African Americans) have already received more than they deserve. (Sears & Henry, 2003)

Modern racism tends to "blame the victim" and place the responsibility for change and improvements on minority groups, not on society.

To illustrate the difference between traditional prejudice and modern racism, consider the results of a recent public opinion survey administered to a representative sample of Americans (National Opinion Research Council, 2010). Respondents were asked to choose from among four explanations of why black people, on the average, have "worse jobs, income, and housing than white people." Respondents could choose as many explanations as they wanted.

One explanation, consistent with traditional anti-black prejudice, attributed racial inequality to the genetic or biological inferiority of African Americans ("The differences are mainly because blacks have less inborn ability to learn"). About 9% of the white respondents chose this explanation. A second explanation attributed continuing racial inequality to discrimination, and a third to the lack of opportunity for an education. Of white respondents, 32% chose the former and 46% chose the latter.

A fourth explanation, consistent with modern racism, attributes racial inequality to a lack of effort by African Americans ("The differences are because most blacks just don't have the motivation or willpower to pull themselves up out of poverty"). Of the white respondents, 49% chose this explanation, the most popular of the four. Thus, support for modern racism—the view that the root of the problem of continuing racial inequality lies in the black community, not in society as a whole—has a great deal of support among white Americans.

What makes this view an expression of prejudice? Besides blaming the victim, it deflects attention away from centuries of oppression and continuing inequality and discrimination in modern society. It stereotypes African Americans and encourages the expression of negative feelings against them (but without invoking the traditional image of innate inferiority).

Researchers consistently have found that modern racism is correlated with opposition to policies and programs intended to reduce racial inequality (Bobo, 2001, p. 292; Quillian, 2006). In the survey summarized earlier, for example, respondents who blamed continuing racial inequality on the lack of motivation or willpower of blacks— the "modern racists"—were the least likely to support government help for African Americans and were comparable to traditional racists (those who choose the "inborn ability" explanation for racial inequality) in their opposition to interracial marriage (see exhibit 5.7).

Exhibit 5.7 Support for Government Help for Blacks and Opposition to Interacial Marriage by Explanation of Racial Inequality, 2010

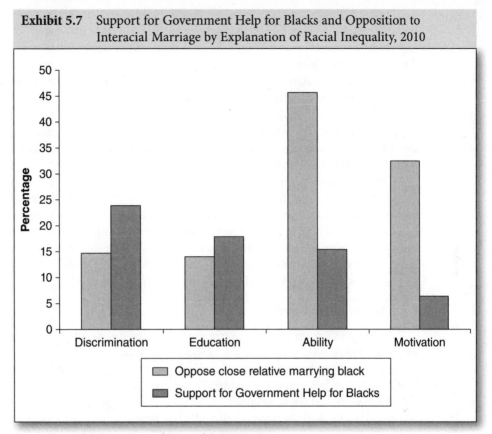

Source: National Opinion Research Council (1972–2010).

In the view of many researchers, modern racism has taken the place of traditional or overt prejudice. If this view is correct, the "report card" on progress in the reduction of racial hostility in the United States must be rather mixed. On one hand, we should not understate the importance of the fading of blatant, overt prejudice. On the other hand, we cannot ignore the evidence that anti-black prejudice has changed in form rather than declined in degree. Subtle and diffuse prejudice is probably preferable to the blunt and vicious variety, but it should not be mistaken for its demise.

Assimilation and Pluralism

Acculturation

The Blauner hypothesis states that the culture of groups created by colonization will be attacked, denigrated, and, if possible, eliminated, and this assertion seems well validated by the experiences of African Americans. African cultures and languages were largely eradicated under slavery. As a powerless, colonized minority group, slaves had few opportunities to preserve their heritage even though traces of African home-lands have been found in black language patterns, kinship systems, music, folk tales, and family legends (see Levine, 1977; and Stuckey, 1987).

Cultural domination continued under the Jim Crow system, albeit through a different structural arrangement. Under slavery, slaves and their owners worked together, and interracial contact was common. Under de jure segregation, intergroup contact diminished, and blacks and whites generally became more separate. After slavery ended, the African American community had somewhat more autonomy (although still few resources) to define itself and develop a distinct culture.

The centuries of cultural domination and separate development have created a unique black experience in America. African Americans share language, religion, values, beliefs, and norms with the dominant society, but have developed distinct variations on the general themes.

The acculturation process may have been slowed (or even reversed) by the Black Power movement. Beginning in the 1960s, on the one hand, there has been an increased interest in African culture, language, clothing, and history, and a more visible celebration of unique African American experiences (e.g., Kwanzaa) and the innumerable contributions of African Americans to the larger society. On the other hand, many of those traditions and contributions have been in existence all along. Perhaps all that really changed was the degree of public recognition.

Secondary Structural Assimilation

As you recall from chapter 2, structural assimilation, or integration, involves two different phases. Secondary structural assimilation refers to integration in more public areas, such as the job market, schools, and political institutions. We can assess integration in this area by comparing residential patterns, income distributions, job profiles, political power, and levels of education of the different groups. Each of these areas is addressed in the next section. We then discuss primary structural assimilation (integration in intimate associations, such as friendship and intermarriage).

Residential Patterns After a century of movement out of the rural South, African Americans today are highly urbanized and much more spread out across the nation. As we saw in chapter 4 (see exhibits 4.2 and 4.3), about 90% of African Americans live in urban areas and a slight majority continue to reside in the South. Between 2000 and 2010, the percentage of African Americans living in the South increased slightly, from 53.6% of all African Americans to 55%. Exhibit 5.8 clearly shows the concentration of African Americans in the states of the old Confederacy; the urbanized East Coast corridor from Washington, DC, to Boston; the industrial centers of the Midwest; and, to a lesser extent, California.

Since Jim Crow segregation ended in the 1960s, residential integration has advanced slowly, if at all. Black and white Americans continue to live in separate areas, and racial residential segregation has been the norm across the nation. This pattern is reinforced by the fact that African Americans are more urbanized than whites and especially concentrated in densely populated center-city areas. Today, the extent of residential segregation varies around the nation, but African Americans continue to be residentially isolated, especially in the older industrial cities of the Northeast and Midwest and in the South.

Exhibit 5.8   Geographical Distribution of the African American Population, 2010

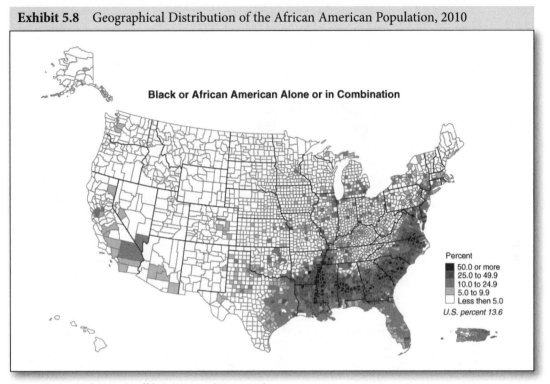

Source: Rastogi, Johnson, Hoeffel, & Drewery (2011, p. 11).

Is racial residential segregation increasing or decreasing? Looking at the nation as a whole, the answer to this question is somewhat unclear, because the studies that have been done use different methodologies, definitions, and databases and come to different conclusions (e.g., see Glaeser & Vigdor, 2001; and Lewis Mumford Center, 2001). One illustrative study (Iceland, Weinberg, & Steinmetz, 2002) examined residential segregation within each of the four major regions of the United States. Exhibit 5.9 presents a measure of segregation called the dissimilarity index for African Americans for 1980, 1990, and 2000. This index indicates the degree to which a group is *not* evenly spread across neighborhoods or census tracts. Specifically, the index is the proportion of each group that would have to move to a different tract or area to achieve residential integration, and scores greater than 0.6 are considered to indicate extreme segregation.

In 1980, all regions scored at or above the 0.6 mark, with the highest levels of segregation found in the Midwest. By 2000, there were declines in all regions, and two (the South and the West) had fallen slightly below the 0.6 mark. Thus, according to this study, racial residential segregation is declining but remains quite high across the nation. As we have seen in chapter 4 and earlier in this chapter, the continuing patterns of residential segregation are reinforced by a variety of practices, including racial steering (guiding clients to same-race housing areas) by realtors and barely disguised discrimination.

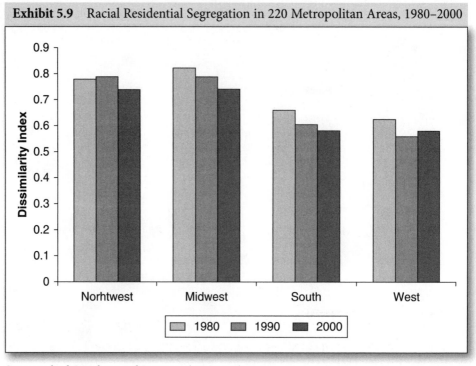

Exhibit 5.9 Racial Residential Segregation in 220 Metropolitan Areas, 1980–2000

Source: Iceland, Weinberg, and Steinmetz (2002, p. 64).

Contrary to a popular belief among whites, an African American preference for living in same-race neighborhoods plays a small role in perpetuating these patterns. For example, one study of representative samples of African Americans from four major American cities (Atlanta, Boston, Detroit, and Los Angeles) found that African Americans overwhelmingly preferred to live in areas split 50–50 between blacks and whites (Krysan & Farley, 2002, p. 949). Finally, the social class and income differences between blacks and whites are also relatively minor factors in perpetuating residential segregation, because the African American middle class is just as likely to be segregated as are the African American poor (Stoll, 2004, p. 26; see also Dwyer, 2010).

Education. In 1954, the year of the landmark Brown desegregation decision, the great majority of African Americans lived in states operating segregated school systems. Compared with white schools, Jim Crow schools were severely underfunded and had fewer qualified teachers, shorter school years, and inadequate physical facilities. School integration was one of the most important goals of the civil rights movement in the 1950s and 1960s, and, aided by pressure from the courts and the federal government, considerable strides were made towards this goal for several decades. More recently, the pressure from the federal government has eased, and one recent report found that schools are being resegregated today at the fastest rate since the 1950s. For example, as

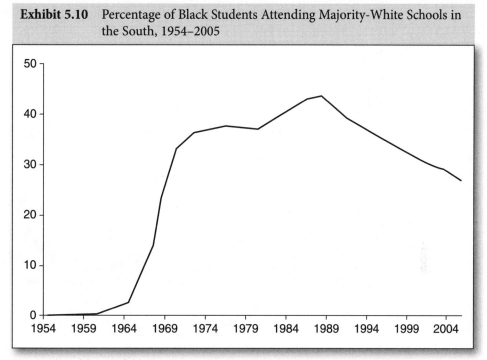

Exhibit 5.10   Percentage of Black Students Attending Majority-White Schools in the South, 1954–2005

Source: Adapted from Orfield, Gary & Lee, Chingmei. 2007. "Historic Reversals, Accelerating Resegregation, and the Need for New Integration Strategies." A Report of the Civil Rights Project.

displayed in exhibit 5.10, schools in the Southern states actually reached their highest levels of racial integration in the late 1980s, when 44% of black students attended white-majority schools. Since that time, this percentage has drifted downward and reached a low of 27% in 2005 (Orfield & Lee, 2007).

Exhibit 5.11 shows the extent of school segregation for black and white students for the nation as a whole in the 1993–1994 and 2005–2006 school years. Three indicators of school segregation are used. The first is the percentage of white and black students in majority-white schools, and the second is the percentage of each in majority-minority schools, or schools in which at least 51% of the student body is non-white. The third indicator is the percentage attending schools that are extremely segregated, in which minorities make up more than 90% of the student body.

Exhibit 5.11 clearly shows that the goal of a racial integration in the public schools has not been achieved. In both school years, the overwhelming majority of white students attended predominantly white schools, whereas the great majority of black students attended schools that were predominantly minority. The percentage of black students in majority-minority schools was higher in the 2005–2006 school year than it had been in the 1993–1994 year, as was the percentage of black students in extremely segregated schools. The degree of racial isolation declined slightly between the two periods as the percentage of white students in majority-white schools dropped from 91% to 87%. According to analyst Richard Fry (2007), this was due to a massive

Exhibit 5.11   School Integration for Black and White Students, 1993–1994 and 2005–2006

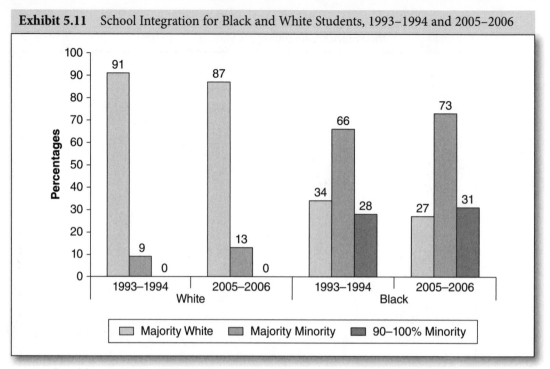

Source: Adapted from Fry, Richard. "The Changing Racial and Ethnic Composition of U.S. Public Schools." Washington, DC: Pew Hispanic Center. August 30, 2007.

increase (55%) in Hispanic students in the schools, not an increase in black–white contacts (p.1).

Underlying and complicating the difficulty of school integration is the widespread residential segregation mentioned previously. The challenges for school integration are especially evident in those metropolitan areas such as Washington, DC, that consist of a largely black-populated inner city surrounded by largely white-populated rings of suburbs. Even with busing, political boundaries would have to be crossed before the school systems could be substantially integrated. Without a renewed commitment to integration, American schools will continue to resegregate. This is a particularly ominous trend, because it directly affects the quality of education. For example, years of research demonstrate that the integration of schools—by social class as well as by race—is related to improved test scores (Orfield & Lee, 2006).

In terms of the quantity of education, the gap between whites and blacks has generally decreased over the past several decades. Exhibit 5.12 displays the percentage of the population older than 25 years, by race and sex, who have high school diplomas. The racial gap has shrunk dramatically at the high school level, even though it has not disappeared. Of course, given the increasing demands for higher educational credentials in the job market, it is ironic that the nation has nearly achieved racial equality in high school education at a time when this credential matters less.

Exhibit 5.12   Percentage of Population Age 25 and Older Completing High School by Race and Sex, 1960–2010

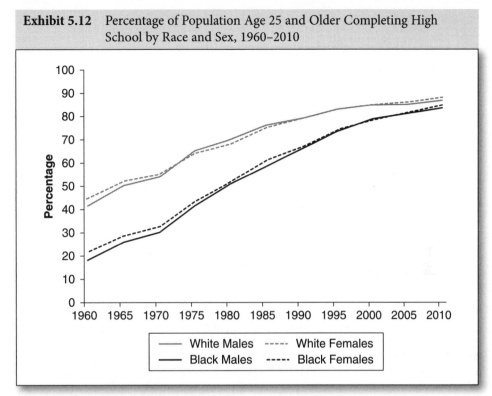

Source: U.S. Census Bureau (2012b, p. 151).

At the college level, the trends somewhat parallel the narrowing gap in levels of high school education, as shown in exhibit 5.13. In 1960, white males held a distinct advantage over all other race or gender groups: they were about three and a half times more likely than African American males to have a college degree. By 2010, the advantage of white males had shrunk, but they were still about 1.7 times more likely than black males and 1.4 times more likely than black females to have a college degree. These racial differences are larger with more-advanced degrees, however, and differences such as these will be increasingly serious in an economy in which jobs more frequently require an education beyond high school. Also, note that black males are lagging behind the other race or gender groups in recent years. What factors discussed in this chapter might help to account for this?

Political Power. Two trends have increased the political power of African Americans since World War II. One is the population movement into urban areas outside the South, a process that concentrated African Americans in areas in which it was easier to get people registered to vote. The effect of the black vote, locally and nationally, began to be felt as early as 1920s. The first African American representative was elected to the U.S. Congress (other than those elected during Reconstruction) in 1928 from the black

Exhibit 5.13 Percentage of the Population 25 Years of Age and Older with College Degree, 1960–2010

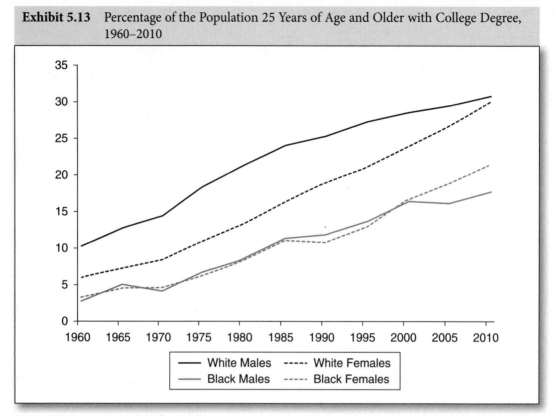

Source: U.S. Census Bureau (2012b, p. 151).

precincts of south Chicago. However, there were still only three African American members in the House of Representatives by 1954 (Franklin, 1967, p. 614), and there are currently 41, about 9% of the total (U.S. Census Bureau, 2012b, p. 259). In 2004, Barack Obama was elected to the U.S. Senate from the State of Illinois, the third African American senator since Reconstruction (the other two were Edward Brooke, R-Mass., who served two terms beginning in 1967, and Carol Mosely-Braun, D-Ill., who served one term beginning in 1993). When Senator Obama became president, his unexpired term was filled by Roland Burris, who also is African American. Burris decided not to seek reelection and there are currently no African Americans in the U.S. Senate.

The number of African American elected officials at all levels of government increased from virtually zero at the turn of the 20th century to more than 9,000 (U.S. Census Bureau, 2011, p. 258). In Virginia in 1989, Douglas Wilder became the first African American to be elected to a state governorship, and both Colin Powell and Condoleezza Rice have served as secretary of state, the highest governmental office—along with Supreme Court justices—ever held by African Americans (other than the presidency). African American communities are virtually guaranteed some political representation by their high degree of geographical concentration at the local level.

Today, most large American cities, including Los Angeles, Chicago, Atlanta, New York, and Washington, DC, have elected African American mayors.

The other trend is the dismantling of the institutions and practices that disenfranchised Southern blacks during Jim Crow segregation (see chapter 4). In particular, the Voting Rights Act of 1965 specifically prohibited many of the practices (poll taxes, literacy tests, and whites-only primaries) traditionally used to keep African Americans politically powerless. The effect of these repressive policies can be seen in the fact that as late as 1962 only 5% of the African American population of Mississippi and 13% of the African American population of Alabama were registered to vote (O'Hare, Pollard, Mann, & Kent, 1991, p. 33).

Since the 1960s, the number of African Americans in the nation's voting age population has increased from slightly less than 10% to about 13%. This increasing potential for political power was not fully mobilized in the past, however, and actual turnout generally has been much lower for blacks than for whites. In the hotly contested presidential races of 2000 and 2004, however, a variety of organizations (such as the NAACP) made a concerted and largely successful effort to increase turnout for African Americans. In both years, black turnout was comparable to that of whites. In the 2008 election, featuring Democrat Barack Obama against Republican John McCain, the black turnout (60.8%) was actually larger than the white turnout (59.6%) (U.S. Census Bureau, 2012b, p. 246). Black voters have been a very important constituency for the Democratic Party and figured prominently in the elections of John F. Kennedy in 1960, Jimmy Carter in 1976, and Bill Clinton in 1992 and 1996.

Overall, black American political power has tended to increase over the past several decades on the national, state, and local levels. One potentially ominous threat to this trend has been the growth of restrictions on voting in many states in recent years. Well over half the states have considered or have passed various measures that could decrease the size of the electorate in general and disproportionately lower the impact of the African American vote. For example, many states may require voters to show a government-issued photo ID—such as a driver's license—before being allowed to cast a ballot.

Proponents of these restrictive measures argue that they prevent voter fraud and the new laws do not, of course, mention African Americans or other minority groups, as is typical of modern institutional discrimination. The result may be a dramatically lower turnout on Election Day for groups that are less likely to have driver's licenses, passports, or similar documentation, including not only African Americans, but also other minority groups of color, low-income groups, senior citizens, and younger voters (Weiser & Norden, 2011).

Jobs and Income. Integration in the job market and racial equality in income follow the trends established in many other areas of social life: on average, the situation of African Americans has improved since the end of de jure segregation but has stopped well short of equality. Among males, whites are much more likely to be employed in the highest-rated and most-lucrative occupational areas, whereas blacks are overrepresented in the service sector and in unskilled labor. Although huge gaps remain, we also should note that the present occupational distribution represents a rapid and significant upgrading, given the fact that as recently as the 1930s the majority of African American males were unskilled agricultural laborers (Steinberg, 1981, pp. 206–207).

A similar improvement has occurred for African American females. In the 1930s, about 90% of employed African American women worked in agriculture or in domestic service (Steinberg, 1981, pp. 206–207). The percentage of African American women in these categories has dropped dramatically, and the majority of African American females are employed in the two highest occupational categories, although typically at the lower levels of these categories. For example, in the top-rated "managerial and professional" category, women are more likely to be concentrated in less-well-paid occupations, such as nurse or elementary school teacher (see exhibit 5.6), whereas men are more likely to be physicians and lawyers.

The racial differences in education and jobs are reflected in a persistent racial income gap, as shown in exhibit 5.14. In the early 1970s, black household income was about 58% of white household income. The gap remained relatively steady through the 1980s, closed during the boom years of the 1990s and, since the turn of the century,

Exhibit 5.14   Median Household Income by Race, 1967–2010 (in 2010 dollars)

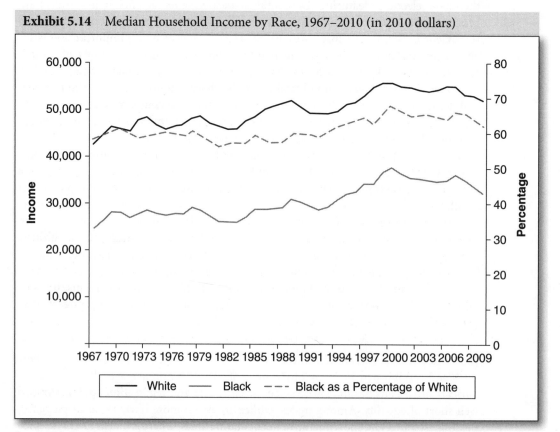

Source: U.S. Census Bureau (2012f).

has widened again. The gap was smallest in 2000 (68%) and, in the most recent year, has grown to 62%, reflecting the differential effects of the recession on minority groups of color, as we discussed previously.

Exhibit 5.14 depicts the racial income gap in terms of the median, an average that shows the difference between "typical" white and black families. Exhibit 5.15 supplements this information by comparing the distribution of income within each racial group for 2010 and highlights the differences in the percentage of each group in low-, middle-, and upper-income categories. To read this graph, note that income categories are arrayed from top to bottom and that the horizontal axis has a zero point in the middle of the graph. The percentage of white households in each income category is represented by the bars to the left of the zero point, and the same information is presented for black households by the bars to the right of the center point.

Starting at the bottom, note that the bars representing black households are considerably wider than those for white households. This reflects the fact that black Americans are more concentrated in the lower income brackets. For example, 26% of black households had incomes less than $15,000, 2.4 times greater than the percentage of white households (11%) in this range.

As we move upward, note that many black and white households have incomes between $50,000 to $124,000, income ranges that would be associated with middle and upper-middle-class lifestyles. In this income range, however, it is the white households that are overrepresented: 39% of white households versus only 27% of black households had incomes in this range. The racial differences are even more dramatic in the highest income ranges: more than 9% of white households had incomes greater than $150,000, versus only 3% of black households. Graphs such as this convincingly refute the notion, common among "modern racists" and many other Americans, that there are no important racial inequalities in the United States today.

Finally, poverty affects African Americans at much higher rates than it does white Americans. Exhibit 5.16 shows the percentage of white and black American families living below the federally established, "official" poverty level from 1967 through 2010. The poverty rate for African American families runs about two and a half to three times greater than the rate for whites.

For most of this period, poverty rates for whites tended to be stable, although they have been rising in the most recent years. For blacks, there was a dramatic decrease in poverty during the 1990s but, since 2000, the rate has drifted upwards, especially in the most recent years. Tragically, the highest rates of poverty continue to be found among children, especially African American children. Note the increases in child poverty for both groups in the most recent years. Again, graphs such as this one convincingly refute the notion that serious racial inequality is a thing of the past for U.S. society.

Primary Structural Assimilation

Interracial contact in the more public areas of society, such as schools or the workplace, is certainly more common today, and as Gordon's model of assimilation predicts, this has led to increases in more intimate contacts across racial lines. For example, the percentage of African Americans who say they have "good friends" who are white

Exhibit 5.15   Distribution of Household Income for Non-Hispanic Whites and Blacks, 2009

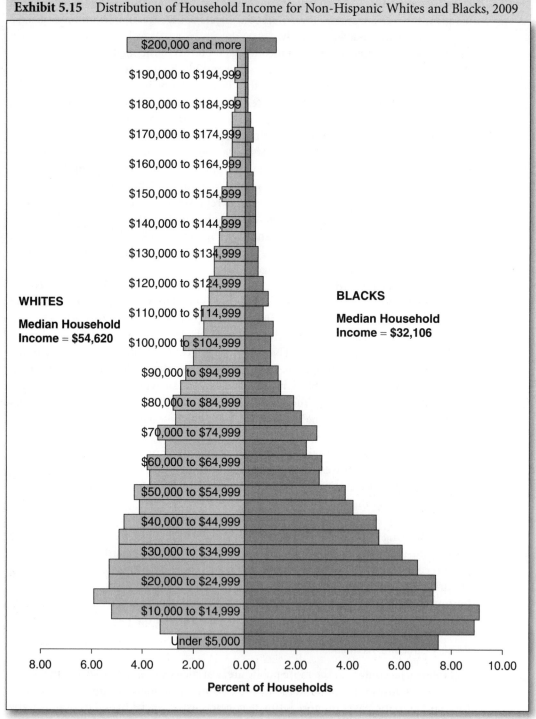

Source: U.S. Census Bureau (2012g).

Exhibit 5.16 Percentage of Children and Families in Poverty by Race, 1967–2010

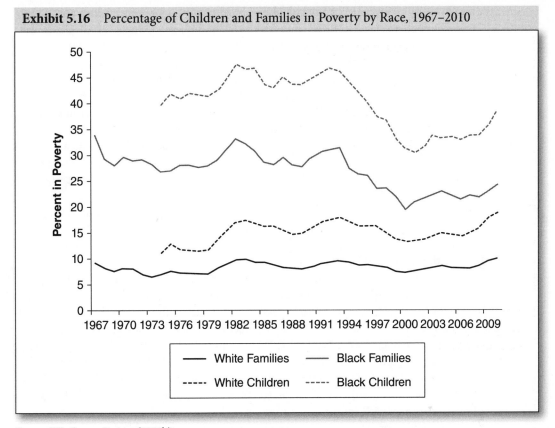

Source: U.S. Census Bureau (2012h).

increased from 21% in 1975 to 78% in 1994. Comparable increases have occurred for whites: in 1975, only 9% said they had "good friends" who were black, and that percentage rose to 73% in 1995 (Thernstrom & Thernstrom, 1997, p. 521).

One study looked at changing intimate relationships among Americans by asking a nationally representative sample about the people with whom they discuss "important matters." Although the study did not focus on black–white relations per se, the researchers did find that the percentage of whites who included African Americans as intimate contacts increased from 9% to more than 15% between 1984 and 2004 (McPherson, Smith-Lovin, & Brashears, 2006). While this increase would be heartening to those committed to a more integrated, racially unified society, these low percentages could also be seen as discouraging because they suggest that about 85% of white Americans maintain racially exclusive interpersonal networks of friends and acquaintances.

Another interesting study (Fisher, 2008) looked at interracial friendships on 27 college campuses across the nation. First-year students were interviewed at the end of their second semester and asked about the group membership of their 10 closest friends on campus. The study found that cross-group friendships were common but that white students had the least diverse circles of friends. For whites, 76% of their friends were also white, a much higher percentage of in-group exclusiveness than Asian students (51%), Hispanic students (56%), and black students (27%). Obviously, these percentages reflect the racial composition of the campuses (all were majority white), but it is significant that cross-group choices were positively related to more tolerant attitudes and a history of having a friend from another group in high school. Most interesting, perhaps, was that cross-group choices were positively related to greater diversity on campus. This finding supports Gordon's assertion that integration at the secondary level leads to integration at the primary level.

Consistent with the decline in traditional, overt prejudice, Americans are much less opposed to interracial dating and marriage today. A Gallup poll, for example, reports that 75% of white Americans express approval of black–white marriage, up from just 20% approval in 1968. The comparable percentage of blacks was 85%, up from 56% in 1968 (Gallup Organization, 2007). Approval of interracial dating and marriage appears to be especially high among younger people: in a 2007 poll, 86% of Americans in the 18 to 29 age range approved of interracial marriage, as opposed to 30% of those aged 65 and older (Wellner, 2007).

Behavior appears to be following attitudes as the rates of interracial dating and marriage are increasing. A number of studies find that interracial dating is increasingly common (see Wellner, 2007); marriages between blacks and whites are also increasing in number, although they are still a tiny percentage of all marriages. According to the U.S. Census Bureau, there were 65,000 black–white married couples in 1970 (including persons of Hispanic origin), about one tenth of 1% (0.1%) of all married couples. By 2010, the number of black–white married couples had increased by a factor of 8.5, to 558,000, but this is still less than 1% (or 0.9%) of all married couples (U.S. Census Bureau, 2012b, p. 54).

One study reports that the rate of out-marriage in the black community has increased substantially over the past 30 years. In 1980, only 2.5% of blacks were married to someone of a different race or ethnicity but this percentage increased to 8.9% in 2010. In 2010, most blacks who out-married were married to whites (58%), with another 23% married to Hispanics (Passel, Wang, & Taylor, 2010, p. 12–13).

FOCUS ON CONTEMPORARY ISSUES:
Does the Election of President Obama Mean that America Is Postracial?

The election of President Barack Obama in 2008 led many people to conclude that the United States had finally and decisively rejected racism and had become "postracial," or a society in which race was irrelevant. Others warned that reports of the death of racism were vastly exaggerated and that the triumph of one person—even one as significant as this—had little relevance for the situation of black Americans in general or for other minority groups.

Which view is most sensible? We won't be able to fully address the issue in these few paragraphs, but consider a few important points that suggest that American society is far from being postracial.

First, race figured prominently in the presidential campaign, although its effects tended to be below the surface. The Obama campaign knew that they had to avoid the third rail of American racism if their candidate was to be successful. They deemphasized his racial identity and presented him as a serious candidate who happened to be black, not as "the black candidate." Obama avoided racially charged issues (e.g., civil rights, affirmative action, or the war on drugs), and stressed issues that were of broad concern (e.g., the economy, the wars in Iraq and Afghanistan, and health care). His strategy was to discuss race "only in the context of other issues" (Ifill, 2009, p. 53).

This strategy, of course, could not defuse all of the concerns, fears, and anxieties triggered by Obama's race. Given the traditional stereotypes about whites and blacks, the mixed-race Obama had to be seen as "more white" and the negativity associated with his blackness had to be contained. The most potentially disastrous racial episode during the campaign linked Obama with the flamboyant Pastor Jeremiah Wright, the minister of a Chicago church that Obama had attended. A YouTube video, in which Wright strongly condemned the United States for its treatment of blacks and other people of color (http://www.youtube.com/watch?v=9hPR5jnjtLo), surfaced and threatened to sink Obama's candidacy by associating him with the angry, militant rhetoric of the African American outsider. Forced to confront American racism openly, Obama crafted an elegant speech in which he acknowledged racism past and present but rejected Reverend Wright's views as distorted, saying that Wright elevated "what is wrong with America above all that we know is right with America" (Obama, 2008).The speech successfully defused the immediate issue but race continued to lurk in the background of the campaign. There was a persistent tendency to see Obama as something other than a "true American"—as a Muslim, a Kenyan, an outsider, a terrorist, a revolutionary, or just an angry black man. His campaign was ultimately successful because it was able to portray him as "white-assimilated, acceptable, mixed-race, and thus less black (or not really black)" (Wingfield & Feagin, 2010, p. 219). The first president of color in American history owed his success to the perception of many that he wasn't "really" black.

Second, support for Obama on Election Day was highly racialized. The candidate built a broad coalition of supporters that included the young, first-time voters, low-income voters, liberals, Democrats, and women. However, his staunchest support came from the black community. Obama actually lost among white voters by a considerable margin (55% voted for McCain, the Republican candidate) but attracted 95% of black voters.

Furthermore, since his election the perceptions of Obama's effectiveness have been highly racialized. Weekly surveys show that the percentage of whites who approve the job the president is doing varies between 30% and 40% while the percentage of

(Continued)

(Continued)

approval among blacks runs between 80% and 90% and sometimes exceeds 90% (Gallup Organization, 2012). Thus, his support in the black community is roughly two to three times his support in the white community.

Finally, and most detrimental to the argument that the United States is postracial, the racial gaps that existed when Obama took office have persisted, and may have grown larger (see the exhibits in this chapter); racial issues regularly animate public discourse. U.S. race relations are arguably the best they have ever been but, given a history that features slavery and segregation, this is far from "postracial."

Is the Glass Half Empty or Half Full?

The contemporary situation of African Americans is perhaps what might be expected for a group so recently "released" from exclusion and subordination. The average situation of African Americans improved vastly during the past 50 years in virtually every area of social life. As demonstrated by the data presented in this chapter, however, racial progress has stopped well short of equality. In assessing the present situation, one might stress the improved situation of the group (the glass is half full) or the challenges that remain before full racial equality and justice are achieved (the glass is half empty). Perhaps the most reasonable approach is to recognize that in many ways the overall picture of racial progress is "different" rather than "better," and that a large percentage of African Americans have traded rural peasantry for urban poverty and now face an array of formidable and deep-rooted problems.

The situation of African Americans is intimately intermixed with the plight of our cities and the changing nature of the labor force. It is the consequence of nearly 400 years of prejudice, racism, and discrimination, but it also reflects broader social forces, such as urbanization and industrialization. Consistent with their origin as a colonized minority group, the relative poverty and powerlessness of African Americans has persisted long after other groups (e.g., the descendants of the European immigrants who arrived between the 1820s and the 1920s) have achieved equality and acceptance. African Americans were enslaved to meet the labor demands of an agrarian economy, became a rural peasantry under Jim Crow segregation, were excluded from the opportunities created by early industrialization, and remain largely excluded from the better jobs in the emerging postindustrial economy.

Progress toward racial equality has slowed considerably since the heady days of the 1960s, and in many areas earlier advances seem hopelessly stagnated. Public opinion polls indicate that there is little support or sympathy for the cause of African Americans. Traditional prejudice has declined, only to be replaced by modern racism. In the court of public opinion, African Americans are often held responsible for their own plight. Biological racism has been replaced by indifference to racial issues or by blaming the victims.

Of course, in acknowledging the challenges that remain, we should not downplay the real improvements that have been made in the lives of African Americans.

Compared with their forebears in the days of Jim Crow, African Americans today are on the average more prosperous and more politically powerful, and some are among the most revered of current popular heroes (the glass is half full). However, the increases in average income and education and the glittering success of the few obscures a tangle of problems for the many, problems that may well grow worse as America moves farther into the postindustrial era. Poverty, unemployment, a failing educational system, residential segregation, subtle racism, and continuing discrimination continue to be inescapable realities for millions of African Americans. In many African American neighborhoods, crime, drugs, violence, poor health care, malnutrition, and a host of other factors compound these problems (the glass is half empty).

Given this gloomy situation, it should not be surprising to find significant strength in pluralistic, nationalistic thinking, as well as resentment and anger in the African American community. Black Nationalism and Black Power remain powerful ideas, but their goals of development and autonomy for the African American community remain largely rhetorical sloganeering without the resources to bring them to actualization.

The situation of the African American community in the early 21st century might be characterized as structural pluralism combined with inequality. The former characterization testifies to the failure of assimilation and the latter to the continuing effects, in the present, of a colonized origin. The problems that remain are less visible (or perhaps just better hidden from the average white middle-class American) than those of previous eras. Responsibility is more diffused, the moral certainties of opposition to slavery or to Jim Crow laws are long gone, and contemporary racial issues must be articulated and debated in an environment of subtle prejudice and low levels of sympathy for the grievances of African Americans. Urban poverty, modern institutional discrimination, and modern racism are less dramatic and more difficult to measure than an overseer's whip, a lynch mob, or a sign that says "Whites Only," but they can be just as real and just as deadly in their consequences.

Main Points

- At the beginning of the 20th century, the racial oppression of African Americans took the form of a rigid competitive system of group relations and de jure segregation. This system ended because of changing economic and political conditions, changing legal precedents, and a mass movement of protest initiated by African Americans.
- The U.S. Supreme Court decision in *Brown v. Board of Education of Topeka* (1954) was the single most powerful blow struck against legalized segregation. A nonviolent direct action campaign was launched in the South to challenge and defeat segregation. The U.S. Congress delivered the final blows to de jure segregation in the 1964 Civil Rights Act and the 1965 Voting Rights Act.
- Outside the South, the concerns of the African American community had centered on access to schooling, jobs, housing, health care, and other opportunities. African Americans' frustration and anger were expressed in the urban riots of the 1960s. The Black Power movement addressed the massive problems of racial inequality remaining after the victories of the civil rights movement.
- Black–white relations since the 1960s have been characterized by continuing inequality, separation, and hostility, along with substantial improvements in status for some African Americans. Class differentiation within the African American community is greater than ever before.

- The African American family has been perceived as weak, unstable, and a cause of continuing poverty. Culture of Poverty Theory attributes poverty to certain characteristics of the poor. An alternative view sees problems such as high rates of family desertion by men as the result of poverty, rather than the cause.
- Anti-black prejudice and discrimination are manifested in more subtle, covert forms (modern racism and institutional discrimination) in contemporary society.
- African Americans are largely acculturated, but centuries of separate development have created a unique black experience in American society.
- Despite real improvements in their status, the overall secondary structural assimilation of African Americans remains low. Evidence of racial inequalities in residence, schooling, politics, jobs, income, unemployment, and poverty is massive and underlines the realities of the urban underclass.
- In the area of primary structural assimilation, interracial interaction and friendships appear to be rising. Interracial marriages are increasing, although they remain a tiny percentage of all marriages.
- Compared with their situation at the start of the 20th century, African Americans have made considerable improvements in quality of life. The distance to true racial equality remains enormous.

Study Site on the Web

Don't forget the interactive quizzes and other resources and learning aids at www.sagepub.com/healeyds4e.

For Further Reading

Feagin, J. (2001). *Racist America: Roots, current realities, and future reparations.* New York: Routledge.
Hacker, A. (1992). *Two nations: Black and white, separate, hostile, unequal.* New York: Scribner's.

Two very readable overviews of contemporary black–white relations.

Massey, D., & Denton, N. (1993). *American apartheid: Segregation and the making of the underclass.* Cambridge, MA: Harvard University Press.

The authors argue powerfully that residential segregation is the key to understanding urban black poverty.

Morris, A. D. (1984). *The origins of the civil rights movement.* New York: Free Press.
Williams, J. (1987). *Eyes on the prize: America's civil rights years, 1954–1965.* New York: Penguin.

Indispensable sources on the Southern civil rights movement.

Smelser, N., Wilson, W., & Mitchell, F. (Eds.). (2001). *America becoming: Racial trends and their consequences.* Washington, DC: National Academy Press.

A two-volume collection of articles by leading scholars that presents a comprehensive analysis of black–white relations in America.

Wingfield, A., & Feagin, J. (2010). *Yes we can? White racial framing and the 2008 presidential campaign.* New York: Routledge.

An important analysis of the racial dynamics of Obama's election campaign.

New York Times. (2001). *How race is lived in America*. New York: Times Books

A comprehensive investigation by reporters of the New York Times *on how race is lived in the everyday lives of ordinary Americans.*

Wilson, W. J. (2009). *More than just race: Being black and poor in the inner city*. New York: W. W. Norton.

The latest publication of one of the most important authorities on race in the United States.

Questions for Review and Study

1. What forces led to the end of de jure segregation? To what extent was this change a result of broad social forces (e.g., industrialization), and to what extent was it the result of the actions of African Americans acting against the system (e.g., the Southern civil rights movement)? By the 1960s and 1970s, how had the movement for racial change succeeded, and what issues were left unresolved? What issues remain unresolved today?

2. Describe the differences between the Southern civil rights movement and the Black Power movement. Why did these differences exist? How are the differences related to the nature of de jure versus de facto segregation? Do these movements remain relevant today? How?

3. How does gender affect contemporary black–white relations and the African American protest movement? Is it true that African American women are a "minority group within a minority group"? How?

4. What are the implications of increasing class differentials among African Americans? Does the greater affluence of middle-class blacks mean that they are no longer a part of a minority group? Will future protests by African Americans be confined only to working-class and lower-class blacks?

5. Regarding contemporary black–white relations, is the glass half empty or half full? Considering the totality of evidence presented in this chapter, which of the following statements would you agree with? Why? (1) American race relations are the best they've ever been; racial equality has been essentially achieved (even though some problems remain); or (2) American race relations have a long way to go before society achieves true racial equality.

Internet Research Project

In this exercise, you will find information in the U.S. census about the total population, African Americans, and two white ethnic groups of your own choosing. You will then use course concepts to assess and analyze this information and place it in the context of this text.

Notes

1. *The numbers you gather for this exercise may vary from those presented in this chapter because of differences in the dates the data was collected or in the nature of the samples used.*

2. *Visit the website for this text to check for updates on the databases available for completing this exercise.*

Get information by following these steps:

1. Go to the official U.S. Census Bureau website at www.census.gov.

2. Click on "Data" in the list of choices at the top of the screen and then click "American Fact Finder" from the drop-down menu.

3. Click the "Race and Ethnic Groups" tab on the left of the next screen. A new window will open. Find the list of "Racial and Ethnic Group Results" on the right of the screen and click on the box next to "Total Population" (Code 001) and the box next to "Black or African American alone or in combination with one or more other races" (Code 005). Next click the "Add" button above the "Racial and Ethnic Group Results" window and these two selections will be added to the "Your selections" box in the top-left-hand corner of the screen.

4. Find the "Race/Ethnic Group Filter Options" window in the middle of the screen and click on "Ancestry Group." Now the "Racial and Ethnic Group Results" window will display a list of ethnic or ancestry groups. Select two groups from this list that trace their origins to a European nation. For example, you might choose German Americans, Irish Americans, or Polish Americans. See exhibits 2.7 and 2.8 for a list of some of the largest white ethnic groups. These groups are listed starting at the bottom of the first screen and then continuing on to screens two and three.

5. When you find a group you would like to include, check the box to the left of the group name and then click the "Add" button at the top of the window.

6. Write the names of your two European-origin groups in the appropriate columns in the table below.

7. Once you have selected your groups, close the "Select Race and Ethnic Groups" window by clicking the "Close" button on the top-right-hand corner of the window. Your groups (the total population, African Americans, and two European-origin groups) will be listed in the "Your Selections" box in the upper-left-hand corner of the screen.

8. The "Search Results" window on the right of the screen lists all of the tables that are currently available from the complete census of 2010 and the yearly American Community Survey (ACS). For this project, we will use the 2011 ACS 1-year estimates. Look in either the "ID" column on the left for Table S0201 or in the Dataset column on the right for the "2011 ACS 1-year estimates." Click the box next to the file name and then click "View" from the menu above the window.

9. The next screen will display a table with your groups listed at the top. Scroll down the table until you find the information needed to fill in the table below.

   a. Under "Total Number of Races Reported," find "Total population."
   b. Follow the instructions below the table to compute "Percent of Total Population."
   c. Under "Educational Attainment," find "Bachelor's degree or higher."
   d. Under "Employment Status," find "Unemployed."
   e. Under "Income in the Past 12 Months," find "Median Household Income."
   f. Under "Poverty Rates for Families and People," find "All Families."
   g. Under "Housing Tenure," find "Owner-Occupied Housing Units."
   h. Select two more variables relevant to this course and fill in the scores for the total population, African Americans, and the two white ethnic groups you selected. (*Note: Your instructor may have different instructions for this step of the project.*)

		Total Population	African Americans	White Ethnic Groups	
				_____	_____
1	Number	311,591,919	42,533,817		
2	Percent of total population*	✕	13.7%		
3	% with BA degree or higher	28.5%			
4	% unemployed.	6.5%			
5	Median household income	$50,502			
6	% of all families in poverty	11.7%			
7	% living in owner-occupied houses	64.6%			
8					
9					

*Divide the number in the group by 311,591,919 and multiply by 100.

Questions

1. What stage of Gordon's model of assimilation (see exhibit 2.1) do these variables measure?

2. Review the Blauner hypothesis (see chapter 3). Do the patterns you observe in the data you have collected conform to the predictions of the hypothesis? How?

3. Review the themes stated at the beginning of chapter 3 and the corollary stated at the beginning of chapter 4. How do the patterns in the table above relate to the contact situation and changing subsistence technologies?

4. Review the concepts of modern institutional discrimination and past-in-present discrimination introduced in chapter 4 and applied in this chapter. How do the patterns you observe in the table above relate to these concepts?

Optional Group Discussion

Bring this information to class and, in groups of four to six people, compare with the information collected by others. Consider the issues raised in the question above and in the chapter and develop some ideas about why African Americans and the two European-origin groups are where they are relative to each other and to the total population. (*Note: Your instructor may have different instructions for this step of the project.*)

6

American Indians: From Conquest to Tribal Survival in a Postindustrial Society

Like most Indian people, I have several names. In Indian Way, names come to you in the course of your life, not just when you're born. Some come during childhood ceremonies; others are given on special occasions throughout your life. Each name gives you a new sense of yourself and your own possibilities. And each name gives you something to live up to. It points out the direction you're supposed to take in this life. One of my names is Tate Wikuwa, which means "Wind Chases the Sun" in the Dakota language.... Another name...is Gwarth-ee-lass, meaning "He Leads the People."

I find special inspiration in both of those names. The first, to me, represents total freedom—a goal even most of those outside prison walls never achieve. When I think that name to myself...I feel free in my heart, able to melt through stone walls and steel bars and ride the wind through pure sunlight to the Sky World. No walls or bars or rolls of razor wire can stop me from doing that. And the second name...to me, represents total commitment, a goal I strive for even within these walls.

Maybe it seems presumptuous, even absurd—a man like me, in prison for two lifetimes, speaking of leading his people. But, like Nelson Mandela, you never know when you will suddenly and unexpectedly be called upon. He, too, knows what it's like to sit here in prison, year after year, decade after decade. I try to keep myself ready if ever I'm needed....

So, in our way, my names tell me and others who I am. Each of my names should be an inspiration to me. Here at Leavenworth—in fact anywhere in the U.S. prison system—my official name is #89637-132. Not much imagination, or inspiration, there.

My Christian name, though I don't consider myself to be a Christian, is Leonard Peltier. The last name's French, from the French fur hunters and voyageurs who came through our country more than a century ago, and I take genuine pride in that holy blood; too.... My first name was given to me by my grandmother, who said I cried so hard as a baby that I sounded like a "little lion": She named me Leonard, she said, because it sounded like "lion-hearted."

Though my bloodline is predominantly Ojibway and Dakota Sioux, I have also married into, and been adopted in the traditional way by, the Lakota Sioux people. All Lakota/Dakota/Nakota people—also known as Sioux—are one great nation of nations. Indians are many nations, but one People. I myself was brought up on both Sioux and Ojibway (Chippewa) reservations in the land known to you as America.

I would like to say with all sincerity—and with no disrespect—that I don't consider myself an American citizen. I am a native of Great Turtle Island. I am of the Ikce Wicasa, the Common People, the Original People. Our sacred land is under occupation, and we are now all prisoners, not just me.

Even so, I love being an Indian, for all of its burdens and all of its responsibilities. Being an Indian is my greatest pride. I thank Wakan Tanka, the Great Mystery, for making me Indian. I love my people. If you must accuse of something, accuse me of that—being Indian. To that crime—and to that crime alone—I plead guilty.

My crime's being an Indian.

What's yours?

—Leonard Peltier (1999, pp. 61–65)*

Leonard Peltier has been in federal prison since 1977. He is serving two consecutive life terms for the murder of two federal agents during a shootout on a Sioux reservation. Many believe that his conviction was unfair or even rigged and was based more on his leadership role in the American Indian Movement (AIM), a protest group he helped to organize, than on his actions during the shootout.

In this excerpt from his autobiographical *Prison Writings* (1999), Peltier reflects on what being an Indian means to him, and in his musings we can hear an authentic Indian voice, reflective of a culture that has survived, even after centuries of attempts to suppress and undermine it. Whatever the merit of his case, voices like Peltier's demonstrate the persistence of a group that is often assumed to have perished in the days of the Wild West. For many people, perhaps the most surprising fact about American Indians is that they are still here.

We discussed the contact period for American Indians in chapter 3. As you recall, this period began in the earliest colonial days and lasted nearly 300 years, ending only with the final battles of the Indian wars in the late 1800s. The Indian nations fought for their land and to preserve their cultures and way of life. The tribes had enough power to win many battles, but they eventually lost all the wars. The superior resources of the burgeoning white society made the eventual defeat of American

---

Indians inevitable, and by 1890 the last of the tribes had been conquered, their leaders had been killed or were in custody, and their people were living on U.S. government–controlled reservations.

Early in the 20th century, American Indians were, in Blauner's (1972) terms, a conquered and colonized minority group. Like the slave plantations, the reservations were paternalistic systems that controlled American Indians with federally mandated regulations and government-appointed Indian agents. For most of the 20th century, as Jim Crow segregation, Supreme Court decisions, industrialization, and urbanization shaped the status of other minority groups, American Indians subsisted on the fringes of development and change, marginalized, relatively powerless, and isolated. Their links to the larger society were weaker and, compared with African Americans, white ethnic groups, and other minorities, they were less affected by the forces of social and political evolution. While other minority groups maintained a regular presence in national headlines, American Indians have been generally ignored and unnoticed, except perhaps as mascots for sports teams, including the Washington Redskins, Atlanta Braves, and Cleveland Indians.

The last decades of the 20th century witnessed some improvement in the status of American Indians in general. Some tribes, especially those with casinos and other gaming establishments, made notable progress toward parity with national standards. Also, the tribes are now more in control of their own affairs, and many have effectively used their increased autonomy and independence to address problems in education, health, joblessness, and other areas. Despite this progress, however, large gaps remain between American Indians and the dominant group in virtually every area of social and economic life and American Indians living on reservations are among the poorest groups in U.S. society.

In this chapter, we will bring the history of American Indians up to the present and explore both recent progress and persisting problems. Some of the questions we address include the following: What accounts for the lowly position of this group for much of the past century? How can we explain the improvements in the most recent decades? Now, early in the 21st century, what problems remain, and how does the situation of American Indians compare with that of other colonized and conquered minority groups? What are the most promising strategies for closing the remaining gaps between American Indians and the larger society?

Size of the Group

How many Indians are there? There are several different answers to this question, partly because of the way census information is collected and partly because of the social and subjective nature of race and group membership. The most current answers come from the 2010 U.S. census.

The task of determining the size of the group is complicated by the way the census collects information on race. As you recall, beginning with the 2000 census people were allowed to claim membership in more than one racial category. If we define "American Indians" as consisting of people who identify themselves as *only* American Indian, we will get one estimate of the size of the group. If we use a broader definition and include people who claim mixed racial ancestry, our estimate of group size will be much larger.

At any rate, exhibit 6.1 shows that there were more than 5 million people who claimed at least some American Indian or Alaska Native ancestry but only about half that number if we confine the group to people who select one race only. By either count, the group is a tiny minority (about 1%) of the total population of the United States. Exhibit 6.1 presents information for American Indians and Alaska Native separately, for the 10 largest tribal groupings of American Indians, and for the four largest tribal groups of Alaska Natives.

American Indians have been growing rapidly over the past several decades, but this fact needs to be seen in the full context of American Indian history. As I mentioned in chapter 3, in 1492 there were anywhere from several million to 10 million or

Exhibit 6.1 American Indians and Alaska Natives

	Alone	*Alone or in combination (2 or more groups)*
ALL AMERICAN INDIANS AND ALASKA NATIVES	2,932,248	5,220,579
AMERICAN INDIANS	2,042,825	3,831,740
ALASKA NATIVE	113,902	162,504
Ten Largest Tribal Groupings for American Indians:		
Cherokee	284,247	819,858
Navajo	286,731	332,129
Choctaw	103,910	195,764
Chippewa	112,757	170,742
Sioux	112,176	170,110
Apache	63,193	118,810
Blackfeet	27,279	105,304
Pueblo	72,270	91,242
Creek	48,352	88,332
Iroquois	40,570	40,432
Largest Tribal Groupings for Alaska Natives		
Yupik	27,329	30,868
Inupiat	20,941	25,687
Tlingit-Haida	8,547	13,486
Alaskan Athabascan	12,318	16,665

Source: Norris, Vines, and Hoeffel (2012).

more American Indians living in what is now the continental ("lower 48") United States (Mann, 2011, 105–109). Losses suffered during the contact period reduced the population to fewer than 250,000 by 1900, a loss of at least 75%, possibly much larger. Recent population growth has perhaps restored the group to its pre-Columbian size. As displayed in exhibit 6.2, growth was slow in the early decades of the 20th century but much more rapid in recent decades. The more-recent growth is largely the result of changing definitions of race in the larger society and a much greater willingness of people to claim Indian ancestry, a pattern that again underscores the basically social nature of race (Thornton, 2001, p. 137).

Exhibit 6.2   American Indian Indian and Alaska Native Population, 1900–2010

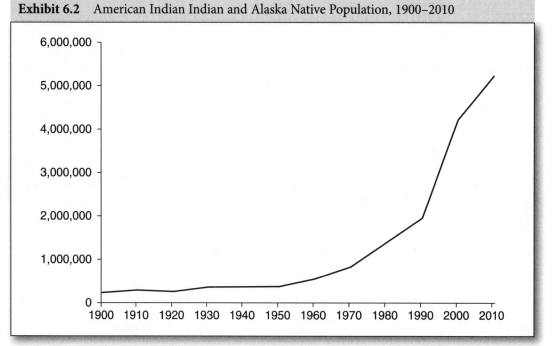

Source: 1900–1990, Thornton (2001, p. 142); 2000: U.S. Census Bureau (2007b, p. 14); 2010: Humes, Jones, and Ramirez (2011, p. 7).

American Indian Cultures

The dynamics of American Indian and Anglo American relationships have been shaped by the vast differences in culture, values, and norms between the two groups. These differences have hampered communication in the past and continue to do so in the present. A comprehensive analysis of American Indian cultures is well beyond the scope of this text, but the past experiences and present goals of the group can be appreciated only with some understanding of their views of the world.

We must note here, as we did in chapter 3, that there were (and are) hundreds of different tribes in what is now the United States, each with its own language and heritage, and that a complete analysis of American Indian culture would have to take this diversity into account. However, some patterns and cultural characteristics are widely shared across the tribes, and we will concentrate on these similarities.

Before exploring the content of their culture, we should note that most Native American tribes that existed in what is now the United States relied on hunting and gathering to satisfy their basic needs, although some cultivated gardens as well. This is important because, as noted by Lenski (see chapter 1), societies are profoundly shaped by their subsistence technology.

Hunting-and-gathering societies often survive on the thin edge of hunger and want. They endure because they stress cultural values such as sharing and cooperation and because they maintain strong bonds of cohesion and solidarity. As you will see, American Indian societies are no exception to this fundamental survival strategy.

The relatively lower level of development of American Indians is reflected in what is perhaps their most obvious difference with Western cultures: their ideas about the relationship between human beings and the natural world. In the traditional view of many American Indian cultures, the universe is a unity. Humans are simply a part of a larger reality, no different from or more important than other animals, plants, trees, and the Earth itself. The goal of many American Indian tribes was to live in harmony with the natural world, not "improve" it, or use it for their own selfish purposes, views that differ sharply from Western concepts of development, commercial farming, and bending the natural world to the service of humans. The gap between the two world-views is evident in the reaction of one American Indian to the idea that his people should become farmers: "You ask me to plow the ground. . . . Shall I take a knife and tear my mother's bosom? You ask me to cut grass and make hay . . . but how dare I cut my mother's hair?" (Brown, 1970, p. 273).

The concept of private property, or the ownership of things, was not prominent in American Indian cultures and was, from the Anglo American perspective, most notably absent in conceptions of land ownership. The land simply existed, and the notion of owning, selling, or buying it was foreign to American Indians. In the words of Tecumseh, a chief of the Shawnee, a man could no more sell the land than the "sea or the air he breathed" (Josephy, 1968, p. 283).

As is typical at the hunting-and-gathering level of development, American Indian cultures and societies also tended to be more oriented toward groups (e.g., the extended family, clan, or tribe) than toward individuals. The interests of the self were subordinated to those of the group, and child-rearing practices strongly encouraged group loyalty (Parke & Buriel, 2002). Cooperative, group activities were stressed over those of a competitive, individualistic nature. The bond to the group was (and is) so strong that "students go hungry rather than ask their parents for lunch money, for in asking they would be putting their needs in front of the group's needs" (Locust, 1990, p. 231).

Many American Indian tribes were organized around egalitarian values that stressed the dignity and worth of every man, woman, and child. Virtually all tribes had a division of labor based on gender, but women's work was valued, and women often occupied far more important positions in tribal society than was typical for women in Anglo American society. In many of the American Indian societies that practiced gardening, women controlled the land. In other tribes, women wielded considerable power and held the most important political and religious offices. Among the Iroquois, for example, a council of older women appointed the chief of the tribe and made decisions about when to wage war (Amott & Matthaei, 1991, pp. 34–35).

These differences in values, compounded by the power differentials that emerged, often placed American Indians at a disadvantage when dealing with the dominant group. The American Indians' conception of land ownership and their lack of experience with deeds, titles, contracts, and other Western legal concepts often made it difficult for them to defend their resources from Anglo Americans. At other times, cultural differences led to disruptions of traditional practices, further weakening American Indian societies. For example, Christian missionaries and government representatives tried to reverse the traditional American Indian division of labor, in which women were responsible for the gardening. In the Western view, only males did farm work. Also, the military and political representatives of the dominant society usually ignored female tribal leaders and imposed Western notions of patriarchy and male leadership on the tribes (Amott & Matthaei, 1991, p. 39).

Relations with the Federal Government after the 1890s

By the end of the Indian wars in 1890, Americans Indians had few resources with which to defend their self-interests. In addition to being confined to reservations, most American Indian groups were scattered throughout the western two-thirds of the United States and split by cultural and linguistic differences. Politically, the power of the group was further limited by the facts that the huge majority of American Indians were not U.S. citizens and that most tribes lacked a cultural basis for understanding representative democracy as practiced in the larger society.

Economically, American Indians were among the most impoverished groups in the United States. Reservation lands were generally of poor quality, traditional food sources such as buffalo and other game had been destroyed, and traditional hunting grounds and gardening plots had been lost to white farmers and ranchers. The tribes had few means of satisfying even their most basic needs. Many became totally dependent on the federal government for food, shelter, clothing, and other necessities.

Prospects for improvement seemed slim. Most reservations were in remote areas, far from sites of industrialization and modernization, and American Indians had few of the skills (knowledge of English, familiarity with Western work habits and routines) that would have enabled them to compete for a place in the increasingly urban and industrial American society of the early 20th century. Off the reservations, racial prejudice and strong intolerance limited them. On the reservations, they were subjected to policies designed either to maintain their powerlessness and poverty or to force them to Americanize. Either way, the future of American Indians was in serious jeopardy, and their destructive relations with white society continued in peace as they had in war.

Reservation Life

As would be expected for a conquered and still hostile group, the reservations were intended to closely supervise American Indians and maintain their powerlessness. Relationships with the federal government were paternalistic and featured a variety of policies designed to coercively acculturate the tribes.

Paternalism and the Bureau of Indian Affairs

The reservations were run not by the tribes, but by an agency of the federal government: the U.S. **Bureau of Indian Affairs (BIA)** of the U.S. Department of the Interior. The BIA and its local superintendent controlled virtually all aspects of everyday life, including the reservation budget, the criminal justice system, and the schools. The BIA (again, not the tribes) even determined tribal membership.

The traditional leadership structures and political institutions of the tribes were ignored as the BIA executed its duties with little regard for, and virtually no input from, the people it supervised. The BIA superintendent of the reservations "ordinarily became the most powerful influence on local Indian affairs, even though he was a government employee, not responsible to the Indians but to his superiors in Washington" (Spicer, 1980, p. 117). The superintendent controlled the food supply and communications to the world outside the reservation. This control was used to reward tribal members who cooperated and to punish those who did not.

Coercive Acculturation: The Dawes Act and Boarding Schools

Consistent with the Blauner hypothesis, American Indians on the reservations were subjected to coercive acculturation or forced Americanization. Their culture was attacked, their languages and religions were forbidden, and their institutions were circumvented and undermined. The centerpiece of U.S. Indian policy was the Dawes Allotment Act of 1887, a deeply flawed attempt to impose white definitions of land ownership and to transform American Indians into independent farmers by dividing their land among the families of each tribe. The intention of the act was to give each Indian family the means to survive like their white neighbors.

Although the law might seem benevolent in intent (certainly thousands of immigrant families would have been thrilled to own land), it was flawed by a gross lack of understanding of American Indian cultures and needs, and in many ways it was a direct attack on those cultures. Most American Indian tribes did not have a strong agrarian tradition, and little or nothing was done to prepare the tribes for their transition to peasant yeomanry. More important, American Indians had little or no concept of land as private property, and it was relatively easy for settlers, land speculators, and others to separate Indian families from the land allocated to them by this legislation. By allotting land to families and individuals, the legislation sought to destroy the broader kinship, clan, and tribal social structures and replace them with Western systems that featured individualism and the profit motive (Cornell, 1988, p. 80).

About 140 million acres were allocated to the tribes in 1887. By the 1930s, the tribes had lost nearly 90 million of those acres—almost 65%. Most of the remaining land was desert or otherwise nonproductive (Wax, 1971, p. 55). From the standpoint of the Indian Nations, the Dawes Allotment Act was a disaster and a further erosion of their already paltry store of resources. (For more details, see Josephy, 1968; Lurie, 1982; McNickle, 1973; and Wax, 1971.)

Coercive acculturation also operated through a variety of other avenues. Whenever possible, the BIA sent American Indian children to boarding schools, sometimes hundreds of miles away from parents and kin, where they were required to speak English, convert to Christianity, and become educated in the ways of Western civilization. Consistent with the Blauner (1972) hypothesis, tribal languages, dress, and religion were forbidden, and to the extent that native cultures were mentioned at all, they were attacked and ridiculed. Children of different tribes were mixed together as roommates to speed the acquisition of English. When school was not in session, children were often boarded with local white families, usually as unpaid domestic helpers or farmhands, and prevented from visiting their families and revitalizing their tribal ties (Hoxie, 1984; Spicer, 1980; Wax, 1971).

American Indians were virtually powerless to change the reservation system or avoid the campaign of acculturation. Nonetheless, they resented and resisted coerced Americanization, and many languages and cultural elements survived the early reservation period, although often in altered form. For example, the traditional tribal religions remained vital through the period, despite the fact that by the 1930s the great majority of Indians had affiliated with one Christian denomination or another. Furthermore, many new religions were founded, some combining Christian and traditional elements (Spicer, 1980, p. 118).

The Indian Reorganization Act

By the 1930s, the failure of the reservation system and the policy of forced assimilation had become obvious to all who cared to observe. The quality of life for American Indians had not improved, and there was little economic development and fewer job opportunities on the reservations. Health care was woefully inadequate, and education levels lagged far behind national standards.

The plight of American Indians eventually found a sympathetic ear in the administration of Franklin D. Roosevelt, who was elected president in 1932, and John Collier, the man he appointed to run the BIA. Collier was knowledgeable about American Indian issues and concerns and was instrumental in securing the passage of the **Indian Reorganization Act (IRA)** in 1934.

This landmark legislation contained a number of significant provisions for American Indians and broke sharply with the federal policies of the past. In particular, the IRA rescinded the Dawes Act of 1887 and the policy of individualizing tribal lands. It also provided means by which the tribes could expand their landholdings. Many of the mechanisms of coercive Americanization in the school system and elsewhere were dismantled. Financial aid in various forms and expertise were made available for the economic development of the reservations. In perhaps the most significant departure from earlier policy, the IRA proposed an increase in American Indian self-governance and a reduction of the paternalistic role of the BIA and other federal agencies.

Although sympathetic to American Indians, the IRA had its limits and shortcomings. Many of its intentions were never realized, and the empowerment of the tribes was not unqualified. The move to self-governance generally took place on the dominant group's terms and in conformity with the values and practices of white society. For example, the proposed increase in the decision-making power of the tribes was contingent on their adoption of Anglo American political forms, including secret ballots, majority rule, and written constitutions. These were alien concepts to those tribes that selected leaders by procedures other than popular election (e.g., leaders might be chosen by councils of elders) or that made decisions by open discussion and consensus building (i.e., decisions required the agreement of everyone with a voice in the process, not a simple majority). The incorporation of these Western forms illustrates the basically assimilationist intent of the IRA.

The IRA had variable effects on American Indian women. In tribes that were male dominated, the IRA gave women new rights to participate in elections, run for office, and hold leadership roles. In other cases, new political structures replaced traditional forms, some of which, as in the Iroquois culture, had accorded women considerable power. Although the political effects were variable, the programs funded by the IRA provided opportunities for women on many reservations to receive education and training for the first time. Many of these opportunities were oriented toward domestic tasks and other traditionally Western female roles, but some prepared American Indian women for jobs outside the family and off the reservation, such as clerical work and nursing (Evans, 1989, pp. 208–209).

In summary, the Indian Reorganization Act (IRA) of 1934 was a significant improvement over prior federal Indian policy, but was bolder and more sympathetic to American Indians in intent than in execution. On the one hand, not all tribes were capable of taking advantage of the opportunities provided by the legislation, and some ended up being further victimized. For example, in the Hopi tribe, located in the Southwest, the Act allowed a Westernized group of American Indians to be elected to leadership roles, with the result that dominant group firms were allowed to have access to the mineral resources, farmland, and water rights controlled by the tribe. The resultant development generated wealth for the white firms and their Hopi allies, not for the tribe: most Hopi continued to languish in poverty (Churchill, 1985, pp. 112–113). On the other hand, some tribes prospered (at least comparatively speaking) under the IRA. One impoverished, landless group of Cherokee in Oklahoma acquired land, equipment, and expert advice through the IRA, and between 1937 and 1949 they developed a prosperous, largely debt-free farming community (Debo, 1970, pp. 294–300). Many tribes remained suspicious of the IRA, and by 1948 fewer than 100 tribes had voted to accept its provisions.

The Termination Policy

The IRA's stress on the legitimacy of tribal identity seemed "un-American" to many. There was constant pressure on the federal government to return to an individualistic policy that encouraged (or required) Americanization. Some viewed the tribal structures and communal-property-holding patterns as relics of an earlier era and as impediments to modernization and development. Not so incidentally, some elements of dominant society still coveted the remaining Indian lands and resources, which could be more easily exploited if property ownership were individualized.

In 1953, the assimilationist forces won a victory when Congress passed a resolution calling for an end to the reservation system and to the special relationships between the tribes and the federal government. The proposed policy, called **termination**, was intended to get the federal government "out of the Indian business." It rejected the IRA and proposed a return to the system of private land ownership imposed on the tribes by the Dawes Act.

Horrified at the notion of termination, the tribes opposed the policy strongly and vociferously. Under this policy, all special relationships—including treaty obligations—between the federal government and the tribes would end. Tribes would no longer exist as legally recognized entities, and tribal lands and other resources would be placed in private hands (Josephy, 1968, pp. 353–355).

About 100 tribes, most of them small, were terminated. In virtually all cases, the termination process was administered hastily, and fraud, misuse of funds, and other injustices were common. The Menominee of Wisconsin and the Klamath on the West Coast were the two largest tribes to be terminated. Both suffered devastating economic losses and precipitous declines in quality of life. Neither tribe had the business or tax base needed to finance the services (e.g., health care and schooling) formerly provided by the federal government, and both were forced to sell land, timber, and other scarce resources to maintain minimal standards of living. Many poor American Indian families were forced to turn to local and state agencies, which placed a severe strain on welfare budgets. The experience of these two tribes was so disastrous that they requested the restoration of their reservation status. The Menominee reservation was restored in 1973 and the Klamath in 1986 (Raymer, 1974; Snipp, 1996, p. 394).

Relocation and Urbanization

At about the same time the termination policy came into being, various programs were established to encourage American Indians to move to urban areas. The movement to the city had already begun in the 1940s, spurred by the availability of factory jobs during World War II. In the 1950s, the movement was further encouraged with programs of assistance and by the declining government support for economic development on the reservation, the most dramatic example of which was the policy of termination (Green, 1999, p. 265). Centers for American Indians were established in many cities, and various services (e.g., job training, housing assistance, English instruction) were offered to assist in the adjustment to urban life. The urbanization of the American Indian population is displayed in exhibit 6.3. Note the rapid increase in the movement to the city that began in the 1950s. Almost 60% of all American Indians are now urbanized, and since 1950 Indians have urbanized faster than the general population. Nevertheless, American Indians are still the least urbanized minority group. The American population as a whole is about 80% urbanized; in contrast, African Americans (see exhibit 4.3) are about 90% urbanized.

Exhibit 6.3   Urbanization of American Indians, 1900–2000

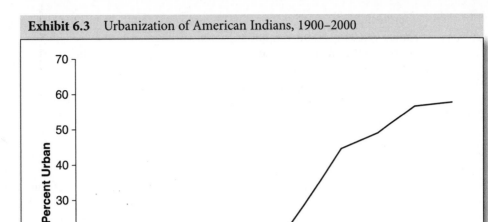

Source: 1900–1990: Thornton (2001, p. 142); 2000: U.S. Census Bureau (2000).

As with African Americans, American Indians arrived in the cities after the mainstream economy had begun to deemphasize blue-collar or manufacturing jobs. Because of their relatively low average levels of educational attainment and their racial and cultural differences, American Indians in the city tended to encounter the same problems experienced by African Americans and other minority groups of color: high rates of unemployment, inadequate housing, and all the other travails of the urban underclass.

American Indian women also migrated to the city in considerable numbers. The discrimination, unemployment, and poverty of the urban environment often made it difficult for the men of the group to fulfill the role of breadwinner, thus the burden of supporting the family tended to fall on the women. The difficulties inherent in combining child rearing and a job outside the home are compounded by isolation from the support networks provided by extended family and clan back on the reservations. Nevertheless, one study found that American Indian women in the city continue to practice their traditional cultures and maintain the tribal identity of their children (Joe & Miller, 1994, p. 186).

American Indians living in the city are, on average, better off than those living on reservations, where unemployment can reach 80% or even 90%. The improvement is relative, however. Although many individual Indians prosper in the urban environment, income figures for urban Indians as a whole are comparable to those for African Americans and well below those for whites. American Indian unemployment rates run much higher than the national average. For example, in the first half of 2010 unemployment for all American Indians was about 15%, comparable to African Americans (see exhibit 5.3) and 67% higher than that for whites (Austin, 2010). Thus, a move to the city often means trading rural poverty for the urban variety, with little net improvement in life chances.

American Indians will probably remain more rural than other minority groups for years to come. Despite the poverty and lack of opportunities for schooling and jobs, the reservation offers some advantages in services and lifestyle. On the reservation, there may be opportunities for political participation and leadership roles that are not available in the cities, where American Indians are a tiny minority. Reservations also offer kinfolk, friends, religious services, and tribal celebrations (Snipp, 1989, p. 84). Lower levels of education, work experience, and financial resources combine with the prejudice, discrimination, and racism of the larger society to lower the chances of success in the city, and will probably sustain a continuing return to the reservations.

Although the economic benefits of urbanization have been slim for the group as whole, other advantages have accrued from life in the city. It is much easier to establish networks of friendship and affiliation across tribal lines in the cities, and urban Indians have been one of the sources of strength and personnel for a movement of protest that began early in the 20th century. Virtually all the organizational vehicles of American Indian protest have had urban roots.

Self-Determination

The termination policy aroused so much opposition from American Indians and was such an obvious disaster that the pressure to push tribes to termination faded in the late 1950s, although the act itself was not repealed until 1975. Since the 1960s, federal Indian policy has generally returned to the tradition set by the IRA. Termination and forced assimilation continue to be officially rejected, and, within limits, the tribes have been granted more freedom to find their own way, at their own pace, of relating to the larger society.

Several federal programs and laws have benefited the tribes during the past few decades, including the antipoverty and Great Society campaigns launched in the 1960s. In 1970, President Richard Nixon affirmed the government's commitment to fulfilling treaty obligations and the right of the tribes to self-governance. The Indian Self-Determination and Education Assistance Act was passed in 1975. This legislation increased aid to reservation schools and American Indian students and increased tribal control over the administration of the reservations, from police forces to schools to road maintenance.

The Self-Determination Act primarily benefited the larger tribes and those that had well-established administrative and governing structures. Smaller and less-well-organized tribes have continued to rely heavily on the federal government (Snipp, 1996, p. 394). Nonetheless, in many cases this new phase of federal policy has allowed American Indian tribes to plot their own courses free of paternalistic regulation, and, just as important, it has given them the tools and resources to address their problems and improve their situations. Decision making was returned to local authorities, who were "held more accountable to local needs, conditions, and cultures than outsiders" (J. Taylor & Kalt, 2005, p. xi).

In the view of many, self-determination is a key reason for the recent improvements in the status of American Indians, and we will look at some of these developments after examining the American Indian protest movement.

Protest and Resistance

Early Efforts

As BIA-administered reservations and coercive Americanization came to dominate tribal life in the 20th century, new forms of Indian activism appeared. The modern protest movement was tiny at first and, with few exceptions, achieved a measure of success only in recent decades. In fact, the American Indian protest movement in the past was not so much unsuccessful as simply ignored. The movement has focused on several complementary goals: protecting American Indian resources and treaty rights, striking a balance between assimilation and pluralism, and finding a relationship with the dominant group that would permit a broader array of life chances without sacrificing tribal identity and heritage.

Formally organized American Indian protest organizations have existed since the 1910s, but the modern phase of the protest movement began during World War II. Many American Indians served in the military or moved to the city to take jobs in aid of the war effort and were thereby exposed to the world beyond the reservation. Also, political activism on the reservation, which had been stimulated by the IRA, continued through the war years, as did American Indians' recognition that many problems were shared across tribal lines grew.

These trends helped stimulate the founding of the National Congress of American Indians (NCAI) in 1944. This organization was pan-tribal (i.e., included members from many different tribes); its first convention was attended by representatives of 50 different tribes and reservations (Cornell, 1988, p. 119). The leadership consisted largely of American Indians educated and experienced in the white world. However, the NCAI's program stressed the importance of preserving the old ways and tribal institutions as well as protecting Indian welfare. An early victory for the NCAI and its allies came in 1946 when the federal government created an Indian Claims Commission. This body was authorized to hear claims brought by the tribes with regard to treaty violations. The commission has settled hundreds of claims, resulting in awards of millions of dollars to the tribes (Weeks, 1988, pp. 261–262).

In the 1950s and 1960s, the protest movement was further stimulated by the threat of termination and by the increasing number of American Indians living in the cities who developed friendships across tribal lines. Awareness of common problems, rising levels of education, and the examples set by the successful protests of other minority groups also increased readiness for collective action.

Red Power

By the 1960s and 1970s, American Indian protest groups were finding ways to express their grievances and problems to the nation. The Red Power movement, like the

Black Power movement (see chapter 5), encompassed a coalition of groups, many considerably more assertive than the NCAI, and a varied collection of ideas, most of which stressed self-determination and pride in race and cultural heritage. Red Power protests included a "fish-in" in Washington State in 1965, an episode that also illustrates the nature of American Indian demands. The State of Washington had tried to limit the fishing rights of several different tribes on the grounds that the supply of fish was diminishing and needed to be protected. The tribes depended on fishing for subsistence and survival and argued that their right to fish had been guaranteed by treaties signed in the 1850s, and that it was the pollution and commercial fishing of the dominant society that had depleted the supply of fish. They organized a "fish-in" in violation of the state's policy and were met by a contingent of police officers and other law officials. Violent confrontations and mass arrests ensued. Three years later, after a lengthy and expensive court battle, the tribes were vindicated, and the U.S. Supreme Court confirmed their treaty rights to fish the rivers of Washington State (Nabakov, 1999, pp. 362–363).

Another widely publicized episode took place in 1969, when American Indians from various tribes occupied Alcatraz Island in San Francisco Bay, the site of a closed federal prison. The protesters were acting on a law that granted American Indians the right to reclaim abandoned federal land. The occupation of Alcatraz was organized in part by the American Indian Movement (AIM), founded in 1968. More militant and radical than the previously established protest groups, AIM aggressively confronted the BIA, the police, and other forces that were seen as repressive. With the backing of AIM and other groups, Alcatraz was occupied for nearly 4 years and generated a great deal of publicity for the Red Power movement and the plight of American Indians.

In 1972, AIM helped organize a march on Washington, DC, called the Trail of Broken Treaties. Marchers came from many tribes and represented both urban and reservation Indians. The intent of the marchers was to dramatize the problems of the tribes. The leaders demanded the abolition of the BIA, the return of illegally taken land, and increased self-governance for the tribes, among other things. When they reached Washington, some of the marchers forcibly occupied the BIA offices. Property was damaged (by which side is disputed), and records and papers were destroyed. The marchers eventually surrendered, but none of their demands was met. The following year, AIM occupied the village of Wounded Knee in South Dakota to protest the violation of treaty rights. Wounded Knee was the site in 1890 of the last armed confrontation between Indians and whites and was selected by AIM for its deep symbolic significance. The occupation lasted more than two months and involved several armed confrontations with federal authorities. Again, the protest ended without achieving any of the demands made by the Indian leadership (Olson & Wilson, 1984, pp. 172–175). Since the early 1970s, the level of protest activity has declined, just as it has for the African American protest movement. Lawsuits and court cases have predominated over dramatic, direct confrontations.

Ironically, the struggle for Red Power encouraged assimilation as well as pluralism. The movement linked members of different tribes and forced Indians of diverse heritages to find common ground, often in the form of a generic American Indian culture. Inevitably, the protests were conducted in English, and the grievances were expressed in ways that were understandable to white society, thus increasing the pressure to acculturate even while arguing for the survival of the tribes. Furthermore, successful protest required that American Indians be fluent in English, trained in the law and other professions, skilled in dealing with bureaucracies, and knowledgeable about the formulation and execution of public policy. American Indians who became proficient in these areas thereby took on the characteristics of their adversaries (Hraba, 1979, p. 235).

As the pan-tribal protest movement forged ties between members of diverse tribes, the successes of the movement and changing federal policy and public opinion encouraged a rebirth of commitment to tribalism and "Indianness." American Indians were simultaneously stimulated to assimilate (by stressing their common characteristics and creating organizational forms that united the tribes) and to retain a pluralistic relationship with the larger society (by working for self-determination and enhanced tribal power and authority). Thus, part of the significance of the Red Power movement was that it encouraged both pan-tribal unity and a continuation of tribal diversity (Olson & Wilson, 1984, p. 206). Today, American Indians continue to seek a way of existing in the larger society that merges assimilation with pluralism.

Exhibit 6.4 summarizes this discussion of federal policy and Indian protest. The four major policy phases since the end of overt hostilities in 1890 are listed on the left.

Exhibit 6.4 Federal Indian Policy and Indian Response

Period	Economic Impact	Political Impact	Indian Response	Government Approach
Reservation late 1800s–1930s	Land loss (Dawes Act) and welfare dependency	Government control of reservation and coerced acculturation	Some resistance; growth of religious movements	Individualistic; creation of self-sufficient farmers
Reorganization (IRA) 1930s and 1940s	Stabilized land base and supported some development of reservation	Establish federally-sponsored tribal governments	Increased political participation in many tribes; some pan-tribal activity	Incorporated tribes as groups; creation of self-sufficient "Americanized" communities
Termination and relocation late 1940s–early 1960s	Withdrawal of government support for reservations. promotion of urbanization	New assault on tribes, new forms of coercive acculturation	Increased pan-tribalism; widespread and intense opposition to termination	Individualistic; dissolved tribal ties and promoted incorporation into the modern, urban labor market
Self-determination 1960s to present	Developed reservation economies; increased integration of Indian labor force	Support for tribal governments	Greatly increased political activity	Incorporated tribes as self-sufficient communities with access to federal programs of support and welfare

Source: From *American Indian Gaming Policy and Its Socio-Economic Effect: A Report to the National Impact Gambling Study Commission* by Stephen Cornell, Joseph Kalt, Matthew Krepps, and Jonathan Taylor. Copyright © July 31, 1998. Reprinted with permission.

The thrust of the government's economic and political policies are listed in the next two columns, followed by a brief characterization of tribal response. The last column shows the changing bases for federal policy, sometimes aimed at weakening tribal structures and individualizing American Indians, and sometimes (including most recently) aimed at working with and preserving tribal structures.

FOCUS ON CONTEMPORARY ISSUES:
Were American Indians the Victims of Genocide?

By 1900, American Indians had lost at least 75% of their population base and numbered fewer than 250,000 people. There is no question that American Indians suffered untold horrors during the contact period (and inflicted horrors of their own), but should this be classified as genocide? Was there a deliberate attempt to destroy American Indians and their culture or was the population loss simply a sad, unavoidable result of a clash of civilizations?

We should begin by defining what is meant by genocide. According to a resolution adopted by the United Nations in 1948, genocide consists of acts "committed with the intent to destroy, in whole or in part, a national, ethnic, racial, or religious group" (United Nations, 1948). Genocide includes actions other than outright killing: inflicting serious bodily or mental harm or creating conditions of life designed to cause the destruction of the group are also included within the definition of the crime.

Some of our core concepts are applicable to this discussion. Genocide almost always involves a dominant-minority group situation and the victimized group is regarded with contempt, racism, and extreme prejudice. Also, power, one of the concepts in the Noel hypothesis, is a key element in genocide; the dominant group must have sufficient power resources to attempt the mass extermination of the minority group.

Before addressing American Indians, let's briefly consider some well-known historical examples of genocide to provide some comparison and context. Unfortunately, there are many instances from which to draw.

The most infamous example of genocide was the effort of German Nazis to exterminate Jews, Slavs, Gypsies, and other "inferior" groups before and during World War II. Millions of people, including 6 million Jews, were systematically slaughtered in the Nazi death camps. This massive, highly bureaucratized, and rationally organized genocide was motivated and "justified" by deep racism and anti-Semitism. Nazi ideology demonized Jews and pictured them as a separate, lower, contemptible race that had to be destroyed for the good of all "proper" Germans and for the health for the Third Reich.

A more recent episode of genocide occurred in the tiny African nation of Rwanda in the early 1990s. The two main Rwandan ethnic groups, Hutus and the Tutsis, had a long history of mutual enmity that had been exacerbated by their German and Belgian colonial ruler's policy of "divide and conquer." The colonizers had given the Hutus a privileged status and their greater power continued after Rwanda became independent in 1962. The sporadic clashes between the tribal groups blossomed into full-blown genocide in 1994, occasioned by a Tutsi-led rebellion and the death of the Hutu president of Rwanda in a plane crash that was thought to have been the result of sabotage and Tutsi treachery.

The slaughter that ensued resulted in the deaths of perhaps 800,000 Tutsis, perhaps many more. No one was spared—not even pregnant women, children, and old people—and much of the killing was done by neighbors and acquaintances with bare hands or machetes. The killing was encouraged by Hutu-controlled radio, which characterized the Tutsi as "cockroaches" and worse (see Gourevitch, 1999). Insults such as these express the prejudice and contempt of the dominant group, but they also abet the slaughter by minimizing the humanity of the victimized group and maximizing their perceived lower status and "otherness."

How does the history of American Indians compare? First, note that international law specifies that acts of genocide must be intentional (United Nations, 1948). The Nazis clearly and openly intended to carry out their "final solution" and exterminate the Jewish people, and the Hutus that led the Rwandan genocide meant to annihilate their Tutsi neighbors. What was the intent of whites with regard to Indians? To be classified as genocide, there must be an intention to exterminate the group as a whole (as opposed to killing enemy combatants in battle).

It is not difficult to find statements that show that some whites clearly wanted to eliminate American Indians. One famous incident can be used to illustrate: In 1864, troops under the command of Colonel John Chivington attacked a Cheyenne village near Sand Creek, Colorado, and killed several hundred Indians, most of them women, children, and old men. The incident is sometimes called the Battle of Sand Creek and sometimes the Massacre at Sand Creek, but what makes it a candidate for genocide is Chivington's motivation as revealed in the following quotations: "My intention is to kill all Indians I come across," including babies and infants because "nits make lice" (Churchill, 1985, p. 229).

However, it is also easy to find white expressions of sympathy for the plight of the Indians and outrage over incidents such as Sand Creek (Lewy, 2004). As many have noted, sympathy for American Indians in the 19th century tended to be most intense in the areas farthest removed from actual battle. Nevertheless, there is no reason to suspect their sincerity (although, as in the case of the Dawes Act, sympathy unalloyed by understanding of Indian culture could have harmful consequences). While it is abundantly clear that some—perhaps many, perhaps most—whites wanted to exterminate all Indians, the sentiment was not universal or unanimous. Certainly, the intent to destroy American Indians was not universal among whites. We also must take account of the reasons for the population loss. Recall that much of the population decline was caused

(Continued)

(Continued)

by the diseases imported by European colonists, not by deliberate attacks. While there were a few instances of "biological warfare" in which Indians were deliberately infected with smallpox, for the most part the diseases simply took their toll unguided by intention or deliberate plan (Lewy, 2004).

Some argue that the intent to exterminate was implicit in the coercive, one-sided assimilation that was the centerpiece of policies such as the Dawes Act and institutions such as the Indian boarding schools. If these policies had succeeded, the American Indian way of life would have been destroyed, even though individual descendants of the tribes might have survived. Also, the deliberate attempts to destroy the Indian food base (e.g., by slaughtering buffalo herds on the Great Plains) and to move Indian tribes from their homelands, and the poor support for reservations could be seen as attempts to create living conditions so desperate and impoverished that they would result in massive loss of life and the disappearance of the group. The intention to exterminate does not have to be overtly stated to be effective or to have that result.

We want to be careful in applying a term like "genocide" and not dilute its power by overuse. We also want to be clear about what actually happened to Indians and not minimize the horror or loss. Was this genocide? Certainly, it looks like genocide, and various authors, scholars, and activists have made that case (see, for example, Churchill, 1997; and Stannard, 1992). Others acknowledge the enormous suffering but argue that the case for genocide is weakened by the fact that most of the population loss was caused by the impersonal spread of disease, not by direct violence or physical assaults (Lewy, 2004).

What would a jury decide? Did American Indians nearly disappear as a group? Yes. Was there intent to exterminate this group? Yes, at least in many members of the dominant group. Did the U.S. government create conditions for the conquered tribes that were so desperate that they resulted—directly or indirectly—in widespread loss of life? Yes, in many instances and for many years. The story of American Indians doesn't feature state-sponsored slaughter like the Nazi Holocaust or the bloody person-to-person violence of Hutus killing Tutsis. Perhaps this was not an instance of genocide by the literal letter of the law. The results for this conquered and colonized group, however, are the same.

The Continuing Struggle for Development in Contemporary American Indian–White Relations

Conflicts between American Indians and the larger society are far from over. Although the days of deadly battle are (with occasional exceptions) long gone, the issues that remain are serious, difficult to resolve, and, in their way, just as much matters of life and death. American Indians face enormous challenges in their struggle to improve their status, but, largely as a result of their greater freedom from stifling federal control since the 1970s, they also have some resources, some opportunities, and a leadership that is both talented and resourceful (Bordewich, 1996, p. 11).

Natural Resources

Ironically, land allotted to American Indian tribes in the 19th century sometimes turned out to be rich in resources that became valuable in the 20th century. These resources include oil, natural gas, coal, and uranium, highly valued sources of energy in the larger society. In addition (and despite the devastation wreaked by the Dawes Act of 1887), some tribes hold title to water rights, fishing rights, woodlands that could sustain a lumbering industry, and wilderness areas that could be developed for camping, hunting, and other forms of recreation. These resources are likely to become more valuable as the Earth's natural resources and undeveloped areas are further depleted in the future.

The challenge faced by American Indians is to retain control of these resources and to develop them for their own benefit. Threats to the remaining tribal lands and assets are common. Mining and energy companies continue to cast envious eyes on American Indian land, and other tribal assets are coveted by real estate developers, fishers (recreational as well as commercial), backpackers and campers, and cities facing water shortages (Harjo, 1996).

Some tribes have succeeded in developing their resources for their own benefit, in part because of their increased autonomy and independence since the passage of the 1975 Indian Self-Determination Act. For example, the White Mountain Apaches of Arizona own a variety of enterprises, including a major ski resort and a casino. (See the tribe's website at http://www.wmat.nsn.us/.) On many other reservations, however, even rich stores of resources lie dormant, awaiting the right combination of tribal leadership, expertise, and development capital.

On a broader level, tribes are banding together to share expertise and negotiate more effectively with the larger society. For example, 25 tribes founded the Council of Energy Resource Tribes in 1975 to coordinate and control the development of the mineral resources on reservation lands. Since its founding, the Council has successfully negotiated a number of agreements with dominant group firms, increasing the flow of income to the tribes and raising their quality of life (Cornell, 1988; Snipp, 1989). The Council now encompasses more than 50 tribes and several Canadian First Nations (see their website at http://74.63.154.129/aboutus-philosophyHistory.html for more information).

Attracting Industry to the Reservation

Many efforts to develop the reservations have focused on creating jobs by attracting industry through such incentives as low taxes, low rents, and a low-wage pool of labor—not unlike the package of benefits offered to employers by less-developed nations in Asia, South America, and Africa. With some notable exceptions, these efforts have not been particularly successful (for a review, see Cornell, 2006; and Vinje, 1996). Reservations are often so geographically isolated that transportation costs become prohibitive. The jobs that have materialized are typically low wage and have few benefits; usually, non-Indians fill the more lucrative managerial positions. Thus, the opportunities for building economic power or improving the standard of living from these jobs are sharply limited. These new jobs may transform "the welfare poor into the working poor" (Snipp, 1996, p. 398), but their potential for raising economic vitality is low.

To illustrate the problems of developing reservations by attracting industry, consider the Navajo, the second-largest American Indian tribe (exhibit 6.5). The Navajo reservation spreads across Arizona, New Mexico, and Utah, and encompasses about 20 million acres, an area a little smaller than either Indiana or Maine (exhibit 6.5). Although the reservation seems huge on a map, much of the land is desert and not suitable for farming or other uses. As they have for the past several centuries, the Navajo today rely heavily on the cultivation of corn and sheepherding for sustenance.

Most wage-earning jobs on the reservation are with the agencies of the federal government (e.g., the BIA) or with the tribal government. Tourism is large but the jobs available in that sector are typically low wage and seasonal. There are reserves of coal, uranium, and oil on the reservation, but these resources have not generated many jobs. In some cases, the Navajo have resisted the damage to the environment that would be caused by mines and oil wells because of their traditional values and respect for the land. When exploitation of these resources has been permitted, the companies involved

Exhibit 6.5 Map of Navajo Reservation

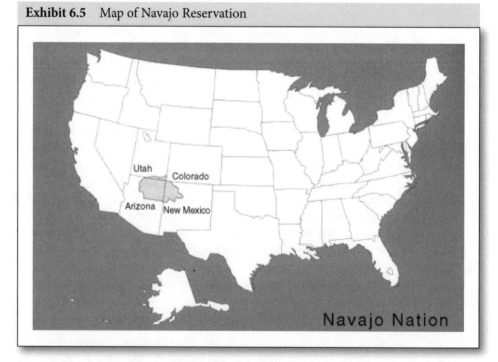

Source: Independent Television Service, Inc., "Companion website for the documentary film, 'Miss Navajo.'" Public Broadcasting Service - Independent Lens (ITVS Interactive), http://www.pbs.org/independentlens/missnavajo/navajo.html. Text written by Lisa Ko.

often use highly automated technologies that generate few jobs (Oswalt & Neely, 1996, pp. 317–351).

Exhibits 6.6 and 6.7 contrast Navajo income, poverty, and education with those for non-Hispanic whites. The poverty rate for the Navajo is about three times greater than the rate for non-Hispanic whites and they are far below national standards in terms of education. Educational achievement is even lower for members of the tribe living on the reservation, where only about 64% have finished high school (versus 73% of all Navajo) (U.S. Census Bureau, 2010). Also, median household income for the Navajo is less than 60% of household income for non-Hispanic whites.

On the other hand, some tribes have managed to achieve relative prosperity by bringing jobs to their people. The Mississippi Band of Choctaw, for example, is one of the 10 largest employers in the state. Tribal leaders have been able to attract companies such as Xerox and Harley-Davidson by promising (and delivering) high-quality labor for relatively low wages. The tribe runs a variety of business enterprises, including two casinos. Incomes have risen, unemployment is relatively low, and the tribe has built schools, hospitals, and a television station, and administers numerous other services for its members (Bordewich, 1996, pp. 300–305). The poverty rate for the Choctaw is 40% lower than the Navajo rate (although still almost double the rate for non-Hispanic whites), and the tribe's educational levels are much closer to national standards.

Exhibit 6.6 Poverty and Education for Non-Hispanic Whites (NHW), All American Indians (AI), Navajo, and Choctaw

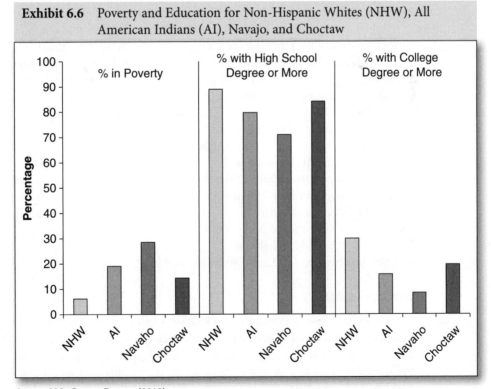

Source: U.S. Census Bureau (2010).

Exhibit 6.7 Median Household Income

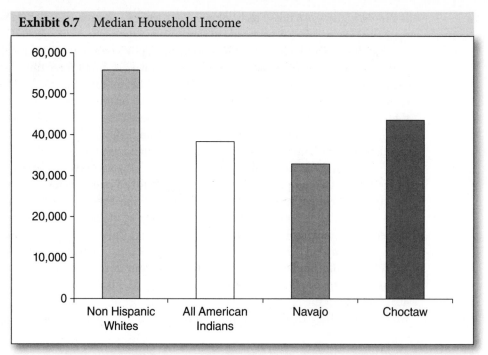

Source: U.S. Census Bureau (2010).

More than 21% of the Choctaw are college educated, more than double the rate for the Navajo. Median household income for the Choctaw is only about 80% of non-Hispanic whites but more than $10,000 greater than median income for the Navajo.

The Choctaw are not the most affluent tribe, and the Navajo are far from being the most destitute. They illustrate the mixture of partial successes and failures that typify efforts to bring prosperity to the reservations; together, these two cases suggest that attracting industry and jobs to the reservations is a possible—but difficult and uncertain—strategy for economic development.

It is worth repeating that self-determination—the ability of tribes to control development on the reservation—seems to be one of the important keys to success. Tribes such as the Choctaw are, in a sense, developing ethnic enclaves (see chapter 2) in which they can capitalize on local networks of interpersonal relationships. As with other groups that have followed this strategy, success in the enclave depends on solidarity and group cohesion, not Americanization and integration (see Cornell, 2006).

Broken Treaties

For many tribes, the treaties signed with the federal government in the 19th century offer another potential resource. These treaties were often violated by white settlers, the military, state and local governments, the BIA, and other elements and agencies of the dominant group, and many tribes are pursuing this trail of broken treaties and seeking compensation for the wrongs of the past. For example, in 1972 the

Passamaquoddy and Penobscot tribes filed a lawsuit demanding the return of 12.5 million acres of land—more than half the state of Maine—and $25 billion in damages. The tribes argued that this land had been illegally taken from them more than 150 years earlier. After 8 years of litigation, the tribes settled for a $25 million trust fund and 300,000 acres of land. Although far less than their original demand, the award gave the tribes control over resources that could be used for economic development, job creation, upgrading educational programs, and developing other programs that would enhance human and financial capital (Worsnop, 1992, p. 391).

Virtually every tribe has similar grievances, and if pursued successfully the long-dead treaty relationship between the Indian nations and the government could be a significant fount of economic and political resources. Of course, lawsuits require considerable (and expensive) legal expertise and years of effort before they bear fruit. Because there are no guarantees of success, this avenue has some sharp limitations and risks.

Gaming and Other Development Possibilities

Another resource for American Indians is the gambling industry, the development of which was made possible by federal legislation passed in 1988. There are currently more than 400 tribally owned gaming establishments (National Indian Gaming Commission, 2012), and the industry has grown many times over, from $212 million in revenues in 1988 (Spilde, 2001) to more than $26 billion in 2010 (National Indian Gaming Commission, 2012). Exhibit 6.8 charts the growth of revenues from gaming

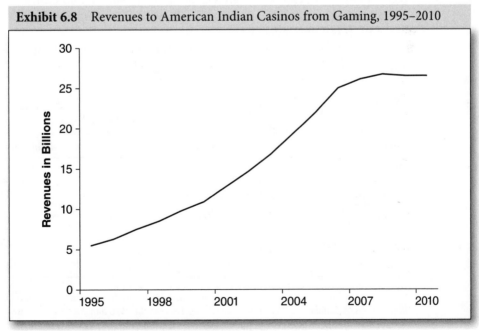

Exhibit 6.8 Revenues to American Indian Casinos from Gaming, 1995–2010

Source: National Indian Gaming Commission (2012).

on American Indian reservations from 1995 to 2010. Revenues have grown more than five times over in this 15-year time frame.

Most operations are relatively small in scale. The 21 largest Indian casinos—about 5% of all Indian casinos—generate almost 40% of the total income from gaming, and the 74 smallest operations—about 18% of all Indian casinos—account for less than 1% of the income (National Indian Gaming Commission, 2012).

The single most profitable Indian gambling operation is the Foxwoods Casino in Connecticut, operated by the Pequot tribe. This casino is one of the largest in the world and generates more revenue than all the casinos of Atlantic City. The profits from the casino are used to benefit tribal members in a variety of ways, including the repurchase of tribal lands, housing assistance, medical benefits, educational scholarships, and public services, such as a tribal police force (Bordewich, 1996, p. 110). Other tribes have used gambling profits to purchase restaurants and marinas and to finance the development of outlet malls, manufacturing plants, and a wide variety of other businesses and enterprises (Spilde, 2001).

The power of gaming to benefit the tribes is suggested by the information displayed in exhibit 6.9. The table shows that on a number of indicators both gaming and nongaming reservations enjoyed significant improvements in their quality of life in the last decade of the 20th century but that gaming reservations improved more rapidly. For example, all reservations increased their per capita income faster than the nation as a whole (+11%), but gaming reservations improved faster (+36%) than nongaming reservations (+21%).

Various tribes have sought other ways to capitalize on their freedom from state regulation and taxes. Some have established small but profitable businesses selling cigarettes tax free. Also, because they are not subject to state and federal environmental regulations, some reservations are exploring the possibility of housing nuclear waste and other refuse of industrialization—a somewhat ironic and not altogether attractive use of the remaining Indian lands.

Clearly, the combination of increased autonomy, treaty rights, natural resources, and gambling means that American Indians today have an opportunity to dramatically

Exhibit 6.9 Various Indicators of Improvement on Gaming vs. Nongaming Reservations and Total United States, 1990–2000

Indicator	Nongaming	Gaming	Total United States
Per capita income	+21%	+36%	+11%
Family poverty	−7%	−12%	−1%
Unemployment	−2%	−5%	−1%
High School Graduates	−1%	+2%	−1%
College Graduates	+2%	+3%	+4%

Source: Adapted from "Changes on Reservations Other Than Navajo," p. xi in *American Indians on Reservations: A Databook of Socioeconomic Change between the 1990 and 2000 Censuses* by Jonathan A. Taylor and Joseph P. Kalt. Copyright © 2005 The Harvard Project on American Indian Economic Development.

raise their standards of living and creatively take control of their own destinies. Some tribes have enjoyed enormous benefits, but for others these assets remain a potential that is waiting to be actualized. Without denying the success stories or the improvements in recent years, the lives of many American Indians continue to be limited by poverty and powerlessness, prejudice, and discrimination. We document these patterns in the next section.

Contemporary American Indian–White Relations

This section uses many of the terms and concepts we have developed over the first five chapters to analyze the contemporary situation of American Indians. Compared with other groups, information about American Indians is scant. Nonetheless, a relatively clear picture emerges. The portrait stresses a mixed picture for this group: improvements for some tribes combined with continued colonization, marginalization, and impoverishment for others. Like African Americans, American Indians can be found at every status and income level, but Indians living on reservations continue as one of the most impoverished, marginalized groups in the United States. American Indians as a group face continuing discrimination and exclusion and continue to search for a meaningful course between assimilation and pluralism.

Prejudice and Discrimination

Anti-Indian prejudice has been a part of American society since first contact. Historically, negative feelings such as hatred and contempt have been widespread and strong, particularly during the heat of war, and various stereotypes of Indians have been common. One stereotype, especially strong during periods of conflict, depicts Indians as bloodthirsty, ferocious, cruel savages capable of any atrocity. The other image of American Indians is that of "the noble Red Man" who lives in complete harmony with nature and symbolizes goodwill and pristine simplicity (Bordewich, 1996, p. 34). Although the first stereotype tended to fade away as hostilities drew to a close, the latter image retains a good deal of strength in modern views of Indians found in popular culture and among environmentalist and "new age" spiritual organizations.

A variety of studies have documented continued stereotyping of American Indians in the popular press, textbooks, the media, cartoons, and various other places (for example, see Aleiss, 2005; Bird, 1999; Meek, 2006; and Rouse & Hanson, 1991). In the tradition of "the noble Red Man," American Indians are often portrayed as bucks and squaws, complete with headdresses, bows, tepees, and other such generic Indian artifacts. These portrayals obliterate the diversity of American Indian culture and lifestyles. American Indians are often referred to in the past tense, as if their present situation were of no importance or, worse, as if they no longer existed. Many history books continue to begin the study of American history in Europe or with the "discovery" of America, omitting the millennia of civilization prior to the arrival of European explorers and colonizers. Contemporary portrayals of American Indians, such as in the movie *Dances With Wolves* (1990), are more sympathetic but still treat the tribes as part of a bucolic past forever lost, not as peoples with real problems in the present.

The persistence of stereotypes and the extent to which they have become enmeshed in modern culture is illustrated by continuing controversies surrounding nicknames for athletic teams (the Washington Redskins, the Cleveland Indians, and the Atlanta Braves) and the use of American Indian mascots, tomahawk "chops," and other practices offensive to many American Indians. Protests have been staged at some athletic events to increase awareness of these derogatory depictions, but as was the case so often in the past, the protests have been attacked, ridiculed, or simply ignored.

There are relatively few studies of anti-Indian prejudices in the social science literature, and it is therefore difficult to characterize changes over the past several decades. We do not know whether there has been a shift to more symbolic or "modern" forms of anti-Indian racism, as there has been for anti-black prejudice, or whether the stereotypes of American Indians have declined in strength or changed in content.

One of the few records of national anti-Indian prejudice over time is that of social distance scale results (see exhibit 1.8). When the scales were first administered in 1926, American Indians were ranked in the middle third of all groups (18th out of 28), at about the same level as Southern and Eastern Europeans and slightly above Mexicans, another colonized group. The ranking of American Indians remained stable until 1977, when there was a noticeable rise in their position relative to other groups. In the most recent polls, the social distance scores of American Indians fell (indicating less prejudice), but the relative ranking still placed them with other racial minority groups. These shifts may reflect a decline in levels of prejudice, a change from more overt forms to more subtle modern racism, or both. Remember, however, that the samples for the social distance research were college students, for the most part, and do not necessarily reflect trends in the general population (see also Hanson & Rouse, 1987; and Smith & Dempsey, 1983).

Research is also unclear about the severity or extent of discrimination against American Indians. Certainly, the group's lower average levels of education limit their opportunities for upward mobility, choice of occupations, and range of income. This is a form of institutional discrimination in the sense that the opportunities to develop human capital are much less available to American Indians than they are to much of the rest of the population. In terms of individual discrimination or more overt forms of exclusion, there is simply too little evidence to sustain clear conclusions (Snipp, 1992, p. 363). The situation of American Indian women is also underresearched, but Snipp reports that, like their counterparts in other minority groups and the dominant group, they "are systematically paid less than their male counterparts in similar circumstances" (p. 363).

The very limited evidence available from social distance scales suggests that overt anti-Indian prejudice has declined, perhaps in parallel with anti-black prejudice. A great deal of stereotyping remains, however, and demeaning, condescending, or negative portrayals of American Indians are common throughout the dominant culture. Institutional discrimination is a major barrier for American Indians, who have not had access to opportunities for education and employment.

Assimilation and Pluralism

In this section, we continue to assess the situation of American Indians today using the same conceptual framework used in chapter 5.

Acculturation

Despite more than a century of coercive Americanization, many tribes have been able to preserve at least a portion of their traditional cultures. For example, many tribal languages continue to be spoken on a daily basis. Almost 20% of American Indians speak a language other than English at home, about the same percentage as the total population. Exhibit 6.10 suggests the extent of language preservation. For 6 of the 10 largest tribes, fewer than 10% of their members speak the tribal language at home. For some tribes, however, the picture is dramatically different. For example, more than 50% of all Navajo and Pueblo Indians speak the tribal language at home.

While some American Indian languages have survived, it seems that even the most widely spoken of these languages is endangered. One study (Krauss, 1996) estimates that only about 11% of the surviving 200 languages are being taught by parents to their

Exhibit 6.10   Percentage of Total Population, All American Indians, and 10 Largest Tribes that Speak a Language Other than English at Home, 2009

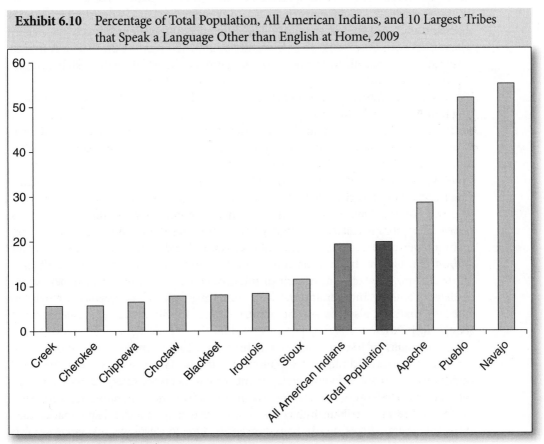

Source: U.S. Census Bureau (2010).

children in the traditional way and that most languages are spoken on a daily basis only by the older generation. If this pattern persists, American Indian languages will disappear as the generations change. A number of tribes have instituted programs to try to renew and preserve their language, along with other elements of their culture, but the success of these efforts is uncertain (Schmid, 2001, p. 25).

Traditional culture is retained in other forms besides language. Religions and value systems, political and economic structures, and recreational patterns have all survived the military conquest and the depredations of reservation life, but each pattern has been altered by contact with the dominant group. Cornell (1987), for example, argues that although American Indians have been affected by the American dream of material success through hard, honest work, their individual values continue to reflect their greater orientation to the group rather than to the individual.

The tendency to filter the impact of the larger society through continuing, vital American Indian culture is also illustrated by the Native American Church. The Native American Church is an important American Indian religion, with more than 100 congregations across the nation. This religion combines elements from both cultures, and church services freely mix Christian imagery and the Bible with attempts to seek personal visions by using peyote, a hallucinogenic drug. The latter practice is consistent with the spiritual and religious traditions of many tribes but clashes sharply with the laws and norms of the larger society. The difference in traditions has generated many skirmishes with the courts, and as recently as 2004 the right of the Native American Church to use peyote was upheld by the Supreme Court of Utah ("Utah Supreme Court Rules," 2004).

American Indians have been more successful than African Americans in preserving their traditional cultures, a pattern that is partly explained by the differences in the relationship between each minority group and the dominant group. African Americans were exploited for labor, whereas the competition with American Indians involved land. African cultures could not easily survive, because the social structures that transmitted the cultures and gave them meaning were destroyed by slavery and sacrificed to the exigencies of the plantation economy.

In contrast, American Indians confronted the dominant group as intact tribal units. The tribes maintained integrity throughout the wars and throughout the reservation period. Tribal culture was indeed attacked and denigrated during the reservation era, but the basic social unit that sustained the culture survived, albeit in altered form. The fact that American Indians were placed on separate reservations, isolated from one another and the "contaminating" effects of everyday contact with the larger society, also abetted the preservation of traditional languages and culture (Cornell, 1990).

The vitality of Indian cultures may have increased in the current atmosphere of greater tolerance and support for pluralism in the larger society, combined with increased autonomy and lower government regulation on the reservations. However, a number of social forces are working against pluralism and the continuing survival of tribal cultures. Pan-tribalism may threaten the integrity of individual tribal cultures as it represents American Indian grievances and concerns to the larger society.

Opportunities for jobs, education, and higher incomes draw American Indians to more developed urban areas and will continue to do so as long as the reservations are underdeveloped. Many aspects of the tribal cultures can be fully expressed and practiced only with other tribal members on the reservations. Thus, many American Indians must make a choice between "Indian-ness" on the reservation and "success" in the city. The younger, more-educated American Indians will be most likely to confront this choice, and the future vitality of traditional American Indian cultures and languages will hinge on which option they choose.

Secondary Structural Assimilation

This section assesses the degree of integration of American Indians into the various institutions of public life, following the general outlines of the parallel section in chapter 5.

Residential Patterns. Since the Indian Removal Act of 1830 (see chapter 3), American Indians have been concentrated in the western two thirds of the nation, as illustrated in exhibit 6.11, although some pockets of population still can be found in the East. California has the largest concentrations of American Indians (14% of the group live there), followed by Oklahoma (10%), Arizona (7%), and Texas (6%) (Nortes, Vines, & Hoeffel, 2012, p. 8). American Indians belong to hundreds of different tribes, the 10 largest of which were listed in exhibit 6.1.

Exhibit 6.11 Percentage of County Populations Choosing AIAN, Alone and in Combination, 2010

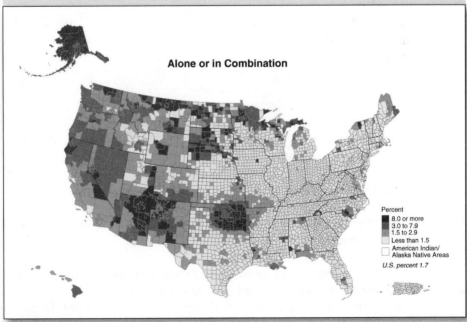

Source: Nortes, Vines, and Hoeffel (2012, p. 9).

Exhibit 6.12 provides some information about the levels of residential segregation of American Indians. The data in the exhibit are limited to metropolitan areas only. Since American Indians are such a small, rural group, exhibit 6.12 is limited to only 13 metropolitan areas, most of them in the West. The Northeast is not included because of the small numbers of American Indians living in the metropolitan areas of that region. Residential segregation is measured using the dissimilarity index, the same statistic used in exhibit 5.9 for African Americans.

Although based on small numbers, the exhibit shows that residential segregation is much lower for American Indians than for African Americans (see exhibit 5.9) and approaches the "high" range (0.6) only in the Western region. Also, the level of residential segregation declined slightly between 1980 and 2000, but remember that more than a third of American Indians live on or near rural reservations where the levels of residential segregation are quite high.

Exhibit 6.12   Residential Segregation of American Indians, 1980–2000

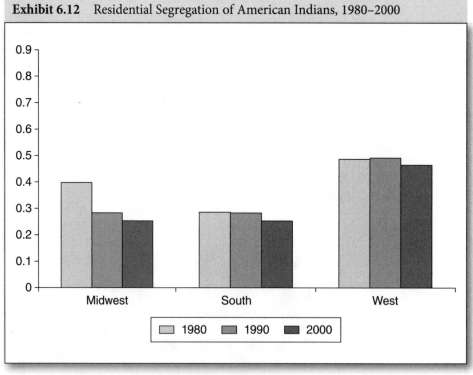

Source: Iceland, Weinberg, and Steinmetz (2002, p. 23).

School Integration and Educational Attainment. As a result of the combined efforts of missionaries and federal agencies, American Indians have had a long but not necessarily productive acquaintance with Western education. Until the past few decades, schools for American Indians were primarily focused on Americanizing children, not so much on educating them. For many tribes, the percentage of high school graduates has increased in the recent past, but American Indians as a whole are still somewhat below national levels. On the other hand, four of the largest tribes now exceed the national standard. The gap in college education is closing as well but remains large. None of the 10 largest tribes approaches the national norm on this variable. The differences in schooling are especially important because the lower levels of educational attainment limit mobility and job opportunities in the postindustrial job market. The educational levels of American Indians are displayed in exhibit 6.13.

One positive development for the education of American Indians is the rapid increase in tribally controlled colleges. There are now 37 tribal colleges: all offer 2-year degrees, six offer 4-year degrees, and two offer master's degrees. These institutions are located on or near reservations; some have been constructed with funds generated in the gaming industry. They are designed to be more sensitive to the educational and cultural needs of the group, and tribal college graduates who transfer to 4-year

Exhibit 6.13   Educational Attainment for the Total Population, All American Indians, and 10 Largest Tribes, 2009

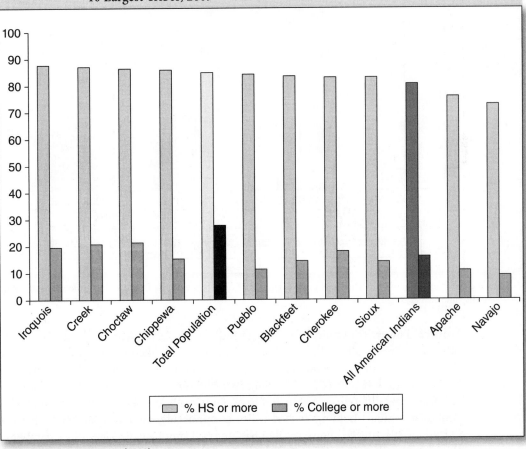

Source: U.S. Census Bureau (2010).

colleges are more likely to graduate than are other American Indian students (see also American Indian Higher Education Consortium, 2008; and Pego, 1998).

Exhibit 6.14 displays the extent of school integration for American Indians in the 1993–1994 and 2005–2006 school years, using the same measures as in exhibit 5.11. American Indian schoolchildren are less segregated than African American school-children, but the degree of racial isolation is still substantial and actually increasing. The percentage of American Indian children attending majority-minority schools increased from 44% to 49% between the 2 school years. The percentage in extremely segregated schools, on the other hand, held steady at 21%, about 10 percentage points lower than the corresponding figure for African American children.

Exhibit 6.14   School Integration, 1993–1994 and 2005–2006

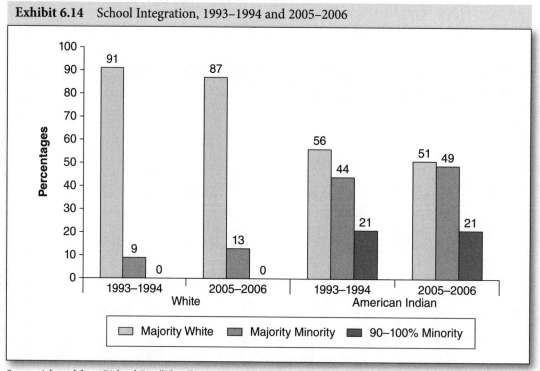

Source: Adapted from Richard Fry, "The Changing Racial and Ethnic Composition of U.S. Public Schools." Washington, DC: Pew Hispanic Center, August 2007.

Political Power. The ability of American Indians to exert power as a voting bloc or to otherwise directly affect the political structure is very limited by group size; they are a tiny percentage of the electorate. Furthermore, their political power is limited by their lower average levels of education, language differences, lack of economic resources, and fractional differences within and between tribes and reservations. The number of American Indians holding elected office is minuscule, far less than 1% (Pollard & O'Hare, 1999). In 1992, however, Ben Nighthorse Campbell, of Colorado, a member of the Northern Cheyenne tribe, was elected to the U.S. Senate and served until 2005.

Jobs and Income. Some of the most severe challenges facing American Indians relate to work and income. The problems are especially evident on the reservations, where jobs traditionally have been scarce and affluence rare. As mentioned previously, the overall unemployment rate for all American Indians is about double the rate for whites. For Indians living on or near reservations, however, the rate is much higher, sometimes rising to 70% to 80% on the smaller, more-isolated reservations (U.S. Census Bureau, 2010).

Nationally, American Indians are underrepresented in the higher-status, more lucrative professions and overrepresented in unskilled labor and service jobs (U.S. Census Bureau, 2010). As is the case for African Americans, American Indians who hold white-collar jobs are more likely than whites to work in relatively low-level occupations, such as typist or retail salesperson (Pollard & O'Hare, 1999).

The income data in exhibit 6.15 show median household income in 2009 for the total U.S. population, all American Indians, and the 10 largest tribes. Overall, income for American Indians is about 75% of the national figure. There is a good deal of variability

Exhibit 6.15 Median Household Income for Total Population, All American Indians, and 10 Largest Tribes, 2009

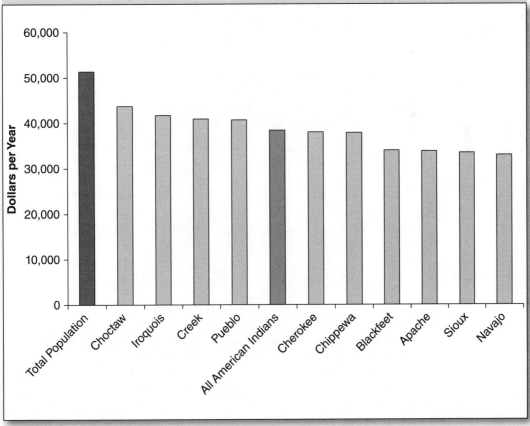

Source: U.S. Census Bureau (2010).

among the 10 largest tribes, but again, none approaches national norms. These incomes reflect lower levels of education as well as the interlocking forces of past discrimination and lack of development on many reservations. The rural isolation of much of the population and their distance from the more urbanized centers of economic growth limit possibilities for improvement and raise the likelihood that many reservations will remain the rural counterparts to urban underclass ghettos.

Exhibit 6.16 supplements the information in exhibit 6.15 by displaying the distribution of income for American Indians and Alaska Natives (AIAN) compared with non-Hispanic whites. This type of graph was introduced in the chapter on African Americans and is similar to the format of exhibit 5.15. In both graphs, the pattern of income inequality is immediately obvious. Starting at the bottom, we see that, like African Americans, AIAN are overrepresented in the lowest income groups. For example,

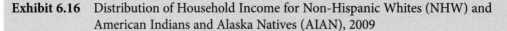

Exhibit 6.16 Distribution of Household Income for Non-Hispanic Whites (NHW) and American Indians and Alaska Natives (AIAN), 2009

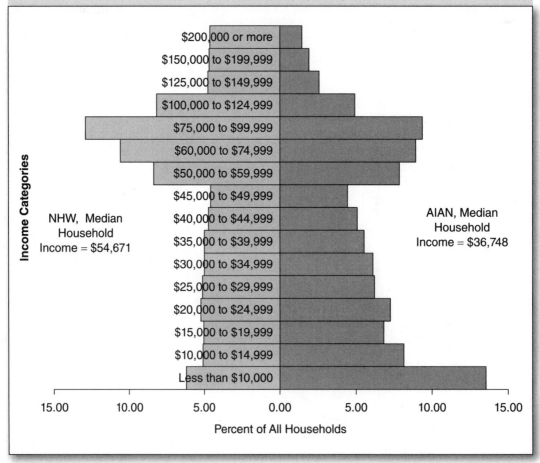

Source: U.S. Census Bureau (2010).

almost 13% of AIAN have incomes less than $10,000, more than double the percentage for non-Hispanic whites (6%) in this range.

Moving up the figure through the lower- and middle-income brackets, we see that AIAN households continue to be overrepresented. There is a notable clustering of both groups in the $50,000 to $100,000 categories, but it is whites who are overrepresented at these higher-income levels: almost a third of white households compared with only 26% of AIAN households are in these categories. The income differences between the groups are especially obvious at the top of the figure. More than 14% of white households versus 6% of AIAN households are in the top three income categories. Exhibit 6.16 also shows the median household income for both groups in 2009, and the difference of almost $18,000 further illustrates the lower socioeconomic level of American Indians.

Finally, exhibit 6.17 shows the poverty levels for the total population, all American Indians, and the 10 largest tribes. The poverty rate for American Indian families is almost double the national rate, and 6 of the 10 largest tribes have an even higher

Exhibit 6.17   Poverty Levels for Families and Children for Total Population, All American Indians, and 10 Largest Tribes, 2009

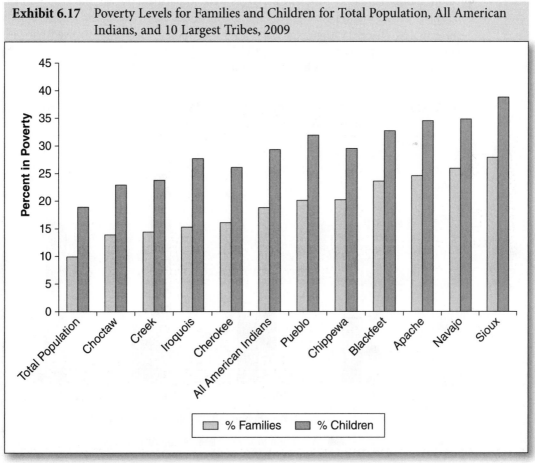

Source: U.S. Census Bureau (2010).

percentage of families living in poverty. The poverty rates for children show a similar pattern, with very high rates for the Apache, Navajo, and Sioux.

Taken together, this information on income and poverty shows that despite the progress American Indians have made over the past several decades, a sizable socio-economic gap persists.

Primary Structural Assimilation

Rates of out-marriage for American Indians are quite high compared with other groups, as displayed in exhibit 6.18. Since the 1980 census, more than half of all married American Indians had spouses from another racial group, a much higher rate than any other group. This pattern is partly the result of the small size of the group. As fewer than 1% of the total population, American Indians are numerically unlikely to find dating and marriage partners within their own group, especially in those regions of the country and urban areas where the group is small in size. For example, an earlier study found that in New England, which has the lowest relative percentage of American Indians of any region, more than 90% of Indian marriages were to partners outside the group. In the mountain states, which have a greater number of American Indians who are also highly concentrated on reservations, only about 40% of Indian marriages involved partners outside the group (Snipp, 1989, pp. 156–159). Also, the social and legal barriers to Indian–white intermarriages have been comparatively weak (Qian & Lichter, 2007).

Exhibit 6.18   Interracial Marriages by Group: Percent of Married People with Spouse of Another Race

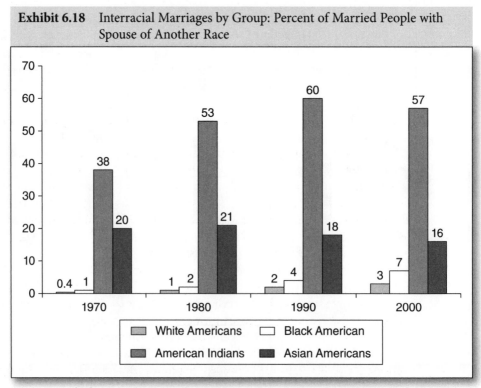

Source: Lee and Edmonston (2005, p. 12).

Comparing Minority Groups

Comparing the experiences of American Indians with those of other groups will further our understanding of the complexities of dominant-minority relationships and permit us to test the explanatory power of the concepts and theories that are central to this text. No two minority groups have had the same experiences, and our concepts and theories should help us understand the differences and the similarities. We will make it a point to compare groups in each of the chapters in this part of the text. We begin by comparing American Indians with African Americans.

First, note the differences in the stereotypes attached to the two groups during the early years of European colonization. While Indians were seen as cruel savages, African Americans under slavery were seen as lazy, irresponsible, and in need of constant supervision. The two stereotypes are consistent with the outcomes of the contact period. The supposed irresponsibility of blacks under slavery helped justify their subordinate, highly controlled status, and the alleged savagery of American Indians helped to justify their near extermination by white society.

Second, both American Indians and African Americans were colonized minority groups, but their contact situations were governed by very different dynamics (competition for labor versus land) and a very different dominant group agenda (the capture and control of a large, powerless workforce versus the elimination of a military threat). These differing contact situations shaped subsequent relationships with the dominant group and the place of the groups in the larger society.

For example, consider the situations of the two groups a century ago. At that time, the most visible enemy for African Americans was de jure segregation, the elaborate system of repression in the South that controlled them politically, economically, and socially (see chapters 4 and 5). In particular, the Southern system of agriculture needed the black population—but only as a powerless, cheap workforce. The goals of African Americans centered on dismantling this oppressive system, assimilation, and equality.

American Indians, in contrast, were not viewed as a source of labor and, after their military defeat, were far too few in number and too dispersed geographically to constitute a political threat. Thus, there was little need to control them in the same way African Americans were controlled. The primary enemies of the tribes were the reservation system, various agencies of the federal government (especially the BIA), rural isolation, and the continuing attacks on their traditional cultures and lifestyles, which are typical for a colonized minority group. American Indians had a different set of problems, different resources at their disposal, and different goals in mind. They always have been more oriented toward a pluralistic relationship with the larger society and toward preserving what they could of their autonomy, their institutions, and their heritage. African Americans spent much of the 20th century struggling for inclusion and equality; American Indians were fighting to maintain or recover their traditional cultures and social structures. This difference in goals reflects the different histories of the two groups and the different circumstances surrounding their colonization.

Progress and Challenges

What does the future hold for American Indians? Their situation has certainly changed over the past 100 years, but is it "better" or just "different," as is the case for large segments of the African American community? The answer seems to be a little of both, as the group grows in size and improves its status. To reach some conclusions, we will look at several aspects of the situation of American Indians and assess the usefulness of our theoretical models and concepts.

Since the 1960s, the decline of intolerance, the growth of pride in ancestry in many groups (e.g., Black Power), and the shift in federal government policy to encourage self-determination have all helped spark a reaffirmation of commitment to tribal cultures and traditions. As was the case with African Americans and the Black Power movement, the Red Power movement asserted a distinct and positive Indian identity, a claim for the equal validity of American Indian cultures within the broad framework of the larger society. During the same period, the favorable settlements of treaty claims, the growth in job opportunities, and the growth of the gambling industry have enhanced the flow of resources and benefits to some reservations. In popular culture, American Indians have enjoyed a strong upsurge of popularity and sympathetic depictions. This enhanced popularity accounts for much of the growth in population size as people of mixed ancestry resurrect and reconstruct their Indian ancestors and their own ethnic identities.

Linear or simplistic views of assimilation do not fit the current situation or the past experiences of American Indians very well. Some American Indians are intermarrying with whites and integrating into the larger society; others strive to retain a tribal culture in the midst of an urbanized, industrialized society; and still others labor to use the profits from gaming and other enterprises for the benefit of the tribe as a whole. Members of the group can be found at every degree of acculturation and integration, and the group seems to be moving toward assimilation in some ways and away from it in others.

From the standpoint of the Noel and Blauner hypotheses, we can see that American Indians have struggled with conquest and colonization, experiences made more difficult by the loss of so much of their land and other resources and by the concerted, unrelenting attacks on their culture and language. The legacy of conquest and colonization was poor health and housing, an inadequate and misdirected education system, and slow (or nonexistent) economic development. For most of the 20th century, American Indians were left to survive as best they could on the margins of the larger society, too powerless to establish meaningful pluralism and too colonized to pursue equality.

Today, one key to further progress for some members of this group is economic development on reservation lands and the further strengthening of the tribes as functioning social units. Some tribes do have assets—natural resources, treaty rights, and the gambling industry—that could fuel development. However, they often do not have the expertise or the finances to exploit these resources. They must rely, in whole or in part, on non-Indian expertise and white-owned companies and businesses. Thus, non-Indians, rather than the tribes, may be the primary beneficiaries of some forms of development (this would, of course, be quite consistent with American history). For those reservations for which gambling is not an option and for those without natural resources, investments in human capital (education) may offer the most compelling direction for future development.

Urban Indians confront the same patterns of discrimination and racism that other minority groups of color confront. Members of the group with lower levels of education and job skills face the prospects of becoming a part of a permanent urban underclass. More-educated and more-skilled American Indians share with African Americans the prospect of a middle-class lifestyle that is more partial and tenuous than that of comparable segments of the dominant group.

The situation of American Indians today is vastly superior to the status of the group a century ago, and this chapter has documented the notable improvements that have occurred, especially since 1990. Given the depressed and desperate conditions of the reservations in the early 20th century, however, it would not take much to show an improvement. American Indians are growing rapidly in numbers and are increasingly diversified by residence, education, and degree of assimilation. Some tribes have made dramatic progress over the past several decades, but enormous problems remain, both on and off the reservations. The challenge for the future, as it was in the past, is to find a course between pluralism and assimilation, pan-tribalism and traditional lifestyles, that will balance the issues of quality of life against the importance of retaining an Indian identity.

COMPARATIVE FOCUS:
Australian Aborigines and American Indians

The history of American Indians—their conquest and domination by a larger, more powerful society—has a number of parallels from around the globe, a reflection of the rise of European societies to power and their frequent conquest of indigenous societies in Africa, North and South America, and Asia. Even though each has its own unique history, similar dynamics seem to be at play. To illustrate, we will use some of the concepts developed in this text to compare the impact of European domination on Australian Aborigines and the indigenous peoples of North America.

Australia came under European domination in the late 1700s, nearly two centuries after the beginning of Anglo American Indian relations. In spite of the difference in when they occurred, however, the two contact situations shared many features. In both cases, the colonial power was Great Britain, and first contacts occurred in the preindustrial era (although Britain had begun to industrialize by the late 1700s). Also, the indigenous peoples of both North America and Australia were thinly spread across vast areas at the time of sustained contact with the British.

(Continued)

(Continued)

The Aboriginal peoples had lived in Australia for 50,000 years by the time the British arrived. They were organized into small, nomadic hunting-and-gathering bands and were less developed than the tribes of North America and much less developed than the British. The Aborigines lacked the population base, social organization, and resources that would have sustained resistance to the invasion of their land. There was plenty of violence in the contact situation, but, unlike the situation in North America, there were no military campaigns pitting large armies against each other.

The initial thrust of colonization was motivated by Great Britain's need for a place to send its convicts after losing the Revolutionary War to the fledgling United States. The European population in Australia grew slowly at first and consisted mostly of prisoners. The early economic enterprises centered on subsistence farming and sheepherding, not large-scale enterprises that required forced labor (at least not on the same scale as in North America).

Early relations centered on competition for land. The British denied that the Aborigines had any claims to the land and simply pushed them aside or killed them if they resisted. As in the Americas, European diseases took their toll, and the indigenous population declined rapidly. Because they were not desired as laborers (although many became semi-unfree servants), they were pushed away from the areas of white settlement into the fringes of development, where they could be ignored. As in North America, they were seen as "savages," members of a culture that would wither away and disappear.

The limited contact with the larger society was often in the form of coercive acculturation. For example, throughout much of the 20th century the Australian government, aided by various church organizations, removed children of mixed parentage from their Aboriginal mothers and placed them in orphanages. The idea behind this program was to give these children a chance to leave their Aboriginal culture behind, marry whites, and enter the larger society. This policy, abandoned only in the 1960s, resulted in the state-sponsored orphaning of thousands of Aboriginal children. Some of the angriest and most militant members of the current generation of Aborigines belong to this "stolen generation." (For a report on this program, see Australian Human Rights and Equal Opportunity Commission, 1997.)

The contemporary situation of Australian Aborigines has many parallels with American Indians, as does their past. The group is largely rural and continues to live on land that is less desirable. After the initial declines, their numbers have been increasing of late, partly because of higher birthrates and partly because of changing perceptions, growing sympathy for their plight, and increased willingness of people to claim their Aboriginal heritage. The population fell to a low of fewer than 100,000 at the start of the 20th century, but is now put at 517,000, or about 2.5% of the total population (Australian Bureau of Statistics, 2008).

Just as in North America, there is a huge gap between the indigenous population and the rest of society in quality of life and access to resources. Life expectancy for

Aborigines is as much as 20 years lower than that of the general population, and their infant mortality rate is two to three times higher. They have much less access to health care, and are much more afflicted with alcoholism, suicide, and malnutrition. Unemployment rates are double the rate in the general population, average income is about 65% of the national average, and only about a third as many Aboriginal people (13.6%) as compared with the national population (34.4%) are in school at age 19 ("Asia: Original Sin," 2007; Brace, 2001; see also Australian Bureau of Statistics, 2002). The issues animating Aboriginal affairs have a familiar ring for anyone familiar with American Indians. They include concerns for the preservation of Aboriginal culture, language, and identity; self-determination and autonomy; the return of lands illegally taken by the Anglo invaders; and an end to discrimination and unequal treatment.

Aboriginal relations are in flux, and the overall picture is mixed. The Aboriginal peoples of Australia, like American Indians, face many—often overwhelming—challenges to securing a better future for themselves and for their children. Their history and their present situation clearly validate both the Blauner and Noel hypotheses: they are a colonized minority group, victims of European domination, with all that status implies.

Main Points

- American Indian and Anglo American cultures are vastly different, and these differences have hampered communication and understanding, usually in ways that harmed American Indians or weakened the integrity of their tribal structures.
- At the beginning of the 20th century, American Indians faced the paternalistic reservation system, poverty and powerlessness, rural isolation and marginalization, and the BIA. American Indians continued to lose land and other resources during the early decades of the 20th century.
- The Indian Reorganization Act (IRA) of 1934 attempted to increase tribal autonomy and to provide mechanisms for improving the quality of life on the reservations. The policy of termination was proposed in the 1950s. The policy was a disaster, and the tribes that were terminated suffered devastating economic losses and drastic declines in quality of life.
- American Indians began to urbanize rapidly in the 1950s but are still less urbanized than is the population as a whole. They are the least urbanized American minority group.
- The Red Power movement rose to prominence in the 1960s and had some successes but was often simply ignored. The Red Power movement was partly assimilationist even though it pursued pluralistic goals and greater autonomy for the tribes.
- Current conflicts between American Indians and the dominant group center on control of natural resources, preservation of treaty rights, and treaties that have been broken in the past. The gaming industry offers another possible source of development (and conflict).
- There is some indication that anti-Indian prejudice has shifted to more modern forms. Institutional discrimination and access to education and employment remain major problems confronting American Indians.

- American Indians have preserved much of their traditional culture, although in altered form. The secondary structural assimilation of American Indians remains relatively low, despite recent improvements in quality of life for many tribes. Primary structural assimilation is comparatively high.
- Over the course of the past 100 years, American Indians have struggled from a position of powerlessness and isolation. Today, the group faces an array of problems similar to those faced by all American colonized minority groups of color as they try to find ways to raise their quality of life and continue their commitment to their tribes and to an Indian identity.

Study Site on the Web

Don't forget the interactive quizzes and other resources and learning aids at www.sagepub.com/healeyds4e.

For Further Reading

Amott, T., & Matthaei, J. (1991). "I am the fire of time: American Indian women." In T. Amott & J. Matthaei (Eds.), *Race, gender, and work: A multicultural history of women in the United States* (pp. 31–62). Boston: South End Press.

Good overview of the history and present situation of American Indian women.

Bordewich, F. (1996). *Killing the white man's Indian.* New York: Doubleday.

A comprehensive, dispassionate analysis of current problems and future possibilities.

Brown, D. (1970). *Bury my heart at Wounded Knee.* New York: Holt, Rinehart & Winston.

A passionately written, highly readable account of the military defeat and the establishment of dominance over American Indians.

Deloria, V. (1969). *Custer died for your sins.* New York: Macmillan.
Deloria, V. (1970). *We talk, you listen.* New York: Macmillan.
Deloria, V. (1995). *Red earth, white lies.* New York: Scribner's.

The three major works of the well-known American Indian activist, writer, and professor of Indian studies.

Harvard Project on American Indian Economic Development, The. (2008). The State of the Native Nations. New York: Oxford University Press.

A comprehensive look at economic development and other issues on reservations across the nation.

Nabakov, P. (Ed.). (1999). *Native American testimony.* New York: Penguin.

A collection of personal accounts by American Indians from pre-Columbian times to the present day.

Snipp, C. M. (1989). *American Indians: The first of this land.* New York: Russell Sage Foundation.

A valuable scholarly study covering a variety of aspects of the American Indian condition.

Treuer, D. (2012). *Rez life.* New York: Atlantic Monthly Press.

A powerful analysis of contemporary reservation life written by an insider.

Mann, Charles C. (2011). *1491: New Revelations of the Americas Before Columbus.* New York: Vintage Books.

An intriguing, eye-opening look at North and South American Indians before the arrival of Europeans

Questions for Review and Study

1. What were the most important cultural differences between American Indian tribes and the dominant society? How did these affect relations between the two groups?

2. Compare and contrast the effects of paternalism and coercive acculturation on American Indians after the end of the contact period with those of African Americans under slavery. What similarities and differences existed in the two situations? Which system was more oppressive and controlling? How? How did these different situations shape the futures of the groups?

3. How did federal Indian policy change over the course of the 20th century? What effects did these changes have on the tribes? Which were more beneficial? Why? What was the role of the Indian protest movement in shaping these policies?

4. What options do American Indians have for improving their position in the larger society and developing their reservations? Which strategies seem to have the most promise? Which seem less effective? Why?

5. Compare and contrast the contact situations of American Indians, African Americans, and Australian Aborigines. What are the most crucial differences in the situations? What implications did these differences have for the development of each group's situation after the initial contact situation?

6. Characterize the present situation of American Indians in terms of acculturation and integration. How do they compare with African Americans? What factors in the experiences of the two groups might help explain contemporary differences?

7. What gender differences can you identify in the experiences of American Indians? How do these compare with the gender differences in the experiences of African Americans?

8. Given the information and ideas presented in this chapter, speculate about the future of American Indians. How likely are American Indian cultures and languages to survive? What are the prospects for achieving equality?

9. Given their small size and marginal status, recognition of their situations and problems continues to be a central struggle for American Indians. What are some ways that the group can build a more realistic, informed, and empathetic relationship with the larger society, the federal government, and other authorities? Are there lessons in the experiences of other groups or in the various protest strategies followed in the Red Power movement?

Internet Research Project

In this exercise, you will use the U.S. census to gather information about the total population of all American Indians and two tribal groups of your own choosing. This project adds to the information you gathered in chapter 5 and the information for the total population is already entered. You can add the information for African Americans from the previous exercise and add data for the new variables in this exercise. You will then use course concepts to assess and analyze this information and place it in the context of this text.

Notes

1. *The numbers you gather for this exercise may vary slightly from those presented in this chapter because of differences in the dates the data were collected or in the nature of the samples used.*

2. *Visit the website for this text to check for updates on the databases available for completing this exercise.*

Get information by following these steps:

1. Go to the official U.S. Census Bureau website at www.census.gov.

2. Click on "Data" in the list of choices at the top of the screen and then click "American Fact Finder" from the drop-down menu.

3. Click the "Race and Ethnic Groups" tab on the left of the next screen. A new window will open. Find the list of "Racial and Ethnic Group Results" on the right of the screen and click on the box next to "Total Population" (Code 001), the box next to "Black or African American alone or in combination with one or more other races" (Code 005), and the box next to "American Indian and Alaska Native alone or in combination with one or more other races" (Code 009). Next click the "Add" button above the "Racial and Ethnic Group Results" window and your selections will be added to the "Your selections" box in the top-left-hand corner of the screen.

4. Select two of the 10 largest American Indian tribes from exhibit 6.1. Find these groups on the list in the "Racial and Ethnic Group Results" window, To do this, you will have to scroll down through three to five screens to find the listing of tribes. When you have a choice, choose the tribal name "alone or in any combination." When you have found your two tribes, click the box next to their names and click the "Add" button to move your selections to the "Your selections" box in the top-left-hand corner of the screen.

5. Check to make sure you have five groups in the "Your selections" box: The total population, black Americans, American Indians and Alaska Natives (AIAN), and two tribal names. Write the names of the tribes in the table below.

6. Close the "Select Race and Ethnic Groups" window by clicking the "Close" button on the top-right-hand corner of the window.

7. For this project, we will again use the 2011 ACS 1-year estimates. As before, look in either the "ID" column on the left for Table S0201 or in the "Dataset" column on the right for the "2011 ACS 1-year estimates." Click the box next to the file name and then click "View" from the menu above the window.

8. The next screen will display a table with your groups listed at the top. Scroll down the table until you find the information needed to fill in the table below.

   a. For "Percent of Total Population," follow the instructions below the table.

   b. Under "Marital Status," find "Percent married, except separated."

   c. Under "Educational Attainment," find "Bachelor's degree."

   d. Under "Language Spoken at Home and Ability to Speak English," find "Speak English less than 'very well.'"

   e. Under "Employment Status," find "% Unemployed."

   f. Under "Income in the Past 12 Months," find "Median Household Income."

   g. Under "Poverty Rates for Families and People," find "All Families."

   h. Under "Housing Tenure," find "Owner-Occupied Housing Units."

   i. Select two more variables relevant to this course and fill in the scores for the total population for African Americans and for AIAN. (*Note: Your instructor may have different instructions for this step of the project.*)

9. Search the Internet using the names of the two tribal groupings as keywords and find out if there is a reservation, if it is federal or state, where it is located, and—if possible—what percentage of the group lives there.

		Total Population	African Americans	AIAN (AOIC)	American Indian tribes	
					_____	_____
1	Number	311,591,919	42,533,817	5,120,813		
2	Percent of total population*	✕	13.7%			
3	Percent married	48.3%				
4	% with BA degree or higher	28.5%				
5	Speak English less than "very well"	8.7%				
6	% unemployed	6.5%				
7	Median household income	$50,502				
8	% of all families in poverty	11.7%				
9	% living in owner-occupied houses	64.6%				
10						
11						

*Divide the number in the group by 311,591,919 and multiply by 100.

Questions

1. Summarize what you found out in your search of the Internet about the two tribal groupings you selected.

2. What stage of Gordon's model of assimilation (see exhibit 2.1) do the variables in the table measure?

3. According to Blauner (see chapter 3), both American Indians and African Americans are "colonized or conquered" minority groups. Is their status in American society similar? What important differences do you see? Are these colonized groups higher or lower than the white ethnic groups you investigated in chapter 5 ? Do these patterns agree with Blauner's predictions? How?

4. Review the themes stated at the beginning of chapter 3 and the "corollary" stated at the beginning of chapter 4. How do the patterns you've observed in the table above relate to the contact situation and changing subsistence technologies?

5. Review the concepts of modern institutional discrimination and past in present discrimination introduced in chapter 4. How do the patterns you've observed in the table above relate to these concepts?

Optional Group Discussion

Bring this information to class and, in groups of four to six people, compare with the information collected by others. Consider the issues raised in the question above and in the chapter and develop some ideas about why American Indians, African Americans, and the individual tribes are where they are relative to each other and to the total population. (*Note: Your instructor may have different instructions for this step of the project.*)

7

Hispanic Americans: Colonization, Immigration, and Ethnic Enclaves

By the spring of 2005, Lucresia was desperate to reunite her family. Her husband had crossed the border, driven by the lack of jobs in Mexico. He had found work in Texas and had sent enough money home to not only support his family, but also to build them a new house. But he had not been home in 2 years, afraid that he would not be able to return to the United States once he crossed the border.

Against the objections of her family, Lucresia arranged to cross the border at Pima County, Arizona, a desolate desert of unending scrub, heat, and sand. She paid the coyotes (smugglers) more than $3,000 to deliver her and her two children to Phoenix, a walk of many days through the unforgiving desert. Three days into the trek, Lucresia collapsed. The smugglers decided to keep the party of 18 migrants moving. They left her in the desert. Her 15-year-old son stayed by her side as she, dehydrated and incoherent, slowly died. Her son survived and eventually was sent back to Mexico.

Upon hearing of her death, Lucresia's father vowed to recover her remains and provide her with a decent burial. He traveled to the United States on a tourist visa and searched the vast desert for his daughter for weeks. He was guided by the memories of his grandson and took pictures of likely landmarks—a particularly shaped tree or a sandy creek bed—and sent them to Lucresia's son in hopes that he would recognize something. He found the remains of several other immigrants who had died in the desert before he found Lucresia. He was able to *identify her skeletal remains by the shoes she wore, her dentures, and three rings still attached to the fleshless fingers of her left hand.*

—Based on Marosi (2005) and communications with members of
the Green Valley Samaritans who regularly patrol the desert of Southern
Arizona to try to prevent other deaths like Lucresia's

Since the early 1990s, globalization has disrupted the Mexican economy and pushed thousands out of work. Desperate to support their families, they cross the border to the United States. They find work in the low-wage, unskilled sector of the economy, live as frugally as they can, and send billions of dollars back to their home villages.

As the volume of immigration from Mexico has increased, U.S. citizens have become increasingly concerned. The Border Patrol was expanded, especially at the most commonly used border crossings, and large walls were built to try to limit the flow of people. In response, the smugglers and coyotes found new crossing points, seeking out the least patrolled areas. These included the Sonoran Desert that straddles the border between Mexico and Arizona. One result of this cat-and-mouse game has been a sharp increase in deaths along the border: Lucresia is one of thousands who have died trying to find a better life for themselves and their families.

The problems associated with the population movement along the Southern border have attracted the attention of a number of groups. Some, like the Green Valley Samaritans, seek to limit the number of deaths and the amount of suffering by providing humanitarian aid, water, and medicine to those trying to cross the desert. Their actions are legal and they coordinate with the Border Patrol and other law enforcement agencies. Others, organized groups and individuals, seek to discourage immigration. While some groups fill water tanks along the most likely migration routes, others vandalize and sabotage these efforts and seek to intimidate the migrants. One member of the Green Valley Samaritans reports finding a noose hanging in a tree next to one of the water tanks her group maintains. The furor over Mexican immigration, like virtually every group conflict in our history, brings out the best and worst of the American spirit: selfless humanitarianism and raw racism.

Hispanic Americans are more than 16% of the total population, which makes them the nation's largest minority group (African Americans are about 13% of the population). The group is concentrated in the Southwest, where there have been large Hispanic Americans communities for many years, but there are nine states—all in the Southeast except South Dakota—where the number of Latinos has more than doubled since 2000 (Passel, Cohn, & Lopez, 2011, p. 2). Communities throughout the nation are, for the first time, hearing Spanish spoken on their streets and finding "exotic" foods—tortillas, salsa, and refried beans—in their grocery stores. America is, once again, being reshaped and remade.

Of course, not all Hispanic American groups are newcomers. Some of these groups were in North America before the Declaration of Independence was signed, before slavery began, even before Jamestown was founded. The label "Hispanic American" includes a number of groups that are diverse and distinct from one another. These groups connect themselves to a variety of traditions; like the larger society, they are dynamic and changeable, unfinished and evolving. Hispanic Americans share a language and some cultural traits but do not generally think of themselves as a single social entity. Many identify with their national origin groups (e.g., Mexican American) rather than broader, more-encompassing labels.

In this chapter, we look at the development of Hispanic American groups over the past century, examine their contemporary relations with the larger society, and assess their current status. We focus on the three largest Hispanic groups: Mexican Americans, Puerto Ricans, and Cuban Americans. Other, smaller groups will be covered in chapter 9. Exhibit 7.1 displays some information on the size and growth of Hispanic Americans and the 10 largest Latino groups from 1990 to 2010. Mexican Americans, the largest

Exhibit 7.1   Size and Growth of All Hispanic Americans and 10 Largest Groups by Nation or Territory of Origin, 1990–2010

Country of Origin	1990	2000	2010	Growth (Number of times larger, 1990–2010)	Percent of Total Population, 2009
Mexico	13,496,000	20,640,711	31,798,258	2.4	10.3%
Puerto Rico*	2,728,000	3,406,178	4,623,716	1.7	1.5%
Cuba	1,044,000	1,241,685	1,785,547	1.7	< 1%
Dominican Republic	520,521	764,945	1,414,703	2.7	< 1%
El Salvador	565,081	655,165	1,648,968	2.9	< 1%
Guatemala	268,779	372,487	1,044,209	3.9	< 1%
Colombia	378,726	470,684	908,734	2.4	< 1%
Honduras	131,066	217,569	633,401	4.8	< 1%
Ecuador	191,198	260,559	564,631	3.0	< 1%
Nicaragua	202,658	177,684	348,202	1.7	< 1%
Total Hispanic	22,355,990	35,305,818	50,477,594	2.3	16.4%
Percentage of U.S. population	9.0%	12.6%	16.4%	—	—
Total U.S. population	248,710,000	281,421,906	308,745,538	1.2	—

Source: 1990: U.S. Census Bureau (1990); 2000: U.S. Census Bureau (2000); 2010: Ennis, Ríos-Vargas, and Albert (2011, p. 3).

Note: *Living on mainland only.

single group, are 10% of the total U.S. population (and about 60% of all Hispanic Americans), but the other groups are small in size. Exhibit 7.2 displays the relative sizes of the major subgroups of Latinos in the United States in 2010, and exhibit 7.3 shows the countries of origin of the three largest Hispanic American groups.

Latinos are growing rapidly, partly because of their relatively high birthrates, but mainly because of immigration. The number of Mexican Americans increased by a factor of 2.4 between 1990 and 2010, and Hispanic groups in general are growing at rates above the national average. This growth is projected to continue well into the century, and Hispanic Americans will become an increasingly important part of life in the United States. Today, 16 out of every 100 Americans is Hispanic, but by 2050 this ratio is projected to almost double to 30 out of every 100 (see exhibit 1.1). One result of these high rates of immigration is that the majority—and often the great majority—of many Hispanic groups are first generation or foreign-born. The percentages are displayed in exhibit 7.4.

Exhibit 7.2 Size of Hispanic American Groups by Nation or Territory of Origin, 2010

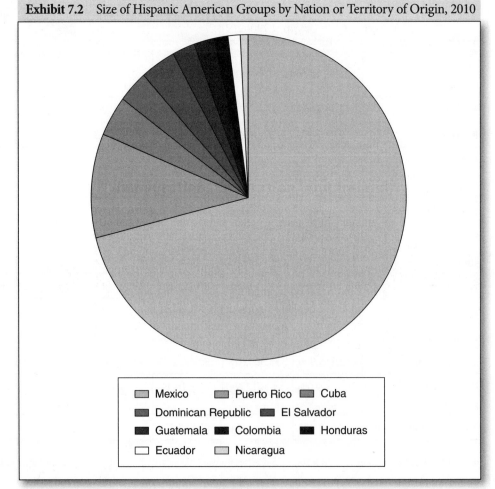

Source: Ennis, Ríos-Vargas, and Albert (2011, p. 3).

Exhibit 7.3   Points of Origin for Mexicans, Cuban Americans, and Puerto Ricans

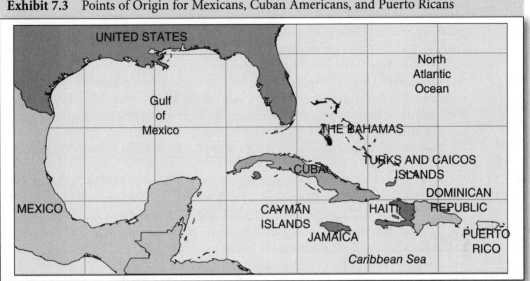

Source: U.S. Bureau of the Census.

Exhibit 7.4   Percent Foreign-Born by Country of Origin

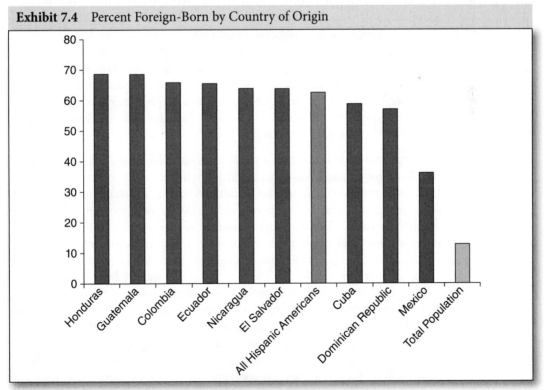

Source: U.S. Census Bureau (2012b).

Note: Puerto Ricans omitted.

It is appropriate to discuss Hispanic Americans at this point because they include both colonized and immigrant groups, and in that sense they combine elements of the polar extremes of Blauner's typology of minority groups. We would expect that the Hispanic groups that were more colonized in the past would have much in common with African Americans and American Indians today. Hispanic groups whose experiences lie closer to the "immigrant" end of the continuum would have different characteristics and follow different pathways of adaptation. We test these ideas by reviewing the histories of the groups and by analyzing their current status and degree of acculturation and integration.

Two additional introductory comments can be made about Hispanic Americans:

• Hispanic Americans are partly an ethnic minority group (i.e., identified by cultural characteristics such as language) and partly a racial minority group (identified by their physical appearance). Latinos bring a variety of racial backgrounds to U.S. society. For example, Mexican Americans combine European and American Indian ancestries and are identifiable by their physical traits as well as by their culture and language. Puerto Ricans, in contrast, are a mixture of white and black ancestry. The original inhabitants of the island of Puerto Rico, the Arawak and Caribe tribes, were decimated by the Spanish conquest, and the proportion of American Indian ancestry is much smaller there than it is in Mexico. Africans were originally brought to the island as slaves, and there has been considerable intermarriage between whites and blacks. The Puerto Rican population today varies greatly in its racial characteristics, combining every conceivable combination of European and African ancestry. Hispanic Americans are often the victims of racial discrimination in the United States. Racial differences often (but not always) overlap with cultural distinctions and reinforce the separation of Hispanic Americans from Anglo American society. Even members of the group who are completely acculturated may still experience discrimination based on their physical appearance.

• As is the case with all American minority groups, labels and group names are important. The term Hispanic American is widely applied to this group and might seem neutral and inoffensive to non-Hispanics. In fact, a recent survey shows that only about 25% of Hispanic Americans use "Hispanic" or "Latino" to describe themselves. Most (51%) identify themselves by their family's country of origin and 21% think of themselves as "American" (Taylor, Lopez, Martinez, & Velasco, 2012, p. 9). Furthermore, the preferred identity varies widely by primary language, generation, and education of the respondent. For example, almost two-thirds of Spanish speakers and first-generation (foreign-born) individuals prefer to identify themselves in terms of their countries of origin, whereas the "American" designation is most popular with the college-educated, the third and higher generation, and English speakers (Taylor et al., 2012, pp. 12–13). At any rate, both the Hispanic and Latino labels are similar to the term "American Indian," in that they were invented and applied by the dominant group and may reinforce the mistaken perception that all Spanish-speaking peoples are the same. Also, the term "Hispanic" highlights Spanish heritage and language but does not acknowledge the roots of these groups in African and Native American civilizations. Furthermore, the label is sometimes mistakenly applied to immigrant groups that bring French, Portuguese, or English traditions (e.g., Haitians, Brazilians, and Jamaicans, respectively). On the other hand, the Latino label stresses the common origins of these groups in Latin America and the fact that each culture is a unique blend of diverse traditions. In this chapter, the terms Latino and Hispanic are used interchangeably.

Mexican Americans

We applied the Noel and Blauner hypotheses to this group in chapter 3. Mexicans were conquered and colonized in the 19th century and used as a cheap labor force in agriculture, ranching, mining, railroad construction, and other areas of the dominant group economy in the Southwest. In the competition for control of land and labor, they became a minority group, and the contact situation left them with few power resources with which to pursue their self-interests.

By the dawn of the 20th century, the situation of Mexican Americans resembled that of American Indians in some ways. Both groups were small, numbering about 0.5% of the total population (Cortes, 1980, p. 702). Both differed from the dominant group in culture and language, and both were impoverished, relatively powerless, and isolated in rural areas distant from the centers of industrialization and modernization.

In other ways, Mexican Americans resembled African Americans in the South in that they also supplied much of the labor power for the agricultural economy of their region and both were limited to low-paying occupations and subordinate status in the social structure. All three groups were colonized and, at least in the early decades of the 20th century, lacked the resources to end their exploitation and protect their cultural heritages from continual attack by the dominant society (Mirandé, 1985, p. 32).

There were also some important differences in the situation of Mexican Americans and the other two colonized minority groups. Perhaps the most crucial difference was the proximity of the sovereign nation of Mexico. Population movement across the border was constant, and Mexican culture and the Spanish language were continually rejuvenated, even as they were attacked and disparaged by Anglo American society.

Cultural Patterns

Besides language differences, Mexican American and Anglo American cultures differ in many ways. Whereas the dominant society is largely Protestant, the overwhelming majority of Mexican Americans are Catholic, and the church remains one of the most important institutions in any Mexican American community. Religious practices also vary: Mexican Americans (especially men) are relatively inactive in church attendance, preferring to express their spiritual concerns in more spontaneous, less-routinized ways.

In the past, everyday life among Mexican Americans was often described in terms of the "culture of poverty" (see chapter 5), an idea originally based on research in several different Hispanic communities (see Lewis, 1959, 1965, 1966). This perspective asserts that Mexican Americans suffer from an unhealthy value system that includes a weak work ethic, fatalism, and other negative attitudes. Today, this characterization is widely regarded as exaggerated or simply mistaken. More-recent research shows that the traits associated with the culture of poverty tend to characterize people who are poor and uneducated, rather than any particular racial or ethnic group. In fact, a number of studies show that there is little difference between the value systems of Mexican Americans and other Americans of similar length of residence in the United States, social class, and educational background (e.g., see Buriel, 1993; Moore & Pinderhughes, 1993; Pew Hispanic Center, 2005, p. 20; Valentine & Mosley, 2000).

A recent survey illustrates the similarity in values systems. The survey found that Hispanic Americans were *more* supportive of "hard work" as a recipe for getting ahead—perhaps the central value in the American creed—than the population in general. About 75% of Hispanic Americans—versus only 58% of the general population—agreed that most people can "get ahead with hard work" (Taylor et al., 2012, pp. 18–19).

Another area of cultural difference involves **machismo**, a value system that stresses male dominance, honor, virility, and violence. The stereotypes of the dominant group exaggerate the negative aspects of machismo and often fail to recognize that machismo can also be expressed through being a good provider and a respected father, as well as in other nondestructive ways. In fact, the concern for male dignity is not unique to Hispanics and can be found in many cultures in varying strengths and expressions, including the Anglo American culture. Thus, this difference is one of degree rather than of kind (Moore & Pachon, 1985).

Compared with Anglo Americans, Mexican Americans tend to place more value on family relations and obligations. Strong family ties can be the basis for support networks and cooperative efforts but can also conflict with the emphasis on individualism and individual success in the dominant culture. For example, strong family ties may inhibit geographical mobility and people's willingness to pursue educational and occupational opportunities distant from their home communities (Moore, 1970, p. 127).

These cultural and language differences have inhibited communication with the dominant group and have served as the basis for excluding Mexican Americans from the larger society. However, they also have provided a basis for group cohesion and unity that has sustained common action and protest activity.

Immigration

Although Mexican Americans originated as a colonized minority group, their situation since the early 1900s (and especially since the 1960s) has been largely shaped by immigration. The numbers of legal Mexican immigrants to the United States are shown in exhibit 7.5. The fluctuations in the rate of immigration can be explained by conditions in Mexico; the varying demand for labor in the low-paying, unskilled sector of the U.S. economy; broad changes in North America and the world; and changing federal immigration policy. As you will see, competition, one of the key variables in Noel's hypothesis, has shaped the relationships between Mexican immigrants and the larger American society.

Exhibit 7.5   Legal Immigration from Mexico, 1905–2011

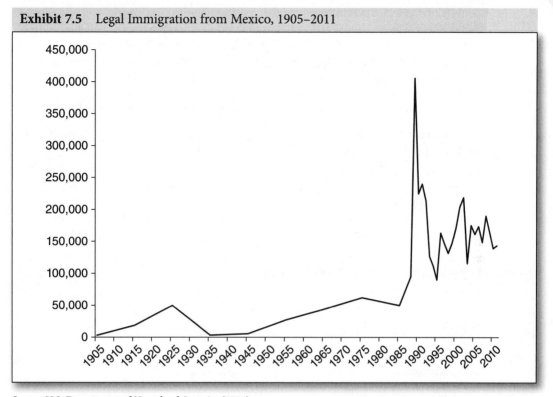

Source: U.S. Department of Homeland Security (2011).

Notes:

1. The very high number of "immigrants" in the late 1980s and early 1990s were the result of people already in the United States legalizing their status under the provisions of the Immigration Reform and Control Act (IRCA).
2. Values are averages per year during each decade until 1989.

Push and Pull

Like the massive wave of immigrants from Europe that arrived between the 1820s and the 1920s (see chapter 2), Mexicans have been **pushed** from their homeland and **pulled** toward the United States by a variety of domestic and global changes. European immigration was propelled by industrialization, urbanization, and rapid population growth. Mexican immigrants have been motivated by similar forces, including continuing industrialization and globalization.

At the heart of the immigration lies a simple fact: the almost 2,000-mile-long border between Mexico and the United States is the longest continuous point of contact between a less-developed nation and a more-developed nation in the world. For the past century, the United States has developed faster than Mexico, moving from an industrial to a postindustrial society and sustaining a substantially higher standard of living. The continuing wage gap between the two nations has made even menial work in the North attractive to millions of Mexicans (and other Central and South

Americans). Mexico has a large number of people who need work, and the United States offers jobs that pay more—often much more—than the wages available south of the border. Just as the air flows from high to low pressure, people move from areas of lower to higher economic opportunities. The flow is not continuous, however, and has been affected by conditions in both the sending and receiving nations.

Conditions in Mexico, Fluctuating Demand for Labor, and Federal Immigration Policy

Generally, for the past 100 years Mexico has served as a reserve pool of cheap labor for the benefit of U.S. businesses, agricultural interests, and other groups, and the volume of immigration largely reflects changing economic conditions in the United States. Immigration increases with good times in the United States and decreases with bad times, a pattern reinforced by the policies and actions of the federal government. The most important events in the complex history of Mexican immigration to the United States are presented in exhibit 7.6, along with some comments regarding the nature of the event and its effects.

Exhibit 7.6   Significant Dates in Mexican Immigration

Dates	Event	Result	Effect on Immigration From Mexico
1910	Mexican Revolution	Political turmoil and unrest in Mexico.	Increased.
Early 20th century	Mexican industrialization	Many groups (especially rural peasants) displaced.	Increased.
1920s	National Origins Act of 1924	Decreased immigration from Europe.	Increased.
1930s	Great Depression	Decreased demand for labor and increased competition for jobs leads to repatriation campaign.	Decreased, many return to Mexico.
1940s	World War II	Increased demand for labor leads to Bracero Guest Worker Program.	Increased.
1950s	Concern over illegal immigrants	Operation Wetback.	Decreased, many return to Mexico.
1965	Repeal of National Origins Act	New immigration policy gives high priority to close family of citizens.	Increased.
1986	IRCA	Illegal immigrants given opportunity to legalize status.	Many undocumented immigrants gain legal status.
1994	NAFTA	Many groups in Mexico (especially rural peasants) displaced.	Increased.
2007	Recession in the United States	Widespread unemployment in the United States, job supply shrinks.	Decreased.

Source: From Healey (2009).

Prior to the early 1900s, the volume of immigration was generally low and largely unregulated. People crossed the border—in both directions—as the need arose, informally and without restriction. The volume of immigration and concern about controlling the border began to rise with the increase of political and economic turmoil in Mexico in the early decades of the 20th century but still remained a comparative trickle.

Immigration increased in the 1920s when federal legislation curtailed the flow of cheap labor from Europe and then decreased in the 1930s when hard times came to the United States (and the world) during the Great Depression. Many Mexicans in the United States returned home during that decade, sometimes voluntarily, often by force. As competition for jobs increased, efforts began to expel Mexican laborers, just as the Noel hypothesis would predict. The federal government instituted a **repatriation** campaign aimed specifically at deporting illegal Mexican immigrants. In many localities, repatriation was pursued with great zeal, and the campaign intimidated many legal immigrants and native-born Mexican Americans into moving to Mexico. The result was that the Mexican American population of the United States declined by an estimated 40% during the 1930s (Cortes, 1980, p. 711).

When the Depression ended and U.S. society began to mobilize for World War II, federal policy toward immigrants from Mexico changed once more as employers again turned to Mexico for workers. In 1942, the Bracero program was initiated to permit contract laborers, usually employed in agriculture and other areas requiring unskilled labor, to work in the United States for a limited time. When their contracts expired, the workers were required to return to Mexico.

The Bracero program continued for several decades after the end of the war and was a crucial source of labor for the American economy. In 1960 alone, **braceros** supplied 26% of the nation's seasonal farm labor (Cortes, 1980, p. 703). The program generated millions of dollars of profit for growers and other employers, because they were paying braceros much less than they would have paid American workers (Amott & Matthaei, 1991, pp. 79–80).

At the same time that the Bracero program permitted immigration from Mexico, other programs and agencies worked to deport undocumented (or illegal) immigrants, large numbers of whom entered the United States with the braceros. Government efforts reached a peak in the early 1950s with **Operation Wetback**, a program under which federal authorities deported almost 4 million Mexicans (Grebler, Moore, & Guzman, 1970, p. 521).

During Operation Wetback, raids on the homes and places of business of Mexican Americans were common, and authorities often ignored their civil and legal rights. In an untold number of cases, U.S. citizens of Mexican descent were deported along with illegal immigrants. These violations of civil and legal rights have been a continuing grievance of Mexican Americans (and other Latinos) for decades (Mirandé, 1985, pp. 70–90).

In 1965, the overtly racist national immigration policy incorporated in the 1924 National Origins Act (see chapter 2) was replaced by a new policy that gave a high priority to immigrants who were family and kin of U.S. citizens. The immediate family (parents, spouses, and children) of U.S. citizens could enter without numerical restriction. Some numerical restrictions were placed on the number of immigrants from each sending country, but about 80% of these restricted visas were reserved for other close relatives of citizens. The remaining 20% of the visas went to people who had skills needed in the labor force (Bouvier & Gardner, 1986, pp. 13–15, 41; Rumbaut, 1991, p. 215).

Immigrants have always tended to move along chains of kinship and other social relationships, and the new policy reinforced those tendencies. The social networks connecting Latin America with the United States expanded, and the rate of immigration from Mexico increased sharply after 1965 (see exhibit 7.5) as immigrants became citizens and sent for other family members.

Most of the Mexican immigrants, documented as well as undocumented, who have arrived since 1965 continue the pattern of seeking work in the low-wage, unskilled sectors of the labor market in the cities and fields of the Southwest. For many, work is seasonal or temporary. When the work ends, they often return to Mexico, commuting across the border as Mexicans have done for decades.

In 1986, Congress attempted to deal with illegal immigrants, most of whom were thought to be Mexican, by passing the Immigration Reform and Control Act. This legislation allowed undocumented immigrants who had been in the country continuously since 1982 to legalize their status. According to the U.S. Immigration and Naturalization Service (1993, p. 17), about 3 million people, 75% of them Mexican, took advantage of this provision, but the program did not slow the volume of illegal immigration. In 1988, at the end of the amnesty application period, there were still almost 3 million undocumented immigrants in the United States. In 2010, the number of undocumented immigrants was estimated at 11.2 million, down from a high of 12 million in 2006 (Passel & Cohn, 2011).

Recent Immigration from Mexico

The population movement from Mexico to the United States continues to reflect the difference in level of development and standard of living between the two societies. Mexico continues to have a much lower standard of living, as measured by average wages, housing quality, health care, or any number of other criteria. To illustrate, according to United Nations (2011) data, the per capita income of the United States ($45,230) is four and a half times greater than the per capita income of Mexico ($9,964). Many Mexicans live in poverty and are drawn to the opportunities for work provided by their affluent northern neighbor. Since the average length of schooling in their homeland is only about 7 years (Nationmaster.com, 2012), Mexican immigrants bring much lower levels of job skills and compete for work in the lower levels of the U.S. job structure.

The impetus to immigrate has been reinforced by the recent globalization of the Mexican economy. In the past, the Mexican government insulated its economy from foreign competition with a variety of tariffs and barriers. These protections have been abandoned over the past several decades, and Mexico, like many less-developed nations, has opened its doors to the world economy. The result has been a flood of foreign agricultural products (cheap corn, in particular), manufactured goods, and capital, which, while helpful in some parts of the economy, has disrupted social life and forced many Mexicans, especially the poor and rural dwellers, out of their traditional way of life.

As we discussed in chapter 1, probably the most significant changes to Mexican society have come from the North American Trade Agreement, or NAFTA. Starting in 1994, this policy united the three nations of North America in a single trading zone. U.S. companies began to move their manufacturing operations to Mexico, attracted by lower wages, less-stringent environmental regulations, and weak labor unions. They built factories (called maquiladoras) along the border and brought many new jobs to the Mexican economy. However, other jobs—no longer protected from global competition—were lost, more than offsetting these gains, and Mexican wages actually declined after the implementation of NAFTA, increasing the already large number of Mexicans living in poverty. One analyst estimates that more than 2.5 million families have been driven out of the rural economy because they cannot compete with U.S. and Canadian agribusinesses (Faux, 2004).

Thus, globalization in general and NAFTA in particular, have reinforced the long-term relationship between the two nations. Mexico, like other nations of the less developed "South," continues to produce a supply of unskilled, less-educated workers, while the United States, like other nations of the more-developed and industrialized North, provides a seemingly insatiable demand for cheap labor. Compared with what is available at home, the wages in *el Norte* (the North) are quite attractive, even when the jobs are at the margins of the mainstream economy or in the irregular, underground economy (e.g., day laborers paid off the books, illegal sweatshop jobs in the garment industry, and sex work) and even when the journey requires Mexican immigrants to break American laws, pay large sums of money to "coyotes" to guide them across the border, and live in constant fear of raids by *la Migra* (the Border Patrol or other immigration authorities).

Predictably, when the U.S. economy faltered recently and the supply of jobs shrunk, the number of Mexicans entering the country declined dramatically. Exhibit 7.7 displays the recent decline based on data compiled for 2002–2009 (Passel & Cohn, 2009).

The Continuing Debate over Immigration Policy

Immigration has once again become a hotly debated issue in the United States. How many immigrants should be admitted? From which nations? With what skills? Should the relatives of U.S. citizens continue to receive a high priority? And, perhaps the issue that generates the most passion, what should be done about illegal immigrants? Virtually all of these questions, even those phrased in general, abstract terms, are mainly about the large volume of immigration from Mexico and the porous U.S. southern border.

The federal government has been attempting to reduce the flow by building a wall on the border with Mexico and beefing up the Border Patrol, with both increased personnel and more high-tech surveillance technology. Still, communities across the nation—not just in border states—are feeling the impact of Mexican immigration and wondering how to respond. Many citizens support extreme measures to close the borders—bigger, thicker walls and even the use of deadly force—while others ponder ways to absorb the newcomers without disrupting or bankrupting local school systems, medical facilities, or housing markets. The nation is divided on many of the

Exhibit 7.7 Population Movement between Mexico and the United States, 2002–2009

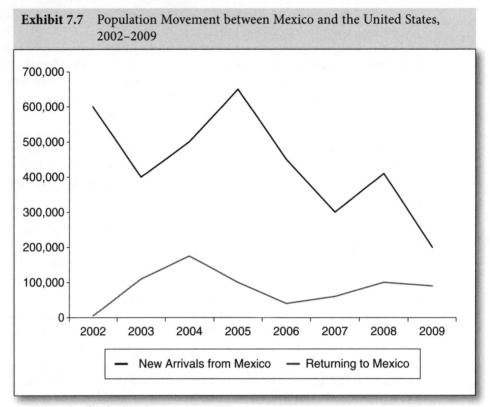

Source: Passel and Cohn (2009).

issues related to immigration. Public opinion polls over the past decade (see exhibit 7.8) show that about 40% to 50% of all Americans would like to lower the volume of immigration but that a large percentage (30% to 40%) favor keeping the present level. A much smaller but steady 10% to 20% favor an increase in the rate of immigration.

Several reforms for immigration policy have been proposed, and the debate on them continues. One key issue is the treatment of illegal immigrants: Should the undocumented be summarily deported, or should some provision be made for them to legalize their status, as was done in the Immigration Reform and Control Act of 1986? If the latter, should the opportunity to attain legal status be extended to all or only to immigrants who meet certain criteria (e.g., those with steady jobs and clean criminal records)? Many believe that amnesty is unjust because immigrants who entered illegally, after all, have broken the law and should be punished. Others point to the economic contributions of these immigrants and the damage to the economy that would result from summary, mass expulsions. Still others worry about the negative impact illegal immigrants might be having on the job prospects for the less-skilled members of the larger population, including the urban underclass that is disproportionately minority. We address some of these issues later in this chapter and in chapters 8 and 9.

Exhibit 7.8   U.S. Public Opinion on Immigration, 1999–2010

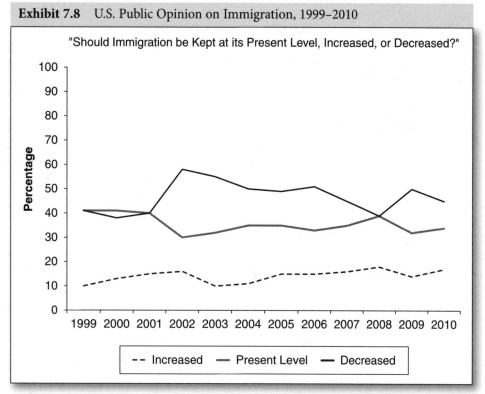

Source: Morales (2010).

Immigration, Colonization, and Intergroup Competition.

Three points can be made about Mexican immigration to the United States. First, the flow of population from Mexico was and is stimulated and sustained by powerful political and economic interests in the United States. Systems of recruitment and networks of communication and transportation have been established to routinize the flow of people and make it a predictable source of labor for the benefit of U.S. agriculture and other employers. The movement of people back and forth across the border was well established long before current efforts to regulate and control it. Depending on U.S. policy, this immigration is sometimes legal and encouraged and sometimes illegal and discouraged. Regardless of the label, the river of people has been steadily flowing for decades in response to opportunities for work in the North.

Second, Mexican immigrants enter a social system in which a colonized status for the group already has been established. The paternalistic traditions and racist systems that were established in the 19th century shaped the positions that were open to Mexican immigrants in the 20th century. Mexican Americans continued to be treated as a colonized group despite the streams of new arrivals, and the history of the group in the 20th century has many parallels with African Americans and American Indians. Thus, Mexican Americans might be thought of as a colonized minority group that happens to have a large number of immigrants or, alternatively, as an immigrant group that incorporates a strong tradition of colonization.

Third, this brief review of the twisting history of U.S. policy on Mexican immigration should serve as a reminder that levels of prejudice, racism, and discrimination increase as competition and the sense of threat between groups increase. The very qualities that make Mexican labor attractive to employers have caused bitter resentment among those segments of the Anglo population that feel that their own jobs and financial security are threatened. Often caught in the middle, Mexican immigrants and Mexican Americans have not had the resources to avoid exploitation by employers or rejection and discrimination by others. The ebb and flow of the efforts to regulate immigration (and sometimes even deport U.S. citizens of Mexican descent) can be understood in terms of competition, differentials in power, and prejudice and racism.

Developments in the United States

As the flow of immigration from Mexico fluctuated with the need for labor, Mexican Americans struggled to improve their status. In the early decades of the 20th century, like other colonized minority groups, they faced a system of repression and control in which they were accorded few rights and had little political power.

Continuing Colonization

Throughout much of the 20th century, Mexican Americans have been limited to less desirable, low-wage jobs. Split labor markets, in which Mexican Americans are paid less than Anglos for the same jobs, have been common. The workforce often has been further split by gender, with Mexican American women assigned to the worst jobs and receiving the lowest wages in both urban and rural areas (Takaki, 1993, pp. 318–319).

Men's jobs often took them away from their families to work in the mines and fields. In 1930, 45% of all Mexican American men worked in agriculture, with another 28% working in unskilled nonagricultural jobs (Cortes, 1980, p. 708). The women were often forced by economic necessity to enter the job market; in 1930, they were concentrated in farm work (21%), unskilled manufacturing jobs (25%), and domestic and other service work (37%) (Amott & Matthaei, 1991, pp. 76–77). They were typically paid less than both Mexican American men and Anglo women. In addition to their job responsibilities, Mexican American women had to maintain their households and raise their children, often facing these tasks without a spouse at home (Baca Zinn & Eitzen, 1990, p. 84).

As the United States industrialized and urbanized during the century, employment patterns became more diversified. Mexican Americans found work in manufacturing, construction, transportation, and other sectors of the economy. Some Mexican Americans, especially those of the third generation or later, moved into middle- and upper-level occupations, and some began to move out of the Southwest. Still, Mexican Americans in all regions (especially recent immigrants) tended to be concentrated at the bottom of the occupational ladder. Women increasingly worked outside the home, but their employment was largely limited to agriculture, domestic service, and the garment industry (Amott & Matthaei, 1991, pp. 76–79; Cortes, 1980, p. 708).

Like African Americans in the segregated South, Mexican Americans were excluded from the institutions of the larger society by law and by custom for much of the 20th century. There were separate (and unequal) school systems for Mexican American children, and in many communities Mexican Americans were disenfranchised and accorded few legal or civil rights. There were "whites only" primary elections modeled after the Jim Crow system, and residential segregation was widespread. The police and the court system generally abetted or ignored the rampant discrimination against the Mexican American community. Discrimination in the criminal justice system and civil rights violations have been continual grievances of Mexican Americans for much of the past 100 years.

Protest and Resistance

Like all minority groups, Mexican Americans have attempted to improve their collective position whenever possible. The beginnings of organized resistance and protest stretch back to the original contact period in the 19th century, when protest was usually organized on a local level. Regional and national organizations made their appearance in the 20th century (Cortes, 1980, p. 709).

As with African Americans, Mexican Americans' early protest organizations were integrationist and reflected the assimilationist values of the larger society. For example, one of the earlier and more significant groups was the League of United Latin American Citizens (LULAC), founded in Texas in 1929. LULAC promoted Americanization and greater educational opportunities for Mexican Americans. The group also worked to expand civil and political rights and to increase equality for Mexican Americans. LULAC fought numerous court battles against discrimination and racial segregation (Moore, 1970, pp. 143–145).

The workplace has been a particularly conflictual arena for Mexican Americans. Split labor market situations increased anti–Mexican American prejudice; some labor unions tried to exclude Mexican immigrants, along with immigrants from Asia and Southern and Eastern Europe (Grebler et al., 1970, pp. 90–93).

At the same time, Mexican Americans played important leadership roles in the labor movement. Since early in the 20th century, Mexican Americans have been involved in union organizing, particularly in agriculture and mining. When excluded by Anglo labor unions, they often formed their own unions to work for the improvement of working conditions. As the 20th century progressed, the number and variety of groups pursuing the Mexican American cause increased. During World War II, Mexican Americans served in the armed forces, and, as with other minority groups, this experience increased their impatience with the constraints on their freedoms and opportunities. After the war ended, a number of new Mexican American organizations were founded, including the Community Service Organization in Los Angeles and the American GI Forum in Texas. Compared with older organizations such as LULAC, the new groups were less concerned with assimilation per se, addressed a broad range of community problems, and attempted to increase Mexican American political power (Grebler et al., 1970, pp. 543–545).

Chicanismo

The 1960s were a time of intense activism and militancy for Mexican Americans. A protest movement guided by an ideology called **Chicanismo** began at about the same time as the Black Power and Red Power movements. Chicanismo encompassed a variety of organizations and ideas, united by a heightened militancy and impatience with the racism of the larger society and strongly stated demands for justice, fairness, and equal rights. The movement questioned the value of assimilation and sought to increase awareness of the continuing exploitation of Mexican Americans; it adapted many of the tactics and strategies (marches, rallies, voter registration drives, etc.) of the civil rights movement of the 1960s.

Chicanismo is similar in some ways to the Black Power ideology (see chapter 5). It is partly a reaction to the failure of U.S. society to implement the promises of integration and equality. It rejected traditional stereotypes of Mexican Americans, proclaimed a powerful and positive group image and heritage, and analyzed the group's past and present situation in American society in terms of victimization, continuing exploitation, and institutional discrimination. The inequalities that separated Mexican Americans from the larger society were seen as the result of deep-rooted, continuing racism and the cumulative effects of decades of exclusion. According to Chicanismo, the solution to these problems lay in group empowerment, increased militancy, and group pride, not in assimilation to a culture that had rationalized and abetted the exploitation of Mexican Americans (Acuna, 1988, pp. 307–358; Grebler et al., 1970, p. 544; Moore, 1970, pp. 149–154).

Some of the central thrusts of the 1960s protest movement are captured in the widespread adoption of **Chicanos**, which had been a derogatory term, as a group name for Mexican Americans. Other minority groups underwent similar name changes at about the same time. For example, African Americans shifted from "Negro" to "black" as a group designation. These name changes were not merely cosmetic—they marked fundamental shifts in group goals and desired relationships with the larger society. The new names came from the minority groups themselves, not from the dominant group, and they expressed the pluralistic themes of group pride, self-determination, militancy, and increased resistance to exploitation and discrimination.

Organizations and Leaders

The Chicano movement saw the rise of many new groups and leaders, one of the most important of which was Reies López Tijerina, who formed the Alianza de Mercedes (Alliance of Land Grants) in 1963. The goal of this group was to correct what Tijerina saw as the unjust and illegal seizure of land from Mexicans during the 19th century. The Alianza was militant and confrontational, and to bring attention to their cause members of the group seized and occupied federal lands. Tijerina spent several years in jail as a result of his activities, and the movement eventually lost its strength and faded from view in the 1970s.

Another prominent Chicano leader was Rodolfo González, who founded the Crusade for Justice in 1965. The crusade focused on abuses of Mexican American civil and legal rights and worked against discrimination by police and the criminal courts. In a 1969 presentation at a symposium on Chicano liberation, Gonzalez expressed some of the nationalistic themes of Chicanismo and the importance of creating a power base within the group (as opposed to assimilating or integrating):

> Where [whites] have incorporated themselves to keep us from moving into their neighborhoods, we can also incorporate ourselves to keep them from controlling our neighborhoods. We . . . have to understand economic revolution. . . . We have to understand that liberation comes from self-determination, and to start to use the tools of nationalism to win over our barrio brothers. . . . We have to understand that we can take over the institutions within our community. We have to create the community of the Mexicano here in order to have any type of power. (Moquin & Van Doren, 1971, pp. 381–382)

A third important leader was José Angel Gutiérrez, organizer of the party La Raza Unida (People United). La Raza Unida offered alternative candidates and ideas to those of Democrats and Republicans. Its most notable success was in Crystal City, Texas, where, in 1973, it succeeded in electing its entire slate of candidates to local office (Acuna, 1988, pp. 332–451).

Without a doubt, the best-known Chicano leader of the 1960s and 1970s was the late César Chávez, who organized the United Farm Workers, the first union to successfully represent migrant workers. Chávez was as much a labor leader as a leader of the Mexican American community, and he also organized African Americans, Filipinos, and Anglo Americans. Migrant farm workers have few economic or political resources, and the migratory nature of their work isolates them in rural areas and makes them difficult to contact. In the 1960s (and still today), many were undocumented immigrants who spoke little or no English and who returned to the cities or to their countries of origin at the end of the season. As a group, farm workers were nearly invisible in the social landscape of the United States in the 1960s, and organizing this group was a demanding task. Chávez's success in this endeavor is one of the more remarkable studies in group protest.

Like Dr. Martin Luther King Jr., Chávez was a disciple of Gandhi and a student of nonviolent direct protest (see chapter 5). His best-known tactic was the boycott; in 1965, he organized a grape-pickers' strike and a national boycott of grapes. The boycott lasted 5 years and ended when the growers recognized the United Farm Workers as the legitimate representative of farm workers. Chávez and his organization achieved a major victory, and the agreement provided for significant improvements in the situation of the workers (for a biography of Chávez, see Levy, 1975).

Gender and the Chicano Protest Movement

Mexican American women were heavily involved in the Chicano protest movement. Jessie Lopez and Dolores Huerta were central figures in the movement to organize farm workers and worked closely with César Chávez. However, as was the case for African American women, Chicano women encountered sexism and gender discrimination within the movement even as they worked for the benefit of the group as a whole. Their dilemmas are described by activist Sylvia Gonzales:

> Along with her male counterpart, she attended meetings, organized boycotts, did everything asked of her. . . . But, if she [tried to assume leadership roles], she was met with the same questioning of her femininity which the culture dictates when a woman is not self-sacrificing and seeks to fulfill her own needs. . . . The Chicano movement seemed to demand self-actualization for only the male members of the group. (Amott & Matthaei, 1991, p. 83)

Despite these difficulties, Chicano women contributed to the movement in a variety of areas. They helped organize poor communities and worked for welfare reform. Continuing issues include domestic violence, childcare, the criminal victimization of women, and the racial and gender oppression that limits women of all minority groups (Amott & Matthaei, 1991, pp. 82–86; see also Mirandé & Enriquez, 1979, pp. 202–243).

Mexican Americans and Other Minority Groups

Like the Black Power and Red Power movements, Chicanismo began to fade from public view in the 1970s and 1980s. The movement could claim some successes, but perhaps the clearest victory was in raising the awareness of the larger society about the grievances and problems of Mexican Americans. Today, many Chicanos continue to face poverty and powerlessness, and exploitation as a cheap agricultural labor force. The less-educated, urbanized segments of the group share the prospect of becoming a permanent urban underclass with other minority groups of color.

Over the past 100 years, the ability of Chicanos to pursue their self-interests has been limited by both internal and external forces. Like African Americans, the group has been systematically excluded from the institutions of the larger society. Continuing immigration from Mexico has increased the size of the group, but these immigrants bring few resources with them that could be directly or immediately translated into economic or political power in the United States.

Unlike immigrants from Europe, who settled in the urban centers of the industrializing East Coast, Mexican Americans tended to work and live in rural areas distant from and marginal to urban centers of industrialization and opportunities for education, skill development, and upward mobility. They were a vitally important source of labor in agriculture and other segments of the economy but only to the extent that they were exploitable and powerless. As Chicanos moved to the cities, they continued to serve as a colonized, exploited labor force concentrated at the lower end of the stratification system. Thus, the handicaps created by discrimination in the past were reinforced by continuing discrimination and exploitation in the present, perpetuating the cycles of poverty and powerlessness.

At the same time, however, the flow of immigration and the constant movement of people back and forth across the border kept Mexican culture and the Spanish language alive. Unlike African Americans under slavery, Chicanos were not cut off from their homeland and native culture, and the culture maintained its integrity even as it was attacked by the larger society.

Clearly, the traditional model of assimilation—which was based largely on the experiences of European immigrant groups—does not describe the experiences of Mexican Americans well. They have experienced less social mobility than European immigrant groups but have maintained their traditional culture and language more completely. Like African Americans, the group is split along lines of social class. Although many Mexican Americans (particularly of the third generation and later) have acculturated and integrated, a large segment of the group continues to fill the same economic role as did their ancestors: an unskilled labor force for the development of the Southwest, augmented with new immigrants at the convenience of U.S. employers. In 2010, more than 17% of employed Mexican Americans—nearly double the percentage for non-Hispanic whites—were in the construction and farm sectors of the labor force (U.S. Census Bureau, 2012a). For the less educated and for recent immigrants, cultural and racial differences combine to increase their social visibility, mark them for exploitation, and rationalize their continuing exclusion from the larger society.

Puerto Ricans

Puerto Rico became a territory of the United States after the defeat of Spain in the Spanish-American War of 1898. The island was small and impoverished, and it was difficult for Puerto Ricans to avoid domination by their new colonial masters. Thus, the initial contact between Puerto Ricans and U.S. society was made in an atmosphere of war and conquest. By the time Puerto Ricans began to migrate to the mainland in large numbers, their relationship to U.S. society was largely that of a colonized minority group, and they generally retained that status on the mainland.

Migration (Push and Pull) and Employment

At the time of initial contact, the population of Puerto Rico was overwhelmingly rural, supporting itself by subsistence farming and by exporting coffee and sugar. As the 20th century wore on, U.S. firms began to invest in and develop the island economy, especially the sugarcane industry. These agricultural endeavors took more and more of the land. Opportunities for economic survival in the rural areas declined, and many peasants were forced to move into the cities (Portes, 1990, p. 163).

Movement to the mainland began gradually and increased slowly until the 1940s. In 1900, there were about 2,000 Puerto Ricans living on the mainland. By the eve of World War II, this number had grown to only 70,000, a tiny fraction of the total population. Then, during the 1940s, the number of Puerto Ricans on the mainland increased more than fourfold, to 300,000, and during the 1950s, it nearly tripled, to 887,000 (U.S. Commission on Civil Rights, 1976, p. 19).

This massive and sudden population growth was the result of a combination of circumstances. First, Puerto Ricans became citizens of the United States in 1917, so their movements were not impeded by international boundaries or immigration restrictions. Second, unemployment was a major problem on the island. The sugarcane industry continued to displace the rural population, urban unemployment was high, and the population continued to grow. By the 1940s, a considerable number of Puerto Ricans were available to seek work off the island and, like Chicanos, could serve as a cheap labor supply for U.S. employers.

Third, Puerto Ricans were pulled to the mainland by the same labor shortages that attracted Mexican immigrants during and after World War II. Whereas the latter responded to job opportunities in the West and Southwest, Puerto Ricans moved to the Northeast. The job profiles of these two groups were similar: both were concentrated in the low-wage, unskilled sector of the job market. However, the Puerto Rican migration began many decades after the Mexican migration, at a time when the United States was much more industrialized and urbanized. As a result, Puerto Ricans were more concentrated than Mexican immigrants in urban labor markets (Portes, 1990, p. 164).

Movement between the island and the mainland was facilitated by the commencement of affordable air travel between San Juan and New York City in the late 1940s. New York had been the major center of settlement for Puerto Ricans on the mainland even before annexation. A small Puerto Rican community had been established in the city, and, as with many groups, organizations and networks were established to ease the transition and help newcomers with housing, jobs, and other issues. Although they eventually dispersed to other regions and cities, Puerto Ricans on the mainland remain centered in New York City. More than half (52.8%) currently reside in the Northeast (Ennis, Ríos-Vargas, & Albert, 2011, p. 7).

Economics and jobs were at the heart of the move to the mainland. The rate of Puerto Rican migration has followed the cycle of boom and bust, just as it has for Mexican immigrants. The 1950s, the peak decade for Puerto Rican migration, was a period of rapid U.S. economic growth. Migration was encouraged, and job recruiters traveled to the island to attract workers. By the 1960s, however, the supply of jobs on the island had expanded appreciably, and the average number of migrants declined from the peak of 41,000 per year in the 1950s to about 20,000 per year. In the 1970s, the U.S. economy faltered, unemployment grew, and the flow of Puerto Rican migration actually reversed itself, with the number of returnees exceeding the number of migrants in various years (U.S. Commission on Civil Rights, 1976, p. 25). The migrations continued: more than 4.6 million Puerto Ricans, 55% of all Puerto Ricans, were living on the mainland in 2010 (Lopez & Velasco, 2011, p. 1).

As the U.S. economy expanded and migration accelerated after World War II, Puerto Ricans moved into a broad range of jobs and locations in the society, and the group grew more economically diversified and more regionally dispersed. Still, the bulk of the group remains concentrated in lower-status jobs in the larger cities of the Northeast. Puerto Rican men have often found work as unskilled laborers or in service occupations, particularly in areas where English language facility is not necessary (e.g., janitorial work). The women often have been employed as domestics or seamstresses for the garment industry in New York City (Portes, 1990, p. 164).

Transitions

Although Puerto Ricans are not "immigrants," the move to the mainland does involve a change in culture and language (Fitzpatrick, 1980, p. 858). Despite nearly a century of political affiliation, Puerto Rican and Anglo cultures differ along many dimensions. Puerto Ricans are overwhelmingly Catholic, but the religious practices and rituals on the mainland are quite different from those on the island. Mainland Catholic parishes often reflect the traditions and practices of other cultures and groups. On the island, "Religious observance reflects the spontaneous and expressive practices of the Spanish and the Italian and not the restrained and well-organized worship of the Irish and Germans" (Fitzpatrick, 1987, pp. 117–138). Also, there are few Puerto Rican priests or even Spanish-speaking clergy on the mainland; thus, members of the group often feel estranged from and poorly served by the church (Fitzpatrick, 1987, pp. 117–138).

A particularly unsettling cultural difference between the island and the mainland involves skin color and perceptions of race. Puerto Rico has a long history of racial intermarriage. Slavery was less monolithic and total than it was on the mainland, and the island had no periods of systematic, race-based segregation like the Jim Crow system. Thus, although skin color prejudice still exists in Puerto Rico, it never has been as categorical as on the mainland. On the island, race is perceived as a continuum of possibilities and combinations, not as a simple dichotomous split between white and black.

Furthermore, in Puerto Rico, other factors, such as social class, are considered to be more important than race as criteria for judging and classifying others. In fact, as we discussed in chapter 4 ("Comparative Focus: Race in Another America"), social class can affect perceptions of skin color, and people of higher status might be seen as lighter skinned. Coming from this background, Puerto Ricans find the rigid racial thinking of U.S. culture disconcerting and even threatening.

The confusion and discomfort that can result was documented and illustrated by a study of Puerto Rican college students in New York City. Dramatic differences were found between the personal racial identification of the students and their perceptions of how Anglos viewed them. When asked for their racial identification, most of the students classified themselves as "tan," with one third labeling themselves "white" and only 7% considering themselves "black." When asked how they thought they were racially classified by Anglos, however, none of the students used the "tan" classification: 58% believed they were seen as "white," and 41% believed they were seen as "black" (Rodriguez, 1989, pp. 60–61; see also Rodriguez & Cordero-Guzman, 1992; and Vargas-Ramos, 2005).

Another study documented dramatic differences in the terms used to express racial identity between women on the mainland and those in Puerto Rico. The latter identified their racial identities primarily in skin color terms: black, white, or *trigueña* (a "mixed-race" category with multiple skin tones), while mainland women identified themselves in nonracial terms, such as Hispanic, Latina, Hispanic American, or American. In the view of the researchers, these labels serve to deflect the stigma associated with black racial status in the United States (Landale & Oropesa, 2002). In the racially dichotomized U.S. culture, many Puerto Ricans feel they have no clear place. They are genuinely puzzled when they first encounter prejudice and discrimination based on skin color and are uncertain about their own identities and self-image. The racial perceptions of the dominant culture can be threatening to Puerto Ricans to the extent that they are victimized by the same web of discrimination and disadvantage that affects African Americans. There are still clear disadvantages to being classified as black in U.S. society. Institutionalized racial barriers can be extremely formidable, and in the case of Puerto Ricans they may combine with cultural and linguistic differences to sharply limit opportunities and mobility.

Puerto Ricans and Other Minority Groups

Puerto Ricans arrived in the cities of the Northeast long after the great wave of European immigrants and several decades after African Americans began migrating from the South. They have often competed with other minority groups for housing, jobs, and other resources. A pattern of ethnic succession can be seen in some neighborhoods and occupational areas in which Puerto Ricans have replaced other groups that have moved out (and sometimes up).

Because of their more recent arrival, Puerto Ricans on the mainland were not subjected to the more repressive paternalistic or rigid competitive systems of race relations such as slavery or Jim Crow. Instead, the subordinate status of the group is manifested in their occupational, residential, and educational profiles and by the institutionalized barriers to upward mobility that they face. Puerto Ricans share many problems with other urban minority groups of color: poverty, failing educational systems, and crime. Like African Americans, Puerto Ricans find their fate to be dependent on the future of the American city, and a large segment of the group is in danger of becoming part of a permanent urban underclass.

Like Mexican Americans, Puerto Ricans on the mainland combine elements of both an immigrant and a colonized minority experience. The movement to the mainland is voluntary in some ways, but in others it is strongly motivated by the transformations in the island economy that resulted from modernization and U.S. domination. Like Chicanos, Puerto Ricans tend to enter the labor force at the bottom of the occupational structure and face similar problems of inequality and marginalization. Also, Puerto Rican culture retains a strong vitality and is continually reinvigorated by the considerable movement back and forth between the island and the mainland.

Cuban Americans

The contact period for Cuban Americans, as for Puerto Ricans, dates back to the Spanish-American War of 1898. Cuba was in revolt against Spain, its colonial master, when the United States intervened on the side of the rebels. Cuba became nominally an independent nation after the war, but the United States remained heavily involved in Cuban politics and economics for decades, and U.S. troops actually occupied the island on two different occasions.

In spite of the continuing close relationship, there was very little population movement from Cuba to the United States during the first half of the 20th century, even during hard times on the island. As recently as the 1950s, Cuban Americans were a very small group, numbering no more than 50,000 (Perez, 1980, p. 256). A Cuban American minority group developed only in the 1960s, and in a manner that bears little resemblance to the experience of either Chicanos or Puerto Ricans.

Immigration (Push and Pull)

The conditions for a mass immigration were created in the late 1950s, when a Marxist revolution brought Fidel Castro to power in Cuba. Castro's government was decidedly anti-American and began to restructure Cuban society along Socialist lines. The middle and upper classes lost political and economic power, and the revolution made it impossible for Cuban capitalists to continue "business as usual." Thus, the first Cuban immigrants to the United States tended to come from the more elite classes and included affluent and powerful people who controlled many resources. The immigration occurred at the height of the Cold War between the United States and Cuba was a client state of the Soviets. Thus, Cuban immigrants were perceived as refugees from Communist oppression and were warmly received by the government and the American public.

The United States, particularly Florida, was a logical destination for those displaced by the revolution. Cuba is only 90 miles from southern Florida, the climates are similar, and the U.S. government, which was as anti-Castro as Castro was anti-American, welcomed the new arrivals. Prior social, cultural, and business ties also pulled the immigrants in the direction of the United States. Since gaining its independence in 1898, Cuba has been heavily influenced by its neighbor to the north, and U.S. companies helped to develop the Cuban economy. At the time of Castro's revolution, the Cuban political leadership and the more affluent classes were profoundly Americanized in their attitudes and lifestyles (Portes, 1990, p. 165). Furthermore, many Cuban exiles viewed southern Florida as an ideal spot from which to launch a counterrevolution to oust Castro.

Immigration was considerable for several years. More than 215,000 Cubans arrived between the end of the revolution and 1962, when an escalation of hostile relations resulted in the cutoff of all direct contact between Cuba and the United States. In 1965, an air link was reestablished, and an additional 340,000 Cubans made the journey. When the air connection was terminated in 1973, immigration slowed to a trickle once more.

In 1980, the Cuban government permitted another period of open immigration. Using boats of every shape, size, and degree of seaworthiness, about 124,000 Cubans crossed to Florida. These immigrants are often referred to as the **Marielitos**, after the port of Mariel from which many of them departed. This wave of immigrants generated a great deal of controversy in the United States, because the Cuban government used the opportunity to rid itself of a variety of convicted criminals and outcasts. The reception for this group was decidedly less favorable than it had been for the original wave of Cuban immigrants. Even the established Cuban American community distanced itself from the Marielitos, who were largely products of the new Cuba, having been born after the revolution, and with whom they lacked kinship or friendship ties (Portes & Shafer, 2006, pp. 16–17.)

Regional Concentrations

The overwhelming majority of Cuban immigrants settled in southern Florida, especially in Miami and the surrounding Dade County. Today, Cuban Americans remain one of the most spatially concentrated minority groups in the United States, with nearly 7 in 10 of all Cuban Americans residing in Florida (Pew Hispanic Center, 2009). This dense concentration has led to a number of disputes and conflicts between the Hispanic, Anglo, and African American communities in the area. Issues have centered on language, jobs, and discrimination by the police and other governmental agencies. The conflicts often have been intense, and on more than one occasion have erupted into violence and civil disorder.

Socioeconomic Characteristics

Compared with other streams of immigrants from Latin America, Cubans are, on the average, unusually affluent and well educated. Among the early immigrants of the 1960s were large numbers of professionals, landowners, and businesspeople. In later years, as Cuban society was transformed by the Castro regime, the stream included fewer elites, largely because there were fewer left in Cuba, and more political dissidents and working-class people. Today (as displayed in the exhibits presented later in this chapter), Cuban Americans rank higher than other Latino groups on a number of dimensions, a reflection of the educational and economic resources they brought with them from Cuba and the favorable reception they enjoyed from the United States (Portes, 1990, p. 169).

These assets gave Cubans an advantage over Chicanos and Puerto Ricans, but the differences between the three Latino groups run deeper and are more complex than a simple accounting of initial resources would suggest. Cubans adapted to U.S. society in a way that is fundamentally different from the experiences of the other two Latino groups.

The Ethnic Enclave

Most of the minority groups we have discussed to this point have been concentrated in the unskilled, low-wage segments of the economy in which jobs are neither secure nor linked to opportunities for upward mobility. Many Cuban Americans have bypassed this sector of the economy and much of the discrimination and limitations associated with it. Like several other groups, such as Jewish Americans, Cuban Americans are an enclave minority (see chapter 2). An ethnic enclave is a social, economic, and cultural subsociety controlled by the group itself. Located in a specific geographical area or neighborhood inhabited solely or largely by members of the group, the enclave encompasses sufficient economic enterprises and social institutions to permit the group to function as a self-contained entity, largely independent of the surrounding community.

The first wave of Cuban immigrants brought with them considerable human capital and business expertise. Although much of their energy was focused on ousting Castro and returning to Cuba, they generated enough economic activity to sustain restaurants, shops, and other small businesses that catered to the exile community.

As the years passed and the hope of a return to Cuba dimmed, the enclave economy grew. Between 1967 and 1976, the number of Cuban-owned firms in Dade

County increased nine-fold, from 919 to about 8,000. Six years later, the number had reached 12,000. Most of these enterprises are small, but some factories employ hundreds of workers (Portes & Rumbaut, 1996, pp. 20–21). By 2001, there were more than 125,000 Cuban-owned firms in the United States and the rate of Cuban-owned firms per 100,00 population was four times greater than the rate for Mexican Americans and 14 times greater than the rate for African Americans (Portes & Shafer, 2006, p. 14).

In addition to businesses serving their own community, Cuban-owned firms are involved in construction, manufacturing, finance, insurance, real estate, and an array of other activities. Over the decades, Cuban-owned firms have become increasingly integrated into local economies and increasingly competitive with firms in the larger society. The growth of economic enterprises has been paralleled by a growth in the number of other types of groups and organizations and in the number and quality of services available (schools, law firms, medical care, funeral parlors, etc.). The enclave has become a largely autonomous community capable of providing for its members from cradle to grave (Logan, Alba, & McNulty, 1994; Peterson, 1995; Portes & Bach, 1985, p. 59).

The fact that the enclave economy is controlled by the group itself is crucial; it separates the ethnic enclave from "the ghetto," or neighborhoods that are both impoverished and segregated. In ghettos, members of other groups typically control the local economy; the profits, rents, and other resources flow out of the neighborhood. In the enclave, profits are reinvested and kept in the neighborhood. Group members can avoid the discrimination and limitations imposed by the larger society and can apply their skills, education, and talents in an atmosphere free from language barriers and prejudice. Those who might wish to venture into business for themselves can use the networks of cooperation and mutual aid for advice, credit, and other forms of assistance. Thus, the ethnic enclave provides a platform from which Cuban Americans can pursue economic success independent of their degree of acculturation or English language ability.

The effectiveness of the ethnic enclave as a pathway for adaptation is illustrated by a study of Cuban and Mexican immigrants, all of whom entered the United States in 1973. At the time of entry, the groups were comparable in levels of skills, education, and English language ability. The groups were interviewed on several different occasions, and although they remained comparable on many variables, there were dramatic differences between the groups that reflected their different positions in the labor market. The majority of the Mexican immigrants were employed in the low-wage job sector. Fewer than 20% were self-employed or employed by another person of Mexican descent. Conversely, 57% of the Cuban immigrants were self-employed or employed by another Cuban (i.e., they were involved in the enclave economy). Among the subjects in the study, self-employed Cubans reported the highest monthly incomes ($1,495), and Cubans otherwise employed in the enclave earned the second-highest monthly incomes ($1,111). The lowest monthly incomes ($880) were earned by Mexican immigrants employed in small, nonenclave firms; many of these immigrants worked as unskilled laborers in seasonal, temporary, or otherwise insecure jobs (Portes, 1990, p. 173; see also Portes & Bach, 1985).

A more recent study confirms the advantages that accrue from forming an enclave. Using 2000 census data, Portes and Shafer (2006) compared the incomes of several groups in the Miami–Fort Lauderdale metropolitan area, including the original Cuban immigrants (who founded the enclave), their children or the second generation, Cuban immigrants who arrived after 1980 (the Marielitos and others), and several other groups. Some of the results of the study for males are presented in exhibit 7.9. The founders and primary beneficiaries of the Cuban enclave are identified as "self-employed, pre-1980 Cuban immigrant," the only group that approximates the income of non-Hispanic whites (the difference in income is about $1,000, quite small and not statistically significant). The sons of the founding generation also enjoy a substantial benefit, both directly (through working in the enclave firms started by their fathers) and indirectly (by translating the resources of their families into human capital, including

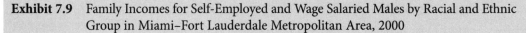

Exhibit 7.9 Family Incomes for Self-Employed and Wage Salaried Males by Racial and Ethnic Group in Miami–Fort Lauderdale Metropolitan Area, 2000

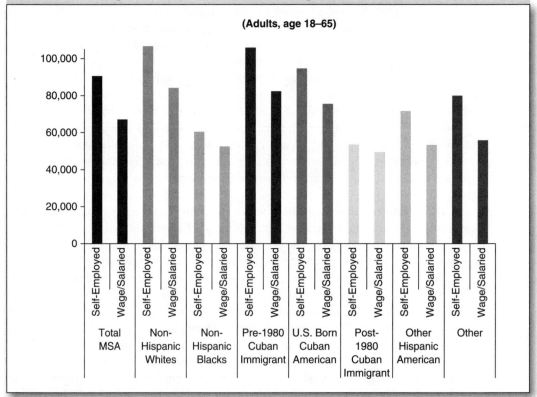

Source: Portes Shafer (2006, p. 42).

Notes: MSA is Metropolitan Statistical Area.

"Others" were mostly first and second generation Asian Americans.

education, for themselves). Note that the incomes of post-1980 Cuban immigrants are comparable to non-Hispanic blacks and much lower than other groups, both self-employed and wage-salaried.

The ability of most Hispanic (and other) immigrants to rise in the class system and compete for place and position is constrained by discrimination and their own lack of economic and political power. Cuban immigrants in the enclave do not need to expose themselves to American prejudices or rely on the job market of the larger society. They constructed networks of mutual assistance and support and linked themselves to opportunities more consistent with their ambitions and their qualifications.

The link between the enclave and economic equality (an aspect of secondary structural integration) challenges the predictions of some traditional assimilation theories and the understandings of many Americans. The pattern long has been recognized by some leaders of other groups, however, and is voiced in many of the themes of Black Power, Red Power, and Chicanismo that emphasize self-help, self-determination, nationalism, and separation.

However, ethnic enclaves cannot be a panacea for all immigrant or other minority groups. They develop only under certain limited conditions—namely, when business and financial expertise and reliable sources of capital are combined with a disciplined labor force willing to work for low wages in exchange for on-the-job training, future assistance and loans, or other delayed benefits. Enclave enterprises usually start on a small scale and cater only to other ethnics. Thus, the early economic returns are small, and prosperity follows only after years of hard work, if at all. Most important, eventual success and expansion beyond the boundaries of the enclave depend on the persistence of strong ties of loyalty, kinship, and solidarity. The pressure to assimilate might easily weaken these networks and the strength of group cohesion (Portes & Manning, 1986, pp. 61–66).

Cuban Americans and Other Minority Groups

The adaptation of Cuban Americans contrasts sharply with the experiences of colonized minority groups and with the common understanding of how immigrants are "supposed" to acculturate and integrate. Cuban Americans are neither the first nor the only group to develop an ethnic enclave, and their success has generated prejudice and resentment from the dominant group and from other minority groups. Whereas Puerto Ricans and Chicanos have been the victims of stereotypes labeling them "inferior," higher-status Cuban Americans have been stereotyped as "too successful," "too clannish," and "too ambitious." The former stereotype commonly emerges to rationalize exploitative relationships; the latter expresses disparagement and rejection of groups that are more successful in the struggle to acquire resources. Nonetheless, the stereotype of Cubans is an exaggeration and a misperception that obscures the fact that poverty and unemployment are major problems for many members of this group, especially for the post-1980 immigrants (see the exhibits at the end of this chapter).

COMPARATIVE FOCUS:
Immigration to Europe vs. Immigration
to the United States

The volume of immigration in the world today is at record levels. As I pointed out in chapter 1 ("Focus on Contemporary Issues: Immigration and Globalization"), about 214 million people, a little more than 3% of the world's population, live outside their countries of birth, and there is hardly a nation or region that has not been affected (United Nations, 2012). Exhibit 7.10 lists, in order of significance, the nations that are projected to be the major destinations and suppliers of immigrants for the next 40 years.

The United States currently hosts 20% of all migrants and has by far the highest number of foreign-born citizens of any nation. However, the United States is only one of many destinations, and the issues of immigration and assimilation that are being debated so fervently here are echoed in many other nations.

In particular, the nations of Western Europe, with their highly developed, advanced industrial economies, are prime destinations for immigrants. Like the United States, these nations have high standards of living, and they offer myriad opportunities for economic survival, even though the price may be to live at the margins of the larger society or to take jobs scorned by the native-born. In addition, a powerful factor that pulls people to this region is that Western European nations have very low birthrates, and in some cases (e.g., Germany and Italy), their populations are projected to actually decline in coming decades (Population Reference Bureau, 2011). The labor force shortages thus created will continue to attract immigrants to Western Europe for decades to come.

The immigrant stream to Western Europe is varied and includes people from all walks of life, from highly educated professionals to peasant laborers. The most prominent

Exhibit 7.10   Major Sending and Receiving Nations for International Migration, in Order of Significance, projected for 2010–2050

Destination Nations	Nations of Origin
United States	Mexico
Canada	China
United Kingdom	India
Spain	The Philippines
Italy	Pakistan
Germany	Indonesia
Australia	Bangladesh
France	

Source: United Nations (2012, p. 32).

flows include movements from Turkey to Germany, from Africa to Spain and Italy, and from many former British colonies (Jamaica, India, Nigeria, etc.) to the United Kingdom. This immigration is primarily an economic phenomenon motivated by the search for jobs and survival, but the stream also includes refugees and asylum seekers spurred by civil war, genocide, and political unrest.

In terms of numbers, the volume of immigration to Western Europe is smaller than the flow to the United States, but its proportional impact is comparable. About 13% of the U.S. population is foreign-born, and many Western European nations (including Belgium, Germany, and Sweden) have a similar profile (Dumont & LeMaitre, 2011). Thus, it is not surprising that in both cases immigration has generated major concerns and debates about handling newcomers and managing a pluralistic society, including national language policy, the limits of religious freedom, and the criteria for citizenship.

To focus on one example, Germany has the largest immigrant community of any Western European nation and has been dealing with a large foreign-born population for decades. Germany began to allow large numbers of immigrants to enter as temporary workers or "guest workers" (*Gastarbeiter*) to help staff its expanding economy beginning in the 1960s. Most of these immigrants came from Turkey, and they were seen by Germans as temporary workers only, people who would return to their homeland when they were no longer needed. Thus, the host society saw no particular need to encourage immigrants to acculturate and integrate.

Contrary to this expectation, many immigrants stayed and settled permanently, and many of their millions of descendants today speak only German and have no knowledge of or experience with their "homeland." Although acculturated, they are not fully integrated, and, in fact—in contrast with the United States—they were denied the opportunity to become citizens until recently. A German law passed a century ago reserved citizenship for ethnic Germans, regardless of place of birth. Under this policy, a recent immigrant from, say, Ukraine was eligible for citizenship if he or she could prove German ancestry—even if he or she spoke no German and was not familiar with German culture or traditions.

In contrast, Turks living in Germany were not eligible for citizenship regardless of how long they or their families had been residents. This law was changed in 2000 to permit greater flexibility in qualifying for citizenship, but still more recently Germany has passed new laws that make it harder for foreigners to enter the country. To gain admission, immigrants from non–European Union nations may have to pass a language test, demonstrate that they earn a minimum of 66,000 euros a year (about $90,000), and have a guaranteed job. The immigrant community sees these new laws as a form of rejection, and there have been bitter (and sometimes violent) demonstrations in response ("Europe: The Integration Dilemma," 2007). Anti-immigrant attitudes seem to be hardening and, in the fall of 2010, German Chancellor Angela Merkel declared that German attempts to create a multicultural society have "utterly failed" (Westervelt, 2010).

(Continued)

(Continued)

Clashes of this sort have been common across Western Europe in recent years, especially with the growing Muslim communities. Many Europeans see Islamic immigrants as unassimilable, too foreign or exotic to ever fit in to the mainstream of their society. These conflicts have been punctuated by violence and riots in France, Germany, the Netherlands, and other countries.

Across Europe, just as in the United States (and Canada), nations are wrestling with issues of inclusion and diversity: What should it mean to be German, or French, or British, or Dutch? How much diversity can be tolerated before national cohesion is threatened? What are the limits of tolerance? What is the best balance between assimilation and pluralism? Struggles over the essential meaning of national identity are increasingly common throughout the developed world.

Contemporary Hispanic–White Relations

As in previous chapters, we will use the central concepts of this text to review the status of Latinos in the United States. Where relevant, comparisons are made between the major Latino groups and the minority groups discussed in previous chapters.

Prejudice and Discrimination

The American tradition of prejudice against Latinos was born in the 19th-century conflicts that created minority group status for Mexican Americans. The themes of the original anti-Mexican stereotypes and attitudes were consistent with the nature of the contact situation: as Mexicans were conquered and subordinated, they were characterized as inferior, lazy, irresponsible, low in intelligence, and dangerously criminal (McWilliams, 1961, pp. 212–214). The prejudice and racism, supplemented with the racist ideas and beliefs brought to the Southwest by many Anglos, helped justify and rationalize the colonized, exploited status of the Chicanos.

These prejudices were incorporated into the dominant culture and transferred to Puerto Ricans when they began to arrive on the mainland. As we have already mentioned, this stereotype does not fit Cuban Americans. Instead, their affluence has been exaggerated and perceived as undeserved or achieved by unfair or "un-American" means, a characterization similar to the traditional stereotype of Jews but just as prejudiced as the perception of Latino inferiority.

There is some evidence that the level of Latino prejudice has been affected by the decline of explicit American racism. For example, social distance scale results show a decrease in the scores of Mexicans, although their group ranking tends to remain stable.

On the other hand, anti-Latino prejudice and racism tend to increase during times of high immigration. In particular, there is considerable, though largely anecdotal, evidence of high levels of anti-Latino prejudice in the "borderlands" or the areas along the United States–Mexico border. Sparked by and deeply intermixed with concerns about undocumented immigration, the levels of prejudice and racism seem extreme, perhaps matching the levels of anti-black prejudice in the tumultuous days of the 1960s. Hate crimes and hate groups such as the Minutemen seem to have increased, and the levels of vitriol and racist rhetoric have approached fever pitch along much of the borderlands. Many observers see racism in the various anti-immigrant bills passed by many states, including Arizona's ban on ethnic studies programs in public schools and its widely publicized Senate Bill 1070 (S.B. 1070), most of which was declared unconstitutional in June 2012. The portion of the bill that survived will allow police to check the citizenship status of anyone they stop (Liptak, 2012b).

At any rate, the level of immigrant-bashing and anti-Latino sentiments along the border demonstrate that American prejudice, although sometimes disguised as subtle modern racism, is alive and well.

In chapter 4, I mentioned that audit studies have documented the persistence of discrimination against blacks in the housing and job market: many of the same studies also demonstrate anti-Hispanic biases (see Quillian, 2006, for a review). Discrimination of all kinds, institutional as well as individual, has been common against Latino groups but it has not been as rigid or as total as the systems that controlled African American labor under slavery and segregation. However, discrimination against Latinos persists across the country. Because of their longer tenure in the United States and their original status as a rural labor force, Mexican Americans probably have been more victimized by the institutionalized forms of discrimination than have other Latino groups.

Assimilation and Pluralism

Acculturation

Latinos are highly variable in their extent of acculturation but are often seen as "slow" to change, learn English, and adopt Anglo customs. Contrary to this perception, research shows that Hispanics are following many of the same patterns of assimilation as did the European groups that immigrated between 1820 and 1920 (see chapter 2). Their rates of acculturation increase with length of residence and are higher for the native-born (Espinosa & Massey, 1997; Goldstein & Suro, 2000; Valentine & Mosley, 2000).

The dominant trend for Hispanic groups, as for immigrants from Europe in the past is that language acculturation increases over the generations, as the length of residence in the United States increases and as education increases. One study, which combines six different surveys conducted since 2000 and which is based on more than 14,000 respondents, illustrates these points. Results are displayed in exhibits 7.11 and 7.12.

A different study shows that the values of Hispanics come to approximate the values of society as a whole as the generations pass. Exhibit 7.13 shows some results of a 2002 survey of Latinos and compares cultural values by English language proficiency, which increases with length of residence and by generation. For example, most Latinos (72%) who speak predominantly Spanish are first generation, while most (78%) who speak predominantly English are third generation. The second generation is most likely to be bilingual.

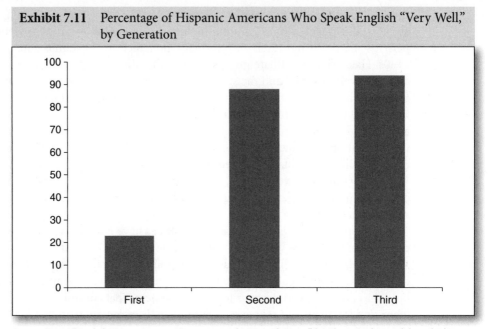

Exhibit 7.11 Percentage of Hispanic Americans Who Speak English "Very Well," by Generation

Source: From "English Usage Among Hispanics in the United States," by Shirin Hakimzadeh and D'Vera Cohn. Pew Hispanic Center, November 29, 2007. Copyright © 2007 Pew Hispanic Center, a Pew Research Center project, www.pewhispanic.org.

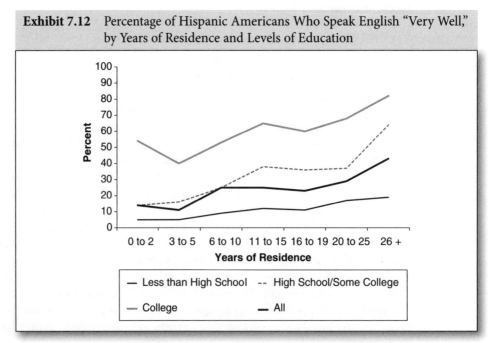

Exhibit 7.12 Percentage of Hispanic Americans Who Speak English "Very Well," by Years of Residence and Levels of Education

Source: From "English Usage Among Hispanics in the United States," by Shirin Hakimzadeh and D'Vera Cohn. Pew Hispanic Center, November 29, 2007. Copyright © 2007 Pew Hispanic Center, a Pew Research Center project, www.pewhispanic.org.

Exhibit 7.13   Percent of Hispanic Americans and Non-Latinos Agreeing by Primary Language

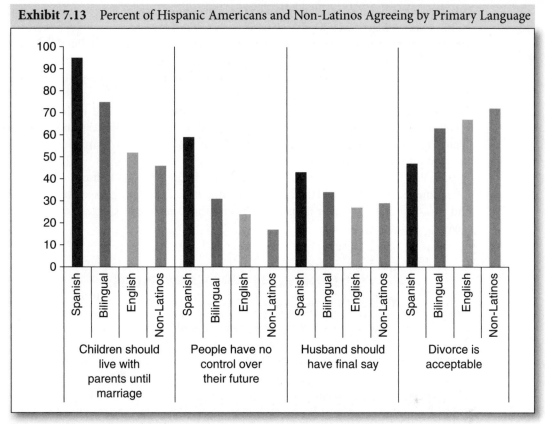

Source: Pew Hispanic Center (2004).

Full Text Of Survey Items:

"It is better for children to live in their parents' home until they are married"

"It doesn't do any good to plan for the future because you don't have any control over it"

"In general, the husband should have the final say in all family matters"

"Divorce is acceptable"

The exhibit shows the results for four different survey items that measure values and opinions. The values of predominantly Spanish speakers are distinctly different from those of non-Latinos, especially on the item that measures support for the statement that "children should live with their parents until they are married." Virtually all the predominantly Spanish speakers supported the statement, but English-speaking Latinos approximate the more individualistic values of Anglos. For each of the other three items, a similar acculturation to American values occurs.

Even while acculturation continues, however, Hispanic culture and the Spanish language are revitalized by immigration. By its nature, assimilation is a slow process that can require decades or generations to complete. In contrast, immigration can be fast, often accomplished in less than a day. Thus, even as Hispanic Americans acculturate and integrate, Hispanic culture and language are sustained and strengthened. What is perceived to be slow acculturation for these groups is mostly the result of fast and continuous immigration.

Furthermore, colonized minority groups such as Chicanos and Puerto Ricans were not encouraged to assimilate in the past. Valued primarily for the cheap labor they supplied, they were seen as otherwise inferior or undesirable and unfit for integration. For much of the 20th century, Latinos were excluded from the institutions and experiences (e.g., school) that could have led to greater equality and higher rates of acculturation. Prejudice, racism, and discrimination combined to keep most Latino groups away from the centers of modernization and change and away from opportunities to improve their situation.

Finally, for Cubans, Dominicans, and other Latino groups, cultural differences reflect the fact that they are largely recent immigrants. Their first generations are alive and well, and as is typical for immigrant groups, they keep the language and traditions alive.

FOCUS ON CONTEMPORARY ISSUES:
Will America Grow "Whiter" or "Browner"?

With Dr. Eileen O'Brien[1]

The United States, virtually since its birth, has been organized into two communities: black and white, separate and unequal. This structural relationship has been reinforced and solidified by the traditional perception that there are only two races. What will happen to these traditions as groups that are *neither* black nor white—Latinos, Asian Americans, and others—continue to grow in numbers and significance in the everyday life of U.S. society?

One possibility, called the whitening thesis, hypothesizes that Latinos (and Asian Americans) eventually will be accepted as white. An opposing position, called the browning thesis, predicts that "peoples of color" will band together and threaten the dominance of whites. We consider each of these views below, as well as a third possible future for the racial order of the United States.

Whitening

In this model, Latinos and Asian Americans will become part of the white American racial group while blacks will remain disproportionately unequal, powerless, and marginalized. The racial identities of Latinos and Asians will become "thinner," declining in salience for them as they increasingly access the privileges of whiteness, much as the Irish and Italian before them. As they assimilate, the "white" racial identity will take primacy over their ethnic connections, and their sense of ethnicity will become largely symbolic. This prediction is based on Gordon's assimilation model, which, as you recall, postulates that immigrants move through a series of stages and become more incorporated into various aspects of the life of the dominant society in a relatively linear fashion. Once a group has completed acculturation, integration, and intermarriage, they will begin to racially identify with the dominant group.

George Yancey (2003) has tested the whitening thesis on a nationally representative data set and his analysis places Latinos and Asian Americans in the middle stages of assimilation because their residential patterns, marital patterns, and several key political beliefs align more closely with white Americans than they do with black Americans. If Gordon's model holds true, these groups will come to identify as white over the next several generations.

Another research project (Murguia & Foreman, 2003) focused on Mexican Americans and found that they tend to prefer spouses, neighbors, coworkers, and friends who are either Puerto Rican or white, not black. The researchers also found that Mexican Americans tend to endorse modern racism (see . . . chapters 1 and 5) and believe that racism . . . is not much of a barrier to success and that people of color are largely responsible for their own hardships. This alignment with the ideology of the dominant group positions Mexican Americans well on the path to whiteness.

Finally, note that an important part of the whitening process is to distance oneself from the perpetually stigmatized black group. To the extent that a whitening process occurs for Latino and Asian Americans, these groups will tend to use both traditional and modern anti-black racism to emphasize their differences and align themselves more with the attitudinal and cultural perspectives of the dominant group. We discussed this type of dynamic in our coverage of the racial identity of Puerto Ricans who come to the mainland.

Browning

The browning thesis argues that whites will gradually lose their dominant status as Latino and Asian American groups grow in numbers. The balance of power will tip towards the non-white groups, who will use their greater numbers to challenge whites for position in the society.

Some theorists see the loss of white dominance as very negative, a threat to the integrity of Anglo American culture. This "doomsday" version of the browning thesis has most notably been presented by political scientist Samuel Huntington (2004) who argues that Latinos are "unassimilable" due to their alleged unwillingness to learn English and absorb other aspects of mainstream U.S. culture. This perspective is based largely on nativism, ethnocentrism, and prejudice, and is not given much credence by most sociologists. Indeed, much of the evidence presented in this and previous chapters

(Continued)

(Continued)

on the assimilation of Hispanic Americans shows that this view is simply wrong (e.g., see exhibits 7.9 and 7.10). Nevertheless, this version of the browning thesis has gained momentum in popular culture and in some talk radio and cable TV shows. It also manifests itself in the political arena in debates over immigration policy and in the movement to make English the "official" language of the nation (see chapter 2).

A different version of the browning thesis has taken hold amongst some sociologists. For example, Feagin and O'Brien (2004) put a positive spin on the idea of the declining white numerical majority. They believe that as "minority groups" grow in size, whites will be forced to share power in a more democratic, egalitarian, and inclusive fashion. This shift will be more likely to the extent that minority groups can forge alliances with each other against the dominant group. These combinations may be foreshadowed by studies of generational differences in the racial attitudes of immigrants, some of which show that native-born or second-generation Latinos and Asian Americans are more likely to express solidarity with African Americans than are the foreign-born and recently arrived members of their group (Murguia & Foreman, 2004). In contrast to the whitening thesis, the browning thesis expects Latinos and Asian Americans to embrace a more color-conscious worldview and find ways to leverage their growing numbers, in alliance with African Americans, to improve their status in American society.

This version of the browning thesis also adopts a more global perspective. It recognizes that the world is occupied by many more "people of color" than by whites of European descent, and that the growing numbers of non-whites in the United States can be an important resource in the global marketplace. For example, people around the world commonly speak several languages on a daily basis, but Americans are almost entirely monolingual, which places them at a disadvantage in a global marketplace that values linguistic diversity. The United States might improve its position if it were to encourage the "fluent bilingualism" of its Latino and Asian American citizens rather than insist on "English only" (see chapter 2).

Something Else?

Still another group of scholars challenges both the browning and the whitening theses and foresees a three-way racial dynamic. These scholars focus on the tremendous diversity within the Latino and Asian American communities in the United States in terms of relative wealth, skin color and other "racial" characteristics, religion, and national origins. This diversity leads them to conclude that only some Latino and Asian Americans will "whiten." Eduardo Bonilla-Silva (2003) sketches out a future racial trichotomy: whites, honorary whites, and the collective black. In this schema, well-off and light-skinned Latinos and Asians would not "become white" but rather would occupy an intermediary "honorary white" status. This status would afford them much of the privileges and esteem not widely accorded to people of color, but it would still be a conditional status, which potentially could be revoked in times of economic crisis or at any other time that those in power would find necessary. Bonilla-Silva predicts (2003) that groups like Chinese Americans and lighter-skinned Latinos would fit into the honorary white category, while darker-skinned Latinos and Asians would fit into the collective black category, along with, of course, American blacks.

Murguia and Foreman (2003) provide some findings from their study of Mexican Americans that can be used to illustrate this process. They point out that skin color and educational level make a difference in whether Latinos ally with blacks. Mexican Americans with darker skin, higher educational levels, and those born in the United States are less likely to buy into the anti-black stereotypes of the larger culture and more likely to recognize the significance of racism in their own lives. Attitudes such as these may form the basis of future alliances between some (but not all) Latinos, Asian Americans, and African Americans.

Conclusion

Will the United States grow browner or whiter? In the face of high levels of immigration and the growing importance of groups that are in the "racial middle"—groups that are neither black nor white—it seems certain that the traditional, dichotomous black–white racial order cannot persist. What will replace it? Whichever thesis proves correct, it seems certain that new understandings of race and new relationships between racial groups will emerge in the coming decades.

Section is based on Dr. Eileen O'Brien, *The Racial Middle: Latinos and Asian Americans Living Beyond the Racial Divide.* New York University Press, 2008.

Secondary Structural Assimilation

In this section, we survey the situation of Latinos in the public areas and institutions of American society, following the same format as the previous two chapters. We begin with where people live.

Residence. Exhibit 7.14 shows the geographic concentrations of Latinos in 2010. The legacies of the varied patterns of entry and settlement for the largest groups are evident. The higher concentrations in the Southwest reflect the presence of Mexican Americans; those in Florida are the result of the Cuban immigration, and those in the Northeast display the settlement patterns of Puerto Ricans.

Exhibit 7.15 highlights the U.S. counties in which Latinos are growing fastest. A quick glance at the map will reveal that many of the high-growth areas are distant from the traditional points of entry for these groups. In particular, the Hispanic American population is growing rapidly in parts of the Northeast and New England, the Southeast, the upper Midwest, the Northwest, and even Alaska. Among many other forces, this population movement is a response to the availability of jobs in factories, mills, chicken-processing plants and slaughterhouses, farms, construction, and other low-skilled areas of the economy.

Exhibit 7.14 Geographic Distribution of Hispanic Americans by County, 2010 (Percentage Share of County Population)

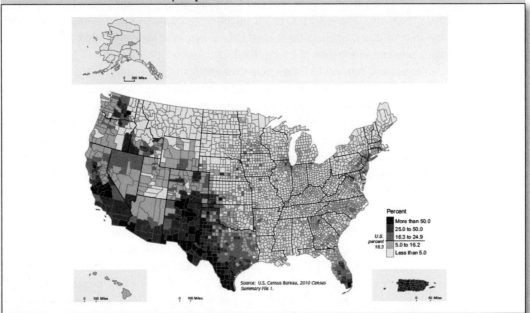

Source: Ennis, Ríos-Vargas, and Albert (2011, p. 10).

Exhibit 7.15 Growth of Hispanic Population by County, 2000–2010

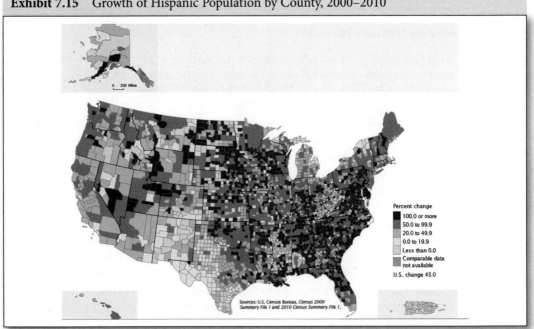

Source: Ennis, Ríos-Vargas, and Albert (2011, p. 12).

Within each of these regions, Latino groups are highly urbanized, as shown in exhibit 7.16. With the exception of Mexican Americans, more than 90% of each of the 10 largest Hispanic American groups lives in urban areas, and this percentage approaches 100% for some groups. Mexican Americans are more rural than the other groups, but in sharp contrast to their historical role as an agrarian workforce, the percentage of the group living in rural areas is tiny today.

The extent of residential segregation for Hispanic Americans is displayed in exhibit 7.17, which shows the average dissimilarity index for 220 metropolitan areas grouped into four regions. Hispanic Americans are less residentially segregated than African Americans (see exhibit 5.9), but in contrast to African Americans their segregation has generally held steady or slightly increased over the 20-year period. Among other factors, this is a reflection of high rates of immigration and "chain" patterns of settlement, which concentrate newcomers in ethnic neighborhoods.

Exhibit 7.16 Percentage of 10 Largest Hispanic American Groups and Non-Hispanic Whites Living in Urbanized Areas, 2000

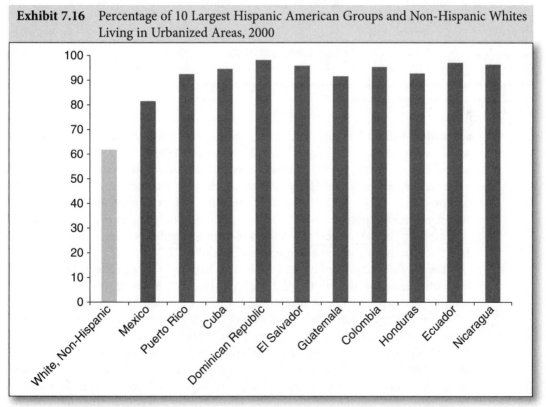

Source: U.S. Census Bureau (2000).

Note: An "urbanized area" is defined as an area with a minimal population density of 1,000 people per square mile and a minimum population of 50,000.

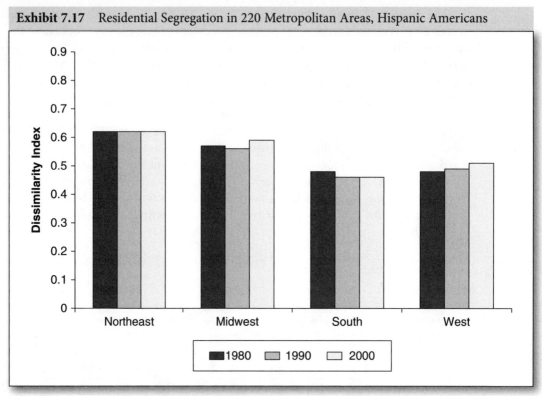

Exhibit 7.17 Residential Segregation in 220 Metropolitan Areas, Hispanic Americans

Source: Iceland, Weinberg, and Steinmetz (2002).

Education. Exhibit 7.18, like Exhibit 5.11 for the black population, shows the extent of school segregation for Hispanic Americans for the 1993–1994 and the 2005–2006 school years. In both years, Hispanic American children were more segregated than either American Indian or African American children. Furthermore, the percentages of Hispanic children in both majority-minority and extremely segregated schools increased over the period. These patterns reflect recent high rates of immigration and the tendency for newcomers to reside in the same neighborhoods as their co-ethnics (see the patterns of residential segregation in exhibit 7.17).

Levels of education for Hispanic Americans have risen in recent years but many are far below national standards (see exhibit 7.19). Hispanic Americans in general and all subgroups, except Colombian Americans, fall well below non-Hispanic whites for high school education. In particular, about 55% of Mexican Americans and only about 45% of Salvadorans and Guatemalans have high school degrees. At the college level, Colombian Americans are on a par with non-Hispanic whites and Cuban Americans approximate national norms, but the other groups and Hispanic Americans as a whole are far below non-Hispanic whites. For all Hispanic groups, there is very little difference by gender: males and females have about the same record of educational attainment.

The lower levels of education are the cumulative results of decades of systematic discrimination and exclusion for Mexican Americans and Puerto Ricans. These levels have been further reduced by the high percentage of recent immigrants from Mexico,

Exhibit 7.18 School Integration for Hispanic Americans, 1993–1994 and 2005–2006

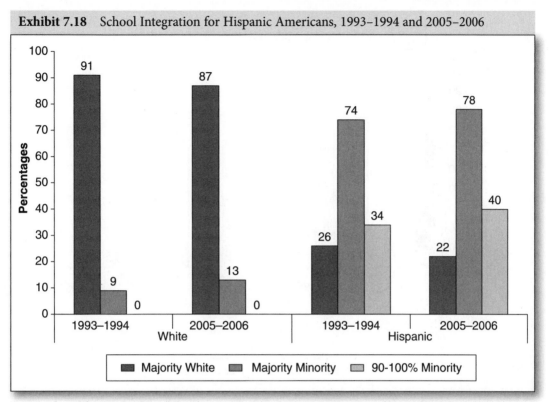

Source: Adapted from Richard Fry, "The Changing Racial and Ethnic Composition of U.S. Public Schools." Washington, DC: Pew Hispanic Center, August 2007.

the Dominican Republic, El Salvador, and other nations that have modest educational backgrounds.

Given the role that educational credentials have come to play in the job market, these figures are consistent with the idea that assimilation may be segmented for some Hispanic groups (see chapters 2 and 9), who may contribute in large numbers, along with African Americans and American Indians, to the growth of an urban underclass.

Political Power. The political resources available to Hispanic Americans have increased over the years, but the group is still proportionally underrepresented. The number of Hispanics of voting age has doubled in the past two decades, and Hispanics today constitute almost 14% of the voting-age population. Yet, because registration rates and actual turnout have been relatively low, Hispanic Americans have not had an impact on the political structure proportionate to its size. For example, in the presidential elections between 1996 and 2004, actual voter turnout for Hispanic Americans was less than 30%, which is less than half of the comparable rate for non-Hispanic whites (U.S. Census Bureau, 2012b, p. 246). In the 2008 presidential election, turnout increased for Hispanic Americans (as well as African Americans and Asian Americans); they accounted for about 9.5% of all voters, up from 8.2% in 2004 (Lopez & Taylor, 2009, p. 1). Clearly, the impact of the Hispanic American vote on national politics will increase as the group . . . grows in size and was considerable in the 2012 presidential election. However, participation is . . . is likely to remain lower than

Exhibit 7.19 Educational Attainment for Non-Hispanic Whites, All Hispanic Americans, and 10 Largest Hispanic American Groups, 2010

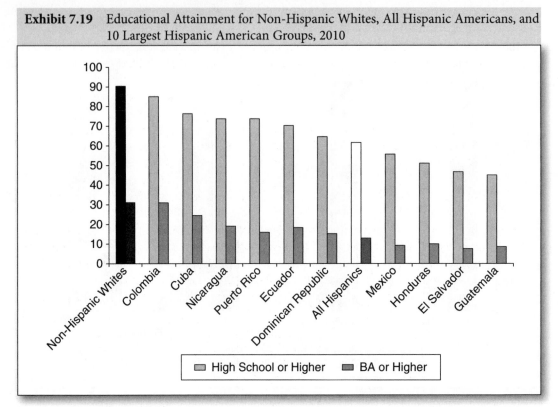

Source: U.S. Census Bureau (2010).

other groups for some time because of the large percentage of recent, non-English-speaking immigrants, and noncitizens in the group.

At the national level, there are now 28 Hispanic Americans in the House of Representatives, more than double the number in 1990 and about 6% of the total. In addition, the 112th Congress includes two Hispanic American senators. Most of these representatives and senators are members of the Democratic Party, but, in a reflection of the diversity of the group, nearly 30% are Republicans. On the local and state level, the number of public officials identified as Hispanic increased by more than 65% between 1985 and 2008, from 3,147 to 5,240 (U.S. Census Bureau, 2011, p. 259).

Although still underrepresented, these figures suggest that Hispanic Americans will become increasingly important in American political life as their numbers continue to grow and their rates of naturalization rise. A preview of their increasing power has been displayed in recent years as Hispanic communities across the nation have mobilized and engaged in massive demonstrations to express their opposition to restrictive immigration policies (e.g., see Aizenman, 2006).

Jobs and Income. The economic situation of Hispanic Americans is quite mixed. Many Latinos, especially those who have been in the United States for several generations, are doing "just fine. They have, in ever increasing numbers, accessed opportunities in education and employment and have carved out a niche of American prosperity for themselves and their children" (Camarillo & Bonilla, 2001, pp. 130–131). For others, however, the picture is not as promising. They face the possibility of becoming members of an impoverished, powerless, and economically marginalized urban underclass, like African Americans and other minority groups of color.

Occupationally, Hispanic Americans who are recent immigrants with modest levels of education and job skills are concentrated in the less-desirable, lower-paid service and unskilled segments of the job market. Those with higher levels of human capital and education compare more favorably with the dominant group.

Unemployment, low income, and poverty continue to be issues for all Hispanic groups. The official unemployment rates for Hispanic Americans run about twice the rate for non-Hispanic whites. Exhibit 7.20 compares median household incomes for whites and all Hispanic Americans across three decades. Read incomes from the left-hand axis and the size of the income gap between Hispanics and whites from the right-hand axis. The size of the income gap fluctuates but is generally between 70% and 75%. In the most recent year, Hispanic American median household income was 73% of white median household income. As a group, Hispanic Americans historically have been intermediate between blacks and whites in the stratification system; this is

Exhibit 7.20   Median Household Incomes for Whites and Hispanics, 1980–2010

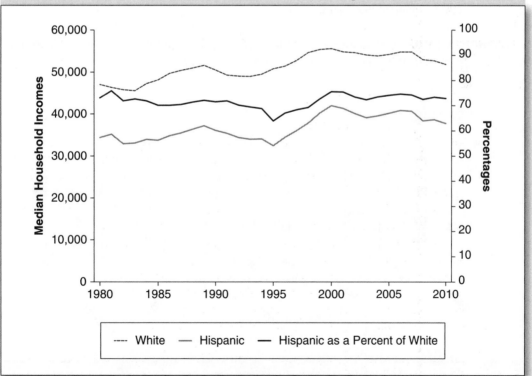

Source: U.S. Census Bureau (2012f).

reflected by the fact that the Hispanic–white income gap is smaller than the black–white income gap (which was 62% in 2010; see exhibit 5.14). This smaller gap also reflects the more favorable economic circumstances of Hispanics (especially those more "racially" similar to the dominant group) who have been in the United States for generations and who are thoroughly integrated into the mainstream economy.

Exhibit 7.21 shows that there is a good deal of income variability from group to group but that Hispanic Americans in general and all subgroups have, on the average, dramatically lower median household incomes than non-Hispanic whites, especially the groups with large numbers of recent immigrants who bring low levels of human capital.

Exhibit 7.22 supplements the information on median income by displaying the overall distribution of income for Hispanic Americans and non-Hispanic whites for 2010. The figure shows a greater concentration (wider bars) of Hispanics in the lower-income categories. Almost 18% of Hispanic households are in the lowest three categories (incomes of $15,000 or less) versus 11% of non-Hispanic white households. In the "upper-middle" income categories, white households outnumber Hispanic 39% to 32%. In the three highest income categories, whites outnumber Hispanic Americans by more than 2.5 to 1 (9.7% to 3.7%). There is less income inequality between Hispanic and whites than between blacks and whites (see exhibit 5.15) and Hispanic Americans can be found at every income level. Nonetheless, information such as that presented in exhibits 7.22 and 5.15 convincingly refutes the notion that no important racial and ethnic inequalities remain.

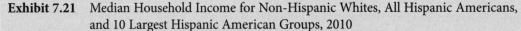

Exhibit 7.21 Median Household Income for Non-Hispanic Whites, All Hispanic Americans, and 10 Largest Hispanic American Groups, 2010

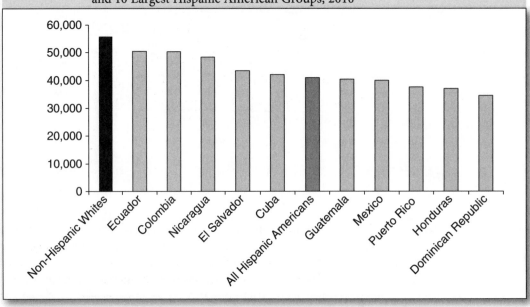

Source: U.S. Census Bureau (2010).

Exhibit 7.22   Distribution of Household Incomes for Non-Hispanic Whites and Hispanic Americans, 2010

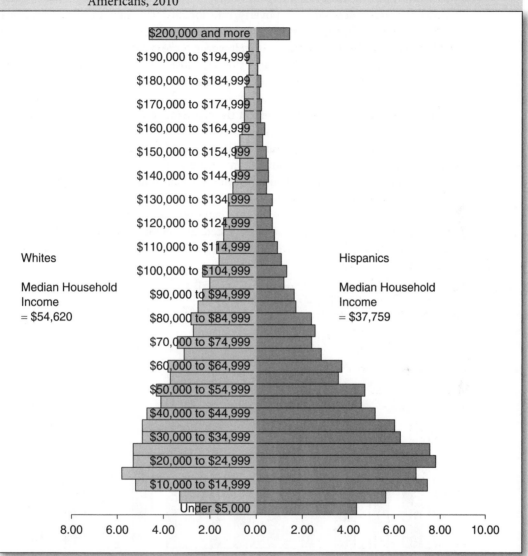

Whites

Median Household
Income
= $54,620

Hispanics

Median Household
Income
= $37,759

Source: U.S. Census Bureau (2012g).

Recent detailed income information is not available for the separate subgroups, but we can assume that, although all groups have members in all income categories, Mexican Americans, Dominican Americans, and Puerto Ricans would be disproportionately represented in the lowest-income categories, and Cuban Americans—especially, as we have seen, those that benefit from the enclave economy—in the higher groups.

Exhibit 7.23 finishes the socioeconomic profile by displaying the varying levels of poverty for Hispanic Americans, a pattern that is consistent with previous information on income and education. The poverty rate for all Hispanic American families is almost three times the rate for non-Hispanic white families and slightly lower than that of African Americans (see exhibit 5.16). However, there is considerable diversity across the subgroups, with Colombians and Cubans closest to non-Hispanic whites and Dominicans the most impoverished. For all groups, children have higher poverty rates than families.

These socioeconomic profiles reflect the economic diversity of Latinos. Some are "doing just fine," but others are concentrated in the low-wage sector of the economy. As a group, Cuban Americans rank higher than Mexican Americans and Puerto Ricans—the two other largest groups—on virtually all measures of wealth and prosperity. This relative prosperity would be even more pronounced for the earlier immigrants from Cuba and their children.

We should also note that the income gap and the picture of economic distress would be much greater if we focused on recent immigrants and, especially, undocumented immigrants, who are concentrated in the informal, irregular economy. These

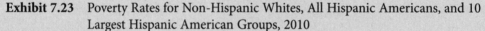

Exhibit 7.23 Poverty Rates for Non-Hispanic Whites, All Hispanic Americans, and 10 Largest Hispanic American Groups, 2010

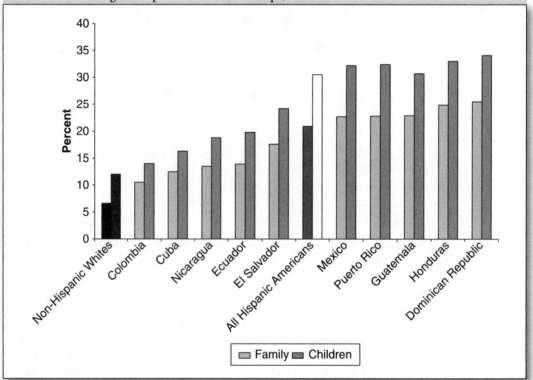

Source: U.S. Census Bureau (2012h).

groups are sometimes paid "off the books" and less than minimum wage. As we have discussed, they tend to be focused on their families and villages back home and live as simply as possible—5 or even 10 to a room, for example—in order to maximize the money they can send home. Since they tend to live "below the radar," they are not as likely to be included in the data-gathering efforts that supply the information for the exhibits in this chapter. If they were, the figures on average wages would be lower and rates of poverty higher for virtually all Latino groups in the United States.

Gender and Inequality. There is a split labor market differentiated by gender within the dual market differentiated by race and ethnicity. Hispanic women—like minority group women in general—are among the lowest-paid, most-exploitable, and least-protected segments of the U.S. labor force. The impact of poverty is especially severe for Latino women because they often find themselves with the responsibility of caring for their children alone. In 2010, about 20% of all Hispanic American households were female-headed (versus about 12% of non-Hispanic households) but this percentage ranged from a low of 14% for Cuban Americans to a high of about 36% for Dominicans (U.S. Census Bureau, 2012a). This pattern is the result of many factors, among them the status of Latino men in the labor force. The jobs available to Latino men often do not pay enough to support a family, and many jobs are seasonal, temporary, or otherwise insecure.

Female-headed Latino families face a triple economic handicap: they have only one wage earner, whose potential income is limited by discrimination against both women and Latinos. The result of these multiple disadvantages is an especially high rate of poverty. Whereas 27% of non-Hispanic white, female-headed households fall below the poverty line, the percentage is about 39% for Hispanic households headed by females (U.S. Census Bureau, 2012a).

Summary. The socioeconomic situation of Latinos is complex, diversified, and segmented. Many Latinos have successfully entered the mainstream economy, but others face poverty and exclusion. Highly concentrated in deteriorated urban areas, segments of these groups, like other minority groups of color, face the possibility of permanent poverty and economic marginality.

Primary Structural Assimilation

Overall, the extent of intimate contact between Hispanic Americans and the dominant group probably has been higher than for either African Americans or American Indians (see, e.g., Quillian & Campbell, 2003; and Rosenfield, 2002). This pattern may reflect the fact that Latinos are partly ethnic minority groups and partly racial minority groups. Some studies report that contact is greater for the more affluent social classes, in the cities, and for the younger generations (who are presumably more Americanized) (Fitzpatrick, 1976; Grebler et al., 1970, p. 397; Rodriguez, 1989, pp. 70–72).

On the other hand, the extent of intimate contact with other groups tends to be dampened by the rapid increase in immigration and the tendency of the first generation to socialize more with their co-ethnics. Between 1980 and 2010, the percentage of Hispanics married to someone of a different group declined slightly from 18% to 17.4% (Passel et al., 2010, p. 14) However, the out-marriage rate varied markedly between the native-born and immigrants. Between 1980 and 2010, out-marriage increased for United States–born Hispanics from 35% to 39% but decreased among the foreign-born from 16% to 12% (Passel et al., 2010, p. 16)

Intermarriage is more common for Latinos than for African Americans, but neither type is a very high percentage of all marriages. Black and white interracial couples make up slightly fewer than 1% of all marriages, and the comparable figure for Latinos is 3.8% of all marriages (U.S. Census Bureau, 2012b, p. 54).

Assimilation and Hispanic Americans

As test cases for what we have called the traditional view of American assimilation, Latinos fare poorly. The group is segmented in many ways: many enjoy high levels of equality and affluence while others are disproportionately impoverished, uneducated, and marginalized.

Almost two centuries after the original contact period, Mexican Americans—especially recent immigrants—continue to be concentrated in the low-wage sector of the labor market, a source of cheap labor for the dominant group's economy. Puerto Ricans, who are more recent arrivals, occupy a similar profile and position.

The fundamental reality faced by both groups, in their histories and in their present situations, is their colonized status in U.S. society. Even while many Mexican Americans and Puerto Ricans have risen in the social class and occupational structure of the larger society, others share many problems with other urban minority groups of color.

The traditional views of assimilation likewise fail to describe the experiences of Cuban Americans. They are more prosperous, on the average, than either Mexican Americans or Puerto Ricans, but they became successful by remaining separate and by developing the enclave in South Florida.

There is no single Hispanic American experience or pattern of adjustment to the larger society. We have focused mainly on three of the many Latino groups in the United States, and the diversity of their experiences suggests the variety and complexity of what it means to be a minority group in U.S. society. Their experiences also illustrate some of the fundamental forces that shape the experiences of minority groups: the split labor market and the U.S. appetite for cheap labor, the impact of industrialization, the dangers of a permanent urban underclass, the relationships between competition and levels of prejudice and rejection, and the persistence of race as a primary dividing line between people and groups.

Note

1. This section based on O'Brien (2008).

Main Points

- Hispanic Americans are a diverse and growing part of U.S. society. There are many distinct groups, but the three largest are Mexican Americans, Puerto Ricans, and Cuban Americans. The various Hispanic groups tend to not think of themselves as a single entity.
- Hispanic Americans have some characteristics of colonized groups and some of immigrant groups. Similarly, these groups are racial minorities in some ways and ethnic minorities in others.
- Since the beginning of the 20th century, Mexico has served as a reserve labor force for the development of the U.S. economy. Immigrants from Mexico entered a social system in which the colonized status of the group was already established. Mexican Americans have been a colonized minority group despite the large numbers of immigrants in the group and have been systematically excluded from opportunities for upward mobility by institutional discrimination and segregation.
- A Mexican American protest movement has been continuously seeking to improve the status of the group. In the 1960s, a more intense and militant movement emerged, guided by the ideology of Chicanismo.
- Puerto Ricans began to move to the mainland in large numbers only in the 1940s and 1950s. The group is concentrated in the urban Northeast, in the low-wage sector of the job market.
- Cubans began immigrating after Castro's revolution in the late 1950s. They settled primarily in southern Florida, where they created an ethnic enclave.
- The overall levels of anti-Hispanic prejudice and discrimination seem to have declined, along with the general decline in explicit, overt racism in American society. Recent high levels of immigration seem to have increased anti-Hispanic prejudice and discrimination, however, especially in the borderlands and other areas with large numbers of immigrants.
- Levels of acculturation are highly variable from group to group and generation to generation. Acculturation increases with length of residence but the vitality of Latino cultures has been sustained by recent immigration.
- Secondary structural assimilation also varies from group to group. Poverty, unemployment, lower levels of educational attainment, and other forms of inequality continue to be major problems for Hispanic groups, even the relatively successful Cuban Americans.
- Primary structural assimilation with the dominant group is greater than for African Americans.

Study Site on the Web

Don't forget the interactive quizzes and other resources and learning aids at www.sagepub.com/healeyds4e.

For Further Reading

Acuna, R. (2010). *Occupied America* (7th ed.). New York: Prentice Hall.

The author reviews Mexican American history and argues that the experiences of this group resemble those of colonized groups.

Garcia, M. C. (1997). *Havana USA: Cuban exiles and Cuban Americans in South Florida, 1959–1994.* Berkeley: University of California Press.

A comprehensive history of the Cuban community in southern Florida.

Acosta-Belen, E., & Santiago, C. (2006). Puerto Ricans in the United States: A contemporary portrait. Boulder, CO: Lynne Reiner.

Good overview of the history and present situation of Puerto Ricans.

Portes, A., & Bach, R. L. (1985). *Latin journey: Cuban and Mexican immigrants in the United States.* Berkeley: University of California Press.

A landmark analysis of Latino immigration, ethnic enclaves, and the United States and assimilation.

Telles, E., & Ortiz, V. (2008). *Generations of exclusion: Mexican Americans, assimilation, and race.* New York: Russell Sage

A very important look at assimilation among Mexicans Americans.

Smith, R. C. (2006). *Mexican New York: Transnational lives of new immigrants.* Berkeley: University of California Press

A ground-breaking study of globalization, transnationalism, and immigration focused on Mexicans in New York and Mexico.

Questions for Review and Study

1. The beginning of this chapter states that Hispanic Americans "combine elements of the polar extremes [immigrant and colonized] of Blauner's typology of minority groups" and that they are "partly an ethnic minority group . . . and partly a racial minority group." Explain these statements in terms of the rest of the material presented in the chapter.

2. What important cultural differences between Mexican Americans and the dominant society shaped the relationships between the two groups?

3. How does the history of Mexican immigration demonstrate the usefulness of Noel's concepts of differentials in power and competition?

4. Compare and contrast the protest movements of Mexican Americans, American Indians, and African Americans. What similarities and differences existed in Chicanismo, Red Power, and Black Power? How do the differences reflect the unique experiences of each group?

5. In what ways are the experiences of Puerto Ricans and Cuban Americans unique compared with those of other minority groups? How do these differences reflect other differences, such as differences in contact situation?

6. The Cuban American enclave has resulted in a variety of benefits for the group. Why don't other minority groups follow this strategy?

7. Describe the situation of the major Hispanic American groups in terms of acculturation and integration. Which groups are closest to equality? What factors or experiences might account for the differences between groups? In what ways might the statement "Hispanic Americans are remaining pluralistic even while they assimilate" be true?

Internet Research Project

In this exercise, you will once again use the U.S. census to gather information about the total population of all Hispanic Americans and two subgroups of your own choosing. This project adds to the information you gathered in chapters 5 and 6 and adds some new variables. The information for the total population is already entered. You can add the information for African Americans and American Indians and Alaska Natives (AIAN) from the previous exercise and add data for the new variables in this exercise. You will then use course concepts to assess and analyze this information and place it in the context of this text.

Notes

1. *The numbers you gather for this exercise may vary slightly from those presented in this chapter because of differences in the dates the data was collected or in the nature of the samples used.*

2. *Visit the website for this text to check for updates on the databases available for completing this exercise.*

Get information by following these steps:

1. Go to the official U.S. Census Bureau website at www.census.gov.

2. Click on "Data" in the list of choices at the top of the screen and then click "American Fact Finder" from the drop-down menu.

3. Click the "Race and Ethnic Groups" tab on the left of the next screen. A new window will open. Find the list of "Racial and Ethnic Group Results" on the right of the screen and click on the box next to "Total Population" (Code 001), the box next to "Black or African American alone or in combination with one or more other races" (Code 005), and the box next to "American Indian and Alaska Native alone or in combination with one or more other races" (Code 009). Next click the "Add" button above the "Racial and Ethnic Group Results" window and your selections will be added to the "Your selections" box in the top-left-hand corner of the screen.

4. In the "Your Race and Ethnic Group Filters" box in the middle of the screen, click on "Race and Hispanic Origin (2010 code based)." In the next box, click "Hispanic Origin" and then click "Hispanic."

5. In the "Race and Ethnic Group Results" window, click the box next to "Hispanic or Latino (of any race)" (Code 400) and click the "Add" button.

6. Next, select two more Hispanic groups from this window. Select at least one of the 10 largest Hispanic groups (see Exhibit 7.1). Once you have selected your two groups, click the "Add" button.

7. You should now have a total of six groups in the "Your Selections" box: The total population, black Americans, AIAN, Hispanic Americans and your two Hispanic subgroups. Write the names of the subgroups in the table below.

8. Close the "Select Race and Ethnic Groups" window by clicking the "Close" button on the top-right-hand corner of the window.

9. For this project, we will again use the 2011 ACS 1-year estimates. As before, look in either the "ID" column on the left for "Table S0201" or in the "Dataset" column on the right for the "2011 ACS 1-year estimates." Click the box next to the file name and then click "View" from the menu above the window.

10. The next screen will display a table with your groups listed at the top. Scroll down the table until you find the information needed to fill in the table below.

   a. For "Percent of Total Population," follow the instructions below the table.
   b. Under "Sex and Age," find "Median age (years)."
   c. Under "Households by Type," find "Average Household size."
   d. Under "Educational Attainment," find "Less than high school diploma."
   e. Under "Language Spoken at Home and Ability to Speak English," find "Speak English less than 'very well.'"
   f. Under "Employment Status," find "% Unemployed."
   g. Under "Income in the Past 12 Months," find "Individuals" and then "Per Capita income" and "Median earnings for full-time, year-round workers for males and females."
   h. Under "Poverty Rates for Families and People," find "All Families."
   i. Select two more variables relevant to this course and fill in the scores for all six groups. (*Note: Your instructor may have different instructions for this step of the project.*)

		Total Population	African Americans	AIAN	All Hispanic Americans	Hispanic American Groups	
1	Number	311,591,919	42,533,817				
2	Percent of total population*	—	13.7%				
3	Median age	37.3					
4	Average household size	2.64					
5	% Less than high school	14.1%					
6	Speak English less than "very well"	8.7%					
7	% unemployed	6.5%					
8	Per capita income	$26,708					
9	Median incomes for full time, year round worker						
	Males	$46,993					
	Females	$37,133					

		Total Population	African Americans	AIAN	All Hispanic Americans	Hispanic American Groups	
						_____	_____
10	Poverty rate, all families	11.7%					
11							
12							

*Divide the number in the group by 311,591,919 and multiply by 100.

Questions

1. What stage of Gordon's model of assimilation (see exhibit 2.1) do the variables in the table measure?

2. Using the Blauner hypothesis (see chapter 3), we can say that both American Indians and African Americans are "colonized or conquered" minority groups. Hispanic Americans, on the other hand, are a mixture of colonized and immigrant origins, as well as a combination of ethnic and racial groups. What would the Blauner hypothesis predict about the relative status of these groups in American society? Does the evidence in the table support the prediction? How?

3. What important differences do you see between your two Hispanic American subgroups? Which is closer to national patterns? To African Americans and American Indians? What are some possible reasons for these patterns? For example, are the differences related to the timing of the group's immigration? What "human capital" does the group bring that might help to account for the differences?

4. What additional concepts from this and previous chapters seem relevant for explaining the patterns you observe in this table? How?

Optional Group Discussion

Bring this information to class and, in groups of four to six people, compare with the information collected by others. Consider the issues raised in the question above and in the chapter and develop some ideas about why these groups are where they are relative to each other and to the total population. (*Note: Your instructor may have different instructions for this step of the project.*)

Asian Americans: "Model Minorities"?

I had flown from San Francisco . . . and was riding a taxi to my hotel to attend a conference on multiculturalism. My driver and I chatted about the weather and the tourists. The rearview mirror reflected a white man in his forties. "How long have you been in this country?" he asked. "All my life," I replied, wincing. "I was born in the United States." With a strong Southern drawl, he remarked: "I was wondering because your English is excellent!" . . . I explained: "My grandfather came here from Japan in the 1880s. My family has been here for over a hundred years." He glanced at me in the mirror. Somehow, I did not look "American" to him; my eyes and complexion looked foreign.

—Ronald Takaki (1993, p. 2)

These few seconds of conversation speak deeply about U.S. perceptions of Asian Americans (and other minority groups). The taxi driver certainly meant no insult, but his casual question reveals his view, widely shared, that the United States is a white European society. At the time of the conversation, Professor Takaki was a distinguished professor at a prestigious West Coast university, a highly respected teacher, and internationally renowned expert in his area. Very possibly, his family had been in the United States longer than the taxi driver's family. Yet, the driver automatically assumed he was an outsider.

Asian Americans, like other peoples of color, continually find themselves set apart, excluded and stigmatized—whether during the 19th century anti-Chinese campaign in California, after the 1922 Supreme Court decision (*Ozawa v. United States*) that declared Asians ineligible for U.S. citizenship, or by a YouTube video that went viral on the Internet in 2011 in which a UCLA student complained bitterly about Asians in the library.[1] The stereotypes might be "positive"—as in the view that Asian Americans are "model minorities"—but the "othering" is real, painful, and consequential. In this chapter, we begin with an overview of Asian American groups and then briefly examine the traditions and customs that they bring with them to America. For much of the chapter, we will focus on the two oldest groups, Chinese Americans and Japanese Americans. Throughout the chapter, we will be especially concerned with the perception that Asian Americans in general and Chinese and Japanese Americans in particular are a "**model minority group**": successful, affluent, highly educated people who do not suffer from the problems usually associated with minority group status. How accurate is this view? Have Asian Americans forged a pathway to upward mobility that could be followed by other groups? Do the concepts and theories that have guided this text (particularly the Blauner and Noel hypotheses) apply? Does the success of these groups mean that the United States is truly an open, fair, and just society? We explore these questions throughout the chapter.

Asian American groups vary in their languages, in their cultural and physical characteristics, and in their experiences in the United States. Some of these groups are truly newcomers to America, but others have roots in this country stretching back for more than 150 years. As was the case with American Indians and Hispanic Americans, the term "Asian American" is a convenient label imposed by the larger society (and by government agencies like the U.S. Census Bureau) that deemphasizes the differences between the groups. Exhibit 8.1 lists information about the size and growth of all Asian Americans and the 10 largest Asian American groups.

Exhibit 8.1   Size and Growth of Asian American* Groups, 1990–2010

Group	1990	2000	2010	Growth (Number of times larger), 1990–2010	Percent of Total Population, 2010
Chinese	1,645,472	2,879,636	4,010,114	2.4	1.3%
Filipino	1,406,770	2,364,815	3,416,840	2.4	1.1%
Asian Indian	815,447	1,899,599	3,183,063	3.9	1.0%
Vietnamese	614,547	1,223,736	1,737,433	2.8	0.6%
Korean	798,849	1,228,427	1,706,822	2.1	0.6%
Japanese	847,562	1,148,932	1,304,286	1.5	0.4%
Pakistani	N/A	204,309	409,163	—	0.1%
Cambodian	147,411	206,052	276,667	1.9	0.1%
Hmong	90,082	186,310	260,073	2.9	0.1%
Laotian	149,014	198,203	232,130	1.6	0.1%
Total Asian American	6,908,638	11,070,913	17,320,856	2.5	5.6%
Percent of U.S. Population	2.8%	3.9%	5.6%		
Total U.S. Population	248,710,000	281,422,000	308,745,538	1.2	

Source: 1990: U.S. Census Bureau (1990); 2000: U.S. Census Bureau (2000); 2010: Hoeffel, Rastogi, Kim, and Shahid (2012, p. 14).

Note: *Asian Americans, alone and in combination with other groups.

Several features of this exhibit are worth noting. First, Asian Americans are a small fraction of the total U.S. population. Even when aggregated, they accounted for less than 6% of all Americans in 2010. In contrast, African Americans are 13% and Hispanic Americans are more than 16%.

Second, most Asian American groups have grown dramatically in recent decades, largely because of high rates of immigration since the 1965 changes in U.S. immigration policy. All the groups listed in exhibit 8.1 grew faster than the total population between 1990 and 2010. The Japanese American population grew at the slowest rate (largely because immigration from Japan has been low in recent decades), but the number of Asian Indians almost quadrupled, and most of the other groups doubled or more than doubled their populations. This rapid growth is projected to continue for decades to come, and the impact of Asian Americans on everyday life and American culture will increase accordingly. Today, 5 out of every 100 Americans are of Asian heritage, but this ratio will grow to nearly 1 out of every 10 by the year 2050 (see exhibit 1.1). The relative sizes of the largest Asian American groups are presented in exhibit 8.2, and their nations of origin are displayed in exhibit 8.3.

Exhibit 8.2   Ten Largest Asian American Groups, 2010

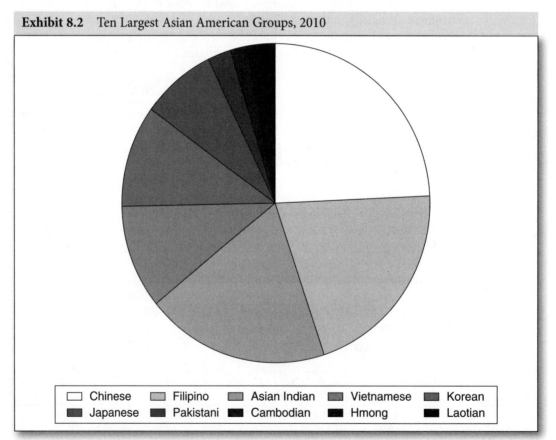

☐ Chinese	▨ Filipino	▨ Asian Indian	▨ Vietnamese	▨ Korean
■ Japanese	■ Pakistani	■ Cambodian	■ Hmong	■ Laotian

Source: Hoeffel, Rastogi, Kim, and Shahid. (2012, p. 14).

Note: The Hmong are from various Southeast Asian nations including Laos and Vietnam.

Exhibit 8.3 Map Showing China, the Philippines, India, South Korea, Vietnam, and Japan

Source: From REGC, 6ed.

Like Hispanic Americans, most Asian American groups have a high percentage of foreign-born members. The majority of most groups listed in exhibit 8.4 are first generation, and even Japanese Americans, the lowest-ranked group, more than double the national norm for foreign-born members. Today, the vast majority of Asian Americans (more than 80%) are either post-1965 immigrants or their second-generation children (Sakamoto, Goyette, & Kim, 2009, p. 269).

Origins and Cultures

Asian Americans have brought a wealth of traditions to the United States. They speak many different languages and practice religions as diverse as Buddhism, Confucianism, Islam, Hinduism, and Christianity. Asian cultures predate the founding of the United States by centuries or even millennia. Although no two of these cultures are the same, some general similarities can be identified. These cultural traits have shaped the behavior of Asian Americans, as well as the perceptions of members of the dominant group, and compose part of the foundation on which Asian American experiences have been built.

Asian cultures tend to stress group membership over individual self-interest. For example, Confucianism, which was the dominant ethical and moral system in traditional

Exhibit 8.4 Percentage Foreign-Born by Group for Total Population, All Asian Americans, and 10 Largest Asian American Groups, 2010

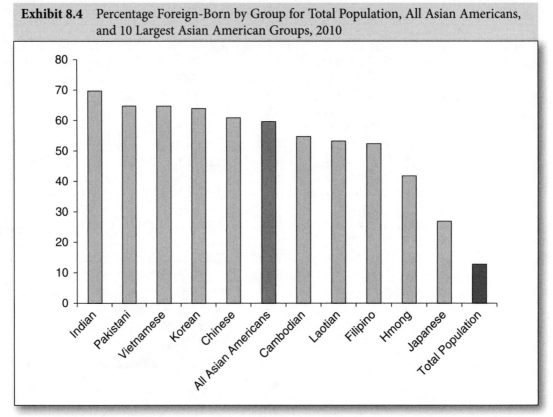

Source: U.S. Census Bureau (2010).

China and which had a powerful influence on many other Asian cultures, counsels people to see themselves as elements in larger social systems and status hierarchies. Confucianism emphasizes loyalty to the group, conformity to societal expectations, and respect for one's superiors. In traditional China, as in other Asian societies, the business of everyday life was organized around kinship relations, and most interpersonal relations were with family members and other relatives (Lyman, 1974, p. 9). The family or the clan often owned the land on which all depended for survival, and kinship ties determined inheritance patterns. The clan also performed a number of crucial social functions, including arranging marriages, settling disputes between individuals, and organizing festivals and holidays.

Asian cultures stress sensitivity to the opinions and judgments of others and the importance of avoiding public embarrassment and not giving offense. Especially when discussing Japanese culture, these cultural tendencies are often contrasted with Western practices in terms of "guilt versus shame" and the nature of personal morality (Benedict, 1946). In Western cultures, individuals are encouraged to develop and abide by a conscience, or an inner moral voice, and behavior is guided by one's personal sense of guilt. In contrast, Asian cultures stress the importance of maintaining the respect and good opinion of others and avoiding shame and public humiliation. Group harmony, or *wa* in Japanese, is a central concern, and displays of individualism are discouraged. These characteristics are reflected in the Japanese proverb, "The nail that sticks up must be hammered down" (Whiting, 1990, p. 70). Asian cultures emphasize proper behavior, conformity to convention and the judgments of others, and avoiding embarrassment and personal confrontations ("saving face").

A possible manifestation of this tendency to seek harmony and avoid confrontation was documented by Chou and Feagin (2008) in interviews with Asian Americans from a variety of groups. They found that their subjects commonly used "compliant conformity" to cope with white racism, discrimination, and rejection (Chou & Feagin, 2008, p. 222). Their respondents often expressed the idea that conformity and hard work would result in recognition and acceptance in the larger society. The parents of the respondents, even those who had experienced substantial discrimination, commonly pressured their children to conform to white expectations and Anglo values in the hope that their success (e.g., in school) would protect them from negative treatment and stereotyping. Chou and Feagin suggest that this strategy has had limited success (at best) and that, ultimately, it sustains white prejudicial values and the conventional racial hierarchy in U.S. society by complying with rather than challenging racism (Chou & Feagin, 2008, p. 222).

Traditional Asian cultures were male dominated, and women were consigned to subordinate roles. A Chinese woman was expected to serve first her father, then her husband, and, if widowed, her eldest son. Confucianism also decreed that women should observe the Four Virtues: chastity and obedience, shyness, a pleasing demeanor, and skill in the performance of domestic duties (Amott & Matthaei, 1991, p. 200). Women of high status in traditional China symbolized their subordination by binding their feet. This painful, crippling practice began early in life and required women to wrap their feet tightly to keep them artificially small. The bones in the arch were broken so that the toes could be bent under the foot, further decreasing the size of the foot. Bound feet were considered beautiful, but they also immobilized women and were intended to prevent them from "wandering away" from domestic and household duties (Jackson, 2000; Takaki, 1993, pp. 209–210).

The experiences of Asian Americans in the United States modified these patriarchal values and traditional traits. For the groups with longer histories in U.S. society, such as Chinese Americans and Japanese Americans, the effects of these values on individual personality may be slight, but for more recently arrived groups, the effects can be more powerful. The cultural and religious differences among the Asian American groups also reflect the recent histories of each of the sending nations. For example, Vietnam was a colony of China for 1,000 years, but for much of the past century it was a colony of France. Although Vietnamese culture has been heavily influenced by China, many Vietnamese are Catholic, a result of the efforts of the French to convert them. The Philippines and India were also colonized by Western nations—the former by Spain and then by the United States and the latter by Great Britain. As a result, many Filipino and Asian Indian immigrants speak English and are familiar with American and Western cultures.

These examples are, of course, the merest suggestion of the diversity of these groups. In fact, Asian Americans, who share little more than a slight physical resemblance and some broad cultural similarities, are much more diverse than Hispanic Americans, who are overwhelmingly Catholic and who share a common language and a historical connection with Spain (Min, 1995, p. 25).

Contact Situations and the Development of the Chinese American and Japanese American Communities

The earliest Asian groups to arrive in substantial numbers were from China and Japan. Their contact situations not only shaped their own histories, but also affected the present situation of all Asian Americans in many ways. As we will see, the contact situations for both Chinese Americans and Japanese Americans featured massive rejection and discrimination. Both groups adapted to the racism of the larger society by forming enclaves, a strategy that eventually produced some major benefits for their descendants.

Chinese Americans

Early Immigration and the Anti-Chinese Campaign.

Immigrants from China to the United States began to arrive in the early 1800s and were generally motivated by the same kinds of social and economic forces that have inspired immigration everywhere for the past two centuries. Chinese immigrants were "pushed" to leave their homeland by the disruption of traditional social relations, caused by the colonization of much of China by more-industrialized European nations, and by rapid population growth (Chan, 1990; Lyman, 1974; Tsai, 1986). At the same time, these immigrants were "pulled" to the West Coast of the United States by the Gold Rush of 1849 and by other opportunities created by the development of the West.

The Noel hypothesis (see chapter 3) provides a useful way to analyze the contact situation that developed between Chinese and Anglo Americans in the mid-19th century. As you recall, Noel argues that racial or ethnic stratification will result when a contact situation is characterized by three conditions: ethnocentrism, competition, and a differential in power. Once all three conditions were met on the West Coast, a vigorous campaign against the Chinese began, and the group was pushed into a subordinate, disadvantaged position.

Ethnocentrism based on racial, cultural, and language differences was present from the beginning of the contact situation. In the early days, however, competition for jobs between Chinese immigrants and native-born workers was muted by a robust, rapidly growing economy and an abundance of jobs. At first, politicians, newspaper editorial writers, and business leaders praised the Chinese for their industriousness and tirelessness (Tsai, 1986, p. 17).

As the century progressed, the economic boom slowed—especially after the American Civil War—and the supply of jobs began to dry up. The Gold Rush petered out, and the transcontinental railroad, which thousands of Chinese workers had helped to build, was completed in 1869. The migration of Anglo Americans from the East continued, and competition for jobs and other resources increased.

As conditions changed, an anti-Chinese campaign of harassment, discrimination, and violent attacks began. In 1871, in Los Angeles, a mob of "several hundred whites shot, hanged, and stabbed 19 Chinese to death" (Tsai, 1986, p. 67). Other attacks against the Chinese occurred in Denver, Seattle, Tacoma, and Rock Springs, Wyoming (Lyman, 1974, p. 77).

As the West Coast economy changed, the Chinese came to be seen as a threat, and elements of the dominant group tried to limit competition. The Chinese were a small group— there were only about 100,000 in the entire country in 1870—and by law, they were not permitted to become citizens. Hence, they controlled few power resources with which to withstand these attacks.

During the 1870s, Chinese workers were forced out of most sectors of the mainstream economy, and in 1882, the anti-Chinese campaign experienced its ultimate triumph when the U.S. Congress passed the **Chinese Exclusion Act**, banning virtually all immigration from China. The Act was one of the first restrictive immigration laws and was aimed solely at the Chinese. It established a "rigid competitive" relationship between the groups (see chapter 4) and eliminated the threat presented by Chinese labor by excluding the Chinese people from American society.

The primary antagonists of Chinese immigrants were native-born workers and organized labor. White owners of small businesses, feeling threatened by Chinese-owned businesses, also supported passage of the Chinese Exclusion Act (Boswell, 1986). Other social classes, such as the capitalists who owned larger factories, might actually have benefited from the continued supply of cheaper labor created by immigration from China. Conflicts such as the anti-Chinese campaign can be especially intense because they can confound racial and ethnic antagonisms with disputes between different social classes.

The ban on immigration from China remained in effect until World War II, when China was awarded a yearly quota of 105 immigrants in recognition of its wartime alliance with the United States. However, large-scale immigration from China did not resume until federal policy was revised in 1965.

Population Trends and the "Delayed" Second Generation

Following the Chinese Exclusion Act in 1882, the number of Chinese in the United States actually declined (see exhibit 8.5), as some immigrants passed away or returned to China and were not replaced by newcomers. The huge majority of Chinese immigrants in the 19th century had been young adult male sojourners who intended to work hard, save money, and return to their home villages in China (Chan, 1990, p. 66). After 1882, it was difficult for anyone from China, male or female, to enter the United States, and the Chinese community in the United States remained overwhelmingly male for many decades. At the end of the 19th century, for example, males outnumbered females by more than 25 to 1, and the sex ratio did not approach parity for decades (Wong, 1995, p. 64; see also Ling, 2000). The scarcity of Chinese women in the United States delayed the second generation (the first born in the United States), and

Exhibit 8.5 Population Growth for Chinese and Japanese Americans, 1850–2010

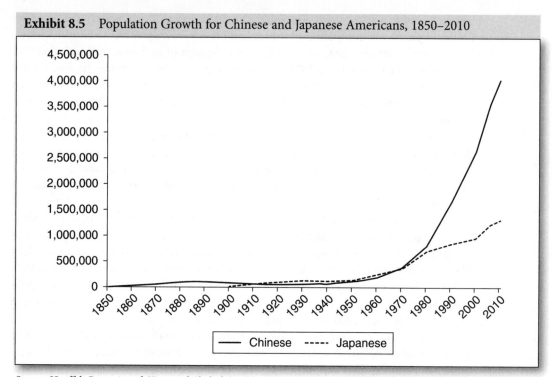

Source: Hoeffel, Rastogi, and Kim, and Shahid (2012); Kitano (1980, p. 562); Lee (1998, p. 15); U.S. Census Bureau (2007a); Xie and Goyette (2004).

it wasn't until the 1920s, 80 years after immigration began, that as many as one third of all Chinese in the United States were native-born (Wong, 1995, p. 64).

The delayed second generation may have reinforced the exclusion of the Chinese American community, which began as a reaction to the overt discrimination of the dominant group (Chan, 1990, p. 66). The children of immigrants are usually much more acculturated, and their language facility and greater familiarity with the larger society often permits them to represent the group and speak for it more effectively. In the case of Chinese Americans (and other Asian groups), members of the second generation were citizens of the United States by birth, a status from which the immigrants were barred, and they had legal and political rights not available to their parents. Thus, the decades-long absence of a more Americanized, English-speaking generation increased the isolation of Chinese Americans.

The Ethnic Enclave

The Chinese became increasingly urbanized as the anti-Chinese campaign and rising racism took their toll. Forced out of towns and smaller cities, they settled in larger urban areas, such as San Francisco, which offered the safety of urban anonymity and ethnic neighborhoods where the old ways could be practiced and contact with the hostile larger society minimized. Chinatowns had existed since the start of the immigration, and they now took on added significance as safe havens from the storm of anti-Chinese venom. The Chinese withdrew to these neighborhoods and became an "invisible minority" (Tsai, 1986, p. 67).

These early Chinatowns were ethnic enclaves like those founded by Jews on the East Coast and the more recently founded Cuban community in Miami, and a similar process formed them. The earliest urban Chinese included merchants and skilled artisans who, like the early wave of Cuban immigrants, were experienced in commerce (Chan, 1990, p. 44). They established businesses and retail stores that were typically small in scope and modest in profits. As the number of urban Chinese increased, the market for these enterprises became larger and more spatially concentrated. New services were required, the size of the cheap labor pool available to Chinese merchants and entrepreneurs increased, and the Chinatowns became the economic, cultural, and social centers of the community.

Within the Chinatowns, elaborate social structures developed that mirrored traditional China in many ways. The enforced segregation of the Chinese in America helped preserve much of the traditional food, dress, language, values, and religions of their homeland from the pressures of Americanization. The social structure was based on a variety of types of organizations, including family and clan groups and ***huiguan***, or associations based on the region or district in China from which the immigrant had come.

These organizations performed various, often overlapping, social and welfare services, including settling disputes, aiding new arrivals from their regions, and facilitating the development of mutual aid networks (Lai, 1980, p. 221; Lyman, 1974, pp. 32–37, 116–118). Life was not always peaceful in Chinatown, and there were numerous disputes over control of resources and the organizational infrastructure. In particular, secret societies called ***tongs*** contested the control and leadership of the merchant-led *huiguan* and the clan associations. These sometimes bloody conflicts were sensationalized in the American press as "Tong Wars," and they contributed to the popular stereotypes of Asians as exotic, mysterious, and dangerous (Lai, 1980, p. 222; Lyman, 1974, pp. 37–50).

Despite these internal conflicts, American Chinatowns evolved into highly organized, largely self-contained communities, complete with their own leadership and decision-making structures. The internal "city government" of Chinatown was the Chinese Consolidated Benevolent Association (CCBA). Dominated by the larger *huiguan* and clans, the CCBA coordinated and supplemented the activities of the various organizations and represented the interests of the community to the larger society.

The local CCBAs, along with other organizations, also attempted to combat the anti-Chinese campaign, speaking out against racial discrimination and filing numerous lawsuits to contest racist legislation (Lai, 1980, p. 223). The effectiveness of the protest efforts was handicapped by the lack of resources in the Chinese community and by the fact that Chinese immigrants could not become citizens. Attempts were made to mobilize international pressure to protest the treatment of the Chinese in the United States. At the time, however, China was itself colonized and dominated by other nations (including the United States). China was further weakened by internal turmoil and could mount no effective assistance for its citizens in the United States (Chan, 1990, p. 62).

Survival and Development

The Chinese American community survived despite the widespread poverty, discrimination, and pressures created by the unbalanced sex ratio. Members of the group began to seek opportunities in other regions, and Chinatowns appeared and grew in New York, Boston, Chicago, Philadelphia, and many other cities.

The patterns of exclusion and discrimination that began during the 19th-century anti-Chinese campaign were common throughout the nation and continued well into the 20th century. Chinese Americans responded by finding economic opportunity in areas where dominant group competition for jobs was weak, continuing their tendency to be an "invisible" minority group. Very often, they started small businesses that either served other members of their own group (e.g., restaurants) or relied on the patronage of the general public (e.g., laundries). The jobs provided by these small businesses were the economic lifeblood of the community but were limited in the amount of income and wealth they could generate. Until recent decades, for example, most restaurants served primarily other Chinese, especially single males. Since their primary clientele was poor, the profit potential of these businesses was sharply limited. Laundries served the more affluent dominant group, but the returns from this enterprise declined as washers and dryers became increasingly widespread in homes throughout the nation. The population of Chinatown was generally too small to sustain more than these two primary commercial enterprises (Zhou, 1992, pp. 92–94).

As the decades passed, the enclave economy and the complex subsociety of Chinatown evolved. However, discrimination, combined with defensive self-segregation, ensured the continuation of poverty, limited job opportunities, and substandard housing. Relatively hidden from general view, Chinatown became the world in which the second generation grew to adulthood.

The Second Generation

Whereas the immigrant generation generally retained its native language and customs, the second generation was much more influenced by the larger culture. The institutional and organizational structures of Chinatown were created to serve the older, mostly male immigrant generation, but younger Chinese Americans tended to look beyond the enclave to fill their needs. They came in contact with the larger society through schools, churches, and voluntary organizations such as the YMCA and YWCA.

They abandoned many traditional customs and were less loyal to and interested in the clan and regional associations that the immigrant generation had constructed. They founded organizations of their own that were more compatible with their Americanized lifestyles (Lai, 1980, p. 225).

As with other minority groups, World War II was an important watershed for Chinese Americans. During the war, job opportunities outside the enclave increased, and after the war many of the 8,000 Chinese Americans who had served in the armed forces were able to take advantage of the GI Bill to further their education (Lai, 1980, p. 226). In the 1940s and 1950s, many second-generation Chinese Americans moved out of the enclave, away from the traditional neighborhoods, and pursued careers in the larger society. This group was mobile and Americanized, and with educational credentials comparable to the general population, they were prepared to seek success outside Chinatown.

In another departure from tradition, the women of the second generation also pursued education, and as early as 1960 median years of schooling for Chinese American women were slightly higher than for Chinese American men (Kitano & Daniels, 1995, p. 48). Chinese American women also became more diverse in their occupational profile as the century progressed. In 1900, three quarters of all employed Chinese American women worked in manufacturing (usually in garment industry sweatshops or in canning factories) or in domestic work. By 1960, fewer than 2% were in domestic work, 32% were in clerical occupations, and 18% held professional jobs, often as teachers (Amott & Matthaei, 1991, pp. 209–211).

An American Success Story?

The men and women of the second generation achieved considerable educational and occupational success and helped establish the idea that Chinese Americans are a "model minority." A closer examination reveals, however, that the old traditions of anti-Chinese discrimination and prejudice continued to limit the life chances of even the best-educated members of this generation. Second-generation Chinese Americans earned less, on the average, and had less-favorable occupational profiles than comparably educated white Americans, a gap between qualifications and rewards that reflects persistent discrimination. Kitano and Daniels (1995, p. 50) conclude, for example, that although well-educated Chinese Americans could find good jobs in the mainstream economy, the highest, most lucrative positions—and those that required direct supervision of whites—were still closed to them (see also Hirschman & Wong, 1984).

Furthermore, many Chinese Americans, including many of those who stayed in the Chinatowns to operate the enclave economy, and the immigrants who began arriving after 1965, do not fit the image of success at all. A large percentage of these Chinese Americans face many of the same problems as do members of colonized, excluded, exploited minority groups of color. For survival, they rely on low-wage jobs in the garment industry, the service sector, and the small businesses of the enclave economy and are beset by poverty and powerlessness, much like the urban underclass segments of other groups.

Thus, Chinese Americans can be found at both ends of the spectrum of success and affluence, and the group is often said to be "bipolar" in its occupational structure (see Barringer, Takeuchi, & Levin, 1995; Min, 2006; Takaki, 1993, pp. 415–416; Wong, 1995, pp. 77–78; and Zhou & Logan, 1989). Although a high percentage of Chinese Americans are found in more desirable occupations—sustaining the idea of Asian success—others, less visible, are concentrated at the lowest levels of society. Later in this chapter, we will again consider the socioeconomic status of Chinese Americans and the accuracy of the image of success and affluence.

Japanese Americans

Immigration from Japan began to increase shortly after the Chinese Exclusion Act of 1882 took effect, in part to fill the gap in the labor supply created by the restrictive legislation (Kitano, 1980). The 1880 census counted only a few hundred Japanese in the United States, but the group increased rapidly over the next few decades. By 1910, the Japanese in the United States outnumbered the Chinese and remained the larger of the two groups until large-scale immigration resumed in the 1960s (see exhibit 8.5).

The Anti-Japanese Campaign

The contact situation for Japanese immigrants resembled that of the Chinese. They immigrated to the same West Coast regions as the Chinese, entered the labor force in a similar position, and were a small group with few power resources. Predictably, the feelings and emotions generated by the anti-Chinese campaign transferred to them. By the early 1900s, an anti-Japanese campaign to limit competition was in full swing. Efforts were being made to establish a rigid competitive system of group relations and to exclude Japanese immigrants in the same way the Chinese had been barred (Kitano, 1980, p. 563; Kitano & Daniels, 1995, pp. 59–60; Petersen, 1971, pp. 30–55).

Japanese immigration was partly curtailed in 1907 when a "gentlemen's agreement" was signed between Japan and the United States limiting the number of laborers Japan would allow to emigrate (Kitano & Daniels, 1995, p. 59). This policy remained in effect until the United States changed its immigration policy in the 1920s and barred immigration from Japan completely. The end of Japanese immigration is largely responsible for the slow growth of the Japanese American population displayed in exhibit 8.5.

Most Japanese immigrants, like the Chinese, were young male laborers who planned to eventually return to their homeland or bring their wives after they were established in their new country (Duleep, 1988, p. 24). The agreement of 1907 curtailed the immigration of men, but because of a loophole, females were able to continue immigrating until the 1920s. Japanese Americans were thus able to maintain a relatively balanced sex ratio, marry, and begin families, and a second generation of Japanese Americans began to appear without much delay. Native-born Japanese numbered about half of the group by 1930 and were a majority of 63% on the eve of World War II (Kitano & Daniels, 1995, p. 59).

The anti-Japanese movement also attempted to dislodge the group from agriculture. Many Japanese immigrants were skilled agriculturists, and farming proved to be their most promising avenue for advancement (Kitano, 1980, p. 563). In 1910, between 30% and 40% of all Japanese in California were engaged in agriculture; from 1900 to 1909, the number of independent Japanese farmers increased from fewer than 50 to about 6,000 (Jibou, 1988, p. 358).

Most of these immigrant farmers owned small plots of land, and they made up only a minuscule percentage of West Coast farmers (Jibou, 1988, pp. 357–358). Nonetheless, their presence and relative success did not go unnoticed and eventually stimulated discriminatory legislation, most notably the **Alien Land Act**, passed by the

California legislature in 1913 (Kitano, 1980, p. 563). This bill made aliens who were ineligible for citizenship (effectively meaning only immigrants from Asia) to be also ineligible to own land. The Act did not achieve its goal of dislodging the Japanese from the rural economy. They were able to dodge the discriminatory legislation by various devices, mostly by putting titles of land in the names of their American-born children, who were citizens by law (Jibou, 1988, p. 359).

The Alien Land Act was one part of a sustained campaign against the Japanese in the United States. In the early decades of this century, the Japanese were politically disenfranchised and segregated from dominant group institutions in schools and residential areas. They were discriminated against in movie houses, swimming pools, and other public facilities (Kitano & Daniels, 1988, p. 56). The Japanese were excluded from the mainstream economy and confined to a limited range of poorly paid occupations (see Yamato, 1994). Thus, there were strong elements of systematic discrimination, exclusion, and colonization in their overall relationship with the larger society.

The Ethnic Enclave

Spurned and disparaged by the larger society, the Japanese, like the Chinese, constructed a separate subsociety. The immigrant generation, called **Issei** (from the Japanese word *ichi*, meaning "one"), established an enclave in agriculture and related enterprises, a rural counterpart of the urban enclaves constructed by other groups we have examined.

By World War II, the Issei had come to dominate a narrow but important segment of agriculture on the West Coast, especially in California. Although the Issei were never more than 2% of the total population of California, Japanese American–owned farms produced as much as 30% to 40% of various fruits and vegetables grown in that state. As late as 1940, more than 40% of the Japanese American population was involved directly in farming, and many more were dependent on the economic activity stimulated by agriculture, including the marketing of their produce (Jibou, 1988, pp. 359–360). Other Issei lived in urban areas, where they were concentrated in a narrow range of businesses and services, such as domestic service and gardening, some of which catered to other Issei and some of which served the dominant group (Jibou, 1988, p. 362).

Japanese Americans in both the rural and urban sectors maximized their economic clout by doing business with other Japanese American–owned firms as often as possible. Gardeners and farmers purchased supplies at Japanese American–owned firms, farmers used other members of the group to haul their products to market, and businesspeople relied on one another and mutual credit associations, rather than dominant group banks, for financial services. These networks helped the enclave economy to grow and also permitted the Japanese to avoid the hostility and racism of the larger society. However, these very same patterns helped sustain the stereotypes that depicted the Japanese as clannish and unassimilable. In the years before World War II, the Japanese American community was largely dependent for survival on their networks of cooperation and mutual assistance, not on Americanization and integration.

The Second Generation (Nisei)

In the 1920s and 1930s, anti-Asian feelings continued to run high, and Japanese Americans continued to be excluded and discriminated against despite (or perhaps because of) their relative success. Unable to find acceptance in Anglo society, the second generation, called **Nisei**, established clubs, athletic leagues, churches, and a multitude of other social and recreational organizations within their own communities (Kitano & Daniels, 1995, p. 63). These organizations reflected the high levels of Americanization of the Nisei and expressed values and interests quite compatible with those of the dominant culture. For example, the most influential Nisei organization was the Japanese American Citizens League, whose creed expressed an ardent patriotism that was to be sorely tested: "I am proud that I am an American citizen. . . . I believe in [American] institutions, ideas and traditions; I glory in her heritage; I boast of her history, I trust in her future" (Kitano & Daniels, 1995, p. 64).

Although the Nisei enjoyed high levels of success in school, the intense discrimination and racism of the 1930s prevented most of them from translating their educational achievements into better jobs and higher salaries. Many occupations in the mainstream economy were closed to even the best-educated Japanese Americans, and anti-Asian prejudice and discrimination did not diminish during the hard times and high unemployment of the Great Depression in the 1930s. Many Nisei were forced to remain within the enclave, and in many cases jobs in the produce stands and retail shops of their parents were all they could find. Their demoralization and anger over their exclusion were eventually swamped by the larger events of World War II.

The Relocation Camps

On December 7, 1941, Japanese forces attacked Pearl Harbor, killing almost 2,500 Americans. President Franklin D. Roosevelt asked Congress for a declaration of war with Japan the next day. The preparations for war stirred up a wide range of fears and anxieties among the American public, including concerns about the loyalty of Japanese Americans. Decades of exclusion and anti-Japanese prejudice had conditioned the dominant society to see Japanese Americans as sinister, clannish, cruel, unalterably foreign, and racially inferior. Fueled by the ferocity of the war itself and fears about a Japanese invasion of the mainland, the tradition of anti-Japanese racism laid the groundwork for a massive violation of civil rights.

Two months after the attack on Pearl Harbor, President Roosevelt signed Executive Order 9066, which led to the relocation of Japanese Americans living on the West Coast. By the late summer of 1942, more than 110,000 Japanese Americans, young and old, male and female—virtually the entire West Coast population—had been transported to **relocation camps**, where they were imprisoned behind barbed-wire fences patrolled by armed guards. Many of these people were American citizens, yet no attempt was made to distinguish between citizen and alien. No trials were held, and no one was given the opportunity to refute the implicit charge of disloyalty.

The government gave families little notice to prepare for evacuation and secure their homes, businesses, and belongings. They were allowed to bring only what they could carry, and many possessions were simply abandoned. Businesspeople sold their establishments and farmers sold their land at panic sale prices. Others locked up their stores and houses and walked away, hoping that the evacuation would be short-lived and their possessions undisturbed.

The internment lasted for nearly the entire war. At first, Japanese Americans were not permitted to serve in the armed forces, but eventually more than 25,000 escaped the camps by volunteering for military service. Nearly all of them served in segregated units or in intelligence work with combat units in the Pacific Ocean. Two all-Japanese combat units served in Europe and became the most decorated units in American military history (Kitano, 1980, p. 567). Other Japanese Americans were able to get out of the camps by means other than the military. Some, for example, agreed to move to militarily nonsensitive areas far away from the West Coast (and their former homes). Still, when the camps closed at the end of the war, about half of the original internees remained (Kitano & Daniels, 1988, p. 64).

The strain of living in the camps affected Japanese Americans in a variety of ways. Lack of activities and privacy, overcrowding, boredom, and monotony were all common complaints. The camps disrupted the traditional forms of family life, as people had to adapt to living in barracks and dining in mess halls. Conflicts flared between those who counseled caution and temperate reactions to the incarceration and those who wanted to protest in more vigorous ways. Many of those who advised moderation were Nisei intent on proving their loyalty by cooperating with the camp administration.

Despite the injustice and dislocations of the incarceration, the camps did reduce the extent to which women were relegated to a subordinate role. Like Chinese women, Japanese women were expected to devote themselves to the care of the males of their family. In Japan, for example, education for females was not intended to challenge their intellect so much as to make them better wives and mothers. In the camps, however, pay for the few jobs available was the same for both men and women, and the mess halls and small living quarters freed women from some of the burden of housework. Many took advantage of the free time to take classes to learn more English and other skills. The younger women were able to meet young men on their own, weakening the tradition of family controlled, arranged marriages (Amott & Matthaei, 1991, pp. 225–229).

Some Japanese Americans protested the incarceration from the start and brought lawsuits to end the relocation program. Finally, in 1944 the Supreme Court ruled that detention was unconstitutional. As the camps closed, some Japanese American individuals and organizations began to seek compensation and redress for the economic losses the group had suffered. In 1948, Congress passed legislation to authorize compensation to Japanese Americans. About 26,500 people filed claims under this legislation. These claims were eventually settled for a total of about $38 million—less than one-tenth of the actual economic losses. Demand for meaningful redress and compensation continued, and in 1988 Congress passed a bill granting reparations of about $20,000 in cash to each of the 60,000 living survivors of the camps. The law also acknowledged that the relocation program had been a grave injustice to Japanese Americans (Biskupic, 1989, p. 2879).

The World War II relocation devastated the Japanese American community and left it with few material resources. The emotional and psychological damage inflicted by this experience is incalculable. The fact that today, only seven decades later, Japanese Americans are equal or superior to national averages on measures of educational achievement, occupational prestige, and income is one of the more dramatic transformations in minority group history.

Japanese Americans After World War II

In 1945, Japanese Americans faced a world very different from the one they had left in 1942. To escape the camps, nearly half of the group had scattered throughout the country and lived everywhere but on the West Coast. As Japanese Americans attempted to move back to their former homes, they found their fields untended, their stores vandalized, their possessions lost or stolen, and their lives shattered. In some cases, there was simply no Japanese neighborhood to return to; the Little Tokyo area of San Francisco, for example, was now occupied by African Americans who had moved to the West Coast to take jobs in the defense industry (Amott & Matthaei, 1991, p. 231).

Japanese Americans themselves had changed as well. In the camps, the Issei had lost power to the Nisei. The English-speaking second generation had dealt with the camp administrators and held the leadership positions. Many Nisei had left the camps to serve in the armed forces or to find work in other areas of the country. For virtually every American minority group, the war brought new experiences and a broader sense of themselves, the nation, and the world. A similar transformation occurred for the Nisei. When the war ended, they were unwilling to rebuild the Japanese community as it had been before.

Like second-generation Chinese Americans, the Nisei had a strong record of success in school, and they also took advantage of the GI Bill to further their education. When anti-Asian prejudice began to decline in the 1950s and the job market began to open, the Nisei were educationally prepared to take advantage of the resultant opportunities (Kitano, 1980, p. 567).

The Issei-dominated enclave economy did not reappear after the war. One indicator of the shift away from an enclave economy was the fact that the percentage of Japanese American women in California who worked as unpaid family laborers (i.e., worked in family-run businesses for no salary) declined from 21% in 1940 to 7% in 1950 (Amott & Matthaei, 1991, p. 231). Also, between 1940 and 1990, the percentage of the group employed in agriculture declined from about 50% to 3%, and the percentage employed in personal services fell from 25% to 5% (Nishi, 1995, p. 116).

By 1960, Japanese Americans had an occupational profile very similar to that of whites except that they were actually overrepresented among professionals. Many were employed in the primary economy, not in the ethnic enclave, but there was a tendency to choose "safe" careers (e.g., in engineering, optometry, pharmacy, and accounting) that did not require extensive contact with the public or supervision of whites (Kitano & Daniels, 1988, p. 70).

Within these limitations, the Nisei, their children (**Sansei**), and their grandchildren (**Yonsei**) have enjoyed relatively high status, and their upward mobility and prosperity have contributed to the perception that Asian Americans are a "model minority group." An additional factor contributing to the high status of Japanese Americans (and to the disappearance of Little Tokyos) is that unlike Chinese Americans, immigrants from Japan have been few in number, and the community has not had to devote many resources to newcomers. Furthermore, recent immigrants from Japan tend to be highly educated professional people whose socioeconomic characteristics add to the perception of success and affluence.

The Sansei and Yonsei are highly integrated into the occupational structure of the larger society. Compared with their parents, their connections with their ethnic past are more tenuous, and in their values, beliefs, and personal goals, they resemble dominant group members of similar age and social class (Kitano & Daniels, 1995, pp. 79–81; also see Spickard, 1996).

Comparing Minority Groups

What factors account for the differences in the development of Chinese Americans and Japanese Americans and other racial minority groups? First, unlike the situation of African Americans in the 1600s and Mexican Americans in the 1800s, the dominant group had no desire to control the labor of these groups. The contact situation featured economic competition (e.g., for jobs) during an era of rigid competition between groups (see exhibit 4.6), and Chinese Americans and Japanese Americans were seen as a threat to security that needed to be eliminated, not as a labor pool that needed to be controlled.

Second, unlike American Indians, Chinese Americans and Japanese Americans in the early 20th century presented no military danger to the larger society, so there was little concern with their activities once the economic threat had been eliminated. Third, Chinese Americans and Japanese Americans had the ingredients and experiences necessary to form enclaves. The groups were allowed to "disappear," but unlike other racial minority groups, the urban location of their enclaves left them with opportunities for starting small businesses and providing an education for the second and later generations. As many scholars argue, the particular mode of incorporation developed by Chinese Americans and Japanese Americans is the key to understanding the present status of these groups.

Contemporary Immigration from Asia

Immigration from Asia has been considerable since the 1960s. Almost 11 million legal Asian immigrants have been admitted, about 30% to 35% of all immigrants. Exhibit 8.6 shows that immigration is heaviest from China, India, and the Philippines but that there also have been sizeable contributions from Korea and Vietnam. As noted previously, immigration from Japan has been relatively low since their initial influx a century ago (see exhibit 8.5).

Exhibit 8.6 Immigration from Asia by Group and Decade, 1950s–2000s

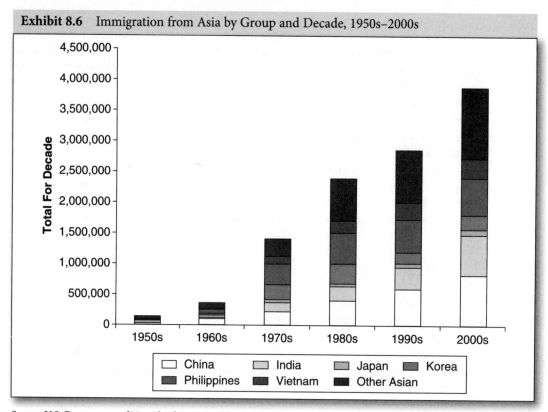

Source: U.S. Department of Homeland Security (2010, pp. 8–9).

As was the case with Hispanic immigrants, the sending nations are considerably less developed than the United States, and the primary motivation for most of these immigrants is economic. However, unlike Hispanic immigration, the Asian immigrant stream also includes a large contingent of highly educated professionals seeking opportunities to practice their careers and expand their skills. While these more elite immigrants contribute to the image of "Asian success," many Asian immigrants are less skilled and educated, and often undocumented. Thus, this stream of immigrants, like Chinese Americans, is "bipolar" and includes a healthy representation of people from both the top and the bottom of the occupational and educational hierarchies.

Of course, other factors besides mere economics attract these immigrants. The United States has maintained military bases throughout the region (including South Korea, Japan, and the Philippines) since the end of World War II, and many Asian immigrants are the spouses of American military personnel. Also, U.S. involvement in the war in Southeast Asia in the 1960s and 1970s created interpersonal ties and governmental programs that drew refugees from Vietnam, Cambodia, and Laos, many of whom lived in camps and relocation centers for years before immigrating to the United States. Because of the conditions of their escape from their homelands, they typically bring little in the way of human or material capital with them.

Among the refugee groups are the Hmong, hill people from Laos and other Southeast Asian nations, who fought with the American forces in the Vietnam War. They are relatively small in number and face some unique challenges in their adjustment to U.S. society. Their culture is very traditional and, in many ways, far removed from the modernized, Western world in which they find themselves. Until recently, they were not much advanced past a hunter–gatherer subsistence technology and bring very little social and cultural capital with them. The scope of the challenges they face in making the transition to the United States are illustrated by anthropologist Anne Fadiman in her account of the fate of an epileptic Hmong girl. According to traditional Hmong cultural understandings, illness is caused by spirits and needs to be treated in the time-honored way, by shamans and traditional healers (see the opening vignette in chapter 2). The girl's parents found it very difficult to accept and follow the instructions of the Western doctors that attempted to treat the girl's epileptic condition. The resultant tragedy underscores the distance between the Hmong and the Western world and illustrates the challenges of acculturation for this group. (Fadiman, 1998; see also Faderman, 1998). Contrary to the image of Asian American success, the Hmong generally display a socioeconomic profile more consistent with America's colonized minority groups.

Another striking contrast is between immigrants from India, many of who are highly educated and skilled, and immigrants from Vietnam, who have a socioeconomic profile that in some ways resembles those of non-Asian racial minorities in the United States. Part of the difference between these two groups relates to their contact situations and can be illuminated by applying the Blauner hypothesis. Immigrants from India are at the "immigrant" end of Blauner's continuum. They bring strong educational credentials and are well equipped to compete for favorable positions in the occupational hierarchy. Immigrants from Vietnam, in contrast, began their American experience as a refugee group fleeing the turmoil of war. Although they do not fit Blauner's "conquered or colonized" category, most Vietnamese Americans had to adapt to American society with few resources and few contacts with an established immigrant community. The consequences of these vastly different contact situations are suggested by the data presented in the exhibits at the end of this chapter. We will address some of these groups in more detail in chapter 9.

Contemporary Relations

In this section, we once more use our guiding concepts to assess the situation of Chinese Americans and Japanese Americans and other Asian groups. This section is organized around the same concepts used in previous case study chapters.

Prejudice and Discrimination

American prejudice against Asians first became prominent during the anti-Chinese movement of the 19th century. The Chinese were believed to be racially inferior, docile, and subservient, but also cruel and crafty, despotic, and threatening (Lai, 1980, p. 220; Lyman, 1974, pp. 55–58). The Chinese Exclusion Act of 1882 was justified by the idea that the Chinese were unassimilable and could never be part of U.S. society. The Chinese were seen as a threat to the working class, to American democracy, and to other American institutions. Many of these stereotypes and fears transferred to the Japanese later in the 19th century and then to other groups as they, in turn, arrived in the United States.

The social distance scores presented in exhibit 1.8 provide the only long-term record of anti-Asian prejudice in the society as a whole. In 1926, the five Asian groups included in the study were grouped in the bottom third of the scale, along with other racial and colonized minority groups. Twenty years later, in 1946, the Japanese had fallen to the bottom of the rankings, and the Chinese had risen seven positions, changes that reflect America's World War II conflict with Japan and alliance with China. This suggests that anti-Chinese prejudice may have softened during the war as distinctions were made between "good" and "bad" Asians. For example, an item published in a December 22, 1941, issue of *Time* magazine, "How to Tell Your Friends From the Japs," provided some tips for identifying "good" Asians: "The Chinese expression is likely to be more placid, kindly, open; the Japanese more positive, dogmatic, arrogant. . . . Japanese are nervous in conversation, laugh loudly at the wrong time."

In more recent decades, the average social distance scores of Asian groups have fallen even though the ranking of the groups has remained relatively stable. The falling scores probably reflect the society-wide increase in tolerance and the shift from blatant prejudice to modern racism that we have discussed previously. However, the relative position of Asians in the American hierarchy of group preferences has remained remarkably consistent since the 1920s. This stability may reflect the cultural or traditional nature of much of American anti-Asian prejudice.

There are numerous reports of violent attacks and other forms of harassment on Asian Americans, especially on recent immigrants. High school and middle school students of Asian descent report that they are stereotyped as "high achieving students who rarely fight back," making them excellent candidates for scapegoating by other groups (Associated Press, 2005). The level of harassment at one high school in New York rose to such severe levels that the U.S. Department of Justice intervened, at the request of school officials (Associated Press, 2005). Incidents such as these suggest that the tradition of anti-Asian prejudice is close to the surface and could be activated under the right combination of competition and threat.

Asian Americans also have been the victims of "positive" stereotypes. The perception of Asian Americans as a "model minority" is exaggerated and, for some Asian American groups, simply false. This label has been applied to these groups by the media, politicians, and others. It is not an image that the Asian American groups themselves developed or particularly advocate. As you might suspect, people who apply these labels to Asian Americans have a variety of hidden moral and political agendas, and we explore these dynamics later in this chapter.

Assimilation and Pluralism

Acculturation

The extent of acculturation of Asian Americans is highly variable from group to group. Japanese Americans represent one extreme. They have been a part of American society for more than a century, and the current generations are highly acculturated. Immigration from Japan has been low and has not revitalized the traditional culture or language. As a result, Japanese Americans are the most acculturated of the Asian American groups, as illustrated in exhibit 8.7, and have the lowest percentage of members who speak English "less than very well."

Filipino and Indian Americans also have low percentages of members who are not competent English speakers, but for different reasons. The Philippines has had a strong American presence since the Spanish-American War of 1898, whereas India is a former British colony in which English remains an important language for higher education and of the educated elite.

Chinese Americans, in contrast, are highly variable in their extent of acculturation. Many are members of families who have been American for generations and are highly acculturated. Others, including many recent undocumented immigrants, are newcomers who have little knowledge of English or of Anglo culture. In this dimen-

Exhibit 8.7 Percent Speaking English Less than "Very Well," for Total Population, All Asian Americans, and 10 Largest Asian American Groups, 2010

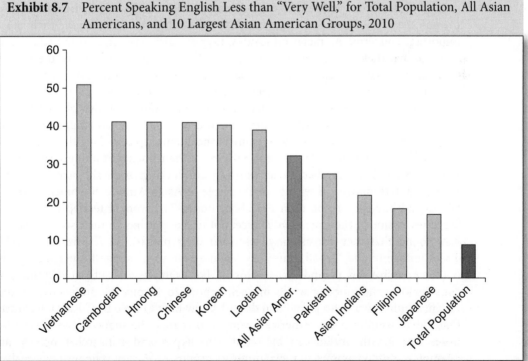

Source: U.S. Census Bureau (2010).

sion, as in occupations, Chinese Americans are "bipolar." This great variability within the group makes it difficult to characterize their overall degree of acculturation. The Hmong, Cambodians, and Vietnamese are among the most recent arrivals in the United States and, characteristically for groups with a high percentage of first generation members, rank lowest on English fluency.

Gender and Physical Acculturation: The Anglo Ideal. Anglo-conformity can happen on levels other than the cultural. A number of studies document the feelings of inadequacy and negative self-images that result when minority group members—especially women—compare themselves with the Anglo standards of attractiveness and beauty that dominate U.S. culture. Some of the studies in this tradition are classics of the social science literature, including the "doll studies" conducted by social psychologists Kenneth and Mamie Clark in the 1930s and 1940s: The Clarks showed pairs of white and black dolls to a sample of young African American children and asked them a series of questions, including "Which doll is pretty?" "Which doll is nice?" "Which doll would you like to play with?" and "Which doll is ugly?" They documented a preference for the white doll, which they interpreted as evidence that the children had internalized white standards of beauty and had developed negative self images as a consequence. Contemporary "replications" of the Clark doll study include a YouTube video entitled *A Girl Like Me* (2005) by then 17-year-old Kiri Davis, and a documentary by comedian Chris Rock entitled *Good Hair* (2009).

Asian American women, like all women in this still paternalistic society, are pressured by the cultural message that physical beauty should be among their most important concerns. As racial minorities, they are also subjected to the additional message that they are inadequate by Anglo standards and that some of their most characteristic physical traits (e.g., their small, "slanted" eyes and flat noses) are devalued— indeed ridiculed—in the larger society (Kaw, 1997). These messages generate pressures for minority women to conform not only culturally, but also physically. For example, African Americans have spent millions of dollars on hair straightening and skin bleachers. For Asian American women, the attempt to comply with Anglo standards of beauty may include cosmetic surgery on their noses or to "open" their eyes. Eugenia Kaw (1997) studied these issues by conducting in-depth interviews with medical practitioners and with a small sample of Asian American women, most of whom had had surgery on their eyelids or noses. The women tended to see their surgeries as simply their personal choice, not unlike putting on make-up. However, Kaw found that they consistently described their presurgical features negatively. They uniformly said "'small, slanty' eyes and a 'flat' nose" suggest a person who is dull and passive and a mind that is "closed." For example, one subject said that she considered eyelid surgery while in high school to "avoid the stereotype of the Oriental bookworm who is dull and doesn't know how to have fun." Kaw concluded that the decision of Asian American women to change the shape of their eyes and noses was greatly influenced by racist stereotypes and patriarchal norms: an attempt—common among all racial minority groups—to acculturate on a physical as well as a cultural level.

Secondary Structural Assimilation

We will cover this complex area in roughly the order followed in previous chapters.

Residence. Exhibit 8.8 shows the regional concentrations of all Asian Americans in 2010. Note the tendency to reside on either coast, especially around San Francisco, Los Angeles, and Seattle on the west coast and in the urban areas centered on New York City, Washington, DC, and Boston on the east coast. Note also the sizable concentrations in a variety of metropolitan areas, including Chicago, Atlanta, Dallas, and Houston.

Exhibit 8.9 shows that Asian Americans, like Hispanic Americans, are moving away from their "traditional" places of residence into new regions. Between 2000 and 2010, the Asian American population increased especially rapidly in North Carolina and other areas of the Southeast, in Arizona, and in some areas of the upper Midwest.

Between 2000 and 2010, thirty of the fifty states increased their Asian populations more than 50%, with eight more closely approaching the 50% mark. Seven states (including Arizona, Nevada, Delaware, and North Carolina) increased their Asian populations by more than 75% (Hoeffel, Rastogi, Kim, & Shahid, 2012, p. 7).

Exhibit 8.8   Distribution of Asian Americans, 2010 (Percent of Country Population)

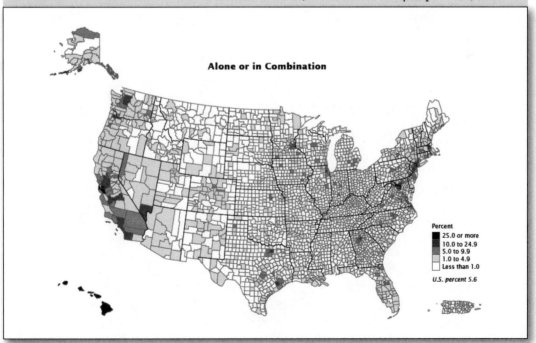

Source: Hoeffel, Rastogi, Kim, and Shahid (2012, p. 10).

Exhibit 8.9 Percent Increase in Asian Population, 2000–2010

Source: Hoeffel, Rastogi, Kim, and Shahid (2012, p. 11).

Exhibit 8.10 Urbanization of 10 Largest Asian American Groups, All Asian Americans, and Total Population, 2000

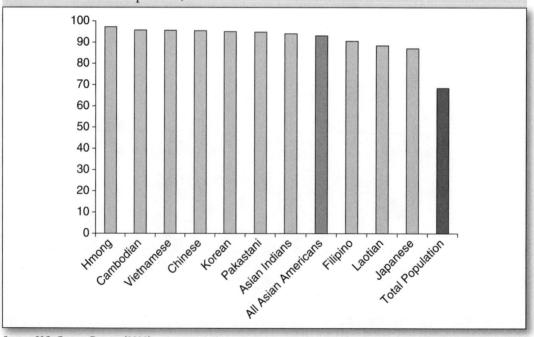

Source: U.S. Census Bureau (2000).

Asian Americans in general are highly urbanized, a reflection of the entry conditions of recent immigrants as well as the appeal of ethnic neighborhoods, such as Chinatowns, with long histories and continuing vitality. As displayed in exhibit 8.10, all but 2 of the 10 largest Asian American groups are more than 90% urbanized, and several approach the 100% mark.

Asian Americans are much less residentially segregated than either African Americans or Hispanic Americans in all four regions of the nation. Exhibit 8.11 shows the average dissimilarity index for 220 metropolitan areas using the same format as in the previous three chapters. Asian Americans are not "extremely" (dissimilarity scores greater than 0.60) segregated in any region, but the level of residential segregation is holding steady or slightly rising, a reflection of high rates of immigration and the tendency for newcomers to settle close to other members of their group.

Asian Americans are also moving away from their traditional neighborhoods and enclaves into the suburbs of metropolitan areas, most notably in the areas surrounding Los Angeles, San Francisco, New York, and other cities where the groups are highly concentrated. For example, Asian Americans have been moving in large numbers to the San Gabriel Valley, just east of downtown Los Angeles. Once a bastion of white, middle-class suburbanites, these areas have taken on a distinctly Asian flavor in recent

Exhibit 8.11   Residential Segregation for Asian and Pacific Islander Americans in 220 Metropolitan Areas, 1980–2000

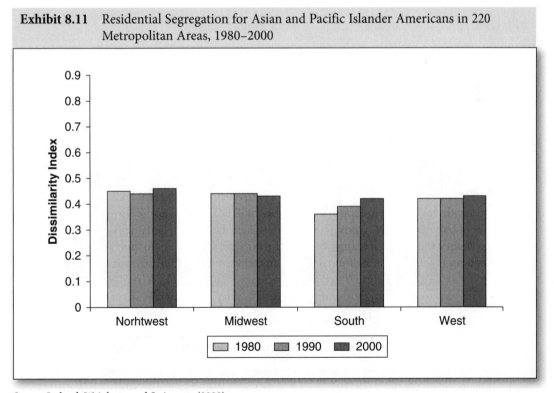

Source: Iceland, Weinberg, and Steinmetz (2002).

years. Monterey Park, once virtually all white, is now majority Chinese American and is often referred to as "America's first suburban Chinatown" or the "Chinese Beverly Hills" (Fong, 2002, p. 49).

Education. The extent of school integration for Asian Americans for the 1993–1994 and 2005–2006 school years is displayed in exhibit 8.12, as was done in previous chapters. In the 2005–2006 school year, Asian American children were much less likely to attend majority-minority or extremely segregated schools than either Hispanic American or African American children. However, the extent of school segregation has increased over the period, a reflection of the pattern of residential segregation in exhibit 8.10.

The extent of schooling for Asian Americans is very different from that for other U.S. racial minority groups. Considered as a whole, Asian Americans compare favorably with society-wide standards for educational achievement, and they are above those standards on many measures. Exhibit 8.13 shows that 4 of the 10 Asian American groups are higher than non-Hispanic whites in high school education and 7 of 10 are higher in college education, a pattern that has been very much reinforced by the high levels of education of many recent Asian immigrants. However, recall that many Asian Americans are first generation immigrants. In these cases, their educational credentials may be from non-U.S. institutions and may not translate into higher-level jobs. Also note that four Asian American groups are far below non-Hispanic whites on both

Exhibit 8.12   School Integration, 1993–1994 and 2005–2006

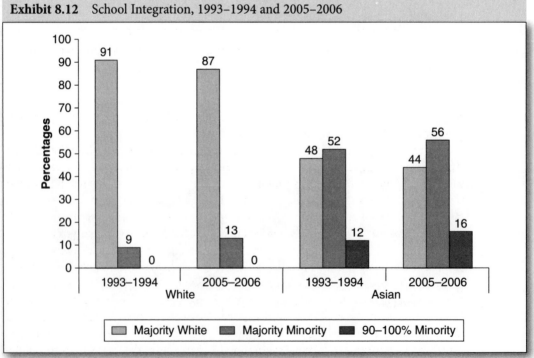

Source: U.S. Bureau of the Census.

Exhibit 8.13 Educational Attainment for All Asian Americans, 10 Largest Asian American Groups, and Non-Hispanic Whites, 2010

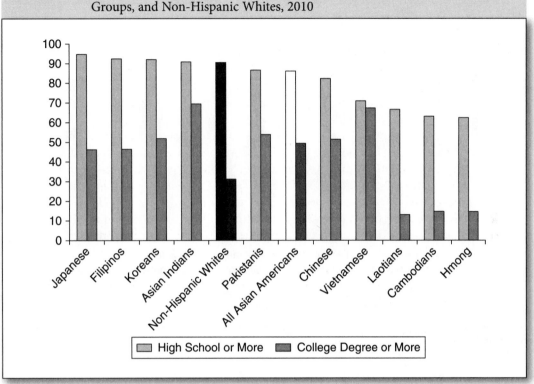

Source: U.S. Census Bureau (2010).

measures of educational attainment. These groups include a large percentage of refugees from the Vietnam War that ended in 1974.

Exhibit 8.13 partially reinforces the "model minority" image, but recall that Chinese Americans (and several other Asian American groups) are "bipolar" and have a sizable underclass group. This reality is captured in exhibit 8.14, which compares the distribution of levels of education for non-Hispanic whites and Chinese Americans. More than 50% of Chinese Americans hold college and graduate degrees, far outnumbering whites (31%) at this level. Many of these highly educated Chinese Americans are recent immigrants seeking to pursue their careers in one of the world's most advanced economies.

Note, however, that Chinese Americans are also disproportionately concentrated at the lowest level of educational achievement. Some 18% of the group has less than a high school diploma, as opposed to just 9.6% of non-Hispanic whites. Many of these less-educated Chinese Americans are also recent immigrants (many of them undocumented), and they supply the unskilled labor force, in retail shops, restaurants, and garment industry "sweatshops," that staffs the lowest levels of the Chinatown economy.

Exhibit 8.14 Educational Levels for Non-Hispanic Whites and Chinese Americans, 2010

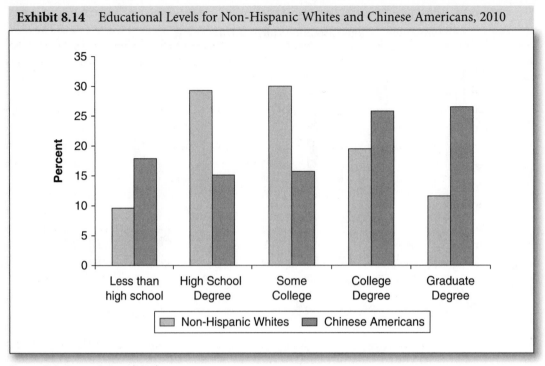

Source: U.S. Census Bureau (2010).

Assessments of Asian American success must also differentiate between the native-born and the foreign-born members of the groups. The native-born are generally better educated and the foreign-born members of the same groups are split between highly educated professionals and those who bring lower levels of human capital. For example, according to the 2000 census, almost all (96%) native-born Chinese American were high school graduates and 66% had college degrees. Comparable percentages among foreign-born Chinese Americans were 79% and 49% (Min, 2006, p. 82)

As illustrated by these examples, the image of achievement and success for Asian Americans needs to be balanced by the recognition that there is a full range of success and failure in the group and by the fact that average levels of achievement are "inflated" for some groups by recent immigrants who are highly educated, skilled professionals.

Political Power. The ability of Asian Americans to pursue their group interests has been sharply limited by a number of factors, including their relatively small size, institutionalized discrimination, and the same kinds of racist practices that have limited the power resources of other minority groups of color. However, and contrary to the perception that Asian Americans are a "quiet" minority, the group has a long history of political action, including a civil rights movement in the 1960s and 1970s (Fong, 2002, pp. 273–281).

The political power of Asian Americans today is also limited by their high percentages of foreign-born members and, for some groups, lack of facility in English. Rates of political participation for the group (e.g., voting in presidential elections) are considerably lower than national norms. For example, fewer than 37% of Asian Americans voted in the last three presidential elections (versus about 64% of all Americans). However, participation has risen since the 2000 presidential election (when only 31% participated) and is much higher when considering only the native-born. For example, in the 2008 presidential election, almost half of native-born Asian Americans (versus 64% of all Americans) voted (U.S. Census Bureau, 2011, p. 259). What this implies is that the participation of the group—and their relative political power—will increase as more members Americanize, learn English, and become citizens.

There are signs of the growing power of the group, especially in areas where they are most residentially concentrated. Of course, Asian Americans have been prominent in Hawaiian politics for decades, but they are increasingly involved in West Coast political life as well. For example, in 1996 the state of Washington elected Gary Locke as governor, the first Chinese American to hold this high office. Governor Locke was reelected in 2000. At present, there are eight Asian and Pacific Islanders in the U.S. House of Representatives (2% of the membership) and one in the Senate (Senator Daniel Inouye of Hawaii, a Japanese American and senator since 1963).

Jobs and Income. The economic situation of Asian Americans is mixed and complex, as is the case for Hispanic Americans. On some measures, Asian Americans as a whole exceed national norms, a reflection of the high levels of academic achievement combined with the impressive educational credential of many new arrivals. However, overall comparisons can be misleading and we must also recognize the economic diversity of Asian Americans.

Starting with occupation profiles, the image of success is again sustained. Both males and females are overrepresented in the highest occupational categories, a reflection of the high levels of educational attainment for the group. Asian American males are underrepresented among manual laborers, but otherwise the occupational profiles of the groups are in rough proportion to the society as a whole (U.S. Census Bureau, 2012a).

Exhibit 8.15 shows median household incomes for Asian Americans and non-Hispanic whites for the past two decades and shows that Asian Americans have averaged *higher* incomes, a picture of general affluence that is in dramatic contrast to the other racial minority groups we have examined in this text. The gap fluctuates, but Asian American's median household income is generally 115% of whites.

This image of success, glittering at first glance, becomes more complicated and nuanced when we look at the separate subgroups within the Asian American community. Exhibit 8.16 displays median household incomes for all non-Hispanic whites, all Asian Americans, and the 10 largest subgroups. We can see immediately that economic success is not universally shared: half of the Asian American groups are below the average income for non-Hispanic whites.

A still more telling picture emerges when we consider income per capita (or per person) as opposed to median incomes for entire households. This is an important comparison because the apparent prosperity of so many Asian American families is

Exhibit 8.15   Median Household Incomes for Non-Hispanic Whites and Asian Americans, 1988–2010

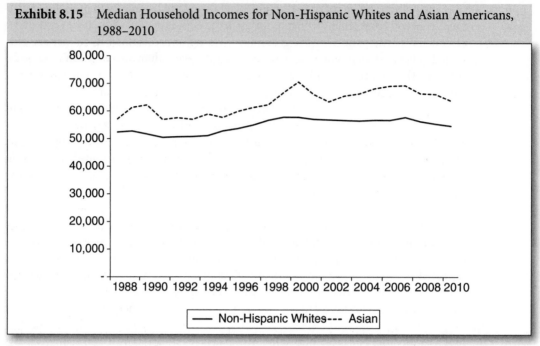

Source: U.S. Census Bureau (2012f).

Exhibit 8.16   Median Household Income for All Asian Americans, 10 Largest Asian American Groups, and Non-Hispanic Whites, 2010

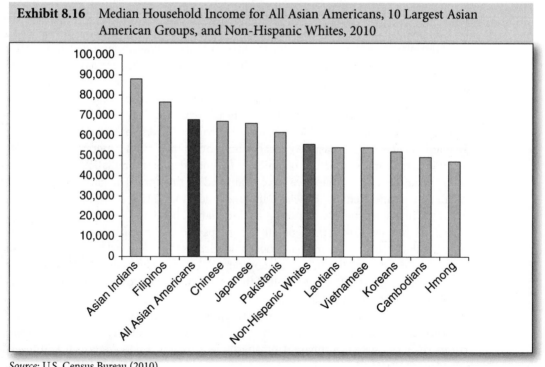

Source: U.S. Census Bureau (2010).

linked to their ownership of small businesses in the enclave. These enterprises typically employ the entire family for many long hours each day, with children adding their labor after school and on weekends and other relatives (many of them new immigrants, a percentage of which are undocumented) contributing as well. The household unit may post a high income as a result of these collective efforts but, when spread across many family members, the glow of "success" is muted.

Exhibit 8.17 shows that, on per capita income, only one Asian American group exceeds non-Hispanic whites. The other nine groups (including Chinese and Korean Americans, the groups most dependent on small business ownership) enjoy much lower levels of relative prosperity. In particular, the Southeast Asian groups with high percentages of refugees from the Vietnam War (especially the Hmong) are far below national norms on this measure.

Exhibit 8.18 provides additional evidence that the image of a "model minority"— uniformly prosperous and successful—is greatly exaggerated. Asian Americans, unlike other racial minority groups, are overrepresented in the highest income categories: 15% of all Asian American households had incomes of $150,000 or more versus only 10% of non-Hispanic whites. However, note that Asian Americans are also overrepresented

Exhibit 8.17   Per Capita Income for All Asian Americans, 10 Largest Asian American Groups, and Non-Hispanic Whites, 2010

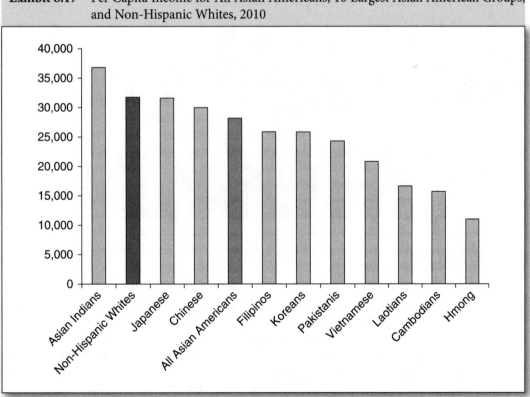

Source: U.S. Census Bureau (2010).

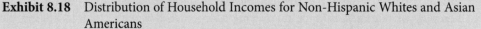

Exhibit 8.18 Distribution of Household Incomes for Non-Hispanic Whites and Asian Americans

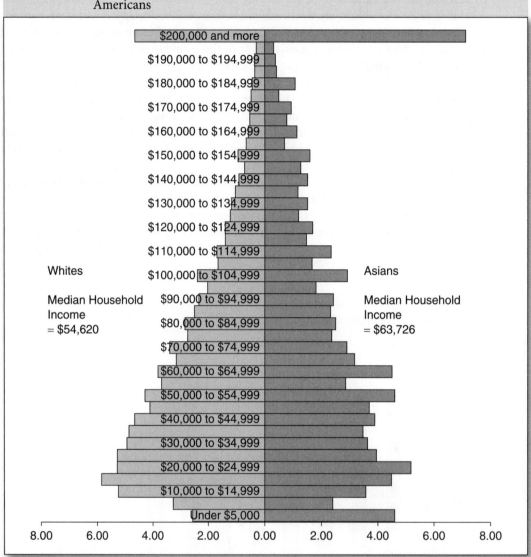

Source: U.S. Census Bureau (2012g).

in the lowest income category, a reflection of the "bipolar" distribution of Chinese Americans and some other groups.

Exhibits 8.19 and 8.20 finish the economic portrait of Asian Americans and reinforce the picture of complexity and diversity. While the poverty levels of all Asian Americans, considered as a single group, are comparable to non-Hispanic whites, several of the groups have much higher rates of poverty, especially for children. As we have seen in other exhibits, Japanese Americans, Filipino Americans, and Asian Indian

Americans are "successful" on this indicator but other groups have poverty levels comparable to colonized racial minority groups.

Exhibit 8.20 examines the situation of Asian Americans in terms of their nativity. Once again, we see the great diversity from group to group, with foreign-born Vietnamese Americans (largely refugees) exhibiting the highest level of poverty—almost three times higher than non-Hispanic whites—and native-born Japanese Americans (largely second generation and later) exhibiting virtually no poverty. Foreign-born Asian Americans generally have higher levels of poverty and native-born Asian Americans generally have lower rates but note the considerable variability from group to group.

These socioeconomic profiles reflect the diversity of Asian American groups. Some are indeed prosperous and successful and exceed national norms, sometimes by a considerable margin. Other groups resemble other American racial minority groups. Japanese Americans and Chinese Americans have the longest histories in the United States and generally rank at the top in measures of wealth and prosperity. Other groups—particularly those that include large numbers of refugees from Southeast Asia—have not fared as well and present pictures of poverty and economic distress. Some "bipolar" groups, like Chinese Americans, fit in both categories. We should also note that the picture of economic distress for these groups would be much greater if we

Exhibit 8.19   Percentage of Families and Children in Poverty for All Asian Americans, 10 Largest Asian American Groups, and Non-Hispanic Whites, 2010

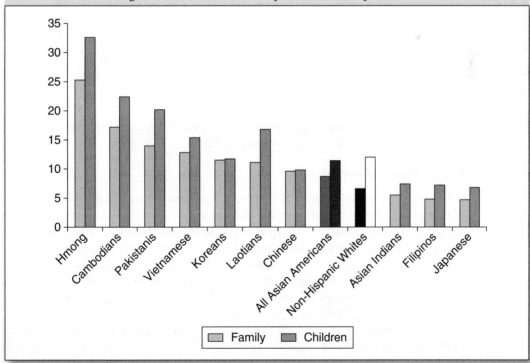

Source: U.S. Census Bureau (2012h).

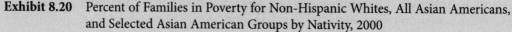

Exhibit 8.20   Percent of Families in Poverty for Non-Hispanic Whites, All Asian Americans, and Selected Asian American Groups by Nativity, 2000

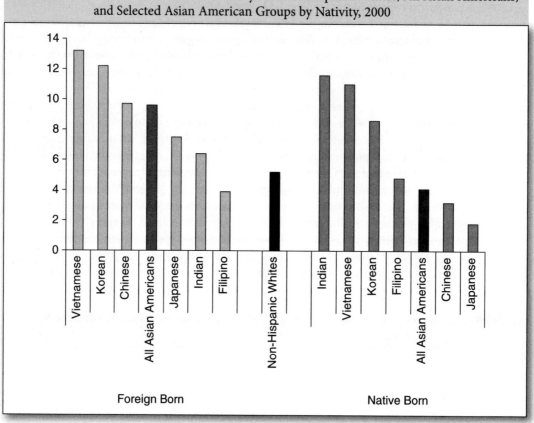

Source: Min (2006, p. 82).

focused on undocumented immigrants, who are numerous in the community and concentrated in the informal, irregular economy.

Primary Structural Assimilation

Studies of integration at the primary level for Asian Americans generally find rates of interracial friendship and marriage that exceed those of other minority groups. A study based on the 1980 census, for example, found intermarriage rates from 15% to 34% for Asian Americans (depending on the specific group) versus rates of only 2% for African Americans and 13% for Hispanic Americans (Lee & Yamanaka, 1990). The same study also found that native-born Asian Americans were much more likely to marry outside their groups than were foreign-born Asian Americans (see also Kitano & Daniels, 1995; Min, 1995; and Sung, 1990).

Studies that are more recent find that rates of primary integration remain relatively high but are declining as the number of Asian Americans grows and the percentage of foreign-born increases. One recent study (Passel et al., 2010) found almost exactly the same percentage of newlywed Asian Americans marrying outside the group in 1980

(32%) and 2008 (31%) but a declining percentage of all currently married Asian Americans with partners outside the group between 1980 and 2008 (see exhibit 8.21). This pattern is a reflection of high rates of immigration and the stronger tendency of newcomers to marry within their group.

Intermarriage trends are highly dependent on gender and nativity. Exhibit 8.22 displays intermarriage trends for newly contracted marriages. Between 1980 and 2010,

Exhibit 8.21 Percentage of All Currently Married Asian Americans Married to Someone of a Different Race or Ethnicity

Year	Percentage
1980	21.0%
1990	17.9%
2000	16.2%
2010	15.8%

Source: Passell, Wang, and Taylor (2010, p. 17).

Exhibit 8.22 Intermarriage Trends among Newlyweds for All Asian Americans, and by Gender and Nativity, 1980–2010

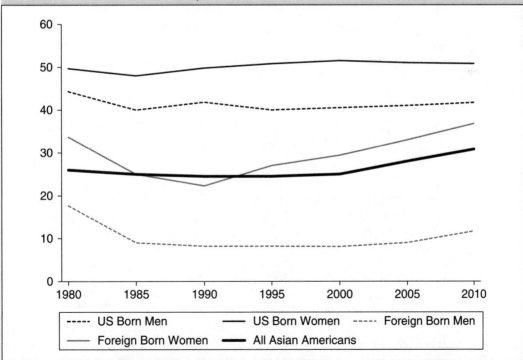

Source: Passell, Wang, and Taylor (2010, p. 36).

native-born females were the most likely to marry outside the group and immigrant males were the least.

Dr. C. N. Le, a sociologist who maintains the Asian Nation website (http://www.asian-nation.org) has analyzed intermarriage patterns using the 2006 U.S. Census Bureau's American Community Survey. His data can be found at http://www.asian-nation.org/interracial.shtml. He found that Japanese Americans, the most acculturated of the groups, are the most likely to marry outside their group. Also, many Japanese Americans are the brides of American GIs who were stationed in Japan. The groups with the highest percentage of foreign-born—Asian Indian Americans, Korean Americans, and Vietnamese Americans—are also the most likely to marry within their groups.

FOCUS ON CONTEMPORARY ISSUES:
How Successful Are Asian Americans? At What Price?

The materials presented in this chapter should make it clear that the view of Asian Americans as "model minorities" is exaggerated and stereotypical. It is true that, as a whole, the group compares favorably to national statistical norms in terms of education and income. However, when we look closer and especially when we take account of the separate subgroups, we find that some Asian American groups are "bipolar" and that others have profiles that closely resemble colonized racial minority groups.

Some further qualifications on the stereotypical view of Asian American success should be noted. First, the group is concentrated in cities where the cost of living is very high. For example, the cities with the largest Asian American populations (e.g., New York, Honolulu, Los Angeles, and San Francisco) are commonly ranked as the most expensive places to live (e.g., see Browne, 2011). Thus, the higher average incomes buy less in the way of housing, food, and other necessities. Second, as illustrated in exhibit 8.18, per capita income for Asian Americans is *lower* than the national average, so the higher average incomes have to be shared across a larger number of people.

Third, researchers commonly find that Asian Americans—especially the foreign-born—get lower income returns for their years of schooling and earn less than whites of the same educational level (see Min, 2006, pp. 82–84 for a review). Also, Asian Americans face a glass ceiling that limits their access to the highest and most lucrative positions in the U.S. status hierarchy and the group is underrepresented on the boards of Fortune 500 companies (Chou & Feagin, 2008, p. 13).

Finally, while it might seem that the "model minority" stereotype is benign and positive, it can have serious negative consequences. The image can create pressure for members of the group, especially children and students, and the resultant stress can impact mental health and result in depression and even suicide. Chou and Feagin (2008) point out the "lose-lose" dilemma faced by many Asian Americans: if they live up to the "model minority" stereotype, they are labeled as "geeks" and "nerds," and if they fail—or enjoy only moderate success in school or work—they can be seen as inferior.

The "model minority" stereotype not only distorts the situation of Asian American groups, but it also can lead to oversimplified and negative views of other minority groups. So-called modern racists sometimes attribute the success of Asian Americans solely to their cultural values, such as a strong work ethic or a traditional respect for education, an argument that implies that other minority groups are less successful because they lack these values, deemphasizing or ignoring the role of structural barriers and past-in-present discrimination. Thus, in the ever-evolving interplay of American group relations, the supposed success of Asian Americans can be used as a way of scolding other minority groups of color, particularly black Americans.

Comparing Minority Groups: Explaining Asian American Success

To conclude this chapter, let's return to a question raised in the opening pages: How can we explain the apparent success of Asian Americans? Relative affluence and high status are not characteristic of the other racial minority groups we have examined, and, at least at first glance, there seems to be little in our theories and concepts to help us understand the situation of Asian Americans. Even after we recognize that the "success" label is simplistic and even misleading, the relatively high status of many Asian Americans begs a closer look.

In this section, we compare Asian Americans with European immigrant groups and with colonized minority groups. What crucial factors differentiate the experiences of these groups? Can we understand these differences in terms of the framework provided by the Blauner and Noel hypotheses and the other concepts developed in this text?

The debate over the causes of Asian American success often breaks down into two different viewpoints. One view offers a cultural explanation, which accepts the evidence of Asian American success at face value and attributes it to the "good values" of traditional Asian cultures that we briefly explored at the beginning of this chapter. These values—including respect for elders and for authority figures, hard work and thriftiness, and conformity and politeness—are highly compatible with U.S. middle-class Protestant value systems and consistent with traditional assimilation theory and human capital theory.

The second point of view stresses the ways in which these groups entered American society and the reactions of Asian Americans to the barriers of racism and exclusion they faced. This approach could be called a "structural explanation," and it emphasizes contact situations, modes of incorporation, enclave economies, group cohesion, position in the labor market, and institutionalized discrimination rather than cultural values. Also, this approach questions the notion that Asian Americans are "successful" and stresses the realities of Asian American poverty and the continuing patterns of racism and exclusion. The structural approach is more compatible with the theories and concepts used throughout this text, and it identifies several of the important pieces needed to solve the puzzle of Asian "success" and put it in perspective. This is not to suggest that the cultural approach is wrong or irrelevant, however. The issues we raise are complex and will probably require many approaches and perspectives before they are fully resolved.

Asian Americans and White Ethnics

Chinese and Japanese immigrants arrived in America at about the same time as immigrants from Southern and Eastern Europe (see chapter 2). Both groups consisted mainly of sojourning young men who were largely unskilled, from rural backgrounds, and not highly educated. European immigrants, like Asian immigrants, encountered massive discrimination and rejection and were also victims of restrictive legislation. Yet the barriers to upward mobility for European immigrants (or at least for their descendants) fell away more rapidly than the barriers for immigrants from Asia. Why?

Some important differences between the two immigrant experiences are clear, the most obvious being the greater racial visibility of Asian Americans. Whereas the cultural and linguistic markers that identified Eastern and Southern Europeans faded with each passing generation, the racial characteristics of the Asian groups continued to separate them from the larger society. Thus, Asian Americans are not "pure immigrant" groups (see Blauner, 1972, p. 55). For most of the 20th century, Chinese Americans and Japanese Americans remained in a less-favorable position than European immigrants and their descendants, excluded by their physical appearance from the mainstream economy until the decades following World War II.

Another important difference relates to position in the labor market. Immigrants from Southern and Eastern Europe entered the industrializing East Coast and Midwest economies, where they took industrial and manufacturing jobs. Although such jobs were poorly paid and insecure, this location in the labor force gave European immigrants and their descendants the potential for upward mobility in the mainstream economy. At the very least, these urban industrial and manufacturing jobs put the children and grandchildren of European immigrants in positions from which skilled, well-paid, unionized jobs were reachable, as were managerial and professional careers.

In contrast, Chinese and Japanese immigrants on the West Coast were forced into ethnic enclaves and came to rely on jobs in the small business and service sector and, in the case of the Japanese, in the rural economy. By their nature, these jobs did not link Chinese and Japanese immigrants or their descendants to the industrial sector or to better-paid, more-secure, unionized jobs. Furthermore, their exclusion from the mainstream economy was reinforced by overt, racially based discrimination from both employers and labor unions (see Fong & Markham, 1991).

Asian Americans and Colonized Racial Minority Groups

Comparisons between Asian Americans and African Americans, American Indians, and Hispanic Americans have generated a level of controversy and a degree of heat and passion that may be surprising at first. An examination of the issues and their implications, however, reveals that the debate involves some thinly disguised political and moral agendas and evokes sharply clashing views on the nature of U.S. society. What might appear on the surface to be merely an academic comparison of different minority groups turns out to be an argument about the quality of American justice and fairness and the very essence of the value system of U.S. society.

What is not in dispute in this debate is that some Asian groups (e.g., Japanese Americans) rank far above other racial minority groups on all the commonly used measures of secondary structural integration and equality. What is disputed is how to interpret these comparisons and assess their meanings. First, we need to recognize that gross comparisons between entire groups can be misleading. If we confine our attention to averages (mean levels of education or median income), the picture of Asian American success is sustained. However, if we also observe the full range of differences within each group (e.g., the "bipolar" nature of occupations among Chinese Americans), we see that the images of success have been exaggerated and need to be placed in a proper context. Even with these qualifications, however, discussion often slides on to more ideological ground, and political and moral issues begin to cloud the debate. Asian American success is often taken as proof that American society is truly the land of opportunity and that people who work hard and obey the rules will get ahead: in America, anyone can be anything they want as long as they work hard enough.

When we discussed modern racism, I pointed out that a belief in the openness and fairness of the United States can be a way of blaming the victim and placing the responsibility for change on the minority groups rather than on the structure of society or on past-in-present or institutionalized discrimination. Asian success is sometimes taken as a "proof" of the validity of this ideology. The none-too-subtle implication is that other groups (African Americans, Hispanic Americans, American Indians) could achieve the same success as Asian Americans but, for various reasons, choose not to. Thus, the relative success of Chinese Americans and Japanese Americans has become a device for criticizing other minority groups.

Structural Explanations of Asian American Success

The structural approach to investigating Asian American success begins with a comparison of the history of the various racial minority groups and their modes of incorporation into the larger society. When Chinese Americans and Japanese Americans were building their enclave economies in the early part of the 20th century, African Americans and Mexican Americans were concentrated in unskilled agricultural occupations, American Indians were isolated from the larger society on their reservations, and Puerto Ricans had not yet begun to arrive on the mainland. The social class differences between these groups today flow from their respective situations in the past.

Many of the occupational and financial advances made by Chinese Americans and Japanese Americans have been due to the high levels of education achieved by the second generations. Although education is traditionally valued in Asian cultures, the decision to invest limited resources in schooling is also quite consistent with the economic niche occupied by these immigrants. Education is one obvious, relatively low-cost strategy to upgrade the productivity and profit of a small-business economy and improve the economic status of the group as a whole. An educated, English-speaking second generation could act as intermediaries with the larger society and bring expertise and business acumen to the family enterprises and lead them to higher levels of performance. Education might also be the means by which the second generation could enter professional careers. This strategy may have been especially attractive to an immigrant generation that was itself relatively uneducated and barred from citizenship (Hirschman & Wong, 1986, p. 23; see also Bonacich & Modell, 1980, p. 152; and Sanchirico, 1991).

The efforts to educate the next generation were largely successful. Chinese Americans and Japanese Americans achieved educational parity with the larger society as early as the 1920s. One study found that for men and women born after 1915, the median years of schooling completed were actually higher for Chinese Americans and Japanese Americans than they were for whites (Hirschman & Wong, 1986, p. 11). Before World War II, both Asian groups were barred from the mainstream economy and from better jobs. When anti-Asian prejudice and discrimination declined in the 1950s, however, the Chinese and Japanese second generations had the educational background necessary to take advantage of the increased opportunities.

Thus, there was a crucial divergence in the development of Chinese Americans and Japanese Americans and the colonized minority groups. At the time that native-born Chinese Americans and Japanese Americans reached educational parity with whites, the vast majority of African Americans, American Indians, and Mexican Americans were still victimized by Jim Crow laws and legalized segregation and excluded from opportunities for anything but rudimentary education. The Supreme Court decision in *Brown v. Board of Education of Topeka* (1954) was decades in the future, and most American Indian schoolchildren were still being subjected to intense Americanization in the guise of a curriculum. Today, these other racial minority groups have not completely escaped from the disadvantages imposed by centuries of institutionalized discrimination. African Americans have approached educational parity with white Americans only in recent years (see chapter 5), and American Indians and Mexican Americans remain far below national averages (see chapters 6 and 7).

The structural explanation argues that the recent upward mobility of Chinese Americans and Japanese Americans is the result of the methods by which they incorporated themselves into American society, and not as much their values and traditions. The logic of their enclave economy led the immigrant generation to invest in the education of their children, who would be better prepared to develop their businesses and seek opportunity in the larger society.

As a final point, note that the structural explanation is not consistent with traditional views of the assimilation process. The immigrant generation of Chinese Americans and Japanese Americans responded to the massive discrimination they faced by withdrawing, developing ethnic enclaves, and becoming "invisible" to the larger society. Like Jewish Americans and Cuban Americans, Chinese Americans and Japanese Americans used their traditional cultures and patterns of social life to create and build their own subcommunities, from which they launched the next generation. Contrary to traditional ideas about how assimilation is "supposed" to happen, we see again that integration can precede acculturation and that the smoothest route to integration may be the creation of a separate subsociety independent of the surrounding community.

COMPARATIVE FOCUS:
Japan's "Invisible" Minority

One of the defining characteristics of a minority group (see chapter 1) is visibility: minority group members must be easy to identify, either culturally (e.g., language) or physically (e.g., skin color). However, there is at least one minority group, the Burakumin of Japan, that is virtually indistinguishable from the general population: there is no physical, cultural, religious, or linguistic difference between the Burakumin and other Japanese. How could such an "invisible" minority come into being? How could the disadvantaged status be maintained through time?

The Burakumin were created centuries ago, during feudal times in Japan. At that time, the society was organized into a caste system (see chapter 3) based on occupation, and the ancestors of today's Burakumin did work that brought them into contact with death (gravediggers, executioners) or required them to handle meat or meat products (leather workers, butchers). These occupations were regarded as very "unclean" and the Burakumin were required to live in separate villages and to wear leather patches for purposes of identification (thus raising their social visibility). They were forbidden to marry outside their caste, and any member of the general population who touched a Burakumin had to be ritually purified or cleansed of pollution (Lamont-Brown, 1993, p. 137).

The caste system was officially abolished in the 19th century, at about the time Japan began to industrialize and most observers today agree the overall situation of the Burakumin has improved (Ball, 2009). Still, the Burakumin maintain their minority group status and prejudice and marginalization continue (Neary, 2003, p. 288).

The Burakumin are a small group, about 2% or 3% of Japan's population. About 1 million still live in the traditional villages and another 2 million or so live in non-Burakumin areas, mostly in larger cities. They continue to be seen as "filthy," "not very bright," and "untrustworthy"—stereotypical traits often associated with minority groups mired in subordinate and unequal positions. Also, as is the case for virtually all American minority groups, the Burakumin have a protest organization—the Burakumin Liberation League (http://www.bll.gr.jp/eng.html)—that is dedicated to improving the conditions of the group.

(Continued)

(Continued)

The situation of the Burakumin might seem puzzling. If the group is indistinguishable from the general population, why don't they blend in and disappear? What keeps them attached to their group?

Some Burakumin are proud of their heritage and refuse to surrender to the dominant culture. They insist on being accepted for who they are, and have no intention of trading their identity for acceptance or opportunity. For others, even those attempting to pass, the tie to the group and a subtle form of social visibility are maintained by the ancient system of residential segregation. The identity of the traditional Burakumin villages are matters of public record, and it is this information—not race or culture—that establishes the boundaries of the group and forms the ultimate barrier to assimilation.

There are reports that Japanese firms keep lists of local Burakumin addresses and use the lists to screen out potential employees. Also, the telltale information may be revealed when applying to rent an apartment (some landlords refuse to rent rooms to Burakumin because of their alleged "filthiness") or purchase a home (banks may be reluctant to make loans to members of a group that is widely regarded as "untrustworthy"). Another line of resistance to the complete integration of the Burakumin arises if they attempt to marry outside the group. It is common for Japanese parents to research the family history of a child's fiancé, and any secret Burakumin connections are very likely to be unearthed by this process. Thus, members of the Burakumin who pass undetected at work and in their neighborhood are likely to be "outed" if they attempt to marry into the dominant group.

This link to the traditional Burakumin residential areas means that this group is not really invisible: There is a way to determine group membership, a mark or sign of who belongs and who doesn't. Consistent with the definition presented in chapter 1, this "birthmark" is the basis for a socially constructed boundary that differentiates "us" from "them" and for the systematic discrimination and prejudice, and all the other disadvantages associated with minority group status.

Note

1. See YouTube: http://www.youtube.com/watch?v=5f71JW2zJTU.

Main Points

- Asian Americans and Pacific Islanders are diverse and have brought many different cultural and linguistic traditions to the United States. These groups are growing rapidly but are still only a tiny fraction of the total population.
- Chinese immigrants were the victims of a massive campaign of discrimination and exclusion and responded by constructing enclaves. Chinatowns became highly organized communities, largely run by

the local CCBAs and other associations. The second generation faced many barriers to employment in the dominant society, although opportunities increased after World War II.

- Japanese immigration began in the 1890s and stimulated a campaign that attempted to oust the group from agriculture and curtail immigration from Japan. The Issei formed an enclave, but during World War II Japanese Americans were forced into relocation camps, and this experience devastated the group economically and psychologically.

- Recent immigration from Asia is diverse in terms of national origins, contact situation, levels of human capital, and mode of incorporation into U.S. society.

- Overall levels of anti-Asian prejudice and discrimination have probably declined in recent years but remain widespread. Levels of acculturation and secondary structural assimilation are variable. Members of these groups whose families have been in the United States longer tend to be highly acculturated and integrated. Recent immigrants from China, however, are "bipolar." Many are highly educated and skilled, but a sizable number are "immigrant laborers" who bring modest educational credentials and are likely to be living in poverty.

- The notion that Asian Americans are a "model minority" is exaggerated, but comparisons with European immigrants and colonized minority groups suggest some of the reasons for the relative "success" of these groups.

Study Site on the Web

Don't forget the interactive quizzes and other resources and learning aids at www.sagepub.com/healeyds4e.

For Further Reading

Espiritu, Y. (2007). *Asian American women and men: Labor, laws, and love (The gender lens)* (2nd ed.). Lanham, MD: Rowman and Littlefield Publishers.

Analyzes the intersections of race, class, and gender among Asian Americans.

Chou, R., & Feagin, J. (2008). *The myth of the model minority: Asian Americans facing racism.* Boulder CO: Paradigm.

Based on in-depth interviews, a comprehensive analysis of Asian Americans, including an analysis of the "model minority" image.

Kitano, H. H. L., & Daniels, R. (2001). *Asian Americans: Emerging minorities* (3rd ed.). Englewood Cliffs, NJ: Prentice Hall.

Min, P. G. (Ed.). (2006). *Asian Americans: Contemporary trends and issues* (2nd ed.). Thousand Oaks, CA: Pine Forge Press.

Two good overviews of the Asian American groups covered in this chapter.

Zhou, M. (1992). *Chinatown.* Philadelphia: Temple University Press.

An excellent analysis of Chinatown, with a behind-the-scenes look at the realities often hidden from outsiders.

Tuan, M. (2005). *Forever foreigners or honorary whites?* New Brunswick, NJ: Rutgers University Press.

A penetrating account of the continuing anti-Asian racism and discrimination

Questions for Review and Study

1. Describe the cultural characteristics of Asian American groups. How did these characteristics shape relationships with the larger society? Did they contribute to the perception of Asian Americans as "successful"? How?

2. Compare and contrast the contact situation for Chinese Americans, Japanese Americans, and Cuban Americans. What common characteristics led to the construction of ethnic enclaves for all three groups? How and why did these enclaves vary from each other?

3. In what sense was the second generation of Chinese Americans "delayed"? How did this affect the relationship of the group with the larger society?

4. Compare and contrast the campaigns that arose in opposition to the immigration of Chinese and Japanese. Do the concepts of the Noel hypothesis help to explain the differences? Do you see any similarities with the changing federal policy toward Mexican immigrants across the 20th century? Explain.

5. Compare and contrast the Japanese relocation camps with Indian reservations in terms of paternalism and coerced acculturation. What impact did this experience have on the Japanese Americans economically? How were Japanese Americans compensated for their losses? Does the compensation paid to Japanese Americans provide a precedent for similar payments (reparations) to African Americans for their losses under slavery? Why or why not?

6. How do the Burakumin in Japan illustrate "visibility" as a defining characteristic of minority group status? How is the minority status of this group maintained?

7. What gender differences characterize Asian American groups? What are some of the important ways in which the experiences of women and men vary?

8. Describe the situation of the Chinese Americans and Japanese Americans in terms of prejudice and discrimination, acculturation, and integration. Are these groups truly "success stories"? How? What factors or experiences might account for this "success"? Are all Asian American groups equally successful? Describe the important variations from group to group. Compare the integration and level of equality of these groups with other American racial minorities. How would you explain the differences? Are the concepts of the Noel and Blauner hypotheses helpful? Why or why not?

Internet Research Project

In this exercise, you will once again use the U.S. census to gather information about the total population of all Asian Americans and two subgroups of your own choosing. This project adds to the information you gathered in chapters 5 through 7. The information for the total population is already entered. You can add the information for African Americans, American Indians and Alaska Natives (AIAN), and Hispanic Americans from previous exercises, but you will need to add information for the new variables and for the variables you select for these groups. You will then use course concepts to assess and analyze this information and place it in the context of this text.

Notes

1. *The numbers you gather for this exercise may vary slightly from those presented in this chapter because of differences in the dates the data were collected or in the nature of the samples used.*

2. *Visit the website for this text to check for updates on the databases available for completing this exercise.*

Get information by following these steps:

1. Go to the official U.S. Census Bureau website at www.census.gov.

2. Click on "Data" in the list of choices at the top of the screen and then click "American Fact Finder" from the drop-down menu.

3. Click the "Race and Ethnic Groups" tab on the left of the next screen. A new window will open. Find the list of "Racial and Ethnic Group Results" on the right of the screen and click on the box next to "Total Population" (Code 001), the box next to "Black or African American alone or in combination with one or more other races" (Code 005), the box next to "American Indian and Alaska Native alone or in combination with one or more other races" (Code 009), and the box next to "Asian alone or in combination with one or more other races" (Code 031). Next click the "Add" button above the "Racial and Ethnic Group Results" window and your selections will be added to the "Your selections" box in the top-left-hand corner of the screen.

4. Next, select two Asian American groups. Select at least one of the 10 largest Asian American groups (see exhibit 8.1). Asian American groups are listed starting on about the fifth or sixth screen. You can use the list of screens on the upper right to move quickly to these screens. Select groups "alone or in any combination." Once you have selected your two groups, click the "Add" button.

5. In the "Your Race and Ethnic Group Filters" box in the middle of the screen, click on "Race and Hispanic Origin (2010 code based)." In the next box, click "Hispanic Origin" and then click "Hispanic." In the "Race and Ethnic Group Results" window, click the box next to "Hispanic or Latino (of any race)" (Code 400) and click the "Add" button.

6. You should now have seven groups in the "Your Selections" box: The total population, black Americans, AIAN, Asian Americans, your two Asian American subgroups, and Hispanic Americans. Write the names of the subgroups in the table below.

7. Close the "Select Race and Ethnic Groups" window by clicking the "Close" button on the top-right-hand corner of the window.

8. We will again use the 2011 ACS 1-year estimates. As before, look in either the "ID" column on the left for "Table S0201" or in the "Dataset" column on the right for the "2011 ACS 1-year estimates." Click the box next to the file name and then click "View" from the menu above the window.

9. The next screen will display a table with your groups listed at the top. Scroll down the table until you find the information needed to fill in the table below.

   a. For "Percent of Total Population," follow the instructions below the table.
   b. Under "Sex and Age," find "median age (years)."
   c. Under "Households by Type," find "Average Household size."
   d. Under "Educational Attainment," find "Less than high school diploma."
   e. Under "Population born outside of the United States," find "Entered 2000 or later."

f. Under "Language Spoken at Home and Ability to Speak English," find "Speak English less than 'very well.'"

g. Under "Employment Status," find "% Unemployed."

h. Under "Income in the Past 12 Months," find "Individuals" and then "Per Capita income" and "Median earnings for full-time, year-round workers for males and females."

i. Under "Poverty Rates for Families and People," find "All Families."

j. Select two more variables relevant to this course and fill in the scores for the total population, African Americans, American Indians and Alaska Natives (AIAN), Hispanic Americans, and all Asian Americans. (*Note: Your instructor may have different instructions for this step of the project.*)

		Total Population	African Americans	AIAN	Hispanic Americans	All Asian Americans	Asian American Groups	
1	Number	311,591,919	42,533,817					
2	Percent of Total Population*	—	13.7%					
3	Median age	37.3						
4	Average household size	2.64						
5	% Less than high school	14.1%						
6	% of the foreign born who entered in 2000	35.7%						
6	Speak English less than "very well"	8.7%						
7	% unemployed	6.5%						
8	Per capita income	$26,708						
9	Median incomes for full-time, year-round workers							
	Males	$46,993						
	Females	$37,133						
10	Poverty rate, all families	11.7%						
11								
12								

*Divide the number in the group by 311,591,919 and multiply by 100.

Questions

1. What stage of Gordon's model of assimilation (see exhibit 2.1) do the variables in the table measure?

2. Using the Blauner hypothesis (see chapter 3), we can say that both American Indians and African Americans are "colonized or conquered" minority groups and that Hispanic Americans are a mixture of colonized and immigrant origin groups. Are Asian Americans more "colonized" or more "immigrant?" What would the Blauner hypothesis predict about the relative status of these groups in American society? Does the evidence in the table support the prediction? How?

3. What important differences do you see between your two Asian American subgroups? Which is closer to national patterns? To African Americans and Hispanic Americans? What are some possible reasons for these patterns? For example, are the differences related to the timing of the group's immigration? What "human capital" does the group bring that might help to account for the differences?

4. What additional concepts from this and previous chapters seem relevant for explaining the patterns you observe in this table? How?

Optional Group Discussion

Bring this information to class and, in groups of four to six people, compare with the information collected by others. Consider the issues raised in the question above and in the chapter and develop some ideas about why these groups are where they are relative to each other and to the total population. (*Note: Your instructor may have different instructions for this step of the project.*)

PART 4

Challenges for the Present and the Future

❧ ❧

Chapter 9 New Americans, Assimilation, and Old Challenges

Chapter 10 Minority Groups and U.S. Society: Themes, Patterns, and the Future

❧ ❧

I n this section, we analyze the new immigration, continuing issues of assimilation, and equality, inclusion, and racism. Many of these issues—as they relate to what it means to be an American—have been discussed throughout this text, as they have been discussed and debated throughout the history of this society. In the final chapter, we summarize the major themes of this text, bring the analysis to a close, and speculate about the future of American race and ethnic relations.

9

New Americans, Assimilation, and Old Challenges

By early 2004, Delfino [an undocumented immigrant] was armed with... phony papers, a car, a shared house, a job, some English. It was then that his attention turned to other things. Back in Mexico, his family's eight-by-twelve-foot shack had been the most visible sign of its... low social standing. The shack had dirt floors, leaked rain, and left them unprotected from the cold. A girl's family once refused Florentino's [Delfino's brother] marriage proposal because that shack was all he could offer her.

Delfino began sending extra money home every month.... In the middle of 2004, the family moved its shack to one side—it took only a few men to lift it. On the site where the shack once stood, Delfino built the first house in his village ever paid for with dollars. It... had an indoor toilet, a kitchen, and concrete floors. The house was fronted by two smoked-glass windows so wide and tall that it looked as if the house wore sunglasses.

"I wanted it to look good when you pass," Delfino said, "and to have a nice view."

In Xocotla, nothing like it had ever been built so quickly by a youth so poor.

A few months later, Florentino [also arranged with his father] to have a house built in the village.... All this helped change their father [Lázaro]. He had stopped drinking and discovered Alcoholics Anonymous. He was now in his forties and tired of waking up in the pig muck.... His sons could now send him money for construction materials and know he wouldn't spend it on booze. So within a year of Delfino's arrival in the United States, Lázaro was not only sober but supervising construction of first Delfino's house, and then Florentino's....

Lázaro had never been the object of anyone's envy. He found that he liked it. He kept building those houses, telling everyone that he'd build until his sons in America told him to stop.

For a time, the Juárez brothers were the village's largest employers—spending close to forty thousand dollars on labor and supplies. As Florentino's house went up, the family of the girl who'd refused his marriage proposal let it be known that they regretted their decision. When Delfino returned to Xocotla for a few months in late 2004, older men, who'd once laughed at his mohawked hair, came to him to borrow money.

> *"Now everyone says hello," said Delfino.*
>
> —Sam Quinones (2007, pp. 284–286)*
>
> Delfino and Florentino represent the experiences of thousands of immigrants—legal as well as undocumented—who have crossed into the United States in recent decades. Driven by the poverty of their home village and attracted by the allure of work in *el Norte*, they pay thousands of dollars to their guides and often risk their lives in pursuit of the dream of earning a decent wage. Many are sojourners who remain focused on the families they have left behind. They send millions of dollars home and are the main—or even the sole—support for their kin, the hope and lifeblood for perhaps scores of relatives. Some are Mexican, like Delfino and Florentino, and others are Chinese, Salvadoran, Filipino, Guatemalan, or Haitian. Their desires are as disparate as their origins, but they share the dream of being able to feed, shelter, and clothe their families.
>
> Are they a threat to U.S. jobs or American culture? Will they bankrupt local welfare and school systems? Should the undocumented be imprisoned? What about their children? What benefits do these immigrants provide? Will they (or their children or grandchildren) enter the middle class, as immigrants have done before?
>
> We address these and other issues in this chapter, but you should be aware that many of these questions will have no easy or obvious answer. The United States is once again grappling with fundamental questions about acceptance and rejection, inclusion and exclusion: about what it means to be an American. In this text, we will study these issues academically, as intellectual matters to be discussed and analyzed. In your everyday life, you will deal with these same issues, probably for your entire life.

The world is on the move as never before and migrant trails connect even the remotest villages of every continent in a global network of population ebb and flow. As we have seen, people are moving everywhere, but the United States remains the single most popular destination. Migrants will pay thousands of dollars—staggering amounts of money in a world where half the population survives on less than $2.50 a day—and undergo enormous hardship to find work in the United States. What motivates this population movement? How does it differ from migrations of the past? What impact will the newcomers have on U.S. society? Will they absorb American culture? What parts? Will they integrate into American society? Which segments?

We have been asking questions like these throughout the text. In this chapter, we focus specifically on current immigrants and the myriad issues stimulated by their presence. We mentioned some groups of new American in chapters 7 and 8. In this chapter, we begin by addressing recent immigration in general terms and then consider some additional groups of new Americans, including Hispanic, Caribbean, and Asian groups, Arab Americans and Middle Easterners, and immigrants from Sub-Saharan Africa. A consideration of these

Antonio's Gun and Delfino's Dream: True Tales of Mexican Migration, by Sam Quinones. Copyright © 2007 by Sam Quinones. Published by University of New Mexico Press, pp. 284–286.

Sam Quinones is a journalist and author of two books of narrative nonfiction about Mexico and Mexican immigration. *True Tales from Another Mexico: the Lynch Mob, the Popsicle Kings, Chalino and the Bronx* (2001) and the book from which this excerpt was taken. He can be contacted at www.samquinones.com.

groups will broaden your understanding of the wide cultural variations, motivations, and human capital of the current immigration stream to the United States.

We will then address the most important and controversial immigration issues facing the United States and conclude with a brief return to the "traditional" minority groups: African Americans, Native American, and other peoples of color that continue to face issues of equality and full integration and must now pursue their long-standing grievances in an atmosphere where public attention and political energy are focused on other groups and newer issues.

Current Immigration

As you are aware, the United States has experienced several different waves of mass immigration. In chapter 2, we discussed the Old Immigration and New Immigration from different parts of Europe in the century between the 1820s and 1920s. During that period, more than 37 million people immigrated to the United States, an average rate of a little fewer than 400,000 per year. This wave of newcomers transformed American society on every level: its neighborhoods and parishes and cities, its popular culture, its accent and dialect, its religion, and its cuisine.

The current mass immigration promises to be equally transformative. This wave began after the 1965 change in U.S. immigration policy and includes people from every corner of the globe. Since the mid-1960s, almost 30 million newcomers have arrived (not counting the undocumented), a rate of more than 600,000 per year, much higher than the earlier period (although the rate is lower as a percentage of the total population).

Exhibit 9.1   Number of Legal Immigrants to the United States, 1960–2010 (Does Not Include IRCA Adjustees)

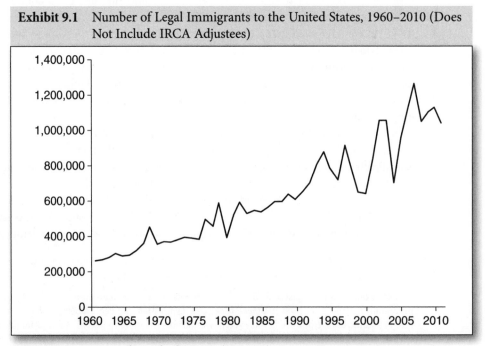

Source: U. S. Department of Homeland Security (2011, p. 5).

Also, exhibit 9.1 shows that the number of legal immigrants per year has been generally increasing over the past five decades. The official record for most immigrants in a year was set in 1907, when almost 1.3 million people arrived on these shores. That number was almost equaled in 2006, and, if undocumented immigrants were included in the count, the 1907 record would have been eclipsed several times since the 1960s.

The more recent wave of immigration is much more global than the first. In 2010 alone, immigrants arrived from more than 200 separate nations, from Afghanistan and Albania to Zambia and Zimbabwe. Only about 9% of the newcomers were from Europe. A third were from North America (most from Mexico), and more than a third were from the nations of Asia, while South America supplied almost 10%. The top 20 sending nations for 2010 are listed in exhibit 9.2. Note that Mexico accounted for more than double the number of immigrants from the next-highest sending nation.

How will this new wave of immigration transform the United States? How will these new immigrants be transformed by the United States? What do they contribute? What do they cost? Will they assimilate and adopt the ways of the dominant society? What are the implications if assimilation fails? We begin by reviewing several case studies of new Americans, focusing on information and statistics comparable to those used in chapters 5 through 8.

Each of the groups covered in this chapter has had some members in the United States for decades, some for more than a century. However, in all cases the groups were

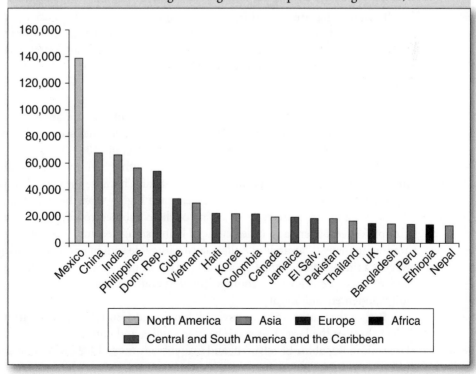

Exhibit 9.2   Number of Legal Immigrants for Top 20 Sending Nations, 2010

Source: U.S. Department of Homeland Security (2011, p. 27–30).

quite small until the latter third of the 20th century. Although they are growing rapidly now, all remain relatively small, and none is larger than 1% of the population. Nonetheless, some will have a greater impact on American culture and society in the future, and some groups—Arab Americans, Muslims, and Middle Easterners—have already become a focus of concern and controversy because of the events of September 11 and the ensuing war on terrorism.

New Hispanic Groups: Immigrants from the Dominican Republic, El Salvador, and Colombia

Immigration from Central America, the Caribbean, and South America, has been considerable, even excluding Mexico. As with other sending nations, the volume of immigration from these regions increased after 1965 and has averaged more than 200,000 per year since the 1980s. Generally, immigrants from these regions—not counting those from Mexico—have been about 25% of all immigrants since the 1960s (U.S. Department of Homeland Security, 2011, pp. 10–11).

The sending nations for these immigrants are economically less developed, and most have long-standing relations with the United States. In chapter 7, we discussed the roles that Mexico and Puerto Rico have historically played as sources of cheap labor and the ties that led Cubans to immigrate to the United States. Each of the other sending nations has been similarly linked to the United States, the dominant economic and political power in the region.

Although the majority of these immigrants bring educational and occupational qualifications that are modest by U.S. standards, they tend to be more educated, more urbanized, and more skilled than the average citizens of the nations from which they come. Contrary to widely held beliefs, these immigrants do not represent the poorest of the poor, the "wretched refuse" of their homelands. They tend to be rather ambitious, as evidenced by their willingness to attempt to succeed in a society that has not been notably hospitable to Latinos or people of color in the past. Most of these immigrants are not only fleeing poverty or joblessness, but also are attempting to pursue their ambitions and seek opportunities for advancement that are simply not available in their countries of origin (Portes & Rumbaut, 1996, pp. 10–11).

This characterization applies to legal and unauthorized immigrants alike. In fact, the latter may illustrate the point more dramatically, because the cost of illegally entering the United States can be considerable, much higher than the cost of a legal entry. The venture may require years of saving or the combined resources of a large kinship group. Forged papers and other costs of being smuggled into the country can easily amount to many thousands of dollars, a considerable sum in nations in which the usual wage is a tiny fraction of the U.S. average. Also, the passage can be extremely dangerous and can require a level of courage (or desperation) not often associated with the undocumented and illegal.

Rather than attempting to cover all South and Central American groups, we will select three of the largest to serve as case studies and consider immigrants from the Dominican Republic, El Salvador, and Colombia (see exhibit 9.3). Together, these three

Exhibit 9.3   Map of Central and South America and the Caribbean Showing the Dominican Republic, El Salvador, and Colombia

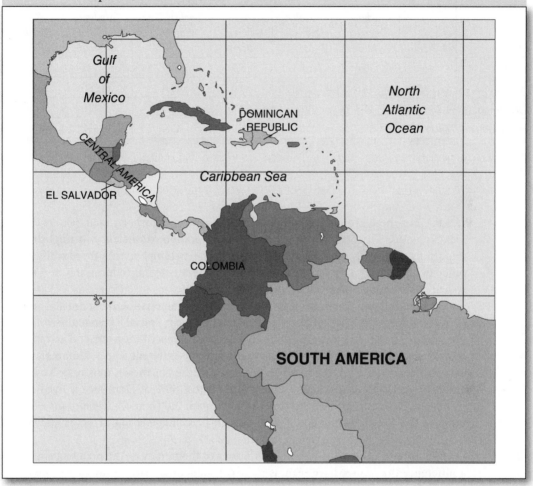

Source: From Healey (2009).

groups have made up 7% to 9% of all immigrants in recent years and about 30% of the immigrants from Central and South America and the Caribbean. These groups had few members in the United States before the 1960s, and all have had high rates of immigration over the past four decades. However, the motivation of the immigrants and the immigration experience has varied from group to group, as we shall see later.

Three Case Studies

Some basic information about these three groups is presented in exhibit 9.4. Some of this information was also presented in chapter 7 but is repeated here to provide a common frame of reference for all the groups covered in this chapter.

Exhibit 9.4   Characteristics of Three Hispanic Groups and Non-Hispanic Whites, 2010

Group	Size	% High School Degree or More	% College Degree or More	% Foreign Born	% That Speak English "Less than Very Well"	Median Household Income	% of Families in Poverty
NHW*	—	90.4	31.1	3.9	1.7	55,747	6.6
Dominicans	1,419,314	64.6	15.3	57.0	45.4	34,560	25.5
Salvadorans	1,735,580	46.8	7.6	63.7	55.1	43,475	17.6
Colombians	929,523	85.1	31.0	65.9	41.4	50,332	10.5

Source: U.S. Census Bureau (2010).

Note: *Non-Hispanic whites.

Each of these groups has a high percentage of foreign-born members, and, predictably with so many members in the first generation, proficiency in English is an important issue. Although Colombians approach national norms in education, the other two groups have relatively low levels of human capital (education), and all are well above national norms in terms of poverty.

Although these groups share some common characteristics, there are also important differences between them. They differ in their "racial" characteristics, with Dominicans more African in appearance, Colombians more European, and Salvadorans more American Indian. The groups tend to settle in different places. Colombians are concentrated in the South, mostly in Florida, and the Northeast, mostly in New York and New Jersey (Dockterman, 2011a, p. 2). Almost 80% of Dominicans lived in the Northeast, half of those in New York (Dockterman, 2011b, p. 2) Salvadorans are split between the West and the South, with a high percentage living in Texas and in the Washington, DC, metro region (Ennis et al., 2011, p. 6)

Finally, the groups differ in the conditions of their entry or their contact situation, a difference that, as we have seen, is quite consequential. Salvadorans are more likely to be political refugees who fled a brutal civil war and political repression, whereas Dominicans and Colombians are more likely to be motivated by economics and the employment possibilities offered in the United States. We will consider each of these groups briefly and explore some of these differences further.

Dominicans. The Dominican Republic shares the Caribbean island of Hispaniola with Haiti. The island economy is still largely agricultural, although the tourist industry has grown in recent years. Unemployment and poverty are major problems, and the adult population averages about 5 years of education (Nationmaster.com, 2012). Dominican immigrants, like those from Mexico, are motivated largely by economics, and they compete for jobs with Puerto Ricans, other immigrant groups, and native-born workers with lower levels of education and jobs skills. Although Dominicans are limited in their job options by the language barrier, they are somewhat advantaged by their willingness to work for lower wages, and they are especially concentrated in the service sector, as day laborers (men) or domestics (women). Dominicans maintain strong ties with their home country, and are a major source of income and support for the families left behind.

In terms of acculturation and integration, Dominicans are roughly similar to Mexican Americans and Puerto Ricans, although some studies suggest that they are possibly the most impoverished immigrant group (e.g., see Camarota, 2002). A high percentage of Dominicans are undocumented, and many spend a great deal of money and take considerable risks to get to the United States. If these less visible members of the community were included in the official, government-generated statistics used in the exhibits presented in this chapter, the portrait of poverty and low levels of education and jobs skills likely would be even more dramatic.

Salvadorans. El Salvador, like the Dominican Republic, is a relatively poor nation, with a high percentage of the population relying on subsistence agriculture for survival. It is estimated that about 50% of the population lives below the poverty level, and there are major problems with unemployment and underemployment. About 80% of the population is literate, and the average number of years of school completed for adults is a little more than five (Nationmaster.com, 2012).

El Salvador, like many sending nations, has a difficult time providing sufficient employment opportunities for its population, and much of the pressure to emigrate is economic. However, El Salvador also suffered through a brutal civil war in the 1980s, and many of the Salvadorans in the United States today are actually political refugees. The United States, under the administration of President Reagan, refused to grant political refugee status to Salvadorans, and many were returned to El Salvador. This federal policy resulted in high numbers of undocumented immigrants and also stimulated a sanctuary movement, led by American clergy, that helped Salvadoran immigrants, both undocumented and legal, to stay in the United States. As is the case with Dominicans, if the undocumented immigrants from El Salvador were included in official government statistics, the picture of poverty would be even more extreme.

Colombians. Colombia is somewhat more developed than most other Central and South American nations but has suffered from more than 40 years of internal turmoil, civil war, and government corruption. The nation is a major center for the production and distribution of drugs to the world in general and the United States in particular, and the drug industry and profits are complexly intertwined with domestic strife. Colombian Americans are closer to U.S. norms of education and income than other Latino groups, and recent immigrants are a mixture of less-skilled laborers and well-educated professionals seeking to further their careers. Colombians are residentially concentrated in urban areas, especially in Florida and the Northeast, and often settle in areas close to other Latino neighborhoods. Of course, the huge majority of Colombian Americans are law-abiding and not connected with the drug trade, but still they must deal with the pervasive stereotype that portrays Colombians as gangsters and drug smugglers (not unlike the Mafia stereotype encountered by Italian Americans).

Non-Hispanic Immigrants from the Caribbean

Immigrants from the western hemisphere bring a variety of traditions to the United States other than Hispanic. Two of the largest non-Latino groups come from Haiti and Jamaica in the Caribbean. Both nations are much less developed than the United States, and this is reflected in the educational and occupational characteristics of their immigrants. A statistical profile of both groups is presented in exhibit 9.5, along with non-Hispanic whites for purposes of comparison.

Two Case Studies

Haitians. Haiti is the poorest country in the western hemisphere, and most of the population relies on small-scale subsistence agriculture for survival. About 80% of the population lives below the poverty line, and only 52% of adults are literate (Central Intelligence Agency [CIA], 2012). Haitians average fewer than 3 years of formal education (Nationmaster.com, 2012). The already difficult conditions in Haiti were intensified by a massive earthquake in January 2010, a disaster from which the tiny nation is still attempting to recover. A map of the Caribbean showing Haiti and Jamaica is found in exhibit 9.6.

Immigration from Haiti was virtually nonexistent until the 1970s and 1980s, when thousands began to flee the brutal political repression of the Duvalier dictatorship, which—counting both father ("Papa Doc") and son ("Baby Doc")—lasted until the mid-1980s. In stark contrast to the treatment of Cuban immigrants (see chapter 7), however, the U.S. government defined Haitians as economic refugees ineligible for asylum, and an intense campaign was commenced to keep Haitians out of the United States. Thousands were returned to Haiti, some to face political persecution, prison, and even death. Others have been incarcerated in the United States, and in the view of some, "During the 1970s and 1980s, no other immigrant group suffered more U.S. government prejudice and discrimination than Haitians" (Stepick, Stepick, Eugene, Teed, & Labissiere, 2001, p. 236).

Exhibit 9.5 Characteristics of Two Non-Hispanic Caribbean Groups and Non-Hispanic Whites, 2010

Group	Size	% High School Degree or More	% College Degree or More	% Foreign Born	% That Speak English "Less than Very Well"	Median Household Income	% of Families in Poverty
NHW*	—	90.4	31.1	3.9	1.7	$55,747	6.6
Haitians	846,032	76.4	19.0	59.7	37.7	$43,001	16.8
Jamaicans	961,929	83.4	24.1	60.6	1.4	$48,558	12.1

Source: U.S. Census Bureau (2010).

Note: *Non-Hispanic whites.

Exhibit 9.6   Map of Caribbean Showing Haiti and Jamaica

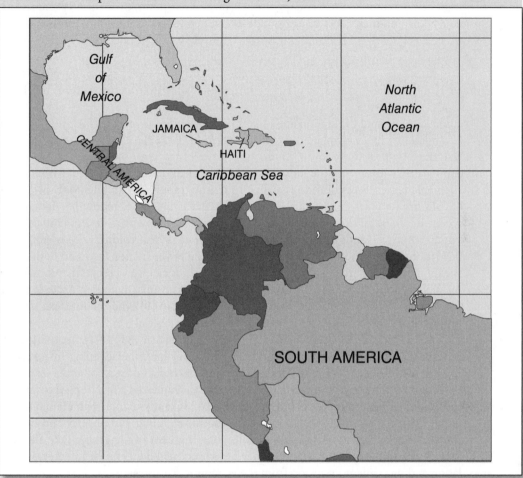

Source: From Healey (2009).

What accounts for this cold, negative reception? Some reasons are not hard to identify. The first Haitian immigrants to come brought low levels of human capital and education. This created concerns about their ability to support themselves in the United States and also meant that they had relatively few resources with which to defend their self-interest. In addition, Haitians speak Creole, a language spoken by almost no one else, and a high percentage of Haitian immigrants speak English poorly or not at all. Perhaps the most important reason for the rejection, however, is that Haitians are black and must cope with the centuries-old traditions of rejection, racism, and prejudice that are such an integral part of American culture (Stepick et al., 2001).

Haitian Americans today are still mostly first generation, and about 30% of the group arrived after 2000. Overall, they are comparable to Hispanic Americans in terms of such measures of equality as level of education, income, and poverty. Still, research shows that some Haitians continue to face the exclusion and discrimination long associated with non-white ancestry. One important study of Haitians in South Florida found that a combination of factors—their hostile reception, their poverty and lack of education, and their racial background—combined to lead the Haitian second generation (the children of the immigrants) to a relatively low level of academic achievement and a tendency to identify with the African American community. "Haitians are becoming American but in a specifically black ethnic fashion" (Stepick et al., 2001, p. 261).

The ultimate path of Haitian assimilation will unfold in the future, but these tendencies—particularly Haitians' low levels of academic achievement—suggest that some of the second generation are unlikely to move into the middle class and that their assimilation will be segmented (Stepick et al., 2001, p. 261).

Jamaicans. The Jamaican economy is more developed than Haiti's, and this is reflected in the higher levels of education of Jamaican immigrants (see exhibit 9.5). However, as is true throughout the less-developed world, the Jamaican economy has faltered in recent decades, and the island nation has been unable to provide full employment opportunities to its population. Jamaica is a former British colony, and its emigrants have journeyed to the United Kingdom in addition to the United States. In both cases, the immigrant stream tends to be more skilled and educated and represents something of a "brain drain," a pattern we have seen with other groups, including Asian Indians. Needless to say, the loss of the more-educated Jamaicans to other nations exacerbates problems of development and growth on the island.

Jamaicans typically settle on the East Coast, particularly in the New York City area. Because they come from a former British colony, they have the advantage of speaking English as their native tongue. On the other hand, they are black, and, like Haitians, they must face the barriers of discrimination and racism faced by all non-white groups in the United States. On the average, they are significantly higher than Haitians (and native-born African Americans) in socioeconomic standing, but poverty and institutionalized discrimination limit the mobility of a segment of the group. Like all other groups of color in the United States, they face a very real danger of segmented assimilation and permanent exclusion from the economic mainstream.

Contemporary Immigration from Asia

Immigration from Asia has been considerable since the 1960s, averaging close to 300,000 people per year and running about 30% to 35% of all immigrants. As was the case with Hispanic immigrants, the sending nations are considerably less developed than the United States, and the primary motivation for most of these immigrants is economic. As I stated in chapter 8, however, the Asian immigrant stream is "bipolar" and includes many highly educated professionals along with the less skilled and less educated. Also, many Asian immigrants are refugees from war and others are spouses of U.S. military personnel who had been stationed throughout the region.

As before, rather than attempting to cover all Asian immigrant groups, we will concentrate on four case studies and consider immigrants from India, the Republic of Korea (South Korea), the Philippines, and Vietnam (see exhibit 9.7). Together, these four groups make up about half of all immigrants from Asia.

Exhibit 9.7 Map of Asia Showing India, Republic of Korea (South Korea), the Philippines, and Vietnam

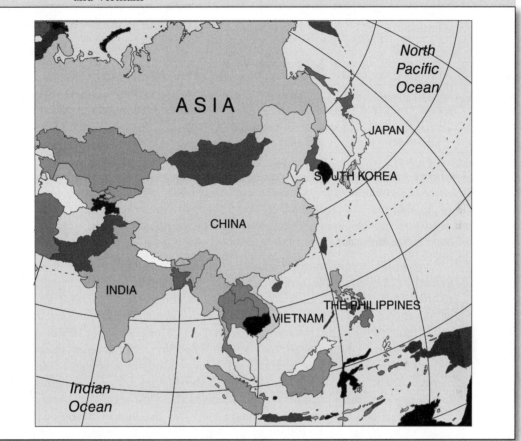

Source: From Healey (2009).

Four Case Studies

The four groups considered here are small, and they all include a high percentage of foreign-born members. They are quite variable in their backgrounds, their occupational profiles, their levels of education, and their incomes. In contrast with Hispanic immigrants, however, they tend to have higher percentages of members who are fluent in English, members with higher levels of education, and relatively more members prepared to compete for good jobs in the American job market. A statistical profile of the groups is presented in exhibit 9.8, along with that of non-Hispanic whites for purposes of comparison.

The four groups vary in their settlement patterns. Most are concentrated along the West Coast, but Asian Indian Americans are roughly equally distributed on both the East and West Coasts, and Vietnamese Americans have a sizable presence in Texas, in part related to the fishing industry along the Gulf Coast.

Exhibit 9.8 Characteristics of Four Asian Groups and Non-Hispanic Whites, 2010

Group	Size	% High School Degree or More	% College Degree or More	% Foreign Born	% That Speak English "Less than Very Well"	Median Household Income	% of Families in Poverty
NHW*	—	90.4	31.1	3.9	1.7	$55,747	6.6
Asian Indian	3,012,554	90.7	69.3	69.7	21.7	$87,996	5.5
Korean	1,686,441	91.9	51.3	63.9	40.2	$52,103	11.5
Filipinos	3,338,531	92.3	46.3	52.3	18.2	$76,592	4.8
Vietnamese	1,727,214	70.8	26.1	64.7	50.9	$54,036	12.8

Source: U.S. Census Bureau (2010).

Note: *Non-Hispanic whites.

Asian Indian Americans

India is the second most populous nation in the world, and its huge population of more than 1 billion people incorporates a wide variety of different languages (India has 19 official languages, including English), religions, and ethnic groups. Overall, the level of education is fairly low: the population averages about 5 years of formal schooling and is about 61% literate (Nationmaster.com, 2012). However, about 10% of the population does reach the postsecondary level of education, which means that there are roughly 100 million (10% of 1 billion) well-educated Indians looking for careers commensurate with their credentials. Because of the relative lack of development in the Indian economy, many members of this educated elite must search for career opportunities abroad, and not just in the United States. It is also important to note that as a legacy of India's long colonization by the British, English is the language of the educated. Thus, Indian immigrants tend to be not only well educated, but also English speaking.

Immigration from India to the United States was low until the mid-1960s, and the group was quite small at that time. The group more than quadrupled in size between 1990 and 2010, and Indians are now the third-largest Asian American group (behind Chinese and Filipinos).

Migrants from India tend to be a select, highly educated, and skilled group. According to the 2000 census, Indians are very overrepresented in some of the most prestigious occupations, including computer engineering, medicine, and college teaching (U.S. Census Bureau, 2000). Immigrants from India are part of a worldwide movement of educated peoples from less-developed countries to more-developed countries. One need not ponder the differences in career opportunities, technology, and compensation for long to get some insight into the reasons for this movement. Other immigrants from India are more oriented to commerce and small business, and there is a sizable Indian ethnic enclave in many cities (Kitano & Daniels, 1995, pp. 96–111; Sheth, 1995).

Korean Americans

Immigration from Korea to the United States began early in the 20th century, when laborers were recruited to help fill the void in the job market left by the 1882 Chinese Exclusion Act. This group was extremely small until the 1950s, when the rate of immigration rose because of refugees and "war brides" after the Korean War. Immigration did not become substantial, however, until the 1960s. The size of the group increased fivefold in the 1970s and doubled between 1990 and 2010 but is still only 0.6% of the total U.S. population.

Recent immigrants from Korea consist mostly of families and include many highly educated people. Although differences in culture, language, and race make Koreans visible targets of discrimination, the high percentage of Christians among them (about 26% of South Koreans are Christian (CIA World Factbook, 2012) may help them appear more "acceptable" to the dominant group. Certainly, Christian church parishes play a number of important roles for the Korean American community, offering assistance to newcomers and the less fortunate, serving as a focal point for networks of mutual assistance, and generally assisting in the completion of the myriad chores to which immigrant communities must attend (e.g., government paperwork, registering to vote, etc.) (Kitano & Daniels, 2001, p. 123).Korean American immigrants have formed an enclave, and the group is heavily involved in small businesses and retail stores, particularly fruit and vegetable retail stores, or greengroceries. According to one study, Koreans had the second-highest percentage of self-employment among immigrant groups (Greeks were the highest), with about 23% of the group in this occupational category (Min, 2006, pp. 238–239). However, Korean Americans are typically more visible than many other entrepreneurial groups because of their size and their concentration in the largest metropolitan areas.

As is the case for other groups that have pursued this course, the enclave allows Korean Americans to avoid the discrimination and racism of the larger society and survive in an economic niche in which lack of English fluency is not a particular problem. However, the enclave has its perils and its costs. For one thing, the success of Korean enterprises depends heavily on the mutual assistance and financial support of other Koreans and the willingness of family members to work long hours for little or no pay. These resources would be weakened or destroyed by acculturation, integration, and the resultant decline in ethnic solidarity. Only by maintaining a distance from the dominant culture and its pervasive appeal can the infrastructure survive.

Furthermore, the economic niches in which Mom-and-Pop greengroceries and other small businesses can survive are often in deteriorated neighborhoods populated largely by other minority groups. There has been a good deal of hostility and resentment expressed against Korean shop owners by African Americans, Puerto Ricans, and other urbanized minority groups. For example, anti-Korean sentiments were widely expressed in the 1992 Los Angeles riots that followed the acquittal of the policemen charged in the beating of Rodney King. Korean-owned businesses were some of the first to be looted and burned, and when asked why, one participant in the looting said simply, "Because we hate 'em. Everybody hates them" (Cho, 1993, p. 199). Thus, part of the price of survival for many Korean merchants is to place themselves in positions in which antagonism and conflict with other minority groups is common (Kitano & Daniels, 1995, pp. 112–129; Light & Bonacich, 1988; Min, 2006; see also Hurh, 1998).

Filipino Americans

Ties between the United States and the Philippines were established in 1898 when Spain ceded the territory after its defeat in the Spanish-American War. The Philippines became independent following World War II, but the United States has maintained a strong military presence there for much of the past 65 years. The nation has been heavily influenced by American culture, and English remains one of two official languages. Thus, Filipino immigrants are often familiar with English, at least as a second language (see exhibit 9.8).

Today, Filipinos are the second-largest Asian American group, but their numbers became sizable only in the past few decades. There were fewer than 1,000 Filipinos in the United States in 1910, and by 1960 the group still numbered fewer than 200,000. Most of the recent growth has come from increased post-1965 immigration. The group more than doubled in size over the past several decades (see exhibit 8.1).

Many of the earliest immigrants were agricultural workers recruited for the sugar plantations of Hawaii and the fields of the West Coast. Because the Philippines was a U.S. territory, Filipinos could enter without regard to immigration quotas until 1935, when the nation became a self-governing commonwealth.

The most recent wave of immigrants is diversified, and, like Chinese Americans, Filipino Americans are "bipolar" in their educational and occupational profiles. Many recent immigrants have entered under the family preference provisions of the U.S. immigration policy. These immigrants are often poor and compete for jobs in the low-wage secondary labor market (Kitano & Daniels, 1995, p. 94). More than half of all Filipino immigrants since 1965, however, have been professionals, many of them in the health and medical fields. Many female immigrants from the Philippines were nurses actively recruited by U.S. hospitals to fill gaps in the labor force. In fact, nurses have become something of an export commodity in the Philippines and thousands leave the Philippines every year to work all over the world. About a third of the world's nurses are Filipino and the United States currently employs more than 50,000 RNs from the Philippines (Kaye, 2010, pp. 30–34). Thus, the Filipino American community includes some members in the higher-wage primary labor market and others who are competing for work in the low-wage secondary sector (Agbayani-Siewart & Revilla, 1995; Espiritu, 1996; Kitano & Daniels, 1995, pp. 83–94; Min, 2006; Posadas, 1999).

Vietnamese Americans

A flow of refugees from Vietnam began in the 1960s as a direct result of the war in Southeast Asia. The war began in Vietnam but expanded when the United States attacked Communist forces in Cambodia and Laos. Social life there was disrupted, and people were displaced throughout the region.

In 1975, when Saigon (the South Vietnamese capital) fell and the U.S. military withdrew, many Vietnamese and other Southeast Asians who had collaborated with the United States and its allies fled in fear for their lives. This group included high-ranking officials and members of the region's educational and occupational elite. Later groups of refugees tended to be less well educated and more impoverished. Many Vietnamese waited in refugee camps for months or years before being admitted to the United States, and they often arrived with few resources or social networks to ease their transition to the new society (Kitano & Daniels, 1995, pp. 151–152). The Vietnamese are the largest of the Asian refugee groups, and, contrary to Asian American success stories and notions of model minorities, they have incomes and educational levels that are somewhat comparable to colonized minority groups (see exhibit 9.8).

Middle Eastern and Arab Americans

Immigration from the Middle East and the Arab world began in the 19th century but has never been particularly large. The earliest immigrants tended to be merchants and traders, and the Middle Eastern community in the United States has been constructed around an ethnic, small-business enclave. The number of Arab Americans and Middle Easterners has grown rapidly over the past several decades but still remains a tiny percentage of the total population. Exhibit 9.9 displays some statistical information on the group, broken down by ancestry group with which individuals identify and exhibit 9.10 shows the nations of origin.

Exhibit 9.9 shows that Middle Eastern and Arab Americans tend to rank relatively high in income and occupation. Most groups are at or above national norms in terms of percentage of high school graduates, and all groups have a higher percentage of college graduates than non-Hispanic whites, with some (Egyptians and Iranians) far more educated. Although poverty is a problem (especially those who identify as Arab American), many of the groups compare quite favorably in terms of income.

Exhibit 9.9 Characteristics of Arab American and Middle Eastern Groups and Non-Hispanic Whites, 2009

Group	Size	% High School Degree or More	% College Degree or More	% Foreign Born	% That Speak English "Less than Very Well"	Median Household Income	% of Families in Poverty
NHW*	—	90.4	31.1	3.9	1.7	$55,747	6.6
Arab	1,597,385	88.8	45.4	41.9	20.2	$55,166	14.8
Egyptian	184,401	95.5	65.7	60.3	24.3	$59,238	12.8
Lebanese	496,504	92.5	47.1	22.7	8.6	$67,298	7.5
Syrian	150,199	90.5	40.0	23.7	11.1	$64,158	7.8
Iranian	448,722	92.3	59.1	64.9	28.7	$68,024	9.0

Source: U.S. Census Bureau (2010).

Note: *Non-Hispanic whites.

Exhibit 9.10 Map of the Middle East Showing Egypt, Iran, Lebanon, and Syria

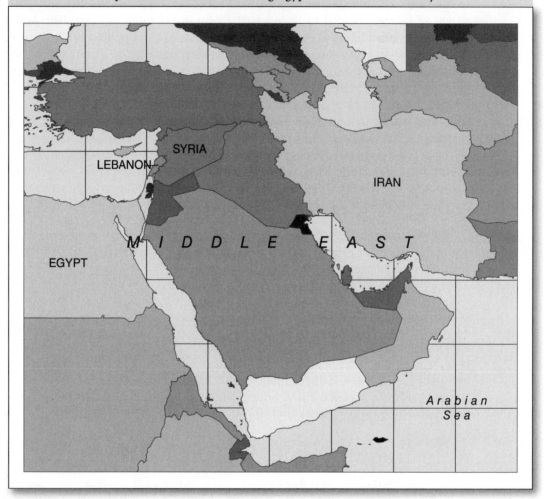

Source: From Healey (2009).

Many recent Middle Eastern immigrants are, like Asian immigrants, highly educated people who take jobs in the highest levels of the American job structure. Also, consistent with the heritage of being an enclave minority, the groups are overrepresented in sales and underrepresented in occupations involving manual labor. One study, using 1990 census data and a survey mailed to a national sample of Arab American women in 2000, found that immigrant Arab American women have a very low rate of employment, the lowest of any immigrant group. The author's analysis strongly suggests that this pattern is due to traditional gender roles and family norms regarding the proper role of women (Read, 2004).

Arab Americans and Middle Easterners are diverse and vary along a number of dimensions. They bring different national traditions and cultures and also vary in religion. Most are Muslim but many are Christian. Also, not all Middle Easterners are Arabic; Iranians, for example, are Persian. Also, about a third of all Muslims in the United States are native-born, and about 20% are African American.

Residentially, Arab Americans and Middle Easterners are highly urbanized, and almost 50% live in just five states (California, Florida, Michigan, New Jersey, and New York). This settlement pattern is not too different from that of other recent immigrant groups except for the heavy concentration in Michigan, especially in the Detroit area. Arab Americans account for 1.2% of the total population of Michigan, a far higher representation than in any other state. Arab Americans make up 30% of the population of Dearborn, Michigan, the highest percentage of any city in the nation. On the other hand, the greatest single concentration is in New York City, which has a population of about 70,000 Arab Americans. These settlement patterns reflect chains of migration, some set up decades ago. Exhibit 9.11 shows the regional distribution of the group in 2000 and clearly displays the clusters in Michigan, Florida, and Southern California.

Exhibit 9.11   Regional Distribution of Arab Americans, 2000

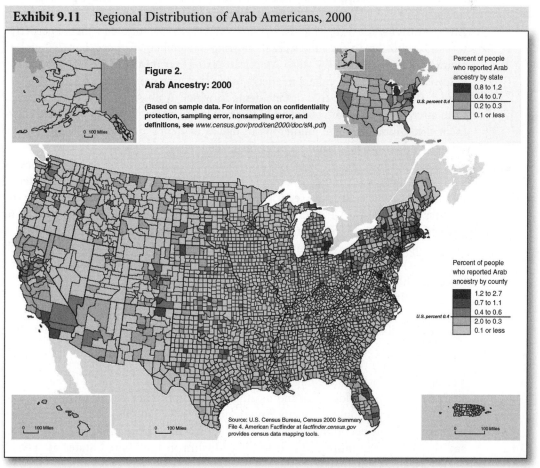

Figure 2.
Arab Ancestry: 2000

(Based on sample data. For information on confidentiality protection, sampling error, nonsampling error, and definitions, see www.census.gov/prod/cen2000/doc/sf4.pdf)

Percent of people who reported Arab ancestry by state

U.S. percent 0.4

- 0.8 to 1.2
- 0.4 to 0.7
- 0.2 to 0.3
- 0.1 or less

Percent of people who reported Arab ancestry by county

U.S. percent 0.4

- 1.2 to 2.7
- 0.7 to 1.1
- 0.4 to 0.6
- 2.0 to 0.3
- 0.1 or less

Source: U.S. Census Bureau, Census 2000 Summary File 4. American Factfinder at factfinder.census.gov provides census data mapping tools.

Source: de la Cruz and Brittingham (2003, p. 6).

9/11 and Arab Americans

There always has been at least a faint strain of prejudice directed at Middle Easterners in American culture (e.g., see the low position of Turks in the 1926 social distance scales presented in chapter 1). These vague feelings have intensified in recent decades as relations with various Middle Eastern nations and groups have worsened. For example, in 1979, the U.S. Embassy in Tehran, Iran, was attacked and occupied, and more than 50 Americans were held hostage for more than a year. The attack stimulated a massive reaction in the United States, in which anti-Arab and anti-Muslim feelings figured prominently. Continuing anti-American activities across the Middle East in the 1980s and 1990s stimulated a backlash of resentment and growing intolerance in the United States.

These earlier events pale in comparison, of course, to the events of September 11, 2001. Americans responded to the attacks on the World Trade Center and the Pentagon by Arab terrorists with an array of emotions that included bewilderment, shock, anger, patriotism, deep sorrow for the victims and their families, and—perhaps predictably in the intensity of the moment—increased prejudicial rejection of Middle Easterners, Arabs, Muslims, and any group that seemed even vaguely associated with the perpetrators of the attacks. In the nine weeks following September 11, more than 700 violent attacks were reported to the Arab American Anti-Discrimination Committee (2002), followed by another 165 violent incidents in the first nine months of 2002. In this same period, there were more than 80 incidents in which Arab Americans were removed from aircraft after boarding because of their ethnicity, more than 800 cases of employment discrimination, and "numerous instances of denial of service, discriminatory service, and housing discrimination" (Ibish, 2003, p. 7).

Anti-Arab passions may have cooled somewhat since the multiple traumas of 9/11, but the Arab American community faces a number of issues and problems, including profiling at airport security checks and greater restrictions on entering the country. Also, the USA Patriot Act, passed in 2001 to enhance the tools available to law enforcement to combat terrorism, allows for long-term detention of suspects, a wider scope for searches and surveillance, and other policies that many (not just Arab Americans) are concerned will encourage violations of due process and suspension of basic civil liberties.

Thus, although the Arab American and Middle Eastern communities are small in size, they have assumed a prominent place in the attention of the nation. The huge majority of these groups denounce and reject terrorism and violence, but, like Colombians and Italians, they are victimized by a strong stereotype that is often applied uncritically and without qualification. A recent survey of Muslim Americans, a category that includes the huge majority of Arab Americans and Middle Easterners, finds them to be "middle class and mostly mainstream." They have a positive view of U.S. society and espouse distinctly American values. At the same time, they are very concerned about becoming scapegoats in the war on terror, and a majority (53%) say that it became more difficult to be a Muslim in the United States after 9/11 (Pew Research Center, 2007).

Relations between Arab Americans and the larger society are certainly among the most tense and problematic of any minority group, and, given the U.S. involvement with wars in Iraq and Afghanistan and the threat of further terrorist attacks, they will not ease anytime soon.

The Arab American Community in Detroit, Michigan

Steve Gold

The events of September 11, 2001, focused attention on Arab American communities. The Detroit area is home to more than 300,000 Arab Americans, one of the largest ethnic enclaves in the United States. Nineteenth-century immigrants from Syria and Lebanon were the first to arrive. With the increased demand for automobiles and the steel to make them at the beginning of the 20th century, more immigrants from the Middle East came to work in Detroit's many factories. By 1916, the Ford motor company counted 555 Arab men among its workforce. The first Islamic mosque in America was established in Highland Park in 1919. The relationship between Arab immigrants and auto manufacturing endures. Next to Ford's famous River Rouge plant is Dearborn's "Arab village."

Immigrants continue to arrive in Detroit, reuniting families that have been divided across borders and continents. Whether from Iraq, Yemen, or Palestine, they seek economic advancement and escape from the Middle East's chronic violence. In 1990, more than one-third of Michigan's residents of Arab origin had been born outside the United States; about 40% had immigrated after 1980. Although all are Arab, their religious affiliations are diverse: Lebanese Christians; Sunni and Shiite Muslims; Palestinians and Jordanians who are Catholic, Protestant, Greek Orthodox, and Sunni Muslims; Eastern rite Catholic Chaldeans; and Yemenis of different Muslim sects.

The Arab community is also socioeconomically diverse, but the 1990 census showed them to be generally well off as a group. College graduation rates are high, and comparatively few are unemployed or struggling on below-poverty incomes. Besides careers in the auto industry, Arab Americans also become professionals, and many are self-employed.

With their new visibility since September 2001, Arab Americans have experienced renewed negative attention. But this, too, has deep roots. Metropolitan Detroit has a long history of racial and ethnic violence, and Arab American residents have become well acquainted with discrimination and stereotyping—from ethnic slurs like being called "camel jockeys" to the more pernicious dominance of European traditions and standards in schools. Neither is this the first conflict in the Middle East for which Arabs were

(Continued)

(Continued)

demonized. With a rich community life, Arab Americans have developed a range of organizational supports that provide succor in the face of the episodic but persistent hostilities they face in America.

Recommended Resources

Abraham, S. Y. (1983). "Detroit's Arab-American community." In S. Y. Abraham & N. Abraham, *Arabs in the New World* (pp. 84–108). Detroit, MI: Wayne State University Center for Urban Studies.

Abraham, N., & Shryock, A. (Eds.). 2000. *Arab Detroit: From margins to mainstream*. Detroit, MI: Wayne State University Press.

Johnson, N. E. 1995. *Health profiles of Michigan populations of color*. Lansing: Michigan Department of Public Health.

Source: From Gold, S. (2002). *The Arab American community in Detroit, Michigan*. Reprinted with permission of the University of California Press.

Immigrants from Africa

Our final group of new Americans consists of immigrants from Africa. Immigration from Africa has been quite low over the past 50 years. However, there was the usual increase after the 1960s, and Africans have made up about 5% of all immigrants in the past few years.

Exhibit 9.12 shows the total number of Sub-Saharan Africans in the United States in 2010, along with the two largest national groups. The number of native Africans in the United States has more than doubled since 1990, and this rapid growth suggests that these groups may have a greater impact on U.S. society in the future. The category

Exhibit 9.12 Characteristics of African Groups

Group	Size	% High School Degree or More	% College Degree or More	% Foreign Born	% That Speak English "Less than Very Well"	Median Household Income	% of Families in Poverty
NHW*	—	90.4	31.1	3.9	1.7	$55,747	6.6
Sub-Saharan African	2,881,735	85.9	29.9	39.2	12.7	$40,738	19.2
Ethiopian	186,923	83.6	26.6	72.2	36.3	$40,044	18.7
Nigerian	260,724	95.9	61.0	60.2	9.6	$59,551	8.9

Source: U.S. Census Bureau (2010).

Note: *Non-Hispanic whites.

"Sub-Saharan African" is extremely broad and encompasses destitute black refugees from African civil wars and relatively affluent white South Africans. In the remainder of this section, we will focus on Nigerians and Ethiopians rather than on this very broad category (see exhibit 9.13).

Clearly, although they are growing, Nigerians and Ethiopians are tiny minorities: neither group is as much as 0.1% of the total population. They are recent immigrants and have a high representation of first-generation members. They both compare favorably to national norms in education, an indication that this is another example of a "brain drain" from the countries of origin (especially from Nigeria). Nigerian and

Exhibit 9.13 Map of Africa Showing Ethiopia and Nigeria

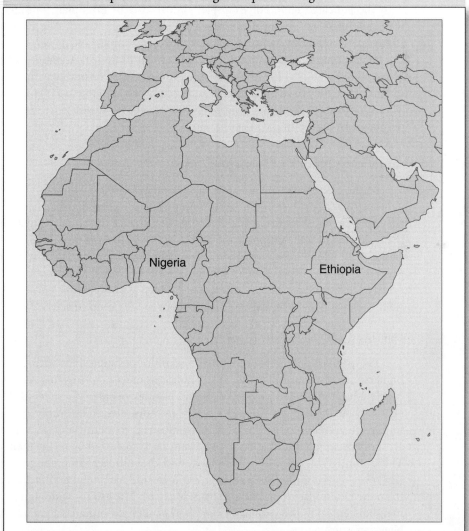

Source: From Healey (2009).

Ethiopian immigrants tend to be highly skilled and educated, and they bring valuable abilities and advanced educational credentials to the United States. Like some other groups, many of the immigrants from Nigeria and Ethiopia are motivated by a search for work, and they compete for more-desirable, higher-prestige occupations.

Nigeria is a former British colony, so the relatively high level of English fluency of the immigrants is not surprising. Exhibit 9.12 shows that members of the group have been able to translate their relatively high levels of human capital and English fluency into a favorable position in the U.S. economy. They compare quite favorably with national norms in their income levels.

Compared with Nigerians, Ethiopians rank lower in their English fluency and are more mixed in their backgrounds. They include refugees from domestic unrest along with the educated elite. For example, almost 20% of Ethiopian immigrants in 2010 were admitted as "refugees and asylees" versus only 1% of Nigerian immigrants. Refugees, virtually by definition, bring fewer resources and lower levels of human capital and thus have a more difficult adjustment to their host nation. These facts are reflected in exhibit 9.12. Although Ethiopians compare favorably with national norms in education, they have much higher rates of poverty and much lower levels of income. These contrasts suggest that Ethiopians are less able to translate their educational credentials into higher-ranked occupations.

Summary: Modes of Incorporation

As the case studies included in this chapter (as well as those in chapters 7 and 8) demonstrate, recent immigrant groups occupy a wide array of different positions in U.S. society. One way to address this diversity is to look at the contact situation, especially the characteristics the groups bring with them (e.g., their race and religion, the human capital with which they arrive) and the reaction of the larger society. There are three main modes of incorporation for immigrants in the United States: entrance through the primary or secondary labor markets (see chapter 4) or the ethnic enclave. We will consider each pathway separately and relate them to the groups discussed in this chapter.

Immigrants and the Primary Labor Market

The primary labor market consists of more desirable jobs with greater security, higher pay, and more benefits, and the immigrants entering this sector tend to be highly educated, skilled professionals and businesspeople. Members of this group are generally fluent in English, and many were educated at U.S. universities. They are highly integrated into the global urban-industrial economy, and, in many cases, they are employees of multinational corporations transferred here by their companies. These immigrants are affluent, urbane, and dramatically different from the peasant laborers so common in the past (e.g., from Ireland and Italy) and in the present (e.g., from the Dominican Republic and from Mexico). The groups with high percentages of members entering the primary labor market include Indian, Egyptian, Iranian, and Nigerian immigrants.

Because they tend to be affluent and enter a growing sector of the labor force, immigrants with professional backgrounds tend to attract less notice and fewer racist reactions than their more unskilled counterparts. Although they come closer to Blauner's pure immigrant group than most other minority groups we have considered, racism can still complicate their assimilation. In addition, Arab American Islamic groups must confront discrimination and prejudice based on their religious affiliation.

Immigrants and the Secondary Labor Market

This mode of incorporation is more typical for immigrants with lower levels of education and fewer job skills. Jobs in this sector are less desirable and command lower pay, little security, and few benefits and are often seasonal or in the underground or informal economy. This labor market includes jobs in construction, landscaping, or the garment industry, in which workers are paid "off the books" and in which working conditions are unregulated by government authorities or labor unions. Other niches in the economy are found in domestic work and some forms of illegal activity, such as drug sales and sex work.

The employers who control these jobs often prefer to hire undocumented immigrants because they are easier to control and less likely to complain to the authorities about abuse and mistreatment. The groups with high percentages of members in the secondary labor market include Dominicans, Haitians, and the less-skilled and less-educated kinfolk of the higher-status immigrants.

Immigrants and Ethnic Enclaves

As we have seen, some immigrant groups—especially those that can bring financial capital and business experience—have established ethnic enclaves. Some members of these groups enter U.S. society as entrepreneurs and become owners of small retail shops and other businesses; their less-skilled and less-educated co-ethnics serve as a source of cheap labor to staff the ethnic enterprises. The enclave provides contacts, financial and other services, and social support for the new immigrants of all social classes. Korean American and Arab Americans, along with Cuban Americans and Jewish Americans in the past, have been particularly likely to follow this path.

This classification suggests some of the variety of relationships between the new Americans and the larger society. The contemporary stream of immigrants entering the United States is extremely diverse and includes people ranging from the most sophisticated and urbane to the most desperate and despairing. The variety is suggested by considering a list of occupations in which recent immigrants are overrepresented. For men, the list includes biologists and other natural scientists, taxi drivers, farm laborers, and waiters. For women, the list includes chemists, statisticians, produce packers, laundry workers, and domestics (Kritz & Girak, 2004).

COMPARATIVE FOCUS:
The Roma: Europe's "True Minority"

Professor Andria D. Timmer

Professor Timmer studies the Roma of Europe and, especially, of Hungary. She lived and worked in Roma communities in Hungary for several years while conducting research.

The European Union is known as a "diverse family of nations," but within this "family" the Roma—sometimes called "Gypsies"—stand out as Europe's true minority. Collectively, the Roma are the most disadvantaged minority group in Europe and present the greatest challenge to integration. Their continued poverty, exclusion, and marginalization challenge the themes of multiculturalism and democracy that are purportedly valued throughout Europe. Furthermore, this is not a new situation and the Roma are by no means newcomers to Europe. According to many historical documents, they have been part of Central and Eastern European society since at least the 14th century. They number approximately 10 million and are present in all European countries, although they are more concentrated in Eastern Europe. Despite the fact that they have lived in Europe for more than half a millennium, they are still treated as recent immigrants in many respects. Thus, the Roma illustrate the point made by Gordon (see chapter 2) and many others that length of residence in a country is not necessarily related to the ability of a group to assimilate and gain acceptance.

Perhaps one of the biggest challenges to integration for the Roma is that they are not a single group or a homogeneous entity. Rather, there are several different ethnic enclaves including the Gitanos of Spain, the Sinti of Germany, the Travelers of England and Ireland, the Kalderash in Romania, and the Beás in Hungary. Members of these groups share little in common and are more similar to the majority members of the country in which they reside than they are to each other. However, from a pan-European perspective, they are often considered a single group. To understand how these different peoples get grouped together, it is necessary to return to the definition of minority provided in chapter 1 of this text. We will use the first two elements of the definition to help us examine the situation of the Roma in Europe.

The first, and most important, defining characteristic of a minority group is disadvantage or inequality, and this is something that all Roma groups have in common. Violence and intolerance towards Roma is not only still very much present, but also on the rise. According to a recent survey (European Union Agency for Fundamental Rights, 2009), 50% of Roma report being discriminated against in the 12 months. Other recent surveys (European Commission, 2007, 2008) found that discrimination has decreased on all grounds except on the basis of ethnic origin and that Europeans are generally comfortable with ethnic diversity except in regards to the Roma. Discriminatory attitudes are especially on the rise in Central and Eastern Europe where the European Roma Rights Center (www.errc.org) reports that, since 2008, there have been at least 48 violent attacks against the Roma in Hungary, 19 in the Czech Republic, and 10 in Slovakia, resulting in at least 11 fatalities. These attacks involved the use of Molotov cocktails, hand grenades, guns, arson, and mob violence.

Even while violence against the Roma is the rise, day-to-day discrimination and patterns of inequality continue everywhere. Roma neighborhoods are often lacking in basic amenities such as running water and regular trash collection. During my field research with Roma groups in Hungary, I visited many segregated villages. In these locales, the Roma and the non-Roma stood in stark contrast to one another. In several cases, the sewerage system stopped at the boundary of the village and the Roma had to contend with standing bodies of polluted water. Garbage dumps were often situated in or near Roma settlements, so flying debris is a constant problem. Roads were often poorly maintained and unpaved so that people had a difficult time traversing them. This often led to injury, and in some cases, prevented individuals from getting to hospital because ambulances could not reach their homes (see also European Roma Rights Center, 2006).

Roma youth are frequently educated separately from their majority peers and receive a lower-quality education that leaves them unable to compete in the job market. In all European countries, the Roma have much lower school attendance and completion rates than majority children. Throughout Hungary, it is common practice for non-Roma parents to transfer their children to other schools when the proportion of Roma children gets too high, largely because of the Roma's reputation for poor grades and behavior problems.

The second defining characteristic of a minority is a visible trait or characteristic. Most researchers claim that the Roma migrated out of northern India sometime between the 10th and 12th centuries and today they look more like contemporary Indians than Europeans, especially in terms of skin color. Apart from skin color, there is little that culturally ties them to India and, as mentioned previously, there are few cultural characteristics that tie all Roma groups together. Very few, apart from Traveler groups of England and Ireland, still practice the stereotypical nomadic lifestyle. Many have lost the use of their native tongue or only use it in the privacy of their homes.

Most European Roma today do not identify with India and they have little or no connection to their ancient homeland. In fact, the Roma today are often considered to be a nation-less people. Cristian Tileagă posits that the Roma constitute the "epitome of foreignness," because "[t]hey have no (national) place, no one wants them and they have no place to go . . . Romanies are the eternal strangers in anybody's land" (2005, 604–605). They are a classic "marginalized" group: they have no home country but, because of their appearance, they are still not considered European.

The deep divide between Roma and non-Roma in Europe is largely the result of a long history of isolation and segregated living. Governments have sometimes helped to build new houses and sponsored environmental clean-up projects but there are few programs to integrate Roma families into the larger national communities. As long as residential segregation, prejudice, and discrimination persist, Europe will remain divided and the Roma will remain isolated and segregated.

Immigration: Issues and Controversies

The Attitudes of Americans

One factor that affects the fate of immigrant groups is the attitude of the larger society, particularly the groups that have the most influence with governmental policymakers. Overall, American public opinion is split on the issue of immigration, as demonstrated in exhibit 9.14. A majority of Americans regard immigration as a positive force but many others are vehemently opposed—and it is the latter whose voices seem to be more prominent in everyday discourse. The history of this nation is replete with anti-immigrant and nativist groups and activities, including those that opposed the immigration from Europe (chapter 2), Mexico (chapter 7), and China and Japan (chapter 8). The present is no exception: as immigration increased over the past several decades, so have the number and visibility of anti-immigrant groups, particularly in the states along the U.S. border with Mexico.

The contemporary anti-immigrant movements have generated a number of state laws. The most controversial and widely publicized of these has been S.B. 1070, passed by the Arizona legislature in the spring of 2010. Among other provisions, the law required law enforcement officers to check the immigration status of anyone they

Exhibit 9.14 American Attitudes on Immigration

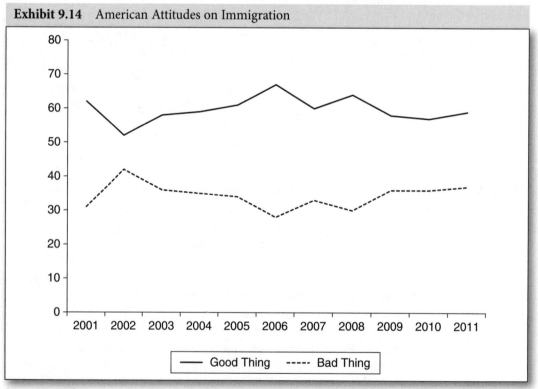

Source: National Opinion Research Council (1972–2008).

Actual question wording: "On the whole, do you think that immigration is a good thing or a bad thing for this country today?"

stopped, detained, or arrested when they had a "reasonable" suspicion that the person might be in the country illegally. Supporters of the legislation argued that it would help control illegal immigrants but opponents raised fears of racial profiling and legalized anti-Hispanic discrimination. There was also considerable concern that the legislation would deter Hispanic Americans from reporting crimes or otherwise cooperating with the police.

Public opinion polls showed that at least a slight majority of Americans supported S.B. 1070. For example, a Gallup poll conducted just days after the bill was passed found that 75% of all Americans had heard of the law and that 51% supported it while 39% opposed it (Jones, 2010). Several other states, including Utah and Georgia, have passed similar legislation. But the fate of these bills is somewhat unclear in view of the Supreme Court decision that declared most of the provision of S.B. 1070 unconstitutional (Liptak, 2012b).

What factors might account for people's view of immigration? One possibility is that negative views of immigrants are linked to fear of job loss and financial insecurity. To illustrate, one survey shows that white Americans who were dissatisfied with their financial situation were more likely to support a reduction in immigration. This relationship is displayed in exhibit 9.15. The table shows that there is a lot of support for decreasing immigration regardless of people's satisfaction with their financial situations but support is strongest for people who are most dissatisfied. This suggests a relationship between opposition to immigrants and prejudice, perhaps motivated by a sense of threat, that is consistent with the Noel hypothesis (see chapter 3) and the outcome of Robber's Cave experiment (see chapter 1). This relationship should come as no surprise at this point in the text.

What other factors might be associated with anti-immigrant attitudes? A recent study (Pettigrew, Wagner, & Christ, 2007) examined attitudes in Germany and compared them with other recent studies of European attitudes and anti-immigration feelings in Canada and the United States. The researchers found similar patterns in all

Exhibit 9.15   Position on Immigration by Satisfaction with Financial Situation

	So far as you and your family are concerned, would you say that you are pretty well satisfied with your present financial situation, more or less satisfied, or not satisfied at all?		
Do you think that the number of immigrants to America should be	*Satisfied*	*More or Less Satisfied*	*Not at all Satisfied*
Increased	12.1%	9.8%	9.4%
Remain the Same	36.6%	37.8%	25.6%
Decreased	51.3%	52.4%	65.0%
	100% (224)	100% (286)	100% (203)

Source: National Opinion Research Council (1972–2008).

locales and concluded that negative views of immigrants were highly correlated with other forms of prejudice. The same forces that produce prejudice—exposure to prejudiced norms and values during childhood, low levels of education—also produce anti-immigrant feelings. We discussed relationships of this sort in chapter 1 when we noted that prejudice is partly cultural and is passed on from generation to generation.

However, remember that prejudice is also related to intergroup conflict. The researchers (Pettigrew et al., 2007, p. 35) found that a sense of collective threat was the single strongest predictor of antiforeigner attitudes, more so than the individual-level threat examined in exhibit 9.15. That is, the most important cause of anti-immigrant attitudes was the sense that newcomers threatened the way of life, political freedoms, and cultural integrity of the nation as a whole, not just jobs or one's personal financial stability. As in so many other instances we have investigated, these forms of prejudice are defensive: they are reactions to the sense that the dominant status of one's group is at risk. As we have seen on numerous occasions (e.g., the Robber's Cave experiment discussed in chapter 1, rigid competitive relations discussed in chapter 4), competition between groups—or even the perception of competition—can stimulate powerful emotions and extreme forms of prejudice and discrimination (see also Hainmueller & Hiscox, 2010; Hopkins, 2010; and Haubert & Fussell, 2006).

Does this mean that everyone who has reservations and questions about immigration is a racist? Emphatically not. While anti-immigrant feelings, prejudice, and a sense of threat are linked, this does not mean that all who oppose immigration are bigots or that all proposals to decrease the flow of immigrants are racist. These are serious and complex issues and it is not helpful simply to label people bigots or dismiss their concerns as prejudiced.

On the other hand, we need to clearly recognize that anti-immigrant feelings—particularly the most extreme—are linked to some of the worst, most negative strains of traditional American culture: the same racist and prejudicial views that helped to justify slavery and the near-genocide of Native Americans. In popular culture, some talk radio and cable TV "news" shows, letters to the editor, and so forth, these views are regularly used to demonize immigrants, blame them for an array of social problems, and stoke irrational fears and rumors, such as the idea that Latino immigrants are aiming to return parts of the Southwest to Mexico. At any rate, when American traditions of prejudice and racism are linked to feelings of group threat and individual insecurity, the possibilities for extreme reactions, hate crimes, and poorly designed policy and law become formidable.

The Immigrants

One survey of immigration issues (National Public Radio, 2004) included a nationally representative sample of immigrant respondents. Not surprisingly, the researchers found that their attitudes and views differed sharply from those of native-born respondents on a number of dimensions. For example, immigrant respondents were more likely to see immigration as a positive force for the larger society and more likely to say that immigrants work hard and pay their fair share of taxes. More relevant for the ultimate impact of the contemporary wave of immigration, the survey found that only about 30% were sojourners (i.e., planning to return to their homelands eventually), a finding that suggests that issues of assimilation and immigration will remain at the forefront of U.S. concerns for many decades.

The survey also showed that immigrants are grateful for the economic opportunities available in the United States, with 84% agreeing that there are more opportunities to get ahead here than in their countries of origin. On the other hand, the immigrant respondents were ambivalent about U.S. culture and values. For example, nearly half (47%) said that the family was stronger in their homelands than in the United States, and only 28% saw U.S. society as having stronger moral values than their homelands.

We have seen that the immigrant stream is highly diversified but it would be helpful to keep in mind the characteristics of the "typical immigrant." The modal or most common immigrant is from Mexico, China, or other Asian or Central American nation and has decided to cross the border largely out of desperation and the absence of viable opportunities at home. These immigrants would prefer to enter legally but their desperation is such that they will enter illegally if necessary. Coming from less-developed nations, they bring little human capital, education, or job skills. Some will come to the United States for a time and then return home, circulating between nations as has been done for decades. Others will stay in the United States, separated from their families and loved ones, because they fear that enhanced border security will prevent them from reentering the United States if they ever visit their homes.

As is typical of the first generation, they tend to be more oriented to their home villages than to the United States, and they are often less interested in acculturation or learning English. Frequently, they don't have the time, energy, or opportunity to absorb much of Anglo culture and are further hampered in their acquisition of English by the fact that they are not very literate in their native language. They are hard-working and frugal, often sharing living quarters with many others to save on rent. They send much of their earnings home to support their family and kin and spend little on themselves. They are generally determined to find a better way of life for their children, even if the cost is to live in poverty at the margins of society and in constant fear of being deported.

Costs and Benefits

Many Americans believe that immigration is a drain on the economic resources of the nation. Common concerns include the ideas that immigrant take jobs from native-born workers, strain societal institutions including schools, housing markets, and medical facilities, and do not pay taxes. These issues are complex and hotly debated at all levels of U.S. society, so much so that passion and intensity of feeling on all sides often compromises the objective analysis of data. The debate is further complicated because conclusions about these economic issues can vary depending on the type of immigrants being discussed and the level of the analysis. For example, conclusions about costs and benefits can be very different depending on whether we focus on less-skilled or undocumented immigrants on the one hand or on the highly educated professional immigrants entering the primary job market on the other. Also, conclusions vary depending the level of the analyses: national studies might lead to different conclusions than studies of local communities.

Contrary to some strains of public opinion, many studies, especially those done at the national level, find that immigrants are not a particular burden. For example, a study conducted by the National Research Council (Smith & Edmonston, 1997) found that immigrants are a positive addition to the economy. They add to the labor supply in areas as disparate as the garment industry, agriculture, domestic work, and college faculty. Other researchers have found that low-skilled immigrants tend to find jobs in areas of the economy in which few U.S. citizens work or in the enclave economies of their own groups, taking jobs that would not have existed without the economic activity of their co-ethnics (Heer, 1996, pp. 190–194; Smith & Edmonston, 1997) and that they do not have a negative effect on the employment of native-born workers (Kochhar, 2006; Meissner, 2010). One important recent study of the economic impact of immigrants concluded that there is a relatively small effect on the wages and employment of native workers, although there may be negative consequences for earlier immigrants and for less-skilled African American workers (Bean & Stevens, 2003).

Another concern is the strain that immigrants place on taxes and services such as schools and welfare programs. Again, these issues are complex and far from settled, but research tends to show that immigrants generally make roughly proportional contributions to local, state, and national budgets in the form of taxes. Taxes are automatically deducted from their paychecks (unless, of course, they are being paid "under the table"), and their use of such services as unemployment compensation, Medicare, food stamps, and Social Security is actually lower than their contributions. This is particularly true for undocumented immigrants, whose use of services is sharply limited by their vulnerable legal status (Marcelli & Heer, 1998; Simon, 1989) but noncitizen immigrants are generally not eligible for government welfare programs. Bean and Stevens (2003, pp. 66–93), in their recent study, found that immigrants are not overrepresented on the welfare rolls. Rather, the key determinant of welfare use is refugee status. Groups such as Haitians, Salvadorans, and Vietnamese—who arrive without resources and, by definition, are in need of assistance on all levels—are the most likely to be on the welfare rolls.

In general, immigrants—undocumented as well as legal—pay local, state, and federal taxes and contribute to Social Security and Medicare. The undocumented are the most likely to be paid "off the books" and receive their wages tax-free, but estimates are that the majority (at least 50%) and probably the huge majority (up to 75%) of them pay federal and state taxes through payroll deduction (White House, 2005). Also, *all* immigrants pay sales taxes and the other taxes (e.g., on gas, cigarettes, and alcohol) that are levied on consumers.

Also, there is evidence that immigrants play a crucial role in keeping the Social Security system solvent. This source of retirement income is being severely strained by the "baby boomers"—the large number of Americans born between 1945 and 1960 who are now retiring. This group is living longer than previous generations and, since the U.S. birth rate has stayed low over the past four decades, there are relatively fewer native-born workers to support them and replace the funds they withdraw as Social

Security and Medicare benefits. Immigrants may supply the much-needed workers to take up the slack in the system and keep it solvent. In particular, most undocumented immigrants pay into the system but (probably) will never draw any money out, because of their illegal status. They thus provide a tidy surplus—perhaps as much as $7 billion a year or more—to help subsidize the retirements of the baby boomers and keep the system functioning (Porter, 2005).

Final conclusions about the impact and costs of immigration must await ongoing research, and many local communities are experiencing real distress as they try to deal with the influx of newcomers in their housing markets, schools, and health-care facilities. Concerns about the economic impact of immigrants are not unfounded, but they may be confounded with and exaggerated by prejudice and racism directed at newcomers and strangers. The current opposition to immigration may be a reaction to "who" as much as to "how many" or "how expensive."

Finally, we can repeat the finding of many studies (e.g., Bean & Stevens, 2003), that immigration is generally a positive force in the economy and that, as has been true for decades, immigrants, legal and illegal, continue to find work and niches in American society in which they can survive. The highly skilled immigrants fill gaps in the primary labor market, in schools and universities, corporations, hospitals, and hundreds of other sectors of the economy. Less-skilled immigrants provide cheap labor for the low-wage secondary job market and, frequently, the primary beneficiaries of this long-established system are not the immigrants (although they are often grateful for the opportunities), but employers, who benefit from a cheaper, more easily exploited workforce, and American consumers, who benefit from lower prices in the marketplace and reap the benefits virtually every time they go shopping, have a meal in a restaurant, pay for home repairs or maintenance, or place a loved one in a nursing home (for an overview, see Griswold, 2012).

Undocumented Immigrants

Americans are particularly concerned with undocumented immigrants but, again, are split in their attitudes. A recent poll (Saad, 2010) asked about people's concerns regarding undocumented immigrants and found that 61% of respondents were concerned with the burden on schools, hospitals, and government services, 55% were concerned that "illegal immigrants might be encouraging others to move here illegally," and 53% were concerned that undocumented immigrants lower wages for native-born workers. At the same time, 64% of respondents proclaimed themselves to be "very" or "somewhat" sympathetic toward undocumented immigrants. Only 17% said they were "very unsympathetic."

The high level of concern is certainly understandable because the volume of illegal immigration has been huge over the past few decades. As displayed in exhibit 9.16, the estimated number of undocumented immigrants increased from 8.4 million in 2000 to a high of 12 million in 2007, an increase of more than 40%. The number has declined during the recession and is now estimated to be about 10.2 million. On the average, about 55% of all unauthorized immigrants are from Mexico.

Exhibit 9.16   Estimated Number of Undocumented Immigrants, 2000–2011

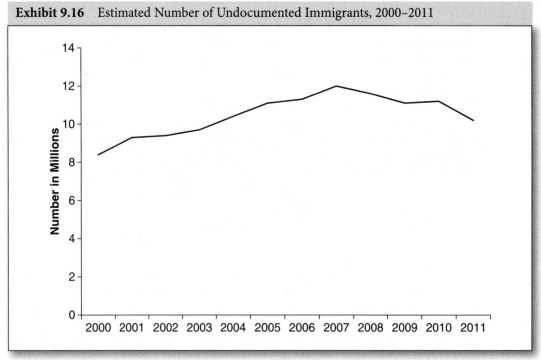

Source: Passel and Cohn (2010); Taylor, Lopez, Passel, and Motel (2011).

Some undocumented immigrants enter the country on tourist, temporary worker, or student visas and simply remain in the nation when their visas expire. In 2010 alone, more than 40 million tourists, businesspeople, temporary workers, and foreign students entered the United States (U.S. Department of Homeland Security, 2011, p. 65) and these numbers suggest how difficult it is to keep tabs on this source of illegal immigrants. Others cross the border illegally in the hopes of evading the Border Patrol, outlaws, kidnappers, criminal gangs, rapists, and thieves, and find their way into some niche in the American economy. The fact that people keep coming suggests that most succeed.

One of the reasons that the supply of unauthorized immigrants has been so high is because of the continuing demand for cheap labor in the U.S. economy. As we have noted on several occasions, the global South—and Mexico in particular—has functioned as a reserve labor force for the U.S. economy for decades. Even in 2010, after several years of economic recession, undocumented immigrants provided a sizeable percentage of the workforce in many states and were as much as 10% of the workers in several (see exhibit 9.17).

The demand for cheap (undocumented) labor varies by the sector of the economy; one of the biggest users has been the agricultural sector. Arturo Rodriguez (2011), the president of the United Farm Workers of America (the union founded by César Chávez and mentioned in chapter 7), estimates that as much as 70% of the 2 million agricultural

Exhibit 9.17   Unauthorized Immigrants as Share of Labor Force, by State, 2010

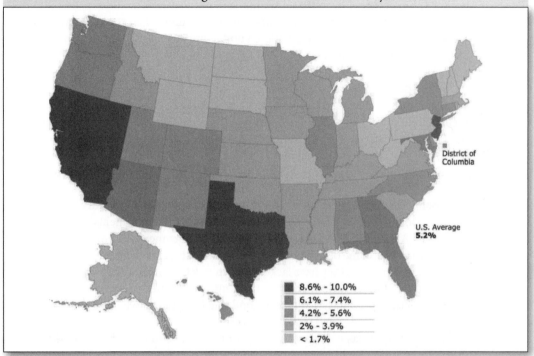

District of
Columbia

U.S. Average
5.2%

■ 8.6% - 10.0%
■ 6.1% - 7.4%
■ 4.2% - 5.6%
■ 2% - 3.9%
■ < 1.7%

Source: Passel and Cohn (2011, p. 28).

workers in the United States—the people who actually pick the crops and prepare them to be shipped to market—are undocumented immigrants. U.S. agriculture and the food supply would collapse without the contributions of undocumented workers.

A variety of efforts continue to be made to curtail and control the flow of illegal immigrants. Various states have attempted to lower the appeal of the United States by limiting benefits and opportunities. Other than the aforementioned S.B. 1070 in Arizona, one of the best known of these attempts occurred in 1994, when California voters passed Proposition 187, which would have denied educational, health, and other services to illegal immigrants. The policy was declared unconstitutional, however, and never implemented. Other efforts to decrease the flow of illegal immigration have included proposals to limit welfare benefits for immigrants, deny in-state college tuition to the children of illegal immigrants, increase the size of the Border Patrol, and construct taller and wider walls along the border with Mexico. Over the past decade, a variety of proposals to reform the national immigration policy have been hotly debated at the highest levels of government but none has been passed.

For much of the past few decades, these efforts to stem the flow of undocumented immigrants seemed futile. Finally, in the past few years, the flow has decreased. Why? The primary reason seems to be the weaker U.S. job market but other important factors include a falling birth rate in Mexico (the major supplier of undocumented immigrants), the dangers associated with crossing the southern border, and increased border enforcement efforts (Passel, Cohn, & Gonzalez-Barrera, 2012, p. 6).

The flow of unauthorized migrants may well resume when the economy recovers. Regardless, there are more than 10 million undocumented immigrants still in the United States, many of them children. What should be done with this population? The issue continues to be hotly debated at all levels of the society. Some advocate punitive policies, including deportation and continuing or expanding the denial of services (as in Proposition 187). Others advocate policies that would allow at least some of the undocumented to legalize their status. Such programs have been implemented in the past (e.g., the Immigration Reform and Control Act of 1987 discussed in chapter 7) and several have support in the present, including the so-called DREAM Act (Development, Relief, and Education for Alien Minors). Some versions of the DREAM Act would permit the children of undocumented immigrants—generally those who came to the United States at a young age and through no choice of their own—a pathway to citizenship. In June 2012, President Obama announced an executive order that implements some provisions of the DREAM Act. The order allows children of undocumented immigrants who meet certain criteria to "come out of the shadows, work legally, and obtain driver's licenses and many other documents they have lacked" (Preston & Cushman, 2012). The order applies to immigrant children who arrived in the United States before they were 16, are high school graduates or military veterans in good standing, and who have lived in the United States for at least 5 years, and who have no criminal record.

President Obama's executive order is controversial and the debate on the undocumented continues. The fate of these immigrants is uncertain and millions may find themselves in legal limbo for decades (or longer). If so, one likely future for much of this population is absorption into the American underclass, a possibility that is discussed in the next section.

FOCUS ON CONTEMPORARY ISSUES:
Birthright Citizenship

Who should be granted American citizenship? Among advanced industrial nations, the United States and Canada alone automatically confer citizenship on any baby born within their borders, including babies born to undocumented immigrants. This policy is based on the 14th Amendment to the U.S. Constitution, which was passed shortly after the Civil War to guarantee the citizenship rights of ex-slaves. The amendment has been interpreted ever since as guaranteeing citizenship for anyone born on American soil.

Birthright citizenship is one of many hotly debated immigration issues. What is at stake here? Does this policy make sense? Is it too broad a definition of who should be an American? What are the costs of maintaining it? What message would be sent by changing it? What are people really saying when they speak about issues like this?

Let's begin with some facts. In 2010 there were about 4.5 million children (about 2% of the total population but about 6% of all children) who had been born in the

United States with at least one parent who was an unauthorized immigrant, more than double the number (2.1 million) in 2000. Each year, between 300,000 and 400,000 additional babies are born to undocumented immigrants: This is as much as 10% of all U.S. births in any given year (Passel & Cohn, 2011, p 12). These few numbers are enough to document the scope of this issue: birthright citizenship has a significant impact, especially on hospital delivery rooms and school systems.

What are the arguments for and against birthright citizenship? We cannot hope to present all relevant points in these few paragraphs but we can consider some of the common arguments.

Arguments for ending birthright citizenship commonly cite the costs to taxpayers (see Federation for American Immigration Reform, 2010). Undocumented immigrants are, virtually by definition, poor, and the costs of delivery and care for newborns amounts to millions—perhaps billions—of dollars per year. These costs are passed on to taxpayers, creating a sizeable strain on local, state, and national treasuries.

On the other hand, ending birthright citizenship would have its own costs. For one thing, if citizenship were made conditional (e.g., granted only to children of U.S. citizens), some procedure would have to be established to check the status of parents. This would suggest the need for additional government bureaucracy, red tape, and expense to tax-payers. There would be other expenses as well, no doubt; the total costs might be difficult to estimate but the point is that a program that limited citizenship would not be free.

Another common argument for eliminating birthright citizenship is that it would reduce the incentive for people to enter illegally. This argument might make sense on its face but if the primary incentive for immigration is work and job opportunities, ending this policy would have little impact on population flows. No European nation grants birthright citizenship, yet they have a sizeable population of unauthorized immigrants.

Furthermore, some research (Van Hook, 2010) argues that repeal of birthright citizenship would increase the size of the unauthorized immigrant population and create a large, permanent class of marginalized people, alien to both the United States and to the native country of their ancestors. In effect, this group would be stateless, without full citizenship rights anywhere, and easily exploited.

These points, of course, just scratch the surface of a complex legal, political, economic, and social issue. It is quite likely that birthright citizenship will be a prominent issue in American politics for some time and that you will encounter strong arguments for and against often. As you consider evidence and opinions, remember to exercise your critical faculties: Is the issue being used to frighten voters or demonize immigrants? Are claims supported by evidence from verifiable sources? Is the language needlessly inflammatory or vague? Do the arguments come from advocacy or special interest groups that are known to favor or oppose immigration reform? It is easy to get swept up in the emotions of the moment, but remember that this issue affects the lives of—literally—millions, and that there is a lot at stake here, both for the migrants and for the United States.

Is Contemporary Assimilation Segmented?

In chapter 2, we reviewed the patterns of acculturation and integration that typified the adjustment of Europeans who immigrated to the United States before the 1930s. Although their process of adjustment was anything but smooth or simple, these groups eventually acculturated and achieved levels of education and affluence comparable to national norms (see exhibits 2.7 and 2.8). Will contemporary immigrants experience similar success? Will their sons and daughters and grandsons and granddaughters rise in the occupational structure to a position of parity with the dominant group? Will the cultures and languages of these groups gradually fade and disappear?

Final answers to these questions must await future developments. In the meantime, there is considerable debate on these issues. Some analysts argue that the success story of the white ethnic groups will not be repeated and that assimilation for contemporary immigrants will be segmented: some will enjoy success and rise to middle-class prosperity, but others—especially, perhaps, the undocumented and their children—will find themselves mired in the urban underclass, beset by crime, drugs, school failure, and marginal, low-paid menial jobs (Haller, Portes, & Lynch, 2011, p. 737). Other analysts find that the traditional perspective on assimilation— particularly the model of assimilation developed by Milton Gordon—continues to be a useful framework for understanding the experience of contemporary immigrants. We will review some of the most important and influential arguments from each side of this debate and, finally, attempt to come to some conclusions about the future of assimilation.

The Case for Segmented Assimilation

This thesis has attracted many advocates, including some of the most important researchers in this area of the social sciences. Here, we will focus on two of the most important works. The first presents an overview and the second is based on an important, continuing research project on the second generation, the children of contemporary immigrants.

Assimilation Now vs. Assimilation Then

Sociologist Douglas Massey (1995) argued that there are three crucial differences between past (before the 1930s) and contemporary (after the mid-1960s) assimilation experiences, each of which calls the traditional perspective into question. First, the flow of immigrants from Europe to the United States slowed to a mere trickle after the 1920s because of restrictive legislation, the worldwide depression of the 1930s, and World War II. Immigration in the 1930s, for example, was less than 10% of the flow of the early 1920s. Thus, as the children and grandchildren of the European immigrants Americanized and grew to adulthood in the 1930s and 1940s, few new immigrants fresh from the old country replaced them in the ethnic neighborhoods. European cultural traditions and languages weakened rapidly with the passing of the first generation and the Americanization of their descendants.

It is unlikely, argues Massey, that a similar hiatus will interrupt contemporary immigration. As we saw in exhibit 9.16, for example, the number of undocumented immigrants remains high in spite of the current recession. Immigration has become continuous, argues Massey, and as some contemporary immigrants (or their descendants) Americanize and rise to affluence and success, new arrivals will replace them and continuously revitalize the ethnic cultures and languages.

Second, the speed and ease of modern transportation and communication will maintain cultural and linguistic diversity. A century ago, immigrants from Europe could maintain contact with the old country only by mail, and many had no realistic expectation of ever returning. Modern immigrants, in contrast, can return to their homes in a day or less and can use telephones, television, e-mail, and the Internet to stay in intimate contact with the families and friends they left behind. Thus, the cultures of modern immigrants can be kept vital and whole in ways that were not available (and not even imagined) 100 years ago.

Third, and perhaps most important, contemporary immigrants face an economy and a labor market that are vastly different from those faced by European immigrants of the 19th and early 20th century. The latter group generally rose in the class system as the economy shifted from manufacturing to service (see exhibit 4.5). Today, rates of upward mobility have decreased, and just when the importance of education has increased, schools available to the children of immigrant laborers have fallen into neglect (Massey, 1995, pp. 645–646).

For the immigrants from Europe a century ago, assimilation meant a gradual rise to middle-class status and suburban comfort, a process often accomplished in three generations. Massey fears that assimilation today is segmented, and that a large percentage of the descendants of contemporary immigrants—especially many of the Hispanic groups, Haitians, and other peoples of color—face permanent membership in a growing underclass population and continuing marginalization and powerlessness.

The Second Generation

An analysis of the second generation of recent immigrant groups (Haller et al., 2011) also found support for the segmented assimilation model. The researchers interviewed the children of immigrants in the Miami and San Diego areas at three different times, when they were average age 14 in the early 1990s, again 3 years later, and a final time when the respondents were an average age 24. The sample was large (more than 5,000 respondents at the beginning) and representative of the second generation in the two metropolitan areas in which the study was conducted. This is an important study because its longitudinal design permits the researchers to track these children of immigrants in precise detail.

The researchers argue, consistent with Massey (1995) and with many of the points made previously in this text, that contemporary immigrants face a number of barriers to successful adaptation, including racial prejudice (since the huge majority are nonwhite), a labor market sharply split between a primary sector that requires high levels of education and a secondary sector that is low paid and insecure, and a widespread criminal subculture based on gangs and drug sales, that provides a sometimes attractive alternative to the conventional pursuit of success through education.

Whether immigrants and their descendants are able to overcome these obstacles depends decisively on three factors, which are listed at the far left of exhibit 9.18. The exhibit also depicts several different projected pathways of mobility across the generations. Immigrants who arrive with high levels of human capital enter the primary labor market and their descendants generally enter the economic and social mainstream by the third generation (see the top row of the exhibit). The descendants of immigrants with lower levels of human capital can succeed if they benefit from strong families and strong co-ethnic communities that reinforce parental discipline. This pathway is depicted in the middle row of exhibit 9.18 and also results in full acculturation and integration in the economic mainstream by the third generation.

The bottom row of the exhibit outlines a very different pathway for a large percentage of some contemporary immigrant groups. The mode of incorporation for these immigrants does not place them in a strong co-ethnic community and they may also experience weaker family structures, sometimes because of their undocumented status or because the family is split between the United States and the home country. The result is lower educational achievement and economic marginalization or assimilation into gangs, the drug subculture, and other deviant lifestyles.

The researchers present a variety of evidence in support of segmented assimilation theory. For example, the second generations of different groups have very different experiences in school, very different income levels, and very different experiences with

Exhibit 9.18   Paths of Immigrant Mobility across Generations

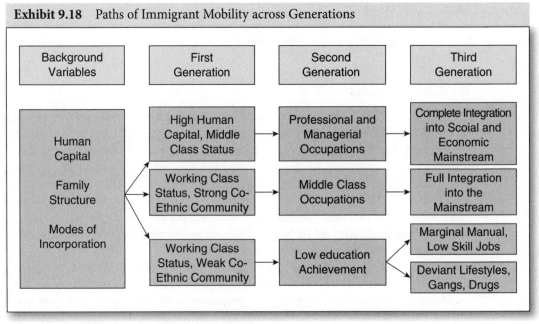

Source: Based on Haller, Portes, and Lynch (2011, p. 738).

the criminal justice system. Some of the differences are presented in exhibit 9.19, which displays large variations in the percentage of second generation individuals who do not pursue education beyond high school, and exhibit 9.20, which shows patterns of incarceration by group.

As the researchers point out, these patterns are not random: they reflect large differences in the human capital of the immigrant generation and variations in modes of incorporation (especially in terms of legal status and racial prejudice). They show that large percentages of the second (and third and later) generations of some groups is destined for assimilation into low-status, marginalized, or deviant sectors of American society, in direct contradiction to the patterns predicted by some versions of traditional assimilation theory.

Another important recent study reinforces some of these points. Sociologists Telles and Ortiz (2008) studied a sample of Mexican Americans who were interviewed in 1965 and again in 2000. They found evidence of strong movements toward acculturation and integration on some dimensions (e.g., language) but not on others. Even fourth-generation members of their sample continued to live in "the barrio" and marry

Exhibit 9.19   Percent of Second Generation Who Are High School Grads or Less

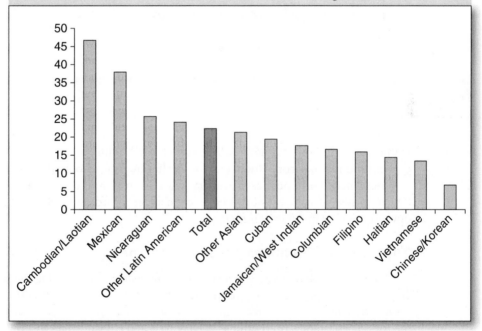

Source: Haller, Portes, and Lynch (2011, p. 742).

Notes:

- Chinese and Korean Americans were combined, as were Cambodians and Laotians because of similar patterns and in order to create groups large enough for statistical analysis.
- "Other Latin" are mostly Salvadoran and Guatemalan.
- "Other Asian" are a diverse group of many nationalities.

Exhibit 9.20   Percent of Second-Generation Males Incarcerated

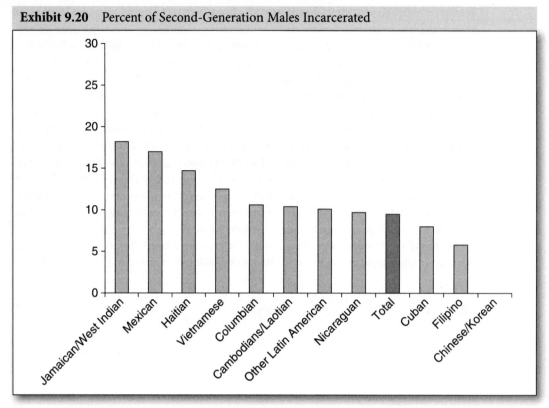

Source: Haller, Portes, and Lynch (2011, p. 742).

Note: See exhibit 9.17.

within the group, and did not reach economic parity with Anglos. The authors single out institutional discrimination (e.g., underfunding of schools that serve Mexican American neighborhoods) as a primary cause of the continuing separation, a point that is consistent with Massey's (1995) conclusion regarding the decreasing rates of upward mobility in American society.

The Case for "Traditional" Assimilation Theory

Other recent studies come to a very different conclusion regarding the second generation: they are generally rising relative to their parents. This contradicts the segmented assimilation thesis and resurrects the somewhat tattered body of traditional assimilation theories. These studies (for example, Alba & Nee, 2003; Bean & Stevens, 2003; Kasinitz, Mollenkopf, Waters, & Holdaway, 2008; and White & Glick, 2009) argue that contemporary assimilation will ultimately follow the same course as that of European immigrant groups 100 years ago and as described in Gordon's theory (see chapter 2).

For example, two recent studies (Alba & Nee, 2003; Bean & Stevens, 2003) find that most contemporary immigrant groups are acculturating and integrating at the "normal" three-generation pace. Those groups (notably Mexicans) that appear to be lagging behind this pace may take as many as four to five generations, but their descendants will eventually find their way onto the primary job market and the cultural mainstream.

Studies of acculturation show that values Americanize and that English language proficiency grows with time of residence and generation (Bean & Stevens, 2003, p. 168). We discussed some of these patterns in chapter 7 (see exhibits 7.11 through 7.13).

In terms of structural integration, contemporary immigrant groups may be narrowing the income gap over time, although many groups (e.g., Dominicans, Mexicans, Haitians, and Vietnamese) are handicapped by very low levels of human capital at the start (Bean & Stevens, 2003, p. 142). Exhibits 9.21 and 9.22 illustrate this process with respect to wage differentials between Mexican American and white non-Hispanic males and females of various generations and levels of education. In these exhibits, complete income equality with non-Hispanic whites would be indicated if the bar touched the 100% line at the top of the graph.

Looking first at males, recent Mexican immigrants earned a little less than half of what white males earned. Income inequality is lower for earlier immigrants, lower still for Mexicans males of the second and third generation, and lowest for the most educated members of those generations. In other words, income equality tends to

Exhibit 9.21 Wage Differential of Mexican Workers, Males

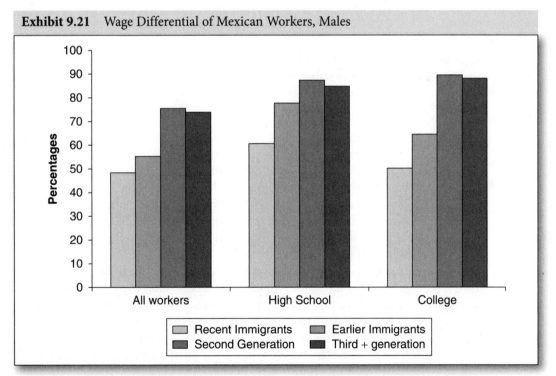

Source: Bean, Frank D. and Gillian Stevens. Figure 6.8, "Hourly Wage Differentials by Ethnicity and Generation, Ages Twenty-Five to Sixty-Four," in *America's Newcomers and the Dynamics of Diversity.* © 2003 Russell Sage Foundation. Reprinted with permission.

Exhibit 9.22   Wage Differentials Relevant to Whites, Females

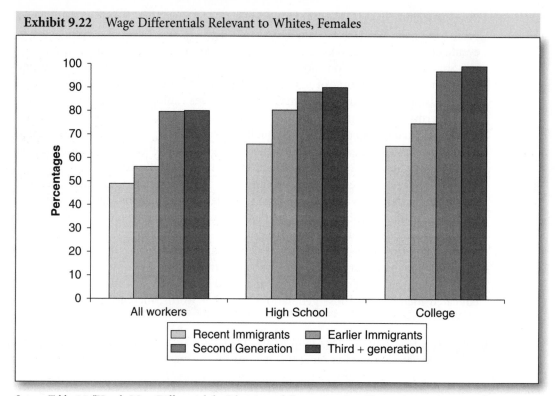

Source: Table 6.8, "Hourly Wage Differentials by Ethnicity and Generation, Ages Twenty-Five to Sixty-Four," in *America's Newcomers and the Dynamics of Diversity,* by Frank D. Bean and Gilliam Stevens. Copyright © 2003 Russell Sage Foundation.

increase over the generations and as education increases. On the other hand, note that third-generation males do not rise relative to their parents' generation. This is contrary to the view that assimilation will proceed in a linear, stepwise fashion across the generations and is reminiscent of the findings of Telles and Ortiz (2008) cited earlier.

For females, the wage differential also shrinks as the generations pass and level of education increases. Note that for third-generation, college-educated females, the wage differential shrinks virtually to zero, indicating integration on this variable.

These patterns generally support the traditional perspective on assimilation. The wage gap shrinks by generation and level of education, and integration is substantial by the third generation (although complete for only one subgroup). This pattern suggests that the movement of Mexican immigrants is toward the economic mainstream, even though they do not close the gap completely. Bean and Stevens (2003) conclude that this pattern is substantially consistent with the "three-generation model": the assimilation trajectory of Mexican Americans and other recent immigrant groups is not into the urban poor, the underclass, or the disenfranchised, disconnected, and marginalized. Assimilation is not segmented, but is substantially repeating the experiences of the European groups on which Gordon (1964) based his theory.

Summary

How can we reconcile the direct contradictions between the segmented and traditional perspectives on assimilation? In large part, this debate concerns the nature of the evidence and judgments about how much weight to give to various facts and trends. On the one hand, Massey's (1995) points about the importance of the postindustrial economy, declining opportunities for less-educated workers, and the neglect that seems typical of inner-city schools are well taken, as is the evidence supplied by other studies that generally support the segmented assimilation thesis. On the other hand, it seems that even the least-educated immigrant groups have been able to find economic niches in which they and their families can survive and eke out an existence long enough for their children and grandchildren to rise in the structure, a pattern that has been at the core of the American immigrant experience for almost two centuries.

Of course, this debate will continue, and new evidence and interpretations will appear. Ultimately, however, these disputes may continue until immigration stops (which is very unlikely to happen, as Massey points out) and the fate of the descendants of the last immigrant groups is measured.

Recent Immigration in Historical and Global Context

The current wave of immigration to the United States is part of a centuries-old process that spans the globe. Underlying this immense and complex population movement is the powerful force of the continuing industrialization, economic development, and globalization. The United States and other advanced industrial nations are the centers of growth in the global economy, and immigrants flow to the areas of greater opportunity. In the 19th century, population moved largely from Europe to the western hemisphere. Over the past 50 years, the movement has been from the global South to the global North. This pattern reflects the geography of industrialization and opportunity and the fact that the more-developed nations are in the northern hemisphere.

The United States has been the world's dominant economic, political, and cultural power for much of the past 100 years and the preferred destination of most immigrants. Newcomers from around the globe continue the collective, social nature of past population movements (see chapter 2). The direction of their travels reflects contemporary global inequalities: labor continues to flow from the less-developed nations to the more-developed nations. The direction of this flow is not accidental or coincidental. It is determined by the differential rates of industrialization and modernization across the globe. Immigration contributes to the wealth and affluence of the more-developed societies and particularly to the dominant groups and elite classes of those societies.

The immigrant flow is also a response to the dynamics of globalization, particularly since the 1980s (Sen & Mamdouh, 2008). The current era of globalization has been guided by the doctrine of neoliberalism, or free trade, which urges nations to eliminate barriers to the free movement of goods and capital. The North American Free Trade Agreement (NAFTA), which we have mentioned on several occasions, is an example of a neoliberal policy. These policies open less-developed nations such as

Mexico to consumer goods manufactured and controlled by large, transnational corporations, which are often able to undersell indigenous goods and drive small-scale local farmers and manufacturers out of business.

Finally, the international agencies that regulate the global economy pressure nations to reduce the size of their governmental sector. This often means that the national budget for health and education is slashed and that services once controlled and subsidized by the government (e.g., water, electricity) are sold to private businesses. The combined result of these global forces may be an increasingly vulnerable population in less-developed nations, unable to provide for themselves, educate their children, or afford the simplest of daily necessities.

Americans tend to see immigrants as individuals acting of their own free will and, often, illegally ("They chose to come to the United States and break the law") but the picture changes when we see immigration as the result of these powerful, global economic and political forces. Globalization today allows for the free movement of capital and goods but not of people. While domestic economies and social systems crumble, the victims of neo-liberal globalization are left with few choices: they cross borders not only to the United States, but also to other advanced industrial nations, illegally if they have to, because "it is the best choice to achieve a dignified life—if not for themselves, then for their children" (Sen & Mamdouh, 2008, p. 7). When viewed through the lens of globalization, it is clear that this population movement will continue because immigrants simply have no choice. It is unlikely that they can be stopped by further militarization of the border or by building bigger and taller walls. Immigrants come to the United States in their numbers, as they did in the past, because the alternatives are unacceptable or nonexistent.

This perspective suggests that the tendency of many citizens of the more-developed world to reject, demonize, and criminalize immigrants is self-defeating. Punitive, militaristic policies will not stem the flow of people from the global South to the global North. Globalization, in its neoliberal form, is incomplete: It allows for the free movement of goods and capital but not of people. It benefits transnational corporations and the megabusinesses that produce consumer goods but victimize the vulnerable citizens of the less-developed nations. As long as these forms of globalization hold, the population pressure from South to North will continue.

New Immigrants and Old Issues

In this chapter, we focused on some of the issues raised by high levels of immigration since the 1960s. As we discuss, debate, and consider these issues, we need to remember a fundamental fact about modern American society: The issues of the "traditional" minority groups—African Americans and American Indians, for example—have not been resolved. As we saw in earlier chapters, these groups have been a part of American society from the beginning, but they remain, in many ways, distant from achieving complete equality and integration.

Many of the current issues facing these groups involve class as well as race. The urban underclass is disproportionately made up of peoples of color and remains marginal to the mainstream society in terms of access to education and job opportunities, decent housing, and reasonable health care. While it is probably true that American society is more open and tolerant than ever before, we must not mistake a decline in blatant racism and overt discrimination for their demise. In fact, as we have seen, there is abundant evidence that shows that racism and discrimination have not declined, but have merely changed form, and that the patterns of exclusion and deprivation sustained in the past continue in the present.

Similarly, gender issues and sexism remain on the national agenda. As we have seen at various points throughout the text, blatant sexism and overt discrimination against women are probably at historic lows, but, again, we cannot mistake change for disappearance. Most important, minority women remain the victims of a double jeopardy and are among the most vulnerable and exploited segments of society. Many female members of the new immigrant groups find themselves in similarly vulnerable positions.

These problems of exclusion and continuing prejudice and sexism are exacerbated by a number of trends in the larger society. For example, the continuing shift in subsistence technology away from manufacturing to the service sector privileges groups that, in the past as well as today, have had access to education. The urban underclass consists disproportionately of groups that have been excluded from education in the past and have less access in the present.

The new immigrant groups have abundant problems of their own, of course, and need to find ways to pursue their self-interests in their new society. Some segments of these groups—the well-educated professionals seeking to advance their careers in the world's most advanced economy—will be much more likely to find ways to avoid the harshest forms of American rejection and exclusion. Similarly, the members of the "traditional" minority groups that have gained access to education and middle-class status will enjoy more opportunities than previous generations could have imagined (although, as we have seen, their middle-class position will be more precarious than that of their dominant-group counterparts).

Will we become a society in which ethnic and racial groups are permanently segmented by class, with the more-favored members enjoying a higher, if partial, level of acceptance while other members of their groups languish in permanent exclusion and segmentation? What does it mean to be an American? What *should* it mean?

Main Points

- Since the mid-1960s, immigrants have been coming to the United States at nearly record rates. Most of these immigrant groups have co-ethnics who have been in the United States for years, but others are "new Americans." How will this new wave of immigration transform America? Will they assimilate? How?

- Various groups of "new Americans" are considered, including Hispanic immigrants, non-Hispanic Caribbean immigrants, Asian, Arab and Middle Eastern, and African immigrants. Some are driven by economic needs, others are political refugees, and some are highly educated. All face multiple issues including racism, institutionalized discrimination, and a changing U.S. economy. Arab Americans remain a special target for hate crimes and for security concerns.

- Contemporary immigrants experience three different modes of incorporation: the primary labor market, the secondary labor market, and the enclave. The pathway of each group is strongly influenced by the amount of human capital they bring, their race, the attitude of the larger society, and many other factors.
- Relations between immigrants and the larger society are animated by a number of issues, including the relative costs and benefits of immigration, concerns about undocumented immigrants, and the speed of assimilation. One important issue currently being debated by social scientists is whether assimilation for new Americans will be segmented or will ultimately follow the pathway established by immigrant groups from Europe in the 19th and 20th centuries.

Study Site on the Web

Don't forget the interactive quizzes and other resources and learning aids at www.sagepub.com/healeyds4e.

For Further Reading

Portes, A., & Rumbaut, R. (2001). *Ethnicities: Children of immigrants in America*. New York: Russell Sage Foundation.

Portes, A., & Rumbaut, R. (2001). *Legacies: The story of the immigrant second generation*. New York: Russell Sage Foundation.

Two landmark studies of new American groups whose findings are generally consistent with the segmented assimilation hypothesis.

Alba, R., & Nee, V. (2003). *Remaking the American mainstream: Assimilation and contemporary immigration*. Cambridge, MA: Harvard University Press.

Bean, F., & Stevens, G. (2003). *America's newcomers and the dynamics of diversity*. New York: Russell Sage Foundation.

Kasinitz, P., Mollenkopf, J. H., Waters, M. C., & Holdaway, J. (2008). *Inheriting the city: The children of immigrants come of age*. New York: Russell Sage Foundation and Harvard University Press.

Three landmark studies of contemporary immigrants that find that assimilation is generally following a course consistent with the "traditional" model of assimilation.

Questions for Review and Study

1. What differences exist between these new Americans in terms of their motivations for coming to the United States? What are the implications of these various "push" factors for their reception and adjustment to the United States?

2. Compare and contrast the Hispanic and Asian immigrant groups discussed in this chapter. What important differences and similarities can you identify in terms of modes of incorporation and human capital? What are the implications of the differences for the experiences of these groups?

3. Compare Arab and Middle Eastern immigrant groups with those from the Caribbean. Which group is more diverse? What differences exist in their patterns of adjustment and assimilation? Why do these patterns exist?

4. Compare and contrast African immigrants with the other groups. How do they differ? What are the implications of these differences for their adjustment to the larger society?

5. What, in your opinion, are the most important issues facing the United States in terms of immigration and assimilation? How are these issues playing out in your community? What are the implications of these issues for the future of the United States?

6. Will assimilation for contemporary immigrants be segmented? After examining the evidence and arguments presented by both sides and using information from this and previous chapters, which side of the debate seems more credible? Why? What are the implications of this debate? What will the United States look like in the future if assimilation is segmented? How would the future change if assimilation follows the "traditional" pathway? Which of these scenarios is more desirable for immigrant groups? For the society as a whole? For various segments of U.S. society (e.g., employers, labor unions, African Americans, consumers, the college educated, the urban underclass, etc.)?

Internet Research Project

In this exercise, you will use information gathered by the U.S. census to learn more about two of the "new American" groups covered in this chapter. This project adds to the information you gathered in chapters 5 through 8. The information for the total population is already entered. You can add the information for African Americans, American Indians and Alaska Natives (AIAN), Hispanic Americans, and Asian American from previous exercises, but you will need to add information for the variables you select. You will then use course concepts to assess and analyze this information and place it in the context of this text.

Notes

1. *The numbers you gather for this exercise may vary slightly from those presented in this chapter because of differences in the dates the data were collected or in the nature of the samples used.*

2. *Visit the website for this text to check for updates on the databases available for completing this exercise*

Get information by following these steps:

1. Choose two of the groups covered in this chapter. There are about 15 different groups and they are listed in exhibits 9.4, 9.5, 9.8, 9.9, and 9.12. Do not choose non-Hispanic whites or Sub-Saharan Africans. Choose groups from two different general categories. For example, you could choose one of the Hispanic groups and one of the Middle Eastern or Arab groups.

2. Go to the official U.S. Census Bureau website at www.census.gov.

3. Click on "Data" in the list of choices at the top of the screen and then click "American Fact Finder" from the drop-down menu.

4. Click the "Race and Ethnic Groups" tab on the left of the next screen. A new widow will open. Find the list of "Racial and Ethnic Group Results" on the right of the screen and click on the box next to "Total Population" (Code 001), the box next to "Black or African American alone or in combination with one or more other races" (Code 005), the box next to "American Indian and Alaska Native alone or in

combination with one or more other races" (Code 009), and the box next to "Asian alone or in combination with one or more other races" (Code 031). Next click the "Add" button above the "Racial and Ethnic Group Results" window and your selections will be added to the "Your selections" box in the top-left-hand corner of the screen.

5. All of the "new American" groups covered in this chapter are listed in the "Racial and Ethnic Group Results" window. To find them, you can scroll through the screens or use the search window in the upper-left-hand corner of the "Select Race and Ethnic Groups" window: Type the name of the group in the window and click "Go." Be sure to click the box beside the group name and click "Add" when you have found your groups.

6. In the "Your Race and Ethnic Group Filters" box in the middle of the screen, click on "Race and Hispanic Origin (2010 code based)." In the next box, click "Hispanic Origin" and then click "Hispanic." In the "Race and Ethnic Group Results" window, click the box next to "Hispanic or Latino (of any race)" (Code 400) and click the "Add" button.

7. Close the "Select Race and Ethnic Groups" window by clicking the "Close" button on the top-right-hand corner of the window.

8. We will again use the 2011 ACS 1-year estimates. As before, look in either the "ID" column on the left for "Table S0201" or in the "Dataset" column on the right for the "2011 ACS 1-year estimates." Click the box next to the file name and then click "View" from the menu above the window.

9. The next screen will display a table with your groups listed at the top. Scroll down the table until you find the information needed to fill in the table below.

   a. Under "Sex and Age," find "median age (years)."
   b. Under "Households by Type," find "Average Household size."
   c. Under "Educational Attainment," find "Less than high school diploma."
   d. Under "Population born outside of the United States," find "Entered 2000 or later."
   e. Under "Language Spoken at Home and Ability to Speak English," find "Speak English less than 'very well.'"
   f. Under "Employment Status," find "% Unemployed."
   g. Under "Income in the Past 12 Months," find "Individuals" and then "Per Capita income" and "Median earnings for full-time, year-round workers for males and females."
   h. Under "Poverty Rates for Families and People," find "All Families."
   i. Select two more variables relevant to this course and fill in the scores for the all groups. (*Note: Your instructor may have different instructions for this step of the project.*)

		Total Population	*African Americans*	*AIAN*	*Hispanic Americans*	*All Asian Americans*	*New American Groups*	
1	Number	311,591,919	42,533,817					
3	Median age	37.3						
4	Average household size	2.64						

		Total Population	African Americans	AIAN	Hispanic Americans	All Asian Americans	New American Groups	
5	% Less than high school	14.1%						
6	% of the foreign born who entered after 2000	35.7%						
6	Speak English less than "very well"	8.6%						
7	% unemployed	6.5%						
8	Per capita income	$26,708						
9	Median incomes for full-time, year-round workers							
	Males	$46,993						
	Females	$37,133						
10	Poverty rate, all families	11.7%						
11								
12								

Questions

1. What stage of Gordon's model of assimilation (see exhibit 2.1) do the variables in the table measure?

2. Describe your groups using the Blauner hypothesis (see chapter 3). Are they closer to the "colonized" or the "immigrant" types? How much human capital do they bring? Are they targeted by racial prejudice? What stereotypes or perceptions dominate how they are perceived? Given this information, what would you predict about their relative status in American society?

3. Use the debate between the segmented assimilation thesis and the traditional (Gordon) assimilation model to compare and contrast your two groups. Are they adjusting successfully to U.S. society? Is there a strong ethnic community to assist new arrivals? Are a large percentage of your groups in danger of falling into the underclass? What are the crucial differences between groups that lead them to different fates?

4. What additional concepts from this and previous chapters seem relevant for explaining the patterns you observe in this table? How?

Optional Group Discussion

Bring this information to class and, in groups of four to six people, compare with the information collected by others. Consider the issues raised in the question above and in the chapter and develop some ideas about why these groups are where they are relative to each other and to the total population. (*Note: Your instructor may have different instructions for this step of the project.*)

10

Minority Groups and U.S. Society: Themes, Patterns, and the Future

O ver the past nine chapters, we have analyzed ideas and theories about dominant-minority relations, examined the historical and contemporary situations of minority groups in U.S. society, and surveyed a variety of dominant-minority situations around the globe. Now it is time to reexamine our major themes and concepts and determine what conclusions can be derived from our analysis. In this final chapter, I restate the general themes of this text and draw conclusions from the material we have covered. I also raise speculative questions about the future. As we look backward to the past and forward to the future, it seems appropriate to paraphrase the words of the historian Oscar Handlin (1951): "Once I thought to write a history of the minority groups in America. Then, I discovered that the minority groups *were* American history" (p. 3).

The Importance of Subsistence Technology

Perhaps the most important sociological idea we have developed is that dominant-minority relations are shaped by large social, political, and economic forces and change as these broad characteristics change. To understand the evolution of America's minority groups is to understand the history of the United States, from the earliest colonial settlement to the modern megalopolis. As we have seen throughout the text, these same broad forces have left their imprint on many societies around the globe.

Subsistence technology is the most basic force shaping a society and the relationships between dominant and minority groups in that society. In the colonial United States, minority relations were bent to the demands of a land-hungry, labor-intensive agrarian technology, and the early relationships between Africans, Europeans, and American Indians flowed from the colonists' desire to control both land and labor. By the mid-1800s, two centuries after Jamestown was founded, the same dynamics that had enslaved African Americans and nearly annihilated American Indians made a minority group out of Mexican Americans.

The agrarian era came to an end in the 19th century as the new technologies of the Industrial Revolution increased the productivity of the economy and eventually changed every aspect of life in the United States. The paternalistic, oppressive systems used to control the labor of minority groups in the agrarian system gave way to competitive systems of group relations. These newer systems evolved from more-rigid forms to more fluid forms as industrialization and urbanization progressed.

As the United States grew and developed, new minority groups were created, and old minority groups were transformed. Rapid industrialization combined with the opportunities available on the frontier made the United States an attractive destination for immigrants from Europe, Asia, Latin America, and other parts of the world. Immigrants helped to farm the Great Plains, mine the riches of the West, and above all, supply the armies of labor required by industrialization.

The descendants of the immigrants from Europe benefited from the continuing industrialization of the economy, rising—sometimes slowly—in the social class structure as the economy grew and matured. Immigrants from Asia and Latin America were not so fortunate. Chinese Americans and Japanese Americans survived in ethnic enclaves on the fringes of the mainstream society, and Mexican Americans and Puerto Ricans supplied low-paid manual labor for both the rural and the urban economies. For much of the 20th century, both Asian Americans and Hispanic Americans were barred from access to dominant group institutions and higher-paid jobs.

The racial minority groups, particularly African Americans, Mexican Americans, and Puerto Ricans, began to enter the urban working class after European American ethnic groups had moved up in the occupational structure, at a time when the supply of manual, unskilled jobs was starting to dwindle. Thus, the processes that created upward mobility for European Americans failed to work for the racial minority groups, who confronted urban poverty and bankrupt cities in addition to the continuing barriers of racial prejudice and institutional discrimination.

Immigration to the United States has been quite high for the past several decades. The stream of newcomers is "bipolar" and includes highly educated professionals who take jobs in the postindustrial economy and undocumented immigrants who work in the secondary labor market and the irregular economy. This stream has evoked the usual American nativism and racism along with very intense debates—in the social sciences as well as in the general public—about the cost and benefits of the immigrants and their ultimate fates in the social structure.

We can only speculate about what the future holds, but the emerging information-based, high-tech society is unlikely to offer many opportunities to people with lower levels of education and few occupational skills. It seems likely that, at least for the near future, a substantial percentage of racial and colonized minority groups and some recent immigrant groups will be participating in the mainstream economy at lower levels than the dominant group, the descendants of the European immigrants, and the more-advantaged recent immigrant groups. This outcome would be consistent with the segmented assimilation thesis, as discussed in chapter 9. Upgraded urban educational systems, job-training programs, and other community development programs might alter the grim scenario of continuing exclusion, but current public opinion about matters of race and discrimination make it unlikely that such programs will be created.

Inaction and perpetuation of the status quo will bar a large percentage of the population from the emerging primary, postindustrial job market. Those segments of the African American, Hispanic American, and Asian American communities currently mired in the urban underclass will continue to compete with some of the newer immigrant groups for jobs in the low-wage, secondary labor market or in alternative opportunity structures, including crime.

The Importance of the Contact Situation, Group Competition, and Power

We have stressed the importance of the contact situation—the conditions under which the minority group and dominant group first come into contact with each other—throughout this text. Blauner's distinction between immigrant and colonized minority groups is fundamental, a distinction so basic that it helps to clarify minority group situations centuries after the initial contact period. In part 3, we used Blauner's distinction as an organizing principle and covered American minority groups in approximate order from "most colonized" to "most immigrant." The groups covered first (African Americans and American Indians) are clearly at a greater disadvantage in contemporary society than the groups covered last (especially immigrants from Asia with high levels of human capital) and the white ethnic groups covered in chapter 2.

For example, prejudice, racism, and discrimination against African Americans remain formidable forces in contemporary America even though they may have softened into more subtle forms. In contrast, prejudice and discrimination against European American groups such as the Irish, Italians, and Polish Americans have nearly disappeared today even though they were quite formidable just a few generations ago. In the same way, contemporary immigrant groups that are non-white and bring few resources and low levels of human capital (e.g., Haitians) may experience segmented assimilation and find themselves in situations resembling those of colonized minority groups. Contemporary immigrant groups that are at the opposite end of the continuum (e.g., Asian Indians) are more likely to approximate the experiences of white ethnics and find themselves in some version of middle-class suburbia. The internet research exercises presented at the ends of chapters 5 to 9 should have given you information to begin to assess some of these patterns.

Noel's hypothesis states that if three conditions are present in the contact situation—ethnocentrism, competition, and the differential in power—ethnic or racial stratification will result. The relevance of ethnocentrism is largely limited to the actual contact situation, but the other two concepts help to clarify the changes occurring after initial contact.

We have examined numerous instances in which group competition—or even the threat of competition—increased prejudice and led to greater discrimination and more repression. Recall, for example, the opposition of the labor movement (dominated by European American ethnic groups) to Chinese immigrants. The anti-Chinese campaign led to the Chinese Exclusion Act of 1882, the first significant restriction on immigration to the United States. There are parallels between campaigns for exclusion in the past and current ideas about ending or curtailing immigration. Clearly, some part of the current opposition to immigration is motivated by a sense of threat and the fear that immigrants are a danger not only to jobs and to the economy, but also to the cultural integrity of U.S. society.

Noel's third variable, the differential in power, determines the outcome of the initial contact situation, and which group becomes dominant and which becomes minority. Following the initial contact, the superior power of the dominant group helps it sustain the inferior position of the minority group. Minority groups by definition have fewer power resources, but they characteristically use what they have in an attempt to improve their situations. The improvements in the situations of American minority groups since the middle of the 20th century have been due in large part to the fact that they (especially African Americans, who typically led the way in protest and demands for change) finally acquired some power resources of their own. For example, one important source of power for the civil rights movement in the South during the 1950s and 1960s was the growth of African American voting strength outside the South. After World War II, the African American electorate became too sizable to ignore, and its political power helped pressure the federal government to take action and pass the legislation that ended the formal Jim Crow system of de jure segregation.

Minority status being what it is, however, each of the groups we have discussed (with the exception of the white ethnic groups) still controls relatively fewer power resources and is limited in its ability to pursue its own self-interests. Many of these limitations are economic and related to social class; many minority groups simply lack the resources to finance campaigns for reform or to exert significant pressure on political institutions. Other limitations include small group size (e.g., Asian American groups), language barriers (e.g., many Hispanic groups), and divided loyalties within the group (e.g., American Indians separated by tribal allegiances).

At any rate, the relative powerlessness of minority groups today is a legacy of the contact situations that created the groups in the first place. In general, colonized groups are at a greater power disadvantage than immigrant groups. Contact situations set agendas for group relations that have impacts centuries after the initial meeting.

Given all that we have examined in this text, it is obvious that competition and differences in power resources will continue to shape intergroup relations (including relations between minority groups themselves) well into the future. Because they are so basic and consequential, jobs will continue to be primary objects of competition, but there will be plenty of other issues to divide the nation. Included on this divisive list will be debates about crime and the criminal justice system, welfare reform, national health-care policy, school integration and multicultural curricula, bilingual education, and immigration policy.

These and other public issues will continue to separate us along ethnic and racial lines because those lines have become so deeply embedded in the economy, in politics, in our schools and neighborhoods, and in virtually every nook and cranny of U.S. society. These deep divisions reflect fundamental realities about who gets what in the United States, and they will continue to reflect the distribution of power and stimulate competition along group lines for generations to come.

Diversity Within Minority Groups

All too often, and this text is probably no exception, minority groups are seen as unitary and undifferentiated. Although overgeneralizations are sometimes difficult to avoid, I want to stress again the diversity within each of the groups we have examined. Minority group members vary from each other by age, sex, region of residence, levels of education, urban versus rural residence, political ideology, and many other variables. The experience of one segment of the group (college-educated, fourth-generation, native-born Chinese American females) may bear little resemblance to the experience of another (unauthorized Chinese male immigrants with less than a high school education), and the problems of some members may not be the problems of others.

I have tried to highlight the importance of this diversity by exploring gender differentiation within each minority group. Study of minority groups by U.S. social scientists has focused predominantly on males, and the experiences of minority women have been described in much less depth. All the cultures examined in this text have strong patriarchal traditions. Women of the dominant group as well as minority women have had much less access to leadership roles and higher-status positions and have generally occupied a subordinate status, even in their own groups. The experiences of minority group women and the extent of their differences from minority group males and dominant group women are only now being fully explored.

One clear conclusion we can make about gender is that minority group females are doubly oppressed and disempowered. Limited by both their minority and their gender roles, they are among the most vulnerable and exploited segments of the society. At one time or another, the women of every minority group have taken the least desirable, lowest-status positions available in the economy, often while trying to raise children and attend to other family needs. They have been expected to provide support for other members of their families, kinship groups, and communities, often sacrificing their own self-interests to the welfare of others. Jade Snow Wong (1993), a Chinese American daughter of immigrant parents, describes the subordinate role and circumscribed world of minority group females in a remembrance of her mother:

> My mother dutifully followed my father's leadership. She was extremely thrifty, but the thrifty need pennies to manage, and the old world had denied her those. Upon arrival in the new world of San Francisco, she accepted the elements her mate had selected to shape her new life: domestic duties, seamstress work in the factory-home, mothering each child in turn, church once a week, and occasional movies. (p. 50)

In their roles outside the family, minority women have encountered discrimination based on their minority group membership, compounded with discrimination based on their gender. The result is, predictably, an economic and social status that is often at the bottom of the social structure. For example, average incomes of black females today are lower than those of white males, white females, and black males (see exhibit 5.5). The same pattern holds for other groups, and the women of many minority groups are highly concentrated in the low-paid secondary labor market and employed in jobs that provide services to members of more privileged groups.

The inequality confronted by minority women extends beyond matters of economics and jobs. Women of color have higher rates of infant mortality and births out of wedlock and a host of other health-related, quality-of-life problems. In short, there is ample evidence to document a pervasive pattern of gender inequality within America's minority groups. Much of this gender inequality is complexly interconnected with rising rates of poverty and female-headed households, teenage pregnancy, and unemployment for minority males in the inner city.

Gender differentiation cuts through minority groups in a variety of ways. Specific issues might unite minority women with women of the dominant group (e.g., sexual harassment in schools and the workplace), and others might unite them with the men of their minority groups (e.g., the enforcement of civil rights legislation). The problems and issues of minority women are complexly tied to the patterns of inequality and discrimination in the larger society and within their own groups. Solving the problems faced by minority groups will not resolve the problems faced by minority women, and neither will resolving the problems of gender inequality alone. Women of color are embedded in structures of inequality and discrimination that limit them in two independent but simultaneous ways. Articulating and addressing these difficulties requires recognition of the complex interactions between gender and minority group status.

Assimilation and Pluralism

It seems fair to conclude that the diversity and complexity of minority group experiences in the United States are not well characterized by some of the traditional, or "melting pot," views of assimilation. For example, the idea that assimilation is a linear, inevitable process has little support. Immigrants from Europe probably fit that model better than other groups, but as the ethnic revival of the 1960s demonstrated (see chapter 2), assimilation and ethnic identity can take surprising turns.

Also without support is the notion that there is always a simple, ordered relationship between the various stages of assimilation: acculturation, integration into public institutions, integration into the private sector, and so forth. We have seen that some groups integrated before they acculturated, others have become more committed to their ethnic or racial identity over the generations, and still others have been acculturated for generations but are no closer to full integration. New expressions of ethnicity come and go, and minority groups emerge, combine, and recombine in unexpected and seemingly unpredictable ways. The 1960s saw a reassertion of ethnicity and loyalty to old identities among some groups, even as other groups developed new coalitions and invented new ethnic identities (for example, pan-tribalism among American Indians). No simple or linear view of assimilation can begin to make sense of the array of minority group experiences.

Indeed, the very desirability of assimilation has been subject to debate. Since the 1960s, many minority spokespersons have questioned the wisdom of becoming a part of a sociocultural structure that was constructed by the systematic exploitation of minority groups. Pluralistic themes increased in prominence as the commitment of the larger society to racial equality faltered. Virtually every minority group proclaimed the authenticity of its own experiences, its own culture, and its own version of history, separate from but as valid as that of the dominant groups. From what might have seemed like a nation on the verge of integration in the 1950s (at least for white ethnic groups), America evolved into what might have seemed like a Tower of Babel in the 1960s. The consensus that assimilation was the best solution and the most sensible goal for all of America's minority groups was shattered (if it ever really existed at all).

Let's review the state of acculturation and integration in the United States on a group-by-group basis, following the order of the case studies in part 3.

African Americans are highly acculturated. Despite the many unique cultural traits forged in America and those that survive from Africa, black Americans share language, values and beliefs, and most other aspects of culture with white Americans of similar class and educational background. In terms of integration, in contrast, African Americans present a mixed picture. For middle-class, more-educated members of the group, American society offers more opportunities for upward mobility and success than ever before. Without denying the prejudice, discrimination, and racism that remain, this segment of the group is in a favorable position to achieve higher levels of affluence and power for their children and grandchildren.

At the same time, a large percentage of African Americans remain mired in urban poverty, and for them, affluence, security, and power are just as distant (perhaps more so) than they were a generation ago. Considering the group as a whole, African Americans are still highly segregated in their residential and school attendance patterns, and their political power, although rising, is not proportional to their size. Unemployment, lower average incomes, and poverty in general remain serious problems and may be more serious than they were a generation ago.

American Indians are less acculturated than African Americans, and some aspects of American Indian culture and language may be increasing in strength and vitality. On measures of integration, there is some indication of improvement, but many American Indian tribes are among the most isolated and impoverished minority groups in the United States. One possible bright spot for some reservations lies in the further development of the gambling industry and the investment of profits in the tribal infrastructure to upgrade schools, health clinics, job training centers, and so forth.

Members of the largest Hispanic American groups are also generally less acculturated than African Americans. Hispanic traditions and the Spanish language have been sustained by the exclusion and isolation of these groups within the United

States and have been continually renewed and revitalized by immigration. Cubans have moved closer to equality than Mexican Americans and Puerto Ricans, but did so by resisting assimilation and building an ethnic enclave economy. Mexican Americans and Puerto Ricans share many of the problems of urban poverty that confront African Americans, and they are below national norms on measures of equality and integration.

The smaller Hispanic groups consist mostly of new immigrants who are just beginning the assimilation process. Many members of these groups, along with Mexican Americans and Puerto Ricans, are less educated and have few occupational skills, and they face the dangers of blending into a permanent urban underclass. Nonetheless, there is some evidence that these groups (or, more accurately, their descendants) may eventually find their way into the American mainstream (recall the debate over segmented assimilation in chapter 9).

As with Hispanic Americans, the extent of assimilation among Asian Americans is highly variable. Some groups (for example, third- and fourth-generation Japanese Americans and Chinese Americans) have virtually completed the assimilation process and are remarkably successful; others (the more elite immigrants from India and the Philippines) seem to be finding a place in the American mainstream. Other Asian American groups consist largely of newer immigrants with occupational and educational profiles that often resemble colonized minority groups, and these groups face the same dangers of permanent marginalization and exclusion. Still other Asian American groups (e.g., Korean Americans) have used their cohesiveness and solidarity to construct ethnic enclaves in which they have achieved relative economic equality by resisting acculturation.

Only European American ethnic groups, covered in chapter 2, seem to approximate the traditional model of assimilation. The development even of these groups, however, has taken unexpected twists and turns, and the pluralism of the 1960s and 1970s suggests that ethnic traditions and ethnic identity, in some form, may withstand the pressures of assimilation for generations to come. Culturally and racially, these groups are the closest to the dominant group. If they still retain a sense of ethnicity, even if merely symbolic, after generations of acculturation and integration, what is the likelihood that the sense of group membership will fade in the racially stigmatized minority groups?

Assimilation is far from accomplished. The group divisions that remain are real and consequential; they cannot be willed away by pretending we are all "just American." Group membership continues to be important because it continues to be linked to fundamental patterns of exclusion and inequality. The realities of pluralism, inequality, and ethnic and racial identity continue to persist to the extent that the American promise of a truly open opportunity structure continues to fail. The group divisions forged in the past and perpetuated over the decades by racism and discrimination will remain, to the extent that racial and ethnic group membership continues to be correlated with inequality and position in the social class structure.

Along with economic and political pressures, other forces help to sustain the pluralistic group divisions. Some argue that ethnicity is rooted in biology and can never be fully eradicated (see van den Berghe, 1981). Although this may be an extreme position, there is little doubt that many people find their ancestry to be a matter of great interest. Some (perhaps most) of the impetus behind the preservation of ethnic and racial identity may be a result of the most vicious and destructive intergroup competition. In other ways, though, ethnicity can be a positive force that helps people locate themselves in time and space and understand their position in the contemporary world. Ethnicity remains an important aspect of self-identity and pride for many Americans from every group and tradition. It seems unlikely that this sense of a personal link to particular groups and heritages within U.S. society will soon fade.

Can we survive as a pluralistic, culturally and linguistically fragmented, racially and ethnically unequal society? What will save us from balkanization and fractionalization? Given our history of colonization and racism, can U.S. society move closer to the relatively harmonious models of race relations found in societies such as Hawaii? As we deal with these questions, we need to remember that in and of itself, diversity is no more "bad" than unity is "good." Our society has grown to a position of global preeminence despite, or perhaps because of, our diversity. In fact, many have argued that our diversity is a fundamental and essential characteristic of U.S. society and a great strength to be cherished and encouraged. Sociologist Ronald Takaki (1993) ended his history of multicultural America, *A Different Mirror*, with an eloquent endorsement of our diversity and pluralism:

> As Americans, we originally came from many different shores and our diversity has been at the center of the making of America. While our stories contain the memories of different communities, together they inscribe a larger narrative. Filled with what Walt Whitman celebrated as the "varied carols" of America, our history generously gives all of us our "mystic chords of memory."
>
> Throughout our past of oppressions and struggles for equality, Americans of different races and ethnicities have been "singing with open mouths their strong melodious songs" in the textile mills of Lowell, the cotton fields of Mississippi, on the Indian reservations of South Dakota, the railroad tracks high in the Sierras of California, in the garment factories of the Lower East Side, the cane fields of Hawaii, and a thousand other places across the country. Our denied history "bursts with telling." As we hear America singing, we find ourselves invited to bring our cultural diversity [into the open], to accept ourselves. (p. 428)

The question for our future might not be as much, "Unity or diversity?" as, "What blend of pluralistic and assimilationist policies will serve us best in the 21st century?" Are there ways in which the society can prosper without repressing our diversity? How can we increase the degree of openness, fairness, and justice without threatening group loyalties? The one-way, Anglo-conformity mode of assimilation of the past is too narrow and destructive to be a blueprint for the future, but the more-extreme forms of minority group pluralism and separatism might be equally dangerous.

How much unity do we need? How much diversity can we tolerate? These are questions you must answer for yourself, and they are questions you will face in a thousand different ways over the course of your life. Let me illustrate by citing some pertinent issues:

- Is it desirable to separate college dormitories by racial or ethnic group? Is this destructive self-segregation or a positive strategy for group empowerment? Will such practices increase prejudice, or will they work like ethnic enclaves and strengthen minority group cohesion and solidarity and permit the groups to deal with the larger society from a stronger position? For the campus as a whole, what good could come from residential separation? In what ways would minority students benefit? Is there a "correct" balance between separation and unity in this situation? Who gets to define what the balance is?

- How much attention should be devoted to minority group experiences in elementary and high school texts and curricula? Who should write and control these curricula? What should they say? How candid and critical should they be about America's often dismal past? How should such topics as slavery, genocide, and the racist exclusion of certain immigrant groups be presented in elementary school texts? In high school texts? Will educating children about the experiences of U.S. minority groups be an effective antidote to prejudice? Is it proper to use classrooms to build respect for the traditions of other groups and an appreciation of their experiences? If the realities of the experiences of minority groups are not addressed in school, what message will children hear? In the absence of minority group voices, what's left?

- What are the limits of free speech with respect to minority relations? When does an ethnic joke become offensive? When are racial and ethnic epithets protected by the First Amendment? As long as lines of ethnicity and race divide the nation and as long as people feel passionately about these lines, the language of dominant-minority relationships will continue to have harsh, crude, and intentionally insulting components. Under what conditions, if any, should a civil society tolerate disparagement of other groups? Should the racial and ethnic epithets uttered by minority group members be treated any differently from those uttered by dominant group members?

- What should the national policy on immigration be? How many immigrants should be admitted each year? How should immigrants be screened? What qualifications should be demanded? Should immigration policy continue to favor the family and close relatives of citizens and permanent residents? What should be done about illegal immigrants? Should they be given an opportunity to legalize their status? Should illegal immigrants or their children receive health care and schooling?

I do not pretend that the ideas presented in this text can fully resolve these issues or others that will arise in the future. As long as immigrants and minority groups are a part of the United States, as long as prejudice and discrimination persist, the debates will continue and new issues will arise as old ones are resolved.

As U.S. society attempts to deal with new immigrants and unresolved minority grievances, we should recognize that it is not diversity per se that threatens stability, but the realities of split labor markets, racial and ethnic stratification, urban poverty, and institutionalized discrimination. We need to focus on the issues that confront us with an honest recognition of the past and the economic, political, and social forces that have shaped us. As the United States continues to remake itself, an informed sense of where we have been will help us decide where we should go. Clearly, the simplistic, one-way, Anglo-conformity model of assimilation of the past does not provide a basis for dealing with these problems realistically and should not be the blueprint for the future of U.S. society.

Minority Group Progress and the Ideology of American Individualism

There is so much sadness, misery, and unfairness in the history of minority groups that evidence of progress sometimes goes unnoticed. Lest we be guilty of ignoring the good news in favor of the bad, let us note some ways in which the situations of American minority groups are better today than they were in the past. Evidence of progress is easy to find for some groups; we need look only to the relative economic, educational, and income equality of European American ethnic groups and some Asian American groups, or recall the election of President Barack Obama. The United States has become more tolerant and open, and minority group members can be found at the highest levels of success, affluence, and prestige.

One of the most obvious changes is the decline of traditional racism and prejudice. The strong racial and ethnic sentiments and stereotypes of the past are no longer the primary vocabulary for discussing race relations among dominant group members, at least not in public. Although the prejudices unquestionably still exist, Americans have become more circumspect and discreet in their public utterances.

The demise of blatant bigotry in polite company is, without doubt, a positive change. However, it seems that negative intergroup feelings and stereotypes have not so much disappeared as changed form. The old racist feelings are now being expressed in other guises, specifically in what has been called "modern" or "symbolic" racism: the view that holds that once Jim Crow–type segregation ended in the 1960s, the opportunity channels and routes of upward mobility of American society were opened to all and, therefore, the remaining inequalities are the fault of the minority group themselves. This individualistic view of social mobility is consistent with the human capital perspective and the traditional, melting-pot view of assimilation. Taken together, these ideologies present a powerful and widely shared perspective on the nature of minority group problems in modern American society. Proponents of these views tend to be unsympathetic to the plight of minorities and to programs such as school busing and affirmative action, which are intended to ameliorate these problems. The overt bigotry of the past has been replaced by blandness and an indifference more difficult to define and harder to measure than "old-fashioned" racism, yet still unsympathetic to racial change.

This text has argued that the most serious problems facing contemporary minority groups, however, are structural and institutional, not individual or personal. For example, the paucity of jobs and high rates of unemployment in the inner cities are the result of economic and political forces beyond the control not only of the minority communities, but also of local and state governments. The marginalization of the minority group labor force is a reflection of the essence of modern American capitalism. The mainstream, higher-paying, blue-collar jobs available to people with modest educational credentials are controlled by national and multinational corporations, which maximize profits by automating their production processes and moving the jobs that remain to areas, often outside the United States, with abundant supplies of cheaper labor.

We have also seen that some of the more effective strategies for pursuing equality require strong in-group cohesion and networks of cooperation, not heroic individual effort. Immigration to this country is (and always has been) a group process that involves extensive, long-lasting networks of communication and chains of population movement, usually built around family ties and larger kinship groups. Group networks continue to operate in America and assist individual immigrants with early adjustments and later opportunities for jobs and upward mobility. A variation on this theme is the ethnic enclave found among so many different groups.

Survival and success in America for all minority groups has had more to do with group processes than with individual will or motivation. The concerted, coordinated actions of the minority community provided support during hard times and, when possible, provided the means to climb higher in the social structure during good times. Far from being a hymn to individualism, the story of U.S. minority groups is profoundly sociological.

A Final Word

U.S. society and its minority groups are linked in fractious unity. They are part of the same structures but are separated by lines of color and culture and by long histories (and clear memories) of exploitation and unfairness. This society owes its prosperity and position of prominence in the world no less to the labor of minority groups than to that of the dominant group. By harnessing the labor and energy of these minority groups, the nation has grown prosperous and powerful, but the benefits have flowed disproportionately to the dominant group.

Since the middle of the 20th century, minority groups have demanded greater openness, fairness, equality, respect for their traditions, and justice. Increasingly, the demands have been made on the terms of the minority groups, not on those of the dominant group. Some of these demands have been met, at least verbally, and the society as a whole has rejected the oppressive racism of the past. Minority group progress has stalled well short of equality, however, and the patterns of poverty, discrimination, marginality, hopelessness, and despair continue to limit the lives of millions.

As the 21st century progresses, the dilemmas of America's minority groups remain perhaps the primary unresolved domestic issue facing the nation. The answers of the past—the simple faith in assimilation and the belief that success in America is open to all who simply try hard enough—have proved inadequate, even destructive and dangerous, because they help to sustain the belief that the barriers to equality no longer exist and that any remaining inequalities are the problems of the minority groups, not the larger society.

These problems of equality and access will not solve themselves or simply fade away. They will continue to manifest themselves in myriad ways: through protest activities, rancorous debates, diffused rage, and pervasive violence. The solutions and policies that will carry us through these coming travails are not clear. Only by asking the proper questions, realistically and honestly, can we hope to find the answers that will help our society fulfill its promises to the millions who are currently excluded from achieving the American dream.

The United States is one of many ethnically and racially diverse nations in the world today. As the globe continues to shrink and networks of communication, immigration, trade, and transportation continue to link all peoples into a single global entity, the problems of diversity will become more international in their scope and implications. Ties will grow between African Americans and the nations of Africa, agreements between the United States and the nations of Latin America will have direct impact on immigration patterns, Asian Americans will be affected by international developments on the Pacific Rim, and so forth. Domestic and international group relations will blend into a single reality. In many ways, the patterns of dominant-minority relations discussed in this text have already been reproduced on the global stage. The mostly Anglo industrialized nations of the northern hemisphere have continuously exploited the labor and resources of the mostly non-white, undeveloped nations of the southern hemisphere. Thus, the tensions and resentments we have observed in U.S. society are mirrored in the global system of societies.

The United States is neither the most nor the least diverse country in the world. Likewise, our nation is neither the most nor the least successful in confronting the problems of prejudice, discrimination, and racism. However, the multigroup nature of our society, along with the present influx of immigrants from around the globe, do present an opportunity to improve on our record and make a lasting contribution. A society that finds a way to deal fairly and humanely with the problems of diversity and difference, prejudice and inequality, and racism and discrimination can provide a sorely needed model for other nations and, indeed, for the world.

References

A changing population. (2010, June 10). *Wall Street Journal*. Retrieved from http://online.wsj .com/public/resources/documents/st_census0610b_20100610.html

Abrahamson, H. (1980). Assimilation and pluralism. In S. Thernstrom, A. Orlov, & O. Handlin (Eds.), *Harvard Encyclopedia of American Ethnic Groups* (pp. 150–160). Cambridge, MA: Harvard University Press.

Acuna, R. (1988). *Occupied America* (3rd ed.). New York: Harper & Row.

Acuna, R. (1999). *Occupied America* (4th ed.). New York: Harper & Row.

Adarand Constructors Inc. v. Peña, 515 U.S. 200. (1995).

Agbayani-Siewert, P., & Revilla, L. (1995). Filipino Americans. In P. G. Min (Ed.), *Asian Americans: Contemporary Issues and Trends* (pp. 134–168). Thousand Oaks, CA: SAGE.

Aizenman, N. C. (2006). Immigration debate wakes a "sleeping Latino giant." *Washington Post*, April 6, p. A1.

Alba, R. (1985). *Italian Americans: Into the twilight of ethnicity*. Englewood Cliffs, NJ: Prentice Hall.

Alba, R. (1990). *Ethnic identity: The transformation of white America*. New Haven, CT: Yale University Press.

Alba, R. (1995). Assimilation's quiet tide. *The Public Interest, 119*, 3–19.

Alba, R. (2004). Language assimilation today: Bilingualism persists more than in the past but English still dominates. Center for Comparative Immigration Studies. Retrieved from http://escholarship.org/uc/item/0j5865nk#page-3

Alba, R., & Nee, V. (1997). Rethinking assimilation theory for a new era of immigration. *International Migration Review, 31*, 826–875.

Alba, R., & Nee, V. (2003). *Remaking the American mainstream: Assimilation and contemporary immigration*. Cambridge, MA: Harvard University Press.

Aleiss, A. (2005). *Making the white man's Indian: Native Americans and Hollywood movies*. Westport, CT: Praeger.

Alexander, M. (2012). *The new Jim Crow*. New York: The New Press.

Almquist, E. M. (1979). Black women and the pursuit of equality. In J. Freeman (Ed.), *Women: A feminist perspective* (pp. 430–450). Palo Alto, CA: Mayfield.

Alvarez, R. (1973). The psycho-historical and socioeconomic development of the Chicano community in the United States. *Social Science Quarterly, 53*, 920–942.

American Sociological Association. (2003). The importance of collecting data and doing scientific research on race. Retrieved from http://www2.asanet.org/media/asa_race_statement .pdf

Amott, T., & Matthaei, J. (1991). *Race, gender, and work: A multicultural history of women in the United States*. Boston: South End.

Andersen, M. L. (1993). *Thinking about women: Sociological perspectives on sex and gender* (3rd ed.). New York: Macmillan.

Anti-Defamation League. (2000). Audit of anti-Semitic incidents. Retrieved from http://www .adl.org/2000audit/2000_audit.pdf

Ashmore, R., & DelBoca, F. (1976). Psychological approaches to understanding group conflict. In P. Katz (Ed.), *Towards the elimination of racism* (pp. 73–123). New York: Pergamon.

Asia: Original sin, Australia's aborigines. (2007, June 2). *Economist,* p. 67.

Associated Press. (2005). Asian youth persistently harassed by U.S. peers. Retrieved from http://www.usatoday.com/news/nation/2005-11-13-asian-teens-bullied_x.htm

Austin, A. (2010). Different race, different recession: American Indian unemployment in 2010. *Economic Policy Institute Issue Brief #289.* Retrieved from http://epi.3cdn.net/94a3394 72e6481485e_hgm6bxpz4.pdf

Australian Bureau of Statistics. (2002). Australian Social Trends 2002, Population, National Summary Tables. Retrieved from http://www.abs.gov.au

Australian Bureau of Statistics. (2008). Aboriginal and Torres Strait Islander population tops half a million: ABS. Retrieved from http://www.abs.gov.au/ausstats/abs@.nsf/Latestproduc ts/3238.0.55.001Media%20Release1Jun%202006?opendocument&tabname=Summary&pr odno=3238.0.55.001&issue=Jun%202006&num=&view=

Australian Human Rights and Equal Opportunity Commission. (1997). Bringing them home: Report of the national inquiry into the separation of aboriginal and Torres Strait Islander children from their families. Retrieved from http://www.hreoc.gov.au/social_justice/bth_ report/report/index.html

Avery, R., & Rendall, M. (2002). Lifetime inheritances of three generations of whites and blacks. *American Journal of Sociology, 107,* 1300–1346

Baca Zinn, M., & Dill, B. T. (1994). *Women of color in U.S. society.* Philadelphia: Temple University Press.

Baca Zinn, M., & Eitzen, D. S. (1990). *Diversity in families.* New York: HarperCollins.

Ball, R. (2009). Social distance in Japan: An exploratory study. *Michigan Sociological Review, 23,* 105–113.

Barringer, H., Takeuchi, D., & Levin, M. (1995). *Asians and Pacific Islanders in the United States.* New York: Russell Sage Foundation.

Bauer, M. (2008). Close to slavery: Guestworker programs in the United States. A report of the Southern Poverty Law Center. Retrieved from http://www.splcenter.org/pdf/static/ SPLCguestworker.pdf

Bean, F., & Stevens, G. (2003). *America's newcomers and the dynamics of diversity.* New York: Russell Sage Foundation.

Becerra, R. (1988). The Mexican American family. In C. H. Mindel, R. W. Habenstein, & R. Wright Jr. (Eds.), *Ethnic families in America: Patterns and variations* (3rd ed., pp. 141–172). New York: Elsevier.

Bell, D. (1973). *The coming of post-industrial society.* New York: Basic Books.

Bell, D. A. (1992). *Race, racism, and American law* (3rd ed.). Boston: Little, Brown.

Benedict, R. (1946). *The chrysanthemum and the sword: Patterns of Japanese culture.* Boston: Houghton Mifflin.

Benjamin, L. (2005). *The black elite.* Lanham, MD: Rowman & Littlefield.

Bertrand, M., & Mullainathan, S. (2004). Are Emily and Greg more employable than Lakisha and Jamal? A field experiment on labor market discrimination. *American Economic Review, 94,* 991–1013.

Bing. (n.d.). Map Navajo reservation. Retrieved from http://www.bing.com/images/search?q=m ap+navajo+reservation&view=detail&id=F7D04C4FE637B3010A4C728D0CE2C1492CA CBFB8&first=0&qpvt=map+navajo+reservation&FORM=IDFRIR

Bird, E. (1999). Gendered construction of the American Indian in popular media. *Journal of Communication, 49,* 60–83.

Biskupic, J. (1989, October 28). House approves entitlement for Japanese-Americans. *Congressional Quarterly Weekly Report,* p. 2879.

Black-Gutman, D., & Hickson, F. (1996). The relationship between racial attitudes and social-cognitive development in children: An Australian study. *Developmental Psychology, 32,* 448–457.

Blackmon, D. (2008). *Slavery by another name.* New York: Anchor Books.

Blassingame, J. W. (1972). *The slave community: Plantation life in the antebellum South.* New York: Oxford University Press.

Blau, P. M., & Duncan, O. D. (1967). *The American occupational structure.* New York: Wiley.

Blauner, R. (1972). *Racial oppression in America.* New York: Harper & Row.

Blessing, P. (1980). Irish. In S. Thernstrom, A. Orlov, & O. Handlin (Eds.), *Harvard encyclopedia of American ethnic groups* (pp. 524–545). Cambridge, MA: Harvard University Press.

Blumer, H. (1965). Industrialization and race relations. In G. Hunter (Ed.), *Industrialization and race relations: A symposium* (pp. 200–253). London: Oxford University Press.

Bobo, L. (1988). Group conflict, prejudice, and the paradox of contemporary racial attitudes. In P. Katz & D. Taylor (Eds.), *Eliminating racism: Profiles in controversy* (pp. 85–114). New York: Plenum Press.

Bobo, L. (2001). Racial attitudes and relations at the close of the twentieth century. In N. Smelser, W. Wilson, & F. Mitchell (Eds.), *America becoming: Racial trends and their consequences* (Vol. 1, pp. 264–301). Washington, DC: National Academy Press.

Bodnar, J. (1985). *The transplanted.* Bloomington: Indiana University Press.

Bogardus, E. (1933). A social distance scale. *Sociology and Social Research, 17,* 265–271.

Bonacich, E., & Modell, J. (1980). The *economic basis of ethnic solidarity: Small business in the Japanese American community.* Berkeley: University of California Press.

Bonilla-Silva, E. (2001). *White supremacy and racism in the post–civil rights era.* Boulder, CO: Lynne Riener.

Bonilla-Silva, E. (2003). "New racism," Color-blind racism, and the future of whiteness in America. In A. Doane & E. Bonilla-Silva (Eds.), *White out: The continuing significance of racism.* New York: Routledge.

Bonilla-Silva, E. (2006). *Racism without racists* (2nd ed.). Lanham, MD: Rowman & Littlefield.

Booth, A., Granger, D., Mazur, A., & Kivligham, K. (2006). Testosterone and social behavior. *Social Forces, 86,* 167–191.

Bordewich, F. (1996). *Killing the white man's Indian.* New York: Doubleday.

Boswell, T. (1986). A split labor market analysis of discrimination against Chinese immigrants, 1850–1882. *American Sociological Review, 51,* 352–371.

Bournay, E., & UNEP/GRID-Arendal. (2012). Skin colour map (indigenous people), 2007. Retrieved from http://maps.grida.no/go/graphic/skin-colour-map-indigenous-people

Bouvier, L. F., & Gardner, R. W. (1986). Immigration to the U.S.: The unfinished story. *Population Bulletin,* November, p. 41.

Brace, M. (2001). A nation divided. *Geographical, 73,* 14–20.

Brittingham, A., & de la Cruz, C. P. (2004). Ancestry: 2000. Retrieved from http://www.census.gov/prod/2004pubs/c2kbr-35.pdf

Brody, D. (1980). Labor. In S. Thernstrom, A. Orlov, & O. Handlin (Eds.), *Harvard encyclopedia of American ethnic groups* (pp. 609–618). Cambridge, MA: Harvard University Press.

Bronson, P., & Merryman, A. (2009, September 14). See baby discriminate. *Newsweek.* Retrieved from http://www.newsweek.com/2009/09/04/see-baby-discriminate.html

Brown, D. (1970). *Bury my heart at Wounded Knee.* New York: Holt, Rinehart & Winston.

Brown, R. (1995). *Prejudice: Its social psychology.* Cambridge, MA: Blackwell.

Brown v. Board of Education of Topeka, 247 U.S. 483 (1954).

Browne, A. (2011). 10 U.S. cities with the most expensive cost of living. *Kiplinger Magazine.* Retrieved from http://www.kiplinger.com/slideshow/cities-with-most-expensive-cost-of-living-2011/1.html

Brunsma, D. (2005). Interracial families and the racial identification of mixed-race children: Evidence from the early childhood longitudinal study. *Social Forces, 84,* 1131–1157.

Bulwa, D. (2010, November 6). Mehserle convicted of involuntary manslaughter. *San Francisco Chronicle.* Retrieved from http://www.sfgate.com/bayarea/article/Mehserle-convicted-of-involuntary-manslaughter-3181861.php

Buriel, R. (1993). Acculturation, respect for cultural differences, and biculturalism among three generations of Mexican American and Euro-American school children. *Journal of Genetic Psychology, 154,* 531–544.

Camarillo, A., & Bonilla, F. (2001). Hispanics in a multicultural society: A new American dilemma? In N. Smelser, W. Wilson, & F. Mitchell (Eds.), *America becoming: Racial trends and their consequences* (Vol. 2, pp. 103–134). Washington, DC: National Academy Press.

Camarota, S. (2002). Immigrants in the United States, 2002. Center for Immigration Studies. Retrieved from http://www.cis.org/articles/2002/back1302.html

Carroll, J. (2007). Hispanics support requiring English proficiency for immigrants. Gallup polls. Retrieved from http://www.gallup.com/poll/28048/Hispanics-Support-Requiring-English-Proficiency-Immigrants.aspx

Carter, N. M., & Silva, C. (2010). Pipeline's broken promise. New York: Catalyst. Retrieved from http://www.catalyst.org/publication/372/pipelines-broken-promise

Central Statistics Office, Ireland. (2011). Population and migration estimates. Retrieved from http://www.cso.ie/en/media/csoie/releasespublications/documents/population/current/Population%20and%20Migration%20Estimates%20April%202011.pdf

Chan, S. (1990). European and Asian immigrants into the United States in comparative perspective, 1820s to 1920s. In V. Yans-McLaughlin (Ed.), *Immigration reconsidered: History, sociology, and politics* (pp. 37–75). New York: Oxford University Press.

Chirot, D. (1994). *How societies change.* Thousand Oaks, CA: Pine Forge Press.

Cho, S. (1993). Korean Americans vs. African Americans: Conflict and construction. In R. Gooding-Williams (Ed.), *Reading Rodney King, Reading urban uprising* (pp. 196–211). New York: Routledge & Kegan Paul.

Chou, R., & Feagin, J. (2008). *The myth of the model minority: Asian Americans facing racism.* Boulder, CO: Paradigm.

Churchill, W. (1985, December). Resisting relocation: Dine and Hopis fight to keep their land. *Dollars and Sense,* 112–115.

Churchill, W. (1997). *A little matter of genocide: Holocaust and denial in the Americas, 1492 to the present.* San Francisco: City Light Books.

CIA World Factbook. (2012). *The CIA World Factbook.* Retrieved from https://www.cia.gov/library/publications/the-world-factbook/

Civil Rights Act of 1964, Pub. L. 88-352, § 42 U.S.C. 2000 (1964).

Cohen, A., & Taylor, E. (2000). *American pharaoh, Mayor Richard J. Daley: His battle for Chicago and the nation.* New York: Little, Brown.

Cohen, S. M. (1985). *The 1984 National Survey of American Jews: Political and social outlooks.* New York: American Jewish Committee.

Conot, R. (1967). *Rivers of blood, years of darkness.* New York: Bantam.

Conzen, K. N. (1980). Germans. In S. Thernstrom, A. Orlov, & O. Handlin (Eds.), *Harvard encyclopedia of American ethnic groups* (pp. 405–425). Cambridge, MA: Harvard University Press.

Cornell, S. (1987). American Indians, American dreams, and the meaning of success. *American Indian Culture and Research Journal, 11,* 59–71.

Cornell, S. (1988). *The return of the native: American Indian political resurgence.* New York: Oxford University Press.

Cornell, S. (1990). Land, labor, and group formation: Blacks and Indians in the United States. *Ethnic and Racial Studies, 13,* 368–388.

Cornell, S. (2006). *What makes First Nations enterprises successful? Lessons from the Harvard Project.* Tucson, AZ: Native Nations Institute for Leadership, Management, and Policy.

Cornell, S., Kalt, J., Krepps, M., & Taylor, J. (1998). American Indian gaming policy and its socio-*economic effects: A report to the National Impact Gambling Study Commission.* Cambridge, MA: Economics Resource Group.

Cortes, C. (1980). Mexicans. In S. Thernstrom, A. Orlov, & O. Handlin (Eds.), *Harvard encyclopedia of American ethnic groups* (pp. 697–719). Cambridge, MA: Harvard University Press.

Cose, E. (1993). *The rage of a privileged class.* New York: HarperCollins.

Cristol, D., & Gimbert, B. (2008). Racial perceptions of young children: A review of literature post-1999. *Early Childhood Education, 36,* 201–207.

Curtin, P. (1990). *The rise and fall of the plantation complex.* New York: Cambridge University Press.

D'Alessio, S., Stolzenberg, L., & Eitle, D. (2002). The effect of racial threat on interracial and intraracial crimes. *Social Science Research, 31,* 392–408.

D'Angelo, R. (2001). *The American civil rights movement: Readings and interpretations.* New York: McGraw-Hill.

Davis, K. (2005). A girl like me. Retrieved from http://www.youtube.com/watch?v=YWyI77Yh1Gg

de la Cruz, P., & Brittingham, A. (2003). The Arab population: 2000. Retrieved from http://www.census.gov/prod/2003pubs/c2kbr-23.pdf

Debo, A. (1970). *A history of the Indians of the United States.* Norman: University of Oklahoma Press.

Dinnerstein, L. (1977). The East European Jewish immigration. In L. Dinnerstein & F. C. Jaher (Eds.), *Uncertain Americans* (pp. 216–231). New York: Oxford University Press.

D'Orso, M. (1996). *Like Judgement Day: The ruin and redemption of a town called Rosewood.* New York: Putnam.

Dockterman, D. (2011a). Hispanics of Colombian origin in the United States, 2009. Pew Hispanic Center. Retrieved from http://www.pewhispanic.org/files/2011/07/77.pdf

Dockterman, D. (2011b). Hispanics of Dominican origin in the United States, 2009. Pew Hispanic Center. Retrieved from http://www.pewhispanic.org/files/2011/07/75.pdf

Doyle, A. B., & Aboud, F. E. (1995). A longitudinal study of white children's racial prejudice as a socio-cognitive development. *Merrill-Palmer Quarterly, 41,* 209–228.

Du Bois, W. E. B. (1961). *The souls of black folk.* Greenwich, CT: Fawcett.

Duleep, H. O. (1988). *Economic status of Americans of Asian descent.* Washington, DC: U.S. Commission on Civil Rights.

Dumont, J.-C., & LeMaitre, G. (2011). Counting immigrants and ex-patriots in OECD countries: A new perspective. Retrieved from http://www.oecd.org/dataoecd/27/5/33868740.pdf

Dwyer, R. (2010). Poverty, prosperity, and place: The shape of class segregation in the age of extremes. *Social Problems, 57,* 114–137.

Egelko, Bob. (2009, January 15). BART shooting draws Rodney King case parallels. *San Francisco Chronicle.* Retrieved from http://www.sfgate.com/cgi-bin/article.cgi?f=/c/a/2009/01/15/MNS8156O8U.DTL

Ehrenreich, B., & Hochschild, A. (2004). *Global women: Nannies, maids and sex workers in the new economy.* New York: Holt Paperbacks.

Elkins, S. (1959). *Slavery: A problem in American institutional and intellectual life.* New York: Universal Library.

Ellsworth, S. (1982). *Death in a promised land: The Tulsa race riot of 1921.* Baton Rouge: Louisiana State University Press.

Encyclopedia of Immigration. (2011). European immigrants. Retrieved from http://immigration-online.org/486-european-immigrants.html

Ennis, S., Ríos-Vargas, M., & Albert, N. (2011). The Hispanic population: 2010. U.S. Census Bureau. Retrieved from http://www.census.gov/prod/cen2010/briefs/c2010br-04.pdf

Espinosa, K., & Massey, D. (1997). Determinants of English proficiency among Mexican migrants to the United States. *International Migration Review, 31,* 28–51.

Espiritu, Y. (1996). Colonial oppression, labour importation, and group formation: Filipinos in the United States. *Ethnic and Racial Studies, 19,* 29–49.

Espiritu, Y. (1997). *Asian American women and men.* Thousand Oaks, CA: SAGE.

Essien-Udom, E. U. (1962). *Black nationalism.* Chicago: University of Chicago Press.

Europe: The integration dilemma: Minorities in Germany. (2007, July 19). *Economist,* p. 39.

Evans, S. M. (1979). *Personal politics.* New York: Knopf.

Evans, S. M. (1989). *Born for liberty: A history of women in America.* New York: Free Press.

Faderman, L. (1998). *I begin my life all over again: The Hmong and the American immigrant experience.* Boston: Beacon Press.

Fadiman, A. (1998). *The spirit catches you and you fall down.* New York: Farrar, Straus & Giroux.

Fanning, B. (2003). *Racism and social change in the Republic of Ireland.* Manchester, UK: Manchester University Press.

European Commission. (2007). *Special Eurobarometer 263: Discrimination in the European Union.* Brussels: Commission of the European Communities.

European Commission. (2008). *Special Eurobarometer 296: Discrimination in the European Union: Perceptions, experiences, and attitudes.* Brussels: Commission of the European Communities.

European Roma Rights Center (ERRC). (2006). *Ambulance not on the way.* Budapest: ERRC.

European Union Agency for Fundamental Rights (FRA). (2009). European Union minorities and discrimination survey The Roma. Retrieved from http://fra.europa.eu/en/project/2011/eu-midis-european-union-minorities-and-discrimination-survey

Farley, J. (2000). *Majority-minority relations* (4th ed.). Englewood Cliffs, NJ: Prentice Hall.

Faux, J. (2004, February 2). NAFTA at 10: Where do we go from here? *Nation,* pp. 11–14.

Feagin, J. (2001). *Racist America: Roots, current realities, and future reparations.* New York: Routledge.

Feagin, J., & Feagin, C. (1986). *Discrimination American style: Institutional racism and sexism.* Malabar, FL: Robert E. Krieger.

Feagin, J., & O'Brien, E. (2004). *White men on race: Power, privilege, and the shaping of cultural consciousness.* Boston: Beacon Press.

Fears, D. (2007, November 20). Hate crime reporting uneven. *Washington Post,* p. A3.

Federal Bureau of Investigation (FBI). (2012). Hate crimes, table 1. Retrieved from http://www.fbi.gov/about-us/cjis/ucr/hate-crime/2010/tables/table-1-incidents-offenses-victims-and-known-offenders-by-bias-motivation-2010.xls

Federal Glass Ceiling Commission. (1995). Good for business: Making full use of the nation's human capital. Retrieved from http://digitalcommons.ilr.cornell.edu/cgi/viewcontent.cgi?article=1117&context=key_workplace

Federation for American Immigration Reform. (2010). Birthright citizenship. Retrieved from http://www.fairus.org/issue/birthright-citizenship?A=SearchResult&SearchID=2723806&ObjectID=5123842&ObjectType=35

Finkelman, P. & Calder, J. (1998) *Macmillan encyclopedia of world slavery.* New York: Macmillan.

Firefighters Local Union No. 1784 v. Stotts, 467 U.S. 561 (1984).

Fisher, M. (2008). Does campus diversity promote friendship diversity? A look at interracial friendships in college. *Social Science Quarterly, 89,* 623–655.

Fitzpatrick, J. P. (1976). The Puerto Rican family. In C. H. Mindel & R. W. Habenstein (Eds.), *Ethnic families in America* (pp. 173–195). New York: Elsevier.

Fitzpatrick, J. P. (1980). Puerto Ricans. In S. Thernstrom, A. Orlov, & O. Handlin (Eds.), *Harvard encyclopedia of American ethnic groups* (pp. 858–867). Cambridge, MA: Harvard University Press.

———. (1987). *Puerto Rican Americans: The meaning of migration to the mainland* (2nd ed.). Englewood Cliffs, NJ: Prentice Hall.

Fong, E., & Markham, W. (1991). Immigration, ethnicity, and conflict: The California Chinese, 1849–1882. *Sociological Inquiry, 61,* 471–490.

Fong, T. (2002). *The contemporary Asian American experience* (2nd ed.). Upper Saddle River, NJ: Prentice Hall.

Forner, P. S. (1980). *Women and the American labor movement: From World War I to the present.* New York: Free Press.

Franklin, J. H. (1967). *From slavery to freedom* (3rd ed.). New York: Knopf.

Franklin, J. H., & Moss, A. (1994). *From slavery to freedom* (7th ed.). New York: McGraw-Hill.

Frazier, E. F. (1957). *Black bourgeoisie: The rise of a new middle class.* New York: Free Press.

Fry, R. (2007). The changing racial and ethnic composition of U.S. public schools. Pew Research. Retrieved from http://pewhispanic.org/files/reports/79.pdf

Gallagher, C. (2001). Playing the ethnic card: How ethnic narratives maintain racial privilege. Paper presented at the Annual Meetings of the Southern Sociological Society, April 4–7, Atlanta, GA.

Gallup Organization. (2007). Americans overwhelmingly favor interracial dating. Retrieved from http://forums.anandtech.com/showthread.php?t=1717425

Gallup Organization. (2010). Race relations. Retrieved from http://www.gallup.com/poll/1687/Race-Relations.aspx

Gallup Organization. (2012). Presidential job approval. Retrieved from http://www.gallup.com/poll/124922/presidential-approval-center.aspx

Gans, H. (1979). Symbolic ethnicity: The future of ethnic groups and cultures in America. *Ethnic and Racial Studies, 2,* 1–20.

Garvey, M. (1969). *Philosophy and opinions of Marcus Garvey* (Vols. 1–2, A. J. Garvey, Ed.). New York: Atheneum.

Genovese, E. D. (1974). *Roll, Jordan, roll: The world the slaves made.* New York: Pantheon.

Gerth, H., & Mills, C. W. (Eds.). (1946). *From Max Weber: Essays in sociology.* New York: Oxford University Press.

Geschwender, J. A. (1978). *Racial stratification in America.* Dubuque, IA: William C. Brown.

Glaeser, E., & Vigdor, J. (2001). *Racial segregation in the 2000 census: Promising news.* Washington, DC: Brookings Institution.

Glazer, N., & Moynihan, D. (1970). *Beyond the melting pot* (2nd ed.). Cambridge: MIT Press.

Gleason, P. (1980). American identity and Americanization. In S. Thernstrom, A. Orlov, & O. Handlin (Eds.), *Harvard encyclopedia of American ethnic groups* (pp. 31–57). Cambridge, MA: Harvard University Press.

Goldstein, A., & Suro, R. (2000, January 16). A journey on stages: Assimilation's pull is still strong but its pace varies. *Washington Post,* p. A1.

Gooding-Williams, R. (1993). *Reading Rodney King, reading urban uprising.* New York: Routledge & Kegan Paul.

Gordon, M. M. (1964). *Assimilation in American life: The role of race, religion and national origins.* New York: Oxford University Press.

Goren, A. (1980). Jews. In S. Thernstrom, A. Orlov, & O. Handlin (Eds.), *Harvard encyclopedia of American ethnic groups* (pp. 571–598). Cambridge, MA: Harvard University Press.

Gourevitch, P. (1999). *We wish to inform you that tomorrow we will be killed with our families: Stories from Rwanda.* New York: Picador.

Gratz v. Bollinger, 539 U.S. 244 (2003).

Grebler, L., Moore, J. W., & Guzman, R. C. (1970). *The Mexican American people.* New York: Free Press.

Greeley, A. M. (1974). *Ethnicity in the United States: A preliminary reconnaissance.* New York: Wiley.

Green, D. (1999). Native Americans. In A. Dworkin & R.Dworkin (Eds.), *The minority report* (pp. 255–277). Orlando, FL: Harcourt-Brace.

Griswold, D. (2012). Immigration and the welfare state. *Cato Journal, 32,* 159–174.

Grutter v. Bollinger, 539 U.S. 306 (2003).

Gutman, H. (1976). *The black family in slavery and freedom, 1750–1925.* New York: Vintage.

Hacker, A. (1992). *Two nations: Black and white, separate, hostile, unequal.* New York: Scribner's.

Hainmueller, J., & Hiscox, M. (2010). Attitudes toward highly skilled and low-skilled immigration: Evidence from a survey experiment. *American Political Science Review, 104,* 61–84.

Hakimzadeh, S., & Cohn, D'V. (2007). English language usage among Hispanics in the United States. Pew Hispanic Center. Retrieved from http://pewhispanic.org/files/reports/82.pdf

Haley, A. (1976). *Roots: The saga of an American family.* New York: Doubleday.

Haller, W., Portes, A., & Lynch, S. (2011). Dreams fulfilled, Dreams shattered: Determinants of segmented assimilation in the second generation. *Social Forces, 89,* 733–762.

Hamer, F. L. (1967). *To praise our bridges: An autobiography of Fannie Lou Hamer.* Jackson, MS: KIPCO.

Handlin, O. (1951). *The uprooted.* New York: Grosset & Dunlap.

Hansen, M. L. (1952). The third generation in America. *Commentary, 14,* 493–500.

Hanson, J., & Rouse, L. (1987). Dimensions of Native American stereotyping. *American Indian Culture and Research Journal, 11,* 33–58.

Harjo, S. (1996). Now and then: Native peoples in the United States. *Dissent, 43,* 58–60.

Hartney, C., & Vuong, L. (2009). Created equal: Racial and ethnic disparities in the U.S. criminal justice system. National Council on Crime and Delinquency. Retrieved from http://www .nccd-crc.org/nccd/pdf/CreatedEqualReport2009.pdf

Haubert, J., & Fussell, E. (2006). Explaining pro-immigrant sentiment in the U.S.: Social class, cosmopolitanism, and perceptions of immigrants. *International Migration Review, 40,* 489–507.

Hawkins, H. (1962). *Booker T. Washington and his critics: The problem of Negro leadership.* Boston: D. C. Heath.

Heaton, T., Chadwick, B., & Jacobson, C. (2000). *Statistical handbook on racial groups in the United States.* Phoenix, AZ: Oryx.

Heer, D. M. (1996). *Immigration in America's future.* Boulder, CO: Westview Press.

Hemispheric Institute. (2006). Deaths in the desert. Retrieved from http://hemisphericinstitute. org/journal/3.2/eng/en32_pg_galvez.html

Herberg, W. (1960). *Protestant-Catholic-Jew: An essay in American religious sociology.* New York: Anchor.

Higham, J. (1963). *Strangers in the land: Patterns of American nativism, 1860–1925.* New York: Atheneum.

Hill-Collins, P. (1991). *Black feminist thought.* New York: Routledge.

Hirschman, C. (1983). America's melting pot reconsidered. *Annual Review of Sociology, 9,* 397–423.

Hirschman, C., & Wong, M. (1984). Socioeconomic gains of Asian Americans, blacks, and Hispanics: 1960–1976 *American Journal of Sociology, 90,* 584–607.

Hirschman, C., & Wong, M. (1986). The extraordinary educational attainment of Asian-Americans: A search for historical evidence and explanations. *Social Forces, 65,* 1–27.

Hoeffel, E., Rastogi, S., Kim, M. O., & Shahid, H. (2012). The Asian population: 2010. U.S. Census Bureau. Retrieved from http://www.census.gov/prod/cen2010/briefs/c2010br-11. pdf

Hopcroft, Rosemary. (2009). Gender inequality in interaction—An evolutionary account. *Social Forces, 87,* 1845–72.

Hopkins, D. (2010). Politicized places: Explaining where and when immigrants provoke local opposition. *American Political Science Review, 104,* 40–60.

Hostetler, J. (1980). *Amish society.* Baltimore: Johns Hopkins University Press.

How to tell your friends from the Japs. (1941, December 22). *Time*, p. 33.

Hoxie, F. (1984). *A final promise: The campaign to assimilate the Indian, 1880–1920*. Lincoln: University of Nebraska Press.

Hraba, J. (1979). *American ethnicity*. Itasca, IL: F. E. Peacock.

Huber, J. (2007). *On the origins of gender inequality*. Colorado Springs, CO: Paradigm Publishers.

Hughes, M., & Thomas, M. (1998). The continuing significance of race revisited: A study of race, class and quality of life in America, 1972 to 1996 *American Sociological Review, 63,* 785–803.

Huntington, S. (2004). *Who are we: The challenges to America's national identity*. New York: Simon & Schuster.

Human Rights Watch. (2009) Decades of disparity: Drug arrests and race in the United States. Retrieved from http://www.hrw.org/en/reports/2009/03/02/decades-disparity-0

Humes, K., Jones, N., & Ramirez, R. (2011). Overview of race and Hispanic origin: 2010. U.S. Census Briefs. Retrieved from http://www.census.gov/prod/cen2010/briefs/c2010br-02.pdf

Hurh, W. M. (1998). *The Korean Americans*. Westport, CT: Greenwood.

Ibish, H. (Ed.). (2003). Report on hate crimes and discrimination against Arab Americans: The post–September 11 backlash. Washington, DC: American-Arab Anti-Discrimination Committee. Retrieved from http://www.adc.org/PDF/hcr02.pdf

Iceland, J., Weinberg, D., & Steinmetz, E. (2002). Racial and ethnic residential segregation in the United States: 1980–2000. U.S. Census Bureau, Series CENSR-3. Washington, DC: U.S. Government Printing Office. Retrieved from http://www.census.gov/prod/2002pubs/censr-3.pdf

Ifill, G. (2009). *The breakthrough: Politics and race in the age of Obama*. New York: Doubleday.

Jackson, B. (2000). *Splendid slippers: A thousand years of an erotic tradition*. Berkeley, CA: Ten Speed Press.

Jacobs, D., & Wood, K. (1999). Interracial conflict and interracial homicide: Do political and economic rivalries explain white killings of blacks or black killings of whites? *American Journal of Sociology, 105,* 157–180.

Jacobs, H. (2012). *Incidents in the life of a slave girl, written by herself*. (Reprinted from edition 1861.) n.p.: Simon & Brown.

Jibou, R. M. (1988). Ethnic hegemony and the Japanese of California. *American Sociological Review, 53,* 353–367.

Joe, J., & Miller, D. (1994). Cultural survival and contemporary American Indian women in the city. In M. Zinn & B. T. Dill (Eds.), *Women of color in U.S. society* (pp. 185–202). Philadelphia: Temple University Press.

Jones, J. (2010). More Americans favor than oppose Arizona immigration law. Gallup Polls. Retrieved from http://www.gallup.com/poll/127598/Americans-Favor-Oppose-Arizona-Immigration-Law.aspx

Jordan, W. (1968). *White over black: American attitudes towards the Negro: 1550–1812*. Chapel Hill: University of North Carolina Press.

Josephy, A. M. (1968). *The Indian heritage of America*. New York: Knopf.

Kallen, H. M. (1915a, February 18). Democracy versus the melting pot. *Nation*, pp. 190–194.

Kallen, H. M. (1915b, February 25). Democracy versus the melting pot. *Nation*, pp. 217–222.

Kasarda, J. D. (1989). Urban industrial transition and the underclass. *Annals of the American Academy, 501,* 26–47.

Kasinitz, P., Mollenkopf, J. H. Waters, M. C.& Holdaway, J. (2008). *Inheriting the city: The children of immigrants come of age*. New York: Russell Sage Foundation and Harvard University Press.

Katz, M., & Stern, M. (2008). *One nation divisible: What America was and what it is becoming*. New York: Russell Sage Foundation.

Katz, P. (1976). The acquisition of racial attitudes in children. In P. Katz (Ed.), *Towards the elimination of racism* (pp. 125–154). New York: Pergamon.

Katz, P. (2003). Racists or tolerant multiculturalists? How do they begin? *American Psychologist, 58,* 897–909.

Katznelson, I. (2005). *When affirmative action was white: An untold history of racial inequality in twentieth-century America.* New York: Norton.

Kaw, E. (1997). Opening faces: The politics of cosmetic surgery and Asian American women. In M. Crawford & R. Under (Eds.), *In our own words: Readings in the psychology of women and gender* (pp. 55–73). New York: McGraw-Hill.

Kaye, J. (2010). *Moving millions: How coyote capitalism fuels global immigration.* Hoboken, NJ: Wiley.

Kennedy, R. (2001). Racial trends in the administration of criminal justice. In N. Smelser, W. Wilson, & F. Mitchell (Eds.), *America becoming: Racial trends and their consequences* (Vol. 2, pp. 1–20). Washington, DC: National Academy Press.

Kennedy, R. J. (1944). Single or triple melting pot: Intermarriage trends in New Haven, 1870–1940. *American Journal of Sociology, 49,* 331–339.

Kephart, W., & Zellner, W. (1994). *Extraordinary groups.* New York: St. Martin's.

Killian, L. (1975). *The impossible revolution, phase 2: Black Power and the American dream.* New York: Random House.

Kinder, D. R., & Sears, D. O. (1981). Prejudice and politics: Symbolic racism versus racial threats to the good life. *Journal of Personality and Social Psychology, 40,* 414–431.

King, M. L. Jr. (1958). *Stride toward freedom: The Montgomery story.* New York: Harper & Row.

King, M. L. Jr. (1963). *Why we can't wait.* New York: Mentor.

King, M. L. Jr. (1968). *Where do we go from here: Chaos or community?* New York: Harper & Row.

Kitano, H. H. L. (1980). Japanese. In S. Thernstrom, A. Orlov, & O. Handlin (Eds.), *Harvard encyclopedia of American ethnic groups* (pp. 561–571). Cambridge, MA: Harvard University Press.

Kitano, H., & Daniels, R. (1988). *Asian Americans: Emerging minorities.* Englewood Cliffs, NJ: Prentice Hall.

Kitano, H., & Daniels, R. (1995). *Asian Americans: Emerging minorities* (2nd ed.). Englewood Cliffs, NJ: Prentice Hall.

Kitano, H., & Daniels, R. (2001). *Asian Americans: Emerging minorities* (3rd ed.). Upper Saddle River, NJ: Prentice Hall.

Kleg, M., & Yamamoto, K. (1998). As the world turns: Ethno-racial distances after 70 years. *Social Science Journal, 35,* 183–191.

Kluegel, J. R., & Smith, E. R. (1982). Whites' beliefs about blacks' opportunities. *American Sociological Review, 47,* 518–532.

Kochhar, R. (2004). The wealth of Hispanic households, 1996–2002. Washington, DC: Pew Hispanic Center. Retrieved from http://www.pewhispanic.org/files/reports/34.pdf

Kochhar, R. (2006). Growth in the foreign-born workforce and employment of the native born. Pew Hispanic Center. Retrieved from http://www.pewhispanic.org/files/reports/69.pdf

Kotlowitz, A. (1991). *There are no children here.* New York: Anchor Books.

Krauss, M. (1996). Status of Native American language endangerment. In G. Cantoni (Ed.) *Stabilizing indigenous languages.* Flagstaff, AZ: Center for Excellence in Education, Northern Arizona University.

Kraybill, D. B., & Bowman, C. F. (2001). *On the backroad to heaven: Old order Hutterites, Mennonites, Amish, and Brethren.* Baltimore: Johns Hopkins University Press.

Kristof, N., & WuDunn, S. (2010). *Half the sky: Turning oppression into opportunity for women worldwide.* New York: Vintage.

Kritz, M., & Girak, D. (2004). *The American people: Immigration and a changing America.* New York: Russell Sage Foundation.

Krysan, M., & Farley, R. (2002). The residential preferences of blacks: Do they explain persistent segregation? *Social Forces, 80,* 937–981.

Kuperman, D. (2001, September). Stuck at the gates of Paradise. *UNESCO Courier,* pp. 24–26

Lacy, D. (1972). *The white use of blacks in America.* New York: McGraw-Hill.

Lai, H. M. (1980). Chinese. In S. Thernstrom, A. Orlov, & O. Handlin (Eds.), *Harvard encyclopedia of American ethnic groups* (pp. 217–234). Cambridge, MA: Harvard University Press.

Lamont-Brown, R. (1993). The Burakumin: Japan's underclass. *Contemporary Review, 263,* 136–140.

Landale, N., & Oropesa, R. S. (2002). White, black, or Puerto Rican? Racial self-identification among mainland and island Puerto Ricans. *Social Forces, 81,* 231–254.

Lee, S. (1998). Asian Americans: Diverse and growing. *Population Bulletin, 53* (2), 1–40. Population Reference Bureau, Washington, DC.

Lee, S., & Edmonston, B. (2005). New marriages, new families: U.S. racial and Hispanic intermarriage. Washington, DC: Population Reference Bureau. Retrieved from http://www.prb.org/pdf05/60.2NewMarriages.pdf

Lee, S. M., & Yamanaka, K. (1990). Patterns of Asian American intermarriage and marital assimilation. *Journal of Comparative Family Studies, 21,* 287–305.

Lenski, G., Nolan, P., & Lenski, J. (1995). *Human societies: An introduction to macrosociology* (7th ed.). New York: McGraw-Hill.

Levine, L. (1977). *Black culture and black consciousness.* New York: Oxford University Press.

Levy, J. (1975). *Cesar Chavez: Autobiography of La Causa.* New York: Norton.

Lewis, O. (1959). *Five families: Mexican case studies in the culture of poverty.* New York: Basic Books.

Lewis, O. (1965). La vida: *A Puerto Rican family in the culture of poverty.* New York: Random House.

Lewis, O. (1966, October). The culture of poverty. *Scientific American,* pp. 19–25.

Lewis Mumford Center. (2001). Ethnic diversity grows, neighborhood integration lags behind. Retrieved from http://mumford1.dyndns.org/cen2000/report.html

Lewy, G.(2004). Were American Indians the victims of genocide? *Commentary,* 118: 55–63.

Lieberson, R. (1998). *Shifting the color line: Race and the American welfare system.* Cambridge, MA: Harvard University Press.

Lieberson, S. (1980). *A piece of the pie: Blacks and white immigrants since 1880.* Berkeley: University of California Press.

Lieberson, S., & Waters, M. C. (1988). *From many strands.* New York: Russell Sage Foundation.

Light, I., & Bonacich, E. (1988). *Immigrant entrepreneurs: Koreans in Los Angeles, 1965–1982.* Berkeley: University of California Press.

Lincoln, C. E. (1961). *The Black Muslims in America.* Boston: Beacon Press.

Ling, H. (2000). Family and marriage of late-nineteenth and early-twentieth century Chinese immigrant women. *Journal of American Ethnic History, 9,* 43–65.

Liptak, A. (2012a, February 22). Justices take up race as a factor in college entry. *New York Times.* Retrieved from http://www.nytimes.com/2012/02/22/us/justices-to-hear-case-on-affirmative-action-in-higher-education.html?pagewanted=all&_moc.semityn.www

Liptak, A. (2012b, June 26). Blocking parts of Arizona law, justices allow its centerpiece. *New York Times.* Retrieved from http://www.nytimes.com/2012/06/26/us/supreme-court-rejects-part-of-arizona-immigration-law.html?pagewanted=all

Locust, C. (1990). Wounding the spirit: Discrimination and traditional American Indian belief systems. In G. Thomas (Ed.), *U.S. race relations in the 1980s and 1990s: Challenges and alternatives* (pp. 219–232). New York: Hemisphere.

Logan, J., Alba, R., & McNulty, T. (1994). Ethnic economies in metropolitan regions: Miami and beyond. *Social Forces, 72,* 691–724.

Lopata, H. Z. (1976). *Polish Americans.* Englewood Cliffs, NJ: Prentice Hall.

Lopez, M. & Taylor, P. (2009). Dissecting the 2008 electorate: Most diverse in U.S. history. Pew Hispanic Center. Retrieved from http://www.pewhispanic.org/files/reports/108.pdf

Lopez, M., & Velasco, G. (2011). A demographic portrait of Puerto Ricans, 2009. Pew Hispanic Center. Retrieved from http://www.pewhispanic.org/files/2011/06/143.pdf

Lurie, N. O. (1982). The American Indian: Historical background. In N. Yetman & C. H. Steele (Eds.), *Majority and minority* (3rd ed., pp. 131–144). Boston: Allyn & Bacon.

Lyman, S. (1974). *Chinese Americans.* New York: Random House.

Malcolm X. (1964). *The autobiography of Malcolm X.* New York: Grove.

Mann, C. (2011). *1491: New revelations of the Americas before Columbus.* New York: Vintage Books.

Mannix, D. P. (1962). *Black cargoes: A history of the Atlantic slave trade.* New York: Viking Press.

Marable, M. (2011). *Malcolm X: A life of reinvention.* New York: Penquin.

Marcelli, E., & Heer, D. (1998). The unauthorized Mexican immigrant population and welfare in Los Angeles County: A comparative statistical analysis. *Sociological Perspectives, 41,* 279–303.

Marosi, R. (2005, August 7) Death and deliverance: The desert swallows another border crosser but her father is determined to find her body. *Los Angeles Times,* p. A1.

Martin, P., & Midgley, E. (1999). Immigration to the United States. *Population Bulletin, 54* (2), 1–44. Population Reference Bureau, Washington, DC.

Massarik, F., & Chenkin, A. (1973). United States national Jewish population study: A first report. In *American Jewish Committee, American Jewish Year Book, 1973* (pp. 264–306). New York: American Jewish Committee.

Massey, D. (1995). The new immigration and ethnicity in the United States. *Population and Development Review, 21,* 631–652.

Massey, D. (2000). Housing discrimination 101. *Population Today, 28,* 1, 4.

Massey, D. (2007). *Categorically unequal: The American stratification system.* New York: Russell Sage.

Massey, D., & Denton, N. (1993). *American apartheid: Segregation and the making of the underclass.* Cambridge, MA: Harvard University Press.

McConahy, J. B. (1986). Modern racism, ambivalence, and the modern racism scale. In J. F. Dovidio & S. Gartner (Eds.), *Prejudice, discrimination and racism* (pp. 91–125). Orlando, FL: Academic Press.

McDowell, A. (2004, September 10). Cracker Barrel settles lawsuit; Black customers, workers reported discrimination. *Washington Post,* p. E1.

McLemore, S. D. (1973). The origins of Mexican American subordination in Texas. *Social Science Quarterly, 53,* 656–679.

McNickle, D. (1973). *Native American tribalism: Indian survivals and renewals.* New York: Oxford University Press.

McPherson, M., Smith-Lovin, L., & Brashears, M. (2006). Social isolation in America: Changes in core discussion networks over two decades. *Social Forces, 71,* 353–375.

McWilliams, C. (1961). *North from Mexico: The Spanish-speaking people of the United States.* New York: Monthly Review Press.

Medoff, M. (1999). Allocation of time and hateful behavior: A theoretical and positive analysis of hate and hate crimes. *American Journal of Economics and Sociology, 58,* 959–973.

Meek, B. (2006). And the Indian goes "How!": Representations of American Indian English in white public space. *Language in Society, 35,* 93–128.

Meissner, D. (2010, May 2). 5 Myths about immigration. *Washington Post,* p. B2.

Mikulak, M. (2011). The symbolic power of color: Constructions of race, skin-color, and identity in Brazil. *Humanity & Society, 35,* 62–99.

Min, P. G. (Ed.). (1995). *Asian Americans: Contemporary trends and issues.* Thousand Oaks, CA: SAGE.

Min, P. G. (Ed.). (2006). *Asian Americans: Contemporary trends and issues.* (2nd ed.). Thousand Oaks, CA: Pine Forge Press.

Mirandé, A. (1985). *The Chicano experience: An alternative perspective.* Notre Dame, IN: University of Notre Dame Press.

Mirandé, A., & Enriquez, E. (1979). *La Chicana: The Mexican-American women.* Chicago: University of Chicago Press.

Moore, J., & Pinderhughes, R. (1993). *In the barrios: Latinos and the underclass debate.* New York: SAGE.

Moore, J. W. (1970). *Mexican Americans.* Englewood Cliffs, NJ: Prentice Hall.

Moore, J. W., & Pachon, H. (1985). *Hispanics in the United States.* Englewood Cliffs, NJ: Prentice Hall.

Moquin, W., & Van Doren, C. (Eds.). (1971). *A documentary history of Mexican Americans.* New York: Bantam.

Morales, L. (2010, July 27). Amid immigration debate, Americans' views ease slightly. Gallup Polls. Retrieved from http://www.gallup.com/poll/141560/Amid-Immigration-Debate-Americans-Views-Ease-Slightly.aspx

Morawska, E. (1990). The sociology and historiography of immigration. In V. Yans-McLaughlin (Ed.), *Immigration reconsidered: History, sociology, and politics* (pp. 187–238). New York: Oxford University Press.

Morgan, E. (1975). *American slavery, American freedom.* New York: Norton.

Morin, R., & Cottman, M. (2001, June 22). Discrimination's lingering sting. *Washington Post,* p. A1.

Morris, A. D. (1984). *The origins of the civil rights movement.* New York: Free Press.

Moynihan, D. (1965). *The Negro family: The case for national action.* Washington, DC: U.S. Department of Labor.

Murguia, E., & Foreman, T. (2003). Shades of whiteness: The Mexican American experience in relation to Anglos and Blacks. In A. Doane & E. Bonilla-Silva (Eds.) *White out: The continuing significance of racism,* (pp. 63–72). New York: Routledge.

Murguia, E., & Foreman, T. (2004). Shades of whiteness. In M. Bush (Ed.), *Breaking the code of good intentions: Everyday forms of whiteness* (pp. 113–122). Lanham, MD: Rowman & Littlefield.

Myrdal, G. (1962). *An American dilemma: The Negro problem and modern democracy.* New York: Harper & Row. (Original work published 1944).

Nabakov, P. (Ed.). (1999). *Native American testimony* (rev. ed.). New York: Penguin.

Nationmaster.com. (2012). Education statistics. Retrieved from http://www.nationmaster.com/graph/edu_ave_yea_of_sch_of_adu-education-average-years-schooling-adults

Nationmaster.com. (n.d.). Map and scores. Retrieved from http://www.nationmaster.com/red/graph/peo_gen_dev-people-gender-development&b_map=1&b_printable=1#

National Advisory Commission. (1968). *Report of the National Advisory Commission on Civil Disorders.* New York: Bantam Books.

National Center for Health Statistics. (2011). Health, United States, 2011. Retrieved from http://www.cdc.gov/nchs/data/hus/hus11.pdf

National Indian Gaming Commission. (2012). NIGC tribal gaming revenues. Retrieved from http://www.nigc.gov/Gaming_Revenue_Reports.aspx

National Opinion Research Council. (1972–2010). *General social survey.* Chicago: Author.

National Public Radio. (2004). Immigration survey. Retrieved from http://www.npr.org/templates/story/story.php?storyId=4062605

Neary, I. (2003). Burakumin at the end of history. *Social Research, 70,* 269–294.

Neissen, J., Schibel, Y., & Thompson, C. (Eds.). (2005). Current immigration debates in Europe: Ireland. Brussels, Belgium: Migration Policy Group. Retrieved from http://www.migpolgroup.org/public/docs/141.EMD_Ireland_2005.pdf

Nelli, H. S. (1980). Italians. In S. Thernstrom, A. Orlov, & O. Handlin (Eds.), *Harvard encyclopedia of American ethnic groups* (pp. 545–560). Cambridge, MA: Harvard University Press.

Nishi, S. (1995). Japanese Americans. In P. G. Min (Ed.), *Asian Americans: Contemporary trends and issues* (pp. 95–133). Thousand Oaks, CA: SAGE.

Noel, D. (1968). A theory of the origin of ethnic stratification. *Social Problems, 16,* 157–172.

Nolan, P., & Lenski, G. (2004). *Human societies.* Boulder, CO: Paradigm.

Norris, T., Vines, P. & Hoeffel, E. (2012). The American Indian and Alaska population: 2010 U.S. Census Bureau. Retrieved from http://www.census.gov/prod/cen2010/briefs/c2010br-10.pdf

Nortes, T., Vines, P., & Hoeffel, E. (2012). The American Indian and Alaska Native population, 2010. U.S. Census Bureau. Retrieved from http://www.census.gov/prod/cen2010/briefs/c2010br-10.pdf

Novak, M. (1973). *The rise of the unmeltable ethnics: Politics and culture in the 1970s.* New York: Collier.

O'Brien, E. (2008). *The racial middle: Latinos and Asian Americans living beyond the racial divide.* New York: New York University Press.

O'Hare, W., Pollard, K., Mann, T., & Kent, M. (1991). *African Americans in the 1990s.* Washington, DC: Population Reference Bureau.

Obama, B. (2008). Barack Obama's speech on race. *New York Times.* Retrieved from http://www.nytimes.com/2008/03/18/us/politics/18text-obama.html?pagewanted=all

Oliver, M., & Shapiro, T. (2001). Wealth and racial stratification. In N. Smelser, W. Wilson, & F. Mitchell (Eds.), *America becoming: Racial trends and their consequences* (Vol. 1, pp. 222–251). Washington, DC: National Academy Press.

Oliver, M., & Shapiro, T. (2006). *Black wealth, white wealth* (2nd ed.). New York: Taylor & Francis.

Oliver, M., & Shapiro, T. (2008). Sub-prime as a black catastrophe. *American Prospect* (October), A9–A11.

Olson, J., & Wilson, R. (1984). *Native Americans in the twentieth century.* Provo, UT: Brigham Young University Press.

Omi, M., & Winant, H. (1986). *Racial formation in the United States from the 1960s to the 1980s.* New York: Routledge & Kegan Paul.

Orfield, G., & Lee, C. (2006). *Racial transformation and the changing nature of segregation.* Cambridge, MA: The Civil Rights Project at Harvard University. Retrieved from http://www.civilrightsproject.ucla.edu/research/deseg/Racial_Transformation.pdf

Orfield, G., & Lee, C. (2007). *Historic reversals, accelerating resegregation, and the need for new integration strategies.* Civil Rights Project, UCLA. Retrieved from http://civilrightsproject.ucla.edu/research/k-12-education/integration-and-diversity/racial-transformation-and-the-changing-nature-of-segregation

Oswalt, W., & Neely, S. (1996). *This land was theirs.* Mountain View, CA: Mayfield.

Ozawa v. United States, 260 (U.S.) 178 (1922)

Parish, P. J. (1989). *Slavery: History and historians.* New York: Harper & Row.

Park, R. E., & Burgess, E. W. (1924). *Introduction to the science of society.* Chicago: University of Chicago Press.

Parke, R., & Buriel, R. (2002). Socialization concerns in African American, American Indian, Asian American, and Latino families. In N. Benokraitis (Ed.), *Contemporary ethnic families in the United States* (pp. 211–218). Upper Saddle Brook, NJ: Prentice Hall.

Parrillo, V. (2003). *Strangers to these shores* (7th ed.). Boston: Allyn & Bacon.

Passel, J., & Cohn, D. (2009). Mexican immigrants: How many come? How many leave? Retrieved from http://www.pewhispanic.org/files/reports/112.pdf

Passel, J., & Cohn, D. (2011). Unauthorized immigrant population: National and state trends, 2011. Pew Hispanic Center. Retrieved from http://pewhispanic.org/files/reports/133.pdf

Passel, J., Cohn, D., & Gonzalez-Barrera, A. (2012). Net migration from Mexico falls to zero—and perhaps less. Pew Hispanic Center. Retrieved from http://www.pewhispanic.org/files/2012/04/Mexican-migrants-report_final.pdf

Passel, J., Cohn, D., & Lopez, M. (2011). Census 2010: 50 million Latinos. Hispanics account for more than half of the nation's growth in the past decade. Pew Hispanic Center. Retrieved from http://pewhispanic.org/files/reports/140.pdf

Passel, J., Wang, W., & Taylor, P. (2010). Marrying out: One-in-seven new U.S. marriages is interracial or interethnic. Pew Research Center. Retrieved from http://pewsocialtrends.org/files/2010/10/755-marrying-out.pdf

PBS. (2003). The power of an illusion. Retrieved from http://www.pbs.org/race/000_General/000_00-Home.htm

Pego, D. (1998). To educate a nation: Native American tribe hopes to bring higher education to an Arizona reservation. *Black Issues in Higher Education, 15,* 60–63.

Peltier, L. (1999). *Prison writings: My life is my sundance.* New York: St. Martin's Press.

Perez, L. (1980). Cubans. In S. Thernstrom, A. Orlov, & O. Handlin (Eds.), *Harvard encyclopedia of American ethnic groups* (pp. 256–261). Cambridge, MA: Harvard University Press.

Petersen, W. (1971). *Japanese Americans.* New York: Random House.

Peterson, M. (1995). Leading Cuban-American entrepreneurs: The process of developing motives, abilities, and resources. *Human Relations, 48,* 1193–1216

Pettigrew, T. (1958). Personality and sociocultural factors in intergroup attitudes: A cross-national comparison. *Journal of Conflict Resolution, 2,* 29–42.

Pettigrew, T. (1971). *Racially separate or together?* New York: McGraw-Hill.

Pettigrew, T., Wagner, U., & Christ, O. (2007). Who opposes immigration? Comparing German and North American findings. *DuBois Review, 4,* 19–39.

Pettit, B., & Western, B. (2004). Mass imprisonment and the life course: Race and class inequality in U.S. incarceration. *American Sociological Review, 69,* 151–169.

Pew Charitable Trust. (2008). *One in a hundred: Behind bars in the United States.* Retrieved from http://www.pewtrusts.org/uploadedFiles/wwwpewtrustsorg/Reports/sentencing_and_corrections/one_in_100.pdf

Pew Hispanic Center. (2004). *Assimilation and language.* Retrieved from http://pewhispanic.org/files/factsheets/11.pdf

Pew Hispanic Center. (2005). *Hispanics: A people in motion.* Washington, DC: Pew Hispanic Center. Retrieved from http://pewhispanic.org/files/reports/40.pdf

Pew Hispanic Center. (2009). Hispanics of Cuban origin in the United States, 2007. Retrieved from http://pewhispanic.org/files/factsheets/50.pdf

Pew Research Center. (2007). *Muslim Americans: Middle class and mostly mainstream.* Retrieved from http://pewresearch.org/assets/pdf/muslim-americans.pdf

Phillips, U. B. (1918). *American Negro slavery.* New York: Appleton.

Pitt, L. (1970). *The decline of the Californios: A social history of the Spanish-speaking Californians, 1846–1890.* Berkeley: University of California Press.

Plessy v. Ferguson, 163 U.S. 537 (1896).

Pollard, K., & O'Hare, W. (1999). America's racial and ethnic minorities. *Population Bulletin, 54* (3), 29–39. Washington, DC: Population Reference Bureau.

Population Reference Bureau. (2011). 2011 World Population Data Sheet. Retrieved from http://www.prb.org/Publications/Datasheets/2011/world-population-data-sheet/data-sheet.aspx

Porter, E. (2005, April 5). Illegal immigrants are bolstering social security with billions. *New York Times,* p. A1.

Portes, A. (1990). From south of the border: Hispanic minorities in the United States. In V. Yans-McLaughlin (Ed.), *Immigration reconsidered* (pp. 160–184). New York: Oxford University Press.

Portes, A., & Bach, R. L. (1985). *Latin journey: Cuban and Mexican immigrants in the United States.* Berkeley: University of California Press.

Portes, A., & Manning, R. (1986). The immigrant enclave: Theory and empirical examples. In S. Olzak & J. Nagel (Eds.), *Competitive ethnic relations* (pp. 47–68). New York: Academic Press.

Portes, A., & Rumbaut, R. (1996). *Immigrant America: A portrait* (2nd ed.). Berkeley: University of California Press.

Portes, A., & Rumbaut, R. (2001). *Legacies: The Story of the Immigrant Second Generation.* New York: Russell Sage Foundation.

Portes, A., & Shafer, S. (2006). Revisiting the enclave hypothesis: Miami twenty-five years later. The Center for Migration and Development, Princeton University. Retrieved from http://www.princeton.edu/cmd/working-papers/papers/wp0610.pdf

Posadas, B. (1999). *The Filipino Americans.* Westport, CT: Greenwood Press.

Potter, G. (1973). *To the golden door: The story of the Irish in Ireland and America.* Westport, CT: Greenwood Press.

Poulan, R. (2003). Globalization and the sex trade: Trafficking and the commodification of women and children. *Canadian Women Studies, 22,* 38–43.

Powlishta, K., Serbin, L., Doyle, A., & White, D. (1994). Gender, ethnic, and body-type biases: The generality of prejudice in childhood. *Developmental Psychology, 30,* 526–537.

Preston, J., & Cushman, J. (2012, June 15). Obama to permit young migrants to remain in U.S. *New York Times.* Retrieved from http://www.nytimes.com/2012/06/16/us/us-to-stop-deporting-some-illegal-immigrants.html?pagewanted=all

Qian, Z., & Lichter, D. T. (2007). Social boundaries and marital assimilation: Interpreting trends in racial and ethnic intermarriage. *American Sociological Review, 72:* 68–94.

Quillian, L. (2006). New approaches to understanding racial prejudice and discrimination. *Annual Review of Sociology, 32,* 299–328.

Quillian, L., & Campbell, M. (2003). Beyond black and white: The present and future of multi-racial friendship segregation. *American Sociological Review, 68,* 540–567.

Quinones, S. (2007). *Antonio's gun and Delfino's dream: True tales of Mexican migration.* Albuquerque: University of New Mexico Press.

Rader, B. G. (1983). *American sports: From the age of folk games to the age of spectators.* Englewood Cliffs, NJ: Prentice Hall.

Rastogi, S., Johnson, T., Hoeffel, E., & Drewery, M. (2011). The black population: 2010. 2010 Census Briefs, U.S. Census Bureau. Retrieved from http://www.census.gov/prod/cen2010/briefs/c2010br-06pdf

Raymer, P. (1974, August). Wisconsin's Menominees: Indians on a seesaw. *National Geographic,* pp. 228–251.

Read, J. G. (2004). Cultural influences on immigrant women's labor force participation: The Arab-American case. *International Migration Review, 38,* 52–77.

Ricci v. DeStafano, 557 U.S. (2009).

Ridgeway, C. (2011). *Framed by gender: How gender inequality persists in the modern world.* New York: Oxford University Press.

Rifkin, J. (1996). *The end of work: The decline of the global labor force and the dawn of the post-market era.* New York: Putnam.

Robertson, C. (1996). Africa and the Americas? Slavery and women, the family, and the gender division of labor. In D. Gaspar & D. Hine (Eds.), *More than chattel: Black women and slavery in the Americas* (pp. 4–40). Bloomington: Indiana University Press.

Rock, C. (2009). *Good hair.* HBO Films.

Rockquemore, K. A., & Brunsma, D. (2008). *Beyond black: Biracial identity in America.* (2nd ed.). Lanham, MD: Rowman & Littlefield.

Rodriguez, A. (2011, April 13). Testimony before the Sub-Committee on Immigration Policy and Enforcement, U.S. House of Representatives. Retrieved from https://www.farmworkerjustice.org/files/immigration-labor/UFW_Statement_-_H2A_hearing_for_4_13_11_FINAL_w_edit.pdf

Rodriguez, C. (1989). *Puerto Ricans: Born in the USA.* Boston: Unwin-Hyman.

Rodriguez, C., & Cordero-Guzman, H. (1992). Placing race in context. *Ethnic and Racial Studies, 15,* 523–542.

Rosenfield, M. (2002). Measures of assimilation in the marriage market: Mexican Americans 1970–1990. *Journal of Marriage and the Family, 64,* 152–163.

Rosich, K. (2007). Race, ethnicity, and the criminal justice system. Washington, DC: American Sociological Association. Retrieved from http://www.asanet.org/images/press/docs/pdf/ASARaceCrime.pdf

Rouse, L., & Hanson, J. (1991). American Indian stereotyping, resource competition, and status-based prejudice. *American Indian Culture and Research Journal, 15,* 1–17.

Royster, D. (2003). *Race and the invisible hand: How white networks exclude black men from blue collar jobs.* Berkeley: University of California Press.

Rumbaut, R. (1991). Passage to America: Perspectives on the new immigration. In A. Wolfe (Ed.), *America at century's end* (pp. 208–244). Berkeley: University of California Press.

Russell, J. W. (1994). *After the fifth sun: Class and race in North America.* Englewood Cliffs, NJ: Prentice Hall.

Saad, L. (2010). Americans value both aspects of immigration reform. Gallup Polls. May 4. Retrieved from http://www.gallup.com/poll/127649/Americans-Value-Aspects-Immigration-Reform.aspx

Saenz, R. (2005). The social and economic isolation of urban African Americans. Population Reference Bureau. Retrieved from http://prb.org/Articles/2005/TheSocialandEconomic IsolationofUrbanAfricanAmericans.aspx

Sakamoto, A., Goyette, K., & Kim, C. (2009). Socioeconomic attainments of Asian Americans. *Annual Review of Sociology, 35,* 255–276

Sanchirico, A. (1991). The importance of small business ownership in Chinese American educational achievement. *Sociology of Education, 64,* 293–304.

Satter, B. (2009). *Family properties: Race, real estate, and the exploitation of black urban America.* New York: Henry Holt.

Schafer, J., & Navarro, J. (2004). The seven stage hate model: The psychopathology of hate groups. *FBI Law Enforcement Bulletin, 72,* 1–9.

Schlesinger, A. M. Jr. (1992). *The disuniting of America: Reflections on a multicultural society.* New York: Norton.

Schmid, C. (2001). *The politics of language: Conflict, identity, and cultural pluralism in comparative perspective.* New York: Oxford University Press.

Schoener, A. (1967). *Portal to America: The Lower East Side, 1870–1925.* New York: Holt, Rinehart & Winston.

Sears, D. (1988). Symbolic racism. In P. Katz & D. Taylor (Eds.), *Eliminating racism: Profiles in controversy* (pp. 53–84). New York: Plenum Press.

Sears, D., & Henry, P. J. (2003). The origins of modern racism. *Journal of Personality and Social Psychology, 85,* 259–275.

See, K. O., & Wilson, W. J. (1988). Race and ethnicity. In N. Smelser (Ed.), *Handbook of sociology* (pp. 223–242). Newbury Park, CA: SAGE.

Selzer, M. (1972). *"Kike": Anti-Semitism in America.* New York: Meridian.

Sen, R., & Mamdouh, F. (2008). *The accidental American: Immigration and citizenship in the age of globalization.* San Francisco: Berrt-Koehler Publications.

Shannon, W. V. (1964). *The American Irish.* New York: Macmillan.

Shapiro, T. (2004). *The hidden cost of being African American.* New York: Oxford University Press.

Sheet Metal Workers v. EEOC, 478 U.S. 421 (1986).

Sherif, M., Harvey, O. J., White, B. J., Hood, W., & Sherif, C. (1961). *Intergroup conflict and cooperation: The Robber's Cave experiment.* Norman, OK: University Book Exchange.

Sheth, M. (1995). Asian Indian Americans. In P. G. Min (Ed.), *Asian American: Contemporary issues and trends* (pp. 168–198). Thousand Oaks, CA: SAGE.

Shinn, H., & Kominski, R. (2010). Language use in the United States, 2007. American Community Survey reports. Retrieved from http://www.census.gov/hhes/socdemo/language/data/acs/ACS-12.pdf

Simon, J. (1989). *The economic consequences of immigration.* Cambridge, MA: Blackwell.

Simpson, G., & Yinger, M. (1985). *Racial and cultural minorities: An analysis of prejudice and discrimination.* New York: Plenum Press.

Skinner, B. (2008). A world enslaved. *Foreign Policy, 165,* 62–68.

Sklare, M. (1971). *America's Jews.* New York: Random House.

Small, M. L., Harding, D. J., & Lamont, M. (2010). Reconsidering culture and poverty. *The annals of the* American Academy of Political and Social Science *629,* 6 Retrieved from http://ann.sagepub.com/content/629/1/6

Smedley, A. (2007). *Race in North America: Origins and evolution of worldview* (3rd ed.). Boulder, CO: Westview Press.

Smith, J., & Edmonston, B. (Eds.). (1997). *The new Americans: Economic, demographic, and fiscal effects of immigration.* Washington, DC: National Academy Press.

Smith, T., & Dempsey, G. (1983). The polls: Ethnic social distance and prejudice. *Public Opinion Quarterly, 47,* 584–600.

Snipp, C. M. (1989). *American Indians: The first of this land.* New York: Russell Sage Foundation.

Snipp, C. M. (1992). Sociological perspectives on American Indians. *Annual Review of Sociology, 18,* 351–371.

Snipp, C. M. (1996). The first Americans: American Indians. In S. Pedraza & R. G. Rumbaut (Eds.), *Origins and destinies: Immigration, race, and ethnicity in America* (pp. 390–403). Belmont, CA: Wadsworth.

Soares, R., Combopiano, J., Regis, A., Shut, Y., & Wong, R. (2010). *2010 catalyst census: Fortune 500 women board directors.* New York: Catalyst. Retrieved from http://www.catalyst.org/publication/460/2010-catalyst-census-fortune-500-women-board-directors

Southern Poverty Law Center (SPLC). (2012). Hate map, 2010. Retrieved from http://splcenter.org/get-informed/hate-map

Spicer, E. H. (1980). American Indians. In S. Thernstrom, A. Orlov, & O. Handlin (Eds.), *Harvard encyclopedia of American ethnic groups* (pp. 58–122). Cambridge, MA: Harvard University Press.

Spickard, P. (1996). *Japanese Americans: The formation and transformations of an ethnic group.* New York: Twayne.

Spilde, K. (2001). The economic development journey of Indian nations. Retrieved from http://indiangaming.org/library/newsletters/index.html

Stampp, K. (1956). *The peculiar institution: Slavery in the ante-bellum South.* New York: Random House.

Stannard, D. (1992). *American Holocaust.* New York: Oxford University Press.

Staples, R. (1988). The black American family. In C. Mindel, R. Habenstein, & R. Wright (Eds.), *Ethnic families in America* (3rd ed., pp. 303–324). New York: Elsevier.

Statistics South Africa. (2008). *Income and expenditures of households, 2005–2006* Retrieved from http://www.statssa.gov.za/publications/P0100/P01002005.pdf

Steinberg, S. (1981). *The ethnic myth: Race, ethnicity, and class in America.* New York: Atheneum.

Steinberg, S. (2011). Poor reason: Culture still doesn't explain poverty. *Boston Review.* Retrieved from http://www.bostonreview.net/BR36.1/steinberg.php

Stepick, A., Stepick, C. D., Eugene, E., Teed, D., & Labissiere, Y. (2001). Shifting identities and intergenerational conflict: Growing up Haitian in Miami. In R. Rumbaut & A. Portes

(Eds.), *Ethnicities: Children of immigrants in America* (pp. 229–266). Berkeley: University of California Press.

Stoddard, E. (1973). *Mexican Americans.* New York: Random House.

Stoll, M. (2004). *African Americans and the color line.* New York: Russell Sage Foundation.

Stuckey, S. (1987). *Slave culture: Nationalist theory and the foundations of black America.* New York: Harper & Row.

Takaki, R. (1993). *A different mirror: A history of multicultural America.* Boston: Little, Brown.

Taylor, J., & Kalt, J. (2005). *American Indians on reservations: A databook of socioeconomic change between the 1990 and 2000 censuses.* Harvard University: The Harvard Project on American Indian Economic Development. Retrieved from http://www.hks.harvard.edu/hpaied/pubs/documentsAmericanIndiansonReservationsADatabookofSocioeconomicChange.pdf

Taylor, P., Lopez, M., Martinez, J., & Velasco, G. (2012). When labels don't fit: Hispanics and their views of identity. Pew Hispanic Center. Retrieved from http://www.pewhispanic.org/files/2012/04/PHC-Hispanic-Identity.pdf

Telles, E. (2004). *Race in another America: The significance of skin color in Brazil.* Princeton, NJ: Princeton University Press.

Telles, E., & Ortiz, V. (2008). *Generations of exclusion: Mexican Americans, assimilation, and race.* New York: Russell Sage Foundation.

Thernstrom, S., & Thernstrom, A. (1997). *America in black and white.* New York: Simon & Schuster.

Thornton, R. (2001). Trends among American Indians in the United States. In N. Smelser, W. Wilson, & F. Mitchell (Eds.), *America becoming: Racial trends and their consequences* (Vol. 1, pp. 135–169). Washington, DC: National Academies Press.

Tileagă, C. (2005). Accounting for extreme prejudice and legitimating blame in talk about the Romanies. *Discourse & Society, 16* (5), 603–624.

Tilly, C. (1990). Transplanted networks. In V. Yans-McLaughlin (Ed.), *Immigration reconsidered: History, sociology, and politics* (pp. 79–95). New York: Oxford University Press.

Tsai, S.-S. H. (1986). *The Chinese experience in America.* Bloomington: Indiana University Press.

Udry, R. (2000). Biological limits of gender construction. *American Sociological Review, 65,* 443–457.

United Nations (UN). (1948). Convention on the prevention and punishment of the crime of genocide. Retrieved from http://www.hrweb.org/legal/genocide.html

United Nations (2010). *The Millennium Development Goals report.* Retrieved from http://www.un.org/millenniumgoals/pdf/MDG%20Report%202010%20En%20r15%20-low%20res%2020100615%20-.pdf

United Nations (2011). Social indicators. Retrieved from http://unstats.un.org/unsd/demographic/products/socind/inc-eco.htm

United Nations (2012). International migrant stock. Retrieved from http://esa.un.org/migration/

United Steelworkers of America, AFL-CIO-CLC v. Weber, 443 U.S. 193 (1979).

U.S. Bureau of Labor. (2012). Table A-4, Employment status of the civilian noninstitutional population by race, Hispanic or Latino ethnicity, sex, and age, seasonally adjusted. Retrieved from http://www.bls.gov/web/empsit/cpseea04.pdf

U.S. Census Bureau. (1978). *Statistical abstract of the United States, 1977.* Washington, DC: Government Printing Office.

U.S. Census Bureau. (1990). Summary file 3. Retrieved from http://factfinder.census.gov/servlet/DatasetMainPageServlet?_program=DEC&_submenuId=datasets_1&_lang=en

U.S. Census Bureau. (1992). *Statistical abstract of the United States, 1992.* Washington, DC: Government Printing Office.

U.S. Census Bureau. (2000). Summary file 4. Retrieved from http://factfinder2.census.gov/faces/nav/jsf/pages/searchresults.xhtml?refresh=t#none

U.S. Census Bureau. (2002). *Statistical abstract of the United States, 2001* (121st ed.). Washington, DC: Government Printing Office.

U.S. Census Bureau. (2004). *Ancestry (2000)*. Retrieved from http://www.census.gov/prod/2004pubs/c2kbr-35.pdf

U.S. Census Bureau. (2005). *Statistical abstract of the United States, 2005*. Washington, DC: Government Printing Office.

U.S. Census Bureau. (2006). 2006 U.S. Census Bureau's American Community Survey.

U.S. Census Bureau. (2007a). American Community Survey, 2006. Retrieved from http://factfinder.census.gov/servlet/DatasetMainPageServlet?_program=ACS&_submenuId=datasets_2&_lang=en&_ts=

U.S. Census Bureau. (2007b). *Statistical abstract of the United States, 2007*. Washington, DC: Government Printing Office. Retrieved from http://www.census.gov/compendia/statab/past_years.html

U.S. Census Bureau. (2008a). 1990 summary tape file 3. Retrieved from http://factfinder.census.gov/servlet/DatasetMainPageServlet?_program=DEC&_tabId=DEC2&_submenuId=datasets_1&_lang=en&_ts=222966429406

U.S. Census Bureau. (2008b) National Population Projections. Retrieved from http://www.census.gov/population/www/projections/summarytables.html

U.S. Census Bureau. (2010). American Community Survey, 2010, 3-year estimates. Retrieved from http://factfinder2.census.gov/faces/nav/jsf/pages/searchresults.xhtml?refresh=t#none

U.S. Census Bureau. (2011). *Statistical abstract of the United States, 2011*. Washington, DC: Government Printing Office. Retrieved from http://www.census.gov/compendia/statab/2011edition.html

U.S. Census Bureau. (2012a). American Community Survey, 2010, 3-year estimates. Retrieved from http://factfinder2.census.gov/faces/tableservices/jsf/pages/productview.xhtml?fpt=table

U.S. Census Bureau. (2012b). *Statistical abstract of the United States, 2012*. Washington, DC: Government Printing Office. Retrieved from http://www.census.gov/compendia/statab/2012edition.html

U.S. Census Bureau. (2012c). Table P-36, Full-time year round workers by median income and sex. Retrieved from http://www.census.gov/hhes/www/income/data/historical/people/index.html

U.S. Census Bureau. (2012d). Table PINC-04, Educational attainment, people 18 years old and over, by total money earnings in 2010. Work experience in 2010, age, race, Hispanic origin, and sex. Retrieved from http://www.census.gov/hhes/www/cpstables/032009/perinc/new04_000.htm

U.S. Census Bureau. (2012e). Table PINC-06, Occupation of longest job in 2009: People 15 years old and over, by total money earnings in 2009, work experience in 2009, race, Hispanic origin, and sex. Retrieved from http://www.census.gov/hhes/www/cpstables/032011/perinc/new06_000.htm

U.S. Census Bureau. (2012f). Table H-5, Race and Hispanic origin of householder: Households by mean and median income. Retrieved from http://www.census.gov/hhes/www/income/data/historical/household/index.html

U.S. Census Bureau. (2012g). Table HINC-01, Selected characteristics of households, by total money income in 2009. Retrieved from http://www.census.gov/hhes/www/cpstables/032010/hhinc/new01_000.htm

U.S. Census Bureau. (2012h). Historical poverty tables, families, table 4. Retrieved from http://www.census.gov/hhes/www/poverty/data/historical/families.html

U.S. Commission on Civil Rights. (1976). *Puerto Ricans in the Continental United States: An Uncertain Future*. Washington, DC: Government Printing Office.

U.S. Department of Homeland Security. (2011). *Yearbook of immigration statistics, 2010*, Washington, DC. Government Printing Office. Retrieved from http://www.dhs.gov/xlibrary/assets/statistics/yearbook/2010/ois_yb_2010.pdf

U.S. Equal Employment Opportunity Commission. (2012). Matrix LLC will pay $450,000 to settle EEOC race discrimination and retaliation lawsuit. Retrieved from http://www.eeoc.gov/eeoc/newsroom/release/1-6-12.cfm

U.S. Immigration and Naturalization Service. (1993). *Statistical yearbook of the Immigration and Naturalization Service, 1992.* Washington, DC: Government Printing Office.

Utah Supreme Court rules that non-Indian members of Native American church can use peyote in church ceremonies. (2004, June 23). *New York Times,* p. A20.

Valentine, S., & Mosley, G. (2000). Acculturation and sex-role attitudes among Mexican Americans: A longitudinal analysis. *Hispanic Journal of Behavioral Sciences, 22,* 104–204.

Van Ausdale, D., & Feagin, J. (2001). *The first R: How children learn race and racism.* Lanham, MD: Rowman & Littlefield.

van den Berghe, P. L. (1967). *Race and racism: A comparative perspective.* New York: Wiley.

van den Berghe, P. L. (1981). *The ethnic phenomenon.* New York: Elsevier.

Van Hook, J. (2010). The demographic impacts of repealing birthright citizenship. Retrieved from http://www.migrationpolicy.org/pubs/BirthrightInsight-2010.pdf

Vargas-Ramos, C. (2005). Black, trigueno, white . . . ? Shifting racial identification among Puerto Ricans. *Du Bois Review 2,* 267–285.

Vincent, T. G. (1976). *Black Power and the Garvey movement.* San Francisco: Ramparts.

Vinje, D. (1996). Native American economic development on selected reservations: A comparative analysis. *American Journal of Economics and Sociology, 55,* 427–442.

Wagley, C., & Harris, M. (1958). *Minorities in the new world: Six case studies.* New York: Columbia University Press.

Wang, W. (2012). The rise of intermarriage. Pew Research Center. Retrieved from http://www.pewsocialtrends.org/files/2012/02/SDT-Intermarriage-II.pdf

Washington, B. T. (1965). *Up from slavery.* New York: Dell.

Waters, M. (1990). *Ethnic options.* Berkeley: University of California Press.

Waters, M., & Jimenez, T. (2005). Assessing immigrant assimilation: New empirical and theoretical challenges. *American Review of Sociology, 31,* 105–125.

Wax, M. (1971). *Indian Americans: Unity and diversity.* Englewood Cliffs, NJ: Prentice Hall.

Weeks, P. (1988). *The American Indian experience.* Arlington Heights, IL: Forum Press.

Weiser, W., & Norden, L. (2011). Voting law changes in 2012. Brennan Center for Justice at New York University School of Law. Retrieved from http://brennan.3cdn.net/92635ddafbc09e8d88_i3m6bjdeh.pdf

Weitzer, R., & Tuch, S. (2005). Racially biased policing: Determinants of citizen perceptions. *Social Forces, 83,* 1009–1030.

Wellner, A. (2007). U.S. attitudes toward interracial dating are liberalizing. Population Reference Bureau. Retrieved from http://www.prb.org/Articles/2005/USAttitudesTowardInterracialDatingAreLiberalizing.aspx

Westervelt, E. (2010). In Germany, voices against immigration grow louder. National Public Radio. Retrieved from http://www.npr.org/templates/story/story.php?storyId=130649146

White, D. G. (1985). *Ar'n't I a woman? Female slaves in the plantation South.* New York: Norton.

White, M., & Glick, J. (2009). *Achieving anew: How new immigrants do in American schools, jobs, and neighborhoods.* New York: Russell Sage.

White House, The. (2005). Economic report of the president. Retrieved from http://www.gpoaccess.gov/eop/download.html

Whiting, R. (1990). *You gotta have wa.* New York: Macmillan.

Wilkens, R. (1992, May 3). L. A.: Images in the flames—looking back in anger: 27 years after Watts, our nation remains divided by racism. *Washington Post,* p. C1.

Williams, G. (1995). *Life on the color line.* New York: Dutton.

Wilson, W. J. (1973). *Power, racism, and privilege: Race relations in theoretical and sociohistorical perspectives.* New York: Free Press.

Wilson, W. J. (1987). *The truly disadvantaged: The inner city, the underclass, and public policy.* Chicago: University of Chicago Press.

Wilson, W. J. (1996). *When work disappears.* New York: Knopf.

Wilson, W. J. (2009). *More than just race.* New York: W.W. Norton.

Wingfield, A., & Feagin, J. (2010). *Yes we can? White racial framing and the 2008 presidential campaign.* New York: Routledge.

Wirth, L. (1945). The problem of minority groups. In R. Linton (Ed.), *The science of man in the world* (pp. 347–372). New York: Columbia University Press.

Wolfenstein, E. V. (1993). *The victims of democracy: Malcolm X.* New York: Guilford Press.

Wong, J. S. (1993). Fifth Chinese daughter. In D. LaGuardia & H. Guth (Eds.), *American voices* (pp. 48–55). Palo Alto, CA: Mayfield.

Wong, M. (1995). Chinese Americans. In P. G. Min (Ed.), *Asian Americans: Contemporary trends and issues* (pp. 58–94). Thousand Oaks, CA: SAGE.

Woodward, C. V. (1974). *The strange career of Jim Crow* (3rd ed.). New York: Oxford University Press.

Worsnop, R. (1992, May 8). Native Americans. *CQ Researcher*, pp. 387–407.

Wright, R. (1940). *Native son.* New York: Harper & Brothers.

Wright, R. (1941). Death on the city pavement. In *Twelve million black voices.* New York: Basic Books.

Wright, R. (1945). *Black boy: A record of childhood and youth.* New York: Harper & Brothers.

Wyman, M. (1993). *Round trip to America.* Ithaca, NY: Cornell University Press.

Xie, Y., & Goyette, K. (2004). *A demographic portrait of Asian Americans.* New York: Russell Sage Foundation.

Yamato, A. (1994). Racial antagonism and the formation of segmented labor markets: Japanese Americans and their exclusion from the work force. *Humboldt Journal of Social Relations, 20,* 31–63.

Yancey, George. (2003). *Who is white? Latinos, Asians, and the new black/non-black divide.* Boulder, CO: Lynne Reinner

Yinger, J. M. (1985). Ethnicity. *Annual Review of Sociology, 11,* 151–180.

Zhou, M. (1992). *Chinatown.* Philadelphia: Temple University Press.

Zhou, M., & Logan, J. R. (1989). Returns on human capital in ethnic enclaves: New York City's Chinatown. *American Sociological Review, 54,* 809–820.

Glossary

Numbers in brackets refer to the chapter in which the term is introduced.

Abolitionism [3] The movement to abolish slavery in the South.

Acculturation [2] The process by which one group (generally a minority or immigrant group) learns the culture of another group (generally the dominant group).

Affective prejudice [1] The emotional or "feeling" dimension of individual prejudice. The prejudiced individual attaches negative emotions to other groups.

Affirmative action [4] Affirmative action programs that are designed to counter the effects of institutional discrimination and the legacy of minority group inequality.

Alien Land Act [8] Bill passed by the California legislature in 1913 that declared aliens who were ineligible for citizenship (effectively meaning only immigrants from Asia) were also ineligible to own land.

Americanization [2] The one-sided process of assimilation that occurred with many immigrant groups in the United States.

Anglo-conformity [2] The model of assimilation by which minority groups conform to Anglo American culture.

Anti-Semitism [2] Prejudice or ideological racism directed specifically at Jews.

Apartheid [4] The policy of extreme racial segregation formerly followed in South Africa.

Ascribed status [1] A position in society that is assigned to the individual, usually at birth. Examples of ascribed status include positions based on ethnicity, race, and gender.

Assimilation [2] The process by which formerly distinct and separate groups merge and become one group.

Black Power movement [5] A coalition of African American groups that rose to prominence in the 1960s. Some central themes of the movement were Black Nationalism, autonomy for African American communities, and pride in race and African heritage.

Black protest movement [4] *See* Civil rights movement.

Blauner hypothesis [3] Minority groups created by colonization will experience more intense prejudice, racism, and discrimination than those created by immigration. The disadvantaged status of colonized groups will persist longer and be more difficult to overcome than the disadvantaged status faced by groups created by immigration.

Border identity [5] The racial identity of people who consider themselves mixed race rather than black or white. This was the most common identity in a study of college students with one black and one white parent.

Bourgeoisie [1] Marxist term for the elite or ruling class in an industrial society that owns or controls the means of production.

Bracero [7] A Mexican laborer in the United States.

Bureau of Indian Affairs (BIA) [6] The agency of the U.S. government that has primary responsibility for the administration of American Indian reservations.

Capital intensive [2] Capital-intensive technology replaces hand labor with machine labor. Large amounts of capital are required to develop, purchase, and maintain the machines.

Caste system [3] A closed system of stratification with no mobility between positions. A person's class at birth is permanent and unchangeable.

Chattel [3] An item of personal property. In a system of chattel slavery, slaves were defined by law not as persons, but as the personal property of their owners.

Chicanismo [7] A militant ideology of the Mexican American protest movement that appeared in the 1960s. The ideology took a critical view of U.S. society, made strong demands for justice and an end to racism, expressed a positive image for the group, and incorporated other pluralistic themes.

Chicanos [7] A group name for Mexican Americans. Associated with the ideology of Chicanismo, which emerged in the 1960s.

Chinese Exclusion Act [8] Legislation passed by the U.S. government in 1882 that banned immigration from China.

Civil rights movement [5] The effort of African Americans in the 1950s and 1960s to win the rights they were entitled to under the U.S. Constitution.

Cognitive prejudice [1] The "thinking" dimension of individual prejudice. The prejudiced individual thinks about other groups in terms of stereotypes.

Colonized minority groups [3] Groups whose initial contact with the dominant group was through conquest or colonization.

Color-blind racism [1] *See* Modern racism.

Competition [3] A situation in which two or more parties struggle for control of some scarce resource.

Core group [1] *See* Dominant group.

Cultural assimilation [2] *See* Acculturation.

Cultural pluralism [2] A situation in which groups have not acculturated, and each maintains a distinct identity.

Culture of Poverty Theory [5] A theory asserting that poverty causes certain personality traits— such as the need for instant gratification—which, in turn, perpetuate poverty.

Culture [2] All aspects of the way of life associated with a group of people. Culture includes language, beliefs, norms, values, customs, technology, and many other components.

De facto segregation [4] A system of racial separation and inequality that appears to result from voluntary choices about where to live, work, and so forth. Often, this form of segregation is really de jure segregation in thin disguise.

De jure segregation [4] The system of rigid competitive race relations that followed Reconstruction in the South. The system lasted from the 1880s until the 1960s and was characterized by laws mandating racial separation and inequality.

Deindustrialization [4] The shift from a manufacturing economy to a service-oriented, information-processing economy.

Differential in power [3] Any difference between two or more groups in their ability to achieve their goals.

Discrimination [1] The unequal or unfair treatment of a person or persons based on their group membership.

Dominant group [1] The group that benefits from and, typically, tries to sustain minority group subordination.

Enclave minority group [2] A group that establishes its own neighborhood and relies on a set of interconnected businesses for economic survival.

Ethclass [2] The group formed by the intersection of social class and racial or ethnic groups.

Ethnic minority groups [1] Minority groups identified primarily by cultural characteristics, such as language or religion.

Ethnic revival [2] The movement toward increased salience for ethnic identity, which began for European Americans in the 1960s.

Ethnic succession [2] The process by which European ethnic groups affected each other's position in the social class structure.

Ethnocentrism [3] Judging other groups, societies, or cultures by the standards of one's own group, society, or culture.

Extractive (primary) occupations [4] Jobs that involve the production of raw materials. Examples include farmer and miner.

Fatalism [5] The view that one's fate is beyond one's control.

Fluid competitive system [4] A system of group relations in which minority group members are freer to compete for jobs and other scarce resources. Associated with advanced industrialization.

Gender roles [1] Expectations about the proper behavior, attitudes, and personality traits for males and females.

Genocide [1] The deliberate attempt to exterminate an entire group of people.

Glass ceiling [4] The informal, "invisible" barrier that keep women and minorities from rising to the highest occupations.

Huiguan [8] An association in Chinese American society based on the region of China from which an individual or his or her family came. The *huiguan* performed a number of social, welfare, and business functions.

Human capital theory [2] Consistent with the traditional view of assimilation, this theory considers success in the United States to be a direct result of individual efforts, personal values and skills, and education.

Ideological racism [1] A belief system asserting that a particular group is inferior. Although individuals may subscribe to racist beliefs, the ideology itself is incorporated into the culture of the society and passed on from generation to generation.

Immigrant minority groups [3] Groups whose initial contact with the dominant group was through immigration.

Indentured servant [3] A contract laborer who is obligated to serve a particular master for a specified length of time.

Indian Reorganization Act (IRA) [6] Federal legislation passed in 1934 that was intended to give Native American tribes more autonomy.

Industrial Revolution [2] The shift in subsistence technology from labor-intensive agriculture to capital-intensive manufacturing.

Institutional discrimination [1] A pattern of unequal treatment based on group membership that is built into the daily operations of society.

Integration [2] The process by which a minority group enters the social structure of the dominant society.

Intermarriage [2] *See* Marital assimilation.

Issei [8] First-generation immigrants from Japan.

Jim Crow system [4] The system of formal, legalized segregation that was created in the American South following the Civil War. Also called de jure segregation.

Labor intensive [2] A form of work in which the bulk of the effort is provided by human beings working by hand. Machines and other labor-saving devices are rare or absent.

Level of development [1] The stage of evolution of society. The stages discussed in this text relate to agrarian and industrial subsistence technology.

Machismo [7] A cultural value stressing male dominance, virility, and honor.

Manufacturing (secondary) occupations [4] Occupations involving the transformation of raw materials into finished products ready for the marketplace. An example is an assembly line worker in an automobile plant.

Marielitos [7] Refugees from Cuba who arrived in the United States in 1980.

Marital assimilation [2] Intermarriage between members of different groups.

Means of production [1] A Marxist term that refers to the materials, tools, resources, and organizations by which the society produces and distributes goods and services.

Melting pot [2] A type of assimilation in which all groups contribute in roughly equal amounts to the creation of a new culture and society.

Mestizo [3] A person of mixed white and Native American ancestry.

Middleman minority groups [2] Groups that rely on small businesses, dispersed throughout a community, for economic survival.

Minority group [1] A group that experiences a pattern of disadvantage or inequality, has a visible identifying trait, and is a self-conscious social unit. Membership is usually determined at birth, and group members have a strong tendency to marry within the group.

Miscegenation [1] Marriage between members of different racial groups.

"Model minority" groups [8] A description often applied to Asian Americans. It exaggerates the relative affluence of these groups and is sometimes used as a rhetorical device for criticizing other minority groups, especially African Americans.

Modern institutional discrimination [4] A more subtle and covert form of institutional discrimination that is often unintentional and unconscious.

Modern racism [1] A subtle form of prejudice that incorporates negative feelings about minority groups but not the traditional stereotypes. Modern racism assumes that (a) discrimination no longer exists, (b) minority groups are responsible for their own disadvantages, and (c) special programs addressing ethnic and racial inequality are unjustified and unnecessary.

Multiculturalism [2] A general term for some versions of pluralism in the United States in the 1990s. Generally, multiculturalism stresses mutual respect for all groups and celebrates the multiplicity of heritages that have contributed to the development of the United States.

New Immigration [2] Immigration from Europe to the United States between the 1880s and the 1920s.

Nisei [8] Second-generation Japanese Americans.

Noel hypothesis [3] A theory about the creation of minority groups that asserts that if two or more groups come together in a contact situation characterized by ethnocentrism, competition, and a differential in power, some form of racial or ethnic stratification will result.

Nonviolent direct action [5] An important tactic used during the civil rights movement in the South to defeat de jure segregation.

Old Immigration [2] Immigration from Europe to the United States between the 1820s and the 1880s.

Operation Wetback [7] A government program developed in the 1950s to deport illegal immigrants from Mexico.

Past-in-present institutional discrimination [4] Patterns of inequality or unequal treatment in the present that are caused by some pattern of discrimination in the past.

Paternalism [3] A form of dominant-minority relations often associated with plantation-based, labor-intensive, agrarian technology. In paternalistic relations, minority groups are extremely unequal and highly controlled. Rates of overt conflict are low.

Patriarchy [1] Male dominance. In a patriarchal society, men have more power than women do.

Plantation system [3] A labor-intensive form of agriculture that requires large tracts of land and a large, cheap labor force. This was a dominant form of agricultural production in the American South before the Civil War.

Pluralism [2] A situation in which groups have separate identities, cultures, and organizational structures.

Power [1] The ability to achieve goals even in the face of opposition from others.

Prejudice [1] The tendency of individuals to think and feel negatively toward others.

Prestige [1] The amount of honor or respect accorded a particular person or group.

Primary labor market [4] The segment of the labor market that encompasses better-paying, higher-status, more-secure jobs, usually in large bureaucracies.

Primary sector of the social structure [2] Relationships and groups that are intimate and personal. Groups in the primary sector are small.

Principle of third-generation interest [2] The notion that the grandchildren of immigrants will stress their ethnicity much more than the second generation will.

Proletariat [1] In Marxist theory, the workers in an industrial society.

Protean [5] The racial identity of people who alter their identity as they move between black and white social settings. This was the least common identity in a study of college students with one black and one white parent.

Pull [7] Factors that cause population movement out of an area.

Push [7] Factors that cause population movement into an area.

Race relations cycle [2] A concept associated with Robert Park, who believed that relations between different groups would go through predictable cycles, from conflict to eventual assimilation.

Race [1] Biologically, an isolated, inbreeding population with a distinctive genetic heritage Socially, the term is used loosely and reflects patterns of inequality and power.

Racial minority groups [1] Minority groups identified primarily by physical characteristics such as skin color (e.g., Asian Americans).

Racism [1] A belief system that asserts the inferiority of a group.

Reconstruction [4] The period of Southern race relations following the Civil War. Reconstruction lasted from 1865 until the 1880s and witnessed many racial reforms, all of which were reversed during de jure segregation, or the Jim Crow era.

Relocation camps [8] The camps in which Japanese Americans were held during World War II.

Repatriation [7] A government campaign begun during the Great Depression of the 1930s to deport illegal immigrants back to Mexico. The campaign also caused legal immigrants and native-born Mexican Americans to leave the United States.

Revolution [2] A minority group goal. A revolutionary group wishes to change places with the dominant group or create a new social order, perhaps in alliance with other groups.

Rigid competitive group [4] A system of group relations in which the dominant group seeks to exclude minority groups or limit their ability to compete for scarce resources such as jobs.

Sansei [8] Third-generation Japanese Americans.

Secondary labor market [4] The segment of the labor market that includes low-paying, low-skilled, insecure jobs.

Secondary sector [2] Relationships and organizations that are public, task oriented, and impersonal. Organizations in the secondary sector can be large.

Segmented assimilation [2] The idea that assimilation in the United States is now fragmented and can have a number of outcomes in addition to eventual entry into mainstream society.

Separatism [2] A minority group goal. A separatist group wishes to sever all ties with the dominant group.

Service (tertiary) occupations [4] Jobs that involve providing services. Examples include retail clerk, janitor, and schoolteacher.

Sharecropping [4] A system of farming often used in the South during de jure segregation. The sharecropper (often black), or tenant, worked the land, which was actually owned by someone else (usually white), in return for a share of the profits at harvest time. The landowner supplied a place to live and credit for food and clothing.

Singular identity [5] The racial identity of people who consider themselves to be either black or white. This was the second most common identity in a study of college students with one black and one white parent.

Social class [1] A group of people who command similar amounts of valued goods and services, such as income, property, and education.

Social construction [1] A perception shared by members of a society or group that reflects habitual routines or institutionalized social processes. Social constructions (such as race or stereotypes) become real to the people who share them.

Social distance [1] The degree of intimacy to which a person is willing to admit members of other groups.

Social mobility [1] Movement from one social class to another.

Social structure [2] The networks of social relationships, groups, organizations, communities, and institutions that organize the work of a society and connect individuals to each other and to the larger society.

Sojourners [2] Immigrants who intend to return to their countries of origin.

Stereotypes [1] Overgeneralizations that are thought to apply to all members of a group.

Stratification [1] The unequal distribution of valued goods and services (e.g., income, job opportunities, prestige and fame, education, health care) in society; the social class system.

Structural assimilation [2] *See* Integration.

Structural mobility [2] Rising occupational and social class standing that is the result of changes in the overall structure of the economy and labor market, as opposed to individual efforts.

Structural pluralism [2] A situation in which a group has acculturated but is not integrated.

Subsistence technology [1] The means by which a society satisfies basic needs. An agrarian society relies on labor-intensive agriculture, whereas an industrial society relies on machines and inanimate fuel supplies.

Symbolic ethnicity [2] A sense of ethnicity that is more superficial, voluntary, and changeable.

Symbolic racism [1] *See* Modern racism.

Termination [6] A policy by which all special relationships between the federal government and American Indians would be abolished.

Tongs [8] Chinese American secret societies in Chinatowns that sometimes fought with other Chinese American groups over control of resources.

Transcendent identity [5] The identity of people who rejected the concept of race and insisted on being seen as unique individuals. This was the third most common identity in a study of college students with one black and one white parent.

Triple melting pot [2] The idea that structural assimilation for European immigrants took place within the context of the three major American religions.

Urban underclass [5] The urban lower classes, consisting largely of African Americans and other minority groups of color, which have been more or less permanently barred from the mainstream economy and the primary labor market.

Vicious cycle of prejudice [1] A process in which a condition is assumed to be true and forces are then set in motion to create and perpetuate that condition.

Yonsei [8] Fourth-generation Japanese Americans.

Index

About the Author

Joseph F. Healey is Professor of Sociology at Christopher Newport University in Virginia. He received his PhD in sociology and anthropology from the University of Virginia. An experienced, innovative teacher of numerous race and ethnicity courses, he has written articles on minority groups, the sociology of sport, social movements, and violence, and he is also the author of *Statistics: A Tool for Social Research* (8th ed., 2008).

⑤SAGE research**methods**

The essential online tool for researchers from the world's leading methods publisher

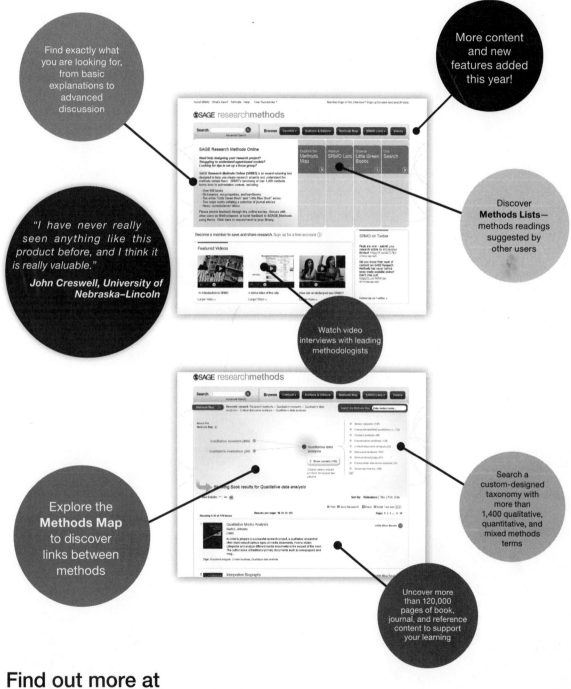

Find exactly what you are looking for, from basic explanations to advanced discussion

More content and new features added this year!

"*I have never really seen anything like this product before, and I think it is really valuable.*"

John Creswell, University of Nebraska–Lincoln

Discover **Methods Lists—** methods readings suggested by other users

Watch video interviews with leading methodologists

Explore the **Methods Map** to discover links between methods

Search a custom-designed taxonomy with more than 1,400 qualitative, quantitative, and mixed methods terms

Uncover more than 120,000 pages of book, journal, and reference content to support your learning

Find out more at
www.sageresearchmethods.com